# Webster's

# *Notebook*

# THESAURUS

*McGraw-Hill*
*Children's Publishing*

*A Division of The* **McGraw·Hill** *Companies*

Copyright © 2003 McGraw-Hill Children's Publishing.

Published by American Education Publishing, an imprint of McGraw-Hill Children's Publishing,
A Division of The McGraw-Hill Companies.

Printed in the United States of America.

Send all inquiries to:
McGraw-Hill Children's Publishing
8787 Orion Place
Columbus, Ohio  43240-4027

ISBN 1-57768-342-0

1 2 3 4 5 6 7 8 9 10 FRY 06 05 04 03 02

# Proofreading Marks

lowercase: / S̸ister

capitalize: ≡ o̲h̲i̲o̲

delete: ℓ w̶o̶r̶d̶e̶

transpose: ∿ sheeps᷍ wool

insert: ∧ a beautiful sunset

## add...

a comma: ⌄

a period: ⊙

a colon: ⌄

a semicolon: ⌄

a quotation mark: ⌄

an apostrophe: ⌄

The thesaurus is a useful tool for expanding vocabulary, which adds variety to speech and writing.

A thesaurus is a compilation of words and phrases that are similar in meaning. The name for these like words is *synonyms*; words that are opposite in meaning are called *antonyms*.

This *Webster's Notebook Thesaurus* from McGraw-Hill Children's Publishing is organized alphabetically, using a base of common words and their variants. Synonyms (*SYN.*) are listed first, followed by antonyms (*ANT.*) when applicable. We believe you will find this to be a handy and reliable reference book.

# A

**a** (SYN.) any, one.

**abandon** (SYN.) relinquish, resign, surrender, leave, give up, cease, forsake, desert, quit, vacate, abjure, discard, evacuate, withdraw. (ANT.) keep, stay, maintain, embrace, adopt, join, engage, retain.

**abandoned** (SYN.) depraved, wicked, deserted, desolate, forsaken, rejected, cast off, degraded, loose, unrestrained, marooned, immoral, evil. (ANT.) befriended, cherished, chaste, moral, respectable, virtuous, righteous.

**abase** (SYN.) humble, reduce, bring down, degrade, demote, mock, scorn, belittle, shame. (ANT.) exalt, cherish, elevate, uplift, dignify.

**abash** (SYN.) disconcert, bewilder, confuse, put off. (ANT.) comfort, relax, hearten.

**abashed** (SYN.) confused, ashamed, embarrassed, mortified, humiliated.

**abate** (SYN.) lessen, curtail, reduce, decrease, restrain, decline, stop, moderate, subside, slow, diminish, slacken. (ANT.) grow, prolong, increase, extend, intensify, quicken, enhance, accelerate.

**abbey** (SYN.) nunnery, convent, cloister.

**abbot** (SYN.) friar, monk.

**abbreviate** (SYN.) shorten, lessen, abridge, condense, curtail, reduce, cut, trim, restrict, clip, contract. (ANT.) lengthen, increase, expand, extend, prolong, enlarge.

**abbreviation** (SYN.) abridgment, reduction, shortening, condensation. (ANT.) expansion, extension, amplification, lengthening dilation.

**abdicate** (SYN.) relinquish, renounce, vacate, waive, desert, forsake, abolish, quit, abandon, surrender, resign. (ANT.) maintain, stay, retain, uphold.

**abdomen** (SYN.) paunch, belly, stomach.

**abduct** (SYN.) carry off, take, kidnap.

**aberrant** (SYN.) capricious, devious, irregular, unnatural, abnormal. (ANT.) regular, usual, fixed, ordinary.

**aberration** (SYN.) oddity, abnormality, irregularity, deviation, monster, abortion, eccentricity. (ANT.) conformity, normality.

**abet** (SYN.) support, connive, encourage, conspire, help, incite, aid, assist. (ANT.) deter, check, hinder, frustrate, oppose, discourage, resist.

**abettor** (SYN.) accomplice, ally, confederate, associate, accessory. (ANT.) opponent, enemy.

**abeyance** (SYN.) cessation, pause, inactivity, rest, suspension, recess, dormancy, remission. (ANT.) ceaseless, continuation.

**abhor** (SYN.) hate, loathe, execrate, avoid, scorn, detest, despise.

**abhorrent** (SYN.) loathsome, horrible, detestable, nauseating, hateful, despicable, disgusting, foul, offensive, terrible, revolting.

**abide** (SYN.) obey, accept, tolerate, endure, dwell, stay, reside.

**ability** (SYN.) aptness, capability, skill, faculty, talent. (ANT.) incapacity, incompetency, weakness, ineptitude, inability.

**abject** (SYN.) sordid, infamous, miserable, wretched, mean, base, contempt.

**abjure** (SYN.) relinquish, renounce, vacate, waive, desert, quit, leave, forsake, foreswear, abdicate, resign, surrender. (ANT.) maintain, uphold, stay.

**able** (SYN.) qualified, competent, fit, capable, skilled, efficient, clever, talented, adequate, skillful. (ANT.) inadequate, trained, incapable, weak, incompetent, unable.

**abnegation** (SYN.) rejection, renunciation, self-denial, abandonment, refusal, relinquishment, abjuration.

**abnormal** (SYN.) uncommon, unnatural, odd, irregular, monstrous. (ANT.) natural, usual, normal, average.

**aboard** (SYN.) on board.

**abode** (SYN.) dwelling, habitat, home, residence, address, quarters, lodging place, domicile.

**abolish** (SYN.) end, eradicate, annul, cancel, revoke, destroy, invalidate, overthrow, obliterate, abrogate, erase, exterminate, wipe out, eliminate. (ANT.) promote, restore, continue, establish, sustain.

**abominable** (SYN.) foul, dreadful, hateful, revolting, vile, odious, loathsome, detestable, bad, horrible, terrible, awful, disgusting. (ANT.) delightful, pleasant, agreeable, commendable, admirable, noble.

**abominate** (SYN.) despise, detest, hate, dislike, abhor, loathe. (ANT.) like, cherish, approve, admire.

**abomination** (SYN.) freak, detestation, hatred, disgust, revulsion, horror.

**abort** (SYN.) flop, fizzle, miscarry, abandon, cancel.

**abortion** (SYN.) miscarriage, fiasco, disaster, failure, defeat.

**abortive** (SYN.) unproductive, vain, unsuccessful, useless, failed, futile. (ANT.) rewarding, effective, profitable, successful.

**abound** (SYN.) swarm, plentiful, filled, overflow, teem. (ANT.) scarce, lack.

**about** (SYN.) relating to, involving, concerning, near, around, upon, almost, approximately, of, nearby, ready to, nearly.

**about-face** (SYN.) reversal, backing out, shift, switch.

**above** (SYN.) higher than, overhead, on, upon, over, superior to. (ANT.) under, beneath, below.

**aboveboard** (SYN.) forthright, open, frank, honest, overt, plain, straightforward, guileless, trustworthy. (ANT.) sneaky, wily.

**abracadabra** (SYN.) voodoo, magic, charm, spell.

**abrasion** (SYN.) rubbing, roughness, scratching, scraping, friction, chap, chafe, chapping, scrape.

**abrasive** (SYN.) rough, hurtful, sharp, galling, annoying, grating, cutting, irritating, caustic. (ANT.) pleasant, soothing, comforting, agreeable, smooth.

**abreast** (SYN.) beside, side by side, alongside.

**abridge** (SYN.) condense, cut, abbreviate, make shorter, contract, shorten, reduce, summarize, curtail. (ANT.) increase, lengthen, expand, extend.

**abridgment** (SYN.) digest, condensation, summary, abbreviation, shortening. (ANT.) lengthening, expansion, enlargement.

**abroad** (SYN.) away, overseas, broadly, widely. (ANT.) at home, privately, secretly.

**abrogate** (SYN.) rescind, withdraw, revoke, annul, cancel, abolish, repeal.

**abrupt** (SYN.) sudden, unexpected, blunt, curt, precipitous, sharp, hasty, unannounced, harsh, precipitate, brusque, rude, rough, short, steep. (ANT.) foreseen, smooth, warm, courteous, gradual, smooth, expected, anticipated.

**abscess** (SYN.) pustule, sore, wound, inflammation.

**absence** (SYN.) nonexistence, deficiency, lack, need, shortcoming. (ANT.) attendance, completeness, existence, presence.

**absent** (SYN.) gone, away, truant, departed, inattentive, lacking, not present, out, off. (ANT.) attending, attentive, present.

**absent-minded** (SYN.) inattentive, daydreaming, preoccupied, absorbed, bemused, dreaming, forgetful. (ANT.) observant, attentive, alert.

**absolute** (SYN.) unconditional, entire, actual, complete, thorough, total, perfect, essential, supreme, ultimate, unrestricted, positive, unqualified, whole. (ANT.) partial, conditional, dependent, accountable, restricted, qualified, limited, fragmentary.

**absolutely** (SYN.) positively, really, doubtlessly. (ANT.) doubtfully, uncertainly.

**absolution** (SYN.) pardon, forgiveness, acquittal, mercy, amnesty, remission.

**absolutism** (SYN.) autarchy, dictatorship, authoritarianism.

**absolve** (SYN.) exonerate, discharge, acquit, pardon, forgive, clear, excuse. (ANT.) blame, convict, charge, accuse.

**absorb** (SYN.) consume, swallow up, engulf, assimilate, imbibe, engage, engross, take in, integrate, incorporate, occupy. (ANT.) discharge, dispense, emit, exude, leak, eliminate, bore, tire, weary, drain.

**absorbent** (SYN.) permeable, spongy, pervious, porous. (ANT.) waterproof, impervious.

**absorbing** (SYN.) interesting, engaging, exciting, engrossing, entertaining, thrilling, intriguing, pleasing, fascinating. (ANT.) dull, boring, tedious, tiresome.

**abstain** (SYN.) forbear, forego, decline, resist, withhold, refrain. (ANT.) pursue.

**abstemious** (SYN.) abstinent, sparing, cautious, temperate, ascetic, self-disciplined, continent, sober. (ANT.) uncontrolled, indulgent, abandoned, excessive.

**abstinence** (SYN.) fasting, self-denial, continence, forbearance, sobriety, refrain. (ANT.) gluttony, greed, excess, self-indulgence.

**abstract** (SYN.) theoretical,

ideal, part, appropriate, steal, separate, purloin, nonconcrete, summarize. *(ANT.) return, concrete, unite, add, replace, specific, clear, particular, restore.*

**abstracted** *(SYN.)* preoccupied, absent-minded, parted, removed, stolen, abridged, taken away. *(ANT.) replaced, returned, alert, united, added.*

**abstraction** *(SYN.)* idea, image, generalization, thought, opinion, impression, notion. *(ANT.) matter, object, substance.*

**abstruse** *(SYN.)* arcane, obscure, complicated, abstract, esoteric, metaphysical. *(ANT.) uncomplicated, direct, obvious, simple.*

**absurd** *(SYN.)* ridiculous, silly, unreasonable, foolish, irrational, nonsensical, impossible, inconsistent, preposterous, self-contradictory, unbelievable. *(ANT.) rational, sensible, sound, meaningful, consistent, reasonable.*

**absurdity** *(SYN.)* foolishness, nonsense, farce, drivel, joke, senselessness, folly.

**abundance** *(SYN.)* ampleness, profusion, copiousness, plenty. *(ANT.) insufficiency, want, absence, dearth, scarcity.*

**abundant** *(SYN.)* ample, overflowing, plentiful, rich, teeming, profuse, abounding. *(ANT.) insufficient, scant, not enough, scarce, deficient, rare, uncommon, absent.*

**abuse** *(SYN.)* maltreatment, misuse, reproach, defamation, dishonor, mistreat, damage, ill-use, reviling, aspersion, desecration, invective, insult, outrage, profanation, perversion, disparagement, misemploy, misapply, hurt, harm, injure, scold, berate. *(ANT.) plaudit, respect, appreciate, commendation, protect, praise, cherish.*

**abusive** *(SYN.)* harmful, insulting, libelous, hurtful, slanderous, nasty, defamatory, injurious, scathing, derogatory. *(ANT.) helpful, laudatory.*

**abut** *(SYN.)* touch, border, meet, join, connect with.

**abutment** *(SYN.)* pier, buttress, bulwark, brace, support.

**abysmal** *(SYN.)* bottomless, unfathomable, yawning, overwhelming.

**abyss** *(SYN.)* depth, chasm, void, infinitude, limbo, unknowable.

**academic** *(SYN.)* learned, scholarly, theoretical, erudite, bookish, formal, pedantic.

*(ANT.) ignorant, practical, simple, uneducated.*

**academy** *(SYN.)* college, school.

**accede** *(SYN.)* grant, agree, comply, consent, yield, endorse, accept, admit. *(ANT.) dissent, disagree, differ, oppose.*

**accelerate** *(SYN.)* quicken, dispatch, facilitate, hurry, rush, speed up, forward, hasten, push, expedite. *(ANT.) hinder, retard, slow, delay.*

**accent** *(SYN.)* tone, emphasis, inflection, stress, consent.

**accept** *(SYN.)* take, approve, receive, allow, consent to, believe, adopt, admit. *(ANT.) ignore, reject, refuse.*

**acceptable** *(SYN.)* passable, satisfactory, fair, adequate, standard, par, tolerable. *(ANT.) poor, substandard.*

**access** *(SYN.)* entrance, approach, course, gateway, door, avenue, gain, enter.

**accessible** *(SYN.)* nearby, attainable, achievable, affable, accommodating. *(ANT.) remote, unobtainable, unachievable, standoffish, forbidding, unfriendly.*

**accessory** *(SYN.)* extra, addition, assistant, supplement, contributory, accomplice.

**accident** *(SYN.)* casualty, disaster, misfortune, mishap, chance, calamity, contingency, fortuity, misadventure, mischance, injury, catastrophe. *(ANT.) purpose, intention, calculation.*

**accidental** *(SYN.)* unintended, chance, casual, fortuitous, contingent, unplanned, unexpected, unforeseen. *(ANT.) calculated, planned, willed, intended, intentional, deliberate.*

**acclaim** *(SYN.)* eminence, fame, glory, honor, reputation, credit, applaud, distinction, approve, notoriety. *(ANT.) infamy, obscurity, disapprove, reject, disrepute.*

**acclimated** *(SYN.)* adapted, habituated, acclimatized, accommodated, seasoned, inured, used to, weathered, reconciled.

**accolade** *(SYN.)* praise, honor, acclaim, recognition, applause, kudos, bouquet, crown, testimonial, acclamation, salute.

**accommodate** *(SYN.)* help, assist, aid, provide for, serve, oblige, hold, house. *(ANT.) inconvenience.*

**accommodating** *(SYN.)* obliging, helpful, willing,

kind, cooperative, gracious, cordial, sympathetic, unselfish. *(ANT.) unfriendly, selfish, hostile.*

**accommodation** *(SYN.)* change, alteration, adaptation, convenience, adjustment, acclimatization, aid, help, boon, kindness, service, courtesy. *(ANT.) inflexibility, rigidity, disservice, stubbornness, disadvantage.*

**accommodations** *(SYN.)* housing, lodgings, room, place, quarters, board.

**accompany** *(SYN.)* chaperon, consort with, escort, go with, associate with, attend, join. *(ANT.) abandon, quit, leave, desert, avoid, forsake.*

**accomplice** *(SYN.)* accessory, ally, associate, partner in crime, assistant, sidekick, confederate. *(ANT.) opponent, rival, enemy, adversary.*

**accomplish** *(SYN.)* attain, consummate, achieve, do, execute, carry out, fulfill, complete, effect, perform, finish. *(ANT.) fail, frustrate, spoil, neglect, defeat.*

**accomplished** *(SYN.)* proficient, skilled, finished, well-trained, gifted, masterly, polished, able. *(ANT.) unskilled, amateurish, crude.*

**accomplishment** *(SYN.)* deed, feat, statute, operation, performance, action, achievement, transaction. *(ANT.) cessation, inhibition, intention, deliberation.*

**accord** *(SYN.)* concur, agree, award, harmony, conformity, agreement, give, tale, sum, statement, record, grant.

**accordingly** *(SYN.)* consequently, therefore, whereupon, hence, so, thus.

**accost** *(SYN.)* approach, greet, speak to, address. *(ANT.) avoid, shun.*

**account** *(SYN.)* description, chronicle, history, narration, reckoning, rate, computation, detail, narrative, relation, recital, consider, believe, deem, record, explanation, report, tale, story, anecdote, reason, statement, tale, ledger.

**accountable** *(SYN.)* chargeable, answerable, beholden, responsible, obliged, liable.

**account for** *(SYN.)* justify, explain, substantiate, illuminate, clarify, elucidate.

**accredited** *(SYN.)* qualified, licensed, deputized, certified, commissioned, vouched for, empowered. *(ANT.) illicit, unofficial, unauthorized.*

**accrue** *(SYN.)* amass, collect,

heap, increase, accumulate, gather, hoard. *(ANT.) disperse, dissipate, waste, diminish.*

**accrued** *(SYN.)* accumulated, totaled, increased, added, enlarged, amassed.

**accumulate** *(SYN.)* gather, collect, heap, increase, accrue, assemble, compile, hoard, amass. *(ANT.) spend, give away, diminish, dissipate.*

**accumulation** *(SYN.)* heap, collection, pile, store, hoard, stack, aggregation.

**accurate** *(SYN.)* perfect, just, truthful, unerring, meticulous, correct. *(ANT.) incorrect, mistaken, false, wrong, inaccurate.*

**accursed** *(SYN.)* ill-fated, cursed, condemned, doomed, bedeviled, ruined. *(ANT.) fortunate, hopeful.*

**accusation** *(SYN.)* charge, incrimination, indictment, arraignment. *(ANT.) pardon, exoneration, absolve.*

**accuse** *(SYN.)* incriminate, indict, censure, tattle, denounce, charge, arraign, impeach, blame. *(ANT.) release, vindicate, exonerate, acquit, absolve, clear.*

**accustom** *(SYN.)* addict, familiarize, condition.

**accustomed** *(SYN.)* familiar with, used to, comfortable with. *(ANT.) strange, unusual, rare, unfamiliar.*

**ace** *(SYN.)* champion, hotshot, pip, one, secret, fighter pilot.

**acerbity** *(SYN.)* bitterness, harshness, unkindness, sourness, acidity, unfriendliness, acrimony, coldness, sharpness. *(ANT.) sweetness, gentleness, kindness, tenderness.*

**ache** *(SYN.)* hurt, pain, throb.

**achieve** *(SYN.)* do, execute, gain, obtain, acquire, accomplish, realize, perform, complete, accomplish, finish, fulfill, reach, attain, secure, procure. *(ANT.) fail, lose, fall short.*

**achievement** *(SYN.)* feat, accomplishment, attainment, exploit, realization, performance, completion, deed. *(ANT.) botch, dud, mess, omission, defeat, failure.*

**acid** *(SYN.)* tart, sour, bitter, mordant, biting. *(ANT.) base, pleasant, friendly, bland, mild, sweet.*

**acknowledge** *(SYN.)* allow, admit, concede, recognize, answer, grant, accept, receive. *(ANT.) reject, refuse, disavow, refute, deny.*

**acme** *(SYN.)* summit, top, zenith, peak, crown. *(ANT.)*

*bottom.*

**acquaint** (SYN.) inform, teach, enlighten, notify, tell.

**acquaintance** (SYN.) fellowship, friendship, cognizance, knowledge, intimacy, familiarity, companionship, associate, colleague, companion. (ANT.) *inexperience, unfamiliarity, ignorance.*

**acquiesce** (SYN.) submit, agree, concur, assent, comply, consent, succumb. (ANT.) *refuse, disagree, rebel, argue.*

**acquire** (SYN.) amass, attain, earn, get, procure, assimilate, obtain, secure, gain, appropriate. (ANT.) *surrender, lose, forego, forfeit.*

**acquirement** (SYN.) training, skill, learning, achievement, attainment, education, information.

**acquisition** (SYN.) procurement, gain, gift, purchase, proceeds, possession, grant.

**acquisitive** (SYN.) greedy, avid, hoarding, covetous.

**acquit** (SYN.) forgive, exonerate, absolve, cleanse, pardon, excuse, discharge, found not guilty. (ANT.) *doom, saddle, sentence, condemn.*

**acrid** (SYN.) bitter, sharp, nasty, stinging, harsh. (ANT.) *pleasant, sweet.*

**acrimonious** (SYN.) sharp, sarcastic, acerb, waspish, cutting, stinging, testy. (ANT.) *soft, kind, sweet, pleasant, soothing.*

**acrobat** (SYN.) athlete, gymnast.

**act** (SYN.) deed, doing, feat, execution, accomplishment, performance, action, operation, transaction, law, decree, statute, edict, achievement, exploit, statute, judgment, routine, pretense. (ANT.) *inactivity, deliberation, cessation.*

**acting** (SYN.) behaving, performing, pretending, officiating, substituting, surrogate, temporary, delegated.

**action** (SYN.) deed, achievement, feat, activity, exploit, movement, motion, behavior, battle, performance, exercise. (ANT.) *idleness, inertia, repose, inactivity, rest.*

**activate** (SYN.) mobilize, energize, start, propel. (ANT.) *paralyze, immobilize, stop, deaden.*

**active** (SYN.) working, operative, alert, agile, nimble, supple, sprightly, busy, brisk, lively, quick, industrious, energetic, vigorous, industrious, occupied, vivacious, dynamic,

engaged. (ANT.) *passive, inactive, idle, dormant, lazy, lethargic.*

**activism** (SYN.) engagement, confrontation, agitation, commitment, aggression, fervor, zeal. (ANT.) *detachment, lethargy, disengagement.*

**activist** (SYN.) militant, doer, enthusiast.

**activity** (SYN.) action, liveliness, motion, vigor, agility, exercise, energy, quickness, enterprise, movement, briskness. (ANT.) *idleness, inactivity, dullness, sloth.*

**actor** (SYN.) performer, trouper, entertainer, thespian.

**actual** (SYN.) true, genuine, certain, factual, authentic, concrete, real. (ANT.) *unreal, fake, bogus, nonexistent, false.*

**actuality** (SYN.) reality, truth, deed, occurrence, fact, certainty. (ANT.) *theory, fiction, falsehood, supposition.*

**acute** (SYN.) piercing, severe, sudden, keen, sharp, perceptive, discerning, shrewd, astute, smart, intelligent. (ANT.) *bland, mild, dull, obtuse, insensitive.*

**adamant** (SYN.) unyielding, firm, obstinate. (ANT.) *yielding.*

**adapt** (SYN.) adjust, conform, accommodate, change, fit, alter, vary, modify. (ANT.) *misapply, disturb.*

**add** (SYN.) attach, increase, total, append, sum, affix, augment, adjoin, put together, unite, supplement. (ANT.) *remove, reduce, deduct, subtract, detach, withdraw.*

**address** (SYN.) greet, hail, accost, speak to, location, residence, home, abode, dwelling, speech, lecture, greeting, oration, presentation. (ANT.) *avoid, pass by.*

**adept** (SYN.) expert, skillful, proficient. (ANT.) *unskillful.*

**adequate** (SYN.) capable, commensurate, fitting, satisfactory, sufficient, enough, ample, suitable, plenty, fit. (ANT.) *lacking, scant, insufficient, inadequate.*

**adhere** (SYN.) stick fast, grasp, hold, keep, retain, cling, stick to, keep, cleave. (ANT.) *surrender, abandon, release, separate, loosen.*

**adherent** (SYN.) follower, supporter. (ANT.) *renegade, dropout, defector.*

**adjacent** (SYN.) next to, near, bordering, adjoining, touching, neighboring. (ANT.) *separate, distant, apart.*

**adjoin** (SYN.) connect, be

close to, affix, attach. (ANT.) *detach, remove,*

**adjoining** (SYN.) touching, bordering, next to, close to. (ANT.) *distant, remote, separate.*

**adjourn** (SYN.) postpone, defer, delay, suspend, discontinue, put off. (ANT.) *begin, convene, assemble.*

**adjust** (SYN.) repair, fix, change, set, regulate, settle, arrange, adapt, suit, accommodate, modify, vary, alter, fit.

**administer** (SYN.) supervise, oversee, direct, manage, rule, govern, control, conduct, provide, give, execute, preside, apply, contribute, help.

**administration** (SYN.) conduct, direction, management, supervision.

**admirable** (SYN.) worthy, fine, praiseworthy, commendable, excellent.

**admiration** (SYN.) pleasure, wonder, esteem, approval. (ANT.) *disdain, disrespect, contempt.*

**admire** (SYN.) approve, venerate, appreciate, respect, revere, esteem, like. (ANT.) *abhor, dislike, despise, loathe, detest, hate.*

**admissible** (SYN.) fair, justifiable, tolerable, allowable, permissible. (ANT.) *unsuitable, unfair, inadmissible.*

**admission** (SYN.) access, admittance, entrance, pass, ticket. (ANT.) *denial.*

**admit** (SYN.) allow, assent, permit, acknowledge, welcome, concede, agree, confess, accept, grant. (ANT.) *deny, dismiss, shun, obstruct.*

**admittance** (SYN.) access, entry, entrance. (ANT.) *refusal.*

**admonish** (SYN.) caution, advise against, warn, rebuke, reprove, censure. (ANT.) *glorify, praise.*

**admonition** (SYN.) advice, warning, caution, reminder, tip.

**ado** (SYN.) trouble, other, fuss, bustle, activity, excitement, commotion, action, upset, confusion, turmoil. (ANT.) *tranquillity.*

**adolescent** (SYN.) young, youthful, immature, teenage. (ANT.) *grown, mature, adult.*

**adoration** (SYN.) veneration, reverence, glorification, worship, homage.

**adore** (SYN.) revere, venerate, idolize, respect, love, cherish, esteem, honor. (ANT.) *loathe, hate, despise.*

**adorn** (SYN.) trim, bedeck, decorate, ornament, beautify, embellish, glamorize, enhance, garnish. (ANT.) *mar, deform, deface, strip, bare.*

**adrift** (SYN.) floating, afloat, drifting, aimless, purposeless, unsettled. (ANT.) *purposeful, stable, secure, well organized.*

**adroit** (SYN.) adept, apt, dexterous, skillful, clever, ingenious, expert. (ANT.) *awkward, clumsy, graceless, unskillful, oafish.*

**adult** (SYN.) full-grown, mature, grown-up. (ANT.) *infantile, immature, baby, child.*

**advance** (SYN.) further, promote, bring forward, propound, proceed, aggrandize, elevate, improve, adduce, propose, progress, move, advancement, improvement, promotion, upgrade. (ANT.) *retard, retreat, hinder, revert, withdraw, flee, retardation.*

**advantage** (SYN.) edge, profit, superiority, benefit, leverage, favor, vantage, gain. (ANT.) *handicap, impediment, obstruction, disadvantage, detriment, hindrance, loss.*

**adventure** (SYN.) undertaking, occurrence, enterprise, happening, event, project, incident, exploit.

**adventurous** (SYN.) daring, enterprising, rash, bold, chivalrous. (ANT.) *cautious, timid, hesitating.*

**adversary** (SYN.) foe, enemy, contestant, opponent, antagonist. (ANT.) *ally, friend.*

**adverse** (SYN.) hostile, counteractive, unfavorable, opposed, disastrous, contrary, antagonistic, opposite, unlucky, unfriendly, unfortunate. (ANT.) *favorable, propitious, fortunate, friendly, beneficial.*

**adversity** (SYN.) misfortune, trouble, calamity, distress, hardship, disaster. (ANT.) *benefit, happiness.*

**advertise** (SYN.) promote, publicize, make known, announce, promulgate.

**advertisement** (SYN.) commercial, billboard, want ad, handbill, flyer, poster, brochure, blurb.

**advice** (SYN.) counsel, instruction, suggestion, warning, information, caution, exhortation, admonition, recommendation, plan, tip, guidance, opinion.

**advisable** (SYN.) wise, sensible, prudent, suitable, fit, proper, fitting. (ANT.) ill-considered, imprudent, inadvisable.

**advise** (SYN.) recommend, suggest, counsel, caution, warn, admonish.

**adviser** (SYN.) coach, guide, mentor, counselor.

**advocate** (SYN.) defend, recommend, support, defender, proponent, lawyer. (ANT.) opponent, adversary, oppose.

**aesthetic** (SYN.) literary, artistic, sensitive, tasteful, well-composed. (ANT.) tasteless, crude, barbaric.

**affable** (SYN.) pleasant, courteous, sociable, friendly, amiable, gracious, approachable, communicative. (ANT.) unfriendly, unsociable.

**affair** (SYN.) event, occasion, happening, party, occurrence, matter, festivity, business, concern, liaison, infidelity.

**affect** (SYN.) alter, modify, concern, regard, move, touch, feign, pretend, influence, sway, transform, change, impress.

**affected** (SYN.) pretended, fake, sham, false, pretentious.

**affection** (SYN.) fondness, kindness, emotion, love, feeling, tenderness, attachment, endearment, liking, friendliness, warmth. (ANT.) aversion, indifference, repulsion, hatred, repugnance, dislike, antipathy.

**affectionate** (SYN.) warm, loving, tender, fond, attached. (ANT.) distant, unfeeling, cold.

**affirm** (SYN.) assert, aver, declare, swear, maintain, endorse, certify, state, ratify, pronounce, say, confirm, establish. (ANT.) deny, dispute, oppose, contradict, demur, disclaim.

**afflict** (SYN.) trouble, disturb, bother, agitate, perturb. (ANT.) soothe.

**affliction** (SYN.) distress, grief, misfortune, trouble, illness. (ANT.) relief, benefit, easement.

**affluent** (SYN.) wealthy, prosperous, rich, abundant, ample, plentiful, bountiful, well-to-do. (ANT.) poor, destitute.

**afford** (SYN.) provide, supply, yield, furnish, manage to buy.

**affront** (SYN.) offense, slur, slight, provocation, insult. (ANT.) compliment.

**afraid** (SYN.) scared, fainthearted, frightened, timid, fearful, apprehensive, cowardly, terrified. (ANT.) assured, composed, courageous,

bold, confident.

**after** (SYN.) following, subsequently, behind, next. (ANT.) before.

**again** (SYN.) anew, repeatedly, afresh.

**against** (SYN.) versus, hostile, opposed to, in disagreement, touching. (ANT.) pro, with, for, promoting.

**age** (SYN.) antiquity, date, period, generation, time, senility, grow old, senescence, mature, dotage, ripen, mature, era, epoch. (ANT.) youth, childhood.

**aged** (SYN.) ancient, elderly, old. (ANT.) youthful, young.

**agency** (SYN.) office, operation.

**agent** (SYN.) performer, doer, worker, operator, instrument, manager.

**aggravate** (SYN.) intensify, magnify, annoy, irritate, increase, nettle, irk, vex, provoke, embitter, worsen. (ANT.) soften, appease, pacify, mitigate, ease, relieve.

**aggregate** (SYN.) collection, entirety, sum, accumulate, total, compile, conglomeration. (ANT.) part, unit, ingredient, element.

**aggression** (SYN.) anger, assault, attack, invasion, offense. (ANT.) defense.

**aggressive** (SYN.) hostile, offensive, belligerent, attacking, militant, pugnacious. (ANT.) timid, withdrawn, passive, peaceful.

**aghast** (SYN.) surprised, astonished, astounded, awed, thunderstruck, flabbergasted, bewildered.

**agile** (SYN.) nimble, graceful, lively, active, alert, fast, quick, athletic, spry. (ANT.) inept, awkward, clumsy.

**agility** (SYN.) quickness, vigor, liveliness, energy, activity, motion. (ANT.) dullness, inertia, idleness, inactivity.

**agitate** (SYN.) disturb, excite, perturb, rouse, shake, arouse, disconcert, instigate, inflame, provoke, jar, incite, shake, stir up, toss. (ANT.) calm, placate, quiet, ease, soothe, steady.

**agitated** (SYN.) jumpy, jittery, nervous, restless, restive, upset, disturbed, ruffled.

**agony** (SYN.) anguish, misery, pain, suffering, torture, ache, distress, throe, woe, torment, grief. (ANT.) relief, ease, comfort.

**agree** (SYN.) comply, coincide, conform, concur, assent, accede, tally, settle, harmonize, unite, yield, consent.

(ANT.) differ, disagree, protest, contradict, argue, refuse.

**agreeable** (SYN.) amiable, charming, gratifying, pleasant, suitable, pleasurable, welcome, pleasing, acceptable, friendly, cooperative.

**agreement** (SYN.) harmony, understanding, unison, contract, pact, stipulation, alliance, deal, bargain, treaty, contract, arrangement, settlement, accord, concord. (ANT.) variance, dissension, discord, disagreement, difference.

**agriculture** (SYN.) farming, gardening, tillage, husbandry, cultivation, agronomy.

**ahead** (SYN.) before, leading, forward, winning, advanced. (ANT.) behind.

**aid** (SYN.) help, remedy, assist, helper, service, support, assistant, relief. (ANT.) obstruct, hinder, obstacle, impede, hindrance.

**ail** (SYN.) bother, trouble, perturb, disturb, suffer.

**ailing** (SYN.) sick, ill. (ANT.) hearty, hale, well.

**ailment** (SYN.) illness, disease, affliction, sickness.

**aim** (SYN.) direction, point, goal, object, target, direct, try, intend, intention, end, objective.

**aimless** (SYN.) directionless, adrift, purposeless.

**air** (SYN.) atmosphere, oxygen, display, reveal, expose, publicize. (ANT.) conceal, hide.

**airy** (SYN.) breezy, light, gay, lighthearted, graceful, fanciful, exposed.

**aisle** (SYN.) corridor, passageway, lane, alley, opening.

**ajar** (SYN.) slightly open.

**akin** (SYN.) alike, related, connected, similar, affiliated, allied.

**alarm** (SYN.) frighten, signal, warning, terror, apprehension, affright, consternation, fear, siren, arouse, startle, bell. (ANT.) tranquility, composure, security, quiet, calm, soothe, comfort.

**alarming** (SYN.) shocking, appalling, daunting. (ANT.) comforting, calming, soothing.

**alcoholic** (SYN.) sot, drunkard, tippler, inebriate.

**alert** (SYN.) attentive, keen, clear-witted, ready, nimble, vigilant, watchful, observant. (ANT.) logy, sluggish, dulled, listless.

**alias** (SYN.) anonym, assumed name.

**alibi** (SYN.) story, excuse.

**alien** (SYN.) foreigner,

stranger, remote, strange, different, extraneous. (ANT.) germane, kindred, relevant, akin, familiar, accustomed.

**alight** (SYN.) land, debark, disembark. (ANT.) embark, board.

**alive** (SYN.) living, existing, breathing, live, lively, vivacious, animated. (ANT.) inactive, dead, moribund.

**allay** (SYN.) soothe, check, lessen, calm, lighten, relieve, soften, moderate, quiet. (ANT.) intensify, worsen, arouse.

**allege** (SYN.) testify, affirm, cite, claim, declare, maintain, state, assert. (ANT.) deny, disprove, refute, contradict, gainsay.

**allegiance** (SYN.) faithfulness, duty.

**allegory** (SYN.) fable, fiction, myth, saga, parable, legend. (ANT.) history, fact.

**alleviate** (SYN.) diminish, soothe, solace, abate, assuage, allay, soften, mitigate, extenuate, relieve, case, slacken, relax, weaken. (ANT.) increase, aggravate, augment, irritate.

**alley** (SYN.) footway, byway, path, passageway, aisle, corridor, opening, lane.

**alliance** (SYN.) combination, partnership, union, treaty, coalition, association, confederacy, marriage, pact, agreement, relation, interrelation, understanding, relationship. (ANT.) separation, divorce, schism.

**allot** (SYN.) divide, mete, assign, give, measure, distribute, allocate, share, grant, dispense, deal, apportion. (ANT.) withhold, retain, keep, confiscate, refuse.

**allow** (SYN.) authorize, grant, acknowledge, admit, let, permit, sanction, consent, concede, mete, allocate. (ANT.) resist, refuse, forbid, object, prohibit.

**allowance** (SYN.) grant, fee, portion, ration, allotment.

**allude** (SYN.) intimate, refer, insinuate, hint, advert, suggest, imply, mention. (ANT.) demonstrate, specify, state, declare.

**allure** (SYN.) attract, fascinate, tempt, charm, infatuate, captivate. (ANT.) repulse.

**ally** (SYN.) accomplice, associate, confederate, abettor, assistant, friend, partner. (ANT.) rival, enemy, opponent, foe, adversary.

**almighty** (SYN.) omnipotent,

powerful.

**almost** (SYN.) somewhat, nearly. (ANT.) completely, absolutely.

**alms** (SYN.) dole, charity, donation, contribution.

**aloft** (SYN.) overhead.

**alone** (SYN.) desolate, unaided, only, isolated, lone, secluded, lonely, deserted, solitary, single, apart, solo, separate. (ANT.) surrounded, attended, accompanied, together.

**aloof** (SYN.) uninterested, uninvolved, apart, away, remote, unsociable, standoffish, separate, distant. (ANT.) warm, outgoing, friendly, cordial.

**also** (SYN.) in addition, likewise, too, besides, furthermore, moreover, further.

**alter** (SYN.) adjust, vary, deviate, modify, change. (ANT.) maintain, preserve, keep.

**alteration** (SYN.) difference, adjustment, change, modification. (ANT.) maintenance, preservation.

**altercation** (SYN.) controversy, dispute, argument, quarrel.

**alternate** (SYN.) rotate, switch, spell, interchange. (ANT.) fix.

**alternative** (SYN.) substitute, selection, option, choice, replacement, possibility.

**although** (SYN.) though, even if, even though, despite.

**altitude** (SYN.) elevation, height. (ANT.) depth.

**altogether** (SYN.) totally, wholly, quite, entirely, thoroughly, completely. (ANT.) partly.

**altruism** (SYN.) benevolence, philanthropy, kindness, tenderness, generosity, charity, liberality. (ANT.) selfishness, unkindness, cruelty.

**always** (SYN.) evermore, forever, perpetually, ever, unceasingly, continually, constantly, eternally, everlastingly. (ANT.) never, rarely, sometimes, occasionally.

**amalgamate** (SYN.) fuse, unify, unite, commingle, merge, blend, combine, consolidate. (ANT.) decompose, disintegrate, separate.

**amass** (SYN.) collect, accumulate, heap up, gather, increase, compile, assemble, store up. (ANT.) disperse, dissipate, spend.

**amateur** (SYN.) beginner, dilettante, learner, dabbler, neophyte, apprentice, novice, nonprofessional, tyro. (ANT.) expert, master, adept,

professional, authority.

**amaze** (SYN.) surprise, flabbergast, stun, dumb-found, astound, bewilder, aghast, thunderstruck, astonish. (ANT.) bore, disinterest, tire.

**ambiguous** (SYN.) vague, uncertain, obscure, dubious, equivocal, unclear, deceptive. (ANT.) plain, clear, explicit, obvious, unequivocal, unmistakable, certain.

**ambition** (SYN.) eagerness, goal, incentive, aspiration, yearning, longing, desire. (ANT.) indifference, satisfaction, indolence, resignation.

**ambitious** (SYN.) aspiring, intent upon. (ANT.) indifferent, content.

**amble** (SYN.) saunter, stroll.

**ambush** (SYN.) trap, surprise, hiding place.

**amend** (SYN.) change, mend, better, correct, improve. (ANT.) worsen.

**amends** (SYN.) compensation, restitution, payment, reparation, remedy, redress.

**amiable** (SYN.) friendly, good-natured, gracious, pleasing, agreeable, outgoing, pleasant. (ANT.) surly, hateful, churlish, disagreeable, ill-natured, ill-tempered, cross, captious, touchy.

**amid** (SYN.) among, amidst, surrounded by.

**amiss** (SYN.) wrongly, improperly, astray, awry. (ANT.) properly, rightly, correct.

**ammunition** (SYN.) shot, powder, shells, bullets.

**among** (SYN.) between, mingled, amidst, amid, betwixt, surrounded by. (ANT.) separate, apart.

**amorous** (SYN.) amatory, affectionate, romantic.

**amount** (SYN.) sum, total, quantity, number, price, value, measure.

**ample** (SYN.) plentiful, large, profuse, spacious, copious, liberal, full, bountiful, abundant, great, extensive, generous, wide, enough, sufficient, roomy. (ANT.) limited, insufficient, meager, small, lacking, cramped, confined, inadequate.

**amplification** (SYN.) magnification, growth, waxing, accrual, enhancement, enlargement, heightening, increase. (ANT.) decrease, diminishing, reduction, contraction.

**amplify** (SYN.) make louder, broaden, develop, expand, enlarge, extend. (ANT.) confine, restrict, abridge, narrow.

**amuse** (SYN.) divert, please, delight, entertain, charm. (ANT.) tire, bore.

**amusement** (SYN.) diversion, pastime, entertainment, pleasure, enjoyment, recreation. (ANT.) tedium, boredom.

**amusing** (SYN.) pleasant, funny, pleasing, entertaining, comical. (ANT.) tiring, tedious, boring.

**analogous** (SYN.) comparable, corresponding, like, similar, correspondent, alike, correlative, parallel, allied, akin. (ANT.) different, opposed, incongruous.

**analysis** (SYN.) examination, separation, investigation.

**analyze** (SYN.) examine, explain, investigate, separate.

**ancestral** (SYN.) hereditary, inherited.

**ancestry** (SYN.) family, line, descent, lineage. (ANT.) posterity.

**anchor** (SYN.) fix, attach, secure, fasten. (ANT.) detach, free, loosen.

**ancient** (SYN.) aged, old-fashioned, archaic, elderly, antique, old, primitive. (ANT.) new, recent, current, fresh.

**anecdote** (SYN.) account, narrative, story, tale.

**anesthetic** (SYN.) opiate, narcotic, sedative, painkiller, analgesic.

**angel** (SYN.) cherub, archangel, seraph. (ANT.) demon, devil.

**angelic** (SYN.) pure, lovely, heavenly, good, virtuous, innocent, godly, saintly. (ANT.) devilish.

**anger** (SYN.) exasperation, fury, ire, passion, rage, resentment, temper, indignation, animosity, irritation, wrath, displeasure, infuriate, arouse, nettle, annoyance, exasperate. (ANT.) forbearance, patience, peace, self-control.

**angry** (SYN.) provoked, wrathful, furious, enraged, incensed, exasperated, maddened, indignant, irate, mad, inflamed. (ANT.) pleased, calm, satisfied, content, tranquil.

**anguish** (SYN.) suffering, torment, torture, distress, pain, heartache, grief, agony, misery. (ANT.) solace, relief, joy, comfort, peace, ecstasy, pleasure.

**animal** (SYN.) beast, creature.

**animate** (SYN.) vitalize, invigorate, stimulate, enliven, alive, vital, vigorous. (ANT.)

dead, inanimate.

**animated** (SYN.) gay, lively, spry, vivacious, active, vigorous, chipper, snappy. (ANT.) inactive.

**animosity** (SYN.) grudge, hatred, rancor, spite, bitterness, enmity, opposition, dislike, hostility, antipathy. (ANT.) goodwill, love, friendliness, kindliness.

**annex** (SYN.) join, attach, add, addition, wing, append.

**annihilate** (SYN.) destroy, demolish, end, wreck, abolish, erase.

**announce** (SYN.) proclaim, give out, make known, notify, publish, report, herald, promulgate, advertise, broadcast, state, tell, declare, publicize. (ANT.) conceal, withhold, suppress, bury, stifle.

**announcement** (SYN.) notification, report, declaration, bulletin, advertisement, broadcast, message.

**annoy** (SYN.) bother, irk, pester, tease, trouble, vex, disturb, inconvenience, molest, irritate, harry, harass. (ANT.) console, gratify, soothe, accommodate, please, calm, comfort.

**annually** (SYN.) yearly.

**anoint** (SYN.) baptize, besprinkle, purify.

**answer** (SYN.) reply, rejoinder, response, retort, rebuttal, respond. (ANT.) summoning, argument, questioning, inquiry, query, ask, inquire.

**antagonism** (SYN.) opposition, conflict, enmity, hostility, animosity. (ANT.) geniality, cordiality, friendliness.

**antagonist** (SYN.) adversary, rival, enemy, foe, opponent. (ANT.) ally, friend.

**antagonize** (SYN.) provoke, counter, oppose, embitter. (ANT.) soothe.

**anthology** (SYN.) treasury, collection.

**anticipate** (SYN.) await, foresee, forecast, hope for, expect.

**anticipated** (SYN.) expected, foresight, hoped, preconceived. (ANT.) dreaded, reared, worried, doubted.

**antics** (SYN.) horseplay, fun, merrymaking, pranks, capers, tricks, clowning.

**antipathy** (SYN.) hatred. (ANT.) sympathy.

**antiquated** (SYN.) old, outdated, old-fashioned.

**antique** (SYN.) rarity, curio, old, ancient, old-fashioned, archaic, out-of-date. (ANT.) new, recent, fresh.

**anxiety** (SYN.) care, disquiet, fear, concern, solicitude, trouble, worry, apprehension, uneasiness, distress, foreboding. (ANT.) nonchalance, assurance, confidence, contentment, peacefulness, placidity, tranquillity.

**anxious** (SYN.) troubled, uneasy, perturbed, apprehensive, worried, concerned, desirous, bothered, agitated, eager, fearful. (ANT.) tranquil, calm, peaceful.

**anyway** (SYN.) nevertheless, anyhow.

**apartment** (SYN.) suite, flat, dormitory.

**apathy** (SYN.) unconcern, indifference, lethargy. (ANT.) interest, feeling.

**aperture** (SYN.) opening, gap, pore, cavity, chasm, abyss, hole, void. (ANT.) connection, bridge, link.

**apex** (SYN.) acme, peak, tip, summit, crown, top.

**apologize** (SYN.) ask forgiveness.

**apology** (SYN.) defense, excuse, confession, justification, alibi, explanation, plea. (ANT.) denial, complaint, dissimulation, accusation.

**apostate** (SYN.) unbeliever, nonconformist, dissenter, heretic, schismatic. (ANT.) saint, conformist, believer.

**appall** (SYN.) shock, stun, dismay, frighten, terrify, horrify. (ANT.) edify, please.

**appalling** (SYN.) fearful, frightful, ghastly, horrid, repulsive, terrible, dire, awful. (ANT.) fascinating, beautiful, enchanting, enjoyable.

**apparatus** (SYN.) rig, equipment, furnishings, gear, tackle.

**apparel** (SYN.) clothing, attire, garb, garments, dress, robes.

**apparent** (SYN.) obvious, plain, self-evident, clear, manifest, transparent, unmistakable, palpable, unambiguous, ostensible, visible, seeming, evident, understandable, illusory. (ANT.) uncertain, indistinct, dubious, hidden, mysterious.

**apparition** (SYN.) illusion, ghost, phantom, vision, fantasy, dream.

**appeal** (SYN.) plea, petition, request, entreaty, plead, beseech, beg, attract. (ANT.) repulse, repel.

**appear** (SYN.) look, arrive, emanate, emerge, arise, seem, turn up. (ANT.) vanish, withdraw, exist, disappear, evaporate.

**appearance** (SYN.) advent,

arrival, aspect, demeanor, fashion, guise, apparition, manner, mien, look, presence. (ANT.) disappearance, reality, departure, vanishing.

**appease** (SYN.) calm, compose, lull, quiet, relieve, assuage, pacify, satisfy, restraint, lessen, soothe, check, ease, alleviate, still, allay, tranquilize. (ANT.) excite, amuse, incense, irritate, inflame.

**append** (SYN.) supplement, attach, add.

**appendage** (SYN.) addition, tail, supplement.

**appetite** (SYN.) zest, craving, desire, liking, longing, stomach, inclination, hunger, thirst, relish, passion. (ANT.) satiety, disgust, distaste, repugnance.

**appetizer** (SYN.) hors d'oeuvre.

**applaud** (SYN.) cheer, clap, hail, approve, praise, acclaim. (ANT.) disapprove, denounce, reject, criticize, condemn.

**appliance** (SYN.) machine, tool, instrument, device, utensil, implement.

**applicable** (SYN.) fitting, suitable, proper, fit, usable, appropriate, suited. (ANT.) inappropriate, inapplicable.

**apply** (SYN.) affix, allot, appropriate, use, employ, petition, request, devote, avail, pertain, attach, ask, administer, petition, assign, relate, utilize. (ANT.) give away, demand, detach, neglect, ignore.

**appoint** (SYN.) name, choose, nominate, designate, elect, establish, assign, place. (ANT.) discharge, fire, dismiss.

**appointment** (SYN.) rendezvous, meeting, designation, position, engagement, assignment. (ANT.) discharge, dismissal.

**appraise** (SYN.) value, evaluate, place a value on.

**appreciate** (SYN.) enjoy, regard, value, prize, cherish, admire, go up, improve, rise, respect, esteem, appraise. (ANT.) belittle, misunderstand, apprehend, degrade, scorn, depreciate, undervalue.

**apprehend** (SYN.) seize, capture, arrest, understand, dread, fear, grasp, perceive. (ANT.) release, lose.

**apprehension** (SYN.) misgiving, fear, dread, uneasiness, worry, fearfulness, anticipation, capture, seizure. (ANT.) confidence, composure, self-assuredness.

**apprehensive** (SYN.)

worried, afraid, uneasy, bothered, anxious, concerned, perturbed, troubled, fearful. (ANT.) relaxed.

**apprentice** (SYN.) amateur, recruit, novice, learner, beginner. (ANT.) experienced, professional, master.

**approach** (SYN.) greet, inlet, come near, advance, access, passageway. (ANT.) avoid, pass by, retreat.

**appropriate** (SYN.) apt, particular, proper, fitting, suitable, applicable, loot, pillage, purloin, rob, steal, embezzle, assign, becoming, apportion, authorize. (ANT.) improper, contrary, inappropriate, buy, repay, restore, return, unfit, inapt.

**approval** (SYN.) commendation, consent, praise, approbation, sanction, assent, endorsement, support. (ANT.) reproach, censure, reprimand, disapprove.

**approve** (SYN.) like, praise, authorize, confirm, endorse, appreciate, ratify, commend, sanction. (ANT.) criticize, nullify, disparage, frown on, disapprove, deny.

**approximate** (SYN.) near, approach, roughly, close. (ANT.) absolute.

**apt** (SYN.) suitable, proper, appropriate, fit, suited, disposed, liable, inclined, prone, clever, bright, alert, intelligent, receptive. (ANT.) illbecoming, unsuitable, unlikely, slow, retarded, dense.

**aptitude** (SYN.) knack, talent, gift, ability.

**aptness** (SYN.) capability, dexterity, qualification, skill, ability, aptitude. (ANT.) incompetence, unreadiness, incapacity.

**aqueduct** (SYN.) gully, pipe, canal, waterway, channel.

**arbitrary** (SYN.) unrestricted, absolute, despotic, willful, unreasonable, unconditional, authoritative. (ANT.) contingent, qualified, fair, reasonable, dependent, accountable.

**arbitrate** (SYN.) referee, settle, mediate, umpire, negotiate.

**architecture** (SYN.) structure, building, construction.

**ardent** (SYN.) fervent, fiery, glowing, intense, keen, impassioned, fervid, hot, passionate, earnest, eager, zealous, enthusiastic. (ANT.) cool, indifferent, nonchalant, apathetic.

**ardor** (SYN.) enthusiasm, rapture, spirit, zeal, fervent,

eager, glowing, eagerness. (ANT.) unconcern, apathy, disinterest, indifference.

**arduous** (SYN.) laborious, hard, difficult, burdensome, strenuous, strained. (ANT.) easy.

**area** (SYN.) space, extent, region, zone, section, expanse, district, neighborhood, size.

**argue** (SYN.) plead, reason, wrangle, indicate, prove, show, dispute, denote, imply, object, bicker, discuss, debate, disagree. (ANT.) reject, spurn, ignore, overlook, agree, concur.

**argument** (SYN.) debate, dispute, discussion, controversy. (ANT.) harmony, accord, agreement.

**arid** (SYN.) waterless, dry, flat, dull, unimaginative, stuffy. (ANT.) fertile, wet, colorful.

**arise** (SYN.) enter, institute, originate, start, open, commence, emerge, appear. (ANT.) terminate, end, finish, complete, close.

**aristocrat** (SYN.) noble, gentleman, peer, lord, nobleman, bourgeoisie. (ANT.) peasant, commoner, proletariat.

**arm** (SYN.) weapon, defend, equip, empower, fortify.

**armistice** (SYN.) truce, pact, deal, understanding, peace, treaty, contract, alliance, agreement.

**army** (SYN.) troops, legion, military, forces, militia.

**aroma** (SYN.) smell, odor, fragrance, perfume, scent.

**arouse** (SYN.) stir, animate, move, pique, provoke, kindle, disturb, excite, foment, stimulate, awaken. (ANT.) settle, soothe, calm.

**arraign** (SYN.) charge, censure, incriminate, indict, accuse. (ANT.) acquit, release, vindicate, exonerate, absolve.

**arraignment** (SYN.) imputation, charge, accusation, incrimination. (ANT.) pardon, exonerate, exculpation.

**arrange** (SYN.) classify, assort, organize, place, plan, prepare, devise, adjust, dispose, regulate, order, group, settle, adapt, catalog, systematize, distribute, prepare. (ANT.) jumble, scatter, disorder, confuse, disturb, disarrange.

**arrangement** (SYN.) display, grouping, order, array, deal.

**array** (SYN.) dress, adorn, attire, clothe, arrange, order, distribute, display, exhibit. (ANT.) disorder, disorganization, disarray.

**arrest** (SYN.) detain, hinder, restrain, seize, withhold, stop, check, obstruct, apprehend, interrupt, catch, capture. *(ANT.) free, release, discharge, liberate.*

**arrival** *(SYN.)* advent, coming. *(ANT.) leaving, departure.*

**arrive** *(SYN.)* come, emerge, reach, visit, land, appear. *(ANT.) exit, leave, depart, go.*

**arrogance** *(SYN.)* pride, insolence. *(ANT.) humbleness, modest, humility.*

**arrogant** *(SYN.)* insolent, prideful, scornful, haughty, cavalier, proud. *(ANT.) modest, humble.*

**art** *(SYN.)* cunning, tact, artifice, skill, aptitude, adroitness, painting, drawing, design, craft, dexterity, composition, ingenuity. *(ANT.) clumsiness, innocence, unskillfulness, honesty.*

**artery** *(SYN.)* aqueduct, pipe, channel.

**artful** *(SYN.)* clever, sly, skillful, knowing, deceitful, tricky, crafty, cunning. *(ANT.) artless.*

**article** *(SYN.)* story, composition, treatise, essay, thing, report, object.

**artifice** *(SYN.)* trick, clever, scheme, device.

**artificial** *(SYN.)* bogus, fake, affected, feigned, phony, sham, unreal, synthetic, assumed, counterfeit, unnatural, man-made, unreal, manufactured, false, feigned, pretended. *(ANT.) genuine, natural, true, real, authentic.*

**artisan** *(SYN.)* worker, craftsman, mechanic.

**artist** *(SYN.)* actor, actress, painter, sculptor, singer, designer.

**artless** *(SYN.)* innocent, open, frank, simple, honest, candid, natural, unskilled, ignorant, truthful, sincere. *(ANT.) artful.*

**ascend** *(SYN.)* rise, scale, tower, mount, go up. *(ANT.) fall, sink, descend, go down.*

**ascertain** *(SYN.)* solve, learn, clear up, answer.

**ascribe** *(SYN.)* attribute, assign.

**ashamed** *(SYN.)* shamefaced, humiliated, abashed, mortified, embarrassed. *(ANT.) proud.*

**ask** *(SYN.)* invite, request, inquire, query, question, beg, solicit, demand, entreat, claim, interrogate, charge, expect. *(ANT.) order, reply, insist, answer.*

**askance** *(SYN.)* sideways.

**askew** *(SYN.)* disorderly, crooked, awry, twisted.

*(ANT.) straight.*

**asleep** *(SYN.)* inactive, sleeping, dormant. *(ANT.) alert, awake.*

**aspect** *(SYN.)* appearance, look, view, outlook, attitude, viewpoint, phase, part, feature, side.

**aspersion** *(SYN.)* dishonor, insult, misuse, outrage, reproach, defamation, abuse, disparagement. *(ANT.) plaudit, respect, approval.*

**asphyxiate** *(SYN.)* suffocate, stifle, smother, choke, strangle, throttle.

**aspiration** *(SYN.)* craving, desire, hope, longing, objective, passion, ambition.

**aspire** *(SYN.)* seek, aim, wish for, strive, desire, yearn for.

**ass** *(SYN.)* mule, donkey, burro, silly, dunce, stubborn, stupid, fool.

**assail** *(SYN.)* assault, attack.

**assassinate** *(SYN.)* purge, kill, murder.

**assault** *(SYN.)* invade, strike, attack, assail, charge, bombard, onslaught. *(ANT.) protect, defend.*

**assemble** *(SYN.)* collect, gather, meet, congregate, connect, manufacture. *(ANT.) disperse, disassemble, scatter.*

**assembly** *(SYN.)* legislature, congress, council, parliament.

**assent** *(SYN.)* consent to, concede, agree, approval, accept, comply, permission. *(ANT.) deny, dissent, refusal, denial, refuse.*

**assert** *(SYN.)* declare, maintain, state, claim, express, defend, press, support, aver, uphold, consent, accept, comply, affirm, allege, emphasize. *(ANT.) deny, refute, contradict, decline.*

**assertion** *(SYN.)* statement, affirmation, declaration. *(ANT.) contradiction, denial.*

**assess** *(SYN.)* calculate, compute, estimate, levy, reckon, tax, appraise.

**asset** *(SYN.)* property, wealth, capitol, resources, goods.

**assign** *(SYN.)* apportion, ascribe, attribute, cast, allot, chose, appropriate, name, elect, appoint, distribute, designate, specify. *(ANT.) release, relieve, unburden, discharge.*

**assignment** *(SYN.)* task, job, responsibility, duty.

**assimilate** *(SYN.)* digest, absorb, blot up.

**assist** *(SYN.)* help, promote, serve, support, sustain, abet, aid, back. *(ANT.) prevent, impede, hamper.*

**assistance** *(SYN.)* backing, help, patronage, relief, succor, support. *(ANT.) hostility, resistance, antagonism, counteraction.*

**assistant** *(SYN.)* accomplice, ally, associate, confederate, abettor. *(ANT.) rival, enemy, adversary.*

**associate** *(SYN.)* affiliate, ally, join, connect, unite, combine, link, mingle, partner, mix. *(ANT.) separate, disconnect, divide, disrupt, estrange.*

**association** *(SYN.)* organization, club, union, society, fraternity, sorority, companionship, fellowship.

**assorted** *(SYN.)* varied, miscellaneous, classified, different, several, grouped, various. *(ANT.) alike, same.*

**assortment** *(SYN.)* collection, variety, mixture, conglomeration.

**assuage** *(SYN.)* calm, quiet, lessen, relieve, ease, allay, moderate, alleviate, restrain.

**assume** *(SYN.)* arrogate, affect, suspect, believe, appropriate, take, pretend, usurp, simulate, understand, postulate, presume, suppose. *(ANT.) doff, demonstrate, prove, grant, concede.*

**assumption** *(SYN.)* presumption, guess, supposition, conjecture, postulate.

**assure** *(SYN.)* promise, convince, warrant, guarantee, pledge. *(ANT.) equivocate, deny.*

**astonish** *(SYN.)* astound, amaze, surprise, shock. *(ANT.) tire, bore.*

**astound** *(SYN.)* shock, amaze, astonish, stun, surprise, floor.

**asunder** *(SYN.)* divided, separate, apart. *(ANT.) together.*

**asylum** *(SYN.)* shelter, refuge, home, madhouse, institution.

**athletic** *(SYN.)* strong, active, able-bodied, gymnastic, muscular, well-built.

**atone** *(SYN.)* repay, make up.

**atrocious** *(SYN.)* horrible, savage, brutal, ruthless, dreadful, awful, horrifying. *(ANT.) good, kind.*

**attach** *(SYN.)* connect, adjoin, annex, join, append, stick, unite, affix. *(ANT.) unfasten, separate, disengage.*

**attack** *(SYN.)* raid, assault, besiege, abuse, censure, offense, siege, denunciation, aggression, push, criticism, invade. *(ANT.) surrender, defense, opposition, aid, defend, protect, repel.*

**attain** *(SYN.)* achieve, acquire, accomplish, gain, get, reach,

win. *(ANT.) discard, abandon, desert.*

**attainment** *(SYN.)* exploit, feat, accomplishment, realization, performance. *(ANT.) omission, defeat, failure, neglect.*

**attempt** *(SYN.)* essay, experiment, trial, try, undertaking, endeavor, effort. *(ANT.) laziness, neglect, inaction.*

**attend** *(SYN.)* accompany, escort, watch, serve, care for, follow, lackey, present, frequent, protect, guard. *(ANT.) desert, abandon, avoid.*

**attendant** *(SYN.)* waiter, servant, valet.

**attention** *(SYN.)* consideration, heed, circumspection, notice, watchfulness, observance, application, reflection, study, care, alertness, mindfulness. *(ANT.) negligence, indifference, omission, oversight, disregard.*

**attentive** *(SYN.)* careful, awake, alive, considerate, heedful, mindful, wary. *(ANT.) unaware, oblivious, apathetic.*

**attest** *(SYN.)* testify, swear, vouch, certify.

**attire** *(SYN.)* apparel, dress, clothe.

**attitude** *(SYN.)* standpoint, viewpoint, stand, pose, aspect, position, posture.

**attract** *(SYN.)* enchant, interest, pull, fascinate, draw, tempt, infatuate, entice. *(ANT.) deter, repel, repulse, alienate.*

**attractive** *(SYN.)* enchanting, winning, engaging, pleasant, pleasing, seductive. *(ANT.) unattractive, obnoxious, repellent, repulsive, forbidding.*

**attribute** *(SYN.)* give, apply, place, trait, characteristic, feature, nature, credit.

**audacious** *(SYN.)* daring, bold, arrogant, foolhardy, cavalier, haughty, insolent. *(ANT.) humble, shy.*

**audacity** *(SYN.)* effrontery, fearlessness, temerity, boldness. *(ANT.) humility, meekness, circumspection, fearfulness.*

**audible** *(SYN.)* distinct, plain, clear. *(ANT.) inaudible.*

**augment** *(SYN.)* enlarge, increase, raise, expand, broaden, extend.

**auspicious** *(SYN.)* lucky, timely, favorable, promising, fortunate. *(ANT.) untimely, unfortunate.*

**austere** *(SYN.)* stern, severe, harsh, strict. *(ANT.) lenient, soft.*

**authentic** *(SYN.)* real, true,

genuine, pure, accurate, reliable, legitimate, factual. (ANT.) false, spurious, artificial, counterfeit, erroneous.

**authenticate** (SYN.) validate, warrant, guarantee, verify, certify.

**author** (SYN.) father, inventor, maker, originator, writer, composer.

**authoritative** (SYN.) certain, secure, commanding, sure, tried, trustworthy, safe, influential, dependable. (ANT.) uncertain, unreliable, dubious, fallible, questionable.

**authority** (SYN.) dominion, justification, power, permission, authorization, importance, domination, supremacy. (ANT.) incapacity, denial, prohibition, weakness, impotence.

**autocrat** (SYN.) monarch, ruler, tyrant.

**autograph** (SYN.) endorse, sign, approve.

**automatic** (SYN.) self-acting, mechanical, spontaneous, uncontrolled, involuntary. (ANT.) hand-operated, intentional, deliberate, manual.

**automobile** (SYN.) auto, car.

**auxiliary** (SYN.) assisting, helping, aiding.

**avail** (SYN.) help, profit, use, value, benefit, serve, advantage.

**available** (SYN.) obtainable, convenient, ready, handy, accessible, prepared. (ANT.) unavailable, out of reach, inaccessible, unobtainable.

**avarice** (SYN.) lust, greed.

**average** (SYN.) moderate, ordinary, usual, passable, fair, intermediate, medium. (ANT.) outstanding, exceptional, extraordinary, unusual.

**averse** (SYN.) unwilling, opposed, forced, against, involuntary. (ANT.) willing.

**avert** (SYN.) avoid, prevent, prohibit. (ANT.) invite.

**avid** (SYN.) greedy, eager.

**avoid** (SYN.) elude, forestall, evade, escape, dodge, avert, forbear, eschew. (ANT.) oppose, meet, confront, encounter, seek.

**award** (SYN.) reward, prize, medal, gift, trophy.

**aware** (SYN.) mindful, perceptive, formed, apprised, realizing, conscious. (ANT.) unaware, ignorant, oblivious.

**away** (SYN.) absent, departed, distracted, gone, not at home. (ANT.) present, attentive, attending.

**awe** (SYN.) surprise, respect, dread, astonishment, alarm.

**awful** (SYN.) frightful, horrible, awe-inspiring, dire, terrible, unpleasant. (ANT.) humble, pleasant, wonderful, commonplace.

**awkward** (SYN.) inept, unpolished, clumsy, gauche, rough, ungraceful. (ANT.) adroit, graceful, polished, skillful.

**awry** (SYN.) askew, wrong, twisted, crooked, disorderly. (ANT.) straight, right.

**axiom** (SYN.) fundamental, maxim, principle, theorem, adage, apothegm, byword, aphorism.

# B

**babble** (SYN.) twaddle, nonsense, gibberish, prattle, balderdash, rubbish, chatter, baby talk, poppycock, jabber, maunder, piffle.

**baby** (SYN.) newborn, infant, neonate, babe, teeny, small, wee, little, undersized, midget, papoose, protect, cosset, pamper.

**babyish** (SYN.) infantile, childish, whiny, unreasonable, immature, puerile, foolish, dependent. (ANT.) mature, adult, sensible, reasonable, grown-up.

**back** (SYN.) help, assist, endorse, support, second, ratify, approve, stand by, posterior, rear. (ANT.) anterior, front, face, undercut, veto, undermine.

**backbiting** (SYN.) gossip, slander, abuse, malice, cattiness, aspersion, derogation, belittling, badmouthing. (ANT.) compliments, praise, loyalty, friendliness, approval.

**backbone** (SYN.) vertebrae, spine, pillar, support, staff, mainstay, basis, courage, determination, toughness, character. (ANT.) timidity, weakness, cowardice, spinelessness.

**backbreaking** (SYN.) exhausting, fatiguing, tough, tiring, demanding, wearying, wearing, difficult. (ANT.) light, relating, undemanding, slight.

**back down** (SYN.) accede, concede, acquiesce, yield, withdraw, renege. (ANT.) persevere, insist.

**backer** (SYN.) underwriter, benefactor, investor, patron, sponsor, supporter.

**backfire** (SYN.) flop, boomerang, fail, founder, disappoint. (ANT.) succeed.

**background** (SYN.) training, practice, knowledge, experience.

**backing** (SYN.) help, support, funds, money, assistance, grant, advocacy, subsidy, sympathy, endorsement. (ANT.) criticism, detraction, faultfinding.

**backlog** (SYN.) inventory, reserve, hoard, amassment, accumulation.

**backslide** (SYN.) relapse, revert, return, weaken, regress, renege.

**backward** (SYN.) dull, sluggish, stupid, loath, regressive, rearward, underdeveloped, slow, retarded. (ANT.) progressive, precocious, civilized, advanced, forward.

**bad** (SYN.) unfavorable, wrong, evil, immoral, sinful, faulty, improper, unwholesome, wicked, corrupt, tainted. (ANT.) good, honorable, reputable, moral, excellent.

**badger** (SYN.) tease, question, annoy, pester, bother, taunt, bait, provoke, torment, harass, hector.

**baffle** (SYN.) confound, bewilder, perplex, puzzle, mystify, confuse, frustrate. (ANT.) inform, enlighten.

**bag** (SYN.) catch, snare, poke, sack.

**bait** (SYN.) enticement, captivate, ensnare, tease, torment, pester, worry, entrap, question, entice, lure, trap, harass, tempt, badger.

**balance** (SYN.) poise, stability, composure, remains, residue, equilibrium, compare, weigh, equalize. (ANT.) unsteadiness, instability.

**bald** (SYN.) bare, hairless, nude, open, uncovered, simple. (ANT.) covered, hairy.

**balk** (SYN.) unwilling, obstinate, stubborn, hesitate, check, stop. (ANT.) willing.

**ball** (SYN.) cotillion, dance, globe, sphere, spheroid.

**ballad** (SYN.) poem, song, ditty.

**balloon** (SYN.) puff up, enlarge, swell. (ANT.) shrivel, shrink.

**ballot** (SYN.) choice, vote, poll.

**balmy** (SYN.) soft, gentle, soothing, fragrant, mild. (ANT.) tempestuous, stormy.

**ban** (SYN.) prohibit, outlaw, disallow, block, bar, exclude, obstruct, prohibition, taboo, forbid. (ANT.) allow, permit.

**banal** (SYN.) hackneyed, corny, vapid, trite, overused, humdrum. (ANT.) striking,

original, fresh, stimulating, novel.

**band** (SYN.) company, association, crew, group, society, belt, strip, unite, gang.

**bandit** (SYN.) thief, robber, highwayman, outlaw, marauder.

**bang** (SYN.) hit, strike, slam.

**banish** (SYN.) drive away, eject, exile, oust, deport, dismiss, expel. (ANT.) receive, accept, shelter, admit, harbor, embrace, welcome.

**bank** (SYN.) barrier, slope, storage, treasury, row, series, string, shore.

**banner** (SYN.) colors, standard, pennant, flag.

**banquet** (SYN.) feast, celebration, festival, dinner, regalement, affair.

**banter** (SYN.) joke, tease, jest.

**bar** (SYN.) counter, impediment, saloon, exclude, obstacle, barricade, obstruct, shut out, hindrance, forbid, block, barrier, obstruction. (ANT.) allow, permit, aid, encouragement.

**barbarian** (SYN.) brute, savage, boor, ruffian, rude, uncivilized, primitive, uncultured, coarse, cruel, barbaric, crude. (ANT.) cultured, civilized.

**barbarous** (SYN.) savage, remorseless, cruel, uncivilized, rude, unrelenting, merciless, crude, ruthless, inhuman. (ANT.) kind, civilized, humane, refined, tasteful.

**barber** (SYN.) coiffeur, hairdresser.

**bare** (SYN.) naked, nude, uncovered, undressed, unclothed, unfurnished, plain, barren, empty, disclose, reveal, publicize, bald, expose, scarce, mere. (ANT.) dressed, garbed, conceal, covered, hide, clothed.

**barefaced** (SYN.) impudent, bold, insolent, brazen, shameless, audacious, impertinent, rude.

**barely** (SYN.) hardly, scarcely, just.

**bargain** (SYN.) agreement, arrangement, deal, contract, arrange, sale.

**baroque** (SYN.) ornamented, elaborate, embellished, ornate.

**barren** (SYN.) unproductive, bare, unfruitful, infertile, sterile, childless. (ANT.) productive, fruitful, fertile.

**barricade** (SYN.) fence, obstruction, shut in, fortification, barrier. (ANT.) free, open, release.

**barrier** (SYN.) fence, wall, bar,

railing, obstacle, hindrance, fortification, restraint, impediment, limit, barricade.
**barter** *(SYN.)* exchange, deal, trade.
**base** *(SYN.)* bottom, rest, foundation, establish, found, immoral, evil, bad, wicked, depraved, selfish, worthless, cheap, debased, poor, support, stand, low, abject, menial. *(ANT.) exalted, righteous, lofty, esteemed, noble, honored, refined, valuable.*
**bashful** *(SYN.)* timorous, abashed, shy, coy, timid, diffident, modest, sheepish, embarrassed, shame-faced, humble, recoiling, uneasy, awkward, ashamed. *(ANT.) fearless, outgoing, adventurous, gregarious, aggressive, daring.*
**basic** *(SYN.)* underlying, chief, essential, main, fundamental. *(ANT.) subsidiary, subordinate.*
**basis** *(SYN.)* presumption, support, base, principle, groundwork, presupposition, foundation, postulate, ground, assumption, premise, essential. *(ANT.) implication, trimming, derivative, superstructure.*
**basket** *(SYN.)* hamper, creel, dossier, bassinet.
**bastion** *(SYN.)* mainstay, support, staff, tower, stronghold.
**bat** *(SYN.)* strike, hit, clout, stick, club, knock, crack.
**batch** *(SYN.)* group, set, collection, lot, cluster, bunch, mass, combination.
**bath** *(SYN.)* washing, shower, tub, wash, dip, soaping.
**bathe** *(SYN.)* launder, drench, swim, cover, medicate, immerse, wet, dip, soak, suffuse, rinse, saturate.
**bathing suit** *(SYN.)* maillot, swimsuit, trunks.
**bathos** *(SYN.)* mawkishness, soppiness, slush, sentimentality.
**bathroom** *(SYN.)* powder room, toilet, bath, lavatory.
**baton** *(SYN.)* mace, rod, staff, billy club, crook, stick, caduceus, fasces.
**battalion** *(SYN.)* mass, army, swarm, mob, drove, horde, gang, legion, regiment.
**batten** *(SYN.)* thrive, flourish, fatten, wax, expand, bloom, boom, grow. *(ANT.) decrease, weaken, fail.*
**batter** *(SYN.)* pound, beat, hit, pommel, wallop, bash, smash, mixture, strike.
**battery** *(SYN.)* series, troop, force, rally, muster, set.
**battle** *(SYN.)* strife, fray, combat, struggle, contest,

skirmish, conflict, fight, war, flight, warfare, action, campaign, strive against. *(ANT.) truce, concord, agreement, settlement, harmony, accept, concur, peace.*
**battlement** *(SYN.)* parapet, crenelation, rampart, fort, bastion, stronghold, escarpment.
**bauble** *(SYN.)* plaything, toy, trinket.
**bawd** *(SYN.)* procuress, prostitute.
**bawdy** *(SYN.)* vulgar, smutty, filthy, dirty, obscene, pornographic.
**bawl** *(SYN.)* sob, shout, wail, cry loudly, bellow, weep, cry.
**bawl out** *(SYN.)* scold, upbraid, censure, berate, reprove, reprimand.
**bay** *(SYN.)* inlet, bayou, harbor, lagoon, cove, sound, gulf.
**bazaar** *(SYN.)* fair, market, marketplace.
**beach** *(SYN.)* sands, seashore, waterfront, seaside, strand, coast, shore.
**beacon** *(SYN.)* light, signal, watchtower, guide, flare, warning, alarm.
**bead** *(SYN.)* globule, drop, pill, blob.
**beak** *(SYN.)* nose, bill, proboscis.
**beam** *(SYN.)* gleam, ray, girder, cross-member, pencil, shine, glisten, smile, glitter, gleam.
**beaming** *(SYN.)* joyful, bright, happy, radiant, grinning. *(ANT.) sullen, gloomy, threatening, scowling.*
**bear** *(SYN.)* carry, support, take, uphold, suffer, convey, allow, stand, yield, endure, tolerate, produce, sustain, brook, transport, undergo, permit, suffer, abide, tolerate. *(ANT.) evade, shun, avoid, refuse, dodge.*
**bearable** *(SYN.)* sufferable, supportable, manageable, tolerable. *(ANT.) terrible, painful, unbearable, awful, intolerable.*
**bearing** *(SYN.)* course, direction, position, posture, behavior, manner, carriage, relation, reference, connection, application, deportment, air, way, conduct.
**bearings** *(SYN.)* orientation, whereabouts, location, direction, position, reading, course.
**bear on** *(SYN.)* affect, relate to.
**bear out** *(SYN.)* confirm, substantiate, justify, verify, prove.
**bear up** *(SYN.)* carry on,

endure.
**bear with** *(SYN.)* tolerate, forbear.
**beast** *(SYN.)* monster, savage, brute, creature, animal.
**beastly** *(SYN.)* detestable, mean, low, hateful, loathsome, nasty, unpleasant, despicable, obnoxious, brutal, brutish, offensive. *(ANT.) considerate, sympathetic, refined, humane, fine, pleasant.*
**beat** *(SYN.)* pulse, buffet, pound, defeat, palpitate, hit, thump, belabor, knock, overthrow, thrash, pummel, rout, smite, throb, punch, subdue, pulsate, dash, strike, overpower, vanquish, conquer, batter, overcome, blow. *(ANT.) stroke, fail, defend, surrender, shield.*
**beaten** *(SYN.)* disheartened, dejected, licked, discouraged, hopeless, downcast, down, depressed. *(ANT.) eager, hopeful, cheerful.*
**beatific** *(SYN.)* uplifted, blissful, elated, happy, wonderful, joyful, divine. *(ANT.) awful, hellish, ill-fated, accursed.*
**beating** *(SYN.)* whipping, drubbing, flogging, lashing, scourging, walloping.
**beau** *(SYN.)* lover, suitor, swain, admirer.
**beautiful** *(SYN.)* pretty, fair, lovely, charming, comely, handsome, elegant, attractive. *(ANT.) repulsive, hideous, unsightly, foul, homely, plainness, unattractive, ugly.*
**beauty** *(SYN.)* handsomeness, fairness, charm, pulchritude, attractiveness, loveliness, comeliness, grace, allegiance. *(ANT.) ugliness, disfigurement, homeliness, plainness, deformity, eyesore.*
**becalm** *(SYN.)* calm, quiet, smooth, still, hush, repose, settle.
**because** *(SYN.)* inasmuch as, as, since, for.
**because of** *(SYN.)* as a result of, as a consequence of.
**beckon** *(SYN.)* call, signal, summon, motion, gesture, wave.
**becloud** *(SYN.)* obfuscate, confuse, befog, confound, obscure, muddle. *(ANT.) illuminate, clarify, solve.*
**become** *(SYN.)* change, grow, suit, be appropriate, befit.
**becoming** *(SYN.)* suitable, meet, befitting, appropriate, fitting, seemly, enhancing, attractive, pleasing, flattering, tasteful, smart, adorning, ornamental. *(ANT.) unsuitable, inappropriate,*

incongruent, ugly, unattractive, improper.
**bed** *(SYN.)* layer, cot, vein, berth, stratum, couch, accumulation, bunk, cradle.
**bedazzle** *(SYN.)* glare, blind, dumbfound, flabbergast, bewilder, furbish, festoon.
**bedeck** *(SYN.)* deck, adorn, beautify, smarten, festoon, garnish.
**bedevil** *(SYN.)* worry, fret, irk, torment, harass, pester, nettle, tease, vex, plague. *(ANT.) soothe, calm, delight, please.*
**bedlam** *(SYN.)* tumult, uproar, madhouse, commotion, confusion, racket, rumpus, pandemonium. *(ANT.) calm, peace.*
**bedraggled** *(SYN.)* shabby, muddy, sodden, messy, sloppy. *(ANT.) dry, neat, clean, well-groomed.*
**bedrock** *(SYN.)* basis, foundation, roots, basics, essentials, fundamentals, bottom, bed, substratum, core. *(ANT.) top, dome, apex, nonessentials.*
**bedroom** *(SYN.)* chamber, bedchamber.
**beef** *(SYN.)* brawn, strength, heft, gripe, sinew, fitness, huskiness, might.
**beef up** *(SYN.)* reinforce, vitalize, nerve, buttress, strengthen. *(ANT.) sap, weaken, enervate, drain.*
**beefy** *(SYN.)* solid, strong, muscular, heavy, stocky.
**befall** *(SYN.)* occur, come about, happen.
**before** *(SYN.)* prior, earlier, in advance, formerly. *(ANT.) behind, following, afterward, latterly, after.*
**befriend** *(SYN.)* welcome, encourage, aid, stand by. *(ANT.) dislike, shun, desert, avoid.*
**befuddle** *(SYN.)* stupefy, addle, confuse, rattle, disorient.
**beg** *(SYN.)* solicit, ask, implore, supplicate, entreat, adjure, petition, beseech, request, importune, entreat, implore. *(ANT.) grant, cede, give, bestow, favor.*
**beget** *(SYN.)* sire, engender, produce, create, propagate, originate, breed, generate, procreate, father. *(ANT.) murder, destroy, kill, abort, prevent, extinguish.*
**beggar** *(SYN.)* scrub, tatterdemalion, pauper, wretch, ragamuffin, vagabond, starveling.
**begin** *(SYN.)* open, enter, arise, initiate, commence, start, inaugurate, originate, institute, create. *(ANT.)*

terminate, complete, finish, close, end, stop.

**beginner** (SYN.) nonprofessional, amateur, apprentice. (ANT.) veteran, professional.

**beginning** (SYN.) outset, inception, origin, source, commencement, start, opening, initiation, inauguration. (ANT.) termination, completion, end, close, consumption, closing, ending, finish.

**begrime** (SYN.) soil, dirty, smear, muddy, splotch, tarnish. (ANT.) wash, clean, freshen, launder.

**begrudge** (SYN.) resent, envy, stint, withhold, grudge.

**begrudging** (SYN.) hesitant, reluctant, resentful, unwilling, forced. (ANT.) willing, eager, quick, spontaneous.

**beguiling** (SYN.) enchanting, interesting, delightful, intriguing, engaging, bewitching, attractive, enthralling, captivating. (ANT.) boring, dull, tedious.

**behalf** (SYN.) benefit, welfare, support, aid, part, interest.

**behave** (SYN.) deport, comport, manage, act, demean, bear, interact, carry, operate, conduct.

**behavior** (SYN.) manners, carriage, disposition, action, deed, bearing, deportment, conduct, demeanor. (ANT.) rebelliousness, misbehavior.

**behead** (SYN.) decapitate, guillotine, decollate.

**behest** (SYN.) order, command, decree, mandate, bidding.

**behind** (SYN.) after, backward, at the back, in back of. (ANT.) frontward, ahead, before.

**behold** (SYN.) look, see, view, notice, observe, perceive, sight. (ANT.) overlook, ignore.

**being** (SYN.) life, existing, existence, living, actuality, organism, individual. (ANT.) death, nonexistence, expiration.

**belabor** (SYN.) repeat, reiterate, pound, explain, expatiate, din.

**belated** (SYN.) late, delayed, overdue, tardy. (ANT.) well-timed, early.

**belch** (SYN.) emit, erupt, gush, disgorge, bubble, eructation, burp.

**beleaguered** (SYN.) bothered, annoyed, beset, harassed, badgered, vexed, plagued, victimized.

**belie** (SYN.) distort, misrepresent, twist, disappoint.

**belief** (SYN.) trust, feeling, certitude, opinion, conviction, persuasion, credence, confidence, reliance, faith, view, creed, assurance. (ANT.) heresy, denial, incredulity, distrust, skepticism, doubt.

**believe** (SYN.) hold, apprehend, fancy, support, accept, conceive, suppose, imagine, trust, credit. (ANT.) doubt, reject, distrust, disbelieve, question.

**believer** (SYN.) adherent, follower, devotee, convert, zealot. (ANT.) doubter, critic, scoffer, skeptic.

**belittle** (SYN.) underrate, depreciate, minimize, decry, disparage, diminish, demean, slight, discredit, militant, depreciate, humiliate. (ANT.) esteem, admire, flatter, overrate, commend.

**bell** (SYN.) pealing, ringing, signal, tolling, buzzer, chime.

**belligerent** (SYN.) aggressive, warlike, hostile, offensive, combative, militant. (ANT.) easygoing, compromising, peaceful.

**bellow** (SYN.) thunder, roar, scream, shout, yell, howl.

**bellwether** (SYN.) leader, pilot, guide, ringleader, boss, shepherd.

**belly** (SYN.) stomach, abdomen, paunch.

**belonging** (SYN.) loyalty, relationship, kinship, acceptance, rapport.

**belongings** (SYN.) property, effects, possessions.

**beloved** (SYN.) adored, sweet, loved, cherished, prized, esteemed, valued, darling.

**below** (SYN.) under, less, beneath, underneath, lower. (ANT.) aloft, overhead, above, over.

**belt** (SYN.) girdle, sash, strap, cummerbund, band, waistband, whack, hit, wallop, punch.

**bemoan** (SYN.) mourn, lament, grieve, sorrow, regret, deplore.

**bend** (SYN.) turn, curve, incline, submit, bow, lean, crook, twist, yield, stoop, crouch, agree, suppress, oppress, mold, kneel, deflect, subdue, influence. (ANT.) resist, straighten, break, stiffen.

**beneath** (SYN.) under, below. (ANT.) above, over.

**benediction** (SYN.) thanks, blessing, prayer.

**beneficial** (SYN.) salutary, good, wholesome, advantageous, useful, helpful, serviceable, profitable. (ANT.) harmful, destructive, injurious, disadvantageous, unwholesome, deleterious, detrimental.

**benefit** (SYN.) support, help, gain, avail, profit, account, favor, aid, good, advantage, serve, interest, behalf, service. (ANT.) handicap, calamity, trouble, disadvantage, distress.

**benevolence** (SYN.) magnanimity, charity, tenderness, altruism, humanity, philanthropy, generosity, liberality, beneficence, goodwill. (ANT.) malevolence, unkindness, cruelty, selfishness, inhumanity.

**benevolent** (SYN.) kindhearted, tender, merciful, generous, altruistic, obliging, kind, good, well-wishing, philanthropy, liberal, unselfish, kindly, disposed, openhearted, humane, benign, friendly. (ANT.) malevolent, greedy, wicked, harsh.

**bent** (SYN.) curved, crooked, resolved, determined, set, inclined, firm, decided. (ANT.) straight.

**berate** (SYN.) scold.

**beseech** (SYN.) appeal, entreat, plead, ask, beg, implore.

**beset** (SYN.) surround, attack.

**besides** (SYN.) moreover, further, except for, also, as well, furthermore.

**besiege** (SYN.) assault, attack, siege, bombard, raid, charge.

**bespeak** (SYN.) engage, reserve, indicate, show, signify, express.

**best** (SYN.) choice, prime, select. (ANT.) worst.

**bestial** (SYN.) brutal, beastly, savage, cruel.

**bestow** (SYN.) confer, place, put, award, give, present. (ANT.) withdraw, withhold.

**bet** (SYN.) gamble, give, stake, wager, pledge, ante.

**betray** (SYN.) reveal, deliver, expose, mislead, trick, deceive, exhibit, show. (ANT.) shelter, protect, safeguard.

**betrothal** (SYN.) marriage, engagement, contract.

**better** (SYN.) superior, preferable, improve. (ANT.) worsen.

**between** (SYN.) among, betwixt.

**beware** (SYN.) take care, watch out, look sharp, be careful.

**bewilder** (SYN.) perplex, confuse, mystify, baffle, puzzle, overwhelm. (ANT.) clarify, enlighten.

**bewitch** (SYN.) captivate, charm, delight, enchant.

**beyond** (SYN.) past, farther, exceeding.

**bias** (SYN.) slant, inclination, proneness, turn, bent, penchant, tendency, disposition, propensity, partiality, predisposition, leaning, proclivity, prejudice, influence, warp, slanting, predilection. (ANT.) fairness, justice, even-handedness, equity, detachment, impartiality.

**bible** (SYN.) guide, handbook, gospel, manual, sourcebook, guidebook.

**bibulous** (SYN.) guzzling, intemperate, winebibbing, sottish, alcoholic. (ANT.) sober, moderate.

**bicker** (SYN.) dispute, argue, wrangle, quarrel. (ANT.) go along with, agree.

**bid** (SYN.) order, command, direct, wish, greet, say, offer, instruct, invite, purpose, tender, proposal.

**bidding** (SYN.) behest, request, decree, call, charge, beck, summons, solicitation, invitation, instruction, mandate.

**bide** (SYN.) stay, tarry, delay, wait, remain.

**big** (SYN.) large, huge, bulky, immense, colossal, majestic, august, monstrous, hulking, gigantic, massive, great, enormous, tremendous, outgoing, important, kind, big-hearted, considerable, generous, grand. (ANT.) small, little, tiny, immature, petite.

**big-hearted** (SYN.) good-natured, liberal, generous, unselfish, open-handed, unstinting, charitable, magnanimous. (ANT.) cold, selfish, mean, uncharitable.

**bigoted** (SYN.) intolerant, partial, prejudiced, biased, unfair, chauvinist.

**bigotry** (SYN.) bias, blindness, intolerance, unfairness, prejudice, ignorance, passion, sectarianism. (ANT.) acceptance, open-mindedness.

**big-shot** (SYN.) somebody, brass hat, big gun. (ANT.) underling, nobody, cipher.

**bijou** (SYN.) gem, bauble, jewel, ornament.

**bile** (SYN.) spleen, rancor, anger, bitterness, peevishness, ill-humor, resentment, discontent, irascibility. (ANT.) cheerfulness, affability, pleasantness.

**bilge** (SYN.) hogwash, drivel, gibberish, rubbish, bosh, foolishness, twaddle.

**bilious** (SYN.) petulant, crabby, ill-natured, cross, peevish, crotchety, cranky. (ANT.) happy, agreeable, pleasant, good-natured.

**bilk** (SYN.) defraud, trick, cheat, hood-wink, deceive, fleece, rook, bamboozle.

**bill** (SYN.) charge, invoice, account, statement, beak.

**billet** (SYN.) housing, quarters, berth, shelter, barrack, installation.

**billingsgate** (SYN.) swearing, scurrility, cursing, abuse, vulgarity, gutter, profanity.

**billow** (SYN.) surge, swell, rise, rush, peaking, magnification, amplification, augmentation, increase, intensification. (ANT.) lowering, decrease.

**bin** (SYN.) cubbyhole, box, container, chest, cubicle, crib, receptacle, can.

**bind** (SYN.) connect, restrain, band, fasten, oblige, obligate, engage, wrap, connect, weld, attach, tie, require, restrict. (ANT.) unlace, loose, unfasten, untie, free.

**binding** (SYN.) compulsory, obligatory, mandatory, compelling, unalterable, imperative, indissoluble, unconditional, unchangeable, hard-and-fast. (ANT.) adjustable, flexible, elastic, changeable.

**binge** (SYN.) fling, spree, carousal, toot.

**birth** (SYN.) origin, beginning, infancy, inception. (ANT.) decline, death, disappearance, end.

**biscuit** (SYN.) bun, roll, cake, muffin, bread, rusk, scone.

**bit** (SYN.) fraction, portion, scrap, fragment, particle, drop, speck, harness, small amount, restraint, morsel.

**bite** (SYN.) gnaw, chew, nip, sting, pierce, mouthful, snack, morsel.

**biting** (SYN.) cutting, sharp, acid, sneering, sarcastic. (ANT.) soothing, kind, gentle, agreeable.

**bitter** (SYN.) distasteful, sour, acrid, pungent, piercing, vicious, severe, biting, distressful, stinging, distressing, ruthless, hostile, grievous, harsh, painful, tart. (ANT.) sweet, mellow, pleasant, delicious.

**bizarre** (SYN.) peculiar, strange, odd, uncommon, queer, unusual. (ANT.) usual, everyday, ordinary, inconspicuous.

**black** (SYN.) sooty, dark, ebony, inky, swarthy, soiled, filthy, dirty, stained, somber, depressing, sad, dismal, gloomy. (ANT.) white, clean, pristine, glowing, pure, cheerful, light-skinned, sunny, bright.

**blackball** (SYN.) turn down, ban, blacklist, exclude, snub, reject, debar. (ANT.) accept, include, invite, ask, bid.

**blacken** (SYN.) tar, ink, black, darken, besoot, smudge, begrime, discredit, defile, dull, dim, tarnish, ebonize, denounce, sully, libel, blemish, defame. (ANT.) exalt, honor, whiten, brighten, shine, bleach.

**blackmail** (SYN.) bribe, payment, bribery, extortion, shakedown, coercion.

**blackout** (SYN.) faint, coma, unconsciousness, oblivion, amnesia, stupor, swoon.

**bladder** (SYN.) saccule, sac, vesicle, pouch, pod, cell, blister, container, cyst.

**blade** (SYN.) cutter, lancet, knife, sword.

**blame** (SYN.) upbraid, criticize, fault, guilt, accuse, rebuke, charge, implicate, impeach, tattle, condemn, indict, responsibility, censure, denounce, reproach. (ANT.) exonerate, credit, honor, absolve.

**blameless** (SYN.) moral, innocent, worthy, faultless. (ANT.) blameworthy, culpable, guilty.

**blanch** (SYN.) whiten, bleach, decolorize, peroxide, fade, wash out, dim, dull.

**bland** (SYN.) soft, smooth, gentle, agreeable, vapid, insipid, mild, polite. (ANT.) harsh, outspoken, disagreeable.

**blandish** (SYN.) praise, compliment, overpraise, cajole, puff, adulate, salve, fawn, court, toady, butter up, please, jolly. (ANT.) insult, deride, criticize, belittle.

**blandisher** (SYN.) adulator, booster, sycophant, eulogist, flunky. (ANT.) knocker, fault-finder, belittler.

**blandishment** (SYN.) applause, cajolery, honor, adulation, plaudits, acclaim, fawning, compliments. (ANT.) criticism, deprecation.

**blank** (SYN.) unmarked, expressionless, uninterested, form, area, void, vacant, empty. (ANT.) marked, filled, alert, animated.

**blanket** (SYN.) quilt, coverlet, cover, comforter, robe, padding, carpet, wrapper, mantle, envelope, housing, coat, comprehensive, universal, across-the-board, panoramic, omnibus. (ANT.) limited, detailed, restricted, precise.

**blare** (SYN.) roar, blast, resound, jar, scream, clang, peal, trumpet, toot, hoot.

**blasphemous** (SYN.) profane, irreverent, impious, godless, ungodly, sacrilegious, irreligious. (ANT.) reverent, reverential, religious, pious.

**blasphemy** (SYN.) profanation, impiousness, cursing, irreverence, sacrilege, abuse, swearing, contempt. (ANT.) respect, piety, reverence, devotion.

**blast** (SYN.) burst, explosion, discharge, blow-out.

**blasted** (SYN.) blighted, withered, ravaged, decomposed, spoiled, destroyed.

**blastoff** (SYN.) launching, expulsion, launch, shot, projection.

**blatant** (SYN.) shameless, notorious, brazen, flagrant, glaring, bold, obvious. (ANT.) deft, subtle, insidious, devious.

**blaze** (SYN.) inferno, shine, flare, marking, fire, outburst, holocaust, notch, flame. (ANT.) die, dwindle.

**bleach** (SYN.) pale, whiten, blanch, whitener. (ANT.) darken, blacken.

**bleak** (SYN.) dreary, barren, cheerless, depressing, gloomy, windswept, bare, cold, dismal, desolate, raw, chilly. (ANT.) lush, hopeful, promising, cheerful.

**bleary** (SYN.) hazy, blurry, fuzzy, misty, clouded, overcast, dim. (ANT.) clear, vivid, precise, clear-cut.

**bleed** (SYN.) pity, lose blood, grieve, sorrow.

**blemish** (SYN.) injury, speck, flaw, scar, disgrace, imperfection, stain, fault, blot. (ANT.) purity, embellishment, adornment, perfection.

**blend** (SYN.) beat, intermingle, combine, fuse, unite, consolidate, amalgamate, conjoin, mix, coalesce, intermix, join, merge, compound, combination, stir, mixture, mingle. (ANT.) separate, decompose, analyze, disintegrate.

**bless** (SYN.) thank, celebrate, extol, glorify, adore, delight, praise, gladden, exalt. (ANT.) denounce, blaspheme, slander, curse.

**blessed** (SYN.) sacred, holy, consecrated, dedicated, hallowed, sacrosanct, beatified, joyful, delighted, joyous, sainted, canonized, blissful. (ANT.) miserable, sad, dispirited, cheerless.

**blessing** (SYN.) sanction, favor, grace, benediction, invocation, approbation, approval, compliment, bounty, windfall, gift, benefit, advantage, kindness, felicitation, invocation. (ANT.) disapproval, execration, curse, denunciation, malediction, rebuke, displeasure, condemnation, adversity, misfortune, mishap, calamity.

**blight** (SYN.) decay, disease, spoil, sickness, wither, ruin, damage, harm, decaying, epidemic, affliction, destroy.

**blind** (SYN.) sightless, unmindful, rash, visionless, ignorant, unsighted, unconscious, discerning, heedless, oblivious, purblind, unknowing, screen, unaware, thoughtless, shade, unthinking, cover, curtain, without thought, headlong. (ANT.) discerning, sensible, calculated, perceiving, perceptive, aware.

**blink** (SYN.) bat, glance, flicker, wink, twinkle.

**bliss** (SYN.) ecstasy, rapture, glee, elation, joy, blessedness, gladness, happiness, delight, felicity, blissfulness. (ANT.) woe, sadness, sorrow, grief, unhappiness, torment, wretchedness, misery.

**blissful** (SYN.) happy, elated, rapturous, ecstatic, paradisiacal, joyous, enraptured.

**blister** (SYN.) swelling, welt, sore, blob, bubble, inflammation, boil, canker.

**blithe** (SYN.) breezy, merry, airy, lighthearted, light, gay, fanciful, graceful. (ANT.) morose, grouchy, low-spirited, gloomy.

**blitz** (SYN.) strike, onslaught, thrust, raid, lunge, drive, incursion, assault, sally.

**blizzard** (SYN.) storm, snowfall, gale, tempest, blast, blow, swirl.

**bloat** (SYN.) distend, puff up, inflate, swell. (ANT.) deflate.

**blob** (SYN.) bubble, blister, pellet, globule.

**block** (SYN.) clog, hinder, bar, impede, close, obstruct, barricade, blockade, obstruction, hindrance, obstacle, impediment, retard, check, stop. (ANT.) forward, promote, aid, clear, advance, advantage, assist, further, open.

**blockade** (SYN.) barrier, fortification, obstruction, barricade.

**blockhead** (SYN.) dunce, dolt, fool, sap, idiot, simpleton, chump, booby, bonehead, woodenhead.

**blood** (SYN.) murder, gore, slaughter, bloodshed, ancestry, lineage, heritage.

**bloodcurdling** (SYN.) hair-raising, terrifying, alarming, chilling, stunning, scary.

**bloodless** (SYN.) dead, torpid, dull, drab, cold, colorless, passionless, lackluster. (ANT.) passionate, vital, ebullient, animated, vivacious.

**bloodshed** (SYN.) murder, killing, slaying, blood bath, massacre, carnage.

**bloodthirsty** (SYN.) murderous, cruel.

**bloody** (SYN.) cruel, pitiless, bloodthirsty, inhuman, ruthless, ferocious, murderous. (ANT.) kind, gentle.

**bloom** (SYN.) thrive, glow, flourish, blossom, flower. (ANT.) wane, decay, dwindle, shrivel, wither.

**blooming** (SYN.) flush, vigorous, thriving, vital, abloom, healthy, fresh, booming. (ANT.) flagging, declining, withering.

**blooper** (SYN.) muff, fluff, error, bungle, botch, blunder, fumble, howler, indiscretion.

**blossom** (SYN.) bloom, flower, flourish. (ANT.) shrink, wither, dwindle, fade.

**blot** (SYN.) stain, inkblot, spot, ink-stain, blemish, dishonor, disgrace, spatter, obliterate, soil, dry.

**blot out** (SYN.) wipe out, destroy, obliterate, abolish, annihilate, cancel, expunge, strike out, shade, darken, shadow, overshadow, obfuscate, cloud, eclipse.

**blow** (SYN.) hit, thump, slap, cuff, box, shock, move, drive, spread, breeze, puff, whistle, inflate, enlarge.

**blowout** (SYN.) blast, explosion, burst.

**blue** (SYN.) sapphire, azure, gloomy, sad, unhappy, depressed, dejected, melancholy. (ANT.) cheerful, optimistic, happy.

**blueprint** (SYN.) design, plan, scheme, chart, draft, prospectus, outline, proposal, conception, project, layout.

**blues** (SYN.) dumps, melancholy, depression, doldrums, despondency, gloominess, moroseness.

**bluff** (SYN.) steep, perpendicular, vertical, abrupt, precipitous, rough, open, frank, hearty, blunt, foot, mislead, pretend, deceive, fraud, lie, fake, deceit.

**blunder** (SYN.) error, flounder, mistake, stumble.

**blunt** (SYN.) solid, abrupt, rough, dull, pointless, plain, bluff, edgeless, unceremonious, obtuse, rude, outspoken, unsharpened, rounded, worn, crude, direct, impolite, short, curt, gruff. (ANT.) tactful, polite, subtle, polished, suave, sharp, keen, pointed, diplomatic.

**blur** (SYN.) sully, dim, obscure, stain, dull, confuse, cloud, smear, stain, smudge. (ANT.) clear, clarify.

**blush** (SYN.) redden.

**board** (SYN.) embark, committee, wood, mount, cabinet, food, get on, lumber.

**boast** (SYN.) vaunt, flaunt, brag, glory, crow, exaggerate. (ANT.) humble, apologize, minimize, deprecate.

**body** (SYN.) remains, bulk, mass, carcass, form, company, corpus, society, firmness, group, torso, substance, collection, cadaver, trunk, group, throng, company, crowd, band. (ANT.) spirit, intellect, soul.

**bogus** (SYN.) counterfeit, false, pretend, fake, phony. (ANT.) genuine.

**boil** (SYN.) seethe, bubble, pimple, fume, cook, swelling, rage, foam, simmer, stew.

**boisterous** (SYN.) rough, violent, rowdy, noisy, tumultuous. (ANT.) serene.

**bold** (SYN.) daring, forward, pushy, striking, brave, dauntless, rude, prominent, adventurous, fearless, insolent, conspicuous, defiant, arrogant, cavalier, brazen, unafraid, intrepid, courageous, valiant, heroic, gallant, disrespectful, impudent, shameless. (ANT.) modest, bashful, cowardly, timid, retiring, flinching, fearful, timorous, polite, courteous, deferential.

**bolt** (SYN.) break away, fastener, floe, take flight, lock.

**bombard** (SYN.) shell, open fire, bomb, rake, assail, attack.

**bond** (SYN.) fastener, rope, tie, cord, connection, attachment, link, tie, promise. (ANT.) sever, separate, untie, disconnect.

**bondage** (SYN.) slavery, thralldom, captivity, imprisonment, servitude, confinement, vassalage, enslavement. (ANT.) liberation, emancipation, free, independence, freedom.

**bonds** (SYN.) chains, cuffs, fetters, shackles, irons, bracelets.

**bone up** (SYN.) learn, master, study, relearn.

**bonus** (SYN.) more, extra, premium, gift, reward, bounty.

**bony** (SYN.) lean, lank, thin, lanky, rawboned, fleshless, skinny, gangling, weight. (ANT.) plump, fleshy, stout.

**book** (SYN.) manual, textbook, work, booklet, monograph, brochure, tract, volume, pamphlet, treatise, publication, hardcover, paperback, novel, workbook, text.

**bookish** (SYN.) formal, scholarly, theoretical, academic, learned, scholastic, erudite. (ANT.) ignorant.

**boom** (SYN.) advance, grow, flourish, progress, gain, roar, beam, rumble, reverberate, thunder, prosper, swell, thrive, pole, rush. (ANT.) decline, fail, recession.

**booming** (SYN.) flourishing, blooming, thriving, vigorous, prospering, exuberant. (ANT.) waning, dying, failing, declining.

**boon** (SYN.) gift, jolly, blessing, pleasant, godsend, windfall.

**boondocks** (SYN.) sticks, backwoods.

**boor** (SYN.) lout, clown, oaf, yokel, rustic, vulgarian, ruffian.

**boorish** (SYN.) coarse, churlish, uncivil, ill-mannered, ill-bred, uncivilized, crude, uncouth. (ANT.) polite, cultivated, well-mannered.

**boost** (SYN.) push, lift, help, hoist, shove. (ANT.) depress, lower, belittle, disparage, decrease, decline, reduction, down turn.

**booster** (SYN.) supporter, fan, rooter, plugger, follower.

**boot** (SYN.) shoe, kick.

**booth** (SYN.) enclosure, cubicle, stand, compartment, box.

**bootless** (SYN.) purposeless, ineffective, profitless, useless. (ANT.) favorable, successful, useful.

**bootlicker** (SYN.) flunky, fawner, toady, sycophant.

**booty** (SYN.) prize, plunder, loot.

**booze** (SYN.) spirits, drink, liquor, alcohol.

**border** (SYN.) fringe, rim, verge, boundary, edge, termination, brink, limit, brim, outskirts, frontier, margin. (ANT.) interior, center, mainland, core, middle.

**borderline** (SYN.) unclassifiable, indeterminate, halfway, obscure, inexact, indefinite, unclear. (ANT.) precise, absolute, definite.

**border on** (SYN.) approximate, approach, resemble, echo, parallel, connect.

**bore** (SYN.) tire, weary, hole, perforate, pierce, drill. (ANT.) arouse, captivate, excite, interest.

**boredom** (SYN.) ennui, doldrums, weariness, dullness, tedium. (ANT.) stimulation, motive, activity, stimulus, excitement.

**boring** (SYN.) monotonous, dull, dead, flat, tedious, wearisome, trite, prosaic, humdrum, long-winded.

**born** (SYN.) hatched, produced.

**borrow** (SYN.) copy, adopt, simulate, mirror, assume, usurp, plagiarize, take. (ANT.) allow, advance, invent, originate, credit, lend.

**bosom** (SYN.) chest, breast, feelings, thoughts, mind, interior, marrow, heart.

**boss** (SYN.) director, employer, oversee, direct, foreman, supervisor, manager.

**bossy** (SYN.) overbearing, arrogant, domineering, lordly, tyrannical. (ANT.) flexible, easygoing, cooperative.

**botch** (SYN.) blunder, bungle, fumble, goof, muff, mishandle, mismanage. (ANT.) perform, realize.

**bother** (SYN.) haunt, molest, trouble, annoy, upset, fleeting, transient, harass, inconvenience, momentary, disturb, passing, pester, tease, irritate, worry, vex. (ANT.) prolonged, extended, long, protracted, lengthy, comfort, solace.

**bothersome** (SYN.) irritating, vexatious, worrisome, annoying, distressing, troublesome, disturbing.

**bottle** (SYN.) container, flask, vessel, decanter, vial, ewer, jar.

**bottleneck** (SYN.) obstacle, obstruction, barrier, block, blockage, detour.

**bottom** (SYN.) basis, fundament, base, groundwork, foot, depths, lowest part, underside, foundation, seat, buttocks, rear, behind. (ANT.) top, peak, apex, summit, topside.

**bough** (SYN.) branch, arm, limb.

**bounce** (SYN.) recoil, ricochet, rebound.

**bound** (SYN.) spring, vault, hop, leap, start, surrounded, jump, limit, jerk, boundary, bounce, skip, tied, shackled, trussed, fettered, certain, sure, destined, compelled, required. (ANT.) unfettered, free.

**boundary** (SYN.) bound,

limit, border, margin, outline, circumference, perimeter, division, frontier, edge.

**boundless** (SYN.) limitless, endless, inexhaustible, unlimited, eternal, infinite. (ANT.) restricted, limited.

**bounteous** (SYN.) plentiful, generous, liberal, abundant. (ANT.) scarce, rare.

**bountiful** (SYN.) bounteous, fertile, plentiful, generous, abundant. (ANT.) sparing, infertile, scarce.

**bounty** (SYN.) generosity, gift, award, bonus, reward, prize, premium.

**bourgeois** (SYN.) common, ordinary, commonplace, middle-class, conventional. (ANT.) upper-class, unconventional, loose, aristocratic.

**bout** (SYN.) round, contest, conflict, test, struggle, match, spell, fight.

**bow** (SYN.) bend, yield, kneel, submit, stoop.

**bowels** (SYN.) entrails, intestines, innards, guts, stomach.

**bowl** (SYN.) container, dish, pot, pottery, crock, jug, vase.

**bowl over** (SYN.) fell, floor, overturn, astound, nonplus, stagger, jar.

**bow out** (SYN.) give up, withdraw, retire, resign, abandon.

**box** (SYN.) hit, fight, crate, case, container.

**boxer** (SYN.) prizefighter, fighter.

**boy** (SYN.) male, youngster, lad, kid, fellow, buddy, youth. (ANT.) girl, man.

**boycott** (SYN.) picket, strike, ban, revolt, blackball.

**boyfriend** (SYN.) date, young man, sweetheart, courtier, beau.

**brace** (SYN.) strengthen, tie, prop, support, tighten, stay, strut, bind, truss, crutch.

**bracelet** (SYN.) armband, bangle, circlet.

**bracing** (SYN.) stimulating, refreshing, restorative, fortifying, invigorating.

**bracket** (SYN.) join, couple, enclose, relate, brace, support.

**brag** (SYN.) boast, flaunt, vaunt, bluster, swagger. (ANT.) demean, debase, denigrate, degrade, depreciate, deprecate.

**braid** (SYN.) weave, twine, wreath, plait.

**brain** (SYN.) sense, intelligence, intellect, common sense, understanding, reason. (ANT.) stupid, stupidity.

**brake** (SYN.) decelerate, stop, curb. (ANT.) accelerate.

**branch** (SYN.) shoot, limb, bough, tributary, offshoot, part, division, expand, department, divide, spread, subdivision.

**brand** (SYN.) make, trademark, label, kind, burn, trade name, mark, stamp, blaze.

**brave** (SYN.) bold, daring, gallant, valorous, adventurous, heroic, magnanimous, chivalrous, audacious, valiant, courageous, fearless, intrepid, unafraid. (ANT.) weak, cringing, timid, cowardly, fearful, craven.

**brawl** (SYN.) racket, quarrel, fracas, riot, fight, melee, fray, disturbance, dispute, disagreement.

**brawn** (SYN.) strength, muscle. (ANT.) weakness.

**brazen** (SYN.) immodest, forward, shameless, bold, brassy, impudent, insolent, rude. (ANT.) retiring, self-effacing, modest, shy.

**breach** (SYN.) rupture, fracture, rift, break, crack, gap, opening, breaking, quarrel, violation.

**break** (SYN.) demolish, pound, rack, smash, burst, rupture, disobey, violate, crack, infringe, crush, squeeze, transgress, fracture, shatter, wreck, crash, atomize, disintegrate, collapse, splinter, gap, breach, opening. (ANT.) restore, heal, join, renovate, mend, repair.

**breed** (SYN.) engender, bear, propagate, father, beget, rear, conceive, train, generate, raise, procreate, nurture, create, mother, produce, originate. (ANT.) murder, abort, kill.

**breeze** (SYN.) air, wind, zephyr, breath. (ANT.) calm.

**breezy** (SYN.) jolly, spry, active, brisk, energetic, lively, carefree, spirited.

**brevity** (SYN.) briefness, conciseness. (ANT.) length.

**brew** (SYN.) plot, plan, cook, ferment, prepare, scheme.

**bribe** (SYN.) buy off.

**bridle** (SYN.) control, hold, restrain, check, harness, curb, restraint, halter. (ANT.) release, free, loose.

**brief** (SYN.) curt, short, fleeting, passing, compendious, terse, laconic, succinct, momentary, transient, temporary, concise, compact, condensed. (ANT.) long, extended, prolonged, lengthy, protracted, comprehensive, extensive, exhaustive.

**brigand** (SYN.) bandit, robber, thief.

**bright** (SYN.) luminous, gleaming, clever, witty, brilliant, lucid, vivid, clear, smart, intelligent, lustrous, clever, shining, shiny, sparkling, shimmering, radiant, cheerful, lively, gay, happy, light-hearted, keen, promising, favorable, encouraging. (ANT.) sullen, dull, murky, dark, gloomy, dim, lusterless, boring, colorless, stupid, backward, slow.

**brilliant** (SYN.) bright, clear, smart, intelligent, sparkling, shining, alert, vivid, splendid, radiant, glittering, talented, ingenious, gifted. (ANT.) mediocre, dull, lusterless, second-rate.

**brim** (SYN.) border, margin, lip, rim, edge. (ANT.) middle, center.

**bring** (SYN.) fetch, take, carry, raise, introduce, propose. (ANT.) remove, withdraw.

**brink** (SYN.) limit, verge, rim, margin, edge.

**brisk** (SYN.) fresh, breezy, cool, lively, refreshing, spirited, jolly, energetic, quick, active, animated, nimble, spry, agile, sharp, keen, stimulating, invigorating. (ANT.) musty, faded, stagnant, decayed, hackneyed, slow, lethargic, sluggish, still, dull, oppressive.

**briskness** (SYN.) energy, exercise, motion, rapidity, agility, action, quickness, activity, vigor, liveliness, movement. (ANT.) inertia, idleness, sloth, dullness, inactivity.

**bristle** (SYN.) flare up, anger, rage, seethe, get mad.

**brittle** (SYN.) crumbling, frail, breakable, delicate, splintery, crisp, fragile, weak. (ANT.) tough, enduring, unbreakable, thick, strong, sturdy, flexible, elastic, supple.

**broach** (SYN.) set afoot, introduce, inaugurate, start, mention, launch, advance.

**broad** (SYN.) large, wide, tolerant, expanded, vast, liberal, sweeping, roomy, expansive, extended, general, extensive, full. (ANT.) restricted, confined, narrow, constricted, slim, tight, limited, negligible.

**broadcast** (SYN.) distribute, announce, publish, scatter, circulate, spread, send, transmit, relay.

**broaden** (SYN.) spread, widen, amplify, enlarge, extend, increase, add to, expand, stretch, deepen, magnify. (ANT.) tighten, narrow, constrict, straiten.

**broad-minded** (SYN.) unprejudiced, tolerant, liberal, unbigoted. (ANT.) prejudiced, petty, narrow-minded.

**brochure** (SYN.) booklet, pamphlet, leaflet, mailing, circular, tract, flier.

**broil** (SYN.) cook, burn, beat, roast, bake, scorch, fire, grill, singe, sear, toast.

**broken** (SYN.) flattened, rent, shattered, wrecked, destroyed, reduced, smashed, crushed, fractured, ruptured, interrupted, burst, separated. (ANT.) whole, integral, united, repaired.

**brokenhearted** (SYN.) disconsolate, forlorn, heartbroken, sad, grieving.

**bromide** (SYN.) banality, platitude, stereotype, commonplace, slogan, proverb.

**brooch** (SYN.) clasp, pin, breast-pin.

**brood** (SYN.) study, consider, ponder, reflect, contemplate, meditate, young, litter, offspring, think, muse, deliberate.

**brook** (SYN.) rivulet, run, branch, stream, creek.

**brother** (SYN.) comrade, man, kinsman, sibling. (ANT.) sister.

**brotherhood** (SYN.) kinship, kindness, fraternity, fellowship, clan, society, brotherliness, bond, association, relationship, solidarity. (ANT.) strife, discard, acrimony, opposition.

**brotherly** (SYN.) affectionate, fraternal, cordial, sympathetic, benevolent, philanthropic, humane, kindred, communal, altruistic.

**brow** (SYN.) forehead, eyebrow.

**browbeat** (SYN.) bully, domineer, bulldoze, intimidate, henpeck, oppress, grind.

**brown study** (SYN.) contemplation, reflection, reverie, musing, thoughtfulness, deliberation, rumination, self-communion.

**browse** (SYN.) scan, graze, read, feed.

**bruise** (SYN.) hurt, injure, wound, damage, abrasion, injury, contusion, mark, harm, wound.

**brunt** (SYN.) force, impact, shock, strain, oppression, severity.

**brush** (SYN.) rub, wipe, clean, bushes, remove, shrubs, broom, whisk, paintbrush, hairbrush, underbrush, thicket.

**brush-off** (SYN.) dismissal, snub, sight, rebuff, turndown.

**brusque** (SYN.) sudden, curt, hasty, blunt, rough, steep, precipitate, rugged, craggy, gruff, surly, abrupt, short, bluff. (ANT.) smooth, anticipated, courteous, expected, gradual, personable.

**brutal** (SYN.) brute, cruel, inhuman, rude, barbarous, gross, sensual, ferocious, brutish, coarse, bestial, carnal, remorseless, ruthless, savage, mean, pitiless, barbaric. (ANT.) kind, courteous, humane, civilized, gentle, kindhearted, mild.

**brute** (SYN.) monster, barbarian, beast, animal, wild, savage.

**bubble** (SYN.) boil, foam, seethe, froth.

**buccaneer** (SYN.) sea robber, privateer, pirate.

**buck** (SYN.) spring, jump, vault, leap.

**bucket** (SYN.) pot, pail, canister, can.

**buckle** (SYN.) hook, fastening, fastener, bend, wrinkle, clip, clasp, distort, catch, strap, fasten, collapse, yield, warp.

**bud** (SYN.) develop, sprout.

**buddy** (SYN.) companion, comrade, friend, partner, pal.

**budge** (SYN.) stir, move.

**budget** (SYN.) schedule, ration.

**buff** (SYN.) shine, polish, burnish, rub, wax.

**buffet** (SYN.) bat, strike, clout, blow, knock, beat, crack, hit, slap, cabinet, counter, server.

**buffoon** (SYN.) jester, fool, clown, jokester, zany, comedian, chump, boor, dolt.

**bug** (SYN.) fault, hitch, defect, catch, snag, failing, rub, flaw, snarl, weakness, annoy, pester, hector, vex, nag, nettle.

**bugbear** (SYN.) bogy, specter, demon, devil, fiend.

**build** (SYN.) found, rear, establish, constructed, raise, set up, erect, assemble. (ANT.) raze, destroy, overthrow, demolish, undermine.

**building** (SYN.) residence, structure, house, edifice.

**buildup** (SYN.) gain, enlargement, increase, praise, commendation, promotion, jump, expansion, uptrend, testimonial, plug, puff, blurb, endorsement, compliment. (ANT.) reduction, decrease, decline.

**bulge** (SYN.) lump, protuberance, bump, swelling, protrusion, extend, protrude.

(ANT.) hollow, shrink, contract, depression.

**bulk** (SYN.) lump, magnitude, volume, size, mass, most, majority.

**bulky** (SYN.) great, big, huge, large, enormous, massive, immense, clumsy, cumbersome, unwieldy. (ANT.) tiny, little, small, petite, handy, delicate.

**bull** (SYN.) push, force, press, drive, thrust, bump.

**bulldoze** (SYN.) cow, bully, coerce, thrust, push.

**bulletin** (SYN.) news, flash, message, statement, newsletter, circular.

**bullheaded** (SYN.) dogged, stiff-necked, stubborn, mulish, rigid, pigheaded, willful, tenacious, unyielding. (ANT.) flexible, submissive, compliant.

**bully** (SYN.) pester, tease, intimidate, harass, domineer.

**bulwark** (SYN.) wall, bastion, abutment, bank, dam, rampart, shoulder, parapet, backing, maintainer, embankment, safeguard, reinforcement, sustainer.

**bum** (SYN.) idler, loafer, drifter, hobo, wretch, dawdler, beggar, vagrant.

**bumbling** (SYN.) bungling, inept, blundering, clumsy, incompetent, awkward, maladroit, lumbering, ungainly. (ANT.) facile, handy, dexterous, proficient.

**bump** (SYN.) shake, push, hit, shove, prod, collide, knock, bang, strike.

**bumpkin** (SYN.) hick, yokel, rustic, yahoo.

**bumptious** (SYN.) arrogant, self-assertive, conceited, forward, overbearing, pushy, boastful, obtrusive. (ANT.) sheepish, self-effacing, retiring, shrinking, unobtrusive, diffident.

**bumpy** (SYN.) uneven, jolting, rough, jarring, rocky, coarse, irregular. (ANT.) flat, smooth, flush, polished, level.

**bunch** (SYN.) batch, bundle, cluster, company, collection, flock, group.

**bundle** (SYN.) package, mass, collection, batch, parcel, packet, box, carton, bunch.

**bungalow** (SYN.) ranch house, cabana, cabin, cottage, lodge, summer house, villa.

**bungle** (SYN.) fumble, botch, foul up, boggle, mess up, louse up, blunder.

**bunk** (SYN.) berth, rubbish, nonsense, couch, bed, cot.

**buoyant** (SYN.) light, jolly, spirited, effervescent, blithe,

sprightly, lively, resilient. (ANT.) hopeless, dejected, sullen, depressed, heavy, despondent, sinking, low, pessimistic, downcast, glum.

**burden** (SYN.) oppress, afflict, trouble, encumber, tax, weight, load, worry, contents, trial, lade, overload. (ANT.) lighten, alleviate, ease, mitigate, console, disburden.

**bureau** (SYN.) office, division, department, unit, commission, chest, dresser.

**bureaucrat** (SYN.) clerk, official, functionary, servant, politician.

**burglar** (SYN.) thief, robber.

**burial** (SYN.) interment, funeral.

**burn** (SYN.) scorch, blaze, scald, sear, char, incinerate, fire, flare, combust. (ANT.) quench, extinguish.

**burrow** (SYN.) tunnel, search, seek, dig, excavate, hunt, den, hole.

**burst** (SYN.) exploded, broken, erupt.

**bury** (SYN.) hide, inhume, conceal, immure, cover, inter, entomb, secrete. (ANT.) reveal, display, open, raise, disinter.

**business** (SYN.) employment, profession, trade, work, art, vocation, occupation, company, concern, firm. (ANT.) hobby, avocation, pastime.

**bustle** (SYN.) noise, flurry, action, fuss, ado, stir, excitement, commotion. (ANT.) calmness, composure, serenity, peacefulness.

**busy** (SYN.) careful, industrious, active, patient, assiduous, diligent, perseverant. (ANT.) unconcerned, indifferent, careless, inactive, unemployed, lazy, indolent.

**busybody** (SYN.) gossip, tattletale, pry, meddler, snoop.

**but** (SYN.) nevertheless, yet, however, though, although, still.

**butcher** (SYN.) kill, murder, slaughter, assassinate, slay, massacre. (ANT.) save, protect, vivify, animate, resuscitate.

**butt** (SYN.) bump, ram, bunt, shove, jam, drive, blow, push, thrust, propulsion.

**buttocks** (SYN.) hind end, rump, posterior, behind, bottom, rear, butt.

**button** (SYN.) clasp, close, fasten, hook, buttress, support, brace, stay, frame, prop, reinforcement, bulwark.

**buy** (SYN.) procure, get, purchase, acquire, obtain. (ANT.)

vend, sell.

**buzz** (SYN.) whir, hum, drone, burr.

**by** (SYN.) near, through, beside, with, from, at, close to.

**bygone** (SYN.) bypast, former, earlier, past, onetime, forgotten. (ANT.) present, current, modern.

**bypass** (SYN.) deviate from, go around, detour around.

**bystander** (SYN.) onlooker, watcher, viewer, observer, witness, kibitzer.

**byway** (SYN.) passage, detour, path.

**byword** (SYN.) adage, proverb, axiom, shibboleth, apothegm, motto, slogan.

# C

**cab** (SYN.) coach, taxi, car, hack, taxicab, carriage.

**cabin** (SYN.) cottage, shack, shanty, hut, dwelling, house.

**cabinet** (SYN.) ministry, council, committee, case, cupboard.

**cable** (SYN.) wire, cord, rope, telegraph.

**cache** (SYN.) bury, hide, cover, store.

**cad** (SYN.) knave, rascal, scoundrel, rogue.

**cafe** (SYN.) coffeehouse.

**cafeteria** (SYN.) cafe, diner, restaurant.

**cagey** (SYN.) cunning, wary, clever, tricky, cautious, shrewd, evasive. (ANT.) innocent, straightforward, guileless, naive.

**calamity** (SYN.) ruin, disaster, casualty, distress, hardship, trouble, misfortune, bad luck, catastrophe. (ANT.) blessing, fortune, welfare.

**calculate** (SYN.) count, compute, figure, estimate, consider, tally, determine, measure, subtract, add, divide, multiply, judge, reckon. (ANT.) guess, miscalculate, assume, conjecture.

**calculating** (SYN.) crafty, shrewd, scheming, cunning. (ANT.) simple, guileless, direct, ingenuous.

**calculation** (SYN.) figuring, reckoning, computation, estimation. (ANT.) guess, assumption.

**calendar** (SYN.) timetable, schedule, diary.

**call** (SYN.) designate, name, yell, cry, ask, shout, speak, cry out, call out, exclaim, command, term, label, phone, ring up, collect, waken, awaken, ring, wake, arouse, rouse, outcry, need, demand, claim, assemble, telephone, occasion, invite.

**calling** (SYN.) occupation, profession, trade.

**callous** (SYN.) insensitive, impenitent, obdurate, unfeeling, indurate, hard, insensible, heartless. (ANT.) soft, compassionate, tender.

**calm** (SYN.) appease, lull, quiet, soothe, alloy, assuage, unruffled, mild, tranquil, smooth, serene, cool, levelheaded, unexcited, aloof, detached, stillness, calmness, serenity, composure. (ANT.) tempestuous, disturbed, emotional, turmoil, incite, inflame, roiled, incense, upheaval, excite, upset, disturb, arouse.

**campaign** (SYN.) movement, cause, crusade.

**can** (SYN.) tin, container.

**canal** (SYN.) gully, tube, duct, waterway.

**cancel** (SYN.) eliminate, obliterate, erase, delete, nullify, repeal, revoke, cross out, expunge, void, recall, set aside, abolish, rescind. (ANT.) perpetuate, confirm, ratify, enforce, enact.

**candid** (SYN.) free, blunt, frank, plain, open, sincere, honest, straightforward, direct, outspoken. (ANT.) sly, contrived, wily, scheming.

**candidate** (SYN.) applicant, aspirant, nominee.

**canine** (SYN.) pooch, dog, puppy.

**canny** (SYN.) artful, skillful, shrewd, clever, cautious, cunning, careful.

**canopy** (SYN.) awning, screen, shelter, cover.

**cant** (SYN.) dissimulation, patois, jargon, shoptalk, deceit, argot, pretense. (ANT.) honesty, candor, frankness, truth.

**cantankerous** (SYN.) crabby, grouchy, irritable, surly, grumpy, irascible.

**canyon** (SYN.) gulch, gully, arroyo, ravine, gorge.

**cap** (SYN.) top, cover, crown, beat, lid, excel.

**capability** (SYN.) aptness, ability, capacity, aptitude, dexterity, power, efficiency, qualification. (ANT.) incapacity, disability, incompetency.

**capable** (SYN.) clever, qualified, able, efficient, competent, skilled, fit, skillful, accomplished, fitted. (ANT.) unfitted, incapable, incompetent,

unskilled, inept, inadequate.

**capacity** (SYN.) capability, power, ability, talent, content, skill, volume, size. (ANT.) inability, stupidity, incapacity, impotence.

**cape** (SYN.) pelisse, cloak, mantle, neck, point, headland, peninsula.

**caper** (SYN.) romp, frisk, cavort, frolic, gambol.

**capital** (SYN.) leading, chief, important, property, wealth, money, city, cash, assets, principal, resources, major, primary, first, funds. (ANT.) unimportant, trivial, secondary.

**capricious** (SYN.) undependable, erratic, inconstant, fickle, changeable, irregular, inconsistent, unstable.

**captain** (SYN.) commander, authority, supervisor, leader, skipper, master, officer.

**caption** (SYN.) heading, title, headline.

**captivate** (SYN.) fascinate, charm, delight.

**captive** (SYN.) convict, prisoner, hostage.

**captivity** (SYN.) detention, imprisonment, custody, confinement, bondage, slavery. (ANT.) liberty, freedom.

**capture** (SYN.) catch, grip, apprehend, clutch, arrest, snare, seize, nab, seizure, catching, grasp, take prisoner, grab, recovery, trap. (ANT.) set free, lose, liberate, throw, free, release.

**car** (SYN.) auto, automobile, motorcar, vehicle.

**carcass** (SYN.) remains, frame, corpse, form, bulk, mass, corpus, association, body, cadaver. (ANT.) mind, intellect, soul.

**cardinal** (SYN.) chief, primary, important, prime, leading, major, essential. (ANT.) subordinate, secondary, auxiliary.

**care** (SYN.) concern, anxiety, worry, caution, solicitude, charge, ward, attention, regard, supervision, consider, consideration, keeping, protection, attend, watch, supervise, keep, guardianship, custody. (ANT.) neglect, disregard, indifference, unconcern, negligence.

**career** (SYN.) occupation, profession, job, calling, vocation, trade.

**carefree** (SYN.) lighthearted, happy, unconcerned, breezy, jolly, uneasy, nonchalant, happy-go-lucky, lively.

**careful** (SYN.) prudent,

thoughtful, attentive, cautious, painstaking, scrupulous, heedful, circumspect, vigilant, guarded, discreet, watchful, wary, concerned, meticulous, thorough. (ANT.) nice, careful, heedless, messy, careless, sloppy.

**careless** (SYN.) imprudent, heedless, unconcerned, inattentive, lax, indiscreet, desultory, reckless, negligent. (ANT.) careful, nice, cautious, painstaking, prudent, accurate.

**caress** (SYN.) hug, fondle, embrace, pet, pat, stroke, kiss, cuddle. (ANT.) spurn, vex, buffet, annoy, tease.

**cargo** (SYN.) freight, load, freight-load, shipment.

**caricature** (SYN.) exaggeration, parody, spoof, takeoff, lampoon, satire, burlesque.

**carnage** (SYN.) massacre, liquidation, slaughter, genocide, butchery, extermination, annihilation.

**carnal** (SYN.) base, corporeal, animal, lustful, worldly, sensual, bodily, gross, fleshy, voluptuous. (ANT.) intellectual, spiritual, exalted, temperate.

**carnival** (SYN.) fete, fair, jamboree, festival.

**carol** (SYN.) hymn, song, ballad.

**carp** (SYN.) pick, praise, complain.

**carpet** (SYN.) mat, rug.

**carping** (SYN.) discerning, exact, captions, accurate, fastidious, important, hazardous. (ANT.) superficial, cursory, approving, encouraging, unimportant, insignificant.

**carriage** (SYN.) bearing, conduct, action, deed, behavior, demeanor, disposition, deportment.

**carry** (SYN.) convey, transport, support, bring, sustain, bear, hold, move, transfer, take. (ANT.) drop, abandon.

**carry off** (SYN.) seize, abduct, capture, kidnap. (ANT.) set free, let go, liberate.

**carry on** (SYN.) go on, continue, proceed, misbehave. (ANT.) stop.

**carry out** (SYN.) succeed, complete, fulfill, win, accomplish, effect.

**carve** (SYN.) hew, shape, cut, whittle, chisel, sculpt.

**case** (SYN.) state, covering, receptacle, condition, instance, example, occurrence, happening, illustration, sample, suit, action, claim, lawsuit, crate, container, carton, box.

**cash** (SYN.) currency, money.

**casket** (SYN.) coffin, box, crate.

**cast** (SYN.) fling, toss, throw, pitch, form, company, shape, sort, mold, hurl, sling, shed, direct, impart, turn, actors, players, type, variety.

**caste** (SYN.) class, grade, order, category, status, elegance, set, rank, station, social standing, denomination, excellence, genre.

**castle** (SYN.) mansion, palace, chateau.

**casual** (SYN.) chance, unexpected, informal, accidental, incidental, offhand, unplanned, relaxed, fortuitous, unintentional, spontaneous. (ANT.) planned, expected, calculated, formal, deliberate, dressy, premeditated, pretentious.

**casualty** (SYN.) calamity, fortuity, mishap, loss, injured, dead, wounded, accident, contingency, victim, sufferer, misfortune. (ANT.) design, purpose, intention, calculation.

**catalog** (SYN.) classify, roll, group, list, inventory, directory, index, record, file.

**catastrophe** (SYN.) mishap, calamity, disaster, adversity, accident, ruin. (ANT.) fortune, boon, triumph, blessing, advantage.

**catch** (SYN.) hook, snare, entrap, ensnare, capture, grip, apprehend, grasp, take, grab, nab, arrest, contract, seize, apprehension, latch, bolt, pin, clasp, trap. (ANT.) lose, free, liberate, throw, release.

**catching** (SYN.) contagious, pestilential, communicable, infectious, virulent. (ANT.) non-communicable, healthful.

**catchy** (SYN.) tricky, misleading, attractive.

**category** (SYN.) class, caste, kind, order, genre, rank, classification, sort, elegance, type, set, excellence.

**cater** (SYN.) coddle, oblige, serve, humor, baby, mollycoddle, pamper, spoil, indulge, provide.

**cause** (SYN.) effect, incite, create, induce, inducement, occasion, incentive, prompt, principle, determinant, reason, origin, motive.

**caustic** (SYN.) bitter, disagreeable, distasteful, acrid, sour, spiteful, pungent, tart, painful, cruel, insulting, peevish, mean, ruthless, malicious, hateful, harsh. (ANT.) mellow, sweet, delicious, pleasant.

**caution** (SYN.) heed, vigilance, care, prudence, counsel, warning, wariness, advice, warn, injunction, admonish, watchfulness. (ANT.) carelessness, heedlessness, incaution, abandon, recklessness.

**cautious** (SYN.) heedful, scrupulous, attentive, prudent, thoughtful, discreet, guarded, circumspect, vigilant, watchful, wary, careful. (ANT.) improvident, headstrong, heedless, foolish, forgetful, indifferent.

**cavalcade** (SYN.) column, procession, parade.

**cavalier** (SYN.) contemptuous, insolent, haughty, arrogant.

**cave** (SYN.) grotto, hole, shelter, lair, den, cavern.

**cave in** (SYN.) fall in, collapse.

**cavity** (SYN.) pit, hole, crater.

**cavort** (SYN.) caper, leap, frolic, hop, prance.

**cease** (SYN.) desist, stop, abandon, discontinue, relinquish, end, terminate, leave, surrender, resign. (ANT.) occupy, continue, persist, begin, endure, stay.

**cede** (SYN.) surrender, relinquish, yield.

**celebrate** (SYN.) honor, glorify, commemorate, keep, solemnize, extol, observe, commend, praise. (ANT.) decry, overlook, profane, disregard, disgrace.

**celebrated** (SYN.) eminent, glorious, distinguished, noted, illustrious, famed, well-known, popular, renowned, famous. (ANT.) obscure, hidden, anonymous, infamous, unknown.

**celebrity** (SYN.) somebody, personage, heroine, hero, dignitary, notable.

**celestial** (SYN.) godlike, holy, supernatural, divine, paradisiacal, utopian, transcendent, superhuman. (ANT.) diabolical, profane, mundane, wicked.

**cement** (SYN.) solidify, weld, fasten, secure.

**cemetery** (SYN.) graveyard.

**censure** (SYN.) denounce, reproach, upbraid, blame, disapproval, reprehend, condemn, criticism, disapprove, criticize, reprove. (ANT.) commend, approval, forgive, approve, praise, applaud, condone.

**center** (SYN.) heart, core, midpoint, middle, nucleus, inside, hub, focus. (ANT.) rim, boundary, edge, border, periphery, outskirts.

**central** (SYN.) chief, necessary, main, halfway, dominant, mid, middle, inner, focal, leading, fundamental, principal. (ANT.) side, secondary, incidental, auxiliary.

**ceremonious** (SYN.) correct, exact, precise, stiff, outward, external, solemn, formal. (ANT.) material, unconventional, easy, heartfelt.

**ceremony** (SYN.) observance, rite, parade, formality, pomp, ritual, protocol, solemnity. (ANT.) informality, casualness.

**certain** (SYN.) definite, assured, fixed, inevitable, sure, undeniable, positive, confident, particular, special, indubitable, secure, unquestionable. (ANT.) probable, uncertain, doubtful, questionable.

**certainly** (SYN.) absolutely, surely, definitely. (ANT.) dubiously, doubtfully, questionably.

**certainty** (SYN.) confidence, courage, security, assuredness, firmness, assertion, statement. (ANT.) humility, bashfulness, modest, shyness.

**certificate** (SYN.) affidavit, document.

**certify** (SYN.) validate, affirm, verify, confirm, authenticate, substantiate.

**certitude** (SYN.) confidence, belief, conviction, feeling, faith, persuasion, trust. (ANT.) doubt, incredulity, denial, heresy.

**cessation** (SYN.) ending, finish, stoppage, termination, conclusion, end.

**chafe** (SYN.) heat, rub, warm, annoy, disturb.

**chagrin** (SYN.) irritation, mortification, embarrassment, annoyance, vexation, worry, bother, shame, annoy, irk, humiliation, irritate, vex, frustrate, humiliate, embarrass, mortify, exasperate, disappoint, disappointment.

**chain** (SYN.) fasten, bind, shackle, restrain.

**chairman** (SYN.) speaker.

**challenge** (SYN.) question, dare, call, summon, threat, invite, threaten, demand.

**chamber** (SYN.) cell, salon, room.

**champion** (SYN.) victor, winner, choice, best, conqueror, hero, support, select.

**chance** (SYN.) befall, accident, betide, disaster, opportunity, calamity, occur, possibility, prospect, happen, luck, fate, take place. (ANT.) design, purpose, inevitability, calculation, certainty, intention.

**change** (SYN.) modification, alternation, alteration, mutation, variety, exchange, shift, alter, transfigure, veer, vary, variation, substitution, substitute, vicissitude. (ANT.) uniformity, monotony, settle, remain, endure, retain, preserve, steadfastness, endurance, immutability, stability.

**changeable** (SYN.) fitful, fickle, inconstant, unstable, shifting, wavering. (ANT.) stable, uniform, constant, unchanging.

**channel** (SYN.) strait, corridor, waterway, artery, duct, canal, way, trough, groove, passageway.

**chant** (SYN.) singing, incantation, hymn, intone, sing, carol, psalm, song, ballad.

**chaos** (SYN.) confusion, jumble, turmoil, anarchy, disorder, muddle. (ANT.) organization, order, tranquility, tidiness, system.

**chaotic** (SYN.) confused, disorganized, disordered, messy. (ANT.) neat, ordered, systematic, organized.

**chap** (SYN.) break, fellow, person, crack, split, man, rough, individual, boy.

**chaperon** (SYN.) associate with, escort, convoy, accompany, consort with. (ANT.) avoid, desert, leave, abandon, quit.

**chapter** (SYN.) part, section, division.

**char** (SYN.) scorch, singe, burn, sear.

**character** (SYN.) description, class, kind, repute, mark, individuality, disposition, traits, personality, reputation, symbol, features, quality, eccentric, nature.

**characteristic** (SYN.) exclusive, distinctive, special, mark, feature, property, typical, unique, attribute, distinguishing, trait, quality.

**charge** (SYN.) arraignment, indictment, accusation, sell for, attack, assail, assault, indict, blame, allegation, care, custody, imputation. (ANT.) pardon, flee, exculpation, excuse, absolve, retreat, exoneration.

**charitable** (SYN.) benevolent, generous, liberal, altruistic, kind, obliging, considerate, unselfish. (ANT.) petty, mean, harsh, wicked, greedy, narrow-minded, stingy, malevolent.

**charity** (SYN.) benevolence, kindness, magnanimity, altruism, generosity. (ANT.) malevolence, cruelty, selfishness.

**charm** (SYN.) allure, spell, enchantment, attractiveness, magic, witchery, amulet, talisman, lure, enchant, bewitch, fascinate, captivate.

**charmer** (SYN.) siren, temptress, enchantress, vamp, seductress, seducer, enchanter.

**charming** (SYN.) attractive, enchanting, fascinating, alluring, appealing, winsome, agreeable, bewitching, winning. (ANT.) revolting, repugnant, repulsive.

**chart** (SYN.) design, plan, cabal, plot, sketch, stratagem, map, diagram, conspiracy, graph, intrigue.

**charter** (SYN.) lease, hire, rent, alliance.

**chase** (SYN.) hunt, run after, pursue, trail, follow, persist, scheme. (ANT.) escape, flee, abandon, elude, evade.

**chasm** (SYN.) ravine, abyss, canyon, gorge.

**chaste** (SYN.) clear, immaculate, innocent, sincere, bare, clean, modest, pure, decent, virtuous, virginal, sheer, absolute, spotless. (ANT.) polluted, tainted, foul, impure, sinful, worldly, sullied, defiled.

**chasten** (SYN.) chastise, restrain, punish, discipline.

**chastise** (SYN.) punish, castigate, correct. (ANT.) release, acquit, free, exonerate.

**chat** (SYN.) argue, jabber, blab, plead, consult, converse, lecture, discuss, talk, conversation, tattle.

**chatter** (SYN.) dialogue, lecture, speech, conference, talk, discourse. (ANT.) silence, correspondence, writing.

**cheap** (SYN.) poor, common, inexpensive, shabby, low-priced, beggary, low-cost, shoddy, mean, inferior. (ANT.) honorable, dear, noble, expensive, costly, well-made, elegant, dignified.

**cheat** (SYN.) deceive, fool, bilk, outwit, victimize, dupe, gull, hoodwink, circumvent, swindler, cheater, trickster, phony, fraud, defraud, charlatan, crook, chiseler, con artist, hoax, swindle.

**check** (SYN.) dissect, interrogate, analyze, contemplate, inquire, question, scrutinize, arrest, stop, halt, block, curb, control, investigate, review, examine, test, counterfoil, stub, barrier, watch. (ANT.) overlook, disregard, advance, foster, continue, promote, omit, neglect.

**checkup** (SYN.) medical examination, physical.

**cheek** (SYN.) nerve, effrontery, impudence, gall, impertinence.

**cheer** (SYN.) console, gladden, comfort, encourage, applause, encouragement, joy, glee, gaiety, mirth, soothe, sympathize, approval, solace. (ANT.) depress, sadden, discourage, derision, dishearten, discouragement, antagonize.

**cheerful** (SYN.) glad, jolly, joyful, gay, happy, cherry, merry, joyous, lighthearted. (ANT.) mournful, sad, glum, depressed, gloomy, sullen.

**cherish** (SYN.) prize, treasure, appreciate, nurse, value, comfort, hold dear, foster, nurture, sustain. (ANT.) disregard, neglect, deprecate, scorn, reject, undervalue, abandon.

**chest** (SYN.) bosom, breast, coffer, box, case, trunk, casket, dresser, commode, cabinet, chiffonier.

**chew** (SYN.) gnaw, munch, bite, nibble.

**chic** (SYN.) fashionable, modish, smart, stylish, trendy.

**chide** (SYN.) admonish, rebuke, scold, reprimand, criticize, reprove. (ANT.) extol, praise, commend.

**chief** (SYN.) chieftain, head, commander, captain, leader, principal, master, boss, leading, ruler. (ANT.) servant, subordinate, secondary, follower, incidental, accidental, auxiliary, attendant.

**chiefly** (SYN.) mainly, especially, mostly.

**childish** (SYN.) immature, childlike, infantile, babyish. (ANT.) mature, grownup.

**chill** (SYN.) coolness, cold, cool, coldness, brisk, frosty. (ANT.) hot, warm, heat, heated, warmth.

**chilly** (SYN.) cold, frigid, freezing, arctic, cool, icy, passionless, wintry, unfeeling. (ANT.) fiery, heated, passionate, ardent.

**chirp** (SYN.) peep, cheep, twitter, tweet, chirrup.

**chivalrous** (SYN.) noble, brave, polite, valorous, gallant, gentlemanly, courteous. (ANT.) crude, rude, impolite, uncivil.

**chivalry** (SYN.) courtesy, nobility, gallantry, knighthood.

**choice** (SYN.) delicate, elegant, file, dainty, exquisite, pure, refined, subtle, splendid, handsome, option, selection, beautiful, minute, pretty, pick, select, uncommon, rare, precious, valuable, thin, small.

**choke** (SYN.) throttle, gag, strangle.

**choose** (SYN.) elect, decide between, pick, select, cull, opt. (ANT.) reject, refuse.

**chop** (SYN.) hew, cut, fell, mince.

**chore** (SYN.) routine, task, job, duty, work.

**chronic** (SYN.) persistent, constant, lingering, continuing, perennial, unending, sustained, permanent. (ANT.) fleeting, acute, temporary.

**chronicle** (SYN.) detail, history, narrative, account, description, narration. (ANT.) misrepresentation, confusion, distortion.

**chuckle** (SYN.) titter, laugh, giggle.

**chum** (SYN.) friend, pal, buddy, companion.

**cinema** (SYN.) effigy, film, etching, appearance, drawing, engraving, illustration, likeness, image, panorama, picture.

**circle** (SYN.) disk, ring, set, group, class, club, surround, encircle, enclose, round.

**circuit** (SYN.) circle, course, journey, orbit, revolution, tour.

**circuitous** (SYN.) distorted, devious, indirect, roundabout, swerving, crooked, tortuous. (ANT.) straightforward, straight, direct, honest.

**circular** (SYN.) complete, curved, bulbous, cylindrical, round, ring-like, globular, entire, rotund. (ANT.) straight.

**circumference** (SYN.) border, perimeter, periphery, edge.

**circumspection** (SYN.) care, worry, solicitude, anxiety, concern, caution, attention, vigilance. (ANT.) neglect, negligence, indifference.

**circumstance** (SYN.) fact, event, incident, condition, happening, position, occurrence, situation.

**circumstances** (SYN.) facts, conditions, factors, situation, background, grounds, means, capital, assets, rank, class.

**cite** (SYN.) affirm, assign, allege, advance, quote, mention, declare, claim, maintain. (ANT.) refute, gainsay, deny, contradict.

**citizen** (SYN.) native, inhabitant, national, denizen, subject, dweller, resident.

**city** (SYN.) metropolis, municipality, town.

**civil** (SYN.) courteous, cultivated, accomplished, public, municipal, respectful, genteel, polite, considerate, gracious, urban. (ANT.) uncouth, uncivil, impertinent, impolite, boorish.

**civilization** (SYN.) cultivation, culture, education, breeding, enlightenment, society, refinement. (ANT.) ignorance, vulgarity.

**civilize** (SYN.) refine, tame, polish, cultivate, instruct, teach.

**claim** (SYN.) aver, declare, allege, assert, affirm, express, state, demand, maintain, defend, uphold. (ANT.) refute, deny, contradict.

**clamor** (SYN.) cry, din, babble, noise, racket, outcry, row, sound, tumult, shouting, shout, uproar. (ANT.) hush, serenity, silence, tranquility, stillness, quiet.

**clan** (SYN.) fellowship, kindness, solidarity, family, brotherhood, association, fraternity. (ANT.) discord, strife, opposition, acrimony.

**clandestine** (SYN.) covert, hidden, latent, private, concealed, secret, unknown. (ANT.) exposed, known, conspicuous, obvious.

**clarify** (SYN.) educate, explain, expound, decipher, illustrate, clear, resolve, define, interpret, unfold. (ANT.) darken, obscure, baffle, confuse.

**clash** (SYN.) clank, crash, clang, conflict, disagreement, opposition, collision, struggle, mismatch, contrast, disagree, collide, interfere. (ANT.) accord, agreement, harmony, blend, harmonize, match, agree.

**clasp** (SYN.) grip, hold, grasp, adhere, clutch, keep, have, maintain, possess, occupy, retain, support, confine, embrace, fastening, check, detain, curb, receive. (ANT.) relinquish, vacate, surrender, abandon.

**class** (SYN.) category, denomination, caste, kind, genre, grade, rank, order, elegance, classification, division, sort, family, species, set, excellence.

**classic** (SYN.) masterpiece.

**classification** (SYN.) order, category, class, arrangement, ordering, grouping, organization.

**classify** (SYN.) arrange, class, order, sort, grade, group, index.

**clause** (SYN.) condition, paragraph, limitation, article.

**claw** (SYN.) hook, talon, nail, scratch.

**clean** (SYN.) mop, tidy, neat, dustless, clear, unsoiled, immaculate, unstained, untainted, pure, dust, vacuum, scour, decontaminate, wipe, sterilize, cleanse, scrub, purify, wash, sweep. (ANT.) stain, soil, pollute, soiled, impure, dirty.

**cleanse** (SYN.) mop, purify, wash, sweep. (ANT.) stain, soil, dirty, pollute.

**clear** (SYN.) fair, sunny, cloudless, transparent, apparent, limpid, distinct, intelligible, evident, unmistakable, understandable, unclouded, light, bright, certain, manifest, lucid, plain, obvious, unobstructed. (ANT.) obscure, unclear, muddled, confused, dark, cloudy, blocked, obstructed, questionable, dubious, blockaded, foul, overcast.

**clearly** (SYN.) plainly, obviously, evidently, definitely, surely, certainly. (ANT.) questionably, dubiously.

**clemency** (SYN.) forgiveness, charity, compassion, grace, mercy, leniency, pity, mildness. (ANT.) punishment, vengeance, retribution.

**clerical** (SYN.) ministerial, pastoral, priestly, celestial, holy, sacred, secretarial.

**clerk** (SYN.) typist, office worker, salesperson, salesclerk.

**clever** (SYN.) apt, dexterous, quick, adroit, quick-witted, talented, bright, skillful, witty, ingenious, smart, intelligent, shrewd, gifted, expert, sharp. (ANT.) unskilled, slow, stupid, backward, maladroit, bungling, dull, clumsy.

**cleverness** (SYN.) intellect, intelligence, comprehension, mind, perspicacity, sagacity, fun. (ANT.) sobriety, stupidity, solemnity, commonplace, platitude.

**client** (SYN.) patron, customer.

**cliff** (SYN.) scar, tor, bluff, crag, precipice, escarpment.

**climate** (SYN.) aura, atmosphere, air, ambience.

**climax** (SYN.) apex, culmination, peak, summit, consummation, height, acme, zenith. (ANT.) depth, base, anticlimax, floor.

**climb** (SYN.) mount, scale, ascend. (ANT.) descend.

**clip** (SYN.) snip, crop, cut, mow, clasp.

**cloak** (SYN.) conceal, cover, disguise, clothe, cape, guard, envelop, hide, mask, protect, shield. (ANT.) *divulge, expose, reveal, bare, unveil.*

**clod** (SYN.) wad, hunk, gobbet, lump, chunk, clot, gob, dunce, dolt, oaf, fool.

**clog** (SYN.) crowd, congest, cram, overfill, stuff.

**cloister** (SYN.) monastery, priory, hermitage, abbey, convent.

**close** (SYN.) adjacent, adjoining, immediate, unventilated, stuffy, abutting, neighboring, dear, oppressive, mean, impending, nearby, near, devoted. (ANT.) *afar, faraway, removed, distant.*

**close** (SYN.) seal, shut, clog, stop, obstruct, cease, conclude, complete, end, terminate, occlude, finish. (ANT.) *unlock, begin, open, unbar, inaugurate, commence, start.*

**closet** (SYN.) cabinet, locker, wardrobe, cupboard.

**cloth** (SYN.) fabric, goods, material, textile.

**clothe** (SYN.) garb, dress, apparel. (ANT.) *strip, undress.*

**clothes** (SYN.) array, attire, apparel, clothing, garb, dress, garments, raiment, drapery, vestments. (ANT.) *nudity, nakedness.*

**clothing** (SYN.) attire, clothes, apparel, array, dress, drapery, garments, garb, vestments. (ANT.) *nudity, nakedness.*

**cloud** (SYN.) fog, mist, haze, mass, collection, obscure, dim, shadow.

**cloudy** (SYN.) dim, dark, indistinct, murky, mysterious, indefinite, vague, sunless, clouded, obscure, overcast, shadowy. (ANT.) *sunny, clear, distinct, limpid, lucid, clarified, cloudless, brilliant, bright.*

**club** (SYN.) society, association, set, circle, organization, bat, cudgel, stick, blackjack.

**clue** (SYN.) sign, trace, hint, suggestion.

**clumsy** (SYN.) bungling, inept, rough, unpolished, bumbling, awkward, ungraceful, gauche, ungainly, unskillful, untoward. (ANT.) *polished, skillful, neat, graceful, dexterous, adroit.*

**cluster** (SYN.) batch, clutch, group, bunch, gather, pack, assemble, crowd.

**clutch** (SYN.) grip, grab, seize, hold.

**coalition** (SYN.) combination, association, alliance, confederacy, entente, league, treaty. (ANT.) *schism, separation, divorce.*

**coarse** (SYN.) unpolished, vulgar, rough, impure, rude, crude, gruff, gross. (ANT.) *delicate, smooth, refined, polished, genteel, cultivated, suave, fine, cultured.*

**coast** (SYN.) seaboard, seashore, beach, shore, drift, glide, ride.

**coax** (SYN.) urge, persuade, wheedle, cajole. (ANT.) *force, bully, coerce.*

**coddle** (SYN.) pamper, baby, spoil, indulge.

**coerce** (SYN.) constrain, compel, enforce, force, drive, oblige, impel. (ANT.) *prevent, persuade, convince, induce.*

**coercion** (SYN.) emphasis, intensity, energy, dint, might, potency, power, vigor, strength, compulsion, force, constraint, violence. (ANT.) *impotence, frailty, feebleness, weakness, persuasion.*

**cognizance** (SYN.) apprehension, erudition, acquaintance, information, learning, knowledge, lore, science, scholarship, understanding. (ANT.) *illiteracy, misunderstanding, ignorance.*

**cognizant** (SYN.) conscious, aware, apprised, informed, mindful, observant, perceptive. (ANT.) *unaware, ignorant, oblivious, insensible.*

**coherent** (SYN.) logical, intelligible, sensible, rational, commonsensical, reasonable.

**coiffeur** (SYN.) hairdresser.

**coiffure** (SYN.) haircut, hairdo.

**coincide** (SYN.) acquiesce, agree, accede, assent, consent, comply, correspond, concur, match, tally, harmonize, conform. (ANT.) *differ, disagree, protest, contradict.*

**coincidence** (SYN.) accident, chance. (ANT.) *plot, plan, prearrangement, scheme.*

**coincident** (SYN.) identical, equal, equivalent, distinguishable, same, like. (ANT.) *distinct, contrary, disparate, opposed.*

**coincidental** (SYN.) unpredicted, unexpected, chance, unforeseen, accidental, fortuitous.

**cold** (SYN.) cool, freezing, chilly, frigid, icy, frozen, wintry, arctic, unfriendly, indifferent, phlegmatic, stoical, passionless, chill, unemotional, heartless, unfeeling. (ANT.) *hot, torrid, fiery, burning, ardent, friendly, temperate, warm, passionate.*

**collapse** (SYN.) descend, decrease, diminish, fail,

downfall, failure, decline, fall, drop, sink, subside, topple. (ANT.) *soar, steady, limb, mount, arise.*

**colleague** (SYN.) companion, attendant, comrade, associate, crony, mate, friend, partner. (ANT.) *enemy, stranger, adversary.*

**collect** (SYN.) assemble, amass, concentrate, pile, accumulate, congregate, obtain, heap, gather, solicit, secure, procure, raise, get, mass, hoard, consolidate. (ANT.) *divide, dole, assort, dispel, distribute, disperse.*

**collected** (SYN.) cool, calm, composed, imperturbable, placid, sedate, quiet. (ANT.) *excited, violent, aroused, agitated.*

**collection** (SYN.) amount, conglomeration, sum, entirety, aggregation, hoard, accumulation, pile, store, aggregate, total, whole. (ANT.) *part, unit, particular, element, ingredient.*

**collide** (SYN.) hit, smash, crash, strike.

**collision** (SYN.) conflict, combat, duel, battle, encounter, crash, smash, fight, contention, struggle, discord. (ANT.) *concord, amity, harmony, consonance.*

**collusion** (SYN.) combination, cabal, intrigue, conspiracy, plot, treachery.

**color** (SYN.) hue, paint, pigment, complexion, dye, shade, tone, tincture, stain, tint, tinge. (ANT.) *paleness, transparency, achromatism.*

**colorful** (SYN.) impressive, vivid, striking, full-color, multicolored, offbeat, weird, unusual. (ANT.) *flat, dull, uninteresting.*

**colossal** (SYN.) enormous, elephantine, gargantuan, huge, immense, gigantic, prodigious. (ANT.) *little, minute, small, miniature, diminutive, microscopic, tiny.*

**combat** (SYN.) conflict, duel, battle, collision, encounter, fight, contest, oppose, war, contention, struggle, discord. (ANT.) *consonance, harmony, concord, yield, surrender, succumb, amity.*

**combination** (SYN.) association, confederacy, alliance, entente, league, compounding, mixture, blend, composite, federation, mixing, compound, blending, union. (ANT.) *separation, division, schism.*

**combine** (SYN.) adjoin,

associate, accompany, conjoin, connect, link, mix, blend, couple, unite, join. (ANT.) *detach, disjoin, divide, separate, disconnect.*

**come** (SYN.) near, approach, reach, arrive, advance. (ANT.) *depart, leave, go.*

**comedian** (SYN.) comic, wit, humorist, gagman, wag.

**comely** (SYN.) charming, elegant, beauteous, beautiful, fine, lovely, pretty, handsome. (ANT.) *hideous, repulsive, foul, unsightly.*

**come-on** (SYN.) lure, inducement, enticement, temptation, premium.

**comfort** (SYN.) contentment, ease, enjoyment, relieve, consolation, relief, cheer, console, calm, satisfaction, soothe, encourage, succor, luxury, solace. (ANT.) *depress, torture, discomfort, upset, misery, disturb, agitate, affliction, discompose, uncertainty, suffering.*

**comfortable** (SYN.) pleasing, agreeable, convenient, cozy, welcome, acceptable, relaxed, restful, cozy, gratifying, easy, contented, rested, satisfying, pleasurable. (ANT.) *miserable, distressing, tense, strained, troubling, edgy, uncomfortable.*

**comical** (SYN.) droll, funny, humorous, amusing, ludicrous, witty, ridiculous, odd, queer. (ANT.) *sober, solemn, sad, serious, melancholy.*

**command** (SYN.) class, method, rank, arrangement, series, sequence, point, aim, conduct, manage, guide, bid, system, succession, bidding, direct, order, demand, direction, rule, dictate, decree. (ANT.) *consent, obey, misdirect, distract, deceive, misguide, license, confusion.*

**commandeer** (SYN.) take possession, seize, confiscate, appropriate.

**commanding** (SYN.) imposing, masterful, assertive, authoritative, positive.

**commence** (SYN.) open, start. (ANT.) *stop, end, terminate, finish.*

**commend** (SYN.) laud, praise, applaud, recommend. (ANT.) *censure, criticize.*

**commendable** (SYN.) deserving, praiseworthy. (ANT.) *bad, deplorable, lamentable.*

**commendation** (SYN.) approval, applause, praise, recommendation, honor, medal. (ANT.) *criticism, condemnation, censure.*

**commensurate** (SYN.) keep,

celebrate, observe, honor, commend, extol, glorify, laud, praise, honor. *(ANT.) decry, disgrace, disregard, overlook, profane, dishonor.*

**comment** *(SYN.)* assertion, declaration, annotation, explanation, review, commentary, report, remark, observation, utterance, criticism, statement.

**commerce** *(SYN.)* business, engagement, employment, art, trade, marketing, enterprise, occupation. *(ANT.) hobby, pastime, avocation.*

**commiseration** *(SYN.)* condolence, empathy, pity. *(ANT.) hardness, brutality, inhumanity, cruelty.*

**commission** *(SYN.)* board, committee, command, permit, order, permission, delegate, authorize, deputize, entrust.

**commit** *(SYN.)* perpetrate, perform, obligate, do, commend, consign, relegate, bind, delegate, empower, pledge, entrust, authorize, trust. *(ANT.) neglect, mistrust, release, free, miscarry, fail.*

**commitment** *(SYN.)* duty, promise, responsibility, pledge.

**committee** *(SYN.)* commission, bureau, board, delegate, council.

**commodious** *(SYN.)* appropriate, accessible, adapted, favorable, handy, fitting, timely. *(ANT.) inconvenient, troublesome, awkward.*

**commodity** *(SYN.)* article, merchandise, wares, goods.

**common** *(SYN.)* ordinary, popular, familiar, mean, low, general, vulgar, communal, mutual, shared, natural, frequent, prevalent, joint, conventional, plain, usual, universal. *(ANT.) odd, exceptional, scarce, noble, extraordinary, different, separate, outstanding, rare, unusual, distinctive, refined.*

**commonplace** *(SYN.)* common, usual, frequent, ordinary, everyday. *(ANT.) distinctive, unusual, original.*

**commonsense** *(SYN.)* perceptible, alive, apprehensible, aware, awake, cognizant, conscious, comprehending, perceptible. *(ANT.) unaware, impalpable, imperceptible.*

**commotion** *(SYN.)* confusion, chaos, disarray, ferment, disorder, stir, tumult, agitation. *(ANT.) tranquillity, peace, order.*

**communicable** *(SYN.)*

infectious, virulent, catching, transferable, contagious. *(ANT.) hygienic, non-communicable.*

**communicate** *(SYN.)* convey, impart, inform, confer, disclose, reveal, relate, tell, advertise, publish, transmit, publicize, divulge. *(ANT.) withhold, hide, conceal.*

**communication** *(SYN.)* disclosure, transmission, declaration, announcement, notification, publication, message, report, news, information.

**communicative** *(SYN.)* unreserved, open, frank, free, straightforward, unrestrained. *(ANT.) close-mouthed, secretive.*

**communion** *(SYN.)* intercourse, fellowship, participation, association, sacrament, union. *(ANT.) nonparticipation, alienation.*

**community** *(SYN.)* public, society, city, town, village, township.

**compact** *(SYN.)* contracted, firm, narrow, snug, close, constricted, packed, vanity, treaty, agreement, tense, taut, tight, niggardly, close-fisted, parsimonious, compressed, stingy. *(ANT.) slack, open, loose, relaxed, unconfined, unfretted, sprawling, lax.*

**companion** *(SYN.)* attendant, comrade, consort, friend, colleague, partner, crony, mate, associate. *(ANT.) stranger, enemy, adversary.*

**companionship** *(SYN.)* familiarity, cognizance, acquaintance, fellowship, knowledge, intimacy. *(ANT.) unfamiliarity, inexperience, ignorance.*

**company** *(SYN.)* crew, group, band, party, throng, house, assemblage, troop, fellowship, association, business, concern, partnership, corporation, companionship, firm. *(ANT.) seclusion, individual, solitude.*

**comparable** *(SYN.)* allied, analogous, alike, akin, like, correspondent, correlative, parallel. *(ANT.) opposed, incongruous, dissimilar, unalike, different, divergent.*

**compare** *(SYN.)* discriminate, match, differentiate, contrast, oppose.

**comparison** *(SYN.)* likening, contrasting, judgment.

**compartment** *(SYN.)* division, section.

**compassion** *(SYN.)* mercy, sympathy, pity.

**compassionate** *(SYN.)*

sympathizing, benign, forbearing, good, tender, affable, humane, indulgent, kind, sympathetic, kindly. *(ANT.) inhuman, merciless, unkind, cold-hearted, unsympathetic, cruel.*

**compatible** *(SYN.)* consistent, agreeing, conforming, accordant, congruous, harmonious, cooperative, agreeable, constant, consonant, correspondent. *(ANT.) discrepant, paradoxical, disagreeable, contradictory.*

**compel** *(SYN.)* drive, enforce, coerce, constrain, force, oblige, impel. *(ANT.) induce, coax, wheedle, persuade, cajole, convince.*

**compensate** *(SYN.)* remunerate, repay, reimburse, recompense, balance.

**compensation** *(SYN.)* fee, earnings, pay, payment, recompense, allowance, remuneration, remittance, settlement, stipend, repayment, salary, wages. *(ANT.) present, gratuity, gift.*

**compete** *(SYN.)* rival, contest, oppose, vie. *(ANT.) reconcile, accord.*

**competence** *(SYN.)* skill, ability, capability.

**competent** *(SYN.)* efficient, clever, capable, able, apt, proficient, skillful, fitted, qualified. *(ANT.) inept, incapable, unfitted, awkward, incompetent, inadequate.*

**competition** *(SYN.)* contest, match, rivalry, tournament.

**competitor** *(SYN.)* rival, contestant, opponent. *(ANT.) ally, friend, colleague.*

**complain** *(SYN.)* lament, murmur, protest, grouch, grumble, regret, moan, remonstrate, whine, repine. *(ANT.) rejoice, praise, applaud, approve.*

**complaint** *(SYN.)* protest, objection, grievance.

**complement** *(SYN.)* supplement, complete. *(ANT.) clash, conflict.*

**complete** *(SYN.)* consummate, entire, ended, thorough, finished, full, whole, concluded, over, done, terminate, unbroken, total, undivided. *(ANT.) unfinished, imperfect, incomplete, start, partial, begin, commence, lacking.*

**completion** *(SYN.)* achievement, attainment, end, conclusion, close, finish, windup, accomplishment, realization. *(ANT.) omission, neglect, failure, defeat.*

**complex** *(SYN.)* sophisticated,

compound, intricate, involved, perplexing, elaborate, complicated. *(ANT.) basic, simple, rudimentary, uncompounded, uncomplicated, plain.*

**complexion** *(SYN.)* paint, pigment, hue, color, dye, stain, tincture, tinge, tint, shade. *(ANT.) paleness, transparency.*

**compliant** *(SYN.)* meek, modest, lowly, plain, submissive, simple, unostentatious, unassuming, unpretentious. *(ANT.) proud, vain, arrogant, haughty, boastful.*

**complicated** *(SYN.)* intricate, involved, complex, compound, perplexing. *(ANT.) simple, plain, uncompounded.*

**compliment** *(SYN.)* eulogy, flattery, praise, admiration, honor, adulation, flatter, commendation, tribute. *(ANT.) taunt, affront, aspersion, insult, disparage, criticism.*

**complimentary** *(SYN.)* gratis, free.

**comply** *(SYN.)* assent, consent, accede, acquiesce, coincide, conform, concur, tally. *(ANT.) differ, dissent, protest, disagree.*

**component** *(SYN.)* division, fragment, allotment, moiety, apportionment, scrap, portion, section, share, segment, ingredient, organ. *(ANT.) whole, entirety.*

**comport** *(SYN.)* carry, conduct, behave, act, deport, interact, operate, manage.

**compose** *(SYN.)* forge, fashion, mold, make, construct, create, produce, shape, form, constitute, arrange, organize, make up, write, invent, devise, frame. *(ANT.) misshape, dismantle, disfigure, destroy.*

**composed** *(SYN.)* calm, cool, imperturbable, placid, quiet, unmoved, sedate, peaceful, collected, tranquil. *(ANT.) aroused, violent, nervous, agitated, perturbed, excited.*

**composer** *(SYN.)* author, inventor, creator, maker, originator.

**composition** *(SYN.)* paper, theme, work, essay, compound, mixture, mix.

**composure** *(SYN.)* calmness, poise, control, self-control, self-possession. *(ANT.) anger, rage, turbulence, agitation.*

**compound** *(SYN.)* blend, confound, jumble, consort, aggregate, complicated, combination, combined, mixture, complex, join.

(ANT.) segregate, separate, divide, simple, sort.

**comprehend** (SYN.) apprehend, discern, learn, perceive, see, grasp, understand. (ANT.) mistake, misunderstand, ignore.

**comprehension** (SYN.) insight, perception, understanding, awareness, discernment. (ANT.) misconception, insensibility.

**comprehensive** (SYN.) wide, inclusive, complete, broad, full. (ANT.) fragmentary, partial, limited, incomplete.

**compress** (SYN.) press, compact, squeeze, pack, crowd. (ANT.) spread, stretch, expand.

**comprise** (SYN.) contain, hold, embrace. (ANT.) emit, encourage, yield, discharge.

**compulsion** (SYN.) might, energy, potency, strength, vigor. (ANT.) persuasion, impotence, frailty.

**compulsory** (SYN.) required, obligatory, necessary, unavoidable. (ANT.) elective, optional, free, unrestricted.

**computation** (SYN.) reckoning, record. (ANT.) misrepresentation.

**compute** (SYN.) count, calculate, determine, figure, reckon. (ANT.) conjecture, guess, miscalculate.

**comrade** (SYN.) attendant, companion, colleague, associate, friend. (ANT.) stranger, enemy, adversary.

**conceal** (SYN.) disguise, cover, hide, mask, screen, secrete, veil, withhold. (ANT.) reveal, show, disclose, expose.

**concede** (SYN.) permit, suffer, tolerate, grant, give, admit, acknowledge, allow, yield. (ANT.) forbid, contradict, protest, refuse, deny, negate, resist.

**conceit** (SYN.) pride, vanity, complacency, conception, idea, egotism, self-esteem, caprice, fancy, whim. (ANT.) humility, meekness, humbleness, modesty.

**conceited** (SYN.) proud, arrogant, vain, smug, egotistical. (ANT.) humble, modest, self-effacing.

**conceive** (SYN.) design, create, imagine, understand, devise, concoct, perceive, frame, grasp, invent. (ANT.) imitate, reproduce, copy.

**concentrate** (SYN.) localize, focus, condense, ponder, meditate, center, scrutinize. (ANT.) scatter, diffuse, dissipate, disperse.

**concentrated** (SYN.) compressed, thick, dense. (ANT.) sparse, quick, dispersed.

**concept** (SYN.) fancy, conception, image, notion, idea, sentiment, thought. (ANT.) thing, matter, substance, entity.

**conception** (SYN.) consideration, deliberation, fancy, idea, notion, regard, thought, view.

**concern** (SYN.) matter, anxiety, affair, disturb, care, business, solicitude, interest, affect, involve, touch, trouble, worry. (ANT.) unconcern, negligence, disinterest, tire, bore, calm, indifference.

**concerning** (SYN.) regarding, about, respecting.

**concerted** (SYN.) united, joint, combined. (ANT.) individual, unorganized, separate.

**concession** (SYN.) admission, yielding, granting. (ANT.) insistence, demand.

**concise** (SYN.) pity, neat, brief, compact, succinct, terse. (ANT.) wordy, lengthy, verbose, prolix.

**conclude** (SYN.) decide, achieve, close, end, finish, terminate, complete, arrange, determine, settle, perfect, perform. (ANT.) start, begin, commence.

**concluding** (SYN.) extreme, final, last, terminal, utmost. (ANT.) first, foremost, opening, initial.

**conclusion** (SYN.) end, finale, termination, deduction, close, settlement, decision, finish, resolution, determination, completion, issue, judgment. (ANT.) commencement, inception, opening, start, beginning.

**conclusive** (SYN.) decisive, eventual, final, terminal, ultimate. (ANT.) original, first, inaugural.

**concord** (SYN.) agreement, unison, understanding, accordance, stipulation. (ANT.) disagreement, discord, dissension.

**concrete** (SYN.) solid, firm, precise, definite, specific. (ANT.) undetermined, vague, general.

**concur** (SYN.) agree, assent, consent, accede. (ANT.) dissent, protest, differ.

**condemn** (SYN.) denounce, reproach, blame, upbraid, convict, rebuke, doom, judge, censure, reprehend, punish, reprobate, sentence. (ANT.) condone, forgive, absolve, praise, applaud, extol, approve, pardon, laud, excuse, commend.

**condense** (SYN.) shorten, reduce, abridge, abbreviate, concentrate, digest, compress, diminish. (ANT.) enlarge, increase, swell, expand.

**condition** (SYN.) circumstance, state, situation, case, plight, requirement, position, necessity, stipulation, predicament, provision, term.

**conditional** (SYN.) dependent, relying. (ANT.) casual, original, absolute.

**condolence** (SYN.) commiseration, concord, harmony, pity, sympathy, warmth. (ANT.) harshness, indifference, unconcern.

**conduct** (SYN.) control, supervise, manage, behavior, deed, actions, act, behave, manners, deportment.

**confederate** (SYN.) ally, abettor, assistant. (ANT.) enemy, rival, opponent, adversary.

**confederation** (SYN.) combination, league, union, marriage, treaty. (ANT.) separation, divorce.

**confer** (SYN.) gossip, grant, speak, tattle, blab, chat, deliberate, consult, award, give, bestow, talk. (ANT.) retrieve, withdraw.

**confess** (SYN.) avow, acknowledge, admit, concede, grant, divulge, reveal. (ANT.) disown, renounce, deny, conceal.

**confession** (SYN.) defense, justification, excuse, apology. (ANT.) dissimulation, denial, complaint.

**confidence** (SYN.) firmness, self-reliance, assurance, faith, trust, pledge, declaration, self-confidence, reliance, self-assurance, courage, statement. (ANT.) distrust, shyness, mistrust, bashfulness, diffidence, doubt, modesty, suspicion.

**confident** (SYN.) certain, sure, dauntless, self-assured. (ANT.) uncertain, timid, shy.

**confine** (SYN.) enclose, restrict, hinder, fence, limit, bound. (ANT.) release, expose, free, expand, open.

**confirm** (SYN.) acknowledge, establish, settle, substantiate, approve, fix, verify, assure, validate, ratify, corroborate, strengthen. (ANT.) disclaim, deny, disavow.

**confirmation** (SYN.) demonstration, experiment, test, trial, verification. (ANT.) fallacy, invalidity.

**confirmed** (SYN.) regular, established, habitual. (ANT.) occasional, infrequent.

**confiscate** (SYN.) capture, catch, gain, purloin, steal, take, clutch, grip, seize, get, obtain, bear.

**conflagration** (SYN.) flame, glow, heat, warmth, fervor, passion, vigor. (ANT.) apathy, cold, quiescence.

**conflict** (SYN.) duel, combat, fight, collision, discord, encounter, interference, inconsistency, contention, struggle, opposition, clash, oppose, battle, controversy, contend, engagement, contest, variance. (ANT.) consonance, harmony, amity.

**conform** (SYN.) adapt, comply, yield, submit, obey, adjust, agree, fit, suit. (ANT.) misapply, misfit, rebel, vary.

**conformity** (SYN.) congruence, accord, agreement, correspondence.

**confound** (SYN.) confuse, baffle, perplex, puzzle, bewilder.

**confront** (SYN.) defy, hinder, resist, thwart, withstand, bar. (ANT.) submit, agree, support, succumb.

**confuse** (SYN.) confound, perplex, mystify, dumbfound, baffle, puzzle, jumble, mislead, mix up, mistake, bewilder. (ANT.) explain, instruct, edify, illumine, enlighten, illuminate, solve.

**confused** (SYN.) deranged, indistinct, disordered, muddled, bewildered, disconcerted, disorganized, perplexed. (ANT.) organized, plain, clear, obvious.

**confusion** (SYN.) commotion, disarray, agitation, disorder, chaos, ferment, stir, perplexity, tumult, bewilderment, disarrangement, uncertainty, muss, mess, turmoil. (ANT.) order, tranquility, enlightenment, comprehension, understanding, tidiness, organization, peace.

**congregate** (SYN.) gather, foregather, meet, convene. (ANT.) scatter, dispel, disperse, dissipate.

**congress** (SYN.) parliament, legislature, assembly.

**congruous** (SYN.) agreeing, conforming, constant, correspondent. (ANT.) incongruous, inconsistent, discrepant.

**conjecture** (SYN.) law, supposition, theory. (ANT.) proof, fact, certainty.

**conjunction** (SYN.) combination, junction, connection, link. (ANT.) separation, disconnection, diversion.

**connect** (SYN.) adjoin, link, combine, relate, join, attach, unite, associate, attribute, affix. (*ANT.*) *detach, separate, disjoin, untie, dissociation, disconnect, disassociation, unfasten.*

**connection** (*SYN.*) conjunction, alliance, link, affinity, bond, tie, association, relationship, union. (*ANT.*) *isolation, dissociation, separation, disassociation, disunion.*

**conquer** (*SYN.*) master, beat, humble, defeat, overcome, rout, win, succeed, achieve, gain, overpower, quell, subdue, crush, vanquish. (*ANT.*) *cede, yield, retreat, surrender.*

**conquest** (*SYN.*) triumph, victory, achievement. (*ANT.*) *surrender, failure, defeat.*

**conscientious** (*SYN.*) upright, straight, honest, incorruptible, scrupulous. (*ANT.*) *careless, irresponsible, slovenly.*

**conscious** (*SYN.*) cognizant, informed, perceptive, aware, intentional, sensible, awake, purposeful, deliberate. (*ANT.*) *unaware, insensible, asleep, comatose, ignorant.*

**consecrate** (*SYN.*) exalt, extol, hallow, honor. (*ANT.*) *mock, degrade, debase, abuse.*

**consecrated** (*SYN.*) holy, divine, devout, spiritual. (*ANT.*) *evil, worldly, secular.*

**consent** (*SYN.*) permission, leave, agree, let, assent, agreement, license, permit. (*ANT.*) *refusal, opposition, denial, dissent, prohibition.*

**consequence** (*SYN.*) outcome, issue, result, effect, significance, importance. (*ANT.*) *impetus, cause.*

**consequential** (*SYN.*) significant, important, weighty. (*ANT.*) *trivial, unimportant, minor, insignificant.*

**consequently** (*SYN.*) hence, thence, therefore.

**conservative** (*SYN.*) conventional, reactionary, cautious, moderate, careful. (*ANT.*) *radical, liberal, foolhardy, reckless.*

**conserve** (*SYN.*) save, retain, reserve, guard, keep, support, sustain. (*ANT.*) *dismiss, neglect, waste, reject, discard.*

**consider** (*SYN.*) heed, ponder, contemplate, examine, study, weigh, reflect, think about, regard, deliberate, respect. (*ANT.*) *ignore, overlook, disdain, disregard, neglect.*

**considerable** (*SYN.*) much, noteworthy, worthwhile, significant, important.

**considerate** (*SYN.*) careful, heedful, prudent, kind, thoughtful, polite, introspective, reflective. (*ANT.*) *thoughtless, heedless, inconsiderate, selfish, rash.*

**consideration** (*SYN.*) kindness, care, heed, politeness, empathy, notice, watchfulness, kindliness, thoughtfulness, courtesy, concern, sympathy, thought, attention, reflection, fee, pay, study. (*ANT.*) *omission, oversight, negligence.*

**consistent** (*SYN.*) conforming, accordant, compatible, agreeing, faithful, constant, harmonious, expected, regular, congruous, correspondent. (*ANT.*) *paradoxical, discrepant, contrary, antagonistic, opposed, eccentric, inconsistent, incongruous.*

**consolation** (*SYN.*) enjoyment, sympathy, relief, ease, contentment, comfort, solace. (*ANT.*) *discomfort, suffering, discouragement, torture, burden, misery.*

**console** (*SYN.*) solace, comfort, sympathize with, assuage, soothe. (*ANT.*) *worry, annoy, upset, disturb, distress.*

**consolidate** (*SYN.*) blend, combine, conjoin, fuse, mix, merge, unite. (*ANT.*) *decompose, separate, analyze, disintegrate.*

**consort** (*SYN.*) companion, comrade, friend. (*ANT.*) *stranger, enemy, adversary.*

**conspicuous** (*SYN.*) distinguished, clear, manifest, salient, noticeable, striking, obvious, prominent, visible. (*ANT.*) *hidden, obscure, neutral, common, inconspicuous.*

**conspiracy** (*SYN.*) machination, combination, treason, intrigue, cabal, treachery, plot, collusion.

**conspire** (*SYN.*) plan, plot, scheme.

**constancy** (*SYN.*) devotion, faithfulness, accuracy, precision, exactness. (*ANT.*) *faithlessness, treachery, perfidy.*

**constant** (*SYN.*) continual, invariable, abiding, permanent, faithful, invariant, true, ceaseless, enduring, unchanging, steadfast, unchangeable, loyal, stable, immutable, staunch, steady, fixed. (*ANT.*) *fickle, irregular, wavering, off-and-on, infrequent, occasional, mutable.*

**constantly** (*SYN.*) eternally, ever, evermore, forever, unceasingly. (*ANT.*) *rarely, sometimes, never, occasionally.*

**consternation** (*SYN.*)

apprehension, dismay, alarm, fear, fright, dread, horror, terror. (*ANT.*) *bravery, courage, boldness, assurance.*

**constitute** (*SYN.*) compose, found, form, establish, organize, create, appoint, delegate, authorize, commission.

**constitution** (*SYN.*) law, code, physique, health, vitality.

**constrain** (*SYN.*) necessity, indigence, need, want, poverty. (*ANT.*) *luxury, freedom, uncertainty.*

**construct** (*SYN.*) build, form, erect, make, fabricate, raise, frame. (*ANT.*) *raze, demolish, destroy.*

**constructive** (*SYN.*) useful, helpful, valuable. (*ANT.*) *ruinous, destructive.*

**construe** (*SYN.*) explain, interpret, solve, render, translate. (*ANT.*) *distort, confuse, misconstrue.*

**consult** (*SYN.*) discuss, chatter, discourse, gossip, confer, report, rumor, deliberate, speech, talk. (*ANT.*) *writing, correspondence, silence.*

**consume** (*SYN.*) engulf, absorb, use up, use, expend, exhaust, devour, devastate, destroy, engross. (*ANT.*) *emit, expel, exude, discharge.*

**consumer** (*SYN.*) user, buyer, purchaser.

**consummate** (*SYN.*) close, conclude, do, finish, perfect, terminate.

**consummation** (*SYN.*) climax, apex, culmination, peak. (*ANT.*) *depth, base, floor.*

**contact** (*SYN.*) meeting, touching.

**contagious** (*SYN.*) infectious, virulent, communicable, catching. (*ANT.*) *noncommunicable, healthful, hygienic.*

**contain** (*SYN.*) embody, hold, embrace, include, accommodate, repress, restrain. (*ANT.*) *emit, encourage, yield, discharge.*

**contaminate** (*SYN.*) corrupt, sully, taint, defile, soil, pollute, dirty, infect, poison. (*ANT.*) *purify.*

**contemplate** (*SYN.*) imagine, recollect, consider, study, reflect upon, observe, deliberate, muse, ponder, plan, intend, view, regard, think about, reflect, think, mean. (*ANT.*) *forget, guess, conjecture.*

**contemplative** (*SYN.*) meditative, thoughtful, pensive, studious. (*ANT.*) *inattentive, indifferent, thoughtless.*

**contemporary** (*SYN.*) modern, present, simultaneous,

fashionable, coexisting, contemporaneous, up-to-date. (*ANT.*) *old, antecedent, past, ancient, succeeding, bygone.*

**contempt** (*SYN.*) detestation, malice, contumely, disdain, derision, scorn. (*ANT.*) *respect, reverence, admiration, esteem, awe.*

**contemptible** (*SYN.*) base, mean, vile, vulgar, nasty, low, detestable, selfish, miserable, offensive. (*ANT.*) *generous, honorable, noble, exalted, admirable.*

**contemptuous** (*SYN.*) disdainful, sneering, scornful, insolent. (*ANT.*) *modest, humble.*

**contend** (*SYN.*) dispute, combat, contest, assert, claim, argue, maintain.

**content** (*SYN.*) pleased, happy, contented, satisfied. (*ANT.*) *restless, dissatisfied, discontented.*

**contented** (*SYN.*) delighted, fortunate, gay, happy, joyous, lucky, merry. (*ANT.*) *gloomy, blue, depressed.*

**contention** (*SYN.*) combat, duel, struggle, discord, battle, variance. (*ANT.*) *concord, harmony, amity, consonance.*

**contentment** (*SYN.*) delight, happiness, gladness, pleasure, satisfaction. (*ANT.*) *misery, sorrow, grief, sadness, despair.*

**contest** (*SYN.*) dispute, debate, competition, tournament, oppose, discuss, quarrel, squabble. (*ANT.*) *allow, concede, agree, assent.*

**continence** (*SYN.*) forbearance, temperance. (*ANT.*) *self-indulgence, excess, intoxication.*

**contingency** (*SYN.*) likelihood, possibility, occasion, circumstance.

**contingent** (*SYN.*) depending, subject. (*ANT.*) *independent, original, casual.*

**continual** (*SYN.*) constant, unceasing, everlasting, unremitting, endless, continuous, uninterrupted, regular, connected, consecutive, ceaseless. (*ANT.*) *periodic, rare, irregular.*

**continue** (*SYN.*) proceed, extend, endure, persist, resume, renew, recommence, last, remain, prolong, pursue. (*ANT.*) *check, cease, discontinue, stop, suspend.*

**continuous** (*SYN.*) continuing, uninterrupted, ceaseless, unceasing, incessant, constant. (*ANT.*) *intermittent, irregular, sporadic.*

**contract** (*SYN.*) condense,

diminish, reduce, bargain, restrict, agreement, compact, pact, shrink, get, treaty, shorten. *(ANT.) lengthen, extend, swell, expand.*

**contraction** *(SYN.)* reduction, shortening. *(ANT.) enlargement, expansion, extension.*

**contradict** *(SYN.)* gainsay, counter, oppose, confute, dispute. *(ANT.) verify, confirm, agree, support.*

**contradictory** *(SYN.)* inconsistent, conflicting, incompatible, paradoxical, unsteady. *(ANT.) congruous, consistent, correspondent.*

**contrary** *(SYN.)* disagreeable, perverse, hostile, stubborn, opposite, opposing, opposed, disagreeing, disastrous, conflicting, headstrong, unlucky. *(ANT.) lucky, agreeable, propitious, favorable, like, obliging, similar, complementary, tractable.*

**contrast** *(SYN.)* differentiate, compare, distinction, disagreement, distinguish, differ, discriminate, difference, oppose. *(ANT.) agreement, similarity, likeness.*

**contribute** *(SYN.)* grant, give, donate, bestow, provide, offer. *(ANT.) deny, withhold.*

**contribution** *(SYN.)* grant, gift, offering, donation.

**contrition** *(SYN.)* grief, regret, self-reproach. *(ANT.) self-satisfaction, complacency.*

**contrive** *(SYN.)* devise, intend, plan, make, invent, plot, hatch, form, project, arrange, manage, maneuver, scheme, sketch.

**control** *(SYN.)* govern, regulate, rule, command, dominate, direct, manage, check, repress, curb, management, mastery, direction, restraint, superintend. *(ANT.) ignore, forsake, follow, submit, abandon.*

**controversy** *(SYN.)* disagreement, dispute, debate. *(ANT.) agreement, harmony, accord, concord, decision.*

**convenience** *(SYN.)* accessibility, aid, benefit, help, service, availability. *(ANT.) inconvenience.*

**convenient** *(SYN.)* adapted, appropriate, fitting, favorable, handy, suitable, accessible, nearby, ready, available, advantageous, timely. *(ANT.) inconvenient, troublesome, awkward.*

**convention** *(SYN.)* meeting, conference, assembly, practice, custom, rule.

**conventional** *(SYN.)* common, regular, usual, everyday, habitual, routine, accustomed. *(ANT.) exotic, unusual, bizarre, extraordinary.*

**conversant** *(SYN.)* aware, intimate, familiar, versed, close, friendly, sociable. *(ANT.) affected, distant, cold, reserved.*

**conversation** *(SYN.)* colloquy, dialogue, chat, parley, discussion, talk.

**converse** *(SYN.)* jabber, talk, argue, comment, harangue, plead, rant, spout, discuss, chat, speak, reason.

**conversion** *(SYN.)* alteration, change, mutation, modification, metamorphosis.

**convert** *(SYN.)* change, alter, turn, transform, shift, modify, exchange, win over, vary, veer. *(ANT.) establish, settle, retain.*

**convey** *(SYN.)* carry, bear, communicate, transport, transmit, support, sustain. *(ANT.) drop, abandon.*

**conveyance** *(SYN.)* van, car, train, truck, plane.

**convict** *(SYN.)* felon, offender, criminal.

**conviction** *(SYN.)* opinion, position, view, faith, belief, confidence, feeling, reliance, trust. *(ANT.) doubt, incredulity, denial.*

**convince** *(SYN.)* persuade, assure, exhort, induce, influence. *(ANT.) deter, compel, restrain, dissuade.*

**convivial** *(SYN.)* jolly, social, jovial, gregarious. *(ANT.) solemn, stern, unsociable.*

**convoy** *(SYN.)* with, attend, chaperone. *(ANT.) avoid, desert, quit, leave.*

**cool** *(SYN.)* frosty, chilly, icy, cold, wintry, quiet, composed, collected, distant, unfriendly, quiet, moderate. *(ANT.) hot, warm, heated, overwrought, excited, hysterical, friendly, outgoing.*

**cooperate** *(SYN.)* unite, combine, help, contribute, support.

**coordinate** *(SYN.)* attune, harmonize, adapt, match, balance.

**copious** *(SYN.)* ample, abundant, bountiful, overflowing, plentiful, profuse, rich. *(ANT.) scant, scarce, insufficient, meager, deficient.*

**copy** *(SYN.)* facsimile, exemplar, imitation, duplicate, reproduction, likeness, print, carbon, transcript. *(ANT.) prototype, original.*

**cordial** *(SYN.)* polite, friendly,

affable, genial, earnest, gracious, warm, ardent, warm-hearted, hearty, sincere. *(ANT.) unfriendly, cool, aloof, hostile, reserved.*

**core** *(SYN.)* midpoint, heart, kernel, center, middle. *(ANT.) outskirts, border, surface, outside, boundary, rim.*

**corporation** *(SYN.)* business, organization, crew, group, troop, society, company, conglomerate, firm. *(ANT.) individual, dispersion, seclusion.*

**corpse** *(SYN.)* cadaver, carcass, remains, body, form. *(ANT.) spirit, soul, mind, intellect.*

**corpulent** *(SYN.)* obese, portly, chubby, stout. *(ANT.) slim, thin, slender, lean.*

**correct** *(SYN.)* true, set right, faultless, impeccable, proper, accurate, precise, mend, right, rebuke, punish, amend, rectify, better, emend, caution, discipline, exact, strict. *(ANT.) condone, aggravate, false, inaccurate, wrong, untrue, faulty.*

**correction** *(SYN.)* order, improvement, regulation, instruction, amendment, emendation, remedy, rectification, repair, training, punishment. *(ANT.) confusion, turbulence, chaos.*

**correlative** *(SYN.)* allied, correspondent, like, similar, parallel. *(ANT.) different, opposed, divergent.*

**correspond** *(SYN.)* compare, coincide, match, agree, suit, fit, write. *(ANT.) differ, diverge, vary.*

**correspondent** *(SYN.)* allied, alike, comparable, like, parallel, similar. *(ANT.) different, opposed, divergent, dissimilar.*

**corridor** *(SYN.)* hallway, hall, foyer, passage, lobby, passageway.

**corrode** *(SYN.)* erode.

**corrupt** *(SYN.)* crooked, untrustworthy, treacherous, debased, unscrupulous, wicked, evil, low, contaminated, perverted, bribe, depraved, corrupted, demoralize, degrade, venal, putrid, tainted, dishonest, impure. *(ANT.) upright, honest, pure, sanctify, edify, purify, sanctified, scrupulous.*

**corrupted** *(SYN.)* crooked, dishonest, impure, spoiled, unsound.

**cost** *(SYN.)* price, value, damage, charge, loss, sacrifice, penalty, worth.

**costly** *(SYN.)* dear, expensive. *(ANT.) cheap, inexpensive.*

**costume** *(SYN.)* dress,

clothes, apparel, clothing, garb.

**couch** *(SYN.)* davenport, sofa, loveseat.

**council** *(SYN.)* caution, instruction, committee, cabinet, board, suggestion.

**counsel** *(SYN.)* guidance, attorney, lawyer, counselor, hint, imply, opinion, advice, offer, advise. *(ANT.) declare, dictate, insist.*

**count** *(SYN.)* consider, number, enumerate, total, figure, compute, tally, estimate. *(ANT.) conjecture, guess, miscalculate.*

**countenance** *(SYN.)* visage, face, aspect, support, appearance, approval, encouragement, favor. *(ANT.) forbid, prohibit.*

**counteract** *(SYN.)* thwart, neutralize, offset, counterbalance, defeat.

**counterfeit** *(SYN.)* false, fraudulent, pretended, pretend, sham, imitate, forgery, artificial, bogus, fake, spurious, imitation, unreal. *(ANT.) authentic, natural, real, genuine, true.*

**country** *(SYN.)* state, nation, forest, farmland. *(ANT.) city.*

**couple** *(SYN.)* team, pair, accompany, associate, attach, combine, connect, brace, join, link, unite. *(ANT.) detach, separate, disjoin, disconnect.*

**courage** *(SYN.)* fearlessness, boldness, chivalry, fortitude, mettle, spirit, daring, bravery, prowess, intrepidity, valor, resolution. *(ANT.) fear, timidity, cowardice.*

**courageous** *(SYN.)* bold, dauntless, brave, daring, intrepid, valorous, plucky, fearless, heroic, valiant. *(ANT.) fearful, weak, timid, cowardly.*

**course** *(SYN.)* passage, advance, path, road, progress, way, direction, bearing, route, street, track, trail, way.

**courteous** *(SYN.)* civil, respectful, polite, genteel, well-mannered, gracious, refined. *(ANT.) discourteous, rude, uncivil, impolite.*

**courtesy** *(SYN.)* graciousness, politeness, respect. *(ANT.) discourtesy, rudeness.*

**covenant** *(SYN.)* agreement, concord, harmony, unison, compact, stipulation. *(ANT.) variance, discord, dissension, difference.*

**cover** *(SYN.)* clothe, conceal, disguise, curtain, guard, envelop, mask, cloak, shield, hide, screen, protect, embrace, top, lid, covering, stopper, protection, refuge, spread, overlay, include, veil. *(ANT.) bare, expose, reveal.*

**covert** *(SYN.)* potential, undeveloped, concealed, dormant. *(ANT.) explicit, visible, manifest.*

**covetous** *(SYN.)* grasping, greedy, acquisitive, avaricious. *(ANT.) generous.*

**coward** *(SYN.)* dastard, milquetoast, cad. *(ANT.) hero.*

**cowardice** *(SYN.)* dread, dismay, fright, dismay, panic, terror, timidity. *(ANT.) fearlessness, courage, bravery.*

**cowardly** *(SYN.)* fearful, timorous, afraid, faint-hearted, yellow, pusillanimous, spineless.

**cower** *(SYN.)* wince, flinch, cringe, quail, tremble.

**coy** *(SYN.)* embarrassed, sheepish, shy, timid. *(ANT.) fearless, outgoing, bold, adventurous, daring.*

**crack** *(SYN.)* snap, break, split.

**cracker** *(SYN.)* wafer, biscuit, saltine.

**craft** *(SYN.)* talent, skill, expertness, ability, cunning, guile, deceit, trade, profession, occupation.

**crafty** *(SYN.)* covert, clever, cunning, skillful, foxy, tricky, sly, underhand, shrewd. *(ANT.) frank, sincere, gullible, open, guileless, ingenuous.*

**craggy** *(SYN.)* rough, rugged, irregular, uneven. *(ANT.) level, sleek, smooth, fine, polished.*

**crank** *(SYN.)* cross, irritable, bad tempered, testy. *(ANT.) cheerful, happy.*

**crash** *(SYN.)* smash, shatter, dash.

**crave** *(SYN.)* want, desire, hunger for. *(ANT.) relinquish, renounce.*

**craving** *(SYN.)* relish, appetite, desire, liking, longing, passion. *(ANT.) renunciation, distaste, disgust.*

**crazy** *(SYN.)* delirious, deranged, idiotic, mad, insane, imbecilic, demented, foolish, maniacal. *(ANT.) sane, sensible, sound, rational, reasonable.*

**creak** *(SYN.)* squeak.

**create** *(SYN.)* fashion, form, generate, engender, formulate, make, originate, produce, cause, ordain, invent, beget, design, construct, constitute. *(ANT.) disband, abolish, terminate, destroy, demolish.*

**creative** *(SYN.)* imaginative, ingenious, original, resourceful, clever, inventive,

innovative, mystical. *(ANT.) unromantic, dull, literal.*

**credence** *(SYN.)* confidence, faith, feeling, opinion, trust. *(ANT.) doubt, incredulity, denial.*

**credible** *(SYN.)* conceivable, believable. *(ANT.) inconceivable, unbelievable.*

**credit** *(SYN.)* believe, accept, belief, trust, faith, merit, honor, apprehend, fancy, hold, support. *(ANT.) doubt, reject, question, distrust, debt.*

**creditable** *(SYN.)* worthy, praiseworthy. *(ANT.) dishonorable, discreditable, shameful.*

**credulous** *(SYN.)* trusting, naive, believing, gullible. *(ANT.) suspicious.*

**creed** *(SYN.)* belief, precept, credo, faith, teaching. *(ANT.) practice, deed, conduct, performance.*

**creek** *(SYN.)* brook, spring, stream, rivulet.

**crime** *(SYN.)* offense, insult, aggression, wrongdoing, wrong, misdeed. *(ANT.) right, gentleness, innocence, morality.*

**criminal** *(SYN.)* unlawful, crook, gangster, outlaw, illegal, convict, delinquent, offender, malefactor, culprit, felonious, felon, transgressor.

**cripple** *(SYN.)* hurt, maim, damage, injure.

**crippled** *(SYN.)* deformed, disabled, maimed, hobbling, limping, unconvincing, unsatisfactory. *(ANT.) robust, sound, vigorous, athletic.*

**crisis** *(SYN.)* conjuncture, emergency, pass, pinch, acme, climax, contingency, juncture, exigency, strait. *(ANT.) calm, normality, stability, equilibrium.*

**crisp** *(SYN.)* crumbling, delicate, frail, brittle. *(ANT.) calm, normality, stability.*

**criterion** *(SYN.)* measure, law, rule, principle, gauge, proof. *(ANT.) fancy, guess, chance, supposition.*

**critic** *(SYN.)* reviewer, judge, commentator, censor, defamer, slanderer, faultfinder.

**critical** *(SYN.)* exact, fastidious, faultfinding, accurate, condemning, reproachful, risky, dangerous, momentous, carping, acute, hazardous, hypercritical, perilous, decisive, important. *(ANT.) shallow, uncritical, approving, insignificant, trivial, unimportant.*

**criticize** *(SYN.)* examine, analyze, inspect, blame, censure, appraise, evaluate, scrutinize,

reprehend. *(ANT.) neglect, overlook, approve.*

**critique** *(SYN.)* criticism, inspection, review.

**crony** *(SYN.)* colleague, companion, chum, buddy, comrade, friend, mate. *(ANT.) stranger, enemy, adversary.*

**crooked** *(SYN.)* twisted, corrupt, hooked, curved, criminal, dishonest, degraded, bent, zigzag, impaired. *(ANT.) improved, raised, straight, honest, vitalized, upright, enhanced.*

**crop** *(SYN.)* fruit, produce, harvest, cut, mow, reaping, result, yield.

**cross** *(SYN.)* mix, mingle, traverse, interbreed, annoyed, irritable, cranky, testy, angry, mean, ill-natured. *(ANT.) cheerful.*

**crouch** *(SYN.)* duck, stoop.

**crow** *(SYN.)* boast, brag.

**crowd** *(SYN.)* masses, flock, host, squeeze, mob, multitude, populace, press, cramp, throng, swarm.

**crown** *(SYN.)* coronet, apex, crest, circlet, pinnacle, tiara, skull, head, top, zenith. *(ANT.) base, bottom, foundation, foot.*

**crude** *(SYN.)* rude, graceless, unpolished, green, harsh, rough, coarse, ill-prepared, unfinished, raw, boorish, unrefined, uncouth. *(ANT.) finished, refined, polished, cultured, genteel, cultivated.*

**cruel** *(SYN.)* ferocious, mean, heartless, unmerciful, malignant, savage, brutal, pitiless, inhuman, ruthless, merciless. *(ANT.) humane, forbearing, kind, compassionate, merciful, benevolent, kindhearted, gentle.*

**cruelty** *(SYN.)* harshness, meanness, savagery, brutality. *(ANT.) compassion, kindness.*

**crumb** *(SYN.)* jot, grain, mite, particle, shred. *(ANT.) mass, bulk, quantity.*

**crunch** *(SYN.)* champ, gnaw, nibble, pierce.

**crush** *(SYN.)* smash, break, crash.

**cry** *(SYN.)* yowl, yell, roar, shout, bellow, scream, wail, weep, bawl, sob.

**cryptic** *(SYN.)* puzzling, mysterious, enigmatic, hidden, secret, vague, obscure, occult, unclear.

**cull** *(SYN.)* elect, choose, pick, select. *(ANT.) reject, refuse.*

**culpable** *(SYN.)* guilty, blameworthy. *(ANT.) innocent.*

**cultivate** *(SYN.)* plant, seed, farm, till, refine, educate,

teach.

**cultivation** *(SYN.)* farming, horticulture, tillage, agriculture.

**cultural** *(SYN.)* civilizing, educational, elevating, instructive.

**cumbersome** *(SYN.)* bulky, clumsy, awkward, unmanageable. *(ANT.) handy.*

**cunning** *(SYN.)* clever, wily, crafty, foxy, skillful, tricky, ingenious, foxiness, ability, skill, wiliness, devious. *(ANT.) gullible, honest, naive, openness, straightforward, simple, direct.*

**curb** *(SYN.)* check, restraint, hinder, hold, limit, control, stop, suppress. *(ANT.) aid, loosen, incite, encourage.*

**cure** *(SYN.)* help, treatment, heal, medicine, restorative, relief, remedy.

**curiosity** *(SYN.)* marvel, rarity, phenomenon, admiration, amazement. *(ANT.) apathy, indifference, expectation.*

**curious** *(SYN.)* interrogative, interested, peculiar, queer, nosy, peeping, prying, inquisitive, snoopy, inquiring, unusual. *(ANT.) unconcerned, ordinary, indifferent, uninterested, common.*

**current** *(SYN.)* up-to-date, contemporary, present, new, tide, stream, modern. *(ANT.) antiquated, old, bygone, ancient, past.*

**curse** *(SYN.)* ban, oath, denounce, swear, condemn. *(ANT.) boon, blessing.*

**cursory** *(SYN.)* frivolous, shallow, slight. *(ANT.) complete, deep, profound, thorough.*

**curt** *(SYN.)* hasty, short, abrupt, brusque, brief, blunt, rude, harsh. *(ANT.) friendly, smooth, gradual, polite, courteous, generous.*

**curtail** *(SYN.)* condense, contract, diminish, reduce, limit, abbreviate. *(ANT.) lengthen, extend.*

**curtain** *(SYN.)* blind, drapery, drape, shade.

**curve** *(SYN.)* crook, deflect, bend, bow, incline, turn, twist. *(ANT.) resist, stiffen, straighten.*

**cushion** *(SYN.)* pillow, pad, absorb.

**custodian** *(SYN.)* guard, keeper, guardian, watchman.

**custody** *(SYN.)* guardianship, care. *(ANT.) neglect, disregard, indifference.*

**custom** *(SYN.)* fashion, rule, routine.

**customary** *(SYN.)* common, usual, regular, everyday,

general. *(ANT.)exceptional, irregular, rare, unusual, abnormal.*

**customer** *(SYN.)* patron, client, buyer.

**cut** *(SYN.)* slash, gash, prick, slit, sever, cleave, mow, incision, chop, lop, slice.

**cutting** *(SYN.)* bitter, stern, caustic, scathing, harsh, acerbic.

**cylindrical** *(SYN.)* circular, curved, plump, rotund, spherical, round.

# D

**dab** *(SYN.)* coat, pat, smear.

**dabble** *(SYN.)* splatter, toy, splash, fiddle, putter.

**dabbler** *(SYN.)* amateur, dilettante, tinkerer, trifler. *(ANT.) master, expert, scholar, specialist, authority.*

**daft** *(SYN.)* crazy, foolish, insane.

**dagger** *(SYN.)* knife, dirk, blade.

**daily** *(SYN.)* every day, diurnal, regularly.

**daily** *(SYN.)* dawdle, linger, lag, delay. *(ANT.) rush, hurry, dash, bustle.*

**dam** *(SYN.)* dike, levee, barrier, slow, stop, check, obstruct, block. *(ANT.) free, release, loose, unleash.*

**damage** *(SYN.)* spoil, deface, impair, mar, hurt, injury, impairment, destruction. *(ANT.) repair, benefit, mend, rebuild, improve, ameliorate.*

**dame** *(SYN.)* woman, lady.

**damn** *(SYN.)* denounce, doom, curse, reprove, blame. *(ANT.) bless, honor, glorify, praise, accept, applaud, commend, consecrate.*

**damp** *(SYN.)* humid, dank, moisture, wetness, humidity. *(ANT.) arid, dry.*

**dampen** *(SYN.)* wet, depressed, moisten, dull, suppress, sprinkle, discouraged, retard, slow, inhibit, deaden, muffle. *(ANT.) dehumidify, increase, encourage.*

**dance** *(SYN.)* bounce, flit, skip, sway, prance, bob, glide, caper, cavort, frisk.

**dandle** *(SYN.)* jounce, joggle, bounce, jiggle, nestle, cuddle, caress.

**dandy** *(SYN.)* coxcomb, fop, swell, great, fine, wonderful, excellent. *(ANT.) rotten, terrible, awful, miserable, slob.*

**danger** *(SYN.)* jeopardy, risk, threat, hazard, uncertainty, peril. *(ANT.) safety, immunity,*

security, defense.

**dangerous** *(SYN.)* risky, insecure, threatening, critical, perilous, unsafe, uncertain, hazardous. *(ANT.) secure, protected, safe.*

**dangle** *(SYN.)* swing, flap, hang, sag.

**dank** *(SYN.)* moist, muggy, wet. *(ANT.) dry.*

**dapper** *(SYN.)* spruce, trim, natty, smart, well-tailored, dashing, neat. *(ANT.) untidy, shabby, messy, unkempt.*

**dappled** *(SYN.)* spotted, flecked, brindled, variegated, piebald, pied. *(ANT.) uniform, solid, unvaried.*

**dare** *(SYN.)* brave, call, question, defy, risk, challenge, summon.

**daredevil** *(SYN.)* lunatic, thrill-seeker, madcap, adventurer.

**daring** *(SYN.)* foolhardy, chivalrous, rash, fearless, courageous, intrepid, valiant, courage, bravery, brave, precipitate, bold. *(ANT.) timid, cowardice, timidity, cautious.*

**dark** *(SYN.)* somber, obscure, gloomy, black, unilluminated, dim, evil, hidden, secret, swarthy, murky, opaque, dismal, mournful, sable, sullen, shadowy, sinister, dusky, mystic, shadowy, unlit, sunless, shaded, wicked, occult. *(ANT.) lucid, light, happy, cheerful, illuminated, pleasant.*

**darling** *(SYN.)* dear, adored, sweetheart, favorite, cherished. *(ANT.) uncherished, unlovable, disagreeable, rejected, forlorn.*

**darn** *(SYN.)* repair, mend.

**dart** *(SYN.)* scurry, arrow, barb, hurry, dash, throw, missile, run, hasten, scamper, toss, rush, cast.

**dash** *(SYN.)* pound, thump, beat, smite, buffet, thrash, smash, break, scurry, run, dart, rush, scamper, hint, pinch, hit, strike. *(ANT.) stroke, hearten, encourage, defend.*

**dashing** *(SYN.)* swashbuckling, dapper, flamboyant, handsome. *(ANT.) dull, colorless, shabby, lifeless.*

**dastardly** *(SYN.)* mean-spirited, craven, cowardly, mean, rotten, villainous, dishonorable. *(ANT.) heroic, brave, high-minded, courageous.*

**data** *(SYN.)* information, statistics, proof, facts, evidence.

**date** *(SYN.)* interview, appointment, commitment, engagement, meeting,

rendezvous, regale, entertain.

**dated** *(SYN.)* out-of-date, old-fashioned, outmoded. *(ANT.) latest, now, current, fashionable, hot.*

**daub** *(SYN.)* coat, grease, soil, scribble, cover, stain, smear, scrawl.

**daunt** *(SYN.)* discourage, dishearten, intimidate, frighten, deter. *(ANT.) enspirit, encourage.*

**dauntless** *(SYN.)* fearless, brave, bold, courageous, intrepid, valiant. *(ANT.) fearful, timid, cowardly.*

**dawn** *(SYN.)* sunrise, start, outset, daybreak, origin, commencement. *(ANT.) dusk, sunset, nightfall, end, conclusion, finish.*

**daydream** *(SYN.)* woolgather, muse.

**daze** *(SYN.)* perplex, stun, puzzle, bewilder, upset, confuse, ruffle, confusion, stupor, bewilderment.

**dazzle** *(SYN.)* surprise, stun, astonish, impress, bewilder, stupefy.

**dead** *(SYN.)* departed, lifeless, deceased, insensible, inanimate, dull, defunct, gone, lifeless, unconscious, inoperative, inactive, inert, motionless, spiritless. *(ANT.) animate, functioning, active, living, alive, stirring.*

**deaden** *(SYN.)* anesthetize, numb, paralyze.

**deadlock** *(SYN.)* standstill, impasse, stalemate.

**deadly** *(SYN.)* lethal, mortal, fatal, deathly.

**deaf** *(SYN.)* unhearing, unheeding, unaware, unheedful, stubborn, oblivious, inattentive. *(ANT.) aware, conscious.*

**deafening** *(SYN.)* vociferous, noisy, stentorian, resounding, loud. *(ANT.) soft, inaudible, subdued.*

**deal** *(SYN.)* act, treat, attend, cope, barter, trade, bargain, apportion, give, distribute, deliver.

**dear** *(SYN.)* valued, esteemed, expensive, beloved, costly, darling, high-priced, loved, precious. *(ANT.) hateful, reasonable, inexpensive, cheap, unwanted.*

**dearth** *(SYN.)* shortage, lack, scarcity.

**death** *(SYN.)* decease, extinction, demise, passing. *(ANT.) life.*

**debase** *(SYN.)* lower, degrade, alloy, adulterate, defile, humiliate, depress, abase, pervert, corrupt. *(ANT.) restore, improve, vitalize, enhance.*

**debate** *(SYN.)* wrangle, discuss, plead, argue, discussion, contend, argument, controversy, dispute. *(ANT.) agreement, accord, ignore, spurn.*

**debonair** *(SYN.)* urbane, sophisticated, refined, dapper, well-bred.

**debris** *(SYN.)* rubbish, litter, junk, wreckage, refuse, detritus, ruins, trash, residue.

**debt** *(SYN.)* amount due, liability, obligation.

**decay** *(SYN.)* decrease, spoil, ebb, decline, waste, disintegrate, wane, dwindle, molder, deteriorate, perish, wither, rot, collapse, rottenness, putrefy, decompose. *(ANT.) progress, rise, increase, grow, flourish.*

**deceased** *(SYN.)* lifeless, departed, dead, insensible, defunct. *(ANT.) living, alive.*

**deceit** *(SYN.)* duplicity, cheat, fraud, chicanery, trick, cunning, deception, guile, beguilement, deceitfulness, dishonesty, wiliness. *(ANT.) truthfulness, openness, forthrightness, honesty, candor.*

**deceitful** *(SYN.)* false, fraudulent, insincere, dishonest, deceptive. *(ANT.) sincere, honest.*

**deceive** *(SYN.)* cheat, defraud, hoodwink, mislead, swindle.

**decency** *(SYN.)* decorum, dignity, propriety, respectability.

**decent** *(SYN.)* befitting, fit, suitable, becoming, respectable, adequate, seemly, fitting, comely, appropriate, proper, tolerable, decorous. *(ANT.) vulgar, gross, improper, unsuitable, indecorous, reprehensible, indecent, coarse.*

**deception** *(SYN.)* trick, cheat, sham, deceit, trickery, craftiness, treachery, beguilement, cunning. *(ANT.) openness, frankness, candor, probity, truthfulness, honesty.*

**deceptive** *(SYN.)* specious, fallacious, deceitful, false, delusive, unreliable, illusive, tricky, dishonest, deceiving, misleading, delusory. *(ANT.) honest, real, genuine, true, truthful, authentic.*

**decide** *(SYN.)* resolve, determine, terminate, conclude, close, settle, adjudicate, choose, end. *(ANT.) waver, hesitate, vacillate, doubt, suspend.*

**decipher** *(SYN.)* render, unravel, construe, solve, decode, translate, elucidate, determine. *(ANT.) misconstrue, distort,* *misinterpret, confuse.*

**decision** *(SYN.)* resolution, determination, settlement.

**decisive** *(SYN.)* determined, firm, decided, unhesitating, resolute.

**declaration** *(SYN.)* pronouncement, notice, affirmation, statement, announcement, assertion.

**declare** *(SYN.)* assert, promulgate, affirm, tell, broadcast, express, proclaim, aver, say, pronounce, profess, announce. *(ANT.)* deny, withhold, conceal, suppress.

**decline** *(SYN.)* descend, decay, dwindle, refuse, incline, wane, sink, depreciate, deny, diminish, weaken. *(ANT.)* accept, ascend, ameliorate, increase.

**decompose** *(SYN.)* rot, disintegrate, molder, decay, crumble.

**decorate** *(SYN.)* trim, paint, deck, enrich, color, beautify, enhance, furbish, furnish, adorn, ornament. *(ANT.)* uncover, mar, deface, defame, debase.

**decoration** *(SYN.)* ornamentation, embellishment, adornment, furnishing, award, citation, medal.

**decoy** *(SYN.)* lure, bait.

**decrease** *(SYN.)* lessen, wane, deduct, diminish, curtail, remove, lessening, decline. *(ANT.)* expansion, increase, enlarge, expand, grow.

**decree** *(SYN.)* order, edict, statute, declaration, announce, act.

**decrepit** *(SYN.)* feeble, puny, weakened, infirm, enfeebled, languid, rickety, weak, run-down, tumble-down, dilapidated, faint. *(ANT.)* strong, forceful, vigorous, energetic, lusty.

**decry** *(SYN.)* lower, belittle, derogate, minimize, undervalue. *(ANT.)* praise, commend, magnify, aggrandize.

**dedicate** *(SYN.)* sanctify, consecrate, hallow, devote, assign.

**dedicated** *(SYN.)* disposed, true, affectionate, fond, wedded. *(ANT.)* indisposed, detached, untrammeled, disinclined.

**deduct** *(SYN.)* lessen, shorten, abate, remove, eliminate, curtail, subtract. *(ANT.)* grow, enlarge, add, increase, amplify, expand.

**deed** *(SYN.)* feat, transaction, action, performance, act, operation, achievement, document, certificate, title, accomplishment. *(ANT.)*

*intention, cessation, inactivity, deliberation.*

**deem** *(SYN.)* hold, determine, believe, regard, reckon, judge, consider, account, expound, view.

**deep** *(SYN.)* bottomless, low, unplumbed, acute, obscure, involved, absorbed. *(ANT.)* shallow.

**deface** *(SYN.)* spoil, impair, damage, mar, hurt, scratch, mutilate, disfigure, injure, harm. *(ANT.)* mend, benefit, repair.

**defamation** *(SYN.)* invective, reproach, upbraiding, abuse, insult, outrage, reviling, desecration. *(ANT.)* respect, approval, laudation, commendation.

**default** *(SYN.)* loss, omission, lack, failure, want, dereliction. *(ANT.)* victory, achievement, sufficiency, success.

**defeat** *(SYN.)* quell, vanquish, beat, overcome, overthrow, subdue, frustrate, spoil, conquest. *(ANT.)* submit, retreat, cede, yield, surrender, capitulate, lose.

**defect** *(SYN.)* shortcoming, fault, omission, blemish, imperfection, forsake, leave, weakness, failure. *(ANT.)* perfection, flawlessness, support, join, completeness.

**defective** *(SYN.)* faulty, imperfect, inoperative, flawed, inoperable. *(ANT.)* flawless, perfect, faultless.

**defend** *(SYN.)* screen, espouse, justify, protect, vindicate, fortify, assert, guard, safeguard, shield. *(ANT.)* oppose, assault, submit, attack, deny.

**defense** *(SYN.)* resistance, protection, bulwark, fort, barricade, trench, rampart, fortress.

**defer** *(SYN.)* postpone, delay. *(ANT.)* speed, hurry, expedite.

**deference** *(SYN.)* fame, worship, adoration, reverence, admiration, respect, fame, dignity, homage. *(ANT.)* dishonor, derision, reproach, contempt.

**defiant** *(SYN.)* rebellious, antagonistic, obstinate. *(ANT.)* yielding, submissive.

**deficient** *(SYN.)* lacking, short, incomplete, defective, scanty, insufficient, inadequate. *(ANT.)* enough, ample, sufficient, adequate.

**defile** *(SYN.)* pollute, corrupt, dirty, debase, contaminate. *(ANT.)* purify.

**define** *(SYN.)* describe, fix, establish, label, designate, set,

name, explain.

**definite** *(SYN.)* fixed, prescribed, certain, specific, exact, determined, distinct, explicit, correct. *(ANT.)* indefinite, confused, undetermined, equivocal.

**definitely** *(SYN.)* certainly, assuredly, absolutely, positively, surely.

**definition** *(SYN.)* sense, interpretation, meaning, explanation.

**deft** *(SYN.)* handy, adroit, clever, adept, dexterous, skillful, skilled. *(ANT.)* inept, clumsy, maladroit, awkward.

**defunct** *(SYN.)* lifeless, dead, departed, expired, extinct, spiritless, inanimate. *(ANT.)* living, alive, stirring.

**defy** *(SYN.)* hinder, oppose, withstand, attack, resist, confront, challenge, flout, dare, thwart. *(ANT.)* yield, allow, relent, surrender, submit, accede.

**degenerate** *(SYN.)* dwindle, decline, weaken, deteriorate, decrease. *(ANT.)* ascend, ameliorate, increase, appreciate.

**degrade** *(SYN.)* crush, reduce, subdue, abash, humble, lower, shame, demote, downgrade, abase, mortify. *(ANT.)* praise, elevate, honor.

**degree** *(SYN.)* grade, amount, step, measure, rank, honor, extent.

**deign** *(SYN.)* condescend, stoop.

**dejected** *(SYN.)* depressed, downcast, sad, disheartened, blue, discouraged. *(ANT.)* cheerful, happy, optimistic.

**delectable** *(SYN.)* tasty, delicious, savory, delightful, sweet, luscious. *(ANT.)* unsavory, distasteful, unpalatable, acrid.

**delegate** *(SYN.)* emissary, envoy, ambassador, representative, commission, deputize, authorize.

**delete** *(SYN.)* erase, cancel, remove. *(ANT.)* add.

**deleterious** *(SYN.)* evil, unwholesome, base, sinful, bad, wicked, immoral, destructive, injurious, hurtful, damaging, detrimental, unsound. *(ANT.)* moral, excellent, reputable, healthful, healthy, helpful, constructive, good.

**deliberate** *(SYN.)* studied, willful, intended, contemplated, premeditated, planned, methodical, designed. *(ANT.)* fortuitous, hasty, accidental.

**delicate** *(SYN.)* frail, critical, slender, dainty, pleasing, fastidious, exquisite, precarious,

demanding, sensitive, savory, fragile, weak. *(ANT.)* tough, strong, coarse, clumsy, hearty, hale, vulgar, rude.

**delicious** *(SYN.)* tasty, luscious, delectable, sweet, savory. *(ANT.)* unsavory, distasteful, unpalatable, unpleasant, acrid.

**delight** *(SYN.)* joy, bliss, gladness, pleasure, ecstasy, happiness, rapture. *(ANT.)* revolt, sorrow, annoyance, displeasure, disgust, displease, revulsion, misery.

**delightful** *(SYN.)* pleasing, pleasant, charming, refreshing, pleasurable. *(ANT.)* nasty, disagreeable, unpleasant.

**delirious** *(SYN.)* raving, mad, giddy, frantic, hysterical, violent.

**deliver** *(SYN.)* impart, publish, rescue, commit, communicate, free, address, offer, save, give, liberate. *(ANT.)* restrict, confine, capture, enslave, withhold, imprison.

**deluge** *(SYN.)* overflow, flood.

**delusion** *(SYN.)* mirage, fantasy, phantasm, vision, dream, illusion, phantom, hallucination. *(ANT.)* substance, actuality.

**delve** *(SYN.)* dig, look, search, scoop, explore, hunt.

**demand** *(SYN.)* claim, inquire, ask, need, require, obligation, requirement, ask for, necessitate. *(ANT.)* tender, give, present, waive, relinquish, offer.

**demean** *(SYN.)* comport, bear, operate, carry, act, manage, deport.

**demeanor** *(SYN.)* manner, way, conduct, actions, behavior.

**demented** *(SYN.)* insane, crazy, mad, mental, psychotic, lunatic.

**demolish** *(SYN.)* ruin, devastate, ravage, annihilate, wreck, destroy, raze, exterminate, obliterate. *(ANT.)* erect, make, save, construct, preserve, build, establish.

**demolition** *(SYN.)* wrecking, destruction. *(ANT.)* erection, construction.

**demon** *(SYN.)* fiend, devil, ogre, spirit.

**demonstrate** *(SYN.)* evince, show, prove, display, illustrate, describe, explain, manifest, exhibit. *(ANT.)* hide, conceal.

**demonstration** *(SYN.)* exhibit, show, presentation, exhibition, display, rally.

**demur** *(SYN.)* waver, falter, delay, stutter, doubt, vacillate, hesitate, scruple. *(ANT.)*

proceed, decide, resolve.

**demure** *(SYN.)* meek, shy, modest, diffident, retiring, bashful, coy.

**den** *(SYN.)* cave, lair, cavern.

**denial** *(SYN.)* disallowance, proscription, refusal, prohibition.

**denounce** *(SYN.)* condemn, blame, reprove, reprehend, censure, reproach, upbraid, reprobate. *(ANT.)* condone, approve, forgive, commend, praise.

**dense** *(SYN.)* crowded, slow, close, obtuse, compact, dull, stupid, compressed, thick, concentrated, packed, solid. *(ANT.)* sparse, quick, dispersed, clever, dissipated, empty, smart, bright.

**dent** *(SYN.)* notch, impress, pit, nick.

**deny** *(SYN.)* refuse, withhold, dispute, disavow, forbid, refute, contradict, abjure, confute, gainsay. *(ANT.)* confirm, affirm, admit, confess, permit, allow, concede, assert.

**depart** *(SYN.)* quit, forsake, withdraw, renounce, desert, relinquish, die, perish, decease. *(ANT.)* tarry, remain, come, abide, stay, arrive.

**departure** *(SYN.)* valediction, farewell.

**depend** *(SYN.)* trust, rely, confide.

**dependable** *(SYN.)* secure, trustworthy, certain, safe, trusty, reliable, tried. *(ANT.)* unreliable, fallible, dubious, uncertain.

**dependent** *(SYN.)* relying, contingent, subordinate, conditional. *(ANT.)* original, casual, absolute, independent.

**depict** *(SYN.)* explain, recount, describe, portray, characterize, relate, narrate.

**deplore** *(SYN.)* repine, lament, bemoan, wail, bewail, weep, grieve, regret.

**deport** *(SYN.)* exile, eject, oust, banish, expel, dismiss, ostracize, dispel, exclude. *(ANT.)* receive, admit, shelter, accept, harbor.

**deportment** *(SYN.)* deed, behavior, manner, action, carriage, disposition, bearing, demeanor.

**deposit** *(SYN.)* place, put, bank, save, store, sediment, dregs, addition, entry. *(ANT.)* withdraw, withdrawal.

**depreciate** *(SYN.)* dwindle, decrease, belittle, disparage, weaken, minimize, descend, deteriorate. *(ANT.)* ascend, ameliorate, praise, increase, applaud, appreciate.

**depress** *(SYN.)* deject, dishearten, sadden, dampen, devaluate, devalue, lessen, lower, cheapen, reduce, dispirit, discourage, sink. *(ANT.)* exalt, cheer, exhilarate.

**depression** *(SYN.)* hopelessness, despondency, pessimism, dip, cavity, pothole, hole, despair, gloom, melancholy, sadness, sorrow, recession, decline, desperation, discouragement. *(ANT.)* elation, optimism, happiness, confidence, elevation, hope.

**deprive** *(SYN.)* bereave, deny, strip. *(ANT.)* provision, supply, provide.

**derelict** *(SYN.)* decrepit, shabby, dilapidated, neglected, forsaken, deserted, remiss, abandoned, lax.

**dereliction** *(SYN.)* want, lack, failure, miscarriage, loss, default, deficiency, omission, fiasco. *(ANT.)* sufficiency, success, achievement, victory.

**derision** *(SYN.)* irony, satire, banter, raillery, sneering, gibe, ridicule.

**derivation** *(SYN.)* source, birth, inception, start, beginning, spring, commencement, foundation, origin. *(ANT.)* issue, end, outcome, harvest, product.

**derive** *(SYN.)* obtain, acquire, get, receive.

**descend** *(SYN.)* wane, lower, move, slope, incline, decline, slant, sink. *(ANT.)* increase, appreciate, ameliorate, ascend.

**descendant** *(SYN.)* child, issue, progeny, offspring.

**describe** *(SYN.)* portray, picture, recount, depict, relate, characterize, represent.

**description** *(SYN.)* history, record, recital, account, computation, chronicle, reckoning, narration, detail, narrative. *(ANT.)* misrepresentation, confusion, caricature.

**desecration** *(SYN.)* profanation, insult, defamation, reviling, abuse, maltreatment, aspersion, perversion, dishonor. *(ANT.)* respect, commendation, approval, laudation.

**desert** *(SYN.)* forsake, wilderness, resign, abjure, abandon, wasteland, waste, leave, surrender, abdicate, quit, barren, uninhabited. *(ANT.)* uphold, defend, stay, maintain, accompany, join, support.

**deserter** *(SYN.)* runaway, renegade, fugitive, defector.

**deserts** *(SYN.)* right, compensation, due, reward, requital, condign.

**deserve** *(SYN.)* earn, warrant, merit.

**design** *(SYN.)* drawing, purpose, outline, devise, intend, draw, contrive, draft, cunning, plan, artfulness, delineation, scheming, sketch, intent, invent, objective, mean, contrivance, plotting, intention, create. *(ANT.)* candor, accident, result, chance.

**designate** *(SYN.)* manifest, indicate, show, specify, denote, reveal, name, appoint, select, assign, disclose, signify, imply, nominate, intimate. *(ANT.)* divert, mislead, conceal, falsify, distract.

**desirable** *(SYN.)* coveted, wanted.

**desire** *(SYN.)* longing, craving, yearning, appetite, lust, long for, crave, covet, want, request, ask, need, wish, aspiration, urge. *(ANT.)* hate, aversion, loathing, abomination, detest, loathe, abhor, distaste.

**desist** *(SYN.)* cork, stop, cease, hinder, terminate, abstain, halt, interrupt, seal, arrest, plug, bar. *(ANT.)* promote, begin, speed, proceed, start.

**desolate** *(SYN.)* forlorn, waste, bare, lonely, abandoned, wild, deserted, uninhabited, empty, sad, miserable, wretched, unhappy, bleak, forsaken. *(ANT.)* crowded, teeming, populous, happy, cheerful, fertile.

**despair** *(SYN.)* discouragement, pessimism, depression, hopelessness, despondency, desperation. *(ANT.)* elation, optimism, hope, joy, confidence.

**desperado** *(SYN.)* criminal, crook, thug, gangster, hoodlum.

**desperate** *(SYN.)* reckless, determined, despairing, wild, daring, hopeless, despondent, audacious. *(ANT.)* optimistic, composed, hopeful, collected, calm, assured.

**despicable** *(SYN.)* vulgar, offensive, base, vile, contemptible, selfish, low, mean, worthless, nasty. *(ANT.)* noble, exalted, admirable, generous, worthy, dignified.

**despise** *(SYN.)* hate, scorn, detest, loath, disdain, abhor, condemn, dislike, abominate. *(ANT.)* love, approve, like, admire.

**despite** *(SYN.)* notwithstanding.

**despoil** *(SYN.)* plunder, rob, loot.

**despondent** *(SYN.)* sad, dismal, depressed, somber, dejected, melancholy, doleful, sorrowful. *(ANT.)* joyous, cheerful, merry, happy.

**despot** *(SYN.)* tyrant, ruler, oppressor, dictator.

**despotic** *(SYN.)* authoritative, unconditional, absolute, tyrannous, entire, unrestricted. *(ANT.)* dependent, conditional, qualified, accountable.

**destiny** *(SYN.)* fate, portion, outcome, consequence, result, fortune, doom, lot.

**destitute** *(SYN.)* poor, penurious, needy, impecunious, poverty-stricken, impoverished, indigent. *(ANT.)* opulent, wealthy, affluent, rich.

**destroy** *(SYN.)* raze, devastate, ruin, end, demolish, wreck, extinguish, annihilate, exterminate, obliterate, waste, slay, kill, eradicate. *(ANT.)* make, construct, start, create, save, establish.

**destroyed** *(SYN.)* rent, smashed, interrupted, flattened, wrecked, broken, ruptured, crushed. *(ANT.)* whole, repaired, integral, united.

**destruction** *(SYN.)* ruin, devastation, extinction, demolition. *(ANT.)* beginning, creation.

**destructive** *(SYN.)* deadly, baneful, noxious, deleterious, injurious, pernicious, fatal, detrimental. *(ANT.)* salutary, beneficial, creative.

**detach** *(SYN.)* deduct, remove, subtract, curtail, divide, shorten, decrease, disengage, reduce, separate, diminish. *(ANT.)* hitch, grow, enlarge, increase, connect, amplify, attack, expand.

**detail** *(SYN.)* elaborate, commission, part, itemize, portion, division, fragment, assign, circumstance, segment.

**detain** *(SYN.)* impede, delay, hold back, retard, arrest, restrain, stay. *(ANT.)* quicken, hasten, expedite, forward, precipitate.

**detect** *(SYN.)* discover, reveal, find, ascertain, determine, learn, originate, devise. *(ANT.)* hide, screen, lose, cover, mask.

**determinant** *(SYN.)* reason, incentive, source, agent, principle, inducement. *(ANT.)* result, effect, consequence, end.

**determine** *(SYN.)* decide, settle, end, conclude, ascertain, induce, fix, verify, resolve, establish, necessitate.

**detest** *(SYN.)* loathe, hate, despise. *(ANT.)* savor, appreciate, like, love.

**detriment** *(SYN.)* injury, harm, disadvantage, damage.

*(ANT.)* benefit.

**detrimental** *(SYN.)* hurtful, mischievous, damaging, harmful. *(ANT.) salutary, advantageous, profitable, beneficial.*

**develop** *(SYN.)* evolve, unfold, enlarge, amplify, expand, create, grow, advance, reveal, unfold, mature, elaborate. *(ANT.) wither, contract, degenerate, stunt, deteriorate, compress.*

**development** *(SYN.)* growth, expansion, progress, unraveling, elaboration, evolution, maturing, unfolding. *(ANT.) compression, abbreviation, curtailment.*

**deviate** *(SYN.)* deflect, stray, divert, diverge, wander, sidetrack, digress. *(ANT.) preserve, follow, remain, continue, persist.*

**device** *(SYN.)* tool, utensil, means, channel, machine, agent, vehicle, gadget, apparatus, instrument, contrivance.

**devilish** *(SYN.)* diabolical, fiendish, diabolic, satanic, demonic.

**devious** *(SYN.)* tortuous, winding, distorted, circuitous, tricky, crooked, roundabout, cunning, erratic, indirect. *(ANT.) straight, direct, straightforward, honest.*

**devise** *(SYN.)* create, concoct, invent, originate.

**devote** *(SYN.)* assign, dedicate, give, apply. *(ANT.) withhold, relinquish, ignore, withdraw.*

**devoted** *(SYN.)* attached, dedicated, prone, wedded, addicted, ardent, earnest, loyal, disposed, inclined, fond, affectionate, faithful. *(ANT.) untrammeled, disinclined, detached, indisposed.*

**devotion** *(SYN.)* piety, zeal, ardor, loyalty, dedication, religiousness, consecration, affection, love, devoutness, fidelity, attachment. *(ANT.) unfaithfulness, aversion, alienation, indifference.*

**devour** *(SYN.)* consume, gulp, gorge, waste, eat, ruin, swallow, destroy.

**devout** *(SYN.)* sacred, religious, spiritual, holy, theological, pietistic, pious, sanctimonious, reverent. *(ANT.) profane, skeptical, atheistic, secular, impious.*

**dexterity** *(SYN.)* talent, capability, qualification, aptness, skill, ability. *(ANT.) unreadiness, incapacity, disability, incompetency.*

**dexterous** *(SYN.)* clever, adroit, handy, deft, facile, skillful, skilled, proficient. *(ANT.) awkward, clumsy.*

**dialed** *(SYN.)* slang, jargon, cant, speech, idiom, tongue, diction, vernacular. *(ANT.) nonsense, drivel, babble, gibberish.*

**dialogue** *(SYN.)* interview, chat, discussion, conference, exchange, talk, conversation.

**diary** *(SYN.)* memo, account, journal.

**dicker** *(SYN.)* haggle, bargain, negotiate.

**dictate** *(SYN.)* deliver, speak, record, command, order, direct.

**dictator** *(SYN.)* oppressor, tyrant, despot, persecutor, overlord, autocrat.

**die** *(SYN.)* fade, wane, cease, depart, wither, decay, decline, sink, expire, perish, decease, go, diminish, fail, languish, decrease. *(ANT.) live, begin, grow, survive, flourish.*

**difference** *(SYN.)* inequality, variety, disparity, discord, distinction, dissension, dissimilarity, disagreement, contrast, separation. *(ANT.) harmony, similarity, identity, agreement, likeness, compatibility, kinship, resemblance.*

**different** *(SYN.)* unlike, various, distinct, miscellaneous, divergent, contrary, differing, diverse, variant, incongruous, unalike, changed, dissimilar, opposite. *(ANT.) similar, congruous, alike, identical.*

**differentiate** *(SYN.)* separate, discriminate, distinguish, perceive, detect, recognize, discern. *(ANT.) confuse, omit, mingle, confound, overlook.*

**difficult** *(SYN.)* involved, demanding, arduous, trying, complicated, hard, laborious, perplexing, hard, intricate. *(ANT.) simple, easy, facile, effortless.*

**difficulty** *(SYN.)* trouble, hardship, fix, predicament, trouble. *(ANT.) ease.*

**diffuse** *(SYN.)* spread, sparse, scattered, scanty, dispersed, thin, rare. *(ANT.) concentrated.*

**dig** *(SYN.)* burrow, excavate, appreciate, understand.

**digest** *(SYN.)* consume, eat, reflect on, study, shorten, consider, summarize, abridge, abstract, abridgment, synopsis.

**dignified** *(SYN.)* serious, solemn, noble, stately, elegant.

**dignify** *(SYN.)* honor, elevate.

*(ANT.)* shame, degrade, humiliate.

**dignity** *(SYN.)* stateliness, distinction, bearing.

**digress** *(SYN.)* divert, wander, bend, stray, deflect, sidetrack, crook. *(ANT.) preserve, continue, remain, follow, persist.*

**dilate** *(SYN.)* increase, widen, amplify, enlarge, augment, expand. *(ANT.) shrink, contract, restrict, abridge.*

**dilemma** *(SYN.)* fix, strait, condition, scrape, difficulty, plight. *(ANT.) ease, calmness, satisfaction, comfort.*

**diligent** *(SYN.)* patient, busy, hardworking, active, perseverant, assiduous, industrious, careful. *(ANT.) unconcerned, indifferent, apathetic, lethargic, careless.*

**dim** *(SYN.)* pale, shadowy, faint, faded, unclear, vague, darken, dull, indistinct. *(ANT.) brighten, brilliant, bright, illuminate, glaring.*

**dimension** *(SYN.)* size, importance, measure, extent.

**diminish** *(SYN.)* suppress, lower, decrease, shrink, wane, abate, reduce, lessen, assuage. *(ANT.) enlarge, revive, amplify, increase.*

**diminutive** *(SYN.)* small, wee, tiny, little, minute. *(ANT.) large, big, gigantic, huge.*

**din** *(SYN.)* tumult, clamor, sound, babble, outcry, row, noise, racket. *(ANT.) quiet, stillness, hush.*

**dine** *(SYN.)* lunch, eat, sup, feed.

**dingy** *(SYN.)* dull, dark, dismal, dirty, drab, murky, gray. *(ANT.) cheerful, bright.*

**dip** *(SYN.)* immerse, plunge, submerge, wet, swim.

**diplomacy** *(SYN.)* knack, dexterity, skill, address, poise, tact, finesse. *(ANT.) vulgarity, blunder, awkwardness, incompetence.*

**diplomatic** *(SYN.)* politic, adroit, tactful, discreet, judicious, gracious, polite, discriminating. *(ANT.) rude, churlish, gruff, boorish, impolite, coarse.*

**dire** *(SYN.)* horrible, terrible, appalling, fearful, harrowing, grievous, ghastly, awful, horrid, terrifying, dreadful, frightful, horrifying, monstrous, horrendous, repulsive. *(ANT.) lovely, enchanting, fascinating, beautiful, enjoyable.*

**direct** *(SYN.)* rule, manage, bid, order, level, command, conduct, regulate, point, indicate, show, aim, control, sight, guide, instruct, train, govern. *(ANT.) swerving, untruthful, misguide, distract, indirect, crooked, deceive.*

**direction** *(SYN.)* way, order, course, instruction, tendency, management, route, trend, guidance, administration, supervision, inclination.

**directly** *(SYN.)* immediately, straight.

**dirt** *(SYN.)* pollution, soil, filthiness, filth. *(ANT.) cleanliness.*

**dirty** *(SYN.)* muddy, base, pitiful, filthy, shabby, foul, soiled, nasty, mean, grimy, low, obscene, untidy, indecent, unclean, messy, squalid, contemptible, sloppy. *(ANT.) pure, neat, wholesome, clean, presentable.*

**disability** *(SYN.)* inability, weakness, handicap, incapacity, injury, unfitness, incompetence, impotence. *(ANT.) power, ability, strength, capability.*

**disable** *(SYN.)* weaken, incapacitate, cripple. *(ANT.) strengthen.*

**disabled** *(SYN.)* deformed, limping, weak, crippled, maimed, defective, unsatisfactory, halt, feeble. *(ANT.) vigorous, athletic, sound, agile, robust.*

**disadvantage** *(SYN.)* drawback, hindrance, handicap, inconvenience, obstacle. *(ANT.) advantage, benefit, convenience.*

**disagree** *(SYN.)* quarrel, dispute, differ, conflict. *(ANT.) agree.*

**disagreement** *(SYN.)* nonconformity, variance, difference, objection, challenge, remonstrance, dissent. *(ANT.) assent, acceptance, compliance, agreement.*

**disappear** *(SYN.)* end, fade out, vanish. *(ANT.) emerge, appear.*

**disappoint** *(SYN.)* fail, displease, mislead, dissatisfy. *(ANT.) please, satisfy, gratify.*

**disappointment** *(SYN.)* dissatisfaction, defeat, discouragement, failure. *(ANT.) pleasure, satisfaction, gratification.*

**disapprove** *(SYN.)* object to, disfavor, oppose. *(ANT.) approve.*

**disarm** *(SYN.)* paralyze, demilitarize.

**disaster** *(SYN.)* casualty, mishap, misfortune, catastrophe, accident, adversity, ruin, calamity. *(ANT.) fortune, advantage.*

# disavow

**disavow** (SYN.) reject, revoke, disclaim, retract, disown. (ANT.) recognize, acknowledge.

**disband** (SYN.) scatter, split, dismiss, separate.

**disbelief** (SYN.) doubt, incredulity, skepticism. (ANT.) certainty, credulity.

**discard** (SYN.) scrap, reject.

**discern** (SYN.) distinguish, see, descry, separate, differentiate, perceive, discriminate, detect, observe, recognize. (ANT.) omit, confuse, overlook, mingle, confound.

**discernment** (SYN.) perception, sharpness, intelligence, perspicacity, acuity, keenness. (ANT.) dullness, stupidity.

**discharge** (SYN.) remove, relieve, dismiss, banish, unburden, shoot, fire, explosion, eject, detonation, liberation, release, unload, discard, send. (ANT.) retain, employ, enlist, hire, accept, recall, detain.

**disciple** (SYN.) learner, follower, student, adherent, supporter, scholar, pupil, votary, devotee. (ANT.) guide, leader.

**discipline** (SYN.) training, order, instruction, drill, restraint, regulation, practice, correction, control, self-control, train, teach, exercise. (ANT.) carelessness, sloppiness, confusion, negligence, messiness, chaos, turbulence.

**disclaim** (SYN.) retract, reject, deny, renounce, disavow, revoke. (ANT.) recognize, acknowledge.

**disclose** (SYN.) show, divulge, betray, uncover, discover, reveal, expose. (ANT.) hide, cloak, mask, cover, obscure, conceal.

**discomfit** (SYN.) malaise, concern, confuse, baffle, perplex, disconcert.

**discomfort** (SYN.) malaise, concern, anxiety, uneasiness.

**disconcerted** (SYN.) disturbed, agitated, upset.

**disconnect** (SYN.) divide, separate, unhook, disengage, detach. (ANT.) connect, bind, attach, unify, engage.

**disconsolate** (SYN.) depressed, downcast, sorrowful, dejected, dismal, sad, unhappy, wretched, somber, cheerless, morose, lugubrious, miserable, mournful. (ANT.) delightful, merry, glad, cheerful, happy.

**discontent** (SYN.) displeased, disgruntled, unhappy, dissatisfied, vexed.

**discontinue** (SYN.) postpone, delay, adjourn, stay, stop, defer, suspend, end, cease, interrupt. (ANT.) prolong, persist, continue, start, begin, proceed, maintain.

**discord** (SYN.) disagreement, conflict. (ANT.) concord, accord, agreement.

**discourage** (SYN.) hamper, obstruct, restrain, block, dishearten, retard, check, dispirit, thwart, depress, hinder, stop. (ANT.) expedite, inspire, encourage, promote, inspirit, assist, further.

**discourteous** (SYN.) gruff, rude, vulgar, blunt, impolite, saucy, uncivil, boorish, rough. (ANT.) stately, courtly, civil, dignified, genteel.

**discover** (SYN.) find out, invent, expose, ascertain, devise, reveal, learn, determine, detect. (ANT.) hide, screen, cover, conceal, lose.

**discredit** (SYN.) disbelieve, dishonor, doubt, disgrace, shame.

**discreet** (SYN.) politic, discriminating, judicious, adroit, prudent, cautious, wise, tactful, careful, diplomatic. (ANT.) incautious, rude, coarse, boorish, tactless, imprudent, indiscreet, careless, gruff.

**discrepant** (SYN.) incompatible, wavering, contrary, irreconcilable, unsteady, illogical, contradictory. (ANT.) correspondent, compatible, consistent.

**discriminating** (SYN.) exact, particular, critical, accurate, discerning. (ANT.) unimportant, shallow, insignificant, superficial.

**discrimination** (SYN.) perspicacity, discernment, racism, wisdom, bias, sagacity, intolerance, prejudice, intelligence, understanding. (ANT.) thoughtlessness, senselessness, arbitrariness.

**discuss** (SYN.) gossip, plead, discourse, blab, lecture, talk, chat, spout, mutter, deliberate, consider, reason, comment.

**discussion** (SYN.) speech, chatter, lecture, conference, talk, dialogue, conversation, rumor. (ANT.) silence, correspondence, writing.

**disdain** (SYN.) derision, hatred, contempt, scorn, contumely, reject, haughtiness, detestation. (ANT.) respect, esteem, reverence, admire, prize, honor, admiration, awe, regard.

**disdainful** (SYN.) haughty, scornful, arrogant, contemptuous. (ANT.) awed, admiring, regardful.

**disease** (SYN.) malady, disorder, ailment, illness, affliction, infirmity, complaint, sickness. (ANT.) soundness, health, vigor.

**disentangle** (SYN.) unwind, untie, clear, unravel, unknot, unsnarl, untangle.

**disfigured** (SYN.) deformed, marred, defaced, scarred.

**disgrace** (SYN.) odium, chagrin, shame, mortification, embarrassment, humiliate, scandal, dishonor, mortification. (ANT.) renown, glory, respect, praise, dignity, honor.

**disgraceful** (SYN.) ignominious, shameful, discreditable, disreputable, scandalous, dishonorable. (ANT.) renowned, esteemed, respectable, honorable.

**disguise** (SYN.) excuse, simulation, pretension, hide, camouflage, make-up, cover-up, mask, conceal, screen, affectation, pretext. (ANT.) show, reality, actuality, display, reveal, sincerity, fact.

**disgust** (SYN.) offend, repulse, nauseate, revolt, sicken. (ANT.) admiration, liking.

**disgusting** (SYN.) repulsive, nauseating, revolting, nauseous, repugnant.

**dish** (SYN.) serve, container, give, receptacle.

**dishearten** (SYN.) depress, sadden, discourage.

**disheveled** (SYN.) mussed, sloppy, rumpled, untidy.

**dishonest** (SYN.) crooked, impure, unsound, false, contaminated, venal, corrupt, putrid, thievish, vitiated, tainted. (ANT.) upright, honest, straightforward.

**dishonor** (SYN.) disrepute, scandal, indignity, chagrin, mortification, shame, obloquy, defamation, humiliation, disgrace, scandal. (ANT.) renown, glory, praise, honor, dignify.

**disinclined** (SYN.) unwilling, reluctant, loath.

**disingenuous** (SYN.) tricky, deceitful, scheming, dishonest, underhanded, cunning, artful, crafty, insidious.

**disintegrate** (SYN.) decompose, dwindle, spoil, decay, wane, ebb, decline, rot. (ANT.) increase, flourish, rise, grow.

**disinterested** (SYN.) unbiased, open-minded, neutral, impartial, unprejudiced.

**dislike** (SYN.) aversion, dread, reluctance, abhorrence, disinclination, hatred, repugnance. (ANT.) devotion, affection, enthusiasm, attachment.

**disloyal** (SYN.) false, treasonable, apostate, unfaithful, recreant, treacherous, untrue, traitorous, faithless. (ANT.) true, devoted, constant, loyal.

**dismal** (SYN.) dark, lonesome, somber, bleak, dull, sad, doleful, sorrowful, cheerless, depressing, dreary, funeral, gloomy, melancholy. (ANT.) lively, gay, happy, lighthearted, charming, cheerful.

**dismantle** (SYN.) take apart, wreck, disassemble.

**dismay** (SYN.) disturb, bother, dishearten, horror, alarm, bewilder, frighten, scare, discourage, confuse. (ANT.) encourage, hearten.

**dismiss** (SYN.) remove, discharge, discard, release, liberate, exile, banish, eject, oust. (ANT.) retain, detain, engage, hire, accept.

**disobedient** (SYN.) refractory, forward, unruly, insubordinate, defiant, rebellious, undutiful. (ANT.) submissive, complaint, obedient.

**disobey** (SYN.) invade, break, violate, infringe, defile.

**disorder** (SYN.) tumult, chaos, jumble, confusion, muddle, turmoil, anarchy. (ANT.) organization, neatness, system, order.

**disorganization** (SYN.) jumble, confusion, muddle, anarchy. (ANT.) system, order.

**disorganized** (SYN.) muddled, confused, indistinct, bewildered, mixed. (ANT.) organized, lucid, clear, plain.

**disown** (SYN.) deny, renounce, reject, repudiate, forsake, disinherit.

**disparage** (SYN.) undervalue, depreciate, lower, belittle, derogate, minimize, decry, discredit. (ANT.) exalting, praise, aggrandize, magnify, commend.

**disparagement** (SYN.) lowering, decrying, undervaluing, belittling, minimizing. (ANT.) praise, exalting, aggrandizement, magnification.

**disparaging** (SYN.) belittling, deprecatory, discrediting, deprecating.

**dispassionate** (SYN.) calm, cool, composed, controlled, unemotional, imperturbable.

**dispatch** (SYN.) throw, impel, transmit, emit, cast, finish, report, message, send, speed, achieve, conclude, communication, promptness, discharge. (ANT.) reluctance, get, redeem, bring, slowness, hold.

**dispel** (SYN.) disseminate, scatter, disperse, separate, diffuse. (ANT.) collect, accumulate, gather.

**dispense** (SYN.) deal, give, allot, assign, apportion, mete, distribute, grant, allocate, measure. (ANT.) refuse, withhold, confiscate, retain, keep.

**disperse** (SYN.) dissipate, scatter, disseminate, diffuse, separate, dispel. (ANT.) collect, amass, gather, assemble, accumulate.

**dispirited** (SYN.) downhearted, unhappy, dejected, disheartened, sad, depressed, melancholy. (ANT.) cheerful, happy, optimistic.

**displace** (SYN.) remove, transport, lodge, shift, move. (ANT.) retain, leave, stay, remain.

**display** (SYN.) parade, exhibit, show, cover, flaunt. (ANT.) hide, cover, conceal.

**displeasure** (SYN.) dislike, disapproval, dissatisfaction, distaste, discontentment.

**disposal** (SYN.) elimination, adjustment, removal, release, arrangement, administration, settlement.

**dispose** (SYN.) settle, adjust, arrange.

**disposition** (SYN.) behavior, character, deed, deportment, action, manner, bearing, temperament, nature, demeanor, personality, carriage.

**dispossess** (SYN.) eject, expel, evict, oust, dislodge.

**disprove** (SYN.) refute, deny, invalidate, controvert.

**dispute** (SYN.) squabble, debate, argument, controversy, contention, disagreement, bicker, contest, argue, contend, quarrel, contradict, discuss, deny, oppose, altercate. (ANT.) harmony, concord, agreement, allow, concur, agree, concede, decision.

**disregard** (SYN.) slight, omit, ignore, inattention, oversight, skip, neglect, overlook. (ANT.) regard, include.

**disrepair** (SYN.) ruin, decay, dilapidation, destruction.

**disreputable** (SYN.) dishonored, notorious, dishonorable, disgraced.

**disrespectful** (SYN.) fresh, impertinent, rude, impolite, impudent. (ANT.) polite, respectful, courteous.

**dissect** (SYN.) examine, cut, analyze.

**disseminate** (SYN.) publish, circulate, spread, publish, broadcast.

**dissent** (SYN.) objection, challenge, disagreement, protest, remonstrance, difference, nonconformity, variance, noncompliance. (ANT.) assent, acceptance, compliance, agreement.

**dissertation** (SYN.) thesis, treatise, disquisition.

**dissimilar** (SYN.) diverse, unlike, various, distinct, contrary, sundry, different, miscellaneous. (ANT.) same, alike, similar, congruous.

**dissimulation** (SYN.) pretense, deceit, sanctimony, hypocrisy, cant. (ANT.) honesty, condone, openness, frankness, truth.

**dissipate** (SYN.) misuse, squander, dwindle, consume, waste, lavish, diminish. (ANT.) save, conserve, preserve, accumulate, economize.

**dissolve** (SYN.) liquefy, end, cease, melt, fade, disappear.

**distant** (SYN.) stiff, cold, removed, far, afar, unfriendly, remote, faraway, separated, aloof, reserved. (ANT.) nigh, friendly, close, cordial, near.

**distasteful** (SYN.) disagreeable, unpleasant, objectionable.

**distend** (SYN.) swell, widen, magnify, expand, enlarge.

**distinct** (SYN.) plain, evident, lucid, visible, apparent, different, separate, individual, obvious, manifest, clear. (ANT.) vague, indistinct, uncertain, obscure, ambiguous.

**distinction** (SYN.) importance, peculiarity, trait, honor, fame, characteristic, repute, quality, renown, prominence, attribute, property. (ANT.) nature, substance, essence, being.

**distinctive** (SYN.) odd, exceptional, rare, individual, eccentric, special, strange. (ANT.) ordinary, general, common, normal.

**distinguish** (SYN.) recognize, differentiate, divide, classify, descry, discern, separate, perceive, detect. (ANT.) mingle, conjoin, blend, found, omit, confuse, overlook.

**distinguished** (SYN.) eminent, illustrious, renowned, celebrated, elevated, noted, important, famous, prominent. (ANT.) ordinary, common, obscure, unimportant.

**distort** (SYN.) contort, falsify, twist, misrepresent.

**distract** (SYN.) occupy, bewilder, disturb, divert, confuse. (ANT.) focus, concentrate.

**distracted** (SYN.) abstracted, preoccupied, absent. (ANT.) attentive, attending, watchful, present.

**distraction** (SYN.) entertainment, confusion, amusement, diversion.

**distress** (SYN.) torment, misery, trouble, worry, pain, agony, torture, anguish, anxiety, disaster, wretchedness, peril, danger, suffering. (ANT.) joy, solace, comfort, relief.

**distribute** (SYN.) deal, sort, allot, mete, classify, share, issue, dole, apportion, allocate, dispense, group.

**district** (SYN.) domain, place, territory, country, region, division, neighborhood, section, area, land.

**distrust** (SYN.) scruple, unbelief, suspect, mistrust, hesitation, suspense, uncertainty, doubt, suspicion, ambiguity. (ANT.) faith, conviction, trust, belief, determination.

**disturb** (SYN.) perturb, vex, confuse, worry, agitate, derange, unsettle, perplex, rouse, bother, trouble, annoy, interrupt, discompose. (ANT.) quiet, order, calm, settle, pacify, soothe.

**disturbance** (SYN.) disorder, commotion, confusion, riot, light, brawl. (ANT.) calm, tranquility, serenity.

**disturbed** (SYN.) neurotic, psychopathic, psychotic. (ANT.) normal.

**diverge** (SYN.) fork, separate. (ANT.) converge, join, merge.

**diverse** (SYN.) unlike, various, different, several.

**diversify** (SYN.) change, modify, alter.

**diversion** (SYN.) entertainment, sport, distraction, amusement, recreation.

**divert** (SYN.) detract, amuse, confuse, distract, deflect, entertain, tickle. (ANT.) tire, bore, weary.

**divide** (SYN.) share, split, detach, cleave, apportion, sunder, part, distribute, allocate, disunite, estrange, separate, allot, sever. (ANT.) merge, unite, convene, join, gather, combine.

**divine** (SYN.) holy, supernatural, godlike, transcendent, celestial, heavenly. (ANT.) mundane, wicked, blasphemous, profane.

**division** (SYN.) partition, separation, sharing, section, segment, part, portion. (ANT.) union, agreement.

**divorce** (SYN.) disjoin, disconnect, separate, divide.

**divulge** (SYN.) discover, release, expose, show, betray, reveal, admit, disclose, uncover. (ANT.) hide, conceal, cloak, cover.

**dizzy** (SYN.) staggering, unsteady, giddy, light-headed, confused. (ANT.) rational, clearheaded, unconfused.

**do** (SYN.) effect, conduct, perform, work, suffice, accomplish, finish, transact, serve, discharge, execute, complete, carry on, make, settle, conclude, fulfill, consummate, produce, terminate, practice.

**docile** (SYN.) pliant, tame, complaint, teachable, obedient, submissive, yielding. (ANT.) unruly, obstinate, ungovernable, mulish.

**dock** (SYN.) moor, clip, anchor, tie.

**doctor** (SYN.) heal, treat, medic, remedy, cure.

**doctrinaire** (SYN.) formal, dogmatic, overbearing, authoritarian, formal, arrogant, magisterial. (ANT.) skeptical, indecisive, fluctuating.

**doctrine** (SYN.) tenet, precept, belief, dogma, teaching, principle, creed. (ANT.) deed, practice, conduct, perform.

**document** (SYN.) report, minute, memorial, vestige, account, note, trace.

**dodge** (SYN.) equivocate, recoil, elude, evade, avoid, duck.

**dogma** (SYN.) tenet, doctrine, belief, teaching, creed. (ANT.) deed, practice, conduct, performance.

**dogmatic** (SYN.) formal, domineering, authoritarian, doctrinaire, opinionated, dictatorial, positive, arrogant, authoritative, overbearing, doctrinal, magisterial. (ANT.) skeptical, indecisive, fluctuating.

**doing** (SYN.) feat, performance, act, deed, action, accomplishment, transaction. (ANT.) intention, inactivity, cessation.

**dole** (SYN.) deal, spread, allot, relief, divide, apportion, alms, welfare, distribute, dispense.

**doleful** (SYN.) dark, depressed, sad, dismal, dejected, bleak, dull, blue, sorrowful, unhappy, morose, lonesome, mournful, somber. (ANT.) gay, lively, cheerful, joyous.

**dolt** (SYN.) blockhead, dunce.

**domain** (SYN.) place, division, region, territory, empire, country, charge, kingdom, realm, quarter, dominion, bailiwick, jurisdiction, land.

**domestic** *(SYN.)* family, tame, native, servant, home-made, household, internal. *(ANT.) alien, foreign, outside.*

**domesticate** *(SYN.)* train, tame, housebreak, teach.

**domicile** *(SYN.)* dwelling, residence, home, abode.

**dominate** *(SYN.)* control, manage, rule, influence, subjugate, command, govern, tyrannize, direct, regulate. *(ANT.) follow, ignore, abandon, submit, forsake.*

**domination** *(SYN.)* mastery, sway, ascendancy, transcendence.

**don** *(SYN.)* wear, slip on.

**donation** *(SYN.)* gift, bequest, present, benefaction, grant, contribution, offering, largess, boon. *(ANT.) earnings, purchase, deprivation, loss.*

**done** *(SYN.)* complete, concluded, finished, over, terminated.

**doom** *(SYN.)* fortune, issue, result, destruction, destiny, consequence, fate, outcome, destine, ruin, death, lot.

**doomed** *(SYN.)* fated, predestined, destined, foreordained.

**dormant** *(SYN.)* unemployed, inert, lazy, unoccupied, idle, indolent. *(ANT.) working, employed, occupied, active, industrious.*

**dose** *(SYN.)* quantity, amount, portion.

**dote** *(SYN.)* indulge, treasure, coddle, pamper, spoil. *(ANT.) ignore.*

**double** *(SYN.)* copy, fold, duplicate.

**doubt** *(SYN.)* distrust, incredulity, suspicion, hesitation, uncertainty, question, scruple, ambiguity, skepticism, suspect, mistrust, unbelief. *(ANT.) conviction, belief, determination, trust, certainty.*

**doubtful** *(SYN.)* uncertain, unsettled, dubious, questionable, unsure.

**doubtless** *(SYN.)* certainly, undoubtedly, assuredly, positively, unquestionably.

**dour** *(SYN.)* gloomy, sulky, crabbed, morose, fretful. *(ANT.) joyous, pleasant, amiable, merry.*

**douse** *(SYN.)* immerse, quench, dip, dunk, extinguish.

**dowdy** *(SYN.)* messy, unkempt, untidy, sloppy, shabby, frowzy.

**downcast** *(SYN.)* sad, disheartened, unhappy, downhearted, dejected, dispirited, discourage, depressed, glum.

**downfall** *(SYN.)* destruction, comedown.

**downgrade** *(SYN.)* reduce, lower, diminish, decrease, depreciate. *(ANT.) improve, upgrade, appreciate.*

**downhearted** *(SYN.)* glum, discouraged, depressed, gloomy, downcast, sad, dejected. *(ANT.) enthusiastic, cheerful, happy.*

**downpour** *(SYN.)* cloudburst, deluge, flood.

**downright** *(SYN.)* totally, positively, completely, definitely.

**dowry** *(SYN.)* endowment, gift, settlement, talent, ability.

**drab** *(SYN.)* flat, dull, lifeless, unattractive.

**draft** *(SYN.)* air, induction, wind, enrollment, drawing, outline.

**drag** *(SYN.)* heave, pull, tug, crawl, draw, tarry, tow, haul, delay.

**drain** *(SYN.)* empty, deprive, dry, filter, spend, tap, exhaust, waste, sap, use. *(ANT.) fulfill, fill.*

**drama** *(SYN.)* show, play, production, piece.

**dramatist** *(SYN.)* playwright.

**drape** *(SYN.)* flow, cover, hang.

**drastic** *(SYN.)* severe, rough, extreme, violent, tough, intense.

**draw** *(SYN.)* tug, obtain, trace, lure, drag, attract, persuade, induce, haul, write, remove, extend, stretch, take out, allure, pull, prolong, extract, tow, draft, delineate, unsheathe, lure, depict, entice, sketch, infer. *(ANT.) shorten, contract, propel, alienate, drive.*

**drawback** *(SYN.)* snag, hitch, disadvantage, handicap, deficiency, difficulty, check, obstacle, hindrance, impediment. *(ANT.) gain, benefit, windfall, advantage.*

**drawing** *(SYN.)* likeness, print, view, engraving, portrait, sketch, illustration, picture, resemblance, scene.

**drawn** *(SYN.)* tired, haggard, taut, strained, harrowed, weary, tense, sapped, spent. *(ANT.) rested, relaxed, energetic, fresh.*

**draw out** *(SYN.)* protract, extend, persist, prolong, lengthen, sustain, continue. *(ANT.) reduce, curtail, shorten, abridge.*

**draw up** *(SYN.)* draft, write out, prepare, compose, indite, formulate, wait, stay.

**dread** *(SYN.)* awe, horror, fear, terror, alarm, apprehension, foreboding. *(ANT.) courage, boldness, assurance, confidence.*

**dreadful** *(SYN.)* dire, inspiring, ghastly, appalling, horrid, impressive, terrible, awful, frightful, horrible, bad, hideous, outrageous, repulsive. *(ANT.) fascinating, beautiful, enjoyable, enchanting, lovely.*

**dream** *(SYN.)* fantasy, wish, hope, vision, daydream, reverie, imagine, fantasize, fancy, invent, muse.

**dream up** *(SYN.)* cook up, create, think up, concoct, contrive, originate, imagine, devise.

**dreary** *(SYN.)* dull, sad, bleak, lonesome, gloomy, chilling, somber, depressing, dismal, cheerless, dark. *(ANT.) lively, hopeful, gay, cheerful, bright, joyous.*

**dregs** *(SYN.)* riffraff, scum, outcasts, dross, leftovers, flotsam.

**drench** *(SYN.)* wet, bathe, flood, soak, saturate.

**dress** *(SYN.)* garb, frock, gown, clothing, costume, apparel, attire, wardrobe, garments, vesture, clothes, habit, wear, don, robe, raiment. *(ANT.) undress, strip, divest, disrobe.*

**dresser** *(SYN.)* dude, clotherhorse, fop, dandy.

**dressing** *(SYN.)* bandage, seasoning, medicine, sauce.

**dressy** *(SYN.)* flashy, swank, showy, dapper. *(ANT.) dowdy, drab, frumpy, shabby, tacky.*

**dribble** *(SYN.)* fall, drip, leak, slaver, slobber.

**drift** *(SYN.)* roam, tendency, meander, sail, float, direction, wander, intention, stray.

**drifter** *(SYN.)* hobo, tramp, vagabond.

**drill** *(SYN.)* employment, lesson, task, use, activity, operation, training. *(ANT.) relaxation, indolence, rest, idleness, repose.*

**drink** *(SYN.)* gulp, swallow, imbibe, beverage, refreshment, potion.

**drip** *(SYN.)* dribble, drop, trickle.

**drive** *(SYN.)* impel, coerce, oblige, force, push, direct, constrain, journey, urge, enforce, trip, handle, ride, propel, control, run, compel.

**drivel** *(SYN.)* slaver, drool, spit, spittle, dribble, slobber, saliva, nonsense, twaddle, rubbish, babble, gibberish.

**driver** *(SYN.)* motorist, operator, teamster, trucker, motorman, pilot, coachman.

**droll** *(SYN.)* laughable, funny, amusing, witty, comical. *(ANT.) sober, sad, solemn, melancholy.*

**drone** *(SYN.)* buzz, hum, loafer, idler, non-worker.

**drool** *(SYN.)* drivel, slaver, dribble, spit, gibber, jabber, twaddle, trickle, salivate.

**droop** *(SYN.)* dangle, weaken, hang, sink, fail, settle, sag, weary, languish, despond. *(ANT.) stand, tower, extend, rise, straighten.*

**drop** *(SYN.)* droop, dribble, topple, collapse, downward, drip, trickle, tumble, gob, droplet, reduction, slump, slip, decrease, fall, dismiss, decline. *(ANT.) ascend, mount, steady, arise, soar.*

**drop out** *(SYN.)* back out, withdraw, stop, forsake, abandon, give up, leave, quit.

**droppings** *(SYN.)* feces, dung, waste, manure, excrement, ordure, guano.

**dross** *(SYN.)* dregs, impurity, leftovers, residue, debris, leavings, remains.

**drove** *(SYN.)* flock, herd.

**drown** *(SYN.)* sink, inundate, submerge, immerse.

**drowse** *(SYN.)* nap, doze, catnap, snooze, sleep, slumber, rest, drop off, repose.

**drowsy** *(SYN.)* dozing, torpid, soothing, dreamy, sleepy, comatose, sluggish, lulling, dull, calming, restful, lethargic. *(ANT.) alert, awake, sharp, keen, acute.*

**drub** *(SYN.)* wallop, thrash, beat, thump, cane, flog, rout, outclass, overcome, belabor, pummel, defeat, outplay.

**drubbing** *(SYN.)* walloping, flogging, beating, pounding, pummeling, thwacking, thrashing, rout, licking, clobbering.

**drudge** *(SYN.)* work, labor, hack, slave, toil, grub, grind, toiler, flunky, menial, servant.

**drudgery** *(SYN.)* toil, travail, effort, task, work, endeavor, labor. *(ANT.) recreation, indolence, leisure.*

**drug** *(SYN.)* remedy, medicine, stupefy, anesthetize, numb, benumb.

**drugged** *(SYN.)* numb, doped, numbed, stupefied, dazed, groggy, benumbed.

**druggist** *(SYN.)* apothecary, chemist, pharmacist.

**drunk** *(SYN.)* tight, intoxicated, soused, drunken, inebriated, alcoholic, sozzled, besotted, sot, toper, boozer, wino, rummy, dipsomaniac, lush, tipsy.

**drunkard** (SYN.) sot, drunk, alcoholic, lush.

**dry** (SYN.) thirsty, dehydrated, vapid, plain and uninteresting, drained, parched, barren, waterless, dull, tedious, boring, desiccated, tiresome. (ANT.) fresh, wet, soaked, fascinating, attractive, lively, moist, interesting.

**dub** (SYN.) nickname, name, christen, call, style, term, confer, bestow, denominate, entitle, characterize, tag, label.

**dubious** (SYN.) unsure, uncertain, undecided, hesitant, spurious, unreliable, puzzling, untrustworthy, questionable, ambiguous. (ANT.) decided, fired, irrefutable, definite, genuine, unquestionable, sound, authentic, trustworthy.

**duct** (SYN.) pipe, tube, passage, vein, funnel, gutter, main, trough, artery.

**due** (SYN.) payable, unpaid, owing, owed, imminent, expected.

**duel** (SYN.) competition, contest, engagement, rivalry, combat, strife, encounter.

**dues** (SYN.) assessment, fees, cost, levy, admission, fare, toll, contribution.

**duffer** (SYN.) bungler, slouch, blunderer, novice, incompetent, fumbler, lummox. (ANT.) master, expert, pro.

**dull** (SYN.) commonplace, slow, sad, dreary, boring, stupid, uninteresting. (ANT.) clear, animated, interesting, lively.

**dullard** (SYN.) dolt, dunce, moron, clod, blockhead, numskull.

**dumb** (SYN.) dull, witless, ignorant, mute, speechless, brainless, dense. (ANT.) bright, alert, clever, intelligent.

**dump** (SYN.) heap, fling down, drop, empty, unload, clear out, dispose of. (ANT.) store, fill, load, hoard, pack.

**dunce** (SYN.) deadhead, nitwit, booby, idiot, ignoramus, numskull, noddy, fool.

**dungeon** (SYN.) jail, prison, keep, cell.

**dunk** (SYN.) plunge, submerge, dip. (ANT.) uplift, elevate, recover.

**dupe** (SYN.) sucker, victim, gull, pushover, fool, cheat, deceive, defraud.

**duplicate** (SYN.) replica, replicate, facsimile, copy, reproduce, clone, double, twin, transcript. (ANT.) prototype.

**duplicity** (SYN.) dissimulation, deception, hypocrisy, deceitfulness, insincerity, artifice, cant, guile. (ANT.) openness, artlessness, candor, straightforwardness, genuineness.

**durability** (SYN.) might, strength, force, sturdiness, intensity, potency, vigor. (ANT.) weakness, frailty, feebleness.

**durable** (SYN.) constant, firm, fixed, unchangeable, enduring, abiding, lasting. (ANT.) unstable, temporary, perishable, transitory.

**duration** (SYN.) time, term, period, while, stage, era, epoch, interim.

**duress** (SYN.) force, demand, compulsion, emergency, pressure.

**dusky** (SYN.) sable, black, dark, darkish, swarthy, tawny, gloomy, overcast, misty, obscure, opaque, shadowy. (ANT.) light, fair, white, pale, shining, clear, bright.

**dutiful** (SYN.) docile, faithful, obedient. (ANT.) disobedient, willful, unruly.

**duty** (SYN.) bond, responsibility, accountability, faithfulness, function, obligation, assignment, engagement. (ANT.) freedom, choice.

**dwarf** (SYN.) midget, runt, reduce, stunt, minimize, tiny. (ANT.) mammoth, colossus, monster, giant.

**dwell** (SYN.) inhabit, roost, settle, abide, live, reside.

**dwindle** (SYN.) wane, decrease, diminish, fade, subside, ebb, shrivel, lessen. (ANT.) enlarge, increase, grow, gain.

**dynamic** (SYN.) active, forceful, kinetic, energetic, motive, mighty, vigorous. (ANT.) sleepy, stable, inert, fixed, dead, still, uninspiring, ineffectual, listless.

# E

**eager** (SYN.) avid, hot, anxious, fervent, enthusiastic, impatient, ardent, impassioned, yearning. (ANT.) unconcerned, apathetic, dull, uninterested, indifferent.

**early** (SYN.) betimes, opportune, first, beforehand, advanced, soon, shortly. (ANT.) retarded, late, tardy, belated, overdue.

**earmark** (SYN.) peculiarity, characteristic, brand, sign, stamp, trademark.

**earn** (SYN.) attain, win, get, achieve, obtain, gain, deserve, realize, collect, net, acquire, merit. (ANT.) lose, waste, forfeit.

**earnest** (SYN.) sincere, decided, determined, intent, serious, eager, resolute. (ANT.) indifferent, frivolous, insincere.

**earnings** (SYN.) wages, pay, salary, income.

**earth** (SYN.) globe, dirt, land, world, turf, soil, sod, ground.

**earthly** (SYN.) mundane, everyday, worldly. (ANT.) heavenly.

**earthy** (SYN.) earthlike, coarse, earthen, crude, unrefined, vulgar. (ANT.) tasteful, elegant, polished, refined.

**ease** (SYN.) lighten, alleviate, pacify, soothe, allay, comfort, contentedness. (ANT.) worry, disturb, confound, trouble, intensify, distress.

**easily** (SYN.) readily, effortlessly, smoothly, naturally, facilely. (ANT.) hardly, arduously, painfully, laboriously.

**easiness** (SYN.) repose, comfort, satisfaction, contentment, liberty, leisure, facility, simplicity. (ANT.) unrest, torment, arduousness, difficulty, discomfort.

**easy** (SYN.) light, simple, facile, gentle, effortless, unhurried, comfortable. (ANT.) hard, demanding, awkward, strict, difficult, formal.

**eat** (SYN.) consume, swallow, dine, corrode, chew, lunch, devour, feast.

**eavesdrop** (SYN.) spy, listen, snoop, overhear.

**ebb** (SYN.) diminish, recede, decline, decrease, retreat, lessen. (ANT.) wax, grow, thrive, increase, swell.

**ebullient** (SYN.) vivacious, buoyant, exuberant. (ANT.) lethargic, sad, gloomy, depressed.

**eccentric** (SYN.) odd, irregular, unusual, abnormal, peculiar. (ANT.) ordinary, conventional, normal.

**eccentricity** (SYN.) kink, idiosyncrasy, whim, freak, caprice, foible, quirk, oddness, strangeness, aberration. (ANT.) conventionality, ordinariness.

**ecclesiastical** (SYN.) religious, churchly, clerical.

**echelon** (SYN.) rank, level, grade, status.

**echo** (SYN.) response, imitation, suggestion, trace, reaction, imitate, repeat.

**eclectic** (SYN.) selective, diverse, broad, liberal, comprehensive. (ANT.) limited,

narrow, rigid, confined.

**eclipse** (SYN.) conceal, screen, hide, cover, obscure, overcast, veil.

**economical** (SYN.) saving, thrifty, careful, frugal, provident, sparing. (ANT.) wasteful, extravagant, lavish, improvident.

**economy** (SYN.) saving, thrift.

**ecstasy** (SYN.) frenzy, gladness, delight, madness, joy, glee, exaltation, pleasure, trance, rapture. (ANT.) misery, melancholy, sadness.

**ecstatic** (SYN.) overjoyed, thrilled, delighted, happy, elated.

**edge** (SYN.) margin, brim, verge, brink, border, keenness, extremity, boundary, trim, periphery, hem, rim, sting. (ANT.) dullness, center, bluntness.

**edgy** (SYN.) tense, touchy, nervous, irritable.

**edict** (SYN.) declaration, order, ruling, decree, pronouncement, command, law, proclamation.

**edifice** (SYN.) construction, building, establishment.

**edit** (SYN.) check, revise, correct, amend.

**educate** (SYN.) instruct, teach, school, train.

**education** (SYN.) training, development, knowledge, learning, cultivation, schooling, instruction, study.

**eerie** (SYN.) weird, fearful, ghastly, spooky, strange.

**efface** (SYN.) obliterate, erase.

**effect** (SYN.) produce, consequence, evoke, cause, make, complete, outcome, result, determine.

**effective** (SYN.) efficient, practical, productive. (ANT.) useless, wasteful, ineffective.

**efficiency** (SYN.) efficacy, capability, effectiveness, competency, ability. (ANT.) wastefulness, inability.

**efficient** (SYN.) efficacious, skillful, capable, adept, competent, useful, effectual, effective, apt, proficient. (ANT.) inefficient, unskilled, ineffectual, incompetent.

**effort** (SYN.) labor, endeavor, pains, essay, trial, exertion, struggle, strain.

**egg** (SYN.) stir, ovum, incite, urge, arouse, embryo, provoke.

**egghead** (SYN.) scholar, intellectual, pedant.

**egoism** (SYN.) self-interest, conceit, pride, selfishness, egotism. (ANT.) modesty, *generosity, selflessness.*

**eject** *(SYN.)* expel, remove, oust, eliminate. *(ANT.) include.*

**elaborate** *(SYN.)* detail, develop, decorated, decorative, ornate, complex. *(ANT.) simplify, simple, unadorned.*

**elapse** *(SYN.)* expire.

**elastic** *(SYN.)* yielding, flexible, adaptable, pliable.

**elated** *(SYN.)* delighted, rejoicing, overjoyed, jubilant. *(ANT.) sad, unhappy.*

**elder** *(SYN.)* senior. *(ANT.) younger.*

**elderly** *(SYN.)* aged, old. *(ANT.) young, youthful.*

**elect** *(SYN.)* pick, appoint, choose.

**electrify** *(SYN.)* shock, charge, stir, upset, generate, agitate.

**elegant** *(SYN.)* tasteful, refined, cultivated, choice, polished, superior, fine. *(ANT.) crude, coarse, unpolished, tasteless.*

**elementary** *(SYN.)* simple, primary, basic, uncomplicated, initial, beginning, fundamental. *(ANT.) involved, complex, sophisticated, complicated.*

**elevate** *(SYN.)* raise, lift. *(ANT.) lower, drop.*

**elf** *(SYN.)* devil, fairy, imp.

**elicit** *(SYN.)* summon.

**eligible** *(SYN.)* fit, suitable, qualified.

**eliminate** *(SYN.)* expel, eject, remove, dislodge, extirpate, erase, oust. *(ANT.) admit, involve.*

**elite** *(SYN.)* nobility, upperclass, aristocracy, gentry. *(ANT.) mob, proletariat.*

**elongate** *(SYN.)* extend, prolong, lengthen.

**elope** *(SYN.)* escape, flee.

**eloquent** *(SYN.)* expressive, fluent, articulate, glib, meaningful. *(ANT.) inarticulate.*

**else** *(SYN.)* different, another, other.

**elude** *(SYN.)* escape, miss, avoid, dodge. *(ANT.) odd, include.*

**emaciated** *(SYN.)* wasted, thin, starved, withered, shriveled, gaunt, shrunken, drawn, undernourished.

**emancipate** *(SYN.)* liberate, free, deliver, save. *(ANT.) restrain.*

**embankment** *(SYN.)* shore, dam, bank, fortification, buttress.

**embargo** *(SYN.)* prohibition, restriction, restraint.

**embark** *(SYN.)* board, depart.

**embarrass** *(SYN.)* discomfit, rattle, distress, hamper, fluster, entangle, abash, mortify, hinder, perplex, confuse, shame, trouble. *(ANT.) relieve, encourage, help.*

**embassy** *(SYN.)* ministry, legation, consulate.

**embed** *(SYN.)* root, inset, enclose, plant.

**embellish** *(SYN.)* adorn, decorate, ornament.

**embezzle** *(SYN.)* pilfer, misuse, rob, misappropriate, steal, take.

**embitter** *(SYN.)* provoke, arouse, alienate, anger, inflame.

**emblem** *(SYN.)* token, mark, symbol, badge.

**embody** *(SYN.)* comprise, cover, embrace, include.

**embrace** *(SYN.)* espouse, accept, receive, comprehend, contain, welcome, comprise, cover, clasp, include, adopt, hug. *(ANT.) spurn, reject, bar, exclude, repudiate.*

**embroider** *(SYN.)* decorate, adorn, stitch, trim, overstate, embellish, ornament, exaggerate, magnify.

**emerge** *(SYN.)* surface, show, appear.

**emergency** *(SYN.)* strait, pass, crisis, urgency, predicament, pinch.

**eminent** *(SYN.)* renowned, glorious, important, conspicuous, prominent, famous. *(ANT.) ordinary, commonplace, unknown, undistinguished, common.*

**emissary** *(SYN.)* envoy, minister, delegate, agent, spy.

**emit** *(SYN.)* expel, breathe, shoot, hurl, ooze, vent, belch, discharge.

**emotion** *(SYN.)* passion, turmoil, perturbation, affection, sentiment, feeling, trepidation, agitation. *(ANT.) dispassion, indifference, tranquillity, calm, restraint.*

**emotional** *(SYN.)* ardent, passionate, stirring, zealous, impetuous, overwrought, enthusiastic. *(ANT.) tranquil, calm, placid.*

**emphasis** *(SYN.)* accent, stress, insistence.

**emphatic** *(SYN.)* positive, definite, forceful, energetic, strong. *(ANT.) lax, quiet, unforceful.*

**employ** *(SYN.)* avail, use, devote, apply, utilize, engage, sign, hire, retain, service, contract. *(ANT.) reject, discard.*

**employee** *(SYN.)* laborer, worker, servant. *(ANT.) boss, employer.*

**employer** *(SYN.)* owner, boss, management, proprietor, manager, superintendent, supervisor. *(ANT.) employee, worker.*

**employment** *(SYN.)* occupation, work, business, position, job, service, engagement. *(ANT.) leisure, idleness, slothfulness.*

**empower** *(SYN.)* enable, sanction, permit, warrant.

**empty** *(SYN.)* void, devoid, unfilled, barren, senseless, unoccupied, unfurnished, vacant, blank, evacuate, unload, hollow. *(ANT.) supplied, full, occupied.*

**emulate** *(SYN.)* follow, imitate, copy.

**enable** *(SYN.)* authorize, empower, sanction, qualify.

**enact** *(SYN.)* legislate, portray, pass, stage.

**enchant** *(SYN.)* charm, titillate, fascinate, bewitch, delight, thrill, captivate. *(ANT.) tire, bore.*

**encircle** *(SYN.)* comprise, include, bound, encompass.

**enclose** *(SYN.)* envelop, confine, bound, surround, encompass, encircle, circumscribe. *(ANT.) open, exclude, distend, expose, develop.*

**encompass** *(SYN.)* include, surround, encircle.

**encore** *(SYN.)* repetition, repeat, again.

**encounter** *(SYN.)* battle, meet, oppose, run into, face, collide.

**encourage** *(SYN.)* incite, favor, cheer, impel, countenance, inspirit, exhilarate, animate, hearten, embolden, support. *(ANT.) deter, dispirit, deject, dissuade.*

**encroach** *(SYN.)* interfere, trespass, intrude, infringe.

**encumber** *(SYN.)* hamper, load, burden.

**end** *(SYN.)* completion, object, close, aim, result, conclusion, finish, extremity, intent, halt, stop, limit, purpose, cessation, expiration, termination. *(ANT.) opening, start, introduction, beginning, launch, inception.*

**endanger** *(SYN.)* imperil, hazard, risk. *(ANT.) secure.*

**endear** *(SYN.)* allure, charm.

**endeavor** *(SYN.)* strive, struggle, exertion, attempt, try, labor.

**endless** *(SYN.)* constant, nonstop, continuous, incessant, everlasting.

**endorse** *(SYN.)* approve, accept, sign, confirm, pass.

**endow** *(SYN.)* provide, furnish, bestow, give, contribute. *(ANT.) divest.*

**endure** *(SYN.)* experience, undergo, sustain, last, bear, continue, remain, undergo, persist, brook, tolerate, suffer. *(ANT.) wane, perish, succumb, fail.*

**enemy** *(SYN.)* foe, antagonist, rival, opponent, competitor, adversary, opposition. *(ANT.) colleague, ally, friend, accomplice.*

**energy** *(SYN.)* strength, vim, force, power, stamina, vigor, might. *(ANT.) feebleness, lethargy.*

**enervate** *(SYN.)* enfeeble, weaken, debilitate, exhaust, devitalize. *(ANT.) invigorate.*

**enfold** *(SYN.)* clasp, surround, wrap, embrace, hug.

**enforce** *(SYN.)* make, drive, compel, execute, force.

**engage** *(SYN.)* absorb, occupy, employ, hold, involve, hire, agree, engross, retain, promise, commit, entangle. *(ANT.) fire, disengage, discharge, dismiss.*

**engaged** *(SYN.)* affianced, betrothed, busy, occupied.

**engaging** *(SYN.)* fascinating, appealing, enticing, interesting, tempting, lovely, beguiling, charming, enchanting, engrossing, delightful, exquisite. *(ANT.) ordinary, boring.*

**engender** *(SYN.)* develop, breed, cause, generate, produce.

**engineer** *(SYN.)* direct, conduct, guide, lead, manage.

**engrave** *(SYN.)* print, cut, impress, inscribe, carve, sketch.

**engross** *(SYN.)* engage, enthrall, occupy, fascinate, absorb.

**engulf** *(SYN.)* flood, swallow.

**enhance** *(SYN.)* better, uplift, improve.

**enigma** *(SYN.)* mystery, stumper, riddle.

**enigmatic** *(SYN.)* perplexing, confusing, puzzling, baffling, mystifying.

**enjoy** *(SYN.)* savor, like, relish.

**enjoyment** *(SYN.)* pleasure, delight, gratification. *(ANT.) abhorrence, displeasure.*

**enlarge** *(SYN.)* widen, distend, amplify, broaden, extend, increase, augment, expand, dilate. *(ANT.) diminish, shrink, contract, decrease, wane, restrict.*

**enlighten** *(SYN.)* inform, illuminate, clarify, teach, instruct. *(ANT.) confuse.*

**enlist** *(SYN.)* enroll, prompt,

join, induce, enter, register, persuade. (ANT.) *quit, leave, abandon.*

**enliven** (SYN.) inspire, brighten, stimulate.

**enmity** (SYN.) antagonism, hatred, animosity, malignity, ill-will, antipathy, hostility, unfriendliness. (ANT.) *love, like, friendliness.*

**enormity** (SYN.) heinousness, wickedness, barbarity, atrociousness.

**enormous** (SYN.) vast, huge, colossal, immense, gargantuan, elephantine, gigantic, stupendous, large. (ANT.) *small, slight, tiny, minute, infinitesimal, diminutive, little.*

**enough** (SYN.) ample, adequate, sufficient, plenty. (ANT.) *inadequate, insufficient.*

**enrage** (SYN.) anger, provoke, madden, inflame. (ANT.) *appease, soothe, calm.*

**enrich** (SYN.) better, improve.

**enroll** (SYN.) record, list, recruit, register, enlist, write, induct. (ANT.) *quit, leave, abandon.*

**enshrine** (SYN.) bury, entomb.

**ensign** (SYN.) banner, colors, flag, officer.

**enslave** (SYN.) keep, hold, capture.

**ensue** (SYN.) arise, succeed, follow.

**ensure** (SYN.) guarantee, assure, protect, defend, cover.

**entangle** (SYN.) confuse, snare, involve, ravel, snarl, tangle, trap.

**enter** (SYN.) join, go inside.

**enterprise** (SYN.) fete, deed, venture, project, adventure, undertaking, ambition, business, exploit.

**enterprising** (SYN.) energetic, resourceful. (ANT.) *lazy, indolent, sluggish, unresourceful.*

**entertain** (SYN.) cheer, gladden, hold, consider, please, contemplate, divert, amuse, harbor, fascinate, interest. (ANT.) *repulse, tire, bore, disgust, annoy.*

**enthrall** (SYN.) captivate, fascinate, enchant, charm, thrill.

**enthusiasm** (SYN.) fervor, fanaticism, zeal, ardor, intensity, devotion, excitement, eagerness, fervency, earnestness. (ANT.) *indifference, ennui, apathy, unconcern, detachment.*

**enthusiastic** (SYN.) earnest, zealous, eager. (ANT.) *aloof, indifferent, unconcerned.*

**entice** (SYN.) lure, attract, seduce.

**entire** (SYN.) complete, intact, whole, undivided. (ANT.) *divided, separated, incomplete, partial.*

**entirely** (SYN.) altogether, thoroughly, wholly, solely.

**entitle** (SYN.) call, label, name, empower, allow, authorize, license, title.

**entourage** (SYN.) train, company, retinue, escort.

**entrance** (SYN.) inlet, portal, doorway, fascinate, entry, intrigue, door, thrill.

**entreat** (SYN.) implore, beg, plead.

**entreaty** (SYN.) plea, appeal.

**entrust** (SYN.) commit, charge, assign, delegate, consign, commission.

**enumerate** (SYN.) count, tally, list, number.

**enunciate** (SYN.) announce, express, speak, state.

**envelop** (SYN.) embrace, cover, conceal, surround, wrap.

**environment** (SYN.) neighborhood, habitat, surroundings, setting.

**envision** (SYN.) picture, imagine, visualize.

**envoy** (SYN.) delegate, emissary, representative, agent, messenger.

**envy** (SYN.) covetousness, jealousy, spitefulness, covet. (ANT.) *indifference, generosity.*

**epicure** (SYN.) gourmand, gourmet, connoisseur, gastronome, Epicurean, aesthete.

**epidemic** (SYN.) prevalent, scourge, plague, catching, widespread, pestilence, infectious.

**episode** (SYN.) happening, affair, occurrence, event, experience.

**epoch** (SYN.) age, era, period, time.

**equal** (SYN.) even, uniform, like, alike, equitable, same, identical, commensurate, equivalent, regular, parallel. (ANT.) *different, unequal, irregular, uneven.*

**equilibrium** (SYN.) stability, steadiness, balance, firmness.

**equip** (SYN.) fit, rig, provide, outfit, prepare, furnish.

**equipment** (SYN.) utensils, material, apparatus.

**equitable** (SYN.) square, rightful, fair, due, just, fit. (ANT.) *partial, biased, unjust, uneven.*

**equity** (SYN.) impartiality, fairness, justness, justice, fair-mindedness, evenhandedness.

**equivalent** (SYN.) match, rival, equal, like, replacement.

**equivocal** (SYN.) oblique, ambiguous, vague, indeterminate, uncertain, obscure. (ANT.) *clear, precise, explicit, certain, clear-cut, definite.*

**equivocate** (SYN.) temporize, evade, hedge, quibble, fudge, waffle, straddle.

**era** (SYN.) epoch, cycle, age, time, period.

**eradicate** (SYN.) remove, demolish, eliminate.

**erase** (SYN.) obliterate, remove, cancel. (ANT.) *add, include.*

**erect** (SYN.) upright, build, straight, raise, construct, vertical. (ANT.) *flat, horizontal, raze, flatten, demolish.*

**erection** (SYN.) building, construction, raising, fabrication.

**erode** (SYN.) rust, consume, disintegrate.

**erotic** (SYN.) carnal, sensual, amatory, prurient, lewd, wanton, passionate, lecherous.

**err** (SYN.) slip, misjudge.

**errand** (SYN.) chore, duty, task, exercise.

**errant** (SYN.) roving, rambling, wandering, vagrant.

**erratic** (SYN.) irregular, abnormal, uneven, occasional, sporadic, changeable, unsteady, odd, eccentric, strange, extraordinary, unconventional, bizarre, peculiar, uncertain, unusual, unstable. (ANT.) *regular, steady, normal, ordinary.*

**erroneous** (SYN.) wrong, mistaken, incorrect, inaccurate, false, untrue. (ANT.) *true, right, correct, accurate.*

**error** (SYN.) inaccuracy, fault, slip, oversight, fallacy, mistake, blunder.

**erudite** (SYN.) sage, wise, learned, deep, profound.

**erupt** (SYN.) vomit.

**escapade** (SYN.) caper, antic, stunt, trick, prank.

**escape** (SYN.) shun, avoid, flee, decamp, elude, flight, avert, departure, abscond, fly, evade. (ANT.) *meet, confront, invite, catch.*

**escort** (SYN.) conduct, lead, attend, accompany, protection, guard, guide, convoy, usher, squire.

**especially** (SYN.) unusually, principally, mainly, particularly, primarily.

**essay** (SYN.) test, thesis, undertake, paper, try.

**essence** (SYN.) substance, character, nature, principle, odor, meaning, basis, smell, perfume.

**essential** (SYN.) vital, intrinsic, basic, requisite, fundamental, indispensable, critical, requirement, necessity, necessary, important. (ANT.) *dispensable, unimportant, inessential.*

**establish** (SYN.) prove, fix, found, settle, institute, raise, verify, conform, form, sanction, ordain, begin, organize. (ANT.) *upset, discontinue, scatter, disperse, refute, abolish, unsettle.*

**esteem** (SYN.) revere, deem, appreciate, honor, value, think, admire, respect, hold, prize, reverence, regard. (ANT.) *scorn, disdain, depreciate, disregard, contempt, abhor.*

**estimate** (SYN.) calculate, gauge, judge, rate, evaluate, compute, value, figure.

**estimation** (SYN.) judgment, viewpoint, opinion.

**etch** (SYN.) stamp, engrave, impress.

**eternal** (SYN.) undying, immortal, ceaseless, infinite, everlasting, deathless, perpetual, endless, timeless. (ANT.) *mortal, transient, finite, brief, temporary, passing.*

**etiquette** (SYN.) decorum, formality.

**evacuate** (SYN.) withdraw, depart, leave, vacate.

**evade** (SYN.) miss, avoid, bypass. (ANT.) *confront, meet, face.*

**evaluate** (SYN.) value, appraise, assay.

**evaporate** (SYN.) disappear, vanish. (ANT.) *condense, appear.*

**even** (SYN.) smooth, level, still, square, same, flat, balanced, equal, parallel, identical. (ANT.) *irregular, bumpy, unbalanced, unequal, divergent.*

**evening** (SYN.) twilight, dusk, sunset. (ANT.) *sunrise, dawn.*

**event** (SYN.) issue, end, result, circumstance, occurrence, incident, consequence, happening, episode, outcome.

**even-tempered** (SYN.) composed, calm, cool. (ANT.) *hotheaded.*

**eventual** (SYN.) consequent, ultimate. (ANT.) *present, current.*

**eventually** (SYN.) ultimately.

**ever** (SYN.) continuously, always, constantly. (ANT.) *never.*

**everlasting** (SYN.) permanent, ceaseless, endless, continual.

**evermore** (*SYN.*) always.

**everyday** (*SYN.*) commonplace, common, usual, ordinary, customary. (*ANT.*) rare.

**evict** (*SYN.*) oust, put out, expel.

**evidence** (*SYN.*) grounds, clue, facts, testimony, data, sign, proof.

**evident** (*SYN.*) apparent, clear, obvious, indubitable, plain, conspicuous, patent, manifest, open, unmistakable. (*ANT.*) hidden, unclear, uncertain, obscure, concealed.

**evil** (*SYN.*) immoral, harmful, badness, sinful, injurious, woe, bad, wicked. (*ANT.*) goodness, moral, useful, upright, virtuous, beneficial, virtue, advantageous.

**evoke** (*SYN.*) summon, prompt.

**evolve** (*SYN.*) grow, advance, develop, result, emerge, unfold.

**exact** (*SYN.*) correct, faultless, errorless, detailed, accurate. (*ANT.*) inaccurate, inexact, faulty.

**exaggerate** (*SYN.*) stretch, expand, amplify, embroider, heighten, overstate, caricature, magnify, enlarge. (*ANT.*) understate, minimize, diminish, depreciate.

**exalt** (*SYN.*) erect, consecrate, raise, elevate, extol, dignify. (*ANT.*) humble, degrade, humiliate.

**examination** (*SYN.*) investigation, inspection, test, scrutiny.

**examine** (*SYN.*) assess, contemplate, question, review, audit, notice, inquire, analyze, check, investigate, dissect, inspect, survey. (*ANT.*) omit, disregard, overlook.

**example** (*SYN.*) pattern, archetype, specimen, illustration, model, instance, prototype, sample. (*ANT.*) rule, principle.

**exasperate** (*SYN.*) aggravate, anger, madden, irritate.

**excavate** (*SYN.*) unearth, dig, burrow.

**exceed** (*SYN.*) excel, beat, surpass, top.

**exceedingly** (*SYN.*) extremely, very, especially, unusually, surprisingly.

**excel** (*SYN.*) better, beat, surpass.

**excellence** (*SYN.*) distinction, superiority. (*ANT.*) poorness, inferiority, badness.

**excellent** (*SYN.*) wonderful, fine, marvelous, superior. (*ANT.*) poor, terrible, bad, inferior.

**except** (*SYN.*) omitting, but, reject, excluding, save, exclude.

**exception** (*SYN.*) affront, offense, exclusion, deviation, omission, anomaly.

**exceptional** (*SYN.*) different, irregular, strange, unusual, abnormal.

**excerpt** (*SYN.*) abstract, extract.

**excess** (*SYN.*) surplus, intemperance, extravagance, immoderation, profusion, abundant, profuse, superfluity. (*ANT.*) want, sparse, lack, dearth.

**exchange** (*SYN.*) barter, interchange, substitute, trade, change, swap.

**excite** (*SYN.*) arouse, incite, agitate, stimulate, awaken, disquiet. (*ANT.*) lull, quiet, bore, pacify.

**exclaim** (*SYN.*) vociferate, cry, call out, cry out, ejaculate, shout.

**exclamation** (*SYN.*) shout, outcry, clamor.

**exclude** (*SYN.*) omit, restrain, hinder, bar, except, prevent. (*ANT.*) welcome, involve, embrace, admit, accept, include.

**exclusion** (*SYN.*) exception, bar, rejection. (*ANT.*) inclusion.

**exclusive** (*SYN.*) restricted, limited, restrictive, choice, selective, fashionable. (*ANT.*) common, general, ordinary, unrestricted, unfashionable.

**excursion** (*SYN.*) voyage, tour, trip.

**excuse** (*SYN.*) exculpate, forgive, remit, acquit, free, pardon, condone, explanation, overlook, exempt, reason, justify, absolve. (*ANT.*) revenge, punish, convict.

**execute** (*SYN.*) complete, accomplish, do, achieve, kill, perform.

**exemplify** (*SYN.*) show, illustrate.

**exempt** (*SYN.*) excuse, free, except, release.

**exercise** (*SYN.*) drill, task, use, activity, lesson, training, exertion, application, gymnastics, operation, practice. (*ANT.*) rest, indolence, repose.

**exertion** (*SYN.*) attempt, effort, strain, endeavor.

**exhale** (*SYN.*) blow, breathe out.

**exhaust** (*SYN.*) drain, tire, empty, wear out, use, finish, fatigue. (*ANT.*) renew, refresh, replace.

**exhaustive** (*SYN.*) comprehensive, thorough, extensive, complete. (*ANT.*) incomplete.

**exhibit** (*SYN.*) demonstrate, display, present, reveal, betray, show, flaunt. (*ANT.*) hide, conceal, disguise.

**exhilarate** (*SYN.*) gladden, refresh, cheer, excite, stimulate.

**exhort** (*SYN.*) advise, coax, press, urge.

**exile** (*SYN.*) expulsion, proscription, deportation, ostracism, expatriation, deport, extradition, expel, banishment. (*ANT.*) retrieval, welcome, recall, admittance.

**exist** (*SYN.*) stand, live, occur, be.

**exit** (*SYN.*) leave, depart.

**exodus** (*SYN.*) leaving, exit, parting, departure.

**exonerate** (*SYN.*) acquit, clear.

**exorbitant** (*SYN.*) unreasonable, outrageous, overpriced, preposterous, excessive. (*ANT.*) normal, reasonable.

**exotic** (*SYN.*) strange, vivid, foreign, gay. (*ANT.*) dull, normal.

**expand** (*SYN.*) unfold, enlarge, broaden, spread, inflate, swell, grow. (*ANT.*) contract, shrivel, shrink.

**expect** (*SYN.*) await, think, hope, anticipate.

**expedient** (*SYN.*) helpful, desirable, rush, hasten, useful, fitting, sensible.

**expedition** (*SYN.*) trek, speed, trip, haste, voyage, journey, hurry.

**expel** (*SYN.*) exile, dislodge, discharge, excommunicate, oust, eject, dismiss, banish, disown. (*ANT.*) recall, invite, admit.

**expend** (*SYN.*) consume, waste, spend, exhaust. (*ANT.*) ration, reserve, conserve.

**expense** (*SYN.*) charge, cost, payment, price.

**expensive** (*SYN.*) costly, dear. (*ANT.*) modest, inexpensive, cheap.

**experience** (*SYN.*) occurrence, episode, sensation, happening, existence, background, feeling, living, encountering, knowledge.

**experienced** (*SYN.*) expert, qualified, accomplished, skilled, practiced. (*ANT.*) untutored, inexperienced, naive.

**experiment** (*SYN.*) trial, test, prove, research, examine, try, verify.

**expert** (*SYN.*) adept, handy, skillful, clever, specialist, authority, skilled, knowledgeable, ingenious. (*ANT.*) untrained, unskilled, inexperienced.

**expire** (*SYN.*) terminate, die, cease, perish, pass, end, disappear. (*ANT.*) commence, continue.

**explain** (*SYN.*) illustrate, decipher, expound, clarify, resolve, define, unravel, elucidate, unfold, justify, interpret. (*ANT.*) darken, baffle, obscure.

**explanation** (*SYN.*) definition, description, interpretation, account, reason, justification, excuse.

**explicit** (*SYN.*) lucid, definitive, specific, express, clear, manifest. (*ANT.*) vague, implicit, ambiguous.

**exploit** (*SYN.*) feat, deed, accomplishment, adventure.

**explore** (*SYN.*) research, hunt, probe, search, investigate, look, examine.

**explosion** (*SYN.*) bang, boom, blowup, flare-up, blast, detonation, outbreak, convulsion, furor, tantrum, paroxysm.

**explosive** (*SYN.*) fiery, rabid, eruptive, volcanic, fulminatory, inflammatory. (*ANT.*) stable, inert, peaceful, calm.

**exponent** (*SYN.*) explicator, spokesman, supporter, expounder, interpreter.

**expose** (*SYN.*) uncover, display, bare, open, unmask, reveal. (*ANT.*) hide, conceal, mask, covered.

**exposition** (*SYN.*) fair, bazaar, show, expo, exhibition.

**expound** (*SYN.*) clarify, present, explain, lecture, demonstrate.

**express** (*SYN.*) voice, tell, send, say, ship, declare, stale, precise, specific, swift, describe.

**expression** (*SYN.*) declaration, statement, look.

**expressive** (*SYN.*) suggestive, meaningful, telling, significant, thoughtful. (*ANT.*) unthinking, meaningless, nondescript.

**expressly** (*SYN.*) precisely, exactly, definitely, clearly. (*ANT.*) tentatively, vaguely, ambiguously.

**expulsion** (*SYN.*) ejection, discharge, removal, elimination.

**expunge** (*SYN.*) blot out, erase, cancel, obliterate, delete, efface, remove.

**expurgate** (*SYN.*) cleanse, purge, censor, edit, emasculate, abridge, blip.

**exquisite** (*SYN.*) delicate, delightful, attractive, dainty, beautiful, elegant, fine, superb, lovely, excellent, perfect. (ANT.) *vulgar, dull, ugly, unattractive.*

**extant** (SYN.) subsisting, remaining, surviving, present, existing. (ANT.) *lost, defunct, extinct, vanished.*

**extemporize** (SYN.) improvise, devise.

**extend** (SYN.) lengthen, stretch, increase, offer, give, grant, magnify, expand. (ANT.) *abbreviate, shorten, curtail.*

**extension** (SYN.) expansion, increase, stretching, enlargement.

**extensive** (SYN.) vast, wide, spacious. (ANT.) *cramped, confined, restricted.*

**extent** (SYN.) length, degree, range, amount, measure, size, compass, reach, magnitude, scope, expanse, area.

**extenuating** (SYN.) exculpating, excusable, qualifying, justifying, softening.

**exterior** (SYN.) surface, face, outside, covering, outer, external. (ANT.) *inside, interior, inner, internal.*

**exterminate** (SYN.) slay, kill, destroy.

**external** (SYN.) outer, exterior, outside. (ANT.) *inner, internal, inside, interior.*

**externals** (SYN.) images, effects, look, appearance, veneer, aspect.

**extinct** (SYN.) lost, dead, gone, vanished. (ANT.) *present, flourishing, alive, extant.*

**extinction** (SYN.) eclipse, annihilation, obliteration, death, extirpation.

**extol** (SYN.) laud, eulogize, exalt, praise. (ANT.) *denounce, discredit, disparage.*

**extra** (SYN.) surplus, spare, additional.

**extract** (SYN.) remove, essence. (ANT.) *penetrate, introduce.*

**extraordinary** (SYN.) unusual, wonderful, marvelous, peculiar, noteworthy. (ANT.) *commonplace, ordinary, usual.*

**extravagant** (SYN.) excessive, exaggerated, lavish, wasteful, extreme. (ANT.) *prudent, frugal, thrifty, economical.*

**extreme** (SYN.) excessive, overdone, outermost, limit, greatest, utmost, furthest. (ANT.) *reasonable, modest, moderate.*

**extricate** (SYN.) rescue, free, clear, release, liberate.

**exuberant** (SYN.) buoyant, ebullient, vivacious. (ANT.) *sad, depressed.*

**exult** (SYN.) rejoice, delight.

**eye** (SYN.) watch, view, stare, look, inspect, glance.

# F

**fable** (SYN.) legend, parable, myth, fib, falsehood, fiction, tale, story.

**fabled** (SYN.) legendary, famous, tamed, historic.

**fabric** (SYN.) goods, textile, material, cloth, yard goods.

**fabricate** (SYN.) assemble, make, construct, produce, create, manufacture, form. (ANT.) *raze, destroy, demolish.*

**fabrication** (SYN.) deceit, lie, falsehood, untruth, forgery, prevarication, deception. (ANT.) *verity, reality, actuality, truth, fact.*

**fabulous** (SYN.) amazing, marvelous, unbelievable, fantastic, astounding, astonishing, striking. (ANT.) *ordinary, commonplace, credible, proven, factual.*

**facade** (SYN.) deception, mask, front, show, pose, veneer, guise, affectation.

**face** (SYN.) cover, mug, front, assurance, countenance, audacity, visage, expression, look, features, facade, encounter, meet, surface. (ANT.) *rear, shun, avoid, evade, back, timidity.*

**facet** (SYN.) perspective, view, side, phase.

**facetious** (SYN.) jocular, pungent, humorous, funny, clever, droll, witty, playful, jesting. (ANT.) *sober, serious, grave, weighty.*

**face to face** (SYN.) opposing, nose to nose, confronting.

**facile** (SYN.) simple, easy, quick, uncomplicated, clever, fluent, skillful. (ANT.) *complex, difficult, complicated, laborious, hard, ponderous, painstaking, arduous.*

**facilitate** (SYN.) help, speed, ease, promote, accelerate, expedite.

**facilities** (SYN.) aid, means, resources, conveniences.

**facility** (SYN.) ability, skill, ease, skillfulness, material. (ANT.) *effort, difficulty.*

**facsimile** (SYN.) reproduction, likeness, replica.

**fact** (SYN.) reality, deed, certainty, act, incident, circumstance, occurrence, event, truth, actuality. (ANT.) *falsehood, fiction, delusion.*

**faction** (SYN.) clique, party, sect.

**factitious** (SYN.) false, sham, artificial, spurious, unnatural, affected. (ANT.) *natural, real, genuine, artless.*

**factor** (SYN.) part, element, basis, cause.

**factory** (SYN.) installation, plant, mill, works.

**factual** (SYN.) true, correct, accurate, sure, genuine, authentic. (ANT.) *incorrect, erroneous, fabricated, invented.*

**faculty** (SYN.) power, capacity, talent, staff, gift, ability, qualification, ability, skill.

**fad** (SYN.) fashion, vogue, mania, rage.

**faddish** (SYN.) ephemeral, modish, temporary, passing, fleeting. (ANT.) *lasting, permanent, enduring, classic.*

**fade** (SYN.) pale, bleach, weaken, dim, decline, sink, discolor, fail, diminish, droop.

**fagged** (SYN.) exhausted, tired, weary, jaded, pooped, worn.

**fail** (SYN.) neglect, weaken, flunk, miss, decline, disappoint, fade. (ANT.) *succeed, achieve, accomplish.*

**failing** (SYN.) fault, foible, imperfection, frailty, defect, peccadillo, shortcoming. (ANT.) *steadiness, strength, integrity.*

**failure** (SYN.) miscarriage, omission, decline, deficiency, fiasco, lack, dereliction, failing, unsuccessfulness, loss, default, want, insufficiency, decay. (ANT.) *conquest, accomplishment, success, triumph, victory, hit, luck, achievement.*

**faint** (SYN.) timid, faded, languid, halfhearted, dim, pale, wearied, feeble, indistinct, weak. (ANT.) *strong, sharp, forceful, glaring, clear, distinct, conspicuous.*

**fainthearted** (SYN.) shy, cowardly, timid, bashful. (ANT.) *fearless, brave, stouthearted, courageous.*

**fair** (SYN.) pale, average, light, sunny, mediocre, just, clear, lovely, market, blond, honest, equitable, impartial, reasonable, comely, exposition. (ANT.) *ugly, fraudulent, foul, outstanding, dishonorable, unfair.*

**fairly** (SYN.) equally, evenly, rather, impartially, passably, justly, squarely, somewhat.

**fair-minded** (SYN.) reasonable, just, open-minded, honest, unprejudiced, impartial, evenhanded. (ANT.) *bigoted, narrow-minded, unjust, close-minded, partisan.*

**fairness** (SYN.) equity, justice, evenhandedness, honesty. (ANT.) *favoritism, partiality, bias, one-sidedness.*

**fairy** (SYN.) leprechaun, gnome, elf, pixie, sprite.

**faith** (SYN.) dependence, trust, reliance, creed, loyalty, doctrine, confidence, dogma, tenet, persuasion, constancy, credence, fidelity, religion, belief. (ANT.) *mistrust, disbelief, doubt, infidelity.*

**faithful** (SYN.) staunch, true, devoted, trusty, loyal, constant, credible, steadfast, strict, trust-worthy, accurate. (ANT.) *untrustworthy, faithless, inaccurate, wrong, false, disloyal, erroneous, treacherous.*

**faithless** (SYN.) treacherous, unfaithful, disloyal, perfidious, untrue. (ANT.) *loyal, true, unwavering, constant, faithful.*

**fake** (SYN.) falsify, distort, pretend, feign, fraud, counterfeit, cheat, false, artificial, phony, imitation, forgery, mock. (ANT.) *honest, pure, real, genuine, authentic.*

**falderol** (SYN.) foolery, jargon, nonsense, gibberish, blather, balderdash.

**fall** (SYN.) drop, decline, diminish, droop, topple, decrease, sink, hang, descend, subside, plunge, collapse. (ANT.) *soar, climb, steady, rise, ascend.*

**fallacious** (SYN.) untrue, false, wrong, erroneous, deceptive, illusory, delusive. (ANT.) *accurate, true, exact, real, factual.*

**fallacy** (SYN.) mistake, error, illusion, sophism, misconception, deception.

**fall back** (SYN.) retreat, recede, retire, withdraw, concede. (ANT.) *progress, advance, gain, prosper, proceed.*

**fallow** (SYN.) idle, unprepared, unproductive, inactive. (ANT.) *prepared, productive, cultivated.*

**false** (SYN.) incorrect, wrong, deceitful, fake, imitation, counterfeit. (ANT.) *genuine, loyal, true, honest.*

**falsehood** (SYN.) untruth, lie, fib, story. (ANT.) *truth.*

**falsify** (SYN.) misquote, distort, misstate, mislead, adulterate.

**falter** (SYN.) stumble, tremble, waver, hesitate, flounder.

**fame** (SYN.) distinction, glory, mane, eminence, credit, reputation, renown, acclaim, notoriety. (ANT.) *infamy, obscurity, anonymity, disrepute.*

**famed** (SYN.) known, renowned, famous. (ANT.)

obscure, unknown, anonymous.

**familiar** (SYN.) informal, intimate, close, acquainted, amicable, knowing, cognizant, well-acquainted, versed, unreserved, friendly, sociable, affable, aware, known, courteous, intimate. (ANT.) unfamiliar, distant, affected, reserved.

**familiarity** (SYN.) sociability, acquaintance, awareness, frankness, intimacy, understanding, knowledge, fellowship. (ANT.) distance, ignorance, reserve, presumption, constraint, haughtiness.

**family** (SYN.) kin, tribe, folks, group, relatives.

**famine** (SYN.) want, deficiency, starvation, need. (ANT.) excess, plenty.

**famous** (SYN.) distinguished, noted, illustrious, famed, celebrated, well-known, eminent, renowned, prominent, esteemed. (ANT.) obscure, hidden, unknown.

**fan** (SYN.) arouse, spread, admirer, enthusiast, devotee, stir, whip, follower.

**fanatic** (SYN.) bigot, enthusiast, zealot.

**fancy** (SYN.) love, dream, ornate, imagine, suppose, imagination, taste, fantasy, ornamented, elaborate, think. (ANT.) plain, undecorated, simple, unadorned.

**fantastic** (SYN.) strange, unusual, odd, wild, unimaginable, incredible, unbelievable, unreal, bizarre, capricious. (ANT.) mundane, ordinary, staid, humdrum.

**fantasy** (SYN.) illusion, dream, whim, hallucination, delusion, caprice, mirage, daydream, fancy. (ANT.) bore.

**far** (SYN.) removed, much, distant, remote, estranged, alienated. (ANT.) close, near.

**fare** (SYN.) prosper, eat, passenger, thrive, toll, progress, succeed.

**farewell** (SYN.) good-by, valediction, departure, leaving. (ANT.) welcome, greeting.

**farm** (SYN.) grow, harvest, cultivate, ranch, hire, charter, plantation.

**fascinate** (SYN.) charm, enchant, bewitch, attract, enthrall.

**fashion** (SYN.) create, shape, style, mode, make, custom, form, manner, method, way, vogue.

**fashionable** (SYN.) chic, smart, stylish, modish, elegant, voguish. (ANT.) dowdy, unfashionable.

**fast** (SYN.) fleet, firm, quick, swift, inflexible, stable, secure, expeditious, rapid, steady, solid, constant, speedy. (ANT.) insecure, sluggish, unstable, loose, slow, unsteady.

**fasten** (SYN.) secure, bind, tie, join, fix, connect, attach, unite. (ANT.) open, loose, free, loosen, release, separate.

**fastidious** (SYN.) choosy, selective, discriminating, picky, meticulous.

**fat** (SYN.) stout, plump, chubby, pudgy, obese, oily, fleshy, greasy, fatty, portly, corpulent, paunchy, wide, thick, rotund. (ANT.) slim, gaunt, emaciated, thin, slender.

**fatal** (SYN.) killing, lethal, doomed, disastrous, deadly, fateful, mortal. (ANT.) nonfatal.

**fate** (SYN.) end, fortune, doom, issue, destiny, necessity, portion, result, lot, chance, luck, outcome, consequence, kismet.

**father** (SYN.) cause, sire, breed, originate, founder, inventor.

**fatherly** (SYN.) protective, paternal, kind, paternalistic.

**fathom** (SYN.) penetrate, understand, interpret, comprehend.

**fatigue** (SYN.) weariness, lassitude, exhaustion, enervation, languor, tiredness. (ANT.) vivacity, rejuvenation, energy, vigor.

**fault** (SYN.) defect, flaw, mistake, imperfection, shortcoming, error, weakness, responsibility, omission, blemish, blame, failure. (ANT.) perfection, completeness.

**faultfinding** (SYN.) carping, censorious, critical, caviling, nitpicking.

**faulty** (SYN.) imperfect, broken, defective, damaged, impaired. (ANT.) flawless, perfect, whole.

**favor** (SYN.) resemble, liking, service, prefer, approval, like, support, patronize, benefit. (ANT.) deplore, disapprove.

**favorite** (SYN.) prized, pet, choice, darling, treasured, preferred.

**favoritism** (SYN.) prejudice, bias, partiality. (ANT.) fairness, impartiality.

**fear** (SYN.) horror, terror, fright, trepidation, alarm, consternation, dismay, cowardice, panic, anxiety, dread, scare, apprehension. (ANT.) fearlessness, boldness, courage, assurance.

**fearless** (SYN.) bold, brave, courageous, gallant, dauntless,

confident. (ANT.) timid, fearful, cowardly.

**feast** (SYN.) dinner, banquet, barbecue.

**feat** (SYN.) performance, act, operation, accomplishment, achievement, doing, transaction, deed. (ANT.) intention, deliberation, cessation.

**feature** (SYN.) trait, quality, characteristic, highlight, attribute.

**fee** (SYN.) payment, pay, remuneration, charge, recompense.

**feeble** (SYN.) faint, puny, exhausted, delicate, weak, enervated, frail, powerless, forceless, sickly, decrepit, ailing. (ANT.) strong, forceful, powerful, vigorous, stout.

**feed** (SYN.) satisfy, nourish, food, fodder, forage.

**feel** (SYN.) sense, experience, perceive.

**feeling** (SYN.) opinion, sensibility, tenderness, affection, impression, belief, sensation, sympathy, thought, passion, sentiment, attitude, emotion. (ANT.) fact, imperturbability, anesthesia, insensibility.

**fellowship** (SYN.) clan, society, brotherhood, fraternity, camaraderie, companionship, comradeship, association. (ANT.) dislike, discord, distrust, enmity, strife, acrimony.

**felonious** (SYN.) murderous, criminal, larcenous.

**feminine** (SYN.) womanly, girlish, ladylike, female, maidenly, womanish. (ANT.) masculine, male, virile.

**ferocious** (SYN.) savage, fierce, wild, blood-thirsty, brutal. (ANT.) playful, gentle, harmless, calm.

**fertile** (SYN.) rich, fruitful, teeming, plenteous, bountiful, prolific, luxuriant, productive, fecund. (ANT.) unproductive, barren, sterile.

**festival** (SYN.) feast, banquet, regalement, celebration.

**festive** (SYN.) joyful, gay, joyous, merry, gala, jovial, jubilant. (ANT.) sad, gloomy, mournful, morose.

**fetching** (SYN.) charming, attractive, pleasing, captivating, winsome.

**feud** (SYN.) dispute, quarrel, strife, argument, conflict, controversy. (ANT.) amity, understanding, harmony, peace.

**fiber** (SYN.) line, strand, thread, string.

**fickle** (SYN.) unstable, capricious, restless, changeable, inconstant, variable. (ANT.) stable, constant, steady, reliable,

dependable.

**fiction** (SYN.) fabrication, romance, falsehood, tale, allegory, narrative, fable, novel, story, invention. (ANT.) verity, reality, fact, truth.

**fictitious** (SYN.) invented, make-believe, imaginary, fabricated, unreal, counterfeit, feigned. (ANT.) real, true, genuine, actual.

**fidelity** (SYN.) fealty, devotion, precision, allegiance, exactness, constancy, accuracy, faithfulness, loyalty. (ANT.) treachery, disloyalty.

**fidget** (SYN.) squirm, twitch, wriggle.

**fiendish** (SYN.) devilish, demonic, diabolical, savage, satanic.

**fierce** (SYN.) furious, wild, savage, violent, ferocious, vehement. (ANT.) calm, meek, mild, gentle, placid.

**fight** (SYN.) contend, scuffle, struggle, battle, wrangle, combat, brawl, quarrel, dispute, war, skirmish, conflict.

**figure** (SYN.) design, pattern, mold, shape, form, frame, reckon, calculate, compute, determine.

**fill** (SYN.) glut, furnish, store, stuff, occupy, gorge, pervade, content, stock, fill up, supply, sate, replenish, satisfy. (ANT.) void, drain, exhaust, deplete, empty.

**filter** (SYN.) screen, strainer, sieve.

**filth** (SYN.) pollution, dirt, sewage, foulness. (ANT.) cleanliness, innocence, purity.

**filthy** (SYN.) foul, polluted, dirty, stained, unwashed, squalid. (ANT.) pure, clean, unspoiled.

**final** (SYN.) ultimate, decisive, concluding, ending, terminal, last, conclusive, eventual, latest. (ANT.) inaugural, rudimentary, beginning, initial, incipient, first, original.

**finally** (SYN.) at last, eventually, ultimately.

**find** (SYN.) observe, detect, discover, locate.

**fine** (SYN.) thin, pure, choice, small, elegant, dainty, splendid, handsome, delicate, nice, powdered, beautiful, minute, exquisite, subtle, pretty, refined. (ANT.) thick, coarse, rough, blunt, large.

**finicky** (SYN.) fussy, meticulous, finical, fastidious, prim.

**finish** (SYN.) consummate, close, get done, terminate, accomplish, conclude, execute, perform, complete, end, achieve, fulfill, do, perfect.

(*ANT.*) *open, begin, start, beginning.*

**fire** (*SYN.*) vigor, glow, combustion, passion, burning, conflagration, ardor, flame, blaze, intensity, fervor. (*ANT.*) *apathy, cold.*

**firm** (*SYN.*) solid, rigid, inflexible, stiff, unchanging, steadfast, dense, hard, unshakable, compact, business, company, corporation, partnership. (*ANT.*) *weak, limp, soft, drooping.*

**first** (*SYN.*) chief, primary, initial, pristine, beginning, foremost, primeval, earliest, prime, primitive, original. (*ANT.*) *subordinate, last, least, hindmost, latest.*

**fishy** (*SYN.*) suspicious, questionable, doubtful. (*ANT.*) *believable, credible.*

**fit** (*SYN.*) adjust, suit, suitable, accommodate, conform, robust, harmonize, belong, seizure, spasm, attack, suited, appropriate, healthy, agree, adapt. (*ANT.*) *misfit, disturb, improper.*

**fitful** (*SYN.*) variable, restless, fickle, capricious, unstable, changeable. (*ANT.*) *trustworthy, stable, constant, steady.*

**fitting** (*SYN.*) apt, due, suitable, proper. (*ANT.*) *improper, unsuitable, inappropriate.*

**fix** (*SYN.*) mend, regulate, affix, set, tie, repair, attach, settle, link, bind, determine, establish, define, rectify, stick, limit, adjust, fasten. (*ANT.*) *damage, change, mistreat, displace, alter, disturb, mutilate.*

**fixation** (*SYN.*) fetish, obsession, infatuation, compulsion.

**flair** (*SYN.*) style, dash, flamboyance, drama, gift, knack, aptitude.

**flamboyant** (*SYN.*) showy, flashy, gaudy, ostentatious.

**flame** (*SYN.*) blaze, fire.

**flash** (*SYN.*) flare, flame, wink, twinkling, instant, gleam.

**flashy** (*SYN.*) tawdry, tasteless, pretentious, garish, flamboyant.

**flat** (*SYN.*) vapid, stale, even, smooth, tasteless, horizontal, dull, level, insipid, uninteresting, lifeless, boring. (*ANT.*) *tasty, racy, hilly, savory, stimulating, interesting, broken, sloping.*

**flattery** (*SYN.*) compliment, praise, applause, blarney, acclaim.

**flaunt** (*SYN.*) exhibit, show off, display, parade. (*ANT.*) *conceal, hide, disguise.*

**flavor** (*SYN.*) tang, taste, savor, essence, quality, character, season, spice.

**flaw** (*SYN.*) spot, imperfection, blemish, fault, deformity, blotch.

**flee** (*SYN.*) fly, abscond, hasten, escape, run away, decamp, evade. (*ANT.*) *remain, appear, stay, arrive.*

**fleece** (*SYN.*) filch, rob, purloin, swindle, defraud, pilfer, cheat.

**fleet** (*SYN.*) rapid, swift, quick, fast. (*ANT.*) *unhurried, sluggish, slow.*

**fleeting** (*SYN.*) brief, swift, passing, temporary. (*ANT.*) *stable, fixed, lasting, permanent.*

**fleshy** (*SYN.*) overweight, chubby, stocky, plump, obese, stout. (*ANT.*) *spare, underweight, skinny.*

**flexible** (*SYN.*) lithe, resilient, pliable, tractable, complaint, elastic, yielding, adaptable, agreeable, supple, pliant, easy, ductile. (*ANT.*) *hard, unbending, firm, brittle, inflexible, rigid, fired.*

**flighty** (*SYN.*) giddy, lightheaded, frivolous, irresponsible. (*ANT.*) *solid, responsible, steady.*

**flimsy** (*SYN.*) wobbly, weak, frail, fragile, unsteady, delicate, thin. (*ANT.*) *durable, stable, firm, strong.*

**fling** (*SYN.*) pitch, throw, toss, fun, celebration, party.

**flippant** (*SYN.*) disrespectful, sassy, insolent, brazen, rude, impertinent. (*ANT.*) *courteous, polite, mannerly.*

**flit** (*SYN.*) flutter, scurry, hasten, dart, skim.

**flock** (*SYN.*) gathering, group, flight, swarm, herd, school.

**flog** (*SYN.*) thrash, lash, switch, strike, paddle.

**flood** (*SYN.*) overflow, deluge, inundate, cascade.

**florid** (*SYN.*) gaudy, fancy, ornate, embellished. (*ANT.*) *spare, simple, plain.*

**flourish** (*SYN.*) succeed, grow, prosper, wave, thrive, bloom. (*ANT.*) *wither, wane, die, decline.*

**flout** (*SYN.*) disdain, scorn, spurn, ignore, taunt, ridicule, mock.

**flow** (*SYN.*) proceed, abound, spout, come, stream, run, originate, emanate, result, pour, squirt, issue, gush, spurt.

**fluctuate** (*SYN.*) vary, oscillate, change, waver, hesitate, vacillate. (*ANT.*) *persist, stick, adhere, resolve.*

**fluent** (*SYN.*) graceful, glib, flowing.

**fluid** (*SYN.*) liquid, running, liquefied.

**flush** (*SYN.*) abundant, flat, even, level.

**fluster** (*SYN.*) rattle, flurry, agitate, upset, perturb, quiver, vibrate.

**fly** (*SYN.*) flee, mount, shoot, decamp, hover, soar, flit, flutter, sail, escape, rush, spring, glide, abscond, dart, float. (*ANT.*) *sink, descend, plummet.*

**foam** (*SYN.*) suds, froth, lather.

**foe** (*SYN.*) opponent, enemy, antagonist, adversary. (*ANT.*) *associate, ally, friend, comrade.*

**fog** (*SYN.*) haze, mist, cloud, daze, confusion, stupor, vapor, smog.

**foible** (*SYN.*) frailty, weakness, failing, shortcoming, kink.

**foist** (*SYN.*) misrepresent, insinuate, falsify.

**fold** (*SYN.*) lap, double, overlap, clasp, pleat, tuck.

**follow** (*SYN.*) trail, observe, succeed, ensue, obey, chase, comply, accompany, copy, result, imitate, heed, adopt. (*ANT.*) *elude, cause, precede, avoid, flee.*

**follower** (*SYN.*) supporter, devotee, henchman, adherent, partisan, votary, attendant, disciple, successor. (*ANT.*) *master, head, chief, dissenter.*

**following** (*SYN.*) public, disciples, supporters, clientele, customers.

**folly** (*SYN.*) silliness, foolishness, indiscretion, absurdity, imprudence, imbecility, stupidity, extravagance. (*ANT.*) *reasonableness, judgment, sense, prudence, wisdom.*

**fond** (*SYN.*) affectionate, loving, attached, tender, devoted. (*ANT.*) *hostile, cool, distant, unfriendly.*

**fondness** (*SYN.*) partiality, liking, affection. (*ANT.*) *hostility, unfriendliness.*

**food** (*SYN.*) viands, edibles, feed, repast, nutriment, sustenance, diet, bread, provisions, meal, rations, victuals, fare. (*ANT.*) *want, hunger, drink, starvation.*

**fool** (*SYN.*) dunce, jester, idiot, simpleton, buffoon, harlequin, dolt, blockhead, numskull, clown, dope, trick, deceive, nincompoop. (*ANT.*) *scholar, genius, sage.*

**foolish** (*SYN.*) senseless, irrational, crazy, silly, brainless, idiotic, simple, nonsensical, stupid, preposterous, asinine. (*ANT.*) *sane, sound, sensible,* rational, judicious, wise, reasonable, prudent.

**footing** (*SYN.*) base, basis, foundation.

**footloose** (*SYN.*) uncommitted, free, detached, independent. (*ANT.*) *engaged, rooted, involved.*

**forbearance** (*SYN.*) moderation, abstinence, abstention, continence. (*ANT.*) *greed, excess, intoxication.*

**forbid** (*SYN.*) disallow, prevent, ban, prohibit, taboo, outlaw. (*ANT.*) *approve, let, allow, permit.*

**forbidding** (*SYN.*) evil, hostile, unfriendly, sinister, scary, repulsive. (*ANT.*) *pleasant, beneficent, friendly.*

**force** (*SYN.*) energy, might, violence, vigor, intensity, dint, power, constraint, coercion, compel, compulsion, oblige, make, coerce, strength. (*ANT.*) *weakness, frailty, persuasion, feebleness, impotence, ineffectiveness.*

**forceful** (*SYN.*) dynamic, vigorous, energetic, potent, drastic, intense. (*ANT.*) *lackadaisical, insipid, weak.*

**foreboding** (*SYN.*) misgiving, suspicion, apprehension, presage, intuition.

**forecast** (*SYN.*) prophesy, predict.

**foregoing** (*SYN.*) above, former, preceding, previous, prior. (*ANT.*) *later, coming, below, follow.*

**foreign** (*SYN.*) alien, strange, exotic, different, unfamiliar. (*ANT.*) *commonplace, ordinary, familiar.*

**foreigner** (*SYN.*) outsider, alien, newcomer, stranger. (*ANT.*) *native.*

**foreman** (*SYN.*) super, boss, overseer, supervisor.

**forerunner** (*SYN.*) harbinger, proclaimer, informant.

**foresee** (*SYN.*) forecast, expect, anticipate, surmise, envisage.

**forest** (*SYN.*) grove, woodland, wood, copse, woods.

**forestall** (*SYN.*) hinder, thwart, prevent, obstruct, repel.

**foretell** (*SYN.*) soothsay, divine, predict.

**forever** (*SYN.*) evermore, always, everlasting, hereafter, endlessly. (*ANT.*) *fleeting, temporarily.*

**forfeit** (*SYN.*) yield, resign, lose, sacrifice.

**forgive** (*SYN.*) exonerate, clear, excuse, pardon. (*ANT.*) *impeach, accuse, blame, censure.*

**forgo** (*SYN.*) relinquish,

release, surrender, waive, abandon. (ANT.) *keep, retain.*

**forlorn** (SYN.) pitiable, desolate, dejected, woeful, wretched. (ANT.) *optimistic, cherished, cheerful.*

**form** (SYN.) frame, compose, fashion, arrange, construct, make up, devise, create, invent, mold, shape, forge, organize, produce, constitute, make. (ANT.) *wreck, dismantle, destroy, misshape.*

**formal** (SYN.) exact, stiff, correct, outward, conformist, conventional, affected, regular, proper, ceremonious, decorous, methodical, precise, solemn, external, perfunctory. (ANT.) *heartfelt, unconstrained, easy, unconventional.*

**former** (SYN.) earlier, previous, erstwhile, prior.

**formidable** (SYN.) alarming, frightful, imposing, terrible, terrifying, dire, fearful, forbidding. (ANT.) *weak, unimpressive, ordinary.*

**forsake** (SYN.) abandon, desert, forgo, quit, discard, neglect.

**forte** (SYN.) gift, capability, talent, specialty, aptitude, bulwark.

**forth** (SYN.) out, onward, forward.

**forthright** (SYN.) honest, direct, candid, outspoken, blunt, sincere, plain, explicit.

**forthwith** (SYN.) instantly, promptly, immediately. (ANT.) *afterward, later, ultimately, slowly.*

**fortify** (SYN.) bolster, strengthen, buttress, barricade, defend.

**fortuitous** (SYN.) successful, benign, lucky, advantageous, propitious, happy, favored, chance. (ANT.) *unlucky, condemned.*

**fortunate** (SYN.) happy, auspicious, fortuitous, successful, favored, advantageous, benign, charmed, lucky, felicitous, blessed, propitious, blissful. (ANT.) *ill-fated, cheerless, unlucky, unfortunate, cursed, condemned.*

**fortune** (SYN.) chance, fate, lot, luck, riches, wealth, kismet, destiny.

**fortuneteller** (SYN.) soothsayer, clairvoyant, forecaster, oracle, medium.

**forward** (SYN.) leading, front, promote, elevate, advance, first, ahead, onward, further, foremost, aggrandize. (ANT.) *withhold, retard, hinder, retreat,*

oppose.

**foul** (SYN.) base, soiled, dirty, mean, unclean, polluted, impure, vile, evil, muddy, wicked, rainy, stormy, despicable, filthy. (ANT.) *pure, neat, wholesome, clean.*

**found** (SYN.) organize, establish.

**foundation** (SYN.) support, root, base, underpinning, groundwork, bottom, establishment, substructure, basis. (ANT.) *top, cover, building.*

**foxy** (SYN.) cunning, sly, artful, crafty, wily, sharp, shrewd, slick.

**fraction** (SYN.) fragment, part, section, morsel, share, piece.

**fracture** (SYN.) crack, break, rupture.

**fragile** (SYN.) delicate, frail, weak, breakable, infirm, brittle, feeble. (ANT.) *tough, hardy, sturdy, strong, stout, durable.*

**fragment** (SYN.) scrap, piece, bit, remnant, part, splinter, segment.

**fragrance** (SYN.) odor, smell, scent, perfume, aroma.

**fragrant** (SYN.) aromatic, scented, perfumed.

**frail** (SYN.) feeble, weak, delicate, breakable, fragile. (ANT.) *sturdy, strong, powerful.*

**frame** (SYN.) support, framework, skeleton, molding, border, mount.

**frank** (SYN.) honest, candid, open, unreserved, direct, sincere, straight-forward. (ANT.) *tricky, dishonest.*

**frantic** (SYN.) frenzied, crazed, raving, panicky. (ANT.) *composed, stoic.*

**fraud** (SYN.) deception, guile, swindle, deceit, artifice, imposture, trick, cheat, imposition, duplicity, chicanery. (ANT.) *sincerity, fairness, integrity.*

**fraudulent** (SYN.) tricky, fake, dishonest, deceitful.

**fray** (SYN.) strife, fight, battle, struggle, tussle, combat, brawl, melee, skirmish. (ANT.) *truce, agreement, peace, concord.*

**freak** (SYN.) curiosity, abnormality, monster, oddity.

**free** (SYN.) munificent, clear, autonomous, immune, open, freed, bountiful, liberated, unfastened, emancipated, unconfined, unobstructed, easy, artless, loose, familiar, bounteous, unrestricted, liberal, independent,

careless, frank, exempt. (ANT.) *stingy, clogged, illiberal, confined, parsimonious.*

**freedom** (SYN.) independence, privilege, familiarity, unrestraint, liberty, exemption, liberation, immunity, license. (ANT.) *servitude, constraint, bondage, slavery, necessity.*

**freely** (SYN.) liberally, generously, unstintingly.

**freight** (SYN.) shipping, cargo, load, shipment.

**frenzy** (SYN.) craze, agitation, excitement.

**frequent** (SYN.) usual, habitual, common, often, customary, general. (ANT.) *unique, rare, solitary, uncommon, exceptional, infrequent, scanty.*

**fresh** (SYN.) recent, new, additional, modern, further, refreshing, natural, brisk, novel, inexperienced, late, current, sweet, pure, cool. (ANT.) *stagnant, decayed, musty, faded.*

**fret** (SYN.) torment, worry, grieve, anguish.

**fretful** (SYN.) testy, irritable, touchy, peevish, short-tempered. (ANT.) *calm.*

**friend** (SYN.) crony, supporter, ally, companion, intimate, associate, comrade, mate, patron, acquaintance, chum, defender. (ANT.) *stranger, adversary.*

**friendly** (SYN.) sociable, kindly, affable, genial, companionable, social, neighborly, amicable. (ANT.) *hostile, antagonistic, reserved.*

**friendship** (SYN.) knowledge, familiarity, fraternity, acquaintance, intimacy, fellowship, comradeship, cognizance. (ANT.) *unfamiliarity, ignorance.*

**fright** (SYN.) alarm, fear, panic, terror.

**frighten** (SYN.) scare, horrify, daunt, affright, appall, terrify, alarm, terrorize, astound, dismay, startle, panic. (ANT.) *soothe, embolden, compose, reassure.*

**frigid** (SYN.) cold, wintry, icy, glacial, arctic, freezing.

**fringe** (SYN.) hem, edge, border, trimming, edging.

**frisky** (SYN.) animated, lively, peppy, vivacious.

**frolic** (SYN.) play, cavort, romp, frisk.

**front** (SYN.) facade, face, start, beginning, border, head. (ANT.) *rear, back.*

**frontier** (SYN.) border, boundary.

**frugal** (SYN.) parsimonious,

saving, stingy, provident, temperate, economical, sparing. (ANT.) *extravagant, wasteful, self-indulgent, intemperate.*

**fruitful** (SYN.) fertile, rich, bountiful, teeming, fecund, productive, luxuriant. (ANT.) *lean, barren, sterile.*

**fruitless** (SYN.) barren, futile, vain, sterile, unproductive. (ANT.) *fertile, productive.*

**frustrate** (SYN.) hinder, defeat, thwart, circumvent, outwit, foil, baffle, disappoint, balk, discourage, prevent. (ANT.) *promote, accomplish, further.*

**fulfill** (SYN.) do, effect, complete, accomplish, realize.

**full** (SYN.) baggy, crammed, entire, satiated, flowing, perfect, gorged, soaked, complete, filled, packed, extensive. (ANT.) *lacking, partial, empty, depleted.*

**full-grown** (SYN.) ripe, adult, mature, developed, grown-up, complete. (ANT.) *green, young, unripe, adolescent.*

**fulsome** (SYN.) disgusting, repulsive, nauseating, repellent, revolting.

**fume** (SYN.) gas, steam, smoke, rage, rave, vapor.

**fun** (SYN.) merriment, pleasure, enjoyment, piety, sport, amusement.

**function** (SYN.) operation, activity, affair, ceremony, gathering, party.

**fundamental** (SYN.) basic, essential, primary, elementary.

**funny** (SYN.) odd, droll, ridiculous, farcical, laughable, comic, curious, amusing. (ANT.) *solemn, sad, sober, melancholy.*

**furious** (SYN.) angry, enraged. (ANT.) *serene, calm.*

**furnish** (SYN.) yield, give, endow, fit, produce, equip, afford, decorate, supply. (ANT.) *divest, denude, strip.*

**furor** (SYN.) commotion, tumult, turmoil.

**furtive** (SYN.) surreptitious, secret, hidden, clandestine. (ANT.) *honest, open.*

**fury** (SYN.) wrath, anger, frenzy, rage, violence, fierceness. (ANT.) *calmness, serenity.*

**fuss** (SYN.) commotion, bother, pester, annoy, irritate.

**futile** (SYN.) pointless, idle, vain, useless, worthless, minor. (ANT.) *weighty, important, worthwhile, serious, valuable.*

**future** (SYN.) approaching, imminent, coming,

impending. (*ANT.*) *former, past.*

**fuzzy** (SYN.) indistinct, blurred. (ANT.) *lucid, clear.*

# G

**gab** (SYN.) jabber, babble, chatter, prattle, gossip.

**gabble** (SYN.) chatter, babble, jabber, blab, prate, gaggle, prattle, gibberish.

**gabby** (SYN.) chatty, talkative, wordy, verbose.

**gad** (SYN.) wander, roam, rove, ramble, meander, cruise.

**gadget** (SYN.) contrivance, device, doodad, jigger, thing, contraption.

**gaffe** (SYN.) blunder, boner, mistake, gaucherie, error, howler.

**gag** (SYN.) witticism, crack, jest, joke.

**gaiety** (SYN.) joyousness, cheerfulness, joyfulness, light-heartedness. (*ANT.*) *melancholy, sadness, depression.*

**gain** (SYN.) acquire, avail, account, good, interest, attain, favor, achieve, get, secure, advantage, earn, profit, procure. (*ANT.*) *trouble, lose, calamity, forfeit, handicap, lose, distress.*

**gainful** (SYN.) lucrative, rewarding, profitable, beneficial, payable, productive. (*ANT.*) *unprofitable, unrewarding.*

**gainsay** (SYN.) refute, contradict, controvert, deny, refuse, impugn, contravene, disavow, differ. (*ANT.*) *aver, affirm, asseverate.*

**gait** (SYN.) stride, walk, tread, step.

**gala** (SYN.) ball, party, carnival, festival.

**gale** (SYN.) burst, surge, outburst.

**gall** (SYN.) nerve, audacity, impudence, annoy, vex, anger, provoke, irritate.

**gallant** (SYN.) bold, brave, courageous, valorous, valiant, noble, polite, fearless, heroic, chivalrous.

**gallantry** (SYN.) valor, daring, courage, prowess, heroism, manliness, dauntlessness, graciousness, attentiveness. (*ANT.*) *poltroonery, timidity, cowardice, cravenness, cloddishness.*

**gallery** (SYN.) passageway, hall, aisle, hallway, passage, corridor.

**galling** (SYN.) vexing, irritating, annoying, distressful, irksome.

**galore** (SYN.) abounding, plentiful, profuse, rich, overflowing.

**gamble** (SYN.) game, wager, bet, hazard, risk, venture, chance.

**gambol** (SYN.) romp, dance, cavort, frolic.

**game** (SYN.) fun, contest, merriment, pastime, match, play, amusement, recreation, diversion, entertainment. (*ANT.*) *labor, hardship, work, business.*

**gamut** (SYN.) extent, scope, sweep, horizon, range.

**gang** (SYN.) group, troop, band, company, horde, crew.

**gangling** (SYN.) rangy, lean, skinny, tall, lanky.

**gangster** (SYN.) crook, hoodlum, gunman, criminal.

**gap** (SYN.) cavity, chasm, pore, gulf, aperture, abyss, interval, space, hole, void, pore, break, opening.

**gape** (SYN.) ogle, stare, gawk.

**garb** (SYN.) clothing, dress, vesture, array, attire, clothes, drapery, apparel, garments, costume, raiment.

**garbage** (SYN.) refuse, waste, trash, rubbish.

**gargantuan** (SYN.) colossal, monumental, giant, huge, large, enormous.

**garments** (SYN.) drapery, dress, garb, apparel, array, attire, clothes, vesture. (*ANT.*) *nakedness, nudity.*

**garnish** (SYN.) decorate, embellish, trim, adorn, enrich, beautify, deck, ornament. (*ANT.*) *expose, strip, debase, uncover, defame.*

**garrulous** (SYN.) chatty, glib, verbose, talkative, communicative, voluble. (*ANT.*) *silent, uncommunicative, laconic, reticent, taciturn.*

**gash** (SYN.) lacerate, slash, pierce, cut, hew, slice.

**gasp** (SYN.) pant, puff, wheeze.

**gather** (SYN.) assemble, collect, garner, harvest, reap, deduce, judge, amass, congregate, muster, cull, glean, accumulate, convene. (*ANT.*) *scatter, disperse, distribute, disband, separate.*

**gathering** (SYN.) meeting, crowd, throng, company, assembly.

**gaudy** (SYN.) showy, flashy, loud, bold, ostentatious.

**gaunt** (SYN.) lank, flimsy, gauzy, narrow, rare, scanty, meager, gossamer, emaciated, scrawny, tenuous, thin, fine, lean, skinny, spare, slim, slight, slender, diluted. (*ANT.*) *wide, fat, thick, broad, bulky.*

**gay** (SYN.) merry, lighthearted, joyful, cheerful, sprightly, jolly, happy, joyous, gleeful, jovial, colorful, bright, glad. (*ANT.*) *glum, mournful, sad, depressed, sorrowful, somber, sullen.*

**gaze** (SYN.) look, stare, view, watch, examine, observe, glance, behold, discern, seem, see, survey, witness, inspect, goggle, appear. (*ANT.*) *hide, overlook, avert, miss.*

**geld** (SYN.) neuter, alter, spay, castrate.

**gem** (SYN.) jewel, semi-precious stone.

**general** (SYN.) ordinary, universal, usual, common, customary, regular, vague, miscellaneous, indefinite, inexact. (*ANT.*) *definite, particular, exceptional, singular, rare, precise, exact, specific.*

**generally** (SYN.) ordinarily, usually, customarily, normally, mainly. (*ANT.*) *seldom, infrequently, rare.*

**generate** (SYN.) produce, bestow, impart, concede, permit, acquiesce, cede, relent, succumb, surrender, pay, supply, grant, bear, afford, submit, waive, allow, breed, accord, accede, abdicate, resign, relinquish, surrender, quit. (*ANT.*) *assert, refuse, smuggle, resist, dissent, oppose, deny, strive.*

**generation** (SYN.) age, date, era, period, seniority, senescence, senility, time, epoch, dotage. (*ANT.*) *infancy, youth, childhood.*

**generosity** (SYN.) magnanimity, benevolence, humanity, kindness, philanthropy, tenderness, altruism, liberality, charity, beneficence. (*ANT.*) *selfishness, malevolence, cruelty, inhumanity, unkindness.*

**generous** (SYN.) giving, liberal, unselfish, magnanimous, bountiful, munificent, charitable, big, noble, beneficent. (*ANT.*) *greedy, stingy, selfish, covetous, mew, miserly.*

**genesis** (SYN.) birth, root, creation, source, origin, beginning.

**genius** (SYN.) intellect, adept, intellectual, sagacity, proficient, creativity, ability, inspiration, faculty, originality, aptitude, brain, gift, prodigy, talent. (*ANT.*) *dullard, stupidity, dolt, shallowness, moron, ineptitude, obtuseness.*

**genre** (SYN.) chaste, order, set, elegance, class, excellence, kind, caste, denomination, grade.

**genteel** (SYN.) cultured, polished, polite, refined, elegant. (*ANT.*) *discourteous, churlish, common.*

**gentle** (SYN.) peaceful, placid, tame, serene, relaxed, docile, benign, soothing, calm, soft, mild, amiable, friendly, kindly, cultivated. (*ANT.*) *nasty, harsh, rough, fierce, mew, violent, savage.*

**genuine** (SYN.) real, true, unaffected, authentic, sincere, bona fide, unadulterated, legitimate, actual, veritable, definite, proven. (*ANT.*) *false, sham, artificial, fake, counterfeit, bogus, pretended, insincere.*

**genus** (SYN.) kind, race, species, type, variety, character, family, breed, sort.

**germ** (SYN.) pest, virus, contamination, disease, pollution, taint, infection, contagion, poison, ailment.

**germinate** (SYN.) vegetate, pullulate, sprout, develop, grow.

**gesture** (SYN.) omen, signal, symbol, emblem, indication, note, token, symptom, movement, sign, motion.

**get** (SYN.) obtain, receive, attain, gain, achieve, acquire, procure, earn, fetch, carry, remove, prepare, take, ready, urge, induce, secure. (*ANT.*) *lose, surrender, forfeit, leave, renounce.*

**ghastly** (SYN.) frightful, horrible, horrifying, frightening, grisly, hideous, dreadful.

**ghost** (SYN.) phantom, spook, apparition, specter, trace, hint, vestige, spirit.

**ghoulish** (SYN.) weird, eerie, horrifying, gruesome, sinister, scary.

**giant** (SYN.) monster, colossus, mammoth, superman, gigantic. (*ANT.*) *small, tiny, dwarf, runt, midget, infinitesimal.*

**gibe** (SYN.) sneer, jeer, mock, scoff, boo, hoot, hiss. (*ANT.*) *approve.*

**giddy** (SYN.) reeling, dizzy, flighty, silly, scatterbrained. (*ANT.*) *serious.*

**gift** (SYN.) endowment, favor, gratuity, bequest, talent, charity, present, largess, donation, grant, aptitude, boon, offering, faculty, genius, benefaction. (*ANT.*) *purchase, loss, ineptitude, deprivation, earnings.*

**gigantic** (SYN.) huge, colossal, immense, large, vast, elephantine, gargantuan, prodigious, mammoth, monumental, enormous. (ANT.) *small, tiny, minute, diminutive, little.*

**giggle** (SYN.) chuckle, jeer, laugh, roar, snicker, titter, cackle, guffaw, mock.

**gild** (SYN.) cover, coat, paint, embellish, sweeten, retouch, camouflage.

**gingerly** (SYN.) gentle, cautiously, carefully, gently. (ANT.) *roughly.*

**gird** (SYN.) wrap, tie, bind, belt, encircle, surround, get set, prepare.

**girl** (SYN.) female, lass, miss, maiden, damsel.

**girth** (SYN.) measure, size, width, dimensions, expanse, proportions.

**gist** (SYN.) connotation, explanation, purpose, significance, acceptation, implication, interpretation, meaning. (ANT.) *redundancy.*

**give** (SYN.) bestow, contribute, grant, impart, provide, donate, confer, deliver, present, furnish, yield, develop, offer, produce, hand over, award, allot, deal out, mete out, bend, sacrifice, supply. (ANT.) *withdraw, take, retain, keep, seize.*

**given** (SYN.) handed over, presented, supposed, stated, disposed, assumed, inclined.

**glacier** (SYN.) frigid, icy, iceberg.

**glad** (SYN.) happy, cheerful, gratified, delighted, joyous, merry, pleased, exulting, charmed, thrilled, satisfied, tickled, gay, bright. (ANT.) *sad, depressed, dejected, melancholy, unhappy, morose, somber, despondent.*

**glade** (SYN.) clearing.

**gladiator** (SYN.) battler, fighter, competitor, combatant, contender, contestant.

**gladness** (SYN.) bliss, contentment, happiness, pleasure, well-being, beatitude, delight, satisfaction, blessedness. (ANT.) *sadness, sorrow, despair, misery, grief.*

**glamorous** (SYN.) spellbinding, fascinating, alluring, charming, bewitching, entrancing, captivating, enchanting, attractive, appealing, enticing, enthralling.

**glamour** (SYN.) charm, allure, attraction, magnetism, fascination.

**glance** (SYN.) eye, gaze, survey, view, examine, inspect, discern, look, see, witness, peek, regard, skim, reflect, glimpse, behold, observe.

**glare** (SYN.) flash, dazzle, stare, glower, glow, shine, glaze, burn, brilliance, flare, blind, scowl.

**glaring** (SYN.) flagrant, obvious, blatant, prominent, dazzling.

**glass** (SYN.) cup, tumbler, goblet, pane, crystal.

**glassy** (SYN.) blank, empty, emotionless, vacant, fixed, expressionless.

**glaze** (SYN.) buff, luster, cover, wax, gloss, coat, polish, shellac.

**gleam** (SYN.) flash, glimmer, glisten, shimmer, sparkle, twinkle, glare, beam, glow, radiate, glimmering, shine, burn, reflection, blaze.

**glean** (SYN.) reap, gather, select, harvest, pick, separate, cull.

**glee** (SYN.) mirth, joy, gladness, enchantment, delight, cheer, bliss, elation, merriment. (ANT.) *depression, misery, dejection.*

**glen** (SYN.) ravine, valley.

**glib** (SYN.) smooth, suave, flat, plain, polished, sleek, urbane. (ANT.) *rough, rugged, blunt, harsh, bluff.*

**glide** (SYN.) sweep, sail, fly, flow, slip, coast, cruise, move easily, skim, slide.

**glimmer** (SYN.) blink, shimmer, flicker, indication, hint, clue, suggestion.

**glimpse** (SYN.) notice, glance, peek, see, impression, look, flash.

**glint** (SYN.) flash, gleam, peek, glance, glimpse, sparkle, glitter.

**glisten** (SYN.) shimmer, shine, glimmer, twinkle, glitter, glister, sparkle.

**glitch** (SYN.) mishap, snag, hitch, malfunction.

**glitter** (SYN.) glisten, glimmer, sparkle, shine, twinkle.

**gloat** (SYN.) triumph, exult, glory, rejoice, revel.

**global** (SYN.) universal, international, worldwide.

**globe** (SYN.) orb, ball, world, earth, map, universe, sphere.

**gloom** (SYN.) bleakness, despondency, misery, sadness, woe, darkness, dejection, obscurity, blackness, shadow, shade, dimness, shadows, melancholy. (ANT.) *joy, mirth, exultation, cheerfulness, light, happiness, brightness, frivolity.*

**gloomy** (SYN.) despondent, dismal, glum, somber, sorrowful, sad, dejected, disconsolate, dim, dark, morose,

dispirited, moody, grave, pensive. (ANT.) *happy, merry, cheerful, high-spirited, bright, sunny, joyous.*

**glorify** (SYN.) enthrone, exalt, honor, revere, adore, dignify, enshrine, consecrate, praise, worship, laud, venerate. (ANT.) *mock, dishonor, debase, abuse, degrade.*

**glorious** (SYN.) exalted, high, noble, splendid, supreme, elevated, lofty, raised, majestic, famous, noted, stately, distinguished, celebrated, renowned, famed, magnificent, grand, proud, impressive, elegant, sublime. (ANT.) *ridiculous, low, base, ignoble, terrible, ordinary.*

**glory** (SYN.) esteem, praise, respect, reverence, admiration, honor, dignity, worship, eminence, homage, deference. (ANT.) *dishonor, disgrace, contempt, reproach, derision.*

**gloss** (SYN.) luster, shine, glow, sheen.

**glossary** (SYN.) dictionary, thesaurus, wordbook, lexicon.

**glossy** (SYN.) smooth, glistening, shiny, sleek, polished. (ANT.) *matte, dull.*

**glow** (SYN.) beam, glisten, radiate, shimmer, sparkle, glare, blaze, scintillate, shine, light, gleam, burn, flare, flame, dazzle, blush, redden, heat, warmth, flicker.

**glower** (SYN.) scowl, stare, frown, glare. (ANT.) *beam, grin, smile.*

**glowing** (SYN.) fiery, intense, passionate, zealous, enthusiastic, ardent, eager, fervent, favorable, impassioned, keen, complimentary, vehement. (ANT.) *cool, indifferent, apathetic, nonchalant.*

**glue** (SYN.) bind, fasten, cement, paste.

**glum** (SYN.) morose, sulky, fretful, crabbed, sullen, dismal, dour, moody. (ANT.) *joyous, merry, amiable, gay, pleasant.*

**glut** (SYN.) gorge, sate, content, furnish, fill, pervade, satiate, stuff, replenish, fill up, satisfy, stock. (ANT.) *empty, exhaust, deplete, void, drain.*

**glutton** (SYN.) pig, hog, greedy eater.

**gluttony** (SYN.) ravenousness, piggishness, devouring, hoggishness, insatiability, voraciousness. (ANT.) *satisfaction, fullness.*

**gnarled** (SYN.) twisted, knotted, rugged, knobby, nodular.

**gnash** (SYN.) gnaw, crunch,

grind.

**gnaw** (SYN.) chew, eat, gnash, grind, erode.

**go** (SYN.) proceed, depart, flee, move, vanish, exit, walk, quit, fade, progress, travel, become, fit, agree, leave, suit, harmonize, pass, travel, function, operate, withdraw. (ANT.) *stay, arrive, enter, stand, come.*

**goad** (SYN.) incite, prod, drive, urge, push, shove, jab, provoke, stimulate.

**goal** (SYN.) craving, destination, desire, longing, objective, finish, end, passion, aim, object, aspiration.

**gobble** (SYN.) devour, eat fast, gorge, gulp, stuff.

**goblet** (SYN.) cup, glass.

**goblin** (SYN.) troll, elf, dwarf, spirit.

**godlike** (SYN.) holy, supernatural, heavenly, celestial, divine, transcendent. (ANT.) *profane, wicked, blasphemous, diabolical, mundane.*

**godly** (SYN.) pious, religious, holy, pure, divine, spiritual, righteous, saintly.

**golden** (SYN.) shining, metallic, bright, fine, superior, nice, excellent, valuable. (ANT.) *dull, inferior.*

**gong** (SYN.) chimes, bells.

**good** (SYN.) honest, sound, valid, cheerful, honorable, worthy, conscientious, moral, genuine, humane, kind, fair, useful, skilful, adequate, friendly, genial, proficient, pleasant, exemplary, admirable, virtuous, reliable, precious, benevolent, excellent, pure, agreeable, gracious, safe, commendable. (ANT.) *bad, imperfect, vicious, undesirable, unfriendly, unkind, evil.*

**good-bye** (SYN.) so long, farewell.

**good-hearted** (SYN.) good, kind, thoughtful, kindhearted, considerate. (ANT.) *evilhearted.*

**good-humored** (SYN.) pleasant, good-natured, cheerful, sunny, amiable. (ANT.) *petulant, cranky.*

**goodness** (SYN.) good, honesty, integrity, virtue, righteousness. (ANT.) *sin, evil, dishonesty, corruption.*

**goods** (SYN.) property, belongings, holdings, possessions, merchandise, wares.

**good will** (SYN.) harmony, willingness, readiness.

**gore** (SYN.) impale, penetrate, puncture, gouge.

**gorge** (SYN.) ravine, devour, stuff, gobble, valley, defile, pass, cram, fill.

**gorgeous** *(SYN.)* grand, ravishing, glorious, stunning, brilliant, divine, splendid, dazzling, beautiful, magnificent. *(ANT.)* homely, ugly, squalid.

**gory** *(SYN.)* bloody.

**gossamer** *(SYN.)* dainty, fine, filmy, delicate, sheer, transparent.

**gossip** *(SYN.)* prate, rumor, prattle, hearsay, meddler, tattler, chatter, talk, chat, blabbermouth.

**gouge** *(SYN.)* scoop, dig, carve, burrow, excavate, chisel, notch.

**gourmet** *(SYN.)* gourmand, gastronome, connoisseur.

**govern** *(SYN.)* manage, oversee, reign, preside over, supervise, direct, command, sway, administer, control, regulate, determine, influence, guide, lead, head, rule. *(ANT.)* assent, submit, acquiesce, obey, yield.

**government** *(SYN.)* control, direction, rule, command, authority.

**governor** *(SYN.)* controller, administrator, director, leader, manager.

**gown** *(SYN.)* garment, robe, frock, dress, costume, attire.

**grab** *(SYN.)* snatch, grip, clutch, seize, grasp, capture, pluck.

**grace** *(SYN.)* charm, beauty, handsomeness, loveliness, dignify, fairness, honor, distinguish, sympathy, attractiveness, elegance, clemency, excuse, pardon, thanks, blessing, prayer, pulchritude. *(ANT.)* eyesore, homeliness, deformity, ugliness.

**graceful** *(SYN.)* elegant, fluid, natural, supple, beautiful, comely, flowing, lithe. *(ANT.)* clumsy, awkward, gawky, ungainly, deformed.

**gracious** *(SYN.)* warm-hearted, pleasing, friendly, engaging, agreeable, kind, amiable, kindly, nice, good, courteous, polite, generous, good-natured. *(ANT.)* surly, hateful, churlish, rude, disagreeable, impolite, thoughtless, discourteous, ill-natured.

**grade** *(SYN.)* kind, rank, elegance, denomination, sort, arrange, category, classify, rate, group, place, mark, incline, slope, excellence, caste, order.

**gradual** *(SYN.)* deliberate, sluggish, dawdling, laggard, slow, leisurely, moderate, easy, delaying. *(ANT.)* quick, swift,

fast, speedy, raid.

**graduate** *(SYN.)* pass, finish, advance.

**graft** *(SYN.)* fraud, theft, cheating, bribery, dishonesty, transplant, corruption.

**grain** *(SYN.)* speck, particle, plant, bit, seed, temper, fiber, character, texture, markings, nature, tendency.

**grand** *(SYN.)* great, elaborate, splendid, royal, stately, noble, considerable, outstanding, distinguished, impressive, prominent, majestic, fine, dignified, large, main, principal. *(ANT.)* unassuming, modest, insignificant, unimportant, humble.

**grandeur** *(SYN.)* resplendence, majesty, distinction, glory.

**grandiose** *(SYN.)* grand, lofty, magnificent, stately, noble, pompous, dignified, imposing, sublime, majestic. *(ANT.)* lowly, ordinary, common, undignified, humble.

**grandstand** *(SYN.)* bleachers, gallery.

**granite** *(SYN.)* stone, rock.

**grant** *(SYN.)* confer, allocate, deal, divide, mete, appropriation, assign, benefaction, distribute, allowance, donate, award, mete out, deal out, consent, bestow, give, measure. *(ANT.)* refuse, withhold, confiscate, keep, retain.

**granular** *(SYN.)* grainy, sandy, crumbly, rough, gritty.

**graph** *(SYN.)* design, plan, stratagem, draw up, chart, sketch, cabal, machination, outline, plot, scheme, diagram.

**graphic** *(SYN.)* vivid, lifelike, significant, meaningful, pictorial, descriptive, representative.

**grapple** *(SYN.)* grip, seize, clutch, clasp, grasp, fight, struggle.

**grasp** *(SYN.)* clutch, grip, seize, apprehend, capture, snare, hold, clasp, comprehend, reach, grab, understand, grapple, possession, control, domination, command, perceive, trap. *(ANT.)* release, lose, throw, liberate.

**grasping** *(SYN.)* possessive, greedy, selfish, acquisitive, mercenary. *(ANT.)* liberal, unselfish, generous.

**grate** *(SYN.)* file, pulverize, grind, scrape, scratch, annoy, irritate.

**grateful** *(SYN.)* beholden, obliged, appreciative, thankful, indebted. *(ANT.)* ungrateful,

unappreciative, grudging.

**gratify** *(SYN.)* charm, gladden, please, satisfy. *(ANT.)* frustrate.

**gratifying** *(SYN.)* contentment, solace, relief, comfort, ease, succor, consolation, enjoyment. *(ANT.)* suffering, torment, affliction, discomfort, torture, misery.

**grating** *(SYN.)* harsh, rugged, severe, stringent, coarse, gruff, jarring, rigorous, strict. *(ANT.)* smooth, melodious, mild, gentle, soft.

**gratis** *(SYN.)* complimentary, free.

**gratitude** *(SYN.)* gratefulness, thankfulness, appreciation. *(ANT.)* ungratefulness.

**gratuity** *(SYN.)* tip, bonus, gift, donation.

**grave** *(SYN.)* sober, grim, earnest, serious, important, momentous, sedate, solemn, somber, imposing, vital, essential, staid, consequential, thoughtful. *(ANT.)* light, flighty, trivial, insignificant, unimportant, trifling, merry, gay, cheery, frivolous.

**gravel** *(SYN.)* stones, pebbles, grain.

**gravitate** *(SYN.)* incline, tend, lean, approach, toward.

**gravity** *(SYN.)* concern, importance, seriousness, pull. *(ANT.)* triviality.

**graze** *(SYN.)* scrape, feed, rub, brush, contact, skim.

**grease** *(SYN.)* fat, oil, lubrication.

**greasy** *(SYN.)* messy, buttery, waxy, fatty.

**great** *(SYN.)* large, numerous, eminent, illustrious, big, gigantic, enormous, immense, vast, weighty, fine, important, countless, prominent, vital, huge, momentous, serious, famed, dignified, excellent, critical, renowned, majestic, august, elevated, noble, grand. *(ANT.)* minute, common, menial, ordinary, diminutive, small, paltry, unknown.

**greed** *(SYN.)* piggishness, lust, desire, greediness, avarice, covetousness. *(ANT.)* unselfishness, selflessness, generosity.

**greedy** *(SYN.)* selfish, devouring, ravenous, avaricious, covetous, rapacious, gluttonous, insatiable, voracious. *(ANT.)* full, generous, munificent, giving, satisfied.

**green** *(SYN.)* inexperienced, modern, novel, recent, further, naive, fresh, natural, raw, unsophisticated, immature,

undeveloped, unripe, additional, brisk, artless. *(ANT.)* hackneyed, musty, decayed, faded, stagnant.

**greenhorn** *(SYN.)* tenderfoot, beginner, apprentice, amateur, novice.

**greenhouse** *(SYN.)* hothouse.

**greet** *(SYN.)* hail, accost, meet, address, talk to, speak to, welcome, approach. *(ANT.)* pass by, avoid.

**gregarious** *(SYN.)* outgoing, civil, affable, communicative, hospitable, sociable. *(ANT.)* inhospitable, antisocial, disagreeable, hermitic.

**grief** *(SYN.)* misery, sadness, tribulation, affliction, heartache, woe, trial, anguish, mourning, distress, lamentation. *(ANT.)* happiness, solace, consolation, comfort, joy.

**grief-stricken** *(SYN.)* heartsick, ravaged, devastated, wretched, forlorn, desolate, wretched. *(ANT.)* joyous, blissful, content.

**grievance** *(SYN.)* injury, wrong, injustice, detriment, complaint, damage, prejudice, evil, objection, protest, accusation, harm. *(ANT.)* improvement, benefit, repair.

**grieve** *(SYN.)* lament, brood over, mourn, weep, wail, sorrow, distress, bemoan, hurt, deplore. *(ANT.)* revel, carouse, celebrate, rejoice, gladden, soothe.

**grieved** *(SYN.)* contrite, remorseful, beggarly, mean, pitiful, shabby, vile, sorrowful, pained, hurt, sorry, contemptible, worthless. *(ANT.)* splendid, delighted, cheerful, impenitent, unrepentant.

**grievous** *(SYN.)* gross, awful, outrageous, shameful, lamentable, regrettable. *(ANT.)* agreeable, comforting, pleasurable.

**grill** *(SYN.)* cook, broil, question, interrogate, barbecue, grating, gridiron, cross-examine.

**grim** *(SYN.)* severe, harsh, strict, merciless, fierce, horrible, inflexible, adamant, ghastly, frightful, unyielding, rigid, stern. *(ANT.)* pleasant, lenient, relaxed, amiable, congenial, smiling.

**grimace** *(SYN.)* expression, sneer, scowl.

**grimy** *(SYN.)* unclean, grubby, soiled.

**grin** *(SYN.)* beam, smile, smirk.

**grind** *(SYN.)* mill, mash, powder, crush, crumble, pulverize, smooth, grate, sharpen, even.

**grip** *(SYN.)* catch, clutch, apprehend, trap, arrest, grasp, hold, bag, suitcase, lay hold of, clench, command, control, possession, domination, comprehension, understanding, seize. *(ANT.) release, liberate, lose, throw.*

**gripe** *(SYN.)* protest, lament, complaint, grumbling.

**grit** *(SYN.)* rub, grind, grate, sand, gravel, pluck, courage, stamina.

**groan** *(SYN.)* sob, wail, howl, moan, whimper, wail, complain.

**groggy** *(SYN.)* dazed, dopey, stupefied, stunned, drugged, unsteady. *(ANT.) alert.*

**groom** *(SYN.)* tend, tidy, preen, curry, spouse, consort.

**groove** *(SYN.)* furrow, channel, track, routine, slot, scratch.

**groovy** *(SYN.)* marvelous, delightful, wonderful.

**grope** *(SYN.)* fumble, feel around.

**gross** *(SYN.)* glaring, coarse, indelicate, obscene, bulky, great, total, whole, brutal, grievous, aggregate, earthy, rude, vulgar, entire, enormous, plain, crass, rough, large. *(ANT.) appealing, delicate, refined, proper, polite, cultivated, slight, comely, trivial, decent.*

**grotesque** *(SYN.)* strange, weird, odd, incredible, fantastic, monstrous, absurd, freakish, bizarre, peculiar, deformed, disfigured, unnatural, queer.

**grotto** *(SYN.)* tunnel, cave, hole, cavern.

**grouch** *(SYN.)* protest, remonstrate, whine, complain, grumble, murmur, mope, mutter, repine. *(ANT.) praise, applaud, rejoice.*

**grouchy** *(SYN.)* cantankerous, grumpy, surly. *(ANT.) cheerful, contented, agreeable, pleasant.*

**ground** *(SYN.)* foundation, presumption, surface, principle, underpinning, premise, base, bottom, fix, basis, soil, land, earth, set, root, support, establish, dirt, presupposition. *(ANT.) implication, superstructure, trimming, derivative.*

**groundless** *(SYN.)* baseless, unfounded, unwarranted, needless.

**grounds** *(SYN.)* garden, lawns, dregs, foundation, leftovers, reason, sediment, cause, basis, premise, motive.

**groundwork** *(SYN.)* support, bottom, base, underpinning, premise, presupposition, principle, basis. *(ANT.) trimming, implication, derivative, superstructure.*

**group** *(SYN.)* crowd, clock, party, troupe, swarm, bunch, brook, assembly, herd, band, mob, brood, class, throng, cluster, flock, lot, collection, pack, horde, gathering, aggregation. *(ANT.) disassemble.*

**grouse** *(SYN.)* mutter, grumble, gripe, scold, growl, complain.

**grovel** *(SYN.)* creep, crawl, cower, cringe, slouch, stoop, scramble.

**groveling** *(SYN.)* dishonorable, lowly, sordid, vile, mean, abject, despicable, ignoble, menial, servile, vulgar, ignominious. *(ANT.) lofty, noble, esteemed, exalted.*

**grow** *(SYN.)* extend, swell, advance, develop, enlarge, germinate, mature, expand, flower, raise, become, cultivate, increase, distend. *(ANT.) wane, shrink, atrophy, decay, diminish, contract.*

**growl** *(SYN.)* complain, snarl, grumble, gnarl, roar, clamor, bellow.

**grown-up** *(SYN.)* full-grown, adult, of age, mature, big, senior. *(ANT.) little, childish, budding, junior, juvenile.*

**growth** *(SYN.)* expansion, development, unfolding, maturing, progress, elaboration, evolution. *(ANT.) degeneration, deterioration, curtailment, abbreviation, compression.*

**grub** *(SYN.)* gouge, dig, scoop out, burrow, tunnel, excavate, plod, toil, drudge.

**grubby** *(SYN.)* unkempt, grimy, slovenly, dirty. *(ANT.) tidy, spruce, neat, clean, well-groomed.*

**grudge** *(SYN.)* malevolence, malice, resentment, bitterness, spite, animosity, enmity, rancor, ill will. *(ANT.) kindness, love, benevolence, affection, good will, friendliness, toleration.*

**grudgingly** *(SYN.)* reluctantly, unwillingly, under protest, involuntarily.

**grueling** *(SYN.)* taxing, exhausting, excruciating, trying, arduous, grinding, crushing. *(ANT.) effortless, easy, light, simple.*

**gruesome** *(SYN.)* hideous, frightful, horrible, loathsome, ghastly, horrifying, grisly.

*(ANT.) agreeable, soothing, delightful, charming.*

**gruff** *(SYN.)* scratchy, crude, incomplete, unpolished, stormy, brusque, rude, rough, uncivil, churlish, violent, harsh, imperfect, craggy, irregular, deep, husky, approximate, tempestuous, blunt. *(ANT.) civil, courteous, polished, calm, even, sleek, smooth, finished, gentle, placid, pleasant, tranquil.*

**grumble** *(SYN.)* protest, mutter, complain.

**grumpy** *(SYN.)* ill-tempered, cranky, grouchy, surly, cross-gained, crabbed, fractious, pettish, disgruntled, moody. *(ANT.) winsome, amiable, pleasant, cheery.*

**guarantee** *(SYN.)* bond, pledge, token, warrant, earnest, surety, bail, commitment, promise, secure, swear, assure, sponsor, certify, warranty, insure, endorse, security.

**guarantor** *(SYN.)* voucher, sponsor, warrantor, signatory, underwriter, surety.

**guaranty** *(SYN.)* warranty, token, deposit, earnest, pledge, gage, collateral, stake.

**guard** *(SYN.)* protect, shield, veil, cloak, conceal, disguise, envelop, preserve, hide, defend, cover, sentry, protector, shroud, curtain. *(ANT.) unveil, expose, ignore, neglect, bare, reveal, disregard, divulge.*

**guarded** *(SYN.)* discreet, cautious, careful. *(ANT.) audacious, reckless, indiscreet, careless.*

**guardian** *(SYN.)* curator, keeper, protector, custodian, patron, champion.

**guess** *(SYN.)* estimate, suppose, think, assume, reason, believe, reckon, speculate, notion, surmise, hypothesis, imagine, consider, opinion, conjecture. *(ANT.) know.*

**guest** *(SYN.)* caller, client, customer, patient, visitor, company. *(ANT.) host.*

**guide** *(SYN.)* manage, supervise, conduct, direct, lead, steer, escort, pilot, show, squire, usher, control, affect, influence, regulate. *(ANT.) follower, follow.*

**guild** *(SYN.)* association, union, society.

**guile** *(SYN.)* deceitfulness, fraud, wiliness, trick, deceit, chicanery, cunning, deception, craftiness, sham, sneakiness, cheat. *(ANT.) sincerity, openness, honesty, truthfulness, candor, frankness.*

**guilt** *(SYN.)* sin, blame, fault, offense.

**guilty** *(SYN.)* culpable, to blame, responsible, at fault, criminal, blameworthy. *(ANT.) blameless, innocent, guileless.*

**guise** *(SYN.)* aspect, pretense, mien, look, air, advent, apparition, appearance.

**gulch** *(SYN.)* gorge, valley, gully, ravine.

**gullible** *(SYN.)* trustful, naive, innocent, deceivable, unsuspicious, believing, *(ANT.) skeptical, sophisticated.*

**gully** *(SYN.)* ditch, gorge, ravine, valley, gulch, gulf.

**gulp** *(SYN.)* devour, swallow, gasp, repress, choke.

**gun** *(SYN.)* fire, shoot, weapon, discharge, pistol, firearm, revolver.

**gust** *(SYN.)* blast, wind, outbreak, outburst, eruption.

**gutter** *(SYN.)* ditch, groove, drain, channel, trench, sewer, trough.

**gymnasium** *(SYN.)* playground, arena, court, athletic field.

**gymnastics** *(SYN.)* drill, exercise, acrobatics, calisthenics.

**gyp** *(SYN.)* swindle, cheat, defraud.

**gypsy** *(SYN.)* nomad.

**gyrate** *(SYN.)* spin, whirl, rotate, revolve.

# H

**habit** *(SYN.)* usage, routine, compulsion, use, wont, custom, disposition, practice, addiction, fashion.

**habitation** *(SYN.)* abode, domicile, lodgings, dwelling, home.

**habitual** *(SYN.)* general, usual, common, typical, frequent, persistent, customary, routine, regular, often. *(ANT.) solitary, unique, exceptional, occasional, unusual, scanty, rare.*

**habituated** *(SYN.)* used, accustomed, adapted, acclimated, comfortable, familiarized, addicted, settled.

**hack** *(SYN.)* cleave, chop, slash, hew, slice, pick, sever, mangle.

**hag** *(SYN.)* beldam, crone, vixen, granny, ogress, harridan, visage.

**haggard** *(SYN.)* drawn, careworn, debilitated, spent, gaunt, worn. *(ANT.) bright, fresh, animated.*

**haggle** *(SYN.)* dicker, bargain.

**hail** (SYN.) welcome, approach, accost, speak to, address, greet. (ANT.) pass by, avoid.

**hair-do** (SYN.) hairstyle, coiffure, haircut.

**hairdresser** (SYN.) beautician, barber.

**hairless** (SYN.) shorn, glabrous, bald, depilated. (ANT.) hirsute, hairy, unshaven.

**hairy** (SYN.) bearded, shaggy, hirsute, bewhiskered.

**hale** (SYN.) robust, well, wholesome, hearty, healthy, sound, strong, vigorous, salubrious. (ANT.) noxious, frail, diseased, delicate, infirm, injurious.

**half-baked** (SYN.) crude, premature, makeshift, illogical, shallow.

**half-hearted** (SYN.) uncaring, indifferent, unenthusiastic, cool. (ANT.) eager, enthusiastic, earnest.

**half-wit** (SYN.) dope, simpleton, nitwit, dunce, idiot, fool.

**hall** (SYN.) corridor, lobby, passage, hallway, vestibule, foyer.

**hallow** (SYN.) glorify, exalt, dignify, aggrandize, consecrate, elevate, ennoble, raise, erect. (ANT.) dishonor, humiliate, debase, degrade.

**hallowed** (SYN.) holy, sacred, sacrosanct, blessed, divine.

**hallucination** (SYN.) fantasy, mirage, dream, vision, phantasm, appearance, aberration, illusion.

**halt** (SYN.) impede, obstruct, terminate, stop, hinder, desist, check, arrest, abstain, discontinue, hold, end, cork, interrupt, bar, cease. (ANT.) start, begin, proceed, speed, beginning, promote.

**halting** (SYN.) imperfect, awkward, stuttering, faltering, hobbling, doubtful, limping, wavering. (ANT.) decisive, confident, smooth, graceful, facile.

**hammer** (SYN.) beat, bang, whack, pound, batter, drive, tap, cudgel.

**hamper** (SYN.) prevent, impede, thwart, restrain, hinder, obstruct. (ANT.) help, assist, expedite, encourage, facilitate.

**hamstrung** (SYN.) disabled, helpless, paralyzed.

**hand** (SYN.) assistant, helper, support, aid, farmhand, laborer.

**handicap** (SYN.) retribution, penalty, disadvantage, forfeiture, hindrance, chastisement.

(ANT.) reward, pardon, compensation, remuneration.

**handily** (SYN.) readily, skillfully, easily, dexterously, smoothly, adroitly, deftly.

**handkerchief** (SYN.) bandanna, kerchief.

**handle** (SYN.) hold, touch, finger, clutch, grip, manipulate, feel, grasp, control, oversee, direct, steer, supervise, run, regulate.

**hand out** (SYN.) disburse, distribute, deal, mete, circulate.

**hand over** (SYN.) release, surrender, deliver, yield, present, fork over.

**handsome** (SYN.) lovely, pretty, fair, comely, beautiful, charming, elegant, good-looking, large, generous, liberal, beauteous, fine. (ANT.) repulsive, ugly, unattractive, stingy, small, mean, petty, unsightly, meager, homely, foul, hideous.

**handy** (SYN.) suitable, adapted, appropriate, favorable, fitting, near, ready, close, nearby, clever, helpful, useful, timely, accessible. (ANT.) inopportune, troublesome, awkward, inconvenient.

**hang** (SYN.) drape, hover, dangle, suspend, kill, sag, execute, lynch.

**hang in** (SYN.) continue, endure, remain, persevere, resist, persist.

**hang-up** (SYN.) inhibition, difficulty, snag, hindrance, block.

**hanker** (SYN.) wish, yearn, long, desire, pine, thirst, covet.

**haphazard** (SYN.) aimless, random, purposeless, casual, indiscriminate, accidental. (ANT.) determined, planned, designed, deliberate.

**hapless** (SYN.) ill-fated, unfortunate, jinxed, luckless, wretched.

**happen** (SYN.) occur, take place, bechance, betide, transpire, come to pass, chance, befall.

**happening** (SYN.) episode, event, scene, incident, affair, experience, phenomenon, transaction.

**happiness** (SYN.) pleasure, gladness, delight, beatitude, bliss, contentment, satisfaction, joy, joyousness, blessedness, joyfulness, felicity, elation. (ANT.) sadness, sorrow, despair, misery, grief.

**happy** (SYN.) gay, joyous, cheerful, fortunate, glad, merry, contented, satisfied,

lucky, blessed, pleased, opportune, delighted. (ANT.) gloomy, morose, sad, sorrowful, miserable, inconvenient, unlucky, depressed, blue.

**happy-go-lucky** (SYN.) easygoing, carefree, unconcerned. (ANT.) prudent, responsible, concerned.

**harangue** (SYN.) oration, diatribe, lecture, tirade, exhortation.

**harass** (SYN.) badger, irritate, molest, pester, taunt, torment, provoke, tantalize, worry, aggravate, annoy, nag, plague, vex. (ANT.) please, soothe, comfort, delight, gratify.

**harbinger** (SYN.) sign, messenger, proclaim, forerunner, herald.

**harbor** (SYN.) haven, port, anchorage, cherish, entertain, protect, shelter.

**hard** (SYN.) difficult, burdensome, arduous, rigid, puzzling, cruel, strict, unfeeling, severe, stern, impenetrable, compact, tough, solid, onerous, rigorous, firm, intricate, harsh, perplexing. (ANT.) fluid, effortless, gentle, tender, easy, simple, plastic, soft, lenient, flabby, elastic.

**hard-boiled** (SYN.) unsympathetic, tough, harsh, unsentimental.

**harden** (SYN.) petrify, solidify. (ANT.) loose, soften.

**hardheaded** (SYN.) stubborn, obstinate, unyielding, headstrong.

**hard-hearted** (SYN.) merciless, hard, unmerciful, callous, pitiless, ruthless.

**hardly** (SYN.) barely, scarcely.

**hard-nosed** (SYN.) shrewd, tough, practical.

**hardship** (SYN.) ordeal, test, effort, affliction, misfortune, trouble, experiment, proof, essay, misery, examination, difficulty, tribulation.

**hardy** (SYN.) sturdy, strong, tough, vigorous. (ANT.) frail, decrepit, feeble, weak, fragile.

**harm** (SYN.) hurt, mischief, misfortune, mishap, damage, wickedness, cripple, injury, evil, detriment, ill, infliction, wrong. (ANT.) favor, kindness, benefit, boon.

**harmful** (SYN.) damaging, injurious, mischievous, detrimental, hurtful, deleterious. (ANT.) helpful, salutary, profitable, advantageous, beneficial.

**harmless** (SYN.) protected, secure, snag, dependable, certain, painless, innocent, trustworthy. (ANT.) perilous, hazardous, insecure,

dangerous, unsafe.

**harmonious** (SYN.) tuneful, melodious, congenial, amicable. (ANT.) dissonant, discordant, disagreeable.

**harmony** (SYN.) unison, bargain, contract, stipulation, pact, agreement, accordance, concord, accord, understanding, unity, coincidence. (ANT.) discord, dissension, difference, variance, disagreement.

**harness** (SYN.) control, yoke.

**harry** (SYN.) vex, pester, harass, bother, plague.

**harsh** (SYN.) jarring, gruff, rugged, severe, stringent, blunt, grating, unpleasant, tough, stern, strict, unkind, rigorous, cruel, coarse. (ANT.) smooth, soft, gentle, melodious, soothing, easy, mild.

**harvest** (SYN.) reap, gather, produce, yield, crop, gain, acquire, fruit, result, reaping, product, proceeds, glean, garner. (ANT.) plant, squander, lose, sow.

**haste** (SYN.) speed, hurry, rush, rapidity, flurry, scramble. (ANT.) sloth, sluggishness.

**hasten** (SYN.) hurry, sprint, quicken, rush, precipitate, accelerate, scurry, run, scamper, dispatch, press, urge, dash, expedite, speed. (ANT.) retard, tarry, detain, linger, dawdle, delay, hinder.

**hasty** (SYN.) quick, swift, irascible, lively, nimble, brisk, active, speedy, impatient, testy, sharp, fast, rapid. (ANT.) slow, dull, sluggish.

**hat** (SYN.) helmet, bonnet, cap.

**hatch** (SYN.) breed, incubate, brood.

**hate** (SYN.) loathe, detest, despise, disfavor, hatred, abhorrence, abominate, abhor, dislike. (ANT.) love, cherish, approve, admire, like.

**hateful** (SYN.) loathsome, detestable, offensive. (ANT.) likable, loving, admirable.

**hatred** (SYN.) detestation, dislike, malevolence, enmity, rancor, ill will, loathing, hate, hostility, abhorrence, aversion, animosity. (ANT.) friendship, love, affection, attraction.

**haughty** (SYN.) proud, stately, vainglorious, arrogant, disdainful, overbearing, supercilious, vain. (ANT.) meek, ashamed, lowly, humble.

**haul** (SYN.) draw, pull, drag, tow.

**have** (SYN.) own, possess, seize, hold, control, occupy,

acquire, undergo, maintain, experience, receive, gain, affect, include, contain, get, take, obtain. (*ANT.*) *surrender, abandon, renounce, lose.*

**havoc** (*SYN.*) devastation, ruin, destruction.

**hazard** (*SYN.*) peril, chance, dare, risk, offer, conjecture, jeopardy, danger. (*ANT.*) *safety, defense, protection, immunity.*

**hazardous** (*SYN.*) perilous, precarious, threatening, unsafe, dangerous, critical, menacing, risky. (*ANT.*) *protected, secure, safe.*

**hazy** (*SYN.*) uncertain, unclear, ambiguous, dim, obscure, undetermined, vague, unsettled, indefinite. (*ANT.*) *specific, clear, lucid, precise, explicit.*

**head** (*SYN.*) leader, summit, top, culmination, director, chief, master, commander, supervisor, start, source, crest, beginning, crisis. (*ANT.*) *foot, base, bottom, follower, subordinate, underling.*

**headstrong** (*SYN.*) obstinate, stubborn, willful. (*ANT.*) *easygoing, amenable.*

**headway** (*SYN.*) movement, progress.

**heady** (*SYN.*) thrilling, intoxicating, exciting, electrifying.

**heal** (*SYN.*) restore, cure.

**healthy** (*SYN.*) wholesome, hale, robust, sound, well, vigorous, strong, hearty, healthful, hygienic, salubrious, salutary. (*ANT.*) *noxious, diseased, unhealthy, delicate, frail, infirm, injurious.*

**heap** (*SYN.*) collection, mound, increase, store, stack, pile, gather, accumulate, amass, accrue, accumulation, collect. (*ANT.*) *dissipate, scatter, waste, disperse.*

**hear** (*SYN.*) heed, listen, detect, hearken, perceive, regard.

**heart** (*SYN.*) middle, center, sympathy, nucleus, midpoint, sentiment, core, feeling, midst. (*ANT.*) *outskirts, periphery, border, rim, boundary.*

**heartache** (*SYN.*) anguish, mourning, sadness, sorrow, affliction, distress, grief, lamentation, tribulation. (*ANT.*) *happiness, joy, solace, comfort, consolation.*

**heartbroken** (*SYN.*) distressed, forlorn, mean, paltry, worthless, contemptible, wretched, crestfallen, disconsolate, downhearted, comfortless, brokenhearted, low.

(*ANT.*) *noble, fortunate, contented, significant.*

**hearten** (*SYN.*) encourage, favor, impel, urge, promote, sanction, animate, cheer, exhilarate. (*ANT.*) *deter, dissuade, deject, discourage, dispirit.*

**heartrending** (*SYN.*) heartbreaking, depressing, agonizing.

**hearty** (*SYN.*) warm, earnest, ardent, cordial, sincere, gracious, sociable. (*ANT.*) *taciturn, aloof, cool, reserved.*

**heat** (*SYN.*) hotness, warmth, temperature, passion, ardor, zeal, inflame, cook, excitement, warm. (*ANT.*) *cool, chill, coolness, freeze, coldness, chilliness, iciness, cold.*

**heated** (*SYN.*) vehement, fiery, intense, passionate.

**heave** (*SYN.*) boost, hoist, raise.

**heaven** (*SYN.*) empyrean, paradise.

**heavenly** (*SYN.*) superhuman, godlike, blissful, saintly, holy, divine, celestial, angelic, blessed. (*ANT.*) *wicked, mundane, profane, blasphemous, diabolical.*

**heavy** (*SYN.*) weighty, massive, gloomy, serious, ponderous, cumbersome, trying, burdensome, harsh, grave, intense, dull, grievous, concentrated, severe, oppressive, sluggish. (*ANT.*) *brisk, light, animated.*

**heckle** (*SYN.*) torment, harass, tease, hector, harry.

**heed** (*SYN.*) care, alertness, circumspection, mindfulness, consider, watchfulness, reflection, study, attention, notice, regard, obey, ponder, respect, meditate, mind, observe, deliberate, examine, contemplate, weigh, esteem, application. (*ANT.*) *negligence, oversight, overlook, neglect, ignore, disregard, indifference, omission.*

**heedless** (*SYN.*) sightless, headlong, rash, unmindful, deaf, unseeing, oblivious, ignorant, inattentive, disregardful, blind. (*ANT.*) *perceiving, sensible, aware, calculated, discerning.*

**height** (*SYN.*) zenith, peak, summit, tallness, mountain, acme, apex, elevation, altitude, prominence, maximum, pinnacle, culmination. (*ANT.*) *base, depth.*

**heighten** (*SYN.*) increase, magnify, annoy, chafe, intensify, amplify, aggravate, provoke, irritate, concentrate,

nettle. (*ANT.*) *soothe, mitigate, palliate, soften, appease.*

**heinous** (*SYN.*) abominable, grievous, atrocious.

**hello** (*SYN.*) greeting, good evening, good afternoon, good morning. (*ANT.*) *farewell, good-bye, so long.*

**help** (*SYN.*) assist, support, promote, relieve, abet, succor, back, uphold, further, remedy, encourage, aid, facilitate, mitigate. (*ANT.*) *afflict, thwart, resist, hinder, impede.*

**helper** (*SYN.*) aide, assistant, supporter.

**helpful** (*SYN.*) beneficial, serviceable, wholesome, useful, profitable, advantageous, good, salutary. (*ANT.*) *harmful, injurious, useless, worthless, destructive, deleterious, detrimental.*

**helpfulness** (*SYN.*) assistance, cooperation, usefulness, serviceability, kindness, neighborliness, willingness, collaboration, supportiveness, readiness. (*ANT.*) *antagonism, hostility, opposition.*

**helpless** (*SYN.*) weak, feeble, dependent, disabled, inept, unresourceful, incapable, incompetent. (*ANT.*) *resourceful, competent, enterprising.*

**helplessness** (*SYN.*) impotence, feebleness, weakness, incapacity, ineptitude, invalidism, shiftless, awkwardness. (*ANT.*) *power, strength, might, potency.*

**helter-skelter** (*SYN.*) haphazardly, chaotically, irregularly.

**hem** (*SYN.*) bottom, border, edge, rim, margin, pale, verge, flounce, boundary, fringe, brim, fence, hedge, frame.

**hem in** (*SYN.*) enclose, shut in, confine, restrict, limit.

**hence** (*SYN.*) consequently, thence, therefore, so, accordingly.

**herald** (*SYN.*) harbinger, crier, envoy, forerunner, precursor, augury, forecast.

**herculean** (*SYN.*) demanding, heroic, titanic, mighty, prodigious, laborious, arduous, overwhelming, backbreaking.

**herd** (*SYN.*) group, pack, drove, crowd, flock, gather.

**heretic** (*SYN.*) nonconformist, sectarian, unbeliever, sectary, schismatic, apostate, dissenter.

**heritage** (*SYN.*) birthright, legacy, patrimony, inheritance.

**hermit** (*SYN.*) recluse, anchorite, eremite.

**hero** (*SYN.*) paladin, champion, idol.

**heroic** (*SYN.*) bold, courageous, fearless, gallant, valiant, valorous, brave, chivalrous, adventurous, dauntless, intrepid, magnanimous. (*ANT.*) *fearful, weak, cringing, timid, cowardly.*

**heroism** (*SYN.*) valor, bravery, gallant, dauntless, bold, courageous, fearless.

**hesitant** (*SYN.*) reluctant, unwilling, disinclined, loath, slow, averse. (*ANT.*) *willing, inclined, eager, ready, disposed.*

**hesitate** (*SYN.*) falter, waver, pause, doubt, demur, delay, vacillate, wait, stammer, stutter, scruple. (*ANT.*) *proceed, resolve, continue, decide, persevere.*

**hesitation** (*SYN.*) distrust, scruple, suspense, uncertainty, unbelief, doubt, incredulity, skepticism. (*ANT.*) *determination, belief, certainty, faith, conviction.*

**hidden** (*SYN.*) undeveloped, unseen, dormant, concealed, quiescent, latent, potential, inactive. (*ANT.*) *visible, explicit, conspicuous, evident.*

**hide** (*SYN.*) disguise, mask, suppress, withhold, veil, cloak, conceal, screen, camouflage, shroud, pelt, skin, leather, cover. (*ANT.*) *reveal, show, expose, disclose, uncover, divulge.*

**hideous** (*SYN.*) frightful, ugly, shocking, frightening, horrible, terrible, horrifying, terrifying, grisly, gross. (*ANT.*) *lovely, beautiful, beauteous.*

**high** (*SYN.*) tall, eminent, exalted, elevated, high-pitched, sharp, lofty, proud, shrill, raised, strident, prominent, important, powerful, expensive, dear, high-priced, costly, grave, serious, extreme, towering. (*ANT.*) *low, mean, tiny, short, base, lowly, deep, insignificant, unimportant, inexpensive, reasonable, trivial, petty, small.*

**highly** (*SYN.*) extremely, very, extraordinarily, exceedingly.

**high-minded** (*SYN.*) lofty, noble, honorable. (*ANT.*) *dishonorable, base.*

**high-priced** (*SYN.*) dear, expensive, costly. (*ANT.*) *economical, cheap.*

**high-strung** (*SYN.*) nervous, tense, wrought-up, intense. (*ANT.*) *calm.*

**highway** (*SYN.*) parkway, speedway, turnpike, superhighway, freeway.

**hilarious** (*SYN.*) funny,

side-splitting, hysterical. (ANT.) depressing, sad.

**hinder** (SYN.) hamper, impede, block, retard, stop, resist, thwart, obstruct, check, prevent, interrupt, delay, slow, restrain. (ANT.) promote, further, assist, expedite, advance, facilitate.

**hindrance** (SYN.) interruption, delay, interference, obstruction, obstacle, barrier.

**hinge** (SYN.) rely, depend, pivot.

**hint** (SYN.) reminder, allusion, suggestion, clue, tip, taste, whisper, implication, intimate, suspicion, mention, insinuation. (ANT.) declaration, affirmation, statement.

**hire** (SYN.) employ, occupy, devote, apply, enlist, lease, rent, charter, rental, busy, engage, utilize, retain, let, avail. (ANT.) reject, banish, discard, fire, dismiss, discharge.

**history** (SYN.) narration, relation, computation, record, account, chronicle, detail, description, narrative, annal, tale, recital. (ANT.) confusion, misrepresentation, distortion, caricature.

**hit** (SYN.) knock, pound, strike, hurt, pummel, beat, come upon, find, discover, blow, smite.

**hitch** (SYN.) tether, fasten, harness, interruption, hindrance, interference.

**hoard** (SYN.) amass, increase, accumulate, gather, save, secret, cache, store, accrue, heap. (ANT.) dissipate, scatter, waste, diminish, squander, spend, disperse.

**hoarse** (SYN.) deep, rough, husky, raucous, grating, harsh. (ANT.) clear.

**hoax** (SYN.) ploy, ruse, wile, device, cheat, deception, antic, imposture, stratagem, stunt, guile, fraud. (ANT.) openness, sincerity, candor, exposure, honesty.

**hobbling** (SYN.) deformed, crippled, lame, unconvincing, unsatisfactory, defective, feeble, disabled, maimed, weak. (ANT.) robust, vigorous, agile, sound, athletic.

**hobby** (SYN.) diversion, pastime, avocation. (ANT.) vocation, profession.

**hobo** (SYN.) derelict, vagrant, vagabond, tramp.

**hoist** (SYN.) heave, lift, elevate, raise, crane, elevator, derrick.

**hold** (SYN.) grasp, occupy, possess, curb, contain, stow, carry, adhere, have, clutch, keep, maintain, clasp, grip, retain, detain, accommodate, restrain, observe, conduct, check, support. (ANT.) vacate, relinquish, surrender, abandon.

**holdup** (SYN.) heist, robbery, stickup, delay, interruption, slowdown.

**hole** (SYN.) cavity, void, pore, opening, abyss, chasm, gulf, aperture, tear, pit, burrow, lair, den, gap.

**hollow** (SYN.) unfilled, vacant, vain, meaningless, flimsy, false, hole, cavity, depression, hypocritical, depressed, empty, pit, insincere. (ANT.) sound, solid, genuine, sincere, full.

**holocaust** (SYN.) fire, burning, extermination, butchery, disaster, massacre.

**holy** (SYN.) devout, divine, blessed, consecrated, sacred, spiritual, pious, sainted, religious, saintly, hallowed. (ANT.) worldly, sacrilegious, unconsecrated, evil, profane, secular.

**homage** (SYN.) reverence, honor, respect.

**home** (SYN.) dwelling, abode, residence, seat, quarters, hearth, domicile, family, house, habitat.

**homely** (SYN.) uncommonly, disagreeable, ill-natured, ugly, vicious, plain, hideous, unattractive, deformed, surly, repellent, spiteful. (ANT.) fair, handsome, pretty, attractive, comely, beautiful.

**homesick** (SYN.) lonely, nostalgic.

**honest** (SYN.) sincere, trustworthy, truthful, fair, ingenuous, candid, conscientious, moral, upright, open, frank, forthright, honorable, just, straightforward. (ANT.) fraudulent, tricky, deceitful, dishonest, lying.

**honesty** (SYN.) frankness, openness, fairness, sincerity, trustworthiness, justice, candor, honor, integrity, responsibility, uprightness. (ANT.) deceit, dishonesty, trickery, fraud, cheating.

**honor** (SYN.) esteem, praise, worship, admiration, homage, glory, respect, admire, heed, dignity, revere, value, deference, venerate, reverence, consider, distinction, character, principle, uprightness, honesty, adoration. (ANT.) scorn, dishonor, despise, neglect, abuse, shame, reproach, disdain, contempt, derision, disgrace.

**honorable** (SYN.) fair, noble, creditable, proper, reputable, honest, admirable, true, trusty, eminent, respectable, esteemed, just, famed, illustrious, noble, virtuous, upright. (ANT.) infamous, disgraceful, shameful, dishonorable, ignominious.

**honorary** (SYN.) gratuitous, complimentary.

**hoodlum** (SYN.) crook, gangster, criminal, hooligan, mobster.

**hop** (SYN.) jump, leap.

**hope** (SYN.) expectation, faith, optimism, anticipation, expectancy, confidence, desire, trust. (ANT.) pessimism, despair, despondency.

**hopeful** (SYN.) optimistic, confident. (ANT.) despairing, hopeless.

**hopeless** (SYN.) desperate, despairing, forlorn, fatal, incurable, disastrous. (ANT.) promising, hopeful.

**hopelessness** (SYN.) gloom, discouragement, depression, pessimism, despondency. (ANT.) hope, optimism, confidence, elation.

**horde** (SYN.) host, masses, press, rabble, swarm, throng, bevy, crush, mob, multitude, crowd, populace.

**horizontal** (SYN.) even, level, plane, flat, straight, sideways. (ANT.) upright, vertical.

**horrendous** (SYN.) awful, horrifying, terrible, dreadful, horrid, ghastly. (ANT.) splendid, wonderful.

**horrible** (SYN.) awful, dire, ghastly, horrid, terrible, repulsive, frightful, appalling, horrifying, dreadful, ghastly, fearful. (ANT.) enjoyable, enchanting, beautiful, lovely, fascinating.

**horrid** (SYN.) repulsive, terrible, appalling, dire, awful, frightful, fearful, shocking, horrible, horrifying, ghastly, dreadful, revolting, hideous. (ANT.) fascinating, enchanting, enjoyable, lovely, beautiful.

**horror** (SYN.) dread, awe, hatred, loathing, foreboding, alarm, apprehension, aversion, terror. (ANT.) courage, boldness, assurance, confidence.

**horseplay** (SYN.) tomfoolery, clowning, shenanigans.

**hospital** (SYN.) infirmary, clinic, sanatorium, rest home, sanitarium.

**hospitality** (SYN.) warmth, liberality, generosity, graciousness, welcome.

**hostile** (SYN.) unfriendly, opposed, antagonistic, inimical, adverse, warlike. (ANT.) friendly, favorable, amicable, cordial.

**hostility** (SYN.) grudge, hatred, rancor, spite, bitterness, enmity, malevolence. (ANT.) love, friendliness, goodwill.

**hot** (SYN.) scorching, fervent, hot-blooded, passionate, peppery, ardent, burning, fiery, impetuous, scalding, heated, sizzling, blazing, frying, roasting, warm, intense, torrid, pungent. (ANT.) indifferent, apathetic, impassive, passionless, bland, frigid, cold, freezing, cool, phlegmatic.

**hot air** (SYN.) bombast, blather, jabber, gabble.

**hotbed** (SYN.) sink, nest, well, den, nursery, cradle, source, incubator, seedbed.

**hot-blooded** (SYN.) passionate, ardent, excitable, wild, fervent, fiery, impetuous, rash, brash, intense, impulsive. (ANT.) stolid, impassive, cold, staid.

**hotel** (SYN.) hostel, motel, inn, hostelry.

**hotheaded** (SYN.) rash, touchy, short-tempered, reckless, unruly. (ANT.) levelheaded, cool-headed, calm.

**hound** (SYN.) harry, pursue, pester, harass.

**hourly** (SYN.) frequently, steadily, constantly, unfailingly, periodically, perpetually, ceaselessly, continually, incessantly. (ANT.) occasionally, seldom.

**house** (SYN.) building, residence, abode, dwelling.

**housebreaker** (SYN.) robber, thief, prowler, cracksman, burglar.

**household** (SYN.) manage, family, home.

**householder** (SYN.) homeowner, occupant.

**housing** (SYN.) lodgings, shelter, dwelling, lodgment, case, casing, quarters, domicile, enclosure, console, bracket.

**hovel** (SYN.) cabin, hut, sty, shack, hole, shed.

**hover** (SYN.) hang, drift, poise, stand by, linger, impend, waver, hand around.

**however** (SYN.) notwithstanding, still, nevertheless, but, yet.

**howl** (SYN.) bellow, yowl, wail, yell, cry.

**hub** (SYN.) pivot, center, core, heart, axis, basis, focus, nucleus.

**hubbub** (SYN.) uproar, tumult, commotion, clamor, bustle, turmoil, racket, confusion. *(ANT.) peacefulness, stillness, silence, quiet.*

**huckster** *(SYN.)* peddler, adman, hawker, salesman, pitchman.

**huddle** *(SYN.)* mass, herd, bunch, crowd, cram, gather, shove, pack, flock, ball, conglomeration, knot, clump, medley, scrum.

**hue** *(SYN.)* pigment, tint, shade, dye, complexion, paint, stain, color, tone, tincture. *(ANT.) transparency, achromatism, paleness.*

**huffy** *(SYN.)* sensitive, vulnerable, testy, offended, thin-skinned, touchy, irascible, cross, offended. *(ANT.) tough, placid, stolid, impassive.*

**hug** *(SYN.)* embrace, coddle, caress, kiss, pet, press, clasp, fondle, cuddle. *(ANT.) tease, vex, spurn, buffet, annoy.*

**huge** *(SYN.)* great, immense, vast, ample, big, capacious, extensive, gigantic, enormous, tremendous, large, wide, colossal. *(ANT.) short, small, mean, little, tiny.*

**hulking** *(SYN.)* massive, awkward, bulky, ponderous, unwieldy, overgrown, lumpish, oafish.

**hullabaloo** *(SYN.)* clamor, uproar, din, racket, tumult, hubbub, commotion, noise, blare. *(ANT.) calm, peace, silence.*

**hum** *(SYN.)* whir, buzz, whiz, purr, croon, murmur, intone, vibrate.

**human** *(SYN.)* manlike, hominid, mortal, fleshly, individual, person, tellurian.

**humane** *(SYN.)* lenient, tender, tolerant, compassionate, clement, forgiving, kind, forbearing, thoughtful, kindhearted, kindly, gentle, merciful. *(ANT.) remorseless, cruel, heartless, pitiless, unfeeling, brutal.*

**humanist** *(SYN.)* scholar, sage, classicist, savant.

**humanitarian** *(SYN.)* benefactor, philanthropist.

**humanitarianism** *(SYN.)* goodwill, beneficence, philanthropy, welfarism, humanism.

**humanity** *(SYN.)* generosity, magnanimity, tenderness, altruism, beneficence, kindness, charity, philanthropy. *(ANT.) selfishness, unkindness, cruelty, inhumanity.*

**humble** *(SYN.)* modest, crush, mortify, simple, shame, subdue, meek, abase, break, plain, submissive, compliant, unpretentious, unassuming, abash,

unostentatious, lowly, polite, courteous, unpretending, degrade. *(ANT.) praise, arrogant, exalt, illustrious, boastful, honor, elevate.*

**humbly** *(SYN.)* deferentially, meekly, respectfully, unassumingly, diffidently, modestly, subserviently, submissively. *(ANT.) insolently, proudly, grandly, arrogantly.*

**humbug** *(SYN.)* drivel, gammon, bosh, nonsense, rubbish, inanity.

**humdrum** *(SYN.)* commonplace, prosy, mundane, insipid, tedious, routine, dull, boring. *(ANT.) interesting, stimulating, arresting, striking, exciting.*

**humid** *(SYN.)* moist, damp, misty, muggy, wet, watery, vaporous. *(ANT.) parched, dry, desiccated.*

**humiliate** *(SYN.)* corrupt, defile, depress, pervert, abase, degrade, disgrace, adulterate, humble, shame, lower, impair, deprave, depress. *(ANT.) restore, raise, enhance, improve, vitalize.*

**humiliation** *(SYN.)* chagrin, dishonor, ignominy, scandal, abasement, mortification, disrepute, odium, disgrace, shame. *(ANT.) honor, praise, glory, dignity, renown.*

**humor** *(SYN.)* jocularity, wit, temperament, sarcasm, irony, joking, amusement, facetiousness, joke, disposition, waggery, fun, clowning, satire, mood. *(ANT.) sorrow, gravity, seriousness.*

**humorous** *(SYN.)* funny, ludicrous, witty, curious, queer, amusing, comical, farcical, laughable, droll. *(ANT.) sober, unfunny, melancholy, serious, sad, solemn.*

**hunger** *(SYN.)* desire, longing, inclination, relish, stomach, zest, craving, liking, passion. *(ANT.) satiety, repugnance, disgust, distaste, renunciation.*

**hungry** *(SYN.)* famished, thirsting, craving, avid, longing, starved, ravenous. *(ANT.) gorged, satisfied, full, sated.*

**hunt** *(SYN.)* pursuit, investigation, examination, inquiry, pursue, track. *(ANT.) cession, abandonment.*

**hurl** *(SYN.)* throw, cast, propel, fling, toss, pitch, thrust. *(ANT.) retain, pull, draw, haul, hold.*

**hurried** *(SYN.)* rushed, hasty, swift, headlong, slipshod, careless, impulsive, superficial. *(ANT.) deliberate, slow,*

dilatory, thorough, prolonged.

**hurry** *(SYN.)* quicken, speed, ado, rush, accelerate, run, hasten, race, urge, bustle, expedite, precipitate. *(ANT.) retard, tarry, hinder, linger, dawdle, delay.*

**hurt** *(SYN.)* damage, harm, grievance, detriment, pain, injustice, injure, abuse, distress, disfigured, mar, afflict, spoil, affront, insult. *(ANT.) improvement, repair, compliment, help, praise, benefit.*

**hurtle** *(SYN.)* charge, collide, rush, crash, lunge, bump, fling.

**husband** *(SYN.)* spouse, mate.

**hush** *(SYN.)* quiet, silence, still.

**husk** *(SYN.)* shell, hull, pod, skin, covering, crust, bark.

**husky** *(SYN.)* strong, brawny, strapping, muscular. *(ANT.) feeble, weak.*

**hustle** *(SYN.)* hasten, run, race, hurry, speed.

**hut** *(SYN.)* cottage, shanty, cabin, shed.

**hutch** *(SYN.)* box, chest, locker, trunk, coffer, bin.

**hybrid** *(SYN.)* mule, mixture, crossbreed, cross, mongrel, mutt.

**hygiene** *(SYN.)* cleanliness, sanitation, health, prophylaxis.

**hygienic** *(SYN.)* robust, strong, clean, well, wholesome, hale, healthy, sound. *(ANT.) frail, noxious, infirm, delicate, diseased.*

**hyperbole** *(SYN.)* puffery, exaggeration, embellishment, overstatement.

**hypercritical** *(SYN.)* fault-finding, captious, censorious, finicky, exacting, carping, querulous, nagging, finical, hairsplitting. *(ANT.) lax, easygoing, indulgent, lenient, tolerant.*

**hypnotic** *(SYN.)* soothing, opiate, sedative, soporific, entrancing, spellbinding, arresting, charming.

**hypnotize** *(SYN.)* entrance, dazzle, mesmerize, fascinate, spellbind.

**hypocrisy** *(SYN.)* pretense, deceit, dissembling, fakery, feigning, sanctimony, cant. *(ANT.) openness, candor, truth, directness, honesty, frankness.*

**hypocrite** *(SYN.)* cheat, deceiver, pretender, dissembler, fake, fraud.

**hypothesis** *(SYN.)* law, theory, supposition, conjecture. *(ANT.) proof, fact, certainty.*

**hypothetical** *(SYN.)*

conjectural, speculative, theoretical. *(ANT.) actual.*

# I

**idea** *(SYN.)* conception, image, opinion, sentiment, concept, fancy, notion, thought, impression. *(ANT.) thing, matter, entity, object, substance.*

**ideal** *(SYN.)* imaginary, supreme, unreal, visionary, perfect, faultless, fancied, exemplary, utopian. *(ANT.) imperfect, actual, material, real, faulty.*

**idealistic** *(SYN.)* extravagant, dreamy, fantastic, fanciful, ideal, maudlin, imaginative, mawkish, sentimental, poetic, picturesque. *(ANT.) practical, literal, factual, prosaic.*

**identify** *(SYN.)* recollect, apprehend, perceive, remember, confess, acknowledge, name, describe, classify. *(ANT.) ignore, forget, overlook, renounce, disown, repudiate.*

**identity** *(SYN.)* uniqueness, personality, character, individuality.

**ideology** *(SYN.)* credo, principles, belief.

**idiom** *(SYN.)* language, speech, vernacular, lingo, dialect, jargon, slang, tongue. *(ANT.) babble, gibberish, drivel, nonsense.*

**idiot** *(SYN.)* buffoon, harlequin, dolt, jester, dunce, blockhead, imbecile, numbskull, simpleton, oaf, nincompoop, fool, moron. *(ANT.) philosopher, genius, scholar, sage.*

**idiotic** *(SYN.)* asinine, absurd, brainless, irrational, crazy, nonsensical, senseless, preposterous, silly, ridiculous, simple, stupid, foolish, inane, moronic, half-witted, simpleminded, dimwitted. *(ANT.) prudent, wise, sagacious, judicious, sane, intelligent, bright, brilliant, smart.*

**idle** *(SYN.)* unemployed, dormant, lazy, inactive, unoccupied, indolent, slothful, inert, unused. *(ANT.) occupied, working, employed, active, industrious, busy, engaged.*

**idolize** *(SYN.)* revere, worship, adore. *(ANT.) despise.*

**ignoble** *(SYN.)* dishonorable, ignominious, lowly, menial, vile, sordid, vulgar, abject, base, despicable, groveling, mean. *(ANT.) righteous, lofty, honored, esteemed, noble, exalted.*

**ignominious** (SYN.) contemptible, abject, despicable, groveling, dishonorable, ignoble, lowly, low, menial, mean, sordid, servile, vulgar, vile. (ANT.) *lofty, noble, esteemed, righteous, exalted.*

**ignorant** (SYN.) uneducated, untaught, uncultured, illiterate, uninformed, unlearned, unlettered, untrained, unaware, unmindful. (ANT.) *cultured, literate, educated, erudite, informed, cultivated, schooled, learned, lettered.*

**ignore** (SYN.) omit, slight, disregard, overlook, neglect, skip. (ANT.) *notice, regard, include.*

**ill** (SYN.) diseased, ailing, indisposed, morbid, infirm, unwell, sick, unhealthy. (ANT.) *robust, healthy, well, sound, fit.*

**ill-advised** (SYN.) injudicious, ill-considered, imprudent.

**ill-at-ease** (SYN.) nervous, uncomfortable, uneasy. (ANT.) *comfortable.*

**illegal** (SYN.) prohibited, unlawful, criminal, illicit, outlawed, illegitimate. (ANT.) *permitted, lawful, honest, legal, legitimate.*

**illiberal** (SYN.) fanatical, bigoted, intolerant, narrow-minded, dogmatic, prejudiced. (ANT.) *progressive, liberal, radical.*

**illicit** (SYN.) illegitimate, criminal, outlawed, unlawful, prohibited, illegal, unauthorized. (ANT.) *legal, honest, permitted, lawful, licit.*

**ill-natured** (SYN.) crabby, cranky, grouchy, cross, irascible.

**illness** (SYN.) complaint, infirmity, ailment, disorder, malady, sickness. (ANT.) *healthiness, health, soundness, vigor.*

**illogical** (SYN.) absurd, irrational, preposterous.

**ill-tempered** (SYN.) crabby, cranky, cross, grouchy.

**ill-treated** (SYN.) harmed, mistreated, abused, maltreated.

**illuminate** (SYN.) enlighten, clarify, irradiate, illustrate, light, lighten, explain, interpret, elucidate, brighten, illumine. (ANT.) *obscure, confuse, darken, obfuscate, shadow, complicate.*

**ill-use** (SYN.) defame, revile, vilify, misemploy, disparage, abuse, traduce, asperse, misapply, misuse. (ANT.) *protect, cherish, respect, honor, praise.*

**illusion** (SYN.) hallucination, vision, phantom, delusion, fantasy, dream, mirage. (ANT.) *substance, actuality, reality.*

**illusive** (SYN.) fallacious, delusive, false, specious, misleading, deceptive, deceitful, delusory. (ANT.) *real, truthful, authentic, genuine, honest.*

**illustrate** (SYN.) decorate, illuminate, adorn, show, picture, embellish, demonstrate.

**illustration** (SYN.) likeness, painting, picture, print, scene, sketch, view, engraving, drawing, panorama, photograph, cinema, etching, effigy, film, appearance, portrayal, resemblance, image, portrait.

**illustrator** (SYN.) painter, artist.

**illustrious** (SYN.) prominent, eminent, renowned, famed, great, vital, elevated, majestic, noble, excellent, dignified, big, gigantic, enormous, immense, huge, vast, large, countless, numerous, celebrated, critical, momentous, august, weighty, grand, fine, magnificent, serious, important. (ANT.) *menial, common, minute, diminutive, small, obscure, ordinary, little.*

**image** (SYN.) reflection, likeness, idea, representation, notion, picture, conception.

**imaginary** (SYN.) fanciful, fantastic, unreal, whimsical. (ANT.) *actual, real.*

**imagination** (SYN.) creation, invention, fancy, notion, conception, fantasy, idea.

**imaginative** (SYN.) inventive, poetical, fanciful, clever, creative, mystical, visionary. (ANT.) *prosaic, dull, unromantic, literal.*

**imagine** (SYN.) assume, surmise, suppose, conceive, dream, pretend, conjecture, fancy, opine, envisage, think, envision, guess, picture.

**imbecile** (SYN.) idiot, numbskull, simpleton, blockhead, dolt, dunce, jester, buffoon, harlequin, nincompoop, clown, fool, oaf. (ANT.) *scholar, genius, philosopher, sage.*

**imbibe** (SYN.) absorb, consume, assimilate, engulf, engage, occupy, engross. (ANT.) *dispense, discharge, emit.*

**imitate** (SYN.) duplicate, mimic, follow, reproduce, mock, ape, counterfeit, copy, simulate, impersonate. (ANT.) *invent, distort, alter, diverge.*

**imitation** (SYN.) replica, reproduction, copy, duplicate, facsimile, transcript, exemplar. (ANT.) *prototype, original.*

**immaculate** (SYN.) clean, spotless, unblemished. (ANT.) *dirty.*

**immature** (SYN.) young, boyish, childish, youthful, childlike, puerile, girlish, juvenile, callow. (ANT.) *old, senile, aged, elderly, mature.*

**immeasurable** (SYN.) unlimited, endless, eternal, immense, interminable, unbounded, boundless, illimitable, infinite. (ANT.) *limited, confined, bounded, finite, circumscribed.*

**immediate** (SYN.) present, instant, instantaneous, near, close, next, prompt, direct. (ANT.) *distant, future.*

**immediately** (SYN.) now, presently, instantly, promptly, straightway, directly, instantaneously, forthwith. (ANT.) *sometime, hereafter, later, shortly, distantly.*

**immense** (SYN.) enormous, large, gigantic, huge, colossal, elephantine, great, gargantuan, vast. (ANT.) *small, diminutive, little, minuscule, minute, petite, tiny.*

**immensity** (SYN.) hugeness, enormousness, vastness.

**immerse** (SYN.) plunge, dip, dunk, sink, submerge, engage, absorb, engross, douse. (ANT.) *uplift, elevate, recover.*

**immigration** (SYN.) settlement, colonization. (ANT.) *exodus, emigration.*

**imminent** (SYN.) nigh, impending, overhanging, approaching, menacing, threatening. (ANT.) *retreating, afar, distant, improbable, remote.*

**immoderation** (SYN.) profusion, surplus, extravagance, excess, intemperance, superabundance. (ANT.) *lack, want, deficiency, dearth, paucity.*

**immoral** (SYN.) sinful, wicked, corrupt, bad, indecent, profligate, unprincipled, antisocial, dissolute. (ANT.) *pure, high-minded, chaste, virtuous, noble.*

**immortal** (SYN.) infinite, eternal, timeless, undying, perpetual, ceaseless, endless, deathless, everlasting. (ANT.) *mortal, transient, finite, ephemeral, temporal.*

**immune** (SYN.) easy, open, autonomous, unobstructed, free, emancipated, clear, independent, unrestricted, exempt, liberated, familiar, loose, unconfined, frank, unfastened, careless, freed. (ANT.) *confined, impeded, restricted, subject.*

**immutable** (SYN.) constant, faithful, invariant, persistent, unchanging, unalterable, continual, ceaseless, enduring, fixed, permanent, abiding, perpetual, unwavering. (ANT.) *mutable, vacillating, wavering, fickle.*

**impact** (SYN.) striking, contact, collision.

**impair** (SYN.) harm, injure, spoil, deface, destroy, hurt, damage, mar. (ANT.) *repair, mend, ameliorate, enhance, benefit.*

**impart** (SYN.) convey, disclose, inform, tell, reveal, transmit, notify, confer, divulge, communicate, relate. (ANT.) *hide, withhold, conceal.*

**impartial** (SYN.) unbiased, just, honest, fair, reasonable, equitable. (ANT.) *fraudulent, dishonorable, partial.*

**impartiality** (SYN.) indifference, unconcern, neutrality, disinterestedness, apathy, insensibility. (ANT.) *passion, ardor, fervor.*

**impasse** (SYN.) standstill, deadlock, stalemate.

**impede** (SYN.) hamper, hinder, retard, thwart, check, encumber, interrupt, bar, clog, delay, obstruct, block, frustrate, restrain, stop. (ANT.) *assist, promote, help, advance, further.*

**impediment** (SYN.) barrier, bar, block, difficulty, check, hindrance, snag, obstruction. (ANT.) *assistance, help, aid.*

**impel** (SYN.) oblige, enforce, drive, coerce, force, constrain. (ANT.) *induce, prevent, convince, persuade.*

**impending** (SYN.) imminent, nigh, threatening, overhanging, approaching, menacing. (ANT.) *remote, improbable, afar, distant, retreating.*

**impenetrable** (SYN.) rigid, tough, harsh, strict, unfeeling, rigorous, intricate, arduous, penetrable, cruel, difficult, severe, stem, firm, hard, compact. (ANT.) *soft, simple, gentle, tender, brittle, fluid, flabby, elastic, lenient, easy, effortless.*

**imperative** (SYN.) critical, instant, important, necessary, serious, urgent, cogent, compelling, crucial, pressing, impelling, importunate, exigent, insistent. (ANT.) *trivial, insignificant, unimportant, petty.*

**imperceptible** (SYN.) invisible, indiscernible, unseen, indistinguishable. (ANT.) seen, evident, visible, perceptible.

**imperfection** (SYN.) flaw, shortcoming, vice, defect, blemish, failure, mistake, omission, fault, error. (ANT.) correctness, perfection, completeness.

**imperil** (SYN.) jeopardize, risk, endanger, hazard, risk. (ANT.) guard, insure.

**impersonal** (SYN.) objective, detached, disinterested. (ANT.) personal.

**impersonate** (SYN.) mock, simulate, imitate, ape, counterfeit, mimic, copy, duplicate. (ANT.) alter, invent, diverge, distort.

**impertinence** (SYN.) impudence, presumption, sauciness, effrontery, audacity, rudeness, assurance, boldness, insolence. (ANT.) truckling, politeness, diffidence, subservience.

**impertinent** (SYN.) rude, offensive, insolent, disrespectful, arrogant, brazen, impudent, insulting, contemptuous, abusive. (ANT.) polite, respectful, considerate, courteous.

**impetuous** (SYN.) rash, heedless, quick, hasty, careless, passionate, impulsive. (ANT.) cautious, reasoning, careful, prudent, thoughtful, calculating.

**implicate** (SYN.) reproach, accuse, blame, involve, upbraid, condemn, incriminate, rebuke, censure. (ANT.) exonerate, absolve.

**implore** (SYN.) beg, pray, request, solicit, crave, entreat, beseech, ask, importune, supplicate, adjure, appeal, petition. (ANT.) give, cede, bestow, favor, grant.

**imply** (SYN.) mean, involve, suggest, connote, hint, mention, indicate, insinuate, signify. (ANT.) state, assert, declare, express.

**impolite** (SYN.) rude, unpolished, impudent, boorish, blunt, discourteous, rough, saucy, surly, savage, insolent, gruff, uncivil, coarse, ignorant, crude, illiterate, raw, primitive, vulgar, untaught. (ANT.) genteel, courteous, courtly, dignified, polite, stately, noble, civil.

**import** (SYN.) influence, significance, stress, emphasis, importance, value, weight. (ANT.) triviality, insignificance.

**important** (SYN.) critical, grave, influential, momentous, well-known, pressing, relevant, prominent, primary, essential, weighty, material, considerable, famous, principle, famed, sequential, notable, significant, illustrious, decisive. (ANT.) unimportant, trifling, petty, trivial, insignificant, secondary, anonymous, irrelevant.

**impose** (SYN.) levy, require, demand.

**imposing** (SYN.) lofty, noble, majestic, magnificent, august, dignified, grandiose, high, grand, impressive, pompous, stately. (ANT.) ordinary, undignified, humble, common, lowly.

**imposition** (SYN.) load, onus, burden.

**impossible** (SYN.) preposterous.

**impregnable** (SYN.) safe, invulnerable, secure, unassailable. (ANT.) vulnerable.

**impress** (SYN.) awe, emboss, affect, mark, imprint, indent, influence.

**impression** (SYN.) influence, indentation, feeling, opinion, mark, effect, depression, guess, thought, belief, dent, sensibility. (ANT.) fact, insensibility.

**impressive** (SYN.) arresting, moving, remarkable, splendid, thrilling, striking, majestic, grandiose, imposing, commanding, affecting, exciting, touching, stirring. (ANT.) regular, unimpressive, commonplace.

**impromptu** (SYN.) casual, unprepared, offhand, extemporaneous.

**improper** (SYN.) unfit, unsuitable, inappropriate, naughty, indecent, unbecoming. (ANT.) fitting, proper, appropriate.

**improve** (SYN.) better, reform, refine, ameliorate, amend, help, upgrade, rectify. (ANT.) debase, vitiate, impair, corrupt, damage.

**improvement** (SYN.) growth, advance, progress, betterment, development, advancement, progression. (ANT.) relapse, regression, decline, retrogression, delay.

**imprudent** (SYN.) indiscreet, thoughtless, desultory, lax, neglectful, remiss, careless, inattentive, heedless, inconsiderate, reckless, ill-advised, irresponsible. (ANT.) careful, meticulous, accurate.

**impudence** (SYN.) boldness, insolence, rudeness, sauciness, assurance, effrontery, impertinence, presumption, audacity. (ANT.) politeness, truckling, subservience, diffidence.

**impudent** (SYN.) forward, rude, abrupt, prominent, striking, bold, fresh, impertinent, insolent, pushy, insulting, brazen. (ANT.) bashful, flinching, polite, courteous, cowardly, retiring, timid.

**impulse** (SYN.) hunch, whim, fancy, urge, caprice, surge, pulse.

**impulsive** (SYN.) passionate, rash, spontaneous, heedless, careless, hasty, quick, impetuous. (ANT.) reasoning, calculating, careful, prudent, cautious.

**impure** (SYN.) dishonest, spoiled, tainted, contaminated, debased, corrupt, profligate, unsound, putrid, corrupted, crooked, depraved, vitiated, venal.

**imputation** (SYN.) diary, incrimination, arraignment, indictment. (ANT.) exoneration, pardon, exculpation.

**inability** (SYN.) incompetence, incapacity, handicap, disability, impotence, weakness. (ANT.) power, strength, ability, capability.

**inaccurate** (SYN.) false, incorrect, mistaken, untrue, askew, wrong, awry, erroneous, fallacious, imprecise, faulty, amiss. (ANT.) right, accurate, true, correct.

**inactive** (SYN.) lazy, unemployed, indolent, motionless, still, inert, dormant, idle, unoccupied. (ANT.) employed, working, active, industrious, occupied.

**inadequate** (SYN.) insufficient, lacking, short, incomplete, defective, scanty. (ANT.) satisfactory, enough, adequate, ample, sufficient.

**inadvertent** (SYN.) careless, negligent, unthinking, thoughtless.

**inane** (SYN.) trite, insipid, banal, absurd, silly, commonplace, vapid, foolish, stupid, hackneyed. (ANT.) stimulating, novel, fresh, original, striking.

**inanimate** (SYN.) deceased, spiritless, lifeless, gone, dull, mineral, departed, dead, insensible, vegetable, unconscious. (ANT.) living, stirring, alive, animate.

**inattentive** (SYN.) absentminded, distracted, abstracted, preoccupied. (ANT.) watchful, attending, attentive.

**inaugurate** (SYN.) commence, begin, open, originate, start, arise, launch, enter, initiate. (ANT.) end, terminate, close, complete, finish.

**incense** (SYN.) anger, enrage, infuriate.

**incentive** (SYN.) impulse, stimulus, inducement, encouragement. (ANT.) discouragement.

**inception** (SYN.) origin, start, source, opening, beginning, outset, commencement. (ANT.) end, termination, close, completion, consummation.

**incessant** (SYN.) perennial, uninterrupted, continual, ceaseless, continuous, unremitting, eternal, constant, unceasing, unending, perpetual, everlasting. (ANT.) rare, occasional, periodic, interrupted.

**incident** (SYN.) happening, situation, occurrence, circumstance, condition, event.

**incidental** (SYN.) casual, contingent, trivial, undesigned, chance, fortuitous, accidental, secondary, unimportant, unintended. (ANT.) intended, fundamental, planned, calculated, willed, decreed.

**incidentally** (SYN.) by the way.

**incinerate** (SYN.) sear, char, blaze, scald, singe, consume, scorch, burn. (ANT.) quench, put out, extinguish.

**incisive** (SYN.) neat, succinct, terse, brief, compact, condensed, neat, summary, concise. (ANT.) wordy, prolix, verbose, lengthy.

**incite** (SYN.) goad, provoke, urge, arouse, encourage, cause, stimulate, induce, instigate, foment. (ANT.) quiet, bore, pacify, soothe.

**inclination** (SYN.) bent, preference, desire, slope, affection, bent, bias, disposition, bending, penchant, incline, attachment, predisposition, predication, tendency, prejudice, slant, lean, leaning. (ANT.) nonchalance, apathy, distaste, aversion, reluctance, disinclination, uprightness, repugnance.

**incline** (SYN.) slope, nod, lean.

**include** (SYN.) contain, hold, accommodate, embody, encompass, involve, comprise, embrace. (ANT.) omit, exclude.

**income** (SYN.) earnings, salary, wages, revenue, pay,

return, receipts.

**incomparable** (SYN.) peerless, matchless, unequaled.

**incompetency** (SYN.) inability, weakness, handicap, impotence, disability, incapacity. (ANT.) strength, ability, power, capability.

**incomprehensible** (SYN.) unintelligible, indecipherable.

**inconceivable** (SYN.) unbelievable, unimaginable, impossible. (ANT.) possible, believable.

**incongruous** (SYN.) inconsistent, contrary, incompatible, irreconcilable, contradictory, unsteady, wavering, paradoxical, vacillating, discrepant, illogical. (ANT.) consistent, compatible, correspondent.

**inconsiderate** (SYN.) unthinking, careless, unthoughtful, unmindful. (ANT.) thoughtful, considerate, kind.

**inconsistency** (SYN.) discord, variance, contention, conflict, controversy, interference. (ANT.) harmony, concord, amity, consonance.

**inconsistent** (SYN.) fickle, wavering, variable, changeable, contrary, unstable, illogical, contradictory, irreconcilable, discrepant, paradoxical, incompatible, self-contradictory, incongruous, unsteady, fitful, shifting. (ANT.) unchanging, steady, logical, stable, uniform, constant.

**inconspicuous** (SYN.) retiring, unnoticed, unostentatious. (ANT.) obvious, conspicuous.

**inconstant** (SYN.) fickle, shifting, changeable, fitful, vacillating, unstable, wavering. (ANT.) stable, constant, steady, uniform, unchanging.

**inconvenient** (SYN.) awkward, inappropriate, untimely, troublesome. (ANT.) handy, convenient.

**incorrect** (SYN.) mistaken, wrong, erroneous, inaccurate. (ANT.) proper, accurate, suitable.

**increase** (SYN.) amplify, enlarge, grow, magnify, multiply, augment, enhance, expand, intensify, swell, raise, greaten, prolong, broaden, lengthen, expansion, accrue, extend, heighten. (ANT.) diminish, reduce, atrophy, shrink, shrinkage, decrease, lessening, lessen, contract.

**incredible** (SYN.) improbable, unbelievable. (ANT.)

plausible, credible, believable.

**incriminate** (SYN.) charge, accuse, indict, arraign, censure. (ANT.) release, exonerate, acquit, absolve, vindicate.

**incrimination** (SYN.) imputation, indictment, accusation, charge, arraignment. (ANT.) exoneration, pardon, exculpation.

**indebted** (SYN.) obliged, grateful, beholden, thankful, appreciative. (ANT.) unappreciative, thankless.

**indecent** (SYN.) impure, obscene, pornographic, coarse, dirty, filthy, smutty, gross, disgusting. (ANT.) modest, refined, decent.

**indeed** (SYN.) truthfully, really, honestly, surely.

**indefinite** (SYN.) unsure, uncertain, vague, confused, unsettled, confusing. (ANT.) decided, definite, equivocal.

**independence** (SYN.) liberation, privilege, freedom, immunity, familiarity, liberty, exemption, license. (ANT.) necessity, constraint, compulsion, reliance, dependence, bondage, servitude.

**independent** (SYN.) free, unrestrained, voluntary, autonomous, self-reliant, uncontrolled, unrestricted. (ANT.) enslaved, contingent, dependent, restricted.

**indestructible** (SYN.) enduring, lasting, permanent, unchangeable, abiding, constant, fixed, stable, changeless. (ANT.) unstable, temporary, transitory, ephemeral.

**indicate** (SYN.) imply, denote, signify, specify, intimate, designate, symbolize, show, manifest, disclose, mean, reveal. (ANT.) mislead, distract, conceal, falsify.

**indication** (SYN.) proof, emblem, omen, sign, symbol, token, mark, portent, gesture, signal.

**indict** (SYN.) charge, accuse, incriminate, censure, arraign. (ANT.) acquit, vindicate, absolve, exonerate.

**indictment** (SYN.) incrimination, arraignment, imputation, charge. (ANT.) pardon, exoneration, exculpation.

**indifference** (SYN.) unconcern, apathy, impartiality, disinterestedness, insensibility, neutrality. (ANT.) ardor, passion, affection, fervor.

**indifferent** (SYN.) uncaring, insensitive, cool, unconcerned. (ANT.) caring, concerned, earnest.

**indigence** (SYN.) necessity,

destitution, poverty, want, need, privation, penury. (ANT.) wealth, abundance, plenty, riches, affluence.

**indigenous** (SYN.) inborn, native, inherent, domestic, aboriginal, plenty, endemic, innate, natural.

**indigent** (SYN.) destitute, covetous, poor, lacking, requiring, wanting, needy, craving.

**indignant** (SYN.) irritated, irate, angry, aroused, exasperated. (ANT.) calm, serene, content.

**indignation** (SYN.) ire, petulance, passion, choler, anger, wrath, temper, irritation, exasperation, animosity, resentment, rage. (ANT.) self-control, peace, forbearance, patience.

**indignity** (SYN.) insolence, insult, abuse, affront, offense. (ANT.) homage, apology.

**indirect** (SYN.) winding, crooked, devious, roundabout, cunning, tricky, tortuous, circuitous, distorted, erratic, swerving, (ANT.) straightforward, direct, straight, honest.

**indiscretion** (SYN.) imprudence, folly, absurdity, extravagance. (ANT.) prudence, sense, wisdom, reasonableness, judgment.

**indispensable** (SYN.) necessary, fundamental, basic, essential, important, intrinsic, vital. (ANT.) optional, expendable, peripheral, extrinsic.

**indistinct** (SYN.) cloudy, dark, mysterious, vague, blurry, ambiguous, cryptic, dim, obscure, enigmatic, abstruse, hazy, blurred, unintelligible. (ANT.) clear, lucid, bright, distinct.

**indistinguishable** (SYN.) identical, like, coincident, equal, same, equivalent. (ANT.) dissimilar, opposed, contrary, disparate, distinct.

**individual** (SYN.) singular, specific, unique, distinctive, single, particular, undivided, human, apart, marked, person, different, special, separate. (ANT.) universal, common, general, ordinary.

**individuality** (SYN.) symbol, description, mark, kind, character, repute, class, standing, sort, nature, disposition, reputation, sign.

**indolent** (SYN.) slothful, lazy, idle, inactive, slow, sluggish, torpid, supine, inert. (ANT.) diligent, active, assiduous, vigorous, zesty, alert.

**indomitable** (SYN.) insurmountable, unconquerable, invulnerable, impregnable, unassailable. (ANT.) weak, puny, powerless, vulnerable.

**induce** (SYN.) evoke, cause, influence, persuade, effect, make, originate, prompt, incite, create.

**inducement** (SYN.) incentive, motive, purpose, stimulus, reason, impulse, cause, principle, spur, incitement. (ANT.) result, attempt, action, effort, deed.

**induct** (SYN.) instate, establish, install. (ANT.) eject, oust.

**indulge** (SYN.) humor, satisfy, gratify.

**indulgent** (SYN.) obliging, pampering, tolerant, easy.

**indurate** (SYN.) impenitent, hard, insensible, tough, obdurate, callous, unfeeling. (ANT.) soft, compassionate, tender, sensitive.

**industrious** (SYN.) hard-working, perseverant, busy, active, diligent, assiduous, careful, patient. (ANT.) unconcerned, indifferent, lethargic, careless, apathetic, lazy, indolent, shiftless.

**inebriated** (SYN.) drunk, tight, drunken, intoxicated, tipsy. (ANT.) sober, clearheaded, temperate.

**ineffective** (SYN.) pliant, tender, vague, wavering, defenseless, weak, inadequate, poor, irresolute, frail, decrepit, delicate, vacillating, assailable, exposed, vulnerable. (ANT.) sturdy, robust, potent, powerful.

**inept** (SYN.) clumsy, awkward, improper, inappropriate. (ANT.) adroit, dexterous, adept, appropriate, proper, apt, fitting.

**inequity** (SYN.) wrong, injustice, unfairness, grievance, injury. (ANT.) righteousness, lawfulness, equity, justice.

**inert** (SYN.) lazy, dormant, slothful, inactive, idle, indolent, motionless, unmoving, fixed, static. (ANT.) working, active, industrious, occupied.

**inertia** (SYN.) indolence, torpidity, idleness, slothfulness, sluggishness. (ANT.) assiduousness, activity, alertness, diligence.

**inevitable** (SYN.) definite, fixed, positive, sure, undeniable, indubitable, certain, assured, unquestionable, secure. (ANT.) uncertain, probable, doubtful, questionable.

**inexpensive** (SYN.) low-priced, cheap, inferior, mean,

beggarly, common, poor, shabby, modest, economical. (ANT.) expensive, costly, dear.

**inexperienced** (SYN.) naive, untrained, uninformed, green. (ANT.) experienced, skilled, sophisticated, trained, seasoned.

**inexplicable** (SYN.) hidden, mysterious, obscure, secret, dark, cryptic, enigmatical, incomprehensible, occult, recondite, inscrutable, dim. (ANT.) plain, simple, clear, obvious, explained.

**infamous** (SYN.) shocking, shameful, scandalous.

**infantile** (SYN.) babyish, naive, immature, childish. (ANT.) mature, grownup, adult.

**infect** (SYN.) pollute, poison, contaminate, defile, sully, taint. (ANT.) purify, disinfect.

**infection** (SYN.) virus, poison, ailment, disease, pollution, pest, germ, taint, contamination, contagion.

**infectious** (SYN.) contagious, virulent, catching, communicable, pestilential, transferable. (ANT.) noncommunicable, hygienic, healthful.

**infer** (SYN.) understand, deduce, extract.

**inference** (SYN.) consequence, result, conclusion, corollary, judgment, deduction. (ANT.) preconception, foreknowledge, assumption, presupposition.

**inferior** (SYN.) secondary, lower, poorer, minor, subordinate, mediocre. (ANT.) greater, superior, better, higher.

**infinite** (SYN.) immeasurable, interminable, unlimited, unbounded, eternal, boundless, illimitable, immense, endless, vast, innumerable, numberless, limitless. (ANT.) confined, limited, bounded, circumscribed, finite.

**infinitesimal** (SYN.) minute, microscopic, tiny, submicroscopic. (ANT.) gigantic, huge, enormous.

**infirm** (SYN.) feeble, impaired, decrepit, forceless, languid, puny, powerless, enervated, weak, exhausted. (ANT.) stout, vigorous, forceful, lusty, strong.

**infirmity** (SYN.) disease, illness, malady, ailment, sickness, disorder, complaint. (ANT.) soundness, health, vigor, healthiness.

**inflame** (SYN.) fire, incite, excite, arouse. (ANT.) soothe, calm.

**inflammation** (SYN.) infection, soreness, irritation.

**inflammatory** (SYN.) instigating, inciting, provocative.

**inflate** (SYN.) expand, swell, distend. (ANT.) collapse, deflate.

**inflexible** (SYN.) firm, stubborn, headstrong, immovable, uncompromising, dogged, contumacious, determined, obstinate, rigid, unbending, unyielding, steadfast. (ANT.) submissive, compliant, docile, amenable, yielding, flexible, giving, elastic.

**inflict** (SYN.) deliver, deal, give, impose, apply.

**influence** (SYN.) weight, control, effect, sway.

**influenced** (SYN.) sway, affect, bias, control, actuate, impel, stir, incite.

**influential** (SYN.) important, weighty, prominent, significant, critical, decisive, momentous, relevant, material, pressing, consequential, grave. (ANT.) petty, irrelevant, mean, trivial, insignificant.

**inform** (SYN.) apprise, instruct, tell, notify, advise, acquaint, enlighten, impart, warn, teach, advise, relate. (ANT.) delude, mislead, distract, conceal.

**informal** (SYN.) simple, easy, natural, unofficial, familiar. (ANT.) formal, distant, reserved, proper.

**informality** (SYN.) friendship, frankness, liberty, acquaintance, sociability, intimacy, unreserved. (ANT.) presumption, constraint, reserve, distance, haughtiness.

**information** (SYN.) knowledge, data, intelligence, facts.

**informative** (SYN.) educational, enlightening, instructive.

**informer** (SYN.) tattler, traitor, betrayer.

**infrequent** (SYN.) unusual, rare, occasional, strange. (ANT.) commonplace, abundant, usual, ordinary, customary, frequent, numerous.

**ingenious** (SYN.) clever, skillful, talented, adroit, dexterous, quick-witted, bright, smart, witty, sharp, apt, resourceful, imaginative, inventive, creative. (ANT.) dull, slow, awkward, bungling, unskilled, stupid.

**ingenuity** (SYN.) cunning, inventiveness, resourcefulness, aptitude, faculty, cleverness, ingenuousness. (ANT.) ineptitude, clumsiness, dullness, stupidity.

**ingenuous** (SYN.) open, sincere, honest, candid, straightforward, plain, frank, truthful, free, naive, simple, innocent, unsophisticated. (ANT.) scheming, sly, contrived, wily.

**ingredient** (SYN.) component, element, constituent.

**inhabit** (SYN.) fill, possess, absorb, dwell, occupy, live. (ANT.) relinquish, abandon, release.

**inherent** (SYN.) innate, native, congenital, intrinsic, inborn, inbred, natural, real. (ANT.) extraneous, acquired, external, extrinsic.

**inhibit** (SYN.) curb, constrain, hold back, restrain, bridle, hinder, repress, suppress, stop, limit. (ANT.) loosen, aid, incite, encourage.

**inhuman** (SYN.) merciless, cruel, brutal, ferocious, savage, ruthless, malignant, barbarous, barbaric, bestial. (ANT.) kind, benevolent, forbearing, gentle, compassionate, merciful, humane.

**inimical** (SYN.) hostile, warlike, adverse, antagonistic, opposed, unfriendly. (ANT.) favorable, amicable, cordial.

**iniquitous** (SYN.) baleful, immoral, pernicious, sinful, wicked, base, bad, evil, noxious, unsound, villainous, unwholesome. (ANT.) moral, good, excellent, honorable, reputable.

**iniquity** (SYN.) injustice, wrong, grievance, unfairness, injury. (ANT.) lawful, equity, righteousness, justice.

**initial** (SYN.) original, first, prime, beginning, earliest, pristine, chief, primeval, primary, foremost, basic, elementary. (ANT.) latest, subordinate, last, least, hindmost, final, terminal.

**initiate** (SYN.) institute, enter, arise, inaugurate, commence, originate, start, open, begin. (ANT.) terminate, complete, end, finish, close, stop.

**initiative** (SYN.) enthusiasm, energy, vigor, enterprise.

**injure** (SYN.) harm, wound, abuse, dishonor, damage, hurt, impair, spoil, disfigure, affront, insult, mar. (ANT.) praise, ameliorate, help, preserve, compliment, benefit.

**injurious** (SYN.) detrimental, harmful, mischievous, damaging, hurtful, deleterious, harmful, destructive. (ANT.) profitable, helpful, advantageous, salutary, beneficial, useful.

**injury** (SYN.) harm, detriment, damage, injustice, wrong, prejudice, grievance, mischief. (ANT.) repair, benefit, improvement.

**injustice** (SYN.) unfairness, grievance, iniquity, wrong, injury. (ANT.) righteousness, justice, equity, lawfulness.

**inmate** (SYN.) patient, prisoner.

**inn** (SYN.) motel, lodge, hotel.

**innate** (SYN.) native, inherent, congenital, real, inborn, natural, intrinsic, inbred. (ANT.) extraneous, acquired, external, extrinsic.

**innocent** (SYN.) pure, sinless, blameless, innocuous, lawful, naive, faultless, virtuous, not guilty. (ANT.) guilty, corrupt, sinful, culpable, sophisticated, wise, worldly.

**innocuous** (SYN.) naive, pure, innocent, blameless, virtuous, lawful, faultless, sinless. (ANT.) sinful, corrupt, unrighteous, culpable, guilty.

**inquire** (SYN.) ask, solicit, invite, demand, claim, entreat, interrogate, query, beg, request, question, investigate, examine. (ANT.) dictate, insist, reply, command, order.

**inquiring** (SYN.) prying, searching, curious, inquisitive, peering, snoopy, peeping, meddling, interrogative. (ANT.) unconcerned, indifferent, uninterested, incurious.

**inquiry** (SYN.) investigation, quest, research, examination, interrogation, exploration, query, question, scrutiny, study. (ANT.) inattention, inactivity, disregard, negligence.

**inquisitive** (SYN.) meddling, peeping, nosy, interrogative, peering, searching, prying, snoopy, inquiring, curious. (ANT.) unconcerned, indifferent, uninterested.

**insane** (SYN.) deranged, mad, foolish, idiotic, demented, crazy, delirious, maniacal, lunatic. (ANT.) sane, rational, reasonable, sensible, coherent.

**insanity** (SYN.) delirium, aberration, dementia, psychosis, lunacy, madness, frenzy, mania, craziness, derangement. (ANT.) stability, rationality, sanity.

**insecure** (SYN.) uneasy, nervous, uncertain, shaky. (ANT.) secure.

**insensitive** (SYN.) unfeeling, impenitent, callous, hard, indurate, obdurate, tough. (ANT.) soft, compassionate, tender, sensitive.

**insight** (SYN.) intuition,

acumen, penetration, discernment, perspicuity. (ANT.) obtuseness.

**insignificant** (SYN.) trivial, paltry, petty, small, frivolous, unimportant, insignificant, trifling. (ANT.) momentous, serious, important, weighty.

**insincere** (SYN.) false, dishonest, deceitful. (ANT.) honest, sincere.

**insinuate** (SYN.) imply, mean, suggest, connote, signify, involve. (ANT.) express, state, assert.

**insipid** (SYN.) tasteless, dull, stale, flat, vapid. (ANT.) racy, tasty, savory, exciting.

**insist** (SYN.) command, demand, require.

**insolence** (SYN.) boldness, presumption, sauciness, effrontery, audacity, assurance, impertinence, rudeness. (ANT.) politeness, truckling, diffidence, subservience.

**insolent** (SYN.) arrogant, impertinent, insulting, rude, brazen, contemptuous, abusive, offensive, disrespectful. (ANT.) respectful, courteous, polite, considerate.

**inspect** (SYN.) observe, discern, survey, view, watch, witness, examine, investigate. (ANT.) overlook, miss, ignore, skip.

**inspection** (SYN.) examination, retrospect, survey, revision, reconsideration, critique, criticism, review.

**inspiration** (SYN.) creativity, aptitude, genius, originality, ability, faculty, sagacity, talent, proficient, master, gift, adept, intellectual, thought, impulse, idea, notion, hunch. (ANT.) dullard, moron, shallowness, ineptitude, stupidity, obtuseness, dolt.

**install** (SYN.) establish.

**instance** (SYN.) occasion, illustration, occurrence, example, case.

**instant** (SYN.) flash, moment.

**instantaneous** (SYN.) hasty, sudden, unexpected, rapid, abrupt, immediate. (ANT.) slowly, anticipated, gradual.

**instantly** (SYN.) now, presently, directly, forthwith, immediately, rapidly, straight-away, at once, instantaneously. (ANT.) sometime, distantly, hereafter, later, shortly.

**instinct** (SYN.) intuition, feeling.

**instinctive** (SYN.) offhand, voluntary, willing, spontaneous, automatic, impulsive, extemporaneous. (ANT.)

rehearsed, planned, compulsory, prepared, forced.

**institute** (SYN.) ordain, establish, raise, form, organize, sanction, fix, found, launch, begin, initiate. (ANT.) overthrow, upset, demolish, abolish, unsettle.

**instruct** (SYN.) teach, tutor, educate, inform, school, instill, train, inculcate, drill. (ANT.) misinform, misguide.

**instruction** (SYN.) advise, warning, information, exhortation, notification, admonition, caution, recommendation, counsel, suggestion, teaching, training, education, command, order.

**instrument** (SYN.) channel, device, utensil, tool, agent, apparatus, means, vehicle, medium, agent, implement. (ANT.) obstruction, hindrance, preventive, impediment.

**insubordinate** (SYN.) rebellious, unruly, defiant, disorderly, disobedient, undutiful, refractory, intractable, mutinous. (ANT.) obedient, compliant, submissive, dutiful.

**insufficient** (SYN.) limited, lacking, deficient, short, inadequate. (ANT.) ample, protracted, abundant, big, extended.

**insulation** (SYN.) quarantine, segregation, seclusion, withdrawal, isolation, loneliness, alienation, solitude. (ANT.) union, communion, association, connection.

**insult** (SYN.) insolence, offense, abuse, dishonor, affront, indignity, offend, humiliate, outrage. (ANT.) compliment, homage, apology, salutation, flatter, praise.

**integrated** (SYN.) mingled, mixed, combined, interspersed, desegregated, nonsectarian, interracial. (ANT.) separated, divided, segregated.

**integrity** (SYN.) honesty, openness, trustworthiness, fairness, candor, justice, rectitude, sincerity, uprightness, soundness, wholeness, honor, principle, virtue. (ANT.) fraud, deceit, cheating, trickery, dishonesty.

**intellect** (SYN.) understanding, judgment.

**intellectual** (SYN.) intelligent.

**intelligence** (SYN.) reason, sense, intellect, understanding, mind, ability, skill, aptitude. (ANT.) feeling, passion, emotion.

**intelligent** (SYN.) clever, smart, knowledgeable,

well-informed, alert, discerning, astute, quick, enlightened, smart, bright, wise. (ANT.) insipid, obtuse, dull, stupid, slow, foolish, unintelligent, dumb.

**intend** (SYN.) plan, prepare, scheme, contrive, outline, design, sketch, plot, project.

**intense** (SYN.) brilliant, animated, graphic, lucid, bright, expressive, vivid, deep, profound, concentrated, serious, earnest. (ANT.) dull, vague, dusky, dim, dreary.

**intensify** (SYN.) accrue, augment, amplify, enlarge, enhance, extend, expand, heighten, grow, magnify, raise, multiply. (ANT.) reduce, decrease, contract, diminish.

**intensity** (SYN.) force, potency, power, toughness, activity, durability, fortitude, vigor, stamina. (ANT.) weakness, feebleness, infirmity, frailty.

**intent** (SYN.) purpose, design, objective, intention, aim. (ANT.) accidental, result, chance.

**intention** (SYN.) intent, purpose, objective, plan, expectation, aim, object. (ANT.) chance, accident.

**intentional** (SYN.) deliberate, intended, studied, willful, contemplated, premeditated, designed, voluntary, purposeful, planned. (ANT.) fortuitous, accidental, chance.

**intentionally** (SYN.) purposefully, deliberately, maliciously. (ANT.) accidentally.

**interest** (SYN.) attention, concern, care, advantage, benefit, profit, ownership, credit, attract, engage, amuse, entertain. (ANT.) apathy, weary, disinterest.

**interested** (SYN.) affected, concerned. (ANT.) unconcerned, indifferent, uninterested.

**interesting** (SYN.) engaging, inviting, fascinating, attractive. (ANT.) boring, tedious, uninteresting, wearisome.

**interfere** (SYN.) meddle, monkey, interpose, interrupt, tamper, butt in, intervene.

**interference** (SYN.) prying, intrusion, meddling, obstacle, obstruction.

**interior** (SYN.) internal, inmost, inner, inward, inside, center. (ANT.) outer, adjacent, exterior, external, outside.

**interject** (SYN.) intrude, introduce, insert, inject, interpose.

**interminable** (SYN.) immense, endless, immeasurable,

unlimited, vast, unbounded, boundless, eternal, infinite. (ANT.) limited, bounded, circumscribed, confined.

**internal** (SYN.) inner, interior, inside, intimate, private. (ANT.) outer, external, surface.

**interpose** (SYN.) arbitrate, inject, intervene, meddle, insert, interject, introduce, intercede, intrude, interfere. (ANT.) overlook, avoid, disregard.

**interpret** (SYN.) explain, solve, translate, construe, elucidate, decode, explicate, render, unravel, define, understand. (ANT.) misinterpret, falsify, confuse, distort, misconstrue.

**interrogate** (SYN.) quiz, analyze, inquire, audit, question, contemplate, assess, dissect, notice, scan, review, view, check, survey, scrutinize, examine. (ANT.) overlook, omit, neglect, disregard.

**interrupt** (SYN.) suspend, delay, postpone, defer, adjourn, stay, discontinue, intrude, interfere. (ANT.) prolong, persist, continue, maintain, proceed.

**interval** (SYN.) pause, gap.

**intervene** (SYN.) insert, intercede, meddle, inject, introduce, interpose, mediate, interfere, interrupt, intrude. (ANT.) overlook, avoid, disregard.

**intimacy** (SYN.) fellowship, friendship, acquaintance, frankness, familiarity, unreserved, liberty. (ANT.) presumption, distance, haughtiness, constraint, reserve.

**intimate** (SYN.) chummy, confidential, friendly, loving, affectionate, close, familiar, near, personal, private, secret. (ANT.) conventional, formal, ceremonious, distant.

**intimation** (SYN.) reminder, implication, allusion, hint, insinuation. (ANT.) declaration, statement, affirmation.

**intolerant** (SYN.) fanatical, narrow-minded, prejudiced, bigoted, illiberal, dogmatic, biased. (ANT.) tolerant, radical, liberal, progressive, broad-minded, fair.

**intoxicated** (SYN.) inebriated, tipsy, drunk, tight, drunken, high. (ANT.) sober, temperate, clearheaded.

**intrepid** (SYN.) brave, fearless, insolent, abrupt, rude, pushy, adventurous, daring, courageous, prominent, striking, forward, imprudent.

*(ANT.) timid, bashful, flinching, cowardly, retiring.*

**intricate** *(SYN.)* compound, perplexing, complex, involved, complicated. *(ANT.) simple, plain, uncompounded.*

**intrigue** *(SYN.)* design, plot, cabal, machination, stratagem, scheme, attract, charm, interest, captivate.

**intrinsic** *(SYN.)* natural, inherent, inbred, congenital, inborn, native. *(ANT.) extraneous, acquired, external, extrinsic.*

**introduce** *(SYN.)* acquaint, present, submit, present, offer, propose.

**introduction** *(SYN.)* preamble, prelude, beginning, prologue, start, preface. *(ANT.) finale, conclusion, end, epilogue, completion.*

**intrude** *(SYN.)* invade, attack, encroach, trespass, penetrate, infringe, interrupt. *(ANT.) vacate, evacuate, abandon.*

**intruder** *(SYN.)* trespasser, thief, prowler, robber.

**intuition** *(SYN.)* insight, acumen, perspicuity, penetration, discernment, instinct, clairvoyance.

**invade** *(SYN.)* intrude, violate, infringe, attack, penetrate, encroach, trespass. *(ANT.) vacate, abandon, evacuate, relinquish.*

**invalidate** *(SYN.)* annul, cancel, abolish, revoke, abrogate. *(ANT.) promote, restore, sustain, establish, continue.*

**invaluable** *(SYN.)* priceless, precious, valuable. *(ANT.) worthless.*

**invasion** *(SYN.)* assault, onslaught, aggression, attack, intrusion. *(ANT.) surrender, opposition, resistance, defense.*

**invective** *(SYN.)* insult, abuse, disparagement, upbraiding, reproach, defamation, aspersion. *(ANT.) laudation, plaudit, commendation.*

**invent** *(SYN.)* devise, fabricate, design, concoct, frame, conceive, contrive, create, originate, devise. *(ANT.) reproduce, copy, imitate.*

**inventive** *(SYN.)* fanciful, imaginative, visionary, poetical, clever, creative. *(ANT.) unromantic, literal, dull, prosaic.*

**inventiveness** *(SYN.)* cunning, cleverness, ingeniousness, aptitude. *(ANT.) ineptitude, clumsiness, dullness, stupidity.*

**invert** *(SYN.)* upset, turn about, transpose, countermand,

revoke, reverse. *(ANT.) maintain, stabilize, endorse.*

**investigate** *(SYN.)* look, probe, ransack, scrutinize, ferret, examine, seek, explore, search, scour, inspect, study.

**investigation** *(SYN.)* exploration, interrogation, quest, question, scrutiny, inquiry, query, examination, study, research. *(ANT.) inattention, disregard, inactivity, negligence.*

**invigorating** *(SYN.)* bracing, fortifying, vitalizing, stimulating.

**invincible** *(SYN.)* insurmountable, unconquerable, impregnable, indomitable, invulnerable, unassailable. *(ANT.) powerless, weak, vulnerable.*

**invisible** *(SYN.)* indistinguishable, unseen, imperceptible, indiscernible. *(ANT.) evident, visible, seen, perceptible.*

**invite** *(SYN.)* bid, ask, encourage, request, urge.

**inviting** *(SYN.)* appealing, attractive, tempting, luring, alluring. *(ANT.) unattractive, uninviting.*

**involuntary** *(SYN.)* reflex, uncontrolled, automatic, unintentional. *(ANT.) voluntary, willful.*

**involve** *(SYN.)* include, embrace, entangle, envelop, incriminate, embroil, implicate, contain, complicate, confuse. *(ANT.) separate, extricate, disengage.*

**involved** *(SYN.)* compound, intricate, complicated, complex, perplexing. *(ANT.) plain, uncompounded, simple.*

**invulnerable** *(SYN.)* indomitable, unassailable, invincible, unconquerable, insurmountable, impregnable. *(ANT.) weak, puny, powerless, vulnerable.*

**irate** *(SYN.)* incensed, enraged, angry.

**ire** *(SYN.)* indignation, irritation, wrath, anger, animosity, fury, passion, temper, exasperation, petulance, rage. *(ANT.) peace, patience, self-control, forbearance.*

**irk** *(SYN.)* irritate, bother, disturb, pester, trouble, vex, tease, chafe, annoy. *(ANT.) console, accommodate, gratify.*

**irrational** *(SYN.)* inconsistent, preposterous, unreasonable, absurd, foolish, nonsensical, ridiculous. *(ANT.) sensible, sound, rational, consistent, reasonable.*

**irregular** *(SYN.)* eccentric,

unusual, aberrant, devious, abnormal, unnatural. *(ANT.) regular, methodical, fired, usual, ordinary, even.*

**irrelevant** *(SYN.)* foreign, unconnected, remote, alien, strange. *(ANT.) germane, relevant, akin, kindred.*

**irresolute** *(SYN.)* frail, pliant, vacillating, ineffective, wavering, weak, yielding, fragile, pliable. *(ANT.) robust, potent, sturdy, strong, powerful.*

**irresponsible** *(SYN.)* unreliable.

**irritable** *(SYN.)* hasty, hot, peevish, testy, irascible, fiery, snappish, petulant. *(ANT.) composed, tranquil, calm.*

**irritate** *(SYN.)* irk, molest, bother, annoy, tease, disturb, inconvenience, vex, trouble, pester, inflame, chafe. *(ANT.) console, gratify, accommodate, soothe, pacify, calm.*

**irritation** *(SYN.)* chagrin, mortification, vexation, annoyance, exasperation, pique. *(ANT.) pleasure, comfort, gratification, appeasement.*

**isolate** *(SYN.)* detach, segregate, separate, disconnect. *(ANT.) happy, cheerful.*

**isolated** *(SYN.)* lone, single, alone, desolate, secluded, solitary, deserted, sole. *(ANT.) surrounded, accompanied.*

**isolation** *(SYN.)* quarantine, seclusion, separation, solitude, alienation, retirement, segregation, detachment. *(ANT.) fellowship, union, association, communion, connection.*

**issue** *(SYN.)* flow, proceed, result, come, emanate, originate, abound, copy, number, edition, problem, question.

**itemize** *(SYN.)* register, detail, record. *(ANT.) generalize, include, summarize.*

# J

**jab** *(SYN.)* thrust, poke, nudge, prod, shove, jolt, boost, tap, slap, rap, thwack, push.

**jabber** *(SYN.)* mumble, gossip, prattle, chatter, gab, palaver.

**jacent** *(SYN.)* level, flatness, plane, proneness, recline.

**jacinth** *(SYN.)* decoration, ornament, embellishment.

**jack** *(SYN.)* fellow, boy, toiler, guy, man, worker.

**jackal** *(SYN.)* puppet, drone, slave, legman, flunky, slavery, tool, servility, vassal.

**jackass** *(SYN.)* fool, idiot, dope, dunce, ignoramus,

imbecile, ninny, simpleton, blockhead.

**jacket** *(SYN.)* wrapper, envelope, coat, sheath, cover, casing, folder, enclosure.

**jack-of-all-trades** *(SYN.)* man friday, expert, proficient, amateur, adept, handyman, dab, master, specialist, mastermind, generalist.

**jade** *(SYN.)* hussy, wanton, trollop, harlot, common, whore, ignoble, wench, hag, shrew.

**jaded** *(SYN.)* exhausted, bored, tired, fatigued, satiated, weary, hardened.

**jag** *(SYN.)* notch, snag, protuberance, barb, dent, cut, nick, serration, indentation, point.

**jagged** *(SYN.)* crooked, bent, ragged, pointy, notched, aquiline, furcated, serrated. *(ANT.) smooth.*

**jail** *(SYN.)* stockade, prison, reformatory, penitentiary, keep, dungeon, brig, confine, lock up, detain, imprison, hold captive, coop, cage, house of detention, incarcerate.

**jailbird** *(SYN.)* convict, parolee, con, inmate, prisoner.

**jailer** *(SYN.)* guard, keeper, turnkey, warden.

**jam** *(SYN.)* force, pack, ram, crowd, push, wedge, squeeze, stuff, load, cram, press, crush, marmalade, jelly, conserve, preserve.

**jamboree** *(SYN.)* celebration, fete, spree, festival, festivity, carousal.

**jangle** *(SYN.)* rattle, vibrate, clank, clatter, dissonance, discord, quarrel, din, discord.

**janitor** *(SYN.)* custodian, doorkeeper, caretaker, superintendent, gatekeeper.

**jape** *(SYN.)* lampoon, banter, joke, jest, tease, ridicule.

**jar** *(SYN.)* rattle, shake, bounce, jolt.

**jargon** *(SYN.)* speech, idiom, dialect, vernacular, diction, argot, phraseology, language, patois, parlance, slang. *(ANT.) gibberish, babble, nonsense, drivel.*

**jaundiced** *(SYN.)* biased, prejudiced. *(ANT.) fair.*

**jaunt** *(SYN.)* journey, trip, tour, excursion, outing, voyage, expedition.

**jaunty** *(SYN.)* lively, vivacious, buoyant, winsome, frisky, showy, dapper, breezy.

**jazzy** *(SYN.)* garish, vivacious, loud, splashy, exaggerated, flashy.

**jealous** *(SYN.)* covetous, desirous of, envious.

**jealousy** (SYN.) suspicion, envy, resentfulness, greed, covetousness. (ANT.) tolerance, indifference, geniality, liberality.

**jeer** (SYN.) taunt, mock, scoff, deride, make fun of, gibe, sneer. (ANT.) flatter, praise, compliment, laud.

**jeering** (SYN.) mockery, sneering, derision, sarcasm, irony, ridicule.

**jell** (SYN.) finalize, congeal, set, solidify, shape up, take form.

**jeopardize** (SYN.) risk, dare, expose, imperil, chance, venture, conjecture, hazard, endanger. (ANT.) know, guard, determine.

**jerk** (SYN.) quiver, twitch, shake, spasm, jolt, yank, fool.

**jerkwater** (SYN.) remote, hick, backwoods, unimportant, one-horse.

**jest** (SYN.) mock, joke, tease, fun, witticism, quip.

**jester** (SYN.) fool, buffoon, harlequin, clown. (ANT.) sage, genius, scholar.

**jet** (SYN.) squirt, spurt, gush, inky, coalblack, nozzle.

**jettison** (SYN.) heave, discharge, throw, eject, cast off, dismiss.

**jetty** (SYN.) pier, breakwater, bulwark, buttress.

**jewel** (SYN.) ornament, gemstone, gem, bauble, stone.

**jib** (SYN.) shrink, shy, dodge, retreat, balk.

**jig** (SYN.) caper, prance, jiggle, leap, skip.

**jiggle** (SYN.) shimmy, agitate, jerk, twitch, wiggle.

**jilt** (SYN.) abandon, get rid of, reject, desert, forsake, leave.

**jingle** (SYN.) chime, ring, tinkle.

**jinx** (SYN.) hex, whammy, nemesis, curse, evil eye.

**jittery** (SYN.) jumpy, nervous, quivering, shaky, skittish.

**job** (SYN.) toil, business, occupation, post, chore, stint, career, duty, employment, profession, trade, work, situation, labor, assignment, position, undertaking, calling, task.

**jobless** (SYN.) idle, unoccupied, inactive, unemployed.

**jocularity** (SYN.) humor, wit, joke, facetiousness, waggery. (ANT.) sorrow, gravity.

**jocund** (SYN.) mirthful, elated, pleasant, cheerful, merry, gay, jovial, frolicsome.

**jog** (SYN.) gait, trot, sprint, run, lope.

**join** (SYN.) conjoin, unite, attach, accompany, associate,

assemble, fit, couple, combine, fasten, unite, clasp, put together, go with, adjoin, link, connect. (ANT.) separate, disconnect, split, sunder, part, divide, detach.

**joint** (SYN.) link, union, connection, junction, coupling, common, combined, mutual, connected. (ANT.) divided, separate.

**joke** (SYN.) game, jest, caper, prank, anecdote, quip, tease, antic, banter, laugh.

**joker** (SYN.) wisecracker, humorist, comedian, trickster, comic, jester, wit, punster.

**jolly** (SYN.) merry, joyful, gay, happy, sprightly, pleasant, jovial, gleeful, spirited, cheerful, glad. (ANT.) mournful, depressed, sullen, glum.

**jolt** (SYN.) sway, waver, startle, rock, jar, totter, jerk, bounce, quake, bump, shake.

**josh** (SYN.) poke fun at, kid, tease, ridicule.

**jostle** (SYN.) shove, push, bump, thrust, jar, shake.

**jot** (SYN.) note, write, record.

**jounce** (SYN.) bounce, jolt, bump, jostle.

**journey** (SYN.) tour, passage, cruise, voyage, pilgrimage, jaunt, trip, outing, expedition, junket, excursion, travel.

**joust** (SYN.) tournament, contest, skirmish, competition, fight.

**jovial** (SYN.) good-natured, kindly, merry, good-humored, good-hearted, joyful, jolly, gleeful. (ANT.) solemn, sad, serious, grim.

**joy** (SYN.) pleasure, glee, bliss, elation, mirth, felicity, rapture, delight, transport, exultation, gladness, happiness, festivity, satisfaction, merriment, ecstasy. (ANT.) grief, depression, unhappiness, sorrow, misery, gloom, sadness, affliction.

**joyful** (SYN.) gay, lucky, opportune, cheerful, happy, blissful, jovial, merry, gleeful, delighted, glad, contented, fortunate. (ANT.) gloomy, sad, blue, solemn, serious, grim, morose, glum, depressed.

**joyous** (SYN.) jolly, gay, blithe, merry, gleeful, cheerful, jovial. (ANT.) sad, gloomy, sorrowful, melancholy.

**jubilant** (SYN.) exulting, rejoicing, overjoyed, triumphant, gay, elated, delighted. (ANT.) dejected.

**jubilee** (SYN.) gala, holiday, celebration, festival, fete.

**judge** (SYN.) umpire, think, estimate, decide, arbitrator,

condemn, decree, critic, appreciate, adjudicator, determine, arbiter, magistrate, arbitrate, justice, consider, mediate, referee, evaluate.

**judgment** (SYN.) wisdom, perspicacity, discernment, decision, common sense, estimation, verdict, understanding, intelligence, discretion, opinion, sense, discrimination. (ANT.) thoughtlessness, senselessness, arbitrariness.

**judicial** (SYN.) legal, judicatory, forensic.

**judicious** (SYN.) sensible, wise, well-advised, thoughtful. (ANT.) ignorant.

**jug** (SYN.) bottle, jar, flask, flagon, pitcher.

**juice** (SYN.) broth, liquid, sap, distillation, serum, fluid.

**jumble** (SYN.) disarrangement, tumult, agitation, ferment, turmoil, commotion, confuse, mix, muddle, scramble, disorder. (ANT.) peace, arrange, compose, certainty, tranquillity.

**jumbo** (SYN.) huge, big, immense, enormous, giant, colossal, monstrous, mammoth, gigantic, tremendous. (ANT.) miniature, midget, dwarf, small, tiny.

**jump** (SYN.) leap, caper, skip, bound, jerk, vault, hop, spring.

**jumpy** (SYN.) touchy, excitable, nervous, sensitive. (ANT.) tranquil, calm, unruffled.

**junction** (SYN.) coupling, joining, union, crossroads, intersection, weld, connection, linking, meeting, tie-up, seam, joint. (ANT.) separation.

**jungle** (SYN.) woods, thicket, undergrowth, forest, bush.

**junior** (SYN.) secondary, inferior, minor, lower, younger.

**junk** (SYN.) rubbish, scraps, trash, waste, dump, discard, castoffs, debris.

**junky** (SYN.) tawdry, ramshackle, tattered, tacky, shoddy.

**jurisdiction** (SYN.) power, commission, warrant, authority, authorization, sovereignty.

**just** (SYN.) fair, trustworthy, precise, exact, candid, upright, honest, impartial, lawful, rightful, proper, legal, truthful, merely, only, conscientious. (ANT.) tricky, dishonest, unjust, corrupt, lying, deceitful.

**justice** (SYN.) justness, rectitude, equity, law, fairness, impartiality, right. (ANT.)

inequity, wrong, partiality.

**justifiable** (SYN.) allowable, tolerable, admissible, warranted. (ANT.) unsuitable, inadmissible.

**justify** (SYN.) uphold, excuse, defend, acquit, exonerate, absolve, clear, vindicate.

**jut** (SYN.) project, protrude, stick out.

**juvenile** (SYN.) puerile, youthful, childish, youngster, youth, young, child. (ANT.) old, aged, adult, mature.

# K

**kaiser** (SYN.) czar, caesar, caliph, mogul, padishah, tycoon, khan.

**kavass** (SYN.) badel, macebearer, constable.

**keck** (SYN.) vomit, belch, retch.

**keen** (SYN.) clever, cunning, acute, penetrating, exact, severe, shrewd, wily, astute, sharp, bright, intelligent, smart, sharp-witted, witty, cutting, fine, quick. (ANT.) stupid, shallow, dull, blunted, slow, bland, gentle, obtuse, blunt.

**keep** (SYN.) maintain, retain, observe, protect, confine, sustain, continue, preserve, save, guard, restrain, reserve, obey, support, honor, execute, celebrate, conserve, have, tend, detain, commemorate, hold. (ANT.) abandon, disobey, dismiss, discard, ignore, neglect, lose, reject, relinquish.

**keeper** (SYN.) warden, jailer, ranger, guard, turnkey, watchman, escort, custodian.

**keeping** (SYN.) congeniality, uniformity, consentaneousness, conformance, congruity, union.

**keepsake** (SYN.) reminder, memorial, relic, souvenir, memento, hint, remembrance.

**keg** (SYN.) container, drum, tub, barrel, receptacle, reservatory, capsule, cask, tank.

**kelpie** (SYN.) sprite, nixie, naiad, pixy.

**kelson** (SYN.) bottom, sole, toe, foot, root, keel.

**kempt** (SYN.) neat, trim, tidy, spruce, cleaned.

**ken** (SYN.) field, view, vision, range, scope.

**kennel** (SYN.) swarm, flock, covy, drove, herd, pound, doghouse.

**kerchief** (SYN.) neckcloth, handkerchief, scarf, headpiece, babushka.

**kern** *(SYN.)* peasant, carle, serf, tike, tyke, countryman.

**kernel** *(SYN.)* marrow, pith, backbone, soul, heart, core, nucleus.

**ketch** *(SYN.)* lugger, cutter, clipper, ship, barge, sloop.

**kettle** *(SYN.)* pan, caldron, vat, pot, teapot, vessel, receptacle, receiver, tureen.

**key** *(SYN.)* opener, explanation, tone, lead, cause, source, note, pitch, answer, clue.

**keynote** *(SYN.)* core, model, theme, pattern, standard, gist.

**keystone** *(SYN.)* backbone, support.

**khan** *(SYN.)* master, czar, kaiser, padishah, caesar.

**kick** *(SYN.)* punt, remonstrate, boot.

**kickback** *(SYN.)* repercussion, backfire, rebound.

**kickoff** *(SYN.)* beginning, opening, commencement, outset, start.

**kid** *(SYN.)* joke, tease, fool, jest, tot, child.

**kidnap** *(SYN.)* abduct, snatch, shanghai.

**kill** *(SYN.)* execute, put to death, slay, butcher, assassinate, murder, cancel, destroy, slaughter, finish, end, annihilate, massacre. *(ANT.)* save, protect, animate, resuscitate, vivify.

**killing** *(SYN.)* massacre, genocide, slaughter, carnage, butchery, bloodshed.

**killjoy** *(SYN.)* wet blanket, sourpuss, party-pooper.

**kin** *(SYN.)* relatives, family, folks, relations.

**kind** *(SYN.)* humane, affable, compassionate, benevolent, merciful, tender, sympathetic, breed, indulgent, forbearing, kindly, race, good, thoughtful, character, benign, family, sort, species, variety, class, type, gentle. *(ANT.)* unkind, cruel, merciless, severe, mean, inhuman.

**kindle** *(SYN.)* fire, ignite, light, arouse, excite, set afire, stir up, trigger, move, provoke, inflame. *(ANT.)* extinguish, calm.

**kindly** *(SYN.)* warm, kindhearted, kind, warm-hearted. *(ANT.)* mean, cruel.

**kindred** *(SYN.)* family, relations, relatives, consanguinity, kinsfolk, affinity. *(ANT.)* strangers, disconnection.

**kinetic** *(SYN.)* vigorous, active, dynamic, energetic, mobile, forceful.

**king** *(SYN.)* sovereign, ruler, chief, monarch, potentate.

**kingdom** *(SYN.)* realm, empire, monarchy, domain.

**kingly** *(SYN.)* kinglike, imperial, regal, royal, majestic.

**kink** *(SYN.)* twist, curl, quirk, complication.

**kinship** *(SYN.)* lineage, blood, family, stock, relationship.

**kismet** *(SYN.)* fate, end, fortune, destiny.

**kiss** *(SYN.)* pet, caress, fondle, cuddle, osculate, embrace. *(ANT.)* vex, spurn, annoy, tease, buffet.

**kit** *(SYN.)* outfit, collection, furnishings, equipment, rig, gear, set.

**knack** *(SYN.)* cleverness, readiness, deftness, ability, ingenuity, skill, talent, aptitude, know-how, art, adroitness, skillfulness. *(ANT.)* inability, clumsiness, awkwardness, ineptitude.

**knave** *(SYN.)* rogue, rascal, villain, scoundrel.

**knead** *(SYN.)* combine, massage, blend.

**knickknack** *(SYN.)* trinket, bric-a-brac, trifle.

**knife** *(SYN.)* sword, blade.

**knightly** *(SYN.)* valiant, courageous, gallant, chivalrous, noble.

**knit** *(SYN.)* unite, join, mend, fasten, connect, combine, heal.

**knob** *(SYN.)* doorknob, handle, protuberance, bump.

**knock** *(SYN.)* thump, tap, rap, strike, hit, jab, punch, beat, pound, bang, hammer.

**knoll** *(SYN.)* hill, elevation, hump, mound, butte.

**knot** *(SYN.)* cluster, gathering, collection, group, crowd, twist, snarl, tangle.

**know** *(SYN.)* perceive, comprehend, apprehend, recognize, understand, discern, discriminate, ascertain, identify, be aware, distinguish. *(ANT.)* doubt, suspect, dispute.

**knowing** *(SYN.)* sage, smart, wise, clever, sagacious, shrewd.

**knowledge** *(SYN.)* information, wisdom, erudition, learning, apprehension, scholarship, lore, cognizance. *(ANT.)* misunderstanding, ignorance, stupidity, illiteracy.

**knurl** *(SYN.)* gnarl, knot, projection, burl, node, lump.

**kosher** *(SYN.)* permitted, okay, fit, proper, acceptable.

**kowtow** *(SYN.)* stoop, bend, kneel, genuflect, bow.

**kudos** *(SYN.)* acclaim, praise, approbation, approval.

# L

**label** *(SYN.)* mark, tag, title, name, marker, stamp, sticker, ticket, docket, identity.

**labor** *(SYN.)* toil, travail, effort, task, childbirth, work, parturition, striving, workers, effort, industry, workingmen, strive, exertion, employment, drudgery, endeavor. *(ANT.)* recreation, indolence, idleness, leisure.

**laboratory** *(SYN.)* lab, workroom, workshop.

**laborer** *(SYN.)* wage earner, helper, worker, toiler, coolie, blue-collar worker.

**laborious** *(SYN.)* tiring, difficult, hard, burdensome, industrious, painstaking. *(ANT.)* simple, easy, relaxing, restful.

**labyrinth** *(SYN.)* complex, maze, tangle.

**lace** *(SYN.)* openwork, fancywork, embroidery, edging.

**lacerate** *(SYN.)* mangle, tear roughly.

**laceration** *(SYN.)* cut, wound, puncture, gash, lesion, injury.

**lack** *(SYN.)* want, need, shortage, dearth, scarcity, require. *(ANT.)* profusion, quantity, plentifulness.

**lackey** *(SYN.)* yes-man, stooge, flatterer, flunky.

**lacking** *(SYN.)* insufficient, short, deficient, incomplete, defective, scanty. *(ANT.)* satisfactory, enough, ample, sufficient, adequate.

**lackluster** *(SYN.)* dull, pallid, flat, lifeless, drab, dim.

**laconic** *(SYN.)* short, terse, compact, brief, curt, succinct, concise.

**lacquer** *(SYN.)* polish, varnish, gild.

**lad** *(SYN.)* youth, boy, fellow, stripling.

**laden** *(SYN.)* burdened, loaded, weighted.

**ladle** *(SYN.)* scoop, dipper.

**lady** *(SYN.)* matron, woman, dame, gentlewoman.

**ladylike** *(SYN.)* feminine, womanly, maidenly, womanish, female. *(ANT.)* masculine, male, virile, mannish, manly.

**lag** *(SYN.)* dawdle, loiter, linger, poke, dilly-dally, straggle, delay, tarry, slowdown.

**laggard** *(SYN.)* idler, lingerer, slowpoke, dawdler.

**lair** *(SYN.)* retreat, burrow, den, nest, mew, hole.

**lambaste** *(SYN.)* berate, castigate, scold, censure.

**lame** *(SYN.)* feeble, maimed, disabled, crippled, deformed, hobbling, unconvincing, weak, poor, inadequate, halt, defective, limping. *(ANT.)* vigorous, convincing, plausible, athletic, robust, agile, sound.

**lament** *(SYN.)* deplore, wail, bemoan, bewail, regret, grieve, mourning, lamentation, moaning, wailing, weep, mourn, sorrow. *(ANT.)* celebrate, rejoice.

**lamentable** *(SYN.)* unfortunate, deplorable.

**lamp** *(SYN.)* light, beam, illumination, shine, insight, knowledge, understanding, radiance, luminosity, incandescence. *(ANT.)* shadow, darkness, obscurity, gloom.

**lampoon** *(SYN.)* skit, tirade, burlesque, parody, satire.

**lance** *(SYN.)* cut, pierce, perforate, stab, puncture, impale, knife.

**land** *(SYN.)* earth, continent, ground, soil, domain, estate, field, realm, plain, surface, arrive, descend, country, island, region, alight, shore, sod, tract, farm.

**landlord** *(SYN.)* owner, landholder, landowner, proprietor.

**landmark** *(SYN.)* keystone, monument, milestone, point, cornerstone.

**landscape** *(SYN.)* panorama, environs, countryside, scenery, scene.

**landslide** *(SYN.)* rockfall, glissade, avalanche.

**lane** *(SYN.)* alley, way, road, path, aisle, pass, channel, avenue, artery, passage.

**language** *(SYN.)* dialect, tongue, speech, lingo, jargon, cant, diction, idiom, patter, phraseology, vernacular, words, lingo, talk, slang. *(ANT.)* gibberish, nonsense, babble, drivel.

**languid** *(SYN.)* feeble, drooping, irresolute, debilitated, dull, lethargic, weak, faint, listless, wearied. *(ANT.)* forceful, strong, vigorous.

**languish** *(SYN.)* decline, sink, droop, wither, waste, fail, wilt, weaken. *(ANT.)* revive, rejuvenate, refresh, renew.

**languor** *(SYN.)* weariness, depression, torpor, inertia, apathy.

**lanky** *(SYN.)* skinny, gaunt, lean, scrawny, slender, thin. *(ANT.)* chunky, stocky, obese.

**lantern** *(SYN.)* torch, light, lamp, flashlight.

**lap** *(SYN.)* drink, lick, fold over.

**lapse** *(SYN.)* decline, sink, go down, slump.

**larceny** *(SYN.)* pillage, robbery,

stealing, theft, burglary, plunder.

**lard** *(SYN.)* grease, fat.

**large** *(SYN.)* great, vast, colossal, ample, extensive, capacious, sizable, broad, massive, grand, immense, big, enormous, huge, giant, mammoth, wide. *(ANT.) tiny, little, short, small.*

**largely** *(SYN.)* chiefly, mainly, principally, mostly.

**lariat** *(SYN.)* lasso, rope.

**lark** *(SYN.)* fling, frolic, play, fun, spree, joke, revel, celebration.

**lascivious** *(SYN.)* lecherous, raunchy, lustful, wanton, lewd.

**lash** *(SYN.)* thong, whip, rod, cane, blow, strike, hit, beat, knout.

**lass** *(SYN.)* maiden, girl, damsel. *(ANT.) woman, lad.*

**lasso** *(SYN.)* lariat, rope, noose, snare.

**last** *(SYN.)* terminal, final, ultimate, remain, endure, concluding, latest, utmost, end, conclusive, hindmost, continue, extreme. *(ANT.) first, initial, beginning, opening, starring, foremost.*

**latch** *(SYN.)* clasp, hook, fastener, lock, closing, seal, catch.

**late** *(SYN.)* overdue, tardy, behind, advanced, delayed, new, slow, recent. *(ANT.) timely, early.*

**lately** *(SYN.)* recently, yesterday.

**latent** *(SYN.)* potential, undeveloped, unseen, dormant, secret, concealed, inactive, hidden, obscured, covered, quiescent. *(ANT.) visible, evident, conspicuous, explicit, manifest.*

**lateral** *(SYN.)* sideways, glancing, tangential, marginal, skirting, side.

**lather** *(SYN.)* suds, foam, froth.

**latitude** *(SYN.)* range, scope, freedom, extent.

**latter** *(SYN.)* more recent, later.

**lattice** *(SYN.)* grating, screen, frame, trellis, openwork, framework, grid.

**laud** *(SYN.)* commend, praise, extol, glorify, compliment. *(ANT.) criticize, belittle.*

**laudable** *(SYN.)* creditable, praiseworthy, commendable, admirable.

**laudation** *(SYN.)* applause, compliment, flattery, praise, commendation, acclaim, extolling, glorification. *(ANT.) criticizing, condemnation,*

reproach, disparagement, censure.

**laugh** *(SYN.)* chuckle, giggle, snicker, cackle, titter, grin, smile, roar, guffaw, jeer, mock.

**laughable** *(SYN.)* funny, amusing, comical, humorous, ridiculous.

**launch** *(SYN.)* drive, fire, propel, start, begin, originate, set afloat, initiate. *(ANT.) finish, stop, terminate.*

**launder** *(SYN.)* bathe, wash, scrub, scour.

**laurels** *(SYN.)* glory, distinction, recognition, award, commendation, reward, honor.

**lavatory** *(SYN.)* toilet, washroom, bathroom, latrine.

**lavish** *(SYN.)* squander, waste, dissipate, scatter, abundant, free, plentiful, liberal, extravagant, ample, wear out, prodigal, generous, spend. *(ANT.) economize, save, conserve, accumulate, sparing, stingy, preserve.*

**law** *(SYN.)* decree, formula, statute, act, rule, ruling, standard, principle, ordinance, proclamation, regulation, order, edict.

**lawful** *(SYN.)* legal, permissible, allowable, legitimate, authorized, constitutional, rightful. *(ANT.) prohibited, criminal, illicit, illegal, illegitimate.*

**lawless** *(SYN.)* uncivilized, uncontrolled, wild, savage, untamed, violent. *(ANT.) obedient, law-abiding, tame.*

**lawlessness** *(SYN.)* chaos, anarchy.

**lawn** *(SYN.)* grass, meadow, turf.

**lawyer** *(SYN.)* counsel, attorney, counselor.

**lax** *(SYN.)* slack, loose, careless, vague, lenient, lazy. *(ANT.) firm, rigid.*

**lay** *(SYN.)* mundane, worldly, temporal, place, dispose, bet, wager, hazard, risk, stake, site, earthly, profane, laic, arrange, location, put, set, ballad, deposit, position, song, secular. *(ANT.) spiritual, unworldly, remove, misplace, disturb, mislay, disarrange, ecclesiastical, religious.*

**lay off** *(SYN.)* discharge, bounce, fire, dismiss.

**layout** *(SYN.)* plan, arrangement, design.

**lazy** *(SYN.)* slothful, supine, idle, inactive, sluggish, inert, indolent, torpid. *(ANT.) alert, ambitious, forceful, diligent, active, assiduous.*

**lea** *(SYN.)* pasture, meadow.

**leach** *(SYN.)* remove, extract, seep, dilute, wash out.

**lead** *(SYN.)* regulate, conduct, guide, escort, direct, supervise, command, come first, steer, control. *(ANT.) follow.*

**leader** *(SYN.)* master, ruler, captain, chief, commander, principal, director, head, chieftain. *(ANT.) follower, servant, disciple, subordinate, attendant.*

**leading** *(SYN.)* dominant, foremost, principal, first, main, primary.

**league** *(SYN.)* entente, partnership, association, confederacy, coalition, society, alliance, federation, union. *(ANT.) separation, schism.*

**leak** *(SYN.)* dribble, flow, drip, opening, perforation.

**lean** *(SYN.)* rely, tilt, slim, slender, slope, incline, tend, trust, bend, tendency, slant, depend, spare, scant, lanky, thin, meager, inclination, narrow, sag. *(ANT.) rise, heavy, fat, erect, straighten, portly, raise.*

**leaning** *(SYN.)* trend, proclivity, bias, tendency, bent, predisposition, proneness. *(ANT.) disinclination, aversion.*

**leap** *(SYN.)* vault, skip, caper, dive, hurdle, jump, bound, start, hop, plunge, spring.

**learn** *(SYN.)* gain, find out, memorize, acquire, determine.

**learned** *(SYN.)* erudite, knowing, enlightened, deep, wise, discerning, scholarly, intelligent, educated, sagacious. *(ANT.) simple, uneducated, ignorant, illiterate, unlettered, foolish.*

**learning** *(SYN.)* science, education, lore, apprehension, wisdom, knowledge, scholarship, erudition. *(ANT.) misunderstanding, ignorance, stupidity.*

**lease** *(SYN.)* charter, let, rent, engage.

**leash** *(SYN.)* chain, strap, shackle, collar.

**least** *(SYN.)* minutest, smallest, tiniest, minimum, fewest, slightest. *(ANT.) most.*

**leave** *(SYN.)* give up, retire, desert, abandon, withdraw, relinquish, will, depart, quit, liberty, renounce, go, bequeath, consent, allowance, permission, freedom, forsake. *(ANT.) come, stay, arrive, tarry, remain, abide.*

**lecherous** *(SYN.)* lustful, sensual, carnal, lascivious.

**lecture** *(SYN.)* talk, discussion, lesson, instruct, speech, conference, sermon, report, recitation, address, oration, discourse. *(ANT.) writing, meditation, correspondence.*

**ledge** *(SYN.)* eaves, ridge, shelf, rim, edge.

**lee** *(SYN.)* shelter, asylum, sanctuary, haven.

**leech** *(SYN.)* barnacle, bloodsucker, parasite.

**leer** *(SYN.)* eye, grimace, ogle, wink, squint.

**leeway** *(SYN.)* reserve, allowance, elbowroom, slack, clearance.

**leftovers** *(SYN.)* scraps, remains, residue, remainder.

**legacy** *(SYN.)* bequest, inheritance, heirloom.

**legal** *(SYN.)* legitimate, rightful, honest, allowable, allowed, permissible, lawful, permitted, authorized. *(ANT.) illicit, illegal, prohibited, illegitimate.*

**legalize** *(SYN.)* authorize, ordain, approve, sanction.

**legate** *(SYN.)* envoy, agent, representative, emissary.

**legend** *(SYN.)* saga, fable, allegory, myth, parable, tale, story, folklore, fiction, chronicle. *(ANT.) history, facts.*

**legendary** *(SYN.)* fictitious, traditional, mythical, imaginary, fanciful.

**legible** *(SYN.)* plain, readable, clear, distinct. *(ANT.) illegible.*

**legion** *(SYN.)* outfit, unit, troop, regiment, company, battalion, force, army, team, division.

**legislation** *(SYN.)* resolution, ruling, lawmaking, regulation, enactment, statute, decree.

**legislator** *(SYN.)* statesman, congressman, senator, politician, lawmaker.

**legitimate** *(SYN.)* true, real, bonafide, lawful, proper, right, valid, correct, unadulterated, authentic, rightful, legal, sincere. *(ANT.) sham, counterfeit, artificial, false.*

**leisure** *(SYN.)* respite, intermission, ease, relaxation, rest, calm, tranquillity, recreation, peace, pause. *(ANT.) motion, commotion, tumult, agitation, disturbance.*

**leisurely** *(SYN.)* sluggish, laggard, unhurried, relaxed, casual, dawdling, slow, deliberate. *(ANT.) hurried, swift, pressed, rushed, forced, fast, speedy, quick.*

**lend** *(SYN.)* entrust, advance, confer.

**length** *(SYN.)* reach, measure,

extent, distance, span, longness, stretch.

**lengthen** *(SYN.)* stretch, prolong, draw, reach, increase, grow, protract, extend. *(ANT.) shrink, contract, shorten.*

**leniency** *(SYN.)* grace, pity, compassion, mildness, charity, mercy, clemency. *(ANT.) vengeance, punishment, cruelty.*

**lenient** *(SYN.)* tender, humane, clement, tolerant, compassionate, merciful, relaxed, forgiving, gentle, mild, lax, kind. *(ANT.) unfeeling, pitiless, brutal, remorseless.*

**leprechaun** *(SYN.)* gnome, imp, goblin, fairy, elf, sprite, banshee.

**lesion** *(SYN.)* wound, blemish, sore, trauma, injury.

**less** *(SYN.)* fewer, smaller, reduced, negative, stinted. *(ANT.) more.*

**lessen** *(SYN.)* shorten, reduce, deduct, subtract, curtail, diminish, shrink, dwindle, decline, instruction, teaching, remove, decrease. *(ANT.) swell, grow, enlarge, increase, expand, multiply, amplify.*

**lesson** *(SYN.)* exercise, session, class, assignment, section, recitation.

**let** *(SYN.)* admit, hire out, contract, allow, permit, consent, leave, grant, rent. *(ANT.) deny.*

**letdown** *(SYN.)* disillusionment, disappointment.

**lethal** *(SYN.)* mortal, dangerous, deadly, fatal, devastating.

**lethargic** *(SYN.)* sluggish, logy, slow, listless, phlegmatic, lazy. *(ANT.) vivacious, energetic.*

**lethargy** *(SYN.)* numbness, stupor, daze, insensibility, torpor. *(ANT.) wakefulness, liveliness, activity, readiness.*

**letter** *(SYN.)* note, mark, message, character, symbol, sign, memorandum.

**letup** *(SYN.)* slowdown, slackening, lessening, abatement, reduction.

**levee** *(SYN.)* dike, breakwater, dam, embankment.

**level** *(SYN.)* smooth, even, plane, equivalent, uniform, horizontal, equal, flatten, equalize, raze, demolish, flat. *(ANT.) uneven, sloping, hilly, broken.*

**level-headed** *(SYN.)* reasonable, sensible, calm, collected, cool.

**leverage** *(SYN.)* clout, power, influence, weight, rank.

**levity** *(SYN.)* humor, triviality, giddiness, hilarity, fun, frivolity.

**levy** *(SYN.)* tax, duty, tribute, rate, assessment, exaction, charge, custom. *(ANT.) wages, remuneration, gift.*

**lewd** *(SYN.)* indecent, smutty, course, gross, disgusting, impure. *(ANT.) pure, decent, refined.*

**liability** *(SYN.)* indebtedness, answerability, obligation, vulnerability.

**liable** *(SYN.)* answerable, responsible, likely, exposed to, subject, amenable, probable, accountable. *(ANT.) immune, exempt, independent.*

**liaison** *(SYN.)* union, coupling, link, connection, alliance.

**liar** *(SYN.)* fibber, falsifier, storyteller, fabricator, prevaricator.

**libel** *(SYN.)* slander, calumny, vilification, aspersion, defamation. *(ANT.) defense, praise, applause, flattery.*

**liberal** *(SYN.)* large, generous, unselfish, openhanded, broad, tolerant, kind, unprejudiced, open-minded, lavish, plentiful, ample, abundant, extravagant, extensive. *(ANT.) restricted, conservative, stingy.*

**liberality** *(SYN.)* kindness, philanthropy, beneficence, humanity, altruism, benevolence, generosity, charity. *(ANT.) selfishness, cruelty, malevolence.*

**liberate** *(SYN.)* emancipate, loose, release, let go, deliver, free, discharge. *(ANT.) subjugate, oppress, jail, confine, restrict, imprison.*

**liberated** *(SYN.)* loose, frank, emancipated, careless, liberal, freed, autonomous, exempt, familiar. *(ANT.) subject, clogged, restricted, impeded.*

**liberty** *(SYN.)* permission, independence, autonomy, license, privilege, emancipation, self-government, freedom. *(ANT.) constraint, imprisonment, bondage, captivity.*

**license** *(SYN.)* liberty, freedom, liberation, permission, exemption, authorization, warrant, allow, consent, permit, sanction, approval, unrestraint. *(ANT.) servitude, constraint, bondage, necessity.*

**lick** *(SYN.)* taste, lap, lave.

**lid** *(SYN.)* top, cover, cap, plug, cork, stopper.

**lie** *(SYN.)* untruth, fib, illusion, delusion, falsehood, fiction, equivocation, prevarication, repose, location, perjury, misinform, site, recline, similitude. *(ANT.) variance, truth, difference.*

**life** *(SYN.)* sparkle, being, spirit, vivacity, animation, buoyancy, vitality, existence, biography, energy, liveliness, vigor. *(ANT.) demise, lethargy, death, languor.*

**lift** *(SYN.)* hoist, pick up, elevate, raise, heft.

**light** *(SYN.)* brightness, illumination, beam, gleam, lamp, knowledge, brilliance, fixture, bulb, candle, fire, ignite, burn, dawn, incandescence, flame, airy, unsubstantial, dainty, luminosity, shine, radiance, giddy, weightless. *(ANT.) darkness, gloom, shadow, extinguish, darken.*

**lighten** *(SYN.)* diminish, unburden, reduce, brighten.

**light-headed** *(SYN.)* giddy, silly, dizzy, frivolous. *(ANT.) sober, clear-headed, rational.*

**lighthearted** *(SYN.)* carefree, merry, gay, cheerful, happy, glad. *(ANT.) somber, sad, serious, melancholy.*

**like** *(SYN.)* fancy, esteem, adore, love, admire, care for, prefer, cherish. *(ANT.) disapprove, loathes, hate, dislike.*

**likely** *(SYN.)* liable, reasonable, probable, possible.

**likeness** *(SYN.)* similarity, resemblance, representation, image, portrait. *(ANT.) difference.*

**likewise** *(SYN.)* besides, as well, also, too, similarly.

**liking** *(SYN.)* fondness, affection, partiality. *(ANT.) antipathy, dislike.*

**limb** *(SYN.)* arm, leg, member, appendage, part, bough.

**limber** *(SYN.)* bending, flexible, elastic, pliable. *(ANT.) inflexible, stiff.*

**limbo** *(SYN.)* exile, banishment, purgatory.

**limelight** *(SYN.)* spotlight, notice, notoriety, fame, prominence.

**limerick** *(SYN.)* jingle, rhyme.

**limit** *(SYN.)* terminus, bound, extent, confine, border, restriction, boundary, restraint, edge, frontier, check, end, limitation. *(ANT.) endlessness, vastness, boundlessness.*

**limn** *(SYN.)* depict, portray, sketch, paint, illustrate.

**limp** *(SYN.)* soft, flabby, drooping, walk, limber, supple, flexible, hobble, stagger. *(ANT.) stiff.*

**limpid** *(SYN.)* clear, open, transparent, unobstructed. *(ANT.) cloudy.*

**line** *(SYN.)* row, file, series, array, sequence, wire, seam, wrinkle, crease, boundary, arrangement, kind, type, division.

**lineage** *(SYN.)* race, family, tribe, nation, strain, folk, people, ancestry, clan.

**linger** *(SYN.)* wait, rest, bide, delay, dawdle, stay, loiter, remain, dilly-dally, tarry. *(ANT.) leave, expedite.*

**lingo** *(SYN.)* vernacular, dialect, language, jargon, speech.

**link** *(SYN.)* unite, connector, loop, couple, attach, connective, connection, coupling, juncture, bond. *(ANT.) separate, disconnect, split.*

**lip** *(SYN.)* edge, brim, rim.

**liquid** *(SYN.)* watery, fluent, fluid, flowing. *(ANT.) solid, congealed.*

**liquidate** *(SYN.)* pay off, settle, defray.

**liquor** *(SYN.)* spirits, alcohol, drink, booze.

**lissome** *(SYN.)* nimble, quick, lively, flexible, agile.

**list** *(SYN.)* roll, register, slate, series.

**listen** *(SYN.)* overhear, attend to, heed, hear, list, hearken. *(ANT.) ignore, scorn, disregard, reject.*

**listless** *(SYN.)* uninterested, tired, lethargic, unconcerned, apathetic. *(ANT.) active.*

**literal** *(SYN.)* exact, verbatim, precise, strict, faithful.

**literally** *(SYN.)* actually, exactly, really.

**literate** *(SYN.)* informed, educated, learned, intelligent, versed, knowledgeable. *(ANT.) unread, illiterate, ignorant, unlettered.*

**literature** *(SYN.)* books, writings, publications.

**lithe** *(SYN.)* supple, flexible, bending, limber, pliable. *(ANT.) stiff.*

**litigious** *(SYN.)* quarrelsome, disputatious, argumentative.

**litter** *(SYN.)* rubbish, trash, scatter, clutter, strew, debris, rubble, disorder.

**little** *(SYN.)* tiny, petty, miniature, diminutive, puny, wee, significant, small, short, brief, bit, trivial. *(ANT.) huge, large, big, long, immense.*

**liturgy** *(SYN.)* ritual, sacrament, worship, service.

**live** *(SYN.)* dwell, reside, abide, survive, exist, alive, occupy, stay, active, surviving. *(ANT.) die.*

**livelihood** *(SYN.)* keep, sustenance, support, subsistence, job, trade, profession, vocation.

**lively** *(SYN.)* blithe,

vivaciousness, clear, vivid, active, frolicsome, brisk, fresh, animated, energetic, live, spry, vigorous, quick, nimble, bright, exciting, supple. (ANT.) stale, dull, listless, slow, vapid.

**livestock** (SYN.) animals, cattle.

**livid** (SYN.) grayish, furious, pale, enraged.

**living** (SYN.) support, livelihood, existent, alive.

**load** (SYN.) oppress, trouble, burden, weight, freight, afflict, encumber, pack, shipment, cargo, lade, tax. (ANT.) lighten, console, unload, mitigate, empty, ease.

**loafer** (SYN.) loiterer, bum, idler, sponger, deadbeat.

**loan** (SYN.) credit, advance, lend.

**loath** (SYN.) reluctant, unwilling, opposed.

**loathe** (SYN.) dislike, despise, hate, abhor, detest, abominate. (ANT.) love, approve, like, admire.

**loathsome** (SYN.) foul, vile, detestable, revolting, abominable, atrocious, offensive, odious. (ANT.) pleasant, commendable, alluring, agreeable, delightful.

**lob** (SYN.) toss, hurl, pitch, throw, heave.

**lobby** (SYN.) foyer, entry, entrance, vestibule, passageway, entryway.

**local** (SYN.) limited, regional, restricted.

**locality** (SYN.) nearness, neighborhood, district, vicinity. (ANT.) remoteness.

**locate** (SYN.) discover, find, unearth, site, situate, place.

**located** (SYN.) found, residing, positioned, situated, placed.

**location** (SYN.) spot, locale, station, locality, situation, place, area, site, vicinity, position, zone, region.

**lock** (SYN.) curl, hook, bolt, braid, ringlet, plait, close, latch, tuft, fastening, bar, hasp, fasten, tress. (ANT.) open.

**locker** (SYN.) wardrobe, closet, cabinet, chest.

**locket** (SYN.) case, lavaliere, pendant.

**locomotion** (SYN.) movement, travel, transit, motion.

**locution** (SYN.) discourse, cadence, manner, accent.

**lodge** (SYN.) cabin, cottage, hut, club, chalet, society, room, reside, dwell, live, occupy, inhabit, abide, board, fix, settle.

**lodger** (SYN.) guest, tenant, boarder, occupant.

**lofty** (SYN.) high, stately, grandiose, towering, elevated, exalted, sublime, majestic, proud, grand, tall, pompous. (ANT.) undignified, lowly, common, ordinary.

**log** (SYN.) lumber, wood, board, register, record, album, account, journal, timber.

**logical** (SYN.) strong, effective, telling, convincing, reasonable, sensible, rational, sane, sound, cogent. (ANT.) crazy, illogical, irrational, unreasonable, weak.

**logy** (SYN.) tired, inactive, lethargic, sleepy, weary.

**loiter** (SYN.) idle, linger, wait, stay, tarry, dilly-dally, dawdle.

**loll** (SYN.) hang, droop, recline, repose, relax.

**lone** (SYN.) lonely, sole, unaided, single, deserted, isolated, secluded, apart, alone, solitary. (ANT.) surrounded, accompanied.

**loneliness** (SYN.) solitude, isolation, seclusion, alienation.

**lonely** (SYN.) unaided, isolated, single, solitary, lonesome, unaccompanied, deserted, alone, desolate. (ANT.) surrounded, attended.

**loner** (SYN.) recluse, maverick, outsider, hermit.

**lonesome** (SYN.) secluded, remote, unpopulated, barren, empty, desolate.

**long** (SYN.) lengthy, prolonged, wordy, elongated, lingering, drawn out, lasting, protracted, extensive, length, prolix, far-reaching, extended. (ANT.) terse, concise, abridged, short.

**long-standing** (SYN.) persistent, established.

**long-winded** (SYN.) boring, dull, wordy. (ANT.) curt, terse.

**look** (SYN.) gaze, witness, seem, eye, behold, see, watch, scan, view, appear, stare, discern, glance, examine, examination, peep, expression, appearance, regard, study, contemplation, survey. (ANT.) overlook, hide, avert, miss.

**loom** (SYN.) emerge, appear, show up.

**loop** (SYN.) ringlet, noose, spiral, fastener.

**loose** (SYN.) untied, unbound, lax, vague, unrestrained, dissolute, limp, undone, baggy, disengaged, indefinite, slack, careless, heedless, unfastened, free, wanton. (ANT.) restrained, steady, fastened, secure, tied, firm, fast, definite, inhibited.

**loosen** (SYN.) untie, undo, loose, unchain. (ANT.) tie, tighten, secure.

**loot** (SYN.) booty, plunder, take, steal, rob, sack, rifle, pillage, ravage, devastate.

**lope** (SYN.) run, race, bound, gallop.

**lopsided** (SYN.) unequal, twisted, uneven, askew, distorted.

**loquacious** (SYN.) garrulous, wordy, profuse, chatty, verbose.

**lord** (SYN.) peer, ruler, proprietor, nobleman, master, owner, boss, governor.

**lore** (SYN.) learning, knowledge, wisdom, stories, legends, beliefs, teachings.

**lose** (SYN.) misplace, flop, fail, sacrifice, forfeit, mislay, vanish, surrender. (ANT.) succeed, locate, place, win, discover, find.

**loss** (SYN.) injury, damage, want, hurt, need, bereavement, trouble, death, failure, deficiency.

**lost** (SYN.) dazed, wasted, astray, forfeited, preoccupied, used, adrift, bewildered, missing, distracted, consumed, misspent, absorbed, confused, mislaid, gone, destroyed. (ANT.) found, anchored.

**lot** (SYN.) result, destiny, bunch, many, amount, fate, cluster, group, sum, portion, outcome, number, doom, issue.

**lotion** (SYN.) cosmetic, salve, balm, cream.

**lottery** (SYN.) wager, chance, drawing, raffle.

**loud** (SYN.) vociferous, noisy, resounding, stentorian, clamorous, sonorous, thunderous, shrill, blaring, roaring, deafening. (ANT.) soft, inaudible, murmuring, subdued, quiet, dulcet.

**lounge** (SYN.) idle, loaf, laze, sofa, couch, davenport, relax, rest, lobby, salon, divan.

**louse** (SYN.) scoundrel, knave, cad, rat.

**lousy** (SYN.) revolting, grimy, rotten, dirty, disgusting.

**lovable** (SYN.) charming, attractive, delightful, amiable, sweet, cuddly, likeable.

**love** (SYN.) attachment, endearment, affection, adoration, liking, devotion, warmth, tenderness, friendliness, adore, worship, like, cherish, fondness. (ANT.) loathing, detest, indifference, dislike, hate, hatred.

**loveliness** (SYN.) grace, pulchritude, elegance, charm, attractiveness, comeliness, fairness, beauty. (ANT.) ugliness, eyesore, disfigurement, deformity.

**lovely** (SYN.) handsome, fair, charming, pretty, attractive, delightful, beautiful, beauteous, exquisite, comely. (ANT.) ugly, unsightly, homely, foul, hideous, repulsive.

**lover** (SYN.) fiancé, suitor, courter, sweetheart, beau.

**loving** (SYN.) close, intimate, confidential, affectionate, friendly. (ANT.) formal, conventional, ceremonious, distant.

**low** (SYN.) mean, vile, despicable, vulgar, abject, groveling, contemptible, lesser, menial. (ANT.) righteous, lofty, esteemed, noble.

**lower** (SYN.) subordinate, minor, secondary, quiet, soften, disgrace, degrade, decrease, reduce, diminish, inferior. (ANT.) greater, superior, increase, better.

**loyal** (SYN.) earnest, ardent, addicted, inclined, faithful, devoted, affectionate, prone, fond, patriotic, dependable, true. (ANT.) indisposed, detached, disloyal, traitorous, untrammeled.

**loyalty** (SYN.) devotion, steadfastness, constancy, faithfulness, fidelity, patriotism, allegiance. (ANT.) treachery, falseness, disloyalty.

**lubricate** (SYN.) oil, grease, anoint.

**lucent** (SYN.) radiant, beaming, vivid, illuminated, lustrous.

**lucid** (SYN.) plain, visible, clear, intelligible, unmistakable, transparent, limpid, translucent, open, shining, light. (ANT.) unclear, vague, obscure.

**luck** (SYN.) chance, fortunate, fortune, lot, fate, fluke, destiny, karma. (ANT.) misfortune.

**lucrative** (SYN.) well-paying, profitable, high-paying, productive, beneficial.

**ludicrous** (SYN.) absurd, ridiculous, preposterous.

**lug** (SYN.) pull, haul, drag, tug.

**luggage** (SYN.) bags, valises, baggage, suitcases, trunks.

**lugubrious** (SYN.) mournful, sad, gloomy, somber, melancholy.

**lukewarm** (SYN.) unenthusiastic, tepid, spiritless, detached, apathetic, mild.

**lull** (SYN.) quiet, calm, soothe, rest, hush, stillness, pause, break, intermission.

**lumber** (SYN.) logs, timber,

wood.

**luminous** *(SYN.)* beaming, lustrous, shining, glowing, gleaming, bright, light. *(ANT.) murky, dull, dark.*

**lummox** *(SYN.)* yokel, oaf, bumpkin, clown, klutz.

**lump** *(SYN.)* swelling, protuberance, mass, chunk, hunk, bump.

**lunacy** *(SYN.)* derangement, madness, aberration, psychosis, craziness. *(ANT.) stability, rationality.*

**lunge** *(SYN.)* charge, stab, attack, thrust, push.

**lurch** *(SYN.)* topple, sway, toss, roll, rock, tip, pitch.

**lure** *(SYN.)* draw, tug, drag, entice, attraction, haul, attract, temptation, persuade, pull, draw on, allure. *(ANT.) drive, alienate, propel.*

**lurid** *(SYN.)* sensational, terrible, melodramatic, startling.

**lurk** *(SYN.)* sneak, hide, prowl, slink, creep.

**luscious** *(SYN.)* savory, delightful, juicy, sweet, pleasing, delectable, palatable, delicious, tasty. *(ANT.) unsavory, nauseous, acrid.*

**lush** *(SYN.)* tender, succulent, ripe, juicy. *(ANT.) dry, arrid, barren.*

**lust** *(SYN.)* longing, desire, passion, appetite, craving, aspiration, urge.

**lusty** *(SYN.)* healthy, strong, mighty, powerful, sturdy, strapping, hale, hardy. *(ANT.) weak.*

**luxuriant** *(SYN.)* abundant, flourishing, dense, lush, rich.

**luxurious** *(SYN.)* rich, lavish, deluxe, elaborate, fancy, opulent, splendid. *(ANT.) simple, crude, sparse.*

**luxury** *(SYN.)* frills, comfort, extravagance, elegance, splendor. *(ANT.) poverty.*

**lyric** *(SYN.)* musical, text, words, libretto.

**lyrical** *(SYN.)* poetic, musical.

**luster** *(SYN.)* shine, gleam, gloss, sparkle, reflection.

# M

**macabre** *(SYN.)* ghastly, grim, horrible, gruesome.

**macala** *(SYN.)* mole, patch, freckle, spot.

**maceration** *(SYN.)* dilution, washing.

**machination** *(SYN.)* hoax, swindle, cardsharking, cunning, plot, cabal, conspiracy.

**machinator** *(SYN.)* strategist, schemer.

**machine** *(SYN.)* motor, mechanism, device, contrivance.

**machinist** *(SYN.)* engineer.

**macilent** *(SYN.)* gaunt, lean, lank, meager, emaciated.

**mactation** *(SYN.)* immolation, self-immolation, infanticide.

**maculate** *(SYN.)* bespot, stipple.

**maculation** *(SYN.)* irritation, striae, iridescence, spottiness.

**mad** *(SYN.)* incensed, crazy, insane, angry, furious, delirious, provoked, enraged, demented, maniacal, exasperated, wrathful, crazy, deranged. *(ANT.) sane, calm, healthy, rational, lucid, cheerful, happy.*

**madam** *(SYN.)* dame, woman, lady, matron, mistress.

**madden** *(SYN.)* anger, annoy, infuriate, enrage, provoke, aspirate, outrage. *(ANT.) please, mollify, calm.*

**madness** *(SYN.)* derangement, delirium, aberration, mania, insanity, craziness, frenzy, psychosis.

**maelstrom** *(SYN.)* surge, rapids, eddy, white water, riptide.

**magazine** *(SYN.)* journal, periodical, arsenal, armory.

**magic** *(SYN.)* sorcery, wizardry, charm, legerdemain, enchantment, black art, necromancy, conjuring.

**magical** *(SYN.)* mystical, marvelous, magic, miraculous, bewitching, spellbinding.

**magician** *(SYN.)* conjuror, sorcerer, wizard, witch, artist, trickster.

**magistrate** *(SYN.)* judge, adjudicator.

**magnanimous** *(SYN.)* giving, bountiful, beneficent, unselfish. *(ANT.) stingy, greedy, selfish.*

**magnate** *(SYN.)* leader, bigwig, tycoon, chief, giant.

**magnet** *(SYN.)* enticer, enticement, lure, temptation.

**magnetic** *(SYN.)* pulling, attractive, alluring, drawing, enthralling, seductive.

**magnetism** *(SYN.)* allure, irresistibility, attraction, appeal.

**magnificence** *(SYN.)* luxury, grandeur, splendor, majesty, dynamic, mesmerizing.

**magnificent** *(SYN.)* rich, lavish, luxurious, splendid, wonderful, extraordinary, impressive. *(ANT.) simple, plain.*

**magnify** *(SYN.)* heighten, exaggerate, amplify, expand, stretch, caricature, increase, enhance. *(ANT.) compress, understate, depreciate, belittle.*

**magnitude** *(SYN.)* mass, bigness, size, area, volume, dimensions, greatness, extent, measure, importance, consequence, significance.

**maid** *(SYN.)* chambermaid, servant, maidservant.

**maiden** *(SYN.)* original, foremost, first, damsel, lass, miss.

**mail** *(SYN.)* dispatch, send, letters, post, correspondence.

**maim** *(SYN.)* disable, cripple, hurt, wound, injure, mangle, mutilate, incapacitate.

**main** *(SYN.)* essential, chief, highest, principal, first, leading, cardinal, supreme, foremost. *(ANT.) supplemental, subordinate, auxiliary.*

**mainstay** *(SYN.)* buttress, pillar, refuge, reinforcement, support, backbone.

**maintain** *(SYN.)* claim, support, uphold, defend, vindicate, sustain, continue, allege, contend, preserve, affirm, keep, justify, keep up. *(ANT.) neglect, oppose, discontinue, resist, deny.*

**maintenance** *(SYN.)* subsistence, livelihood, living, support, preservation, upkeep.

**majestic** *(SYN.)* magnificent, stately, noble, august, grand, imposing, sublime, lofty, high, grandiose, dignified, royal, kingly, princely, regal. *(ANT.) humble, lowly, undignified, common, ordinary.*

**majesty** *(SYN.)* grandeur, dignity, nobility, splendor, distinction, eminence.

**major** *(SYN.)* important, superior, larger, chief, greater, uppermost. *(ANT.) inconsequential, minor.*

**make** *(SYN.)* execute, cause, produce, establish, assemble, create, shape, compel, fashion, construct, build, fabricate, manufacture, form, become. *(ANT.) unmake, break, undo, demolish.*

**make-believe** *(SYN.)* pretend, imagined, simulated, false, fake, unreal.

**maker** *(SYN.)* inventor, creator, producer, builder, manufacturer, originator.

**makeshift** *(SYN.)* proxy, deputy, understudy, expedient, agent, lieutenant, alternate, substitute, equivalent. *(ANT.) sovereign, head, principal.*

**make-up** *(SYN.)* composition, formation, structure, cosmetics.

**malady** *(SYN.)* disease, illness, sickness, ailment, infirmity, disorder, affliction. *(ANT.) vigor, healthiness, health.*

**malaise** *(SYN.)* anxiety, apprehension, dissatisfaction, uneasiness, nervousness, disquiet, discontent.

**malcontent** *(SYN.)* displeased, ill-humored, querulous, discontented, quarrelsome.

**male** *(SYN.)* masculine, virile. *(ANT.) female, womanly, feminine.*

**malefactor** *(SYN.)* perpetrator, gangster, hoodlum, wrongdoer, troublemaker, criminal, scoundrel, evildoer, lawbreaker.

**malevolence** *(SYN.)* spite, malice, enmity, rancor, animosity. *(ANT.) love, affection, toleration, kindness.*

**malfunction** *(SYN.)* flaw, breakdown, snag, glitch, failure.

**malice** *(SYN.)* spite, grudge, enmity, ill will, malignity, animosity, rancor, resentment, viciousness, grudge, bitterness. *(ANT.) love, affection, toleration, benevolence, charity.*

**malicious** *(SYN.)* hostile, malignant, virulent, bitter, rancorous, evil-minded, malevolent, spiteful, wicked. *(ANT.) kind, benevolent, affectionate.*

**malign** *(SYN.)* misuse, defame, revile, abuse, traduce, asperse, misapply, disparage. *(ANT.) praise, cherish, protect, minor.*

**malignant** *(SYN.)* harmful, deadly, killing, lethal, mortal, destructive, hurtful, malicious. *(ANT.) benign, harmless.*

**malingerer** *(SYN.)* quitter, idler, goldbrick.

**malleable** *(SYN.)* meek, tender, soft, lenient, flexible, mild, compassionate, supple. *(ANT.) tough, rigid, unyielding, hard.*

**malodorous** *(SYN.)* reeking, fetid, smelly, noxious, vile, rancid, offensive.

**malpractice** *(SYN.)* wrongdoing, misdeed, abuse, malfeasance, error, mismanagement, dereliction, fault, sin, misconduct.

**maltreat** *(SYN.)* mistreat, ill-treatment, abuse.

**maltreatment** *(SYN.)* disparagement, perversion, aspersion, invective, defamation, profanation. *(ANT.) respect, approval, laudation, commendation.*

**mammoth** *(SYN.)* enormous,

immense, huge, colossal, gigantic, gargantuan, ponderous. (*ANT.*) *minuscule, tiny, small.*

**man** (*SYN.*) person, human being, society, folk, soul, individual, mortal, fellow, male, gentleman. (*ANT.*) *woman.*

**manacle** (*SYN.*) chain, shackle, cuff, handcuff, bond.

**manage** (*SYN.*) curb, govern, direct, bridle, command, regulate, repress, check, restrain, dominate, guide, lead, supervise, superintend, control, rule. (*ANT.*) *forsake, submit, abandon, mismanage, bungle.*

**manageable** (*SYN.*) willing, obedient, docile, controllable, tractable, submissive, governable, wieldy, untroublesome. (*ANT.*) *recalcitrant, unmanageable, wild.*

**management** (*SYN.*) regulation, administration, supervision, direction, control.

**manager** (*SYN.*) overseer, superintendent, supervisor, director, boss, executive.

**mandate** (*SYN.*) order, injunction, command, referendum, dictate, writ, directive, commission.

**mandatory** (*SYN.*) compulsory, required, obligatory, imperative, necessary. (*ANT.*) *optional.*

**maneuver** (*SYN.*) execution, effort, proceeding, enterprise, working, action, operation, agency, instrumentality. (*ANT.*) *rest, inaction, cessation.*

**mangle** (*SYN.*) tear apart, cut, maim, wound, mutilate, injure, break, demolish.

**mangy** (*SYN.*) shoddy, frazzled, seedy, threadbare, shabby, ragged, sordid.

**manhandle** (*SYN.*) maltreat, maul, abuse, ill-treat.

**manhood** (*SYN.*) maturity, manliness. (*ANT.*) *youth.*

**mania** (*SYN.*) insanity, enthusiasm, craze, desire, madness.

**manic** (*SYN.*) excited, hyped up, agitated.

**manifest** (*SYN.*) open, evident, lucid, clear, distinct, unobstructed, cloudless, apparent, intelligible, apparent. (*ANT.*) *vague, overcast, unclear, cloudy, hidden, concealed.*

**manifesto** (*SYN.*) pronouncement, edict, proclamation, statement, declaration.

**manifold** (*SYN.*) various, many, multiple, numerous, abundant, copious, profuse. (*ANT.*) *few.*

**manipulate** (*SYN.*) manage, feel, work, operate, handle, touch, maneuver.

**manly** (*SYN.*) strong, brave, masculine, manful, courageous, stalwart.

**man-made** (*SYN.*) artificial. (*ANT.*) *natural.*

**manner** (*SYN.*) air, demeanor, custom, style, method, deportment, mode, habit, practice, way, behavior, fashion.

**mannerism** (*SYN.*) eccentricity, quirk, habit, peculiarity, idiosyncrasy, trait.

**mannerly** (*SYN.*) well-bred, gentlemanly, courteous, suave, polite, genteel.

**manor** (*SYN.*) land, mansion, estate, domain, villa, castle, property, palace.

**manslaughter** (*SYN.*) murder, killing, assassination, homicide, elimination.

**mantle** (*SYN.*) serape, garment, overgarment, cover, cloak, wrap.

**manual** (*SYN.*) directory, guidebook, handbook, physical, laborious, menial.

**manufacture** (*SYN.*) construct, make, assemble, fabricate, produce, fashion, build.

**manure** (*SYN.*) fertilizer, droppings, waste, compost.

**manuscript** (*SYN.*) copy, writing, work, paper, composition, document.

**many** (*SYN.*) numerous, various, diverse, multitudinous, sundry, multifarious, manifold, abundant, plentiful. (*ANT.*) *infrequent, meager, few, scanty.*

**map** (*SYN.*) sketch, plan, chart, graph.

**mar** (*SYN.*) spoil, hurt, damage, impair, harm, deface, injure. (*ANT.*) *repair, benefit, mend.*

**marathon** (*SYN.*) relay, race, contest.

**maraud** (*SYN.*) invade, plunder, loot, ransack, ravage, raid.

**march** (*SYN.*) promenade, parade, pace, hike, walk, tramp.

**margin** (*SYN.*) boundary, border, rim, edge.

**marginal** (*SYN.*) unnecessary, nonessential, borderline, noncritical. (*ANT.*) *essential.*

**marine** (*SYN.*) naval, oceanic, nautical, ocean, maritime.

**mariner** (*SYN.*) seafarer, gob, seaman, sailor.

**marionette** (*SYN.*) doll, puppet.

**maritime** (*SYN.*) shore, coastal, nautical.

**mark** (*SYN.*) stain, badge, stigma, vestige, sign, feature, label, characteristic, trace,

brand, trait, scar, indication, impression, effect, imprint, stamp, brand.

**marked** (*SYN.*) plain, apparent, noticeable, evident, decided, noted, special, noteworthy.

**market** (*SYN.*) supermarket, store, bazaar, mart, stall, marketplace, plaza, emporium.

**maroon** (*SYN.*) desert, leave behind, forsake, abandon, jettison.

**marriage** (*SYN.*) wedding, matrimony, nuptials, espousal, union, alliance, association. (*ANT.*) *divorce, celibacy, separation.*

**marrow** (*SYN.*) center, core, gist, essential.

**marry** (*SYN.*) wed, espouse, betroth.

**marsh** (*SYN.*) bog, swamp, mire, everglade, estuary.

**marshal** (*SYN.*) adjutant, officer, order, arrange, rank.

**mart** (*SYN.*) shop, market, store.

**martial** (*SYN.*) warlike, combative, militant, belligerent. (*ANT.*) *peaceful.*

**martyr** (*SYN.*) victim, sufferer, tortured, torment, plague, harass, persecute.

**marvel** (*SYN.*) phenomenon, wonder, miracle, astonishment, sensation.

**marvelous** (*SYN.*) rare, wonderful, extraordinary, unusual, exceptional, miraculous, wondrous, amazing, astonishing, astounding. (*ANT.*) *usual, common, ordinary.*

**mascot** (*SYN.*) pet, amulet, charm.

**masculine** (*SYN.*) robust, manly, virile, strong, bold, male, lusty, vigorous, hardy, mannish. (*ANT.*) *weak, emasculated, feminine, effeminate, womanish, female.*

**mash** (*SYN.*) mix, pulverize, crush, grind, crumble, granulate.

**mask** (*SYN.*) veil, disguise, cloak, secrete, withhold, hide, cover, protection, protector, camouflage, conceal, screen. (*ANT.*) *uncover, reveal, disclose, show, expose.*

**masquerade** (*SYN.*) pretend, disguise, pose, impersonate, costume party.

**mass** (*SYN.*) society, torso, body, remains, association, carcass, bulk, company, pile, heap, quantity, aggregation. (*ANT.*) *spirit, mind, intellect.*

**massacre** (*SYN.*) butcher, murder, carnage, slaughter, execute, slay, genocide, killing, butchery, extermination.

(*ANT.*) *save, protect, vivify, animate.*

**massage** (*SYN.*) knead, rub, stroke.

**masses** (*SYN.*) populace, crowd, multitude, people.

**massive** (*SYN.*) grave, cumbersome, heavy, sluggish, ponderous, serious, burdensome, huge, immense, tremendous, gigantic. (*ANT.*) *light, animated, small, tiny, little.*

**mast** (*SYN.*) pole, post.

**master** (*SYN.*) owner, employer, leader, ruler, chief, head, lord, teacher, manager, holder, commander, overseer, expert, maestro, genius, captain, director, boss. (*ANT.*) *slave, servant.*

**masterful** (*SYN.*) commanding, bossy, domineering, dictatorial, cunning, wise, accomplished, skillful, sharp.

**masterly** (*SYN.*) adroit, superb, skillful, expert. (*ANT.*) *awkward, clumsy.*

**mastermind** (*SYN.*) prodigy, sage, guru.

**masterpiece** (*SYN.*) prizewinner, classic, perfection, model.

**mastery** (*SYN.*) sway, sovereignty, domination, transcendence, ascendancy, influence, jurisdiction, prestige.

**masticate** (*SYN.*) chew.

**mat** (*SYN.*) cover, rug, pallet, bedding, pad.

**match** (*SYN.*) equivalent, equal, contest, balance, resemble, peer, mate.

**matchless** (*SYN.*) peerless, incomparable, unequaled, unrivaled, excellent. (*ANT.*) *ordinary, unimpressive.*

**mate** (*SYN.*) friend, colleague, associate, partner, companion, comrade. (*ANT.*) *stranger, adversary.*

**material** (*SYN.*) sensible, momentous, germane, bodily, palpable, important, physical, essential, corporeal, tangible, substance, matter, fabric. (*ANT.*) *metaphysical, spiritual, insignificant, mental, immaterial, irrelevant, intangible.*

**materialize** (*SYN.*) take shape, finalize, embody, incarnate, emerge, appear.

**maternal** (*SYN.*) motherly. (*ANT.*) *fatherly.*

**mathematics** (*SYN.*) measurements, computations, numbers, calculation, figures.

**matrimony** (*SYN.*) marriage, wedding, espousal, union. (*ANT.*) *virginity, divorce.*

**matrix** (*SYN.*) template, stamp, negative, stencil,

mold, form, die, cutout.

**matron** *(SYN.)* lady.

**matted** *(SYN.)* tangled, clustered, rumpled, shaggy, knotted, gnarled, tousled.

**matter** *(SYN.)* cause, thing, substance, occasion, material, moment, topic, stuff, concern, theme, subject, consequence, affair, business, interest. *(ANT.)* spirit, immateriality.

**mature** *(SYN.)* ready, matured, complete, ripe, consummate, mellow, aged, seasoned, full-grown. *(ANT.) raw, crude, undeveloped, young, immature, innocent.*

**maudlin** *(SYN.)* emotional, mushy, sentimental, mawkish.

**maul** *(SYN.)* pummel, mistreat, manhandle, beat, batter, bruise, abuse.

**mausoleum** *(SYN.)* shrine, tomb, vault.

**maverick** *(SYN.)* nonconformist, oddball, outsider, dissenter, loner.

**mawkish** *(SYN.)* sentimental, emotional, nostalgic.

**maxim** *(SYN.)* rule, code, law, proverb, principle, saying, adage, motto.

**maximum** *(SYN.)* highest, largest, head, greatest, climax. *(ANT.) minimum.*

**may** *(SYN.)* can, be able.

**maybe** *(SYN.)* feasibly, perchance, perhaps, possibly. *(ANT.) definitely.*

**mayhem** *(SYN.)* brutality, viciousness, ruthlessness.

**maze** *(SYN.)* complex, labyrinth, network, muddle, confusion, snarl, tangle.

**meadow** *(SYN.)* field, pasture, lea, range, grassland.

**meager** *(SYN.)* sparse, scanty, mean, frugal, slight, paltry, inadequate. *(ANT.) ample, plentiful, abundant, bountiful.*

**meal** *(SYN.)* refreshment, dinner, lunch, repast, breakfast.

**mean** *(SYN.)* sordid, base, intend, plan, propose, expect, indicate, denote, say, signify, suggest, express, average, nasty, middle, contemptible, offensive, vulgar, unkind, cruel, despicable, vile, low, medium. *(ANT.) dignified, noble, exalted, thoughtful, gentle, openhanded, kind, generous, admirable.*

**meander** *(SYN.)* wind, stray, wander, twist.

**meaning** *(SYN.)* gist, connotation, intent, purport, drift, acceptation, implication, sense, import, interpretation, denotation, signification, explanation, purpose, significance.

**meaningful** *(SYN.)* profound, deep, expressive, important, crucial.

**meaningless** *(SYN.)* nonsensical, senseless, unreasonable, preposterous.

**means** *(SYN.)* utensil, channel, agent, money, riches, vehicle, apparatus, device, wealth, support, medium, instrument. *(ANT.) preventive, impediment, hindrance.*

**measly** *(SYN.)* scanty, puny, skimpy, meager, petty.

**measure** *(SYN.)* law, bulk, rule, criterion, size, volume, weight, standard, dimension, breadth, depth, test, touchstone, trial, length, extent, gauge.

**measureless** *(SYN.)* immeasurable, immense, boundless, limitless, infinite, vast. *(ANT.) figurable, ascertainable, measurable.*

**meat** *(SYN.)* lean, flesh, food.

**mecca** *(SYN.)* target, shrine, goal, sanctuary, destination.

**mechanic** *(SYN.)* repairman, machinist.

**mechanism** *(SYN.)* device, contrivance, tool, machine, machinery.

**medal** *(SYN.)* decoration, award, badge, medallion, reward, ribbon, prize, honor.

**meddle** *(SYN.)* tamper, interpose, pry, snoop, intrude, interrupt, interfere, monkey.

**meddlesome** *(SYN.)* forward, bothersome, intrusive, obtrusive.

**mediate** *(SYN.)* settle, intercede, umpire, intervene, negotiate, arbitrate, referee.

**medicinal** *(SYN.)* helping, healing, remedial, therapeutic, corrective.

**medicine** *(SYN.)* drug, medication, remedy, cure, prescription, potion.

**mediocre** *(SYN.)* medium, mean, average, moderate, fair, ordinary. *(ANT.) outstanding, exceptional.*

**meditate** *(SYN.)* remember, muse, think, judge, mean, conceive, contemplate, deem, suppose, purpose, consider, picture, reflect, believe, plan, reckon.

**medium** *(SYN.)* modicum, average, middling, median. *(ANT.) extreme.*

**medley** *(SYN.)* hodgepodge, mixture, assortment, conglomeration, mishmash, miscellany.

**meek** *(SYN.)* subdued, dull, tedious, flat, docile, domesticated, tame, insipid, domestic. *(ANT.) spirited, exciting,*
savage, wild.

**meet** *(SYN.)* fulfill, suffer, find, collide, gratify, engage, connect, converge, encounter, unite, join, satisfy, settle, greet, answer, undergo, meeting, contest, match, assemble, discharge, gather, convene, congregate, confront, intersect. *(ANT.) scatter, disperse, separate, cleave.*

**melancholy** *(SYN.)* disconsolate, dejected, despondent, glum, somber, pensive, moody, dispirited, depressed, gloomy, dismal, doleful, depression, downcast, gloom, sadness, sad, grave, downhearted, sorrowful. *(ANT.) happy, cheerful, merry.*

**meld** *(SYN.)* unite, mix, combine, fuse, merge, blend, commingle, amalgamate.

**melee** *(SYN.)* battle royal, fight, brawl, free-for-all, fracas.

**mellow** *(SYN.)* mature, ripe, aged, cured, full-flavored, sweet, smooth, melodious, develop, soften. *(ANT.) unripened, immature.*

**melodious** *(SYN.)* lilting, musical, lyric, dulcet, mellifluous, tuneful, melodic.

**melodramatic** *(SYN.)* dramatic, ceremonious, affected, stagy, histrionic, overwrought, sensational, stagy. *(ANT.) unemotional, subdued, modest.*

**melody** *(SYN.)* strand, concord, music, air, song, tune, harmony.

**melt** *(SYN.)* dissolve, liquefy, blend, fade out, vanish, dwindle, disappear, thaw. *(ANT.) freeze, harden, solidify.*

**member** *(SYN.)* share, part, allotment, moiety, element, concern, interest, lines, faction, role, apportionment.

**membrane** *(SYN.)* layer, sheath, tissue, covering.

**memento** *(SYN.)* keepsake, token, reminder, trophy, sign, souvenir, remembrance.

**memoirs** *(SYN.)* diary, reflections, experiences, autobiography, journal, confessions.

**memorable** *(SYN.)* important, historic, significant, unforgettable, noteworthy, momentous, crucial, impressive. *(ANT.) passing, forgettable, transitory, commonplace.*

**memorandum** *(SYN.)* letter, mark, token, note, indication, remark, message.

**memorial** *(SYN.)* monument, souvenir, memento, remembrance, commemoration, reminiscent, ritual, testimonial.

**memorize** *(SYN.)* study, remember.

**memory** *(SYN.)* renown, remembrance, reminiscence, fame, retrospection, recollection, reputation. *(ANT.) oblivion.*

**menace** *(SYN.)* warning, threat, intimidation, warn, threaten, imperil, forebode.

**menagerie** *(SYN.)* collection, zoo, kennel.

**mend** *(SYN.)* restore, better, refit, sew, remedy, patch, correct, repair, rectify, ameliorate, improve, reform, recover, fix. *(ANT.) hurt, deface, rend, destroy.*

**mendacious** *(SYN.)* dishonest, false, lying, deceitful, deceptive, tricky. *(ANT.) honest, truthful, sincere, creditable.*

**mendicant** *(SYN.)* ragamuffin, vagabond, beggar.

**menial** *(SYN.)* unskilled, lowly, degrading, tedious, humble, routine.

**mental** *(SYN.)* reasoning, intellectual, rational, thinking, conscious, reflective, thoughtful. *(ANT.) physical.*

**mentality** *(SYN.)* intellect, reason, understanding, liking, disposition, judgment, brain, inclination, faculties, outlook. *(ANT.) materiality, corporeality.*

**mention** *(SYN.)* introduce, refer to, reference, allude, enumerate, speak of.

**mentor** *(SYN.)* advisor, tutor, sponsor, guru, teacher, counselor, master, coach.

**mercenary** *(SYN.)* sordid, corrupt, venal, covetous, grasping, avaricious, greedy. *(ANT.) liberal, generous.*

**merchandise** *(SYN.)* stock, wares, goods, sell, commodities, promote, staples, products.

**merchant** *(SYN.)* retailer, dealer, trader, storekeeper, salesman, businessman.

**merciful** *(SYN.)* humane, kindhearted, tender, clement, sympathetic, forgiving, tolerant, forbearing, lenient, compassionate, tenderhearted, kind. *(ANT.) remorseless, cruel, unjust, mean, harsh, unforgiving, vengeful, brutal, unfeeling, pitiless.*

**merciless** *(SYN.)* carnal, ferocious, brute, barbarous, gross, ruthless, cruel, remorseless, bestial, savage, rough, pitiless, inhuman. *(ANT.) humane, courteous, merciful, openhearted, kind, civilized.*

**mercurial** *(SYN.)* fickle,

unstable, volatile, changeable, inconstant, capricious, flighty.

**mercy** (SYN.) grace, consideration, kindness, clemency, mildness, forgiveness, pity, charity, sympathy, leniency, compassion. (ANT.) punishment, retribution, ruthlessness, cruelty, vengeance.

**mere** (SYN.) only, simple, scant, bare. (ANT.) substantial, considerable.

**merely** (SYN.) only, barely, simply, hardly.

**meretricious** (SYN.) gaudy, sham, bogus, tawdry, flashy.

**merge** (SYN.) unify, fuse, combine, amalgamate, unite, blend, commingle. (ANT.) separate, decompose, analyze.

**merger** (SYN.) cartel, union, conglomerate, trust, incorporation, combine, pool.

**meridian** (SYN.) climax, summit, pinnacle, zenith, peak, acme, apex, culmination.

**merit** (SYN.) worthiness, earn, goodness, effectiveness, power, value, virtue, goodness, quality, deserve, excellence, worth. (ANT.) sin, fault, lose, consume.

**merited** (SYN.) proper, deserved, suitable, adequate, earned. (ANT.) unmerited, improper.

**meritorious** (SYN.) laudable, excellent, commendable, good, praiseworthy, deserving.

**merry** (SYN.) hilarious, lively, festive, joyous, sprightly, mirthful, blithe, gay, cheery, joyful, jolly, happy, gleeful, jovial, cheerful. (ANT.) sorrowful, doleful, morose, gloomy, sad, melancholy.

**mesh** (SYN.) grid, screen, net, complex.

**mesmerize** (SYN.) enthrall, transfix, spellbind, bewitch, charm, fascinate, hypnotize.

**mess** (SYN.) dirtiness, untidiness, disorder, confusion, muddle, trouble, jumble, difficulty, predicament, confuse, dirty.

**message** (SYN.) letter, annotation, memo, symbol, indication, sign, note, communication, memorandum, observation, token.

**messenger** (SYN.) bearer, agent, runner, courier, liaison, delegate, page.

**messy** (SYN.) disorderly, dirty, confusing, confused, disordered, sloppy, untidy, slovenly. (ANT.) orderly, neat, tidy.

**metallic** (SYN.) grating, harsh, clanging, brassy, brazen.

**metamorphosis** (SYN.) transfiguration, change, alteration, rebirth, mutation.

**mete** (SYN.) deal, assign, apportion, divide, give, allocate, allot, measure. (ANT.) withhold, keep, retain.

**meteoric** (SYN.) flashing, blazing, swift, brilliant, spectacular, remarkable.

**meter** (SYN.) record, measure, gauge.

**method** (SYN.) order, manner, plan, way, mode, technique, fashion, approach, design, procedure. (ANT.) disorder.

**methodical** (SYN.) exact, definite, ceremonious, stiff, accurate, distinct, unequivocal. (ANT.) easy, loose, informal.

**meticulous** (SYN.) precise, careful, exacting, fastidious, fussy, perfectionist.

**metropolitan** (SYN.) civic, city, municipal.

**mettle** (SYN.) intrepidity, resolution, boldness, prowess, bravery, fearlessness. (ANT.) fear, timidity, cowardice.

**microscopic** (SYN.) tiny, precise, fine, detailed, minute, infinitesimal, minimal. (ANT.) general, huge, enormous.

**middle** (SYN.) midpoint, nucleus, center, midst, median, central, intermediate, core. (ANT.) end, rim, outskirts, beginning, border, periphery.

**middleman** (SYN.) dealer, agent, distributor, broker, representative, intermediary.

**midget** (SYN.) gnome, shrimp, pygmy, runt, dwarf. (ANT.) giant.

**midst** (SYN.) center, heart, middle, thick.

**midway** (SYN.) halfway, midmost, inside, central, middle.

**mien** (SYN.) way, semblance, manner, behavior, demeanor, expression, deportment.

**miff** (SYN.) provoke, rile, chagrin, irk, irritate, affront, offend, annoy, exasperate.

**might** (SYN.) force, power, vigor, potency, ability, strength. (ANT.) frailty, vulnerability, weakness.

**mighty** (SYN.) firm, fortified, powerful, athletic, potent, muscular, robust, strong, cogent. (ANT.) feeble, weak, brittle, insipid, frail, delicate.

**migrant** (SYN.) traveling, roaming, straying, roving, rambling, transient, meandering.

(ANT.) stationary.

**migrate** (SYN.) resettle, move, emigrate, immigrate, relocate, journey. (ANT.) stay, remain, settle.

**migratory** (SYN.) itinerant, roving, mobile, vagabond, unsettled, nomadic, wandering.

**mild** (SYN.) soothing, moderate, gentle, tender, bland, pleasant, kind, meek, calm, amiable, compassionate, temperate, peaceful, soft. (ANT.) severe, turbulent, stormy, excitable, violent, harsh, bitter.

**milieu** (SYN.) environment, background, locale, setting, scene, circumstances.

**militant** (SYN.) warlike, belligerent, hostile, fighting, pugnacious, aggressive, combative. (ANT.) peaceful.

**military** (SYN.) troops, army, service, soldiers.

**milksop** (SYN.) namby-pamby, weakling, sissy, coward.

**mill** (SYN.) foundry, shop, plant, factory, manufactory.

**millstone** (SYN.) load, impediment, burden, encumbrance, hindrance.

**mimic** (SYN.) simulate, duplicate, copy, imitate, mock, counterfeit, simulate. (ANT.) invent, distort, alter.

**mince** (SYN.) shatter, fragment, chop, smash.

**mind** (SYN.) intelligence, psyche, disposition, intention, understanding, intellect, spirit, brain, inclination, mentality, soul, wit, liking, brain, sense, watch, faculties, judgment, reason.

**mindful** (SYN.) alert, aware, cognizant, watchful, sensible, heedful.

**mine** (SYN.) shaft, lode, pit, excavation, drill, dig, quarry, source.

**mingle** (SYN.) unite, coalesce, fuse, merge, combine, amalgamate, unify, conjoin, mix, blend, commingle. (ANT.) separate, analyze, sort, disintegrate.

**miniature** (SYN.) small, little, tiny, midget, minute, minuscule, wee, petite, diminutive. (ANT.) outsize.

**minimize** (SYN.) shorten, deduct, belittle, decrease, reduce, curtail, lessen, diminish, subtract. (ANT.) enlarge, increase, amplify.

**minimum** (SYN.) lowest, least, smallest, slightest. (ANT.) maximum.

**minister** (SYN.) pastor, clergyman, vicar, parson, curate, preacher, prelate, chaplain, cleric, deacon, reverend.

**minor** (SYN.) poorer, lesser, petty, youth, inferior, secondary, smaller, unimportant, lower. (ANT.) higher, superior, major, greater.

**minority** (SYN.) youth, childhood, immaturity.

**minstrel** (SYN.) bard, musician.

**mint** (SYN.) stamp, coin, strike, punch.

**minus** (SYN.) lacking, missing, less, absent, without.

**minute** (SYN.) tiny, particular, fine, precise, jiffy, instant, moment, wee, exact, detailed, microscopic. (ANT.) large, huge, enormous.

**miraculous** (SYN.) spiritual, supernatural, wonderful, marvelous, incredible, preternatural. (ANT.) commonplace, natural, common, plain, everyday, human.

**mirage** (SYN.) vision, illusion, fantasy, dream, phantom. (ANT.) reality, actuality.

**mire** (SYN.) marsh, slush, slime, mud.

**mirror** (SYN.) glass, reflector, reflect.

**mirth** (SYN.) joy, glee, jollity, joyousness, gaiety, joyfulness, laughter, merriment. (ANT.) sadness, gloom, seriousness.

**misadventure** (SYN.) accident, adversity, reverse, calamity, catastrophe, hardship, mischance, setback.

**misappropriate** (SYN.) embezzle, steal, purloin, plunder, cheat, filch, defraud.

**misbehave** (SYN.) trespass, act badly. (ANT.) behave.

**miscalculate** (SYN.) miscount, blunder, confuse, err, mistake, misconstrue.

**miscarriage** (SYN.) omission, want, decay, fiasco, default, deficiency, loss, abortion, prematurity. (ANT.) success, sufficiency, achievement.

**miscarry** (SYN.) flounder, fall short, falter, go wrong, fail. (ANT.) succeed.

**miscellaneous** (SYN.) diverse, motley, indiscriminate, assorted, sundry, heterogeneous, mixed, varied. (ANT.) classified, selected, homogeneous, alike, ordered.

**miscellany** (SYN.) medley, gallimaufry, jumble, potpourri, mixture, collection.

**mischief** (SYN.) injury, harm, damage, evil, prankishness, rascality, roguishness, playfulness, wrong, detriment, hurt. (ANT.) kindness, boon, benefit.

**mischievous** (SYN.) roguish, prankish, naughty, playful.

*(ANT.)* well-behaved, good.

**misconduct** *(SYN.)* transgression, delinquency, wrongdoing, negligence.

**miscreant** *(SYN.)* rascal, wretch, rogue, sinner, criminal, villain, scoundrel.

**miscue** *(SYN.)* blunder, fluff, mistake, error, lapse.

**misdemeanor** *(SYN.)* infringement, transgression, violation, offense, wrong.

**miser** *(SYN.)* cheapskate, tightwad, skinflint. *(ANT.)* philanthropist.

**miserable** *(SYN.)* abject, forlorn, comfortless, low, worthless, pitiable, distressed, heartbroken, disconsolate, despicable, wretched, uncomfortable, unhappy, poor, unlucky, paltry, contemptible, mean. *(ANT.)* fortunate, happy, contented, joyful, content, wealthy, honorable, lucky, noble.

**miserly** *(SYN.)* stingy, greedy, acquisitive, tight, tightfisted, cheap, mean, parsimonious, avaricious. *(ANT.)* bountiful, generous, spendthrift, munificent, extravagant, openhanded, altruistic.

**misery** *(SYN.)* suffering, woe, evil, agony, torment, trouble, distress, anguish, grief, unhappiness, tribulation, calamity, sorrow. *(ANT.)* fun, pleasure, delight, joy.

**misfit** *(SYN.)* crank, loner, deviate, fifth wheel, individualist.

**misfortune** *(SYN.)* adversity, distress, mishap, calamity, accident, catastrophe, hardship, ruin, disaster, affliction. *(ANT.)* success, blessing, prosperity.

**misgiving** *(SYN.)* suspicion, doubt, mistrust, hesitation, uncertainty.

**misguided** *(SYN.)* misdirected, misled.

**misinformed** *(SYN.)* wrong, unwise, foolish, erroneous, unwarranted, ill-advised, misguided.

**mishap** *(SYN.)* misfortune, casualty, accident, disaster, adversity, reverse. *(ANT.)* intention, calculation, purpose.

**mishmash** *(SYN.)* medley, muddle, gallimaufry, hodgepodge, hash.

**misjudge** *(SYN.)* err, mistake, miscalculate.

**mislay** *(SYN.)* misplace, lose. *(ANT.)* discover, find.

**mislead** *(SYN.)* misdirect, misinform, deceive, delude.

**misleading** *(SYN.)* fallacious, delusive, deceitful, false,

deceptive, illusive. *(ANT.)* real, genuine, truthful, honest.

**mismatched** *(SYN.)* unfit, unsuitable, incompatible, unsuited.

**misplace** *(SYN.)* lose, mislay, miss. *(ANT.)* find.

**misrepresent** *(SYN.)* misstate, distort, falsify, twist, belie, garble, disguise.

**miss** *(SYN.)* lose, want, crave, yearn for, fumble, drop, error, slip, default, omit, lack, need, desire, fail. *(ANT.)* suffice, have, achieve, succeed.

**misshapen** *(SYN.)* disfigured, deformed, grotesque, malformed, ungainly, gnarled, contorted.

**missile** *(SYN.)* grenade, shot, projectile.

**missing** *(SYN.)* wanting, lacking, absent, lost, gone, vanished.

**mission** *(SYN.)* business, task, job, stint, work, errand, assignment, delegation.

**missionary** *(SYN.)* publicist, evangelist, propagandist.

**mist** *(SYN.)* cloud, fog, haze, steam, haze.

**mistake** *(SYN.)* slip, misjudge, fault, blunder, misunderstand, confuse, inaccuracy, misinterpret, error. *(ANT.)* truth, accuracy.

**mistaken** *(SYN.)* false, amiss, incorrect, awry, wrong, misinformed, confused, inaccurate, askew. *(ANT.)* true, correct, suitable, right.

**mister** *(SYN.)* young man, gentleman, esquire, fellow, buddy.

**mistreat** *(SYN.)* wrong, pervert, oppress, harm, maltreat, abuse.

**mistrust** *(SYN.)* suspect, doubt, distrust, dispute, question, skepticism, apprehension. *(ANT.)* trust.

**misunderstand** *(SYN.)* misjudge, misinterpret, jumble, confuse, mistake. *(ANT.)* perceive, comprehend.

**misunderstanding** *(SYN.)* clash, disagreement, dispute, conflict, misinterpretation.

**misuse** *(SYN.)* defame, malign, abuse, misapply, traduce, asperse, revile, vilify. *(ANT.)* protect, honor, respect, cherish.

**mite** *(SYN.)* particle, mote, smidgen, trifle, iota, corpuscle.

**mitigate** *(SYN.)* soften, soothe, abate, assuage, relieve, allay, diminish. *(ANT.)* irritate, agitate, increase.

**mix** *(SYN.)* mingle, blend, consort, fuse, alloy, combine,

jumble, fraternize, associate, concoct, commingle, amalgamate, confound, compound, join. *(ANT.)* divide, sort, segregate, dissociate, separate.

**mixture** *(SYN.)* diversity, variety, strain, change, kind, confusion, heterogeneity, jumble, mess, assortment, breed, mix, hodge-podge, subspecies. *(ANT.)* likeness, sameness, homogeneity, monotony.

**moan** *(SYN.)* wail, groan, cry, lament.

**moat** *(SYN.)* fortification, ditch, trench, entrenchment.

**mob** *(SYN.)* crowd, host, populace, swarm, rot, bevy, horde, rabble, throng, multitude.

**mobile** *(SYN.)* free, movable, portable. *(ANT.)* stationary, immobile, fixed.

**mock** *(SYN.)* taunt, jeer, deride, scoff, scorn, ridicule, tease, fake, imitation, sham, gibe, sneer, fraudulent, flout. *(ANT.)* praise, applaud, real, genuine, honor, authentic, compliment.

**mockery** *(SYN.)* gibe, ridicule, satire, derision, sham, banter, irony, sneering, scorn, travesty, jeering. *(ANT.)* admiration, praise.

**mode** *(SYN.)* method, fashion, procedure, design, manner, technique, way, style, practice, plan. *(ANT.)* disorder, confusion.

**model** *(SYN.)* copy, prototype, type, example, ideal, imitation, version, facsimile, design, style, archetype, pattern, standard, mold. *(ANT.)* reproduction, imitation.

**moderate** *(SYN.)* lower, decrease, average, fair, reasonable, abate, medium, conservative, referee, umpire, suppress, judge, lessen, assuage. *(ANT.)* intensify, enlarge, amplify.

**moderation** *(SYN.)* sobriety, forbearance, self-control, restraint, continence, temperance. *(ANT.)* greed, excess, intoxication.

**moderator** *(SYN.)* referee, leader, arbitrator, chairman, chairperson, master of ceremonies, emcee.

**modern** *(SYN.)* modish, current, recent, novel, fresh, contemporary, new. *(ANT.)* old, antiquated, past, bygone, ancient.

**modernize** *(SYN.)* refurnish, refurbish, improve, rebuild, renew, renovate.

**modest** *(SYN.)* unassuming, virtuous, bashful, meek, shy,

humble, decent, demure, unpretentious, prudish, moderate, reserved. *(ANT.)* forward, bold, ostentatious, conceited, immodest, arrogant.

**modesty** *(SYN.)* decency, humility, propriety, simplicity, shyness. *(ANT.)* conceit, vanity, pride.

**modicum** *(SYN.)* particle, fragment, grain, trifle, smidgen, bit.

**modification** *(SYN.)* alternation, substitution, variety, change, alteration. *(ANT.)* uniformity, monotony.

**modify** *(SYN.)* shift, vary, alter, change, convert, adjust, temper, moderate, curb, exchange, transform, veer. *(ANT.)* settle, establish, retain, stabilize.

**modish** *(SYN.)* current, fashionable, chick, stylish, voguish.

**modulate** *(SYN.)* temper, align, balance, correct, regulate, adjust, modify.

**module** *(SYN.)* unit, measure, norm, dimension, component, gauge.

**modus operandi** *(SYN.)* method, technique, system, means, process, workings, procedure.

**mogul** *(SYN.)* bigwig, personage, figure, tycoon, magnate, potentate.

**moiety** *(SYN.)* part, scrap, share, allotment, piece, division, portion.

**moist** *(SYN.)* damp, humid, dank, muggy, clammy.

**moisten** *(SYN.)* wet, dampen, sponge. *(ANT.)* dry.

**moisture** *(SYN.)* wetness, mist, dampness, condensation, evaporation, vapor, humidity. *(ANT.)* aridity, dryness.

**mold** *(SYN.)* make, fashion, organize, produce, forge, constitute, create, combine, construct, form, pattern, format. *(ANT.)* wreck, dismantle, destroy, misshape.

**moldy** *(SYN.)* dusty, crumbling, dank, old, deteriorating.

**molest** *(SYN.)* irk, disturb, trouble, annoy, pester, bother, vex, inconvenience. *(ANT.)* console, accommodate.

**mollify** *(SYN.)* soothe, compose, quiet, humor, appease, tranquilize, pacify.

**molt** *(SYN.)* slough off, shed, cast off.

**molten** *(SYN.)* fusible, melted, smelted, redhot.

**moment** *(SYN.)* flash, jiffy, instant, twinkling, gravity, importance, consequence, seriousness.

**momentary** *(SYN.)* concise, pithy, brief, curt, terse, laconic, compendious. *(ANT.)* long, extended, prolonged.

**momentous** *(SYN.)* critical, serious, essential, grave, material, weighty, consequential, decisive, important. *(ANT.)* unimportant, trifling, mean, trivial, insignificant.

**momentum** *(SYN.)* impetus, push, thrust, force, impulse, drive, vigor, propulsion, energy.

**monarch** *(SYN.)* ruler, king, queen, empress, emperor, sovereign.

**monastery** *(SYN.)* convent, priory, abbey, hermitage, cloister.

**monastic** *(SYN.)* withdrawn, dedicated, austere, unworldly, celibate, abstinent, ascetic.

**money** *(SYN.)* cash, bills, coin, notes, currency, funds, specie, capital.

**monger** *(SYN.)* seller, hawker, huckster, trader, merchant, shopkeeper, retailer, vendor.

**mongrel** *(SYN.)* mixed-breed, hybrid, mutt.

**monitor** *(SYN.)* director, supervisor, advisor, observe, watch, control.

**monkey** *(SYN.)* tamper, interfere, interrupt, interpose.

**monogram** *(SYN.)* mark, stamp, signature.

**monograph** *(SYN.)* publication, report, thesis, biography, treatise, paper, dissertation.

**monologue** *(SYN.)* discourse, lecture, sermon, talk, speech, address, soliloquy, oration.

**monomania** *(SYN.)* obsessiveness, passion, single-mindedness, extremism.

**monopoly** *(SYN.)* corner, control, possession.

**monotonous** *(SYN.)* dull, slow, tiresome, boring, humdrum, dilatory, tiring, irksome, tedious, burdensome, wearisome. *(ANT.)* interesting, riveting, quick, fascinating, exciting, amusing.

**monsoon** *(SYN.)* storm, rains.

**monster** *(SYN.)* brute, beast, villain, demon, fiend, wretch.

**monstrous** *(SYN.)* tremendous, huge, gigantic, immense, enormous, revolting, repulsive, shocking, horrible, hideous, terrible. *(ANT.)* diminutive, tiny, miniature, small.

**monument** *(SYN.)* remembrance, memento, commemoration, souvenir, statue, shrine.

**monumental** *(SYN.)* enormous, huge, colossal, immense, gigantic, important, significant. *(ANT.)* trivial, insignificant, tiny, miniature.

**mood** *(SYN.)* joke, irony, waggery, temper, disposition, temperament, sarcasm. *(ANT.)* sorrow, gravity.

**moody** *(SYN.)* morose, fretful, crabbed, changeable, sulky, dour, short-tempered, testy, temperamental, irritable, peevish, glum. *(ANT.)* good-natured, even-tempered, merry, gay, pleasant, joyous.

**moor** *(SYN.)* tether, fasten, tie, dock, anchor, bind.

**moorings** *(SYN.)* marina, slip, harbor, basin, landing, dock, wharf, pier, anchorage.

**moot** *(SYN.)* unsettled, questionable, problematical, controversial, contestable.

**mop** *(SYN.)* wash, wipe, swab, scrub.

**mope** *(SYN.)* gloom, pout, whine, grumble, grieve, sulk, fret. *(ANT.)* rejoice.

**moral** *(SYN.)* just, right, chaste, good, virtuous, pure, decent, honest, upright, ethical, righteous, honorable, scrupulous. *(ANT.)* libertine, immoral, unethical, licentious, amoral, sinful.

**morale** *(SYN.)* confidence, spirit, assurance.

**morality** *(SYN.)* virtue, strength, worth, chastity, probity, force, merit. *(ANT.)* fault, sin, corruption, vice.

**morals** *(SYN.)* conduct, scruples, guidelines, behavior, life style, standards.

**morass** *(SYN.)* fen, march, swamp, mire.

**morbid** *(SYN.)* sickly, unwholesome, unhealthy, ghastly, awful, horrible, shocking. *(ANT.)* pleasant, healthy.

**more** *(SYN.)* further, greater, farther, extra, another. *(ANT.)* less.

**moreover** *(SYN.)* further, in addition, also, furthermore, besides.

**mores** *(SYN.)* standards, rituals, rules, customs, conventions, traditions.

**moron** *(SYN.)* subnormal, dunce, blockhead, imbecile, retardate, simpleton.

**morose** *(SYN.)* gloomy, moody, fretful, crabbed, sulky, glum, dour, surly, downcast, sad, unhappy. *(ANT.)* merry, gay, amiable, joyous, pleasant.

**morsel** *(SYN.)* portion, fragment, bite, bit, scrap, amount, piece, taste, tidbit. *(ANT.)* whole, all, sum.

**mortal** *(SYN.)* fatal, destructive, human, perishable, deadly, temporary, momentary, final. *(ANT.)* superficial, immortal.

**mortgage** *(SYN.)* stake, post, promise, pledge.

**mortician** *(SYN.)* funeral director, embalmer.

**mortified** *(SYN.)* embarrassed, humiliated, abashed, ashamed.

**mortify** *(SYN.)* humiliate, crush, subdue, abase, degrade, shame. *(ANT.)* praise, exalt, elevate.

**mortuary** *(SYN.)* morgue, crematory, funeral parlor.

**most** *(SYN.)* extreme, highest, supreme, greatest, majority. *(ANT.)* least.

**mostly** *(SYN.)* chiefly, generally, largely, mainly, principally, especially, primarily.

**mother** *(SYN.)* bring about, produce, breed, mom, mama, watch, foster, mind, nurse, originate, nurture. *(ANT.)* father.

**motif** *(SYN.)* keynote, topic, subject, theme.

**motion** *(SYN.)* change, activity, movement, proposition, action, signal, gesture, move, proposal. *(ANT.)* stability, immobility, equilibrium, stillness.

**motionless** *(SYN.)* still, undisturbed, rigid, fixed, stationary, unresponsive, immobilized.

**motivate** *(SYN.)* move, prompt, stimulate, induce, activate, propel, arouse.

**motive** *(SYN.)* inducement, purpose, cause, incentive, reason, incitement, idea, ground, principle, stimulus, impulse, spur. *(ANT.)* deed, result, attempt, effort.

**motley** *(SYN.)* heterogeneous, mixed, assorted, sundry, diverse, miscellaneous. *(ANT.)* ordered, classified.

**motor** *(SYN.)* engine, generator, machine.

**mottled** *(SYN.)* streaked, flecked, dappled, spotted, speckled.

**motto** *(SYN.)* proverb, saying, adage, byword, saw, slogan, catchword, aphorism.

**mound** *(SYN.)* hillock, hill, heap, pile, stack, knoll, accumulation, dune.

**mount** *(SYN.)* scale, climb, increase, rise, prepare, ready, steed, horse, tower. *(ANT.)* sink, descend.

**mountain** *(SYN.)* alp, mount, pike, peak, ridge, height, range.

**mountebank** *(SYN.)* faker, rascal, swindler, cheat, fraud.

**mounting** *(SYN.)* backing, pedestal, easel, support, framework, background.

**mourn** *(SYN.)* suffer, grieve, bemoan, sorrow, lament, weep, bewail. *(ANT.)* revel, celebrate, carouse.

**mournful** *(SYN.)* gloomy, sorrowful, sad, melancholy, woeful, disconsolate. *(ANT.)* joyful, cheerful, happy.

**mourning** *(SYN.)* misery, trial, distress, affliction, tribulation, sorrow, woe. *(ANT.)* happiness, solace, comfort, joy.

**mousy** *(SYN.)* quiet, reserved, dull, colorless, withdrawn, shy, bashful.

**move** *(SYN.)* impel, agitate, persuade, induce, push, instigate, advance, stir, progress, propel, shift, drive, retreat, proceed, stir, transfer, budge, actuate. *(ANT.)* halt, stop, deter, rest.

**moving** *(SYN.)* stirring, touching.

**mow** *(SYN.)* prune, cut, shave, crop, clip.

**much** *(SYN.)* abundance, quantity, mass, ample, plenty, sufficient, substantial.

**mucilage** *(SYN.)* adhesive, glue, paste.

**muck** *(SYN.)* filth, mire, dirt, rot, sludge.

**muddle** *(SYN.)* disorder, chaos, mess.

**muddled** *(SYN.)* disconcerted, confused, mixed, bewildered, perplexed. *(ANT.)* plain, lucid, organized.

**muff** *(SYN.)* blunder, spoil, mess, fumble.

**muffle** *(SYN.)* soften, deaden, mute, quiet, drape, shroud, veil, cover. *(ANT.)* louden, amplify.

**mug** *(SYN.)* cup, stein, goblet, tankard.

**muggy** *(SYN.)* damp, warm, humid, stuffy, sticky, dank.

**mulct** *(SYN.)* amerce, punish, penalize.

**mulish** *(SYN.)* obstinate, stubborn, headstrong, rigid, tenacious, willful.

**multifarious** *(SYN.)* various, many, numerous, diversified, several, manifold. *(ANT.)* scanty, infrequent, scarce, few.

**multiply** *(SYN.)* double, treble, increase, triple, propagate, spread, expand. *(ANT.)* lessen, decrease.

**multitude** *(SYN.)* crowd, throng, mass, swarm, host,

mob, army, legion. (*ANT.*) *scarcity, handful.*

**mumble** (*SYN.*) stammer, whisper, hesitate, mutter. (*ANT.*) *shout, yell.*

**mundane** (*SYN.*) temporal, earthly, profane, worldly, lay, secular, common. (*ANT.*) *unworldly, religious.*

**municipal** (*SYN.*) urban, metropolitan.

**munificent** (*SYN.*) bountiful, full, generous, forthcoming, satisfied. (*ANT.*) *voracious, insatiable, grasping, ravenous.*

**murder** (*SYN.*) homicide, kill, slay, slaughter, butcher, killing, massacre, assassinate, execute. (*ANT.*) *save, protect, vivify, animate.*

**murky** (*SYN.*) gloomy, dark, obscure, unclear, impenetrable. (*ANT.*) *cheerful, light.*

**murmur** (*SYN.*) mumble, whine, grumble, whimper, lament, mutter. (*ANT.*) *praise, applaud, rejoice.*

**muscle** (*SYN.*) brawn, strength, power, fitness, vigor, vim, stamina, robustness.

**muse** (*SYN.*) ponder, brood, think, meditate, ruminate, reflect.

**museum** (*SYN.*) exhibit hall, treasure house, gallery, repository.

**mushroom** (*SYN.*) multiply, proliferate, flourish, spread, grow, pullulate.

**musical** (*SYN.*) tuneful, melodious, dulcet, lyrical, harmonious.

**muss** (*SYN.*) mess, disarray, rumple, litter, clutter, disarrange. (*ANT.*) *fix, arrange.*

**must** (*SYN.*) ought to, should, duty, obligation, ultimatum.

**muster** (*SYN.*) cull, pick, collect, harvest, accumulate, garner, reap, deduce. (*ANT.*) *separate, disband, scatter.*

**musty** (*SYN.*) mildewed, rancid, airless, dank, stale, decayed, rotten, funky.

**mute** (*SYN.*) quiet, noiseless, dumb, taciturn, hushed, peaceful, speechless, uncommunicative, silent. (*ANT.*) *raucous, clamorous, noisy.*

**mutilate** (*SYN.*) tear, cut, clip, amputate, lacerate, dismember, deform, castrate.

**mutinous** (*SYN.*) revolutionary, rebellious, unruly, turbulent, riotous. (*ANT.*) *dutiful, obedient, complaint.*

**mutiny** (*SYN.*) revolt, overthrow, rebellion, rebel, coup, uprising, insurrection.

**mutter** (*SYN.*) complain, mumble, whisper, grumble, murmur.

**mutual** (*SYN.*) correlative, interchangeable, shared, alternate, joint, common. (*ANT.*) *unshared, unrequited, separate, dissociated.*

**muzzle** (*SYN.*) restrain, silence, bridle, bind, curb, suppress, gag, stifle, censor.

**myopia** (*SYN.*) incomprehension, folly, shortsightedness, obtuseness.

**myriad** (*SYN.*) considerable, many.

**mysterious** (*SYN.*) hidden, mystical, secret, cryptic, incomprehensible, occult, dim, dark, inexplicable, enigmatical. (*ANT.*) *simple, obvious, clear, plain.*

**mystery** (*SYN.*) riddle, difficulty, enigma, puzzle, strangeness, conundrum. (*ANT.*) *solution, key, answer, resolution.*

**mystical** (*SYN.*) secret, cryptic, hidden, dim, obscure, dark, cabalistic. (*ANT.*) *simple, explained, plain, clear.*

**mystify** (*SYN.*) puzzle, confound, bewilder, stick, get, bamboozle.

**myth** (*SYN.*) fable, parable, allegory, fiction, tradition, lie, saga, legend. (*ANT.*) *history.*

# N

**nag** (*SYN.*) badger, harry, provoke, tease, bother, annoy, molest, taunt, vex, torment, worry, annoy, pester, irritate, pick on, horse. (*ANT.*) *please, comfort, soothe.*

**nail** (*SYN.*) hold, fasten, secure, fix, seize, catch, snare, hook, capture. (*ANT.*) *release.*

**naive** (*SYN.*) frank, unsophisticated, natural, artless, ingenuous, simple, candid, open, innocent. (*ANT.*) *worldly, cunning, crafty.*

**naked** (*SYN.*) uncovered, unfinished, nude, bare, open, unclad, stripped, exposed, plain, mere, simple, barren, unprotected, bald, defenseless, unclothed. (*ANT.*) *covered, protected, dressed, clothed, concealed.*

**name** (*SYN.*) title, reputation, appellation, style, fame, repute, renown, denomination, appoint, character, designation, surname, distinction, christen, denominate, mention, specify, epithet, entitle, call, label. (*ANT.*) *anonymity, hint, misname.*

**nap** (*SYN.*) nod, doze, sleep, snooze, catnap, slumber, drowse.

**narcissistic** (*SYN.*) egotistical, egocentric, self-centered, egotistic.

**narcotics** (*SYN.*) opiates, drugs, sedatives, tranquilizers, barbiturates.

**narrate** (*SYN.*) recite, relate, declaim, detail, rehearse, deliver, review, tell, describe, recount.

**narrative** (*SYN.*) history, relation, account, record, chronicle, detail, recital, description, story, tale. (*ANT.*) *distortion, caricature, misrepresentation.*

**narrow** (*SYN.*) narrow-minded, illiberal, bigoted, fanatical, prejudiced, close, restricted, slender, cramped, confined, meager, thin, tapering, tight. (*ANT.*) *progressive, liberal, wide.*

**narrow-minded** (*SYN.*) close-minded, intolerant, partisan, arbitrary, bigoted. (*ANT.*) *tolerant, liberal, broadminded.*

**nascent** (*SYN.*) prime, introductory, emerging, elementary.

**nasty** (*SYN.*) offensive, malicious, selfish, mean, disagreeable, unpleasant, foul, dirty, filthy, loathsome, disgusting, polluted, obscene, indecent, sickening, nauseating, obnoxious, revolting. (*ANT.*) *generous, dignified, noble, admirable, pleasant.*

**nation** (*SYN.*) state, community, realm, nationality, commonwealth, kingdom, country, republic, land, society, tribe.

**native** (*SYN.*) domestic, inborn, inherent, natural, aboriginal, endemic, innate, inbred, indigenous, hereditary. (*ANT.*) *alien, stranger, foreigner, outsider, foreign.*

**natty** (*SYN.*) chic, well-dressed, sharp, dapper.

**natural** (*SYN.*) innate, genuine, real, unaffected, characteristic, native, normal, regular, inherent, original, simple, inbred, inborn, hereditary, typical, authentic, honest, legitimate, pure, customary. (*ANT.*) *irregular, false, unnatural, formal, abnormal.*

**naturally** (*SYN.*) typically, ordinarily, usually, indeed, normally, plainly, of course, surely, certainly. (*ANT.*) *artificially.*

**nature** (*SYN.*) kind, disposition, reputation, character, repute, world, quality, universe, essence, variety, features, traits.

**naught** (*SYN.*) zero, nothing.

**naughty** (*SYN.*) unmanageable, insubordinate, disobedient, mischievous, unruly, bad, misbehaving, disorderly, wrong, evil, rude, improper, indecent. (*ANT.*) *obedient, good, well-behaved.*

**nausea** (*SYN.*) sickness, vomiting, upset, queasiness, seasickness.

**nauseated** (*SYN.*) unwell, sick, queasy, squeamish.

**nautical** (*SYN.*) naval, oceanic, marine.

**naval** (*SYN.*) oceanic, marine, nautical, maritime.

**navigate** (*SYN.*) sail, cruise, pilot, guide, steer.

**near** (*SYN.*) close, nigh, dear, adjacent, familiar, at hand, neighboring, approaching, impending, proximate, imminent, bordering. (*ANT.*) *removed, distant, far, remote.*

**nearly** (*SYN.*) practically, close to, approximately, almost.

**neat** (*SYN.*) trim, orderly, precise, clear, spruce, nice, clean, well-kept, clever, skillful, adept, apt, dapper, smart, proficient, expert, handy, well-done, shipshape, elegant, well-organized. (*ANT.*) *unkempt, sloppy, dirty, slovenly, messy, sloppy, disorganized.*

**nebulous** (*SYN.*) fuzzy, indistinct, indefinite, clouded, hazy. (*ANT.*) *definite, distinct, clear.*

**necessary** (*SYN.*) needed, expedient, unavoidable, required, essential, indispensable, urgent, imperative, inevitable, compelling, compulsory, obligatory, needed, exigent. (*ANT.*) *optional, nonessential, contingent, casual, accidental, unnecessary, dispensable, unneeded.*

**necessity** (*SYN.*) requirement, fate, destiny, constraint, requisite, poverty, exigency, compulsion, want, essential, prerequisite. (*ANT.*) *option, luxury, freedom, choice, uncertainty.*

**necromancy** (*SYN.*) witchcraft, charm, sorcery, conjuring, wizardry.

**need** (*SYN.*) crave, want, demand, claim, desire, covet, wish, lack, necessity, requirement, poverty, require, pennislessness.

**needed** (*SYN.*) necessary, indispensable, essential, requisite. (*ANT.*) *optional, contingent.*

**needle** *(SYN.)* goad, badger, tease, nag, prod, provoke.

**needless** *(SYN.)* nonessential, unnecessary, superfluous, useless, purposeless.

**needy** *(SYN.)* poor, indigent, impoverished, penniless, destitute. *(ANT.)* affluent, well-off, wealthy, well-to-do.

**nefarious** *(SYN.)* detestable, vicious, wicked, atrocious, horrible, vile.

**negate** *(SYN.)* revoke, void, cancel, nullify.

**neglect** *(SYN.)* omission, default, heedlessness, carelessness, thoughtlessness, disregard, negligence, oversight, omission, ignore, slight, failure, overlook, omit, skip, pass over, be inattentive, miss. *(ANT.)* diligence, do, protect, watchfulness, care, attention, careful, attend, regard, concern.

**negligent** *(SYN.)* imprudent, thoughtless, lax, careless, inattentive, indifferent, remiss, neglectful. *(ANT.)* careful, nice, accurate, meticulous.

**negligible** *(SYN.)* trifling, insignificant, trivial, inconsiderable. *(ANT.)* major, vital, important.

**negotiate** *(SYN.)* intervene, talk over, mediate, transact, umpire, referee, arbitrate, arrange, settle, bargain.

**neighborhood** *(SYN.)* environs, nearness, district, vicinity, area, section, locality. *(ANT.)* remoteness.

**neighboring** *(SYN.)* bordering, near, adjacent, next to, surrounding, adjoining.

**neighborly** *(SYN.)* friendly, sociable, amiable, affable, companionable, congenial, kind, cordial, amicable. *(ANT.)* distant, reserved, cool, unfriendly, hostile.

**neophyte** *(SYN.)* greenhorn, rookie, amateur, beginner, apprentice, tyro, student.

**nepotism** *(SYN.)* bias, prejudice, patronage, favoritism.

**nerve** *(SYN.)* bravery, spirit, courage, boldness, rudeness, strength, stamina, bravado, daring, impudence, mettle, impertinence. *(ANT.)* frailty, cowardice, weakness.

**nervous** *(SYN.)* agitated, restless, excited shy, timid, upset, disturbed, shaken, rattle, high-strung, flustered, tense, jittery, strained, edgy, perturbed, fearful. *(ANT.)* placid, courageous, confident, calm, tranquil, composed, bold.

**nest** *(SYN.)* den, refuge, hideaway.

**nestle** *(SYN.)* cuddle, snuggle.

**net** *(SYN.)* snare, trap, mesh, earn, gain, web, get, acquire, secure, obtain.

**nettle** *(SYN.)* irritate, vex, provoke, annoy, disturb, irk, needle, pester.

**neurotic** *(SYN.)* disturbed, psychoneurotic.

**neutral** *(SYN.)* nonpartisan, uninvolved, detached, impartial, cool, unprejudiced, indifferent, inactive. *(ANT.)* involved, biased, partisan.

**neutralize** *(SYN.)* offset, counteract, nullify, negate.

**nevertheless** *(SYN.)* notwithstanding, however, although, anyway, but, regardless.

**new** *(SYN.)* modem, original, newfangled, late, recent, novel, young, firsthand, fresh, unique, unusual. *(ANT.)* antiquated, old, ancient, obsolete, outmoded.

**newborn** *(SYN.)* baby, infant, cub, suckling.

**news** *(SYN.)* report, intelligence, information, copy, message, advice, tidings, knowledge, word, story, data.

**next** *(SYN.)* nearest, following, closest, successive, succeeding, subsequent.

**nibble** *(SYN.)* munch, chew, bit.

**nice** *(SYN.)* pleasing, pleasant, agreeable, thoughtful, satisfactory, friendly, enjoyable, gratifying, desirable, fine, good, cordial. *(ANT.)* nasty, unpleasant, disagreeable, unkind, inexact, careless, thoughtless.

**niche** *(SYN.)* corner, nook, alcove, cranny, recess.

**nick** *(SYN.)* cut, notch, indentation, dash, score, mark.

**nickname** *(SYN.)* byname, sobriquet.

**nigh** *(SYN.)* close, imminent, near, adjacent, approaching, bordering, neighboring, impending. *(ANT.)* removed, distant.

**nightmare** *(SYN.)* calamity, horror, torment, bad dream.

**nil** *(SYN.)* zero, none, naught, nothing.

**nimble** *(SYN.)* brisk, quick, active, supple, alert, lively, spry, light, fast, speedy, swift, agile. *(ANT.)* slow, heavy, sluggish, clumsy.

**nincompoop** *(SYN.)* nitwit, idiot, fool, moron, blockhead, ninny, idiot, simpleton.

**nip** *(SYN.)* bite, pinch, chill, cold, squeeze, crispness, sip, small.

**nippy** *(SYN.)* chilly, sharp, bitter, cold, penetrating.

**nit-picker** *(SYN.)* fussbudget, precise, purist, perfectionist.

**nitty-gritty** *(SYN.)* essentials, substance, essence.

**noble** *(SYN.)* illustrious, exalted, dignified, stately, eminent, lofty, grand, elevated, honorable, honest, virtuous, great, distinguished, majestic, important, prominent, magnificent, grandiose, aristocratic, upright, well-born. *(ANT.)* vile, low, base, mean, dishonest, common, ignoble.

**nod** *(SYN.)* bob, bow, bend, tip, signal.

**node** *(SYN.)* protuberance, growth, nodule, cyst, lump, wen.

**noise** *(SYN.)* cry, sound, din, babel, racket, uproar, clamor, outcry, tumult, sounds, hubbub, bedlam, commotion, rumpus, clatter. *(ANT.)* quiet, stillness, hush, silence, peace.

**noisome** *(SYN.)* repulsive, disgusting, revolting, obnoxious, malodorous, rotten, rancid.

**noisy** *(SYN.)* resounding, loud, clamorous, vociferous, stentorian, tumultuous. *(ANT.)* soft, dulcet, subdued, quiet, silent, peaceful.

**nomad** *(SYN.)* gypsy, rover, traveler, roamer, migrant, vagrant, wanderer.

**nominate** *(SYN.)* propose, choose, select.

**nomination** *(SYN.)* appointment, naming, choice, selection, designation.

**nominee** *(SYN.)* contestant, candidate.

**nonbeliever** *(SYN.)* skeptic, infidel, atheist, heathen.

**nonchalant** *(SYN.)* unconcerned, indifferent, cool, casual, easygoing.

**noncommittal** *(SYN.)* neutral, tepid, undecided, cautious, guarded, uncommunicative.

**nonconformist** *(SYN.)* protester, rebel, radical, dissenter, renegade, dissident, eccentric.

**nondescript** *(SYN.)* unclassifiable, indescribable, indefinite.

**nonentity** *(SYN.)* nothing, menial, nullity.

**nonessential** *(SYN.)* needless, unnecessary.

**nonpareil** *(SYN.)* unsurpassed, exceptional, paramount, unrivaled.

**nonplus** *(SYN.)* confuse, perplex, dumfound, mystify, confound, puzzle, baffle, bewilder. *(ANT.)* illumine, clarify, salve, explain.

**nonsense** *(SYN.)* balderdash, rubbish, foolishness, folly, ridiculousness, stupidity, absurdity, poppycock, trash.

**nonsensical** *(SYN.)* silly, preposterous, absurd, unreasonable, foolish, irrational, ridiculous, stupid, senseless. *(ANT.)* sound, consistent, reasonable.

**nonstop** *(SYN.)* constant, continuous, unceasing, endless.

**nook** *(SYN.)* niche, corner, recess, cranny.

**noose** *(SYN.)* snare, rope, lasso, loop.

**normal** *(SYN.)* ordinary, uniform, natural, unvaried, customary, regular, healthy, sound, whole, usual, typical, characteristic, routine, standard. *(ANT.)* rare, erratic, unusual, abnormal.

**normally** *(SYN.)* regularly, frequently, usually, customarily.

**nosy** *(SYN.)* inquisitive, meddling, peering, searching, prying, snooping. *(ANT.)* unconcerned, incurious, uninterested.

**notable** *(SYN.)* noted, unusual, uncommon, noteworthy, remarkable, conspicuous, distinguished, distinctive, celebrity, starts, important, striking, special, memorable, extraordinary, rare, exceptional, personality. *(ANT.)* commonplace, ordinary, usual.

**notch** *(SYN.)* cut, nick, indentation, gash.

**note** *(SYN.)* sign, annotation, letter, indication, observation, mark, symbol, comment, remark, token, message, memorandum, record, memo, write, list, inscribe, notice.

**noted** *(SYN.)* renowned, glorious, celebrated, famous, illustrious, well-known, distinguished, famed, notable. *(ANT.)* unknown, hidden, infamous, ignominious.

**noteworthy** *(SYN.)* consequential, celebrated, exceptional, prominent.

**notice** *(SYN.)* heed, perceive, hold, mark, behold, descry, recognize, observe, attend to, remark, note, regard, see, sign, announcement, poster, advertisement, observation, warning. *(ANT.)* overlook, disregard, skip.

**notify** *(SYN.)* apprise, acquaint, instruct, tell, advise, warn, teach, inform, report, remind, announce, mention, reveal. *(ANT.)* mislead, delude, conceal.

**notion** *(SYN.)* image, conception, sentiment, abstraction, thought, idea, impression, fancy, understanding, view, opinion, concept. (*ANT.*) *thing, matter, substance, entity.*

**notorious** *(SYN.)* celebrated, renowned, famous, well-known, popular, infamous.

**nourish** *(SYN.)* strengthen, nurse, feed, supply, nurture, sustain, support.

**nourishment** *(SYN.)* nutriment, food, sustenance, support. (*ANT.*) *starvation, deprivation.*

**novel** *(SYN.)* fiction, narrative, allegory, tale, fable, story, romance, invention, different, unusual, strange, original. (*ANT.*) *verity, history, truth, fact.*

**novice** *(SYN.)* beginner, amateur, newcomer, greenhorn, learner, apprentice, freshman, dilettante. (*ANT.*) *expert, professional, adept, master.*

**now** *(SYN.)* today, at once, right away, immediately, at this time, present. (*ANT.*) *later.*

**noxious** *(SYN.)* poisonous, harmful, damaging, toxic, detrimental. (*ANT.*) *harmless.*

**nucleus** *(SYN.)* core, middle, heart, focus, hub, kernel.

**nude** *(SYN.)* naked, unclad, plain, open, defenseless, mere, bare, exposed, unprotected, simple, stripped, uncovered. (*ANT.*) *dressed, protected, clothed, covered.*

**nudge** *(SYN.)* prod, push, jab, shove, poke, prompt.

**nugget** *(SYN.)* clump, mass, lump, wad, chunk, hunk.

**nuisance** *(SYN.)* annoyance, bother, irritation, pest.

**nullify** *(SYN.)* abolish, cross out, delete, invalidate, obliterate, cancel, expunge, repeal, annul, revoke, quash, rescind. (*ANT.*) *perpetuate, confirm, enforce.*

**numb** *(SYN.)* unfeeling, dull, insensitive, deadened, anesthetized, stupefied.

**numeral** *(SYN.)* figure, symbol, digit.

**numerous** *(SYN.)* many, several, manifold, multifarious, various, multitudinous, diverse, abundant, sundry. (*ANT.*) *infrequent, meager, few, scarce.*

**nuptials** *(SYN.)* marriage, wedding, espousal, wedlock, matrimony. (*ANT.*) *virginity, divorce, celibacy.*

**nurse** *(SYN.)* tend, care for, nourish, nurture, feed, train, mind, attend.

**nurture** *(SYN.)* hold dear, foster, sustain, appreciate, prize, rear, value, treasure. (*ANT.*) *dislike, disregard, abandon.*

**nutriment** *(SYN.)* food, diet, sustenance, repast, meal, fare, edibles. (*ANT.*) *hunger, want, starvation.*

**nutrition** *(SYN.)* nourishment, sustenance, food, nutriment.

**oaf** *(SYN.)* boor, clod, clown, lummox, fool, lout, dunce, bogtrotter.

**oasis** *(SYN.)* shelter, haven, retreat, refuge.

**oath** *(SYN.)* promise, pledge, vow, profanity, curse, agreement, commitment.

**obdurate** *(SYN.)* insensible, callous, hard, rough, unfeeling, insensitive. (*ANT.*) *soft, compassionate, tender.*

**obedience** *(SYN.)* docility, submission, subservience, compliance. (*ANT.*) *rebelliousness, disobedience.*

**obedient** *(SYN.)* dutiful, yielding, tractable, compliant, submissive. (*ANT.*) *rebellious, intractable, insubordinate, obstinate.*

**obese** *(SYN.)* portly, fat, pudgy, chubby, plump, rotund, stout, thickset, corpulent, stocky. (*ANT.*) *slim, lean, thin, slender.*

**obey** *(SYN.)* submit, yield, mind, comply, listen to, conform. (*ANT.*) *resist, disobey.*

**obfuscate** *(SYN.)* bewilder, complicate, fluster, confuse.

**object** *(SYN.)* thing, aim, intention, design, end, objective, particular, mark, purpose, goal, target, article. (*ANT.*) *assent, agree, concur, approve, acquiesce.*

**objection** *(SYN.)* disagreement, protest, rejection, dissent, challenge, noncompliance, difference, nonconformity, recusancy, disapproval, criticism. (*ANT.*) *acceptance, compliance, agreement, assent.*

**objectionable** *(SYN.)* improper, offensive, unbecoming, deplorable.

**objective** *(SYN.)* aspiration, goal, passion, desire, aim, hope, purpose, drift, design, ambition, end, object, intention, intent, longing, craving. (*ANT.*) *biased, subjective.*

**objectivity** *(SYN.)* disinterest, neutrality, impartiality.

**obligate** *(SYN.)* oblige, require, pledge, bind, force, compel.

**obligation** *(SYN.)* duty, bond, engagement, compulsion, account, contract, ability, debt. (*ANT.*) *freedom, choice, exemption.*

**oblige** *(SYN.)* constrain, force, impel, enforce, coerce, drive, gratify. (*ANT.*) *persuade, convince, allure, free, induce, disoblige, prevent.*

**obliging** *(SYN.)* considerate, helpful, thoughtful, well-meaning, accommodating. (*ANT.*) *discourteous.*

**obliterate** *(SYN.)* terminate, destroy, eradicate, raze, extinguish, exterminate, annihilate, devastate, wipe out, ravage. (*ANT.*) *make, save, construct, establish, preserve.*

**oblivious** *(SYN.)* sightless, unmindful, headlong, rash, blind, senseless, ignorant, forgetful, undiscerning, preoccupied, unconscious, heedless. (*ANT.*) *sensible, aware, calculated, perceiving, discerning.*

**obloquy** *(SYN.)* defamation, rebuke, censure.

**obnoxious** *(SYN.)* hateful, offensive, nasty, disagreeable, repulsive, loathsome, vile, disgusting, detestable, wretched, terrible, despicable, dreadful.

**obscene** *(SYN.)* indecent, filthy, impure, dirty, gross, lewd, pornographic, coarse, disgusting, bawdy, offensive, smutty. (*ANT.*) *modest, pure, decent, refined.*

**obscure** *(SYN.)* cloudy, enigmatic, mysterious, abstruse, cryptic, dim, dusky, ambiguous, dark, indistinct, unintelligible, unclear, shadowy, fuzzy, blurred, vague. (*ANT.*) *clear, famous, distinguished, noted, illumined, lucid, bright, distinct.*

**obsequious** *(SYN.)* fawning, flattering.

**observance** *(SYN.)* protocol, ritual, ceremony, rite, parade, pomp, solemnity. (*ANT.*) *omission.*

**observant** *(SYN.)* aware, alert, mindful, watchful, heedful, considerate, attentive, anxious, circumspect, cautious, wary. (*ANT.*) *unaware, indifferent, oblivious.*

**observation** *(SYN.)* attention, watching, comment, opinion, remark, notice.

**observe** *(SYN.)* note, behold, discover, notice, perceive, eye, detect, inspect, keep, commemorate, mention, utter, watch, examine, mark, view, express, see, celebrate. (*ANT.*) *neglect, overlook, disregard, ignore.*

**observer** *(SYN.)* examiner, overseer, lookout, spectator, bystander, witness, watcher.

**obsession** *(SYN.)* preoccupation, mania, compulsion, passion, fetish, infatuation.

**obsolete** *(SYN.)* old, out-of-date, ancient, archaic, extinct, old-fashioned, discontinued, obsolescent, venerable, dated, antiquated. (*ANT.*) *modern, stylish, current, recent, fashionable, extant.*

**obstacle** *(SYN.)* block, hindrance, barrier, impediment, snag, check, deterrent, stoppage, hitch, bar, difficulty, obstruction. (*ANT.*) *help, aid, assistance, encouragement.*

**obstinate** *(SYN.)* firm, headstrong, immovable, stubborn, determined, dogged, intractable, uncompromising, inflexible, willful, bullheaded, contumacious, obdurate, unbending, unyielding, pertinacious. (*ANT.*) *yielding, docile, amenable, submissive, pliable, flexible, compliant.*

**obstruct** *(SYN.)* clog, barricade, impede, block, delay, hinder, stop, close, bar. (*ANT.*) *promote, clear, aid, help, open, further.*

**obstruction** *(SYN.)* block, obstacle, barrier, blockage, interference.

**obtain** *(SYN.)* get, acquire, secure, win, procure, attain, earn, gain, receive, assimilate. (*ANT.*) *surrender, forfeit, lose, forego, miss.*

**obtrusive** *(SYN.)* blatant, garish, conspicuous.

**obtuse** *(SYN.)* blunt, dull, slow-witted, unsharpened, stupid, dense, slow. (*ANT.*) *clear, interesting, lively, bright, animated, sharp.*

**obviate** *(SYN.)* prevent, obstruct, forestall, preclude, intercept, avert, evade.

**obvious** *(SYN.)* plain, clear, evident, palpable, patent, self-evident, apparent, distinct, understandable, manifest, unmistakable. (*ANT.*) *concealed, hidden, abstruse, obscure.*

**obviously** *(SYN.)* plainly, clearly, surely, evidently, certainly.

**occasion** *(SYN.)* occurrence, time, happening, excuse, opportunity, chance.

**occasional** *(SYN.)* random, irregular, sporadic, infrequent, periodically, spasmodic. (*ANT.*) *chronic, regular, constant.*

**occasionally** *(SYN.)* seldom, now and then, infrequently, sometimes, irregularly.

(ANT.) regularly, often.

**occlude** (SYN.) clog, obstruct, choke, throttle.

**occupant** (SYN.) tenant, lodger, boarder, dweller, resident, inhabitant.

**occupation** (SYN.) employment, business, enterprise, job, trade, vocation, work, profession, matter, interest, concern, affair, activity, commerce, trading, engagement. (ANT.) hobby, pastime, avocation.

**occupy** (SYN.) dwell, have, inhabit, absorb, hold, possess, fill, busy, keep. (ANT.) relinquish, abandon, release.

**occur** (SYN.) take place, bechance, come about, befall, chance, transpire, betide, happen.

**occurrence** (SYN.) episode, event, issue, end, result, consequence, happening, circumstance, outcome.

**ocean** (SYN.) deep, sea, main, briny.

**odd** (SYN.) strange, bizarre, eccentric, unusual, single, uneven, unique, queer, quaint, peculiar, curious, unmatched, remaining, singular. (ANT.) matched, common, typical, normal, familiar, even, usual.

**odious** (SYN.) obscene, depraved, vulgar, despicable, mean, wicked, sordid, foul, base, loathsome, vicious, displeasing, hateful, revolting, offensive, repulsive, horrible, obnoxious, vile. (ANT.) decent, upright, laudable, attractive, honorable.

**odor** (SYN.) fume, aroma, fragrance, redolence, smell, stink, scent, essence, stench.

**odorous** (SYN.) scented, aromatic, fragrant.

**odyssey** (SYN.) crusade, quest, journey, voyage.

**offbeat** (SYN.) uncommon, eccentric, strange, unconventional, peculiar.

**off-color** (SYN.) rude, improper, earthy, suggestive, salty.

**offend** (SYN.) annoy, anger, vex, irritate, displease, provoke, hurt, grieve, pain, disgust, wound, horrify, stricken, insult, outrage. (ANT.) flatter, please, delight.

**offender** (SYN.) criminal, culprit, lawbreaker, miscreant.

**offense** (SYN.) indignity, injustice, transgression, affront, outrage, misdeed, sin, insult, atrocity, aggression, crime. (ANT.) morality, gentleness, innocence, right.

**offensive** (SYN.) attacking, aggressive, unpleasant, revolting, disagreeable, nauseous, disgusting. (ANT.) pleasing, defending, defensive, pleasant, attractive, agreeable.

**offer** (SYN.) suggestion, overture, proposal, present, suggest, propose, try, submit, attempt, tender. (ANT.) withdrawal, denial, rejection.

**offhand** (SYN.) informal, unprepared, casual, impromptu, spontaneous. (ANT.) considered, planned, calculated.

**office** (SYN.) position, job, situation, studio, berth, incumbency, capacity, headquarters, duty, task, function, work, post.

**officiate** (SYN.) regulate, administer, superintend, oversee, emcee.

**offset** (SYN.) compensate, counterbalance, cushion, counteract, neutralize, soften, balance.

**offshoot** (SYN.) outgrowth, addition, byproduct, supplement, appendage, accessory, branch.

**offspring** (SYN.) issue, children, progeny, descendants.

**often** (SYN.) frequently, repeatedly, commonly, generally, many times, recurrently. (ANT.) seldom, infrequently, rarely, occasionally, sporadically.

**ogle** (SYN.) gaze, stare, eye, leer.

**ogre** (SYN.) fiend, monster, devil, demon.

**ointment** (SYN.) lotion, pomade, balm, emollient.

**old** (SYN.) antique, senile, ancient, archaic, old-fashioned, superannuated, obsolete, venerable, antiquated, elderly, discontinued, abandoned, aged. (ANT.) new, youthful, recent, modern, young.

**old-fashioned** (SYN.) outmoded, old, dated, ancient. (ANT.) modern, fashionable, current, new.

**olio** (SYN.) potpourri, variety, mixture, jumble.

**omen** (SYN.) sign, gesture, indication, proof, portent, symbol, token, emblem, signal.

**ominous** (SYN.) unfavorable, threatening, sinister, menacing.

**omission** (SYN.) failure, neglect, oversight, default. (ANT.) inclusion, notice, insertion.

**omit** (SYN.) exclude, delete, cancel, eliminate, ignore, neglect, skip, leave out, drop, miss, bar, overlook, disregard.

(ANT.) insert, notice, enter, include, introduce.

**omnipotent** (SYN.) all-powerful, almighty, divine.

**oncoming** (SYN.) imminent, approaching, arriving, nearing.

**onerous** (SYN.) intricate, arduous, hard, perplexing, difficult, burdensome, puzzling. (ANT.) simple, easy, facile, effortless.

**one-sided** (SYN.) unfair, partial, biased, prejudiced. (ANT.) impartial, neutral.

**ongoing** (SYN.) advancing, developing, continuing, progressive.

**onlooker** (SYN.) witness, spectator, observer, bystander.

**only** (SYN.) lone, sole, solitary, single, merely, but, just.

**onset** (SYN.) commencement, beginning, opening, start, assault, attack, charge, offense, onslaught. (ANT.) end.

**onslaught** (SYN.) invasion, aggression, attack, assault, offense, drive, criticism, onset, charge, denunciation. (ANT.) vindication, defense, surrender, opposition, resistance.

**onus** (SYN.) load, weight, burden, duty.

**onward** (SYN.) ahead, forward, frontward. (ANT.) backward.

**ooze** (SYN.) seep, leak, drip, flow, filter.

**opacity** (SYN.) obscurity, thickness, imperviousness.

**opaque** (SYN.) murky, dull, cloudy, filmy, unilluminated, dim, obtuse, indistinct, shadowy, dark, obscure. (ANT.) light, clear, bright.

**open** (SYN.) uncovered, overt, agape, unlocked, passable, accessible, unrestricted, candid, plain, clear, exposed, unclosed, unobstructed, free, disengaged, frank, unoccupied, public, honest, ajar, available.

**open** (SYN.) unbar, unfold, exhibit, spread, unseal, expand, unfasten. (ANT.) close, shut, conceal, hide.

**open-handed** (SYN.) kind, generous, charitable, lavish, extravagant, bountiful. (ANT.) mean, stingy.

**openhearted** (SYN.) frank, honest, candid, sincere, ingenuous, straightforward. (ANT.) insincere, devious.

**opening** (SYN.) cavity, hole, void, abyss, aperture, chasm, pore, gap, loophole.

**openly** (SYN.) sincerely, frankly, freely. (ANT.) secretly.

**open-minded** (SYN.) tolerant, fair, just, liberal, impartial, reasonable, unprejudiced. (ANT.) prejudiced, bigoted.

**operate** (SYN.) comport, avail, behave, interact, apply, manage, utilize, demean, run, manipulate, employ, act, exploit, exert, exercise, practice, conduct. (ANT.) neglect, waste.

**operation** (SYN.) effort, enterprise, mentality, maneuver, action, instrumentality, performance, working, proceeding, agency. (ANT.) inaction, cessation, rest, inactivity.

**operative** (SYN.) busy, active, industrious, working, effective, functional. (ANT.) inactive, dormant.

**opiate** (SYN.) hypnotic, tranquilizer, narcotic.

**opinion** (SYN.) decision, feeling, notion, view, idea, conviction, belief, judgment, sentiment, persuasion, impression. (ANT.) knowledge, fact, misgiving, skepticism.

**opinionated** (SYN.) domineering, overbearing, arrogant, dogmatic, positive, magisterial, obstinate, pertinacious. (ANT.) questioning, fluctuating, indecisive, skeptical, open-minded, indecisive.

**opponent** (SYN.) competitor, foe, adversary, contestant, enemy, rival, contender, combatant, antagonist. (ANT.) comrade, team, ally, confederate.

**opportune** (SYN.) fitting, suitable, appropriate, proper, favorable, felicitous.

**opportunity** (SYN.) possibility, chance, occasion, time, contingency, opening. (ANT.) obstacle, disadvantage, hindrance.

**oppose** (SYN.) defy, resist, withstand, combat, bar, counteract, confront, thwart, struggle, fight, contradict, hinder, obstruct. (ANT.) submit, support, agree, cooperate, succumb.

**opposed** (SYN.) opposite, contrary, hostile, adverse, counteractive, unlucky, antagonistic, unfavorable, disastrous. (ANT.) lucky, benign, propitious, fortunate, favorable.

**opposite** (SYN.) reverse, contrary, different, unlike, opposed. (ANT.) like, same, similar.

**opposition** (SYN.) combat, struggle, discord, collision, conflict, battle, fight, encounter, discord, controversy, inconsistency, variance. (ANT.) harmony, amity, concord, consonance.

**oppress** *(SYN.)* harass, torment, vex, afflict, annoy, harry, pester, hound, worry, persecute. *(ANT.) encourage, support, comfort, assist, aid.*

**oppression** *(SYN.)* cruelty, tyranny, persecution, injustice, despotism, brutality, abuse. *(ANT.) liberty, freedom.*

**oppressive** *(SYN.)* difficult, stifling, burdensome, severe, domineering, harsh, unjust, overbearing, overwhelming.

**oppressor** *(SYN.)* bully, scourge, slave-driver.

**opprobrium** *(SYN.)* disgrace, contempt, reproach, shame, discredit.

**opt** *(SYN.)* choose, prefer, pick, select.

**optical** *(SYN.)* seeing, visual.

**optimism** *(SYN.)* faith, expectation, optimism, anticipation, trust, expectancy, confidence, hope. *(ANT.) despair, pessimism, despondency.*

**optimistic** *(SYN.)* happy, cheerful, bright, glad, pleasant, radiant, lighthearted. *(ANT.) pessimistic.*

**option** *(SYN.)* preference, choice, selection, alternative, election, self-determination.

**optional** *(SYN.)* selective, elective, voluntary. *(ANT.) required.*

**opulence** *(SYN.)* luxury, abundance, fortune, riches, wealth, plenty, affluence. *(ANT.) need, indigence, want, poverty.*

**opulent** *(SYN.)* wealthy, rich, prosperous, well-off, affluent, well-heeled.

**oracle** *(SYN.)* authority, forecaster, wizard, seer, mastermind, clairvoyant.

**oral** *(SYN.)* voiced, sounded, vocalized, said, uttered, verbal, vocal, spoken. *(ANT.) recorded, written, documentary.*

**orate** *(SYN.)* preach, lecture, sermonize.

**oration** *(SYN.)* address, lecture, speech, sermon, discourse, recital, declamation.

**orb** *(SYN.)* globe, sphere, ball, moon.

**orbit** *(SYN.)* path, lap, course, circuit, revolution, revolve, circle.

**orchestra** *(SYN.)* ensemble, band.

**orchestrate** *(SYN.)* coordinate, direct, synchronize, organize.

**ordain** *(SYN.)* constitute, create, order, decree, decide, dictate, command, rule, bid, sanction, appoint. *(ANT.) terminate, disband.*

**ordeal** *(SYN.)* hardship, suffering, test, affliction, trouble, fortune, proof, examination, trial, experiment, tribulation, misery. *(ANT.) consolation, alleviation.*

**order** *(SYN.)* plan, series, decree, instruction, command, system, method, aim, arrangement, class, injunction, mandate, instruct, requirement, dictate, guide, rule, direct, govern, manage, regulate, bid, conduct *(ANT.) consent, license, confusion, disarray, irregularity, permission.*

**orderly** *(SYN.)* regulated, neat, well-organized, disciplined, methodical, shipshape. *(ANT.) sloppy, messy, haphazard, disorganized.*

**ordinarily** *(SYN.)* commonly, usually, generally, mostly, customarily, normally.

**ordinary** *(SYN.)* common, habitual, normal, typical, usual, conventional, familiar, accustomed, customary, average, standard, everyday, inferior, mediocre, regular, vulgar, plain. *(ANT.) uncommon, marvelous, extraordinary, remarkable, strange.*

**ordnance** *(SYN.)* munitions, artillery.

**organ** *(SYN.)* instrument, journal, voice.

**organic** *(SYN.)* living, biological, animate.

**organism** *(SYN.)* creature, plant, microorganism.

**organization** *(SYN.)* order, rule, system, arrangement, method, plan, regularity, scheme, mode, process. *(ANT.) irregularity, chaos, disarrangement, chance, disorder.*

**organize** *(SYN.)* assort, arrange, plan, regulate, systematize, devise, categorize, classify, prepare. *(ANT.) jumble, disorder, disturb, confuse, scatter.*

**organized** *(SYN.)* planned, neat, orderly, arranged.

**orient** *(SYN.)* align, fit, accustom, adjust.

**orifice** *(SYN.)* vent, slot, opening, hole.

**origin** *(SYN.)* birth, foundation, source, start, commencement, inception, beginning, derivation, infancy, parentage, spring, cradle. *(ANT.) product, issue, outcome, end.*

**original** *(SYN.)* primary, fresh, new, initial, pristine, creative, first, primordial, inventive, primeval, novel, introductory.

*(ANT.) banal, trite, subsequent, derivative, later, modern, terminal.*

**originality** *(SYN.)* unconventionality, genius, novelty, creativity, imagination.

**originate** *(SYN.)* fashion, invent, cause, create, make, initiate, inaugurate, organize, institute, produce, engender, commence, found, establish, form, begin, arise, generate, formulate. *(ANT.) demolish, terminate, annihilate, disband, destroy.*

**originator** *(SYN.)* creator, inventor, discoverer. *(ANT.) follower, imitator.*

**ornament** *(SYN.)* decoration, ornamentation, adornment, embellishment, trimming, garnish.

**ornamental** *(SYN.)* ornate, decorative.

**ornate** *(SYN.)* florid, overdone, elaborate, showy, flowery, pretentious.

**ornery** *(SYN.)* disobedient, firm, unruly, stiff, rebellious, stubborn, headstrong, willful, contrary, rigid, mean, difficult, malicious, cross, disagreeable. *(ANT.) pleasant.*

**orthodox** *(SYN.)* customary, usual, conventional, correct, proper, accepted. *(ANT.) different, unorthodox.*

**oscillate** *(SYN.)* vary, change, hesitate, waver, undulate, fluctuate, vacillate. *(ANT.) persist, resolve, adhere, stick, decide.*

**ostentation** *(SYN.)* parade, show, boasting, pageantry, vaunting, pomp, display, flourish. *(ANT.) reserve, humility, unobtrusiveness, modesty.*

**ostentatious** *(SYN.)* flashy, showy, overdone, fancy, pretentious, garish.

**ostracize** *(SYN.)* hinder, omit, bar, exclude, blackball, expel, prohibit, shout out, prevent, except. *(ANT.) welcome, accept, include, admit.*

**other** *(SYN.)* distinct, different, extra, further, new, additional, supplementary.

**ought** *(SYN.)* must, should, be obliged.

**oust** *(SYN.)* eject, banish, exclude, expatriate, ostracize, dismiss, exile, expel. *(ANT.) shelter, accept, receive, admit, harbor.*

**ouster** *(SYN.)* expulsion, banishment, ejection, overthrow.

**outbreak** *(SYN.)* riot, revolt, uprising, disturbance, torrent, eruption, outburst.

**outburst** *(SYN.)* outbreak,

eruption, torrent, ejection, discharge.

**outcast** *(SYN.)* friendless, homeless, deserted, abandoned, forsaken, disowned, derelict, forlorn, rejected.

**outclass** *(SYN.)* outshine, surpass.

**outcome** *(SYN.)* fate, destiny, necessity, doom, portion, consequence, result, end, fortune, effect, issue, aftermath.

**outcry** *(SYN.)* scream, protest, clamor, noise, uproar.

**outdated** *(SYN.)* old-fashioned, unfashionable, old, outmoded. *(ANT.) stylish.*

**outdo** *(SYN.)* outshine, defeat, excel, beat, surpass.

**outer** *(SYN.)* remote, exterior, external.

**outfit** *(SYN.)* garb, kit, gear, furnish, equip, rig, clothing, provisions.

**outgoing** *(SYN.)* leaving, departing, friendly, congenial, amicable. *(ANT.) unfriendly, incoming.*

**outgrowth** *(SYN.)* effect, outcome, upshot, fruit, result, consequence, product.

**outing** *(SYN.)* journey, trip, excursion, jaunt, expedition, junket.

**outlandish** *(SYN.)* peculiar, odd, weird, curious, strange, queer, exotic, bazaar. *(ANT.) ordinary, common.*

**outlast** *(SYN.)* survive, endure, outlive.

**outlaw** *(SYN.)* exile, bandit, outcast, bad-man, convict, criminal, fugitive, desperado.

**outlay** *(SYN.)* expense, costs, spending, disbursement, expenditure, charge.

**outlet** *(SYN.)* spout, opening, passage.

**outline** *(SYN.)* form, sketch, brief, draft, figure, profile, contour, chart, diagram, skeleton, delineation, plan, silhouette.

**outlook** *(SYN.)* viewpoint, view, prospect, opportunity, position, attitude, future.

**outlying** *(SYN.)* external, remote, outer, out-of-the-way, suburban, rural.

**outmoded** *(SYN.)* unfashionable, old-fashioned. *(ANT.) up-to-date, modern.*

**outnumber** *(SYN.)* exceed.

**output** *(SYN.)* yield, crop, harvest, proceeds, productivity, production.

**outrage** *(SYN.)* aggression, transgression, vice, affront, offense, insult, indignity, atrocity, misdeed, trespass, wrong. *(ANT.) morality, right, gentleness, innocence.*

**outrageous** *(SYN.)* shameful, shocking, disgraceful, insulting, nonsensical, absurd, foolish, crazy, excessive, ridiculous, bizarre, preposterous, offensive. *(ANT.) prudent, reasonable, sensible.*

**outright** *(SYN.)* entirely, altogether, completely, quite, fully, thoroughly.

**outset** *(SYN.)* inception, origin, start, commencement, opening, source. *(ANT.) end, completion, termination, consummation, close.*

**outside** *(SYN.)* covering, exterior, surface, facade, externals, appearance. *(ANT.) intimate, insider.*

**outsider** *(SYN.)* immigrant, stranger, foreigner, alien, newcomer, bystander. *(ANT.) countryman, friend, acquaintance, neighbor, associate.*

**outsmart** *(SYN.)* outmaneuver, outwit.

**outspoken** *(SYN.)* rude, impolite, unceremonious, brusque, unrestrained, vocal, open, straight-forward, blunt, unreserved, frank, forthright, rough. *(ANT.) suave, tactful, shy, polished, polite, subtle.*

**outstanding** *(SYN.)* well-known, important, prominent, leading, eminent, distinguished, significant, conspicuous. *(ANT.) insignificant, unimportant.*

**outward** *(SYN.)* apparent, outside, exterior, visible.

**outweigh** *(SYN.)* predominate, supersede, counteract, dwarf.

**outwit** *(SYN.)* baffle, trick, outsmart, bewilder, outdo, outmaneuver, confuse.

**oval** *(SYN.)* egg-shaped, elliptical, ovular.

**ovation** *(SYN.)* fanfare, homage, applause, tribute, cheers, acclamation.

**overall** *(SYN.)* comprehensive, complete, general, extensive, wide-spread, entire.

**overbearing** *(SYN.)* domineering, masterful, autocratic, dictatorial, arrogant, bossy, imperious, haughty. *(ANT.) humble.*

**overcast** *(SYN.)* dim, shadowy, cloudy, murky, dark, mysterious, gloomy, somber, dismal, hazy, indistinct. *(ANT.) sunny, bright, limpid, clear.*

**overcome** *(SYN.)* quell, beat, crush, surmount, rout, humble, conquer, subjugate, defeat, subdue, upset, vanquish. *(ANT.) retreat, surrender, capitulate, cede, lose.*

**overconfident** *(SYN.)* egotistical, presumptuous, arrogant, conceited.

**overdo** *(SYN.)* stretch, exaggerate, enlarge, magnify, exhaust, overexert.

**overdue** *(SYN.)* tardy, advanced, slow, delayed, new. *(ANT.) timely, early, beforehand.*

**overflow** *(SYN.)* run over, flood, spill, cascade, inundate.

**overflowing** *(SYN.)* ample, plentiful, teeming, abundant, copious, profuse. *(ANT.) insufficient, deficient, scarce.*

**overhang** *(SYN.)* protrude, extend.

**overhaul** *(SYN.)* recondition, rebuild, service, repair, condition, revamp.

**overhead** *(SYN.)* high, above, aloft, expenses, costs.

**overjoyed** *(SYN.)* enchanted, delighted, ecstatic, enraptured, elated, blissful. *(ANT.) depressed.*

**overlap** *(SYN.)* overhang, extend, superimpose.

**overload** *(SYN.)* burden, weight, oppress, afflict, weigh, trouble, encumber, tax. *(ANT.) ease, lighten, console, alleviate.*

**overlook** *(SYN.)* miss, disregard, exclude, cancel, omit, skip, ignore, drop, delete, neglect, exclude, watch, eliminate. *(ANT.) notice, include, introduce, inset.*

**overly** *(SYN.)* exceedingly, unreasonably.

**overpass** *(SYN.)* span, bridge, viaduct.

**overpower** *(SYN.)* overcome, conquer, defeat, surmount, vanquish, overwhelm. *(ANT.) surrender.*

**overrule** *(SYN.)* disallow, nullify, cancel, override, repeal, revoke.

**overrun** *(SYN.)* spread, exceed, beset, infest, flood, abound.

**oversee** *(SYN.)* direct, run, operate, administer, boss, manage, supervise.

**overseer** *(SYN.)* leader, ruler, master, teacher, chief, commander, lord, employer, manager, head. *(ANT.) slave, servant.*

**overshadow** *(SYN.)* dominate, control, outclass, surpass, domineer.

**oversight** *(SYN.)* omission, charge, superintendence, surveillance, inattention, error, inadvertence, neglect, mistake, inspection, control, slip, management. *(ANT.) scrutiny, attention, observation.*

**overstep** *(SYN.)* surpass, exceed, trespass, transcend, impinge, violate, intrude.

**overt** *(SYN.)* honest, candid, frank, plain, open, apparent, straightforward.

**overtake** *(SYN.)* outdistance, reach, catch, pass.

**overthrow** *(SYN.)* defeat, demolish, overcome, destroy, ruin, rout, vanquish, subvert, reverse, supplant, overturn, overpower, upset. *(ANT.) revive, restore, construct, regenerate, reinstate.*

**overturn** *(SYN.)* demolish, overcome, vanquish, upset, supplant, destroy. *(ANT.) uphold, construct, build, preserve, conserve.*

**overweight** *(SYN.)* pudgy, stout, heavy, obese, fat.

**overwhelm** *(SYN.)* crush, surmount, vanquish, conquer, astonish, surprise, bewilder, astound, startle, overcome.

**overwrought** *(SYN.)* distraught, hysterical.

**owe** *(SYN.)* be liable, be indebted.

**own** *(SYN.)* monopolize, hold, possess, maintain, have.

**owner** *(SYN.)* landholder, partner, proprietor, possessor.

# P

**pace** *(SYN.)* rate, gait, step.

**pacify** *(SYN.)* appease, lull, relieve, quell, soothe, allay, assuage, calm, satisfy, compose, placate, alleviate. *(ANT.) incense, inflame, arouse, excite.*

**pack** *(SYN.)* prepare, stow, crowd, stuff, bundle, parcel, load, crowd, gang, mob.

**package** *(SYN.)* parcel, packet, load, bundle, box, bottle, crate.

**packed** *(SYN.)* filled, complete, plentiful, crammed, fall, replete, gorged, satiated. *(ANT.) lacking, depleted, devoid, vacant, insufficient, partial, empty.*

**pageant** *(SYN.)* show, display, spectacle.

**pain** *(SYN.)* twinge, ache, pang, agony, distress, grief, anguish, throe, paroxysm. *(ANT.) happiness, pleasure, comfort, relief, solace, ease, delight, joy.*

**painful** *(SYN.)* hurting, galling, poignant, bitter, grievous, agonizing, aching. *(ANT.) sweet, pleasant, soothing.*

**painting** *(SYN.)* image, picture, portrayal, scene, view, sketch, illustration, panorama, likeness, representation.

**pair** *(SYN.)* team, couple, mate, match.

**palatial** *(SYN.)* majestic, magnificent, sumptuous, luxurious.

**pale** *(SYN.)* colorless, white, pallid, dim, faint, whiten, blanch. *(ANT.) flushed, ruddy, bright, dark.*

**pamphlet** *(SYN.)* leaflet, brochure.

**pang** *(SYN.)* throb, pain, hurt.

**panic** *(SYN.)* fear, terror, fright, alarm, apprehension, trembling, horror, dread. *(ANT.) tranquillity, composure, calmness, serenity, calm, soothe.*

**pant** *(SYN.)* wheeze, puff, gasp.

**pantry** *(SYN.)* cupboard, storeroom.

**paper** *(SYN.)* journal, newspaper, document, article, essay.

**parable** *(SYN.)* fable, saga, legend, myth, allegory, chronicle, fiction.

**parade** *(SYN.)* procession, cavalcade, succession, train, file, cortege, retinue, sequence, march, review, pageant, strut.

**paradise** *(SYN.)* utopia, heaven.

**paradoxical** *(SYN.)* unsteady, contradictory, discrepant, incompatible, inconsistent, vacillating, wavering, illogical. *(ANT.) correspondent, compatible, congruous, consistent.*

**parallel** *(SYN.)* allied, analogous, comparable, corresponding, akin, similar, correlative, alike, like, resembling, equal, counterpart, likeness, correspondence, resemble, equal, match. *(ANT.) opposed, different, incongruous.*

**paralyze** *(SYN.)* numb, deaden.

**paraphernalia** *(SYN.)* effect, gear, belonging, equipment.

**parcel** *(SYN.)* packet, package, bundle.

**parched** *(SYN.)* dry, arid, thirsty, drained, dehydrated, desiccated. *(ANT.) moist, damp.*

**pardon** *(SYN.)* absolution, amnesty, excuse, exoneration, forgive, acquit, condone, overlook, absolve, remit. *(ANT.) punish, chastise, accuse, sentence, penalty, conviction, condemn, convict.*

**pare** *(SYN.)* skin, peel, reduce, trim, shave.

**parley** *(SYN.)* interview, talk, conference, chat, dialogue,

# paroxysm

colloquy.

**paroxysm** *(SYN.)* twinge, pang, ache, pain. *(ANT.)* ease, relief, comfort.

**parsimonious** *(SYN.)* avaricious, miserly, penurious, stingy, acquisitive, greedy. *(ANT.)* munificent, extravagant, bountiful, altruistic, generous.

**part** *(SYN.)* piece, section, allotment, portion, segment, element, member, concern, side, interest, lines, role, apportionment, division, share, fragment, ingredient, organ, party, moiety, section, fraction, participation, divide, separate, sever, sunder. *(ANT.)* whole, entirety, join, combine, unite, convene.

**partake** *(SYN.)* dispense, parcel, allot, assign, distribute, partition, appropriate, divide, portion, share. *(ANT.)* condense, aggregate, combine.

**partial** *(SYN.)* unfinished, undone, incomplete, prejudiced, unfair. *(ANT.)* comprehensive, complete.

**partiality** *(SYN.)* preconception, bias, predisposition, bigotry. *(ANT.)* reason, fairness, impartiality.

**participant** *(SYN.)* associate, colleague, partner, shareholder.

**participate** *(SYN.)* join, share, partake.

**participation** *(SYN.)* communion, sacrament, union, intercourse, association, fellowship. *(ANT.)* nonparticipation, alienation.

**particle** *(SYN.)* mite, crumb, scrap, atom, corpuscle, grain, iota, shred, smidgen, grain, speck, bit, spot. *(ANT.)* quantity, bulk, mass.

**particular** *(SYN.)* peculiar, unusual, detailed, specific, fastidious, individual, distinctive, singular, circumstantial, exact, careful, squeamish, special. *(ANT.)* general, rough, universal, comprehensive, undiscriminating.

**partisan** *(SYN.)* follower, successor, adherent, attendant, henchman, devotee, disciple, votary. *(ANT.)* leader, chief, master, head.

**partition** *(SYN.)* distribution, division, separation, screen, barrier, separator, divider, wall. *(ANT.)* unification, joining.

**partly** *(SYN.)* comparatively, partially, somewhat.

**partner** *(SYN.)* colleague, comrade, friend, crony, consort, associate, companion,

mate, participant. *(ANT.)* stranger, enemy, adversary.

**party** *(SYN.)* company, gathering, crowd, group.

**pass** *(SYN.)* proceed, continue, move, go, disregard, ignore, exceed, gap, permit, permission, admission, throw, toss. *(ANT.)* note, consider, notice.

**passable** *(SYN.)* fair, average, mediocre, acceptable, adequate, satisfactory. *(ANT.)* worst, excellent, first-rate, exceptional, extraordinary, superior.

**passage** *(SYN.)* section, passageway, corridor, section, voyage, tour, crossing.

**passenger** *(SYN.)* traveler, tourist, rider, voyager, commuter.

**passion** *(SYN.)* feeling, affection, turmoil, sentiment, perturbation, agitation, emotion, trepidation, zeal, rapture, excitement, desire, love, liking, fondness, enthusiasm. *(ANT.)* tranquillity, indifference, calm, restraint, dispassion, apathy, coolness.

**passionate** *(SYN.)* fiery, ardent, burning, glowing, irascible, fervid, excitable, hot, impetuous, emotional, impulsive, excited, zealous, enthusiastic, earnest, sincere. *(ANT.)* calm, cool, apathetic, deliberate.

**passive** *(SYN.)* relaxed, idle, stoical, enduring, inert, inactive, patient, submissive. *(ANT.)* dynamic, active, aggressive.

**password** *(SYN.)* code word.

**past** *(SYN.)* done, finished, gone, over, former. *(ANT.)* future, present, ahead.

**pastime** *(SYN.)* match, amusement, diversion, fun, play, sport, contest, merriment, recreation, entertainment, hobby. *(ANT.)* quiescence, labor, apathy, business.

**patch** *(SYN.)* restore, fix, repair, ameliorate, correct, rectify, remedy, sew, mend, better. *(ANT.)* rend, deface, destroy, hurt, injure.

**patent** *(SYN.)* conspicuous, apparent, obvious, clear, evident, unmistakable, open, overt, manifest, indubitable, protection, control, copyright, permit. *(ANT.)* hidden, concealed, obscure, coven.

**path** *(SYN.)* avenue, street, trail, walk, course, route, thoroughfare, channel, way, track, lane, footpath, pathway, walkway.

**pathetic** *(SYN.)* piteous, sad,

affecting, moving, poignant, pitiable, touching, pitiful, touching. *(ANT.)* funny, comical.

**patience** *(SYN.)* perseverance, composure, endurance, fortitude, long-suffering, forbearance, calmness, passiveness, serenity, courage, persistence. *(ANT.)* restlessness, nervousness, impatience, impetuosity.

**patient** *(SYN.)* indulgent, stoical, forbearing, composed, assiduous, passive, uncomplaining, resigned, persistent, untiring, persevering, submissive, resigned, serene, calm, quiet, unexcited, unruffled. *(ANT.)* turbulent, high-strung, chafing, clamorous, hysterical.

**patrol** *(SYN.)* inspect, watch, guard.

**patron** *(SYN.)* purchaser, buyer, client, customer.

**patronize** *(SYN.)* support.

**pattern** *(SYN.)* guide, example, original, model, design, figure, decoration.

**paunchy** *(SYN.)* fat, pudgy, stout, plump, portly, rotund, corpulent, obese, stocky. *(ANT.)* slim, slender, gaunt, lean, thin.

**pause** *(SYN.)* falter, hesitate, waver, demur, doubt, scruple, delay, vacillate, hesitation, rest, interruption, break, delay, intermission, recess. *(ANT.)* proceed, continue, decide, resolve, persevere, continuity.

**pawn** *(SYN.)* tool, puppet, stooge.

**pay** *(SYN.)* earnings, salary, allowance, stipend, wages, payment, compensation, recompense. *(ANT.)* gratuity, present, gift.

**payable** *(SYN.)* unpaid, due, owed, owing.

**peace** *(SYN.)* hush, repose, serenity, tranquillity, silence, stillness, calmness, quiescence, calm, quietude, rest, quiet, peacefulness, pact. *(ANT.)* noise, tumult, agitation, disturbance, excitement.

**peaceable** *(SYN.)* mild, calm, friendly, peaceful, amiable, gentle, pacific. *(ANT.)* aggressive, hostile, warlike.

**peaceful** *(SYN.)* pacific, calm, undisturbed, quiet, serene, mild, placid, gentle, tranquil, peaceable. *(ANT.)* noisy, violent, agitated, turbulent, disturbed, disrupted, riotous.

**peak** *(SYN.)* climax, culmination, summit, zenith, height, acme, consummation, apex, top, point, crest. *(ANT.)*

depth, floor, base, anticlimax, base, bottom.

**peculiar** *(SYN.)* odd, eccentric, extraordinary, unusual, individual, particular, striking, rare, exceptional, distinctive, strange, unfamiliar, uncommon, queer, curious, outlandish. *(ANT.)* ordinary, common, normal, general, regular.

**peculiarity** *(SYN.)* characteristic, feature, mark, trait, quality, attribute, property, distinctiveness.

**pedantic** *(SYN.)* formal, scholastic, erudite, academic, learned, bookish, theoretical, scholarly. *(ANT.)* simple, commonsense, ignorant, practical, unlearned.

**peddle** *(SYN.)* sell, vend, hawk.

**pedestrian** *(SYN.)* stroller, walker.

**pedigree** *(SYN.)* descent, line, parentage, lineage, ancestry, family.

**peek** *(SYN.)* glimpse, look, peer, peep.

**peel** *(SYN.)* rind, skin, peeling.

**peep** *(SYN.)* squeak, cheep, chirp.

**peer** *(SYN.)* match, rival, equal, parallel, peep, glimpse, examine, peek, scrutinize.

**peeve** *(SYN.)* nettle, irk, irritate, annoy.

**peevish** *(SYN.)* ill-natured, irritable, waspish, touchy, petulant, snappish, fractious, ill-tempered, fretful. *(ANT.)* pleasant, affable, good-tempered, genial, good-natured.

**pen** *(SYN.)* coop, enclosure, cage.

**penalize** *(SYN.)* dock, punish.

**penalty** *(SYN.)* fine, retribution, handicap, punishment, chastisement, disadvantage, forfeiture, forfeit. *(ANT.)* remuneration, compensation, reward, pardon.

**penchant** *(SYN.)* disposition, propensity, tendency, partiality, inclination, bent, tendency, slant, bias. *(ANT.)* justice, fairness, equity, impartiality.

**penetrate** *(SYN.)* bore, hole, pierce, enter.

**penetrating** *(SYN.)* profound, recondite, abstruse, deep, solemn, piercing, puncturing, boring, sharp, acute. *(ANT.)* superficial, trivial, shallow, slight.

**peninsula** *(SYN.)* spit, headland, neck, point.

**penitent** *(SYN.)* remorseful, sorrowful, regretful, contrite, sorry, repentant. *(ANT.)* remorseless, objurgate.

**penniless** (SYN.) poor, destitute, impecunious, poverty-stricken, needy. (ANT.) rich, wealthy, affluent, opulent, prosperous, well-off.

**pensive** (SYN.) dreamy, meditative, thoughtful, introspective, reflective, contemplative. (ANT.) thoughtless, heedless, inconsiderate, precipitous, rash.

**penurious** (SYN.) avaricious, greedy, parsimonious, miserly, stingy, acquisitive, tight. (ANT.) munificent, extravagant, bountiful, generous, altruistic.

**penury** (SYN.) poverty, want, destitution, necessity, indigence, need, privation. (ANT.) riches, affluence, abundance, plenty.

**people** (SYN.) humans, person.

**perceive** (SYN.) note, conceive, see, comprehend, understand, discern, recognize, apprehend, notice, observe, distinguish, grasp. (ANT.) overlook, ignore, miss.

**perceptible** (SYN.) sensible, appreciable, apprehensible. (ANT.) imperceptible, absurd, impalpable.

**perception** (SYN.) understanding, apprehension, conception, insight, comprehension, discernment. (ANT.) misconception, ignorance, misapprehension.

**perceptive** (SYN.) informed, observant, apprised, cognizant, aware, conscious, sensible, mindful, discerning, sharp, acute, observant. (ANT.) unaware, ignorant, oblivious, insensible.

**perfect** (SYN.) ideal, whole, faultless, immaculate, complete, superlative, absolute, unqualified, utter, sinless, holy, finished, blameless, entire, excellent, pure, flawless, ideal. (ANT.) incomplete, defective, imperfect, deficient, blemished, lacking, faulty, flawed.

**perfectionist** (SYN.) purist, pedant.

**perform** (SYN.) impersonate, pretend, act, play, do, accomplish, achieve, complete.

**performance** (SYN.) parade, entertainment, demonstration, movie, show, production, ostentation, spectacle, presentation, offering.

**performer** (SYN.) entertainer, actress, actor.

**perfume** (SYN.) cologne, scent, essence.

**perfunctory** (SYN.) decorous, exact, formal, external, correct, affected, methodical, precise, stiff, outward, proper, solemn. (ANT.) unconventional, easy, unconstrained, natural, heartfelt.

**perhaps** (SYN.) conceivable, possible, maybe. (ANT.) absolutely, definitely.

**peril** (SYN.) jeopardy, risk, danger, hazard. (ANT.) safety, protection, defense, security.

**perilous** (SYN.) menacing, risky, hazardous, critical, dangerous, precarious, unsafe, insecure, threatening. (ANT.) safe, firm, protected, secure.

**period** (SYN.) era, age, interval, span, tempo, time, epoch, duration, spell, date.

**periodical** (SYN.) uniform, customary, orderly, systematic, regular, steady. (ANT.) exceptional, unusual, abnormal, rare, erratic.

**perish** (SYN.) die, sink, cease, decline, decay, depart, wane, wither, languish, expire, cease, pass away. (ANT.) grow, survive, flourish, begin, live.

**perishable** (SYN.) decomposable.

**permanent** (SYN.) constant, durable, enduring, abiding, fixed, changeless, unchangeable, lasting, indestructible, stable, continuing, long-lived, persistent, persisting, everlasting, unchanging, unaltered. (ANT.) unstable, transient, ephemeral, temporary, transitory, passing, inconstant, fluctuating.

**permeate** (SYN.) penetrate, pervade, run through, diffuse, fill, saturate, infiltrate.

**permissible** (SYN.) allowable, fair, tolerable, admissible, justifiable, probable, warranted. (ANT.) unsuitable, inadmissible.

**permission** (SYN.) authorization, liberty, permit, authority, consent, leave, license, freedom. (ANT.) refusal, prohibition, denial, opposition.

**permissive** (SYN.) easy, tolerant, open-minded. (ANT.) restrictive.

**permit** (SYN.) let, tolerate, authorize, sanction, allow, grant, give. (ANT.) refuse, resist, forbid, protest, object, prohibit, disallow.

**perpendicular** (SYN.) standing, upright, vertical. (ANT.) horizontal.

**perpetrate** (SYN.) commit, perform, do. (ANT.) neglect, fail, miscarry.

**perpetual** (SYN.) everlasting, immortal, ceaseless, endless, timeless, undying, infinite, eternal, unceasing, continuing, continual, continuous, permanent, constant, eternal. (ANT.) transient, mortal, finite, temporal, ephemeral, inconstant, intermittent, fluctuating.

**perpetually** (SYN.) continually, ever, incessantly, eternally, forever, always, constantly. (ANT.) rarely, sometimes, never, occasionally, fitfully.

**perplex** (SYN.) confuse, dumbfound, mystify, puzzle, bewilder, confound, nonplus. (ANT.) solve, explain, illumine, instruct, clarify.

**perplexed** (SYN.) confused, disorganized, mixed, bewildered, deranged, disordered, muddled, disconcerted. (ANT.) plain, obvious, clear, lucid, organized.

**perplexing** (SYN.) intricate, complex, involved, compound, complicated. (ANT.) uncompounded, plain, simple.

**persecute** (SYN.) harass, hound, torment, worry, vex, torture, harry, afflict, annoy, oppress, pester, ill-treat, victimize, maltreat. (ANT.) support, comfort, assist, encourage, aid.

**persevere** (SYN.) remain, abide, endure, last, persist, continue. (ANT.) vacillate, desist, discontinue, cease, waver, lapse.

**perseverance** (SYN.) persistency, constancy, pertinacity, steadfastness, tenacity, industry. (ANT.) sloth, cessation, laziness, idleness, rest.

**persist** (SYN.) endure, remain, abide, persevere, continue, last. (ANT.) vacillate, waver, desist, cease, discontinue, stop.

**persistence** (SYN.) persistency, constancy, perseverance, steadfastness, tenacity. (ANT.) cessation, rest, sloth, idleness.

**persistent** (SYN.) lasting, steady, obstinate, stubborn, fixed, enduring, immovable, constant, indefatigable, dogged. (ANT.) wavering, unsure, hesitant.

**person** (SYN.) human, individual, somebody, someone.

**personal** (SYN.) secret, private. (ANT.) general, public.

**personality** (SYN.) make-up, nature, disposition, character.

**perspicacity** (SYN.) intelligence, understanding, discernment, judgment, wisdom, sagacity. (ANT.) thoughtlessness, stupidity, arbitrariness, senselessness.

**persuade** (SYN.) entice, coax, exhort, prevail upon, urge, allure, induce, influence, win over, convince. (ANT.) restrain, deter, compel, dissuade, coerce, discourage.

**persuasion** (SYN.) decision, feeling, notion, view, sentiment, conviction, belief, opinion. (ANT.) knowledge, skepticism, fact, misgiving.

**persuasive** (SYN.) winning, alluring, compelling, convincing, stimulating, influential. (ANT.) dubious, unconvincing.

**pertain** (SYN.) refer, relate, apply.

**pertinacious** (SYN.) firm, obstinate, contumacious, head-strong, dogged, inflexible, obdurate, uncompromising, determined, immovable, unyielding. (ANT.) yielding, docile, amenable, submissive, compliant.

**pertinent** (SYN.) apt, material, relevant, relating, applicable, to the point, germane, apropos, apposite, appropriate. (ANT.) unrelated, foreign, alien, extraneous.

**perturbed** (SYN.) agitated, disturbed, upset, flustered.

**pervade** (SYN.) penetrate, saturate, fill, diffuse, infiltrate, run through, permeate.

**perverse** (SYN.) obstinate, ungovernable, sinful, contrary, fractious, peevish, forward, disobedient, wicked, intractable, petulant. (ANT.) docile, agreeable, tractable.

**perversion** (SYN.) maltreatment, outrage, desecration, abuse, profanation, misuse, reviling. (ANT.) respect.

**pervert** (SYN.) deprave, humiliate, impair, debase, corrupt, degrade, abase, defile. (ANT.) improve, raise, enhance.

**perverted** (SYN.) wicked, perverse, sinful.

**pest** (SYN.) annoyance, bother, nuisance, bother, irritant, irritation.

**pester** (SYN.) disturb, annoy, irritate, tease, bother, chafe, inconvenience, molest, trouble, vex, harass, torment, worry. (ANT.) console, soothe, accommodate, gratify.

**pet** (SYN.) darling, favorite, caress.

**petition** (SYN.) invocation, prayer, request, appeal, entreaty, supplication, suit, plea, application, solicitation, entreaty.

**petty** (SYN.) paltry, trivial, frivolous, small, unimportant, trifling, insignificant. (*ANT.*) *important, serious, weighty, momentous, grand, vital, significant, generous.*

**petulant** (*SYN.*) irritable, ill-natured, fretful, snappish, peevish, ill-tempered, waspish, touchy. (*ANT.*) *pleasant, affable, good-tempered, genial, good-natured.*

**phantom** (*SYN.*) apparition, ghost, specter.

**phase** (*SYN.*) period, stage, view, condition.

**phenomenon** (*SYN.*) occurrence, fact, happening, incident.

**philanthropy** (*SYN.*) kindness, benevolence, charity, generosity, tenderness, liberality, humanity, magnanimity, altruism. (*ANT.*) *unkindness, inhumanity, cruelty, malevolence, selfishness.*

**phlegmatic** (*SYN.*) unfeeling, passionless, listless, cold, lethargic, sluggish, slow, lazy. (*ANT.*) *passionate, ardent, energetic.*

**phony** (*SYN.*) counterfeit, artificial, ersatz, fake, synthetic, unreal, spurious, feigned, assumed, bogus, sham, false, forged. (*ANT.*) *real, genuine, natural, true.*

**phrase** (*SYN.*) expression, term, word, name.

**physical** (*SYN.*) material, bodily, carnal, corporeal, natural, somatic, corporal. (*ANT.*) *spiritual, mental.*

**pick** (*SYN.*) cull, opt, select, elect, choose. (*ANT.*) *reject, refuse.*

**picture** (*SYN.*) etching, image, painting, portrait, print, representation, sketch, appearance, cinema, effigy, engraving, scene, view, illustration, panorama, resemblance, likeness, drawing, photograph.

**piece** (*SYN.*) portion, bit, fraction, morsel, scrap, fragment, amount, part, quantity, unit, section, portion. (*ANT.*) *sum, whole, entirety, all, total.*

**piecemeal** (*SYN.*) gradually, partially. (*ANT.*) *whole, complete, entire.*

**pierce** (*SYN.*) puncture, perforate.

**pigheaded** (*SYN.*) inflexible, stubborn, obstinate.

**pigment** (*SYN.*) shade, tint, color, dye, hue, complexion, tincture, stain, tinge. (*ANT.*) *transparency, paleness.*

**pile** (*SYN.*) accumulation, heap, collection.

**pilgrim** (*SYN.*) wanderer, traveler.

**pilgrimage** (*SYN.*) trip, journey, tour, expedition.

**pillar** (*SYN.*) support, prop, column, shaft.

**pillow** (*SYN.*) bolster, cushion, pad.

**pilot** (*SYN.*) helmsman, aviator, steersman.

**pin** (*SYN.*) clip, fastening, peg, fastener.

**pinch** (*SYN.*) squeeze, nip.

**pinnacle** (*SYN.*) crown, zenith, head, summit, chief, apex, crest, top. (*ANT.*) *bottom, foundation, base, foot.*

**pioneer** (*SYN.*) guide, pilgrim, pathfinder, explorer.

**pious** (*SYN.*) devout, religious, spiritual, consecrated, divine, hallowed, holy, saintly, reverent. (*ANT.*) *worldly, sacrilegious, evil, secular, profane, irreligious, impious.*

**pirate** (*SYN.*) plunderer, buccaneer, privateer.

**pistol** (*SYN.*) gun, revolver, weapon, handgun.

**pit** (*SYN.*) well, cavity, hole, excavation.

**pitch** (*SYN.*) throw, cast, toss, propel, hurl, fling, thrust, establish. (*ANT.*) *retain, draw, hold, pull, haul.*

**pitcher** (*SYN.*) jug.

**piteous** (*SYN.*) poignant, touching, affecting, moving, pitiable, sad, pathetic. (*ANT.*) *funny, ludicrous, comical.*

**pitfall** (*SYN.*) lure, snare, wile, ambush, bait, intrigue, trick, trap, artifice, net, snare.

**pitiable** (*SYN.*) poignant, touching, moving, affecting, sad. (*ANT.*) *ludicrous, funny, comical.*

**pitiful** (*SYN.*) distressing, pathetic, pitiable.

**pitiless** (*SYN.*) unmerciful, mean, unpitying, merciless, cruel. (*ANT.*) *gentle, kind.*

**pity** (*SYN.*) sympathy, commiseration, condolence, mercy, compassion, charity, mercy. (*ANT.*) *ruthlessness, hardness, cruelty, inhumanity, brutality, vindictiveness.*

**pivotal** (*SYN.*) crucial, critical, essential, central. (*ANT.*) *peripheral, unimportant.*

**place** (*SYN.*) lay, arrange, dispose, put, deposit, space, region, location, plot, area, spot. (*ANT.*) *mislay, remove, disarrange, disturb, misplace.*

**placid** (*SYN.*) pacific, serene, tranquil, calm, imperturbable, composed, peaceful, quiet, still, undisturbed, unruffled. (*ANT.*) *wild, frantic, turbulent, stormy, excited.*

**plagiarize** (*SYN.*) recite, adduce, cite, quote, paraphrase, repeat, extract. (*ANT.*) retort, contradict, misquote, refute.*

**plague** (*SYN.*) hound, pester, worry, harass, annoy, persecute, torment, vex, afflict, badger, torture, epidemic, trouble. (*ANT.*) *encourage, aid, comfort, assist, support.*

**plain** (*SYN.*) candid, simple, flat, smooth, clear, evident, sincere, unpretentious, level, distinct, absolute, visible, open, frank, palpable, undecorated, ordinary, unembellished, unadorned. (*ANT.*) *embellished, abstruse, abrupt, rough, insincere, adorned, fancy, elaborate, beautiful, ornamented.*

**plan** (*SYN.*) design, purpose, sketch, devise, invent, contrive, intend, draw, create, scheme, plot, method, procedure.

**plane** (*SYN.*) level, airplane.

**plastic** (*SYN.*) pliable, moldable, supple, flexible, synthetic.

**platform** (*SYN.*) stage, pulpit.

**plausible** (*SYN.*) likely, practical, credible, feasible, possible, probable. (*ANT.*) *impracticable, impossible, visionary.*

**play** (*SYN.*) entertainment, amusement, pastime, sport, game, fun, diversion, recreation, show, performance, drama, theatrical. (*ANT.*) *work, labor, boredom, toil.*

**playful** (*SYN.*) sportive, frolicsome, frisky.

**plaything** (*SYN.*) game, trinket, toy, gadget.

**playwright** (*SYN.*) scriptwriter, dramatist.

**plea** (*SYN.*) invocation, request, appeal, entreaty, supplication, petition, suit.

**plead** (*SYN.*) beseech, defend, rejoin, supplicate, discuss, beg, appeal, ask, implore, argue, entreat. (*ANT.*) *deny, refuse.*

**pleasant** (*SYN.*) agreeable, welcome, suitable, charming, pleasing, amiable, gratifying, acceptable, pleasurable, enjoyable, nice, satisfying, satisfactory, acceptable, affable, mild, friendly. (*ANT.*) *offensive, disagreeable, obnoxious, unpleasant, horrid, sour, difficult, nasty.*

**please** (*SYN.*) satisfy, suffice, fulfill, content, appease, gratify, satiate, compensate, remunerate. (*ANT.*) *dissatisfy, annoy, tantalize, frustrate, displease, vex.*

**pleasing** (*SYN.*) luscious, melodious, sugary, delightful, agreeable, honeyed, mellifluous, engaging, pleasant, charming, engaging. (*ANT.*) *repulsive, sour, acrid, bitter, offensive, irritating, annoying.*

**pleasure** (*SYN.*) felicity, delight, amusement, enjoyment, gratification, happiness, joy, satisfaction, gladness, well-being. (*ANT.*) *suffering, pain, vexation, trouble, affliction, discomfort, torment.*

**pledge** (*SYN.*) promise, statement, assertion, declaration, assurance, agreement, oath, commitment, agree, vow, swear; bind, obligate, commit. (*ANT.*) *renounce, release, neglect, mistrust.*

**plentiful** (*SYN.*) ample, profuse, replete, bountiful, abundant, plenteous, luxurious, fullness, fruitful, copious. (*ANT.*) *rare, scanty, deficient, scarce, insufficient.*

**plenty** (*SYN.*) fruitfulness, bounty, fullness, abundance. (*ANT.*) *want, scarcity, need.*

**pliable** (*SYN.*) elastic, supple, flexible, compliant, pliant, resilient, ductile. (*ANT.*) *rigid, unbending, hard, brittle, stiff.*

**plight** (*SYN.*) dilemma, situation, difficulty, condition, predicament, fix, scrape, state. (*ANT.*) *satisfaction, ease, comfort, calmness.*

**plot** (*SYN.*) design, plan, scheme, cabal, conspiracy, diagram, sketch, graph, chart, machination, intrigue.

**plotting** (*SYN.*) cunning, scheming, objective, artfulness, contrivance, purpose, intent, design. (*ANT.*) *accident, chance, result, candor, sincerity.*

**ploy** (*SYN.*) ruse, guile, antic, deception, hoax, subterfuge, wile, cheat, artifice, fraud, trick. (*ANT.*) *honesty, sincerity, openness, exposure, candor.*

**pluck** (*SYN.*) yank, snatch, jerk, pull.

**plug** (*SYN.*) cork, stopper.

**plump** (*SYN.*) obese, portly, stout, thickset, rotund, chubby, fat, paunchy, stocky, corpulent, pudgy, fleshy. (*ANT.*) *slim, thin, gaunt, lean, slender, skinny.*

**plunder** (*SYN.*) ravage, strip, sack, rob, pillage, raid, loot.

**plunge** (*SYN.*) immerse, dip, submerge.

**pocketbook** (*SYN.*) purse, handbag.

**poem** (*SYN.*) lyric, verse, poetry, rhyme.

**pogrom** (*SYN.*) massacre, carnage, slaughter, butchery.

**poignant** (*SYN.*) pitiable,

touching, affecting, impressive, sad, tender, moving, heart-rending.

**point** *(SYN.)* direct, level, train, aim, locality, position, spot, location. *(ANT.) distract, misguide, deceive, misdirect.*

**pointed** *(SYN.)* keen, sharp, shrewd, witty, quick, acute, penetrating, cutting, piercing, astute, severe. *(ANT.) shallow, stupid, bland, blunt, gentle.*

**pointless** *(SYN.)* vain, purposeless.

**poise** *(SYN.)* composure, self-possession, equanimity, equilibrium, carriage, calmness, balance, self-control, assurance, control, dignity. *(ANT.) rage, turbulence, agitation, anger, excitement.*

**poison** *(SYN.)* corrupt, sully, taint, infect, befoul, defile, contaminate, venom, toxin, virus. *(ANT.) purify, disinfect.*

**poke** *(SYN.)* punch, stab, thrust, jab.

**policy** *(SYN.)* procedure, system, rule, approach, tactic.

**polish** *(SYN.)* brighten, shine, finish, brightness, gloss. *(ANT.) tarnish, dull.*

**polished** *(SYN.)* glib, diplomatic, urbane, refined, sleek, suave, slick. *(ANT.) rough, blunt, bluff, harsh, rugged.*

**polite** *(SYN.)* civil, refined, well-mannered, accomplished, courteous, genteel, urbane, well-bred, cultivated, considerate, thoughtful, mannerly, respectful. *(ANT.) uncouth, impertinent, rude, boorish, uncivil, discourteous.*

**pollute** *(SYN.)* contaminate, poison, taint, sully, infect, befoul, defile, dirty. *(ANT.) purify, disinfect, clean, clarify.*

**pomp** *(SYN.)* flourish, pageantry, vaunting, show, boasting, ostentation, parade, display. *(ANT.) reserve, humility, modesty.*

**pompous** *(SYN.)* high, magnificent, stately, august, dignified, grandiose, noble, majestic, lofty, imposing, arrogant, vain, pretentious. *(ANT.) lowly, undignified, humble, common, ordinary.*

**ponder** *(SYN.)* examined, study, contemplate, investigate, meditate, muse, scrutinize, cogitate, reflect, weigh, deliberate, consider.

**ponderous** *(SYN.)* burdensome, trying, gloomy, serious, sluggish, massive, heavy, cumbersome, grievous, grave, dull, weighty. *(ANT.) light, animated, brisk.*

**poor** *(SYN.)* penniless, bad, deficient, destitute, inferior, shabby, wrong, scanty, indigent, needy, poverty-stricken, unfavorable, impoverished. *(ANT.) wealthy, prosperous, rich, fortunate, good, excellent.*

**poppycock** *(SYN.)* rubbish, babble, twaddle, nonsense.

**popular** *(SYN.)* favorite, general, common, familiar, prevalent, liked, prevailing, well-liked, approved, accepted, celebrated, admired, ordinary. *(ANT.) unpopular, esoteric, restricted, exclusive.*

**populous** *(SYN.)* dense, thronged, crowded.

**porch** *(SYN.)* patio, veranda.

**pornographic** *(SYN.)* impure, indecent, obscene, coarse, dirty, filthy, lewd, smutty, offensive, disgusting. *(ANT.) refined, modest, pure, decent.*

**port** *(SYN.)* harbor, refuge, anchorage.

**portable** *(SYN.)* transportable, movable.

**portal** *(SYN.)* entry, doorway, opening, inlet, entrance. *(ANT.) exit, departure.*

**portend** *(SYN.)* foreshadow, presage, foretoken.

**portentous** *(SYN.)* significant, critical, momentous. *(ANT.) trivial.*

**portion** *(SYN.)* share, bit, parcel, part, piece, section, fragment, division, quota, segment, allotment. *(ANT.) whole, bulk.*

**portly** *(SYN.)* majestic, grand, impressive, dignified, stout, fat, heavy, obese. *(ANT.) slender, thin, slim.*

**portrait** *(SYN.)* painting, representation, picture, likeness.

**portray** *(SYN.)* depict, picture, represent, sketch, describe, delineate, paint. *(ANT.) misrepresent, caricature, suggest.*

**position** *(SYN.)* caste, site, locality, situation, condition, standing, incumbency, office, bearing, posture, berth, place, job, pose, rank, attitude, location, spot, station, situation, occupation.

**positive** *(SYN.)* sure, definite, fixed, inevitable, undeniable, indubitable, assured, certain, unquestionable, unmistakable. *(ANT.) uncertain, doubtful, questionable, unsure, dubious, confused, negative, adverse.*

**positively** *(SYN.)* unquestionably, surely, certainly, absolutely.

**possess** *(SYN.)* own, obtain, have, seize, hold, occupy, affect, control. *(ANT.)* surrender, abandon, lose, renounce.

**possessed** *(SYN.)* entranced, obsessed, consumed, haunted, enchanted.

**possession** *(SYN.)* custody, ownership, occupancy.

**possessions** *(SYN.)* commodities, effects, goods, property, merchandise, wares, wealth, belongings, stock.

**possible** *(SYN.)* likely, practical, probable, achievable, feasible, plausible, credible, practicable. *(ANT.) implausible, impossible, improbable.*

**possibility** *(SYN.)* opportunity, chance, contingency, occasion. *(ANT.) obstacle, disadvantage, hindrance.*

**possibly** *(SYN.)* perchance, perhaps, maybe.

**post** *(SYN.)* position, job, berth, incumbency, situation, shaft, pole, fort, base, station.

**postpone** *(SYN.)* delay, stay, suspend, discontinue, defer, adjourn, interrupt, put off. *(ANT.) persist, maintain, continue, proceed.*

**postulate** *(SYN.)* principle, adage, saying, proverb, truism, byword, aphorism, axiom, fundamental, maxim.

**potency** *(SYN.)* effectiveness, capability, skillfulness, efficiency, competency, ability. *(ANT.) wastefulness, inability, ineptitude.*

**potent** *(SYN.)* mighty, influential, convincing, effective. *(ANT.) feeble, weak, powerless, impotent.*

**potential** *(SYN.)* likely, possible, dormant, hidden, latent.

**pouch** *(SYN.)* container, bag, sack.

**pound** *(SYN.)* buffet, beat, punch, strike, thrash, defeat, subdue, pulse, smite, belabor, knock, thump, overpower, palpitate, rout, vanquish. *(ANT.) fail, surrender, stroke, defend, shield.*

**pour** *(SYN.)* flow.

**pout** *(SYN.)* brood, sulk, mope.

**poverty** *(SYN.)* necessity, need, want, destitution, privation, indigence, distress. *(ANT.) plenty, abundance, wealth, riches, affluence, richness, comfort.*

**power** *(SYN.)* potency, might, authority, control, predominance, capability, faculty, validity, force, vigor, command, influence, talent, ability, dominion, competency. *(ANT.) incapacity, fatigue, weakness, disablement, impotence, ineptitude.*

**powerful** *(SYN.)* firm, strong, concentrated, enduring, forcible, robust, sturdy, tough, athletic, forceful, hale, impregnable, hardy, mighty, potent. *(ANT.) feeble, insipid, brittle, delicate, fragile, weak, ineffectual, powerless.*

**practical** *(SYN.)* sensible, wise, prudent, reasonable, sagacious, sober, sound, workable, attainable. *(ANT.) stupid, unaware, impalpable, absurd, impractical.*

**practically** *(SYN.)* almost, nearly.

**practice** *(SYN.)* exercise, habit, custom, manner, wont, usage, drill, tradition, performance, action, repetition. *(ANT.) inexperience, theory, disuse, idleness, speculation.*

**practiced** *(SYN.)* able, expert, skilled, adept. *(ANT.) inept.*

**prairie** *(SYN.)* plain, grassland.

**praise** *(SYN.)* applaud, compliment, extol, laud, glorify, commend, acclaim, eulogize, flatter, admire, celebrate, commendation, approval. *(ANT.) criticize, censure, reprove, condemn, disparage, disapprove, criticism.*

**pray** *(SYN.)* supplicate, importune, beseech, beg.

**prayer** *(SYN.)* plea, suit, appeal, invocation, supplication, petition, entreaty, request.

**preach** *(SYN.)* teach, moralize, lecture.

**preamble** *(SYN.)* overture, prologue, beginning, introduction, prelude, start, foreword, preface. *(ANT.) end, finale, completion, conclusion, epilogue.*

**precarious** *(SYN.)* dangerous, perilous, threatening, menacing, critical, risky, unsafe, hazardous. *(ANT.) secure, firm, protected, safe.*

**precaution** *(SYN.)* foresight, forethought, care.

**precedence** *(SYN.)* preference, priority.

**precedent** *(SYN.)* model, example.

**precept** *(SYN.)* doctrine, tenet, belief, creed, teaching, dogma. *(ANT.) practice, conduct, performance, deed.*

**precious** *(SYN.)* dear, useful, valuable, costly, esteemed, profitable, expensive, priceless, dear. *(ANT.) poor, worthless, cheap, mean, trashy.*

**precipice** *(SYN.)* bluff, cliff.

**precipitate** *(SYN.)* speedy, swift, hasty, sudden.

**precipitous** *(SYN.)* unannounced, sudden, harsh,

rough, unexpected, sharp, abrupt, hasty, craggy, steep, precipitate. *(ANT.) expected, smooth, anticipated, gradual.*

**precise** *(SYN.)* strict, exact, formal, rigid, definite, unequivocal, prim, ceremonious, distinct, accurate, correct. *(ANT.) loose, easy, vague, informal, careless, erroneous.*

**precisely** *(SYN.)* specifically, exactly.

**precision** *(SYN.)* correction, accuracy, exactness.

**preclude** *(SYN.)* hinder, prevent, obstruct, forestall, obviate, thwart, impede. *(ANT.) permit, aid, expedite, encourage, promote.*

**preclusion** *(SYN.)* omission, exception, exclusion. *(ANT.) standard, rule, inclusion.*

**predicament** *(SYN.)* dilemma, plight, situation, condition, fix, difficulty, strait, scrape. *(ANT.) satisfaction, comfort, ease.*

**predict** *(SYN.)* forecast, foretell.

**prediction** *(SYN.)* forecast, prophecy.

**predilection** *(SYN.)* attachment, inclination, affection, bent, desire, penchant, disposition, preference. *(ANT.) repugnance, aversion, apathy, distaste, nonchalance.*

**predominant** *(SYN.)* highest, paramount, cardinal, foremost, main, first, leading, supreme, principal, essential, prevalent, dominant, prevailing. *(ANT.) subsidiary, auxiliary, supplemental, minor, subordinate.*

**predominate** *(SYN.)* prevail, outweigh, rule.

**preface** *(SYN.)* foreword, introduction, preliminary, prelude, prologue, preamble.

**prefer** *(SYN.)* select, favor, elect, fancy.

**preference** *(SYN.)* election, choice, selection, alternative, option.

**prejudice** *(SYN.)* bias, favoritism, unfairness, partiality.

**prejudiced** *(SYN.)* fanatical, narrow-minded, dogmatic, bigoted, illiberal, intolerant. *(ANT.) radical, liberal, tolerant, progressive.*

**preliminary** *(SYN.)* introductory, preparatory, prelude, preface.

**premature** *(SYN.)* early, untimely, unexpected. *(ANT.) timely.*

**premeditated** *(SYN.)* intended, voluntary, contemplated,

designed, intentional, willful, deliberate, studied. *(ANT.) fortuitous, accidental.*

**premeditation** *(SYN.)* intention, deliberation, forethought, forecast. *(ANT.) hazard, accident, impromptu, extemporization.*

**premise** *(SYN.)* basis, presupposition, assumption, postulate, principle, presumption. *(ANT.) superstructure, derivative, trimming, implication.*

**preoccupied** *(SYN.)* abstracted, distracted, absorbed, meditative, inattentive, absent, absent-minded. *(ANT.) attentive, alert, conscious, present, attending, watchful.*

**prepare** *(SYN.)* contrive, furnish, ready, predispose, condition, fit, arrange, plan, qualify, make ready, get ready.

**preposterous** *(SYN.)* foolish, nonsensical, silly, contradictory, unreasonable, absurd, inconsistent, irrational, self-contradictory. *(ANT.) sensible, rational, consistent, sound.*

**prerequisite** *(SYN.)* essential, requirement, necessity, condition, demand.

**prerogative** *(SYN.)* grant, right, license, authority, privilege. *(ANT.) violation, encroachment, wrong, injustice.*

**prescribe** *(SYN.)* order, direct, designate.

**presence** *(SYN.)* nearness, attendance, closeness, vicinity, appearance, bearing, personality.

**present** *(SYN.)* donation, gift, today, now, existing, current, largess, donate, acquaint, introduce, being, give, gratuity, boon, grant. *(ANT.) reject, spurn, accept, retain, receive.*

**presentable** *(SYN.)* polite, well-bred, respectable, well-mannered.

**presently** *(SYN.)* shortly, soon, directly, immediately.

**preserve** *(SYN.)* protect, save, conserve, maintain, secure, rescue, uphold, spare, keep, can, safeguard, defend, rescue. *(ANT.) impair, abolish, destroy, abandon, squander, injure.*

**preside** *(SYN.)* officiate, direct, administrate.

**press** *(SYN.)* impel, shove, urge, hasten, push, compress, squeeze, hug, crowd, propel, force, drive, embrace, smooth, iron, insist on, pressure, promote, urgency, jostle. *(ANT.) oppose, pull, falter, drag, retreat.*

**pressing** *(SYN.)* impelling, insistent, necessary, urgent, compelling, imperative,

instant, serious, important, cogent, exigent, importunate. *(ANT.) unimportant, trifling, insignificant, petty, trivial.*

**pressure** *(SYN.)* force, influence, stress, press, compulsion, urgency, constraint, compression. *(ANT.) relaxation, leniency, ease, recreation.*

**prestige** *(SYN.)* importance, reputation, influence, renown, fame, distinction.

**presume** *(SYN.)* guess, speculate, surmise, imagine, conjecture, apprehend, believe, think, assume, suppose, deduce. *(ANT.) prove, ascertain, demonstrate, know.*

**presumption** *(SYN.)* boldness, impertinence, insolence, rudeness, assurance, effrontery, impudence, assumption, audacity, supposition, sauciness. *(ANT.) politeness, diffidence.*

**presumptuous** *(SYN.)* bold, impertinent, fresh, imprudent, rude, forward, arrogant.

**presupposition** *(SYN.)* basis, principle, premise, assumption, postulate. *(ANT.) superstructure, derivative, implication.*

**pretend** *(SYN.)* feign, stimulate, act, profess, make believe, imagine, fake, sham, affect. *(ANT.) expose, reveal, display.*

**pretense** *(SYN.)* mask, pretext, show, affection, disguise, garb, semblance, simulation, fabrication, lie, excuse, falsification, deceit, subterfuge. *(ANT.) sincerity, actuality, truth, fact, reality.*

**pretentious** *(SYN.)* gaudy, ostentatious. *(ANT.) simple, humble.*

**pretty** *(SYN.)* charming, handsome, lovely, beauteous, fair, comely, attractive, beautiful, elegant. *(ANT.) repulsive, foul, unsightly, homely, plain, hideous.*

**prevail** *(SYN.)* win, succeed, predominate, triumph. *(ANT.) yield, lose.*

**prevailing** *(SYN.)* common, current, general, habitual, steady, regular, universal.

**prevalent** *(SYN.)* ordinary, usual, common, general, familiar, popular, prevailing, widespread, universal, frequent. *(ANT.) odd, scarce, exceptional, extraordinary.*

**prevent** *(SYN.)* impede, preclude, forestall, stop, block, check, halt, interrupt, deter, slow, obviate, hinder, obstruct, thwart. *(ANT.) expedite, help, allow, abet, aid,

permit, encourage, promote.*

**previous** *(SYN.)* former, anterior, preceding, prior, antecedent, earlier, aforesaid, foregoing. *(ANT.) subsequent, following, consequent, succeeding, later.*

**prey** *(SYN.)* raid, seize, victimize.

**price** *(SYN.)* worth, cost, expense, charge, value.

**pride** *(SYN.)* self-respect, vanity, glory, superciliousness, haughtiness, conceit, arrogance, self-importance, pretension, egotism, satisfaction, fulfillment, enjoyment, self-esteem. *(ANT.) modesty, shame, humbleness, lowliness, meekness, humility.*

**prim** *(SYN.)* formal, puritanical, priggish, prudish.

**primarily** *(SYN.)* mainly, chiefly, firstly, essentially, originally. *(ANT.) secondarily.*

**primary** *(SYN.)* first, principal, primeval, pristine, beginning, original, initial, fundamental, elementary, chief, foremost, earliest, main, prime. *(ANT.) subordinate, last, secondary, least, hindmost, latest.*

**prime** *(SYN.)* first, primary, chief, excellent, best, superior, ready.

**primeval** *(SYN.)* fresh, primary, novel, inventive, creative, primordial, original, first, new, initial. *(ANT.) modern, subsequent, banal, later, terminal, derivative.*

**primitive** *(SYN.)* antiquated, early, primeval, prehistoric, uncivilized, uncultured, simple, pristine, old, aboriginal, unsophisticated, rude, rough, primary. *(ANT.) sophisticated, modish, civilized, cultured, cultivated, late.*

**primordial** *(SYN.)* pristine, inventive, novel, creative, original, first, initial, new, primary. *(ANT.) trite, terminal, banal, modern, derivative, subsequent, later.*

**principal** *(SYN.)* first, leading, main, supreme, predominant, chief, foremost, highest, prime, primary, leader, headmaster, paramount, essential, cardinal. *(ANT.) supplemental, secondary, auxiliary, subsidiary, accessory, minor, subordinate.*

**principle** *(SYN.)* law, method, axiom, rule, propriety, regulation, maxim, formula, order, statute. *(ANT.) exception, hazard, chance, deviation.*

**print** *(SYN.)* issue, reprint, publish, letter, sign, fingerprint, mark, picture, lithograph, engraving, etching.

**prior** (SYN.) previous, aforesaid, antecedent, sooner, earlier, preceding, former, foregoing. (ANT.) succeeding, following, later, consequent, subsequent.

**prison** (SYN.) brig, jail, stockade, penitentiary.

**pristine** (SYN.) primordial, creative, first, original, fresh, inventive, novel, primary, initial. (ANT.) trite, terminal, derivative, modem, banal, subsequent, plagiarized, later.

**private** (SYN.) concealed, hidden, secret, clandestine, unknown, personal, surreptitious, covert, individual, particular, special, latent. (ANT.) exposed, known, closed, general, public, conspicuous, disclosed.

**privation** (SYN.) necessity, penury, destitution, need, poverty, want. (ANT.) wealth, affluence, abundance, plenty, riches.

**privilege** (SYN.) liberty, right, advantage, immunity, freedom, license, favor, sanction. (ANT.) restriction, inhibition, prohibition, disallowance.

**prize** (SYN.) compensation, bonus, award, premium, remuneration, reward, bounty, esteem, value, rate, recompense, requital. (ANT.) charge, punishment, wages, earnings, assessment.

**probable** (SYN.) presumable, likely.

**probe** (SYN.) stretch, reach, investigate, examine, examination, scrutiny, scrutinize, inquire, explore, inquiry, investigation, extend. (ANT.) miss, short.

**problem** (SYN.) dilemma, question, predicament, riddle, difficulty, puzzle.

**procedure** (SYN.) process, way, fashion, form, mode, conduct, practice, manner, habit, system, operation, management, plan.

**proceed** (SYN.) progress, continue, issue, result, spring, thrive, improve, advance, emanate, rise. (ANT.) retard, withhold, withdraw, hinder, retreat, oppose.

**proceeding** (SYN.) occurrence, business, affair, deal, negotiation, transaction, deed.

**proceedings** (SYN.) account, record, document.

**proceeds** (SYN.) result, produce, income, reward, intake, fruit, profit, store, yield,

product, return, harvest, crop.

**process** (SYN.) method, course, system, procedure, operation, prepare, treat.

**procession** (SYN.) cortege, parade, sequence, train, cavalcade, file, retinue, succession.

**proclaim** (SYN.) declare, assert, make known, promulgate, state, assert, broadcast, express, announce, aver, advertise, tell, publish, profess.

**proclamation** (SYN.) declaration, announcement, promulgation.

**procrastinate** (SYN.) waver, vacillate, defer, hesitate, delay, postpone.

**procreate** (SYN.) generate, produce, beget, engender, originate, propagate, sire, create, father. (ANT.) murder, destroy, abort, kill, extinguish.

**procure** (SYN.) secure, gain, win, attain, obtain, get, acquire, earn. (ANT.) lose.

**prod** (SYN.) goad, nudge, jab, push.

**prodigious** (SYN.) astonishing, enormous, immense, monstrous, remarkable, marvelous, huge, amazing, astounding, stupendous, monumental. (ANT.) insignificant, commonplace, small.

**produce** (SYN.) harvest, reaping, bear, result, originate, bring about, store, supply, make, create, crop, proceeds, bring forth, occasion, breed, generate, cause, exhibit, show, demonstrate, fabricate, hatch, display, manufacture, exhibit, give, yield. (ANT.) conceal, reduce, destroy, consume, waste, hide.

**product** (SYN.) outcome, result, output, produce, goods, commodity, stock, merchandise.

**productive** (SYN.) fertile, luxuriant, rich, bountiful, fruitful, creative, fecund, teeming, plenteous, prolific. (ANT.) wasteful, unproductive, barren, useless, sterile.

**profanation** (SYN.) dishonor, insult, outrage, aspersion, defamation, invective, misuse, abuse, reviling, maltreatment, desecration, perversion. (ANT.) plaudit, commendation, laudation, respect, approval.

**profane** (SYN.) deflower, violate, desecrate, pollute, dishonor, ravish, debauch.

**profess** (SYN.) declare, assert, make known, state, protest, announce, aver, express,

broadcast, avow, tell. (ANT.) suppress, conceal, repress, withhold.

**profession** (SYN.) calling, occupation, vocation, employment. (ANT.) hobby, avocation, pastime.

**proffer** (SYN.) extend, tender, volunteer, propose, advance. (ANT.) reject, spurn, accept, receive, retain.

**proficient** (SYN.) competent, adept, clever, able, cunning, practiced, skilled, versed, ingenious, accomplished, skillful, expert. (ANT.) untrained, inexpert, bungling, awkward, clumsy.

**profit** (SYN.) gain, service, advantage, return, earnings, emolument, improvement, benefit, better, improve, use, avail. (ANT.) waste, loss, detriment, debit, lose, damage, mum.

**profitable** (SYN.) beneficial, advantageous, helpful, wholesome, useful, gainful, favorable, beneficial, serviceable, salutary, productive, good. (ANT.) harmful, destructive, injurious, deleterious, detrimental.

**profligate** (SYN.) corrupt, debased, tainted, unsound, vitiated, contaminated, crooked, depraved, impure, venal.

**profound** (SYN.) deep, serious, knowing, wise, intelligent, knowledgeable, recondite, solemn, abstruse, penetrating. (ANT.) trivial, slight, shallow, superficial.

**profuse** (SYN.) lavish, excessive, extravagant, improvident, luxuriant, prodigal, wasteful, exuberant, immoderate, plentiful. (ANT.) meager, poor, economical, sparse, skimpy.

**profusion** (SYN.) immoderation, superabundance, surplus, extravagance, intemperance, superfluity. (ANT.) lack, paucity, death, want, deficiency.

**program** (SYN.) record, schedule, plan, agenda, calendar.

**progress** (SYN.) advancement, improvement, development, betterment, advance, movement, improve, progression. (ANT.) regression, relapse, retrogression, decline.

**progression** (SYN.) gradation, string, train, chain, arrangement, following, arrangement, order.

**prohibit** (SYN.) hinder, forbid, disallow, obstruct, prevent, stop, ban, interdict,

debar. (ANT.) help, tolerate, allow, sanction, encourage, permit.

**prohibition** (SYN.) prevention, ban, embargo, restriction. (ANT.) allowance, permission.

**prohibitive** (SYN.) forbidding, restrictive.

**project** (SYN.) design, proposal, scheme, contrivance, outline, homework, activity, purpose, bulge, protrude, throw, cast, device, plan. (ANT.) production, accomplishment, performance.

**prolific** (SYN.) fertile, rich, fruitful, teeming, fecund, bountiful, luxuriant, productive, plenteous. (ANT.) unproductive, barren, sterile, impotent.

**prolong** (SYN.) extend, increase, protract, draw, stretch, lengthen. (ANT.) shorten.

**prominent** (SYN.) distinguished, illustrious, outstanding, renowned, influential, famous, well-known, noted, notable, important, conspicuous, eminent, leading, celebrated. (ANT.) low, vulgar, ordinary, common.

**promise** (SYN.) assurance, guarantee, pledge, undertaking, agreement, bestowal, word, contract, oath, vow.

**promote** (SYN.) advance, foster, encourage, assist, support, further, aid, help, elevate, raise, facilitate, forward. (ANT.) obstruct, demote, hinder, impede.

**prompt** (SYN.) punctual, timely, exact, arouse, evoke, occasion, induce, urge, effect, cite, suggest, hint, cause, mention, propose, make, precise, originate. (ANT.) laggardly, slow, tardy, dilatory.

**promptly** (SYN.) immediately, instantly, straightaway, forthwith, directly, instantaneously, presently. (ANT.) later, sometime, hereafter, distantly, shortly.

**promulgate** (SYN.) declare, known, protest, affirm, broadcast, profess, assert, proclaim, state, aver, tell. (ANT.) repress, conceal, withhold.

**prone** (SYN.) apt, inclined, disposed, likely, predisposed.

**pronounce** (SYN.) proclaim, utter, announce, articulate, enunciate.

**pronounced** (SYN.) clear, definite. (ANT.) minor, unnoticeable.

**proof** (SYN.) evidence, verification, confirmation,

experiment, demonstration, testimony, trial, protected, impenetrable, corroboration, test. (*ANT.*) *fallacy, invalidity, failure.*

**propagate** (*SYN.*) create, procreate, sire, beget, breed, father, originate, produce. (*ANT.*) *extinguish, kill, abort, destroy.*

**propel** (*SYN.*) drive, push, transfer, actuate, induce, shift, persuade, move. (*ANT.*) *stay, deter, halt, rest, stop.*

**propensity** (*SYN.*) leaning, proneness, trend, drift, aim, inclination, bias, proclivity, tendency, predisposition. (*ANT.*) *disinclination, aversion.*

**proper** (*SYN.*) correct, suitable, decent, peculiar, legitimate, right, conventional.

**property** (*SYN.*) real estate, effects, possessions, quality, characteristic, merchandise, stock, possession, land. (*ANT.*) *poverty, destitution, want, deprivation.*

**prophecy** (*SYN.*) augury, prediction.

**prophesy** (*SYN.*) foretell, predict, augur.

**prophet** (*SYN.*) fortuneteller, oracle, seer, soothsayer, clairvoyant.

**propitious** (*SYN.*) lucky, opportune, advantageous, favorable, fortunate, promising, happy.

**proportion** (*SYN.*) steadiness, poise, composure, relation, balance, equilibrium. (*ANT.*) *unsteadiness, imbalance, fall.*

**proposal** (*SYN.*) plan, proposition, tender, scheme, program, offer, suggestion, overture. (*ANT.*) *rejection, acceptance, denial.*

**propose** (*SYN.*) offer, proffer, recommend, plan, mean, expect, move, design, propound, present, tender. (*ANT.*) *fulfill, perform, effect.*

**proposition** (*SYN.*) proposal, motion.

**propound** (*SYN.*) bring forward, offer, advance, allege, propose, assign. (*ANT.*) *retreat, hinder, withhold, retard.*

**proprietor** (*SYN.*) master, owner. (*ANT.*) *slave, servant.*

**prosaic** (*SYN.*) commonplace, common, everyday, ordinary, routine. (*ANT.*) *exciting, different, extraordinary.*

**proscribe** (*SYN.*) forbid, ban, prohibit. (*ANT.*) *permit, allow.*

**prospect** (*SYN.*) anticipation, expectation, candidate, buyer,

explore, search.

**prospective** (*SYN.*) planned, proposed.

**prosper** (*SYN.*) succeed, win, achieve, gain, rise, prevail, flourish, thrive. (*ANT.*) *miscarry, wane, miss, fail.*

**prosperous** (*SYN.*) rich, wealthy, affluent, well-to-do, sumptuous, well-off, flourishing, thriving, opulent, luxurious. (*ANT.*) *impoverished, indigent, beggarly, needy, destitute, poor.*

**prostrate** (*SYN.*) prone, supine, overcome, recumbent, crushed.

**protect** (*SYN.*) defend, preserve, save, keep, conserve, safeguard, maintain, guard, shield, secure. (*ANT.*) *impair, abandon, destroy, abolish, injure.*

**protest** (*SYN.*) dissent, noncompliance, disagree, objection, disagreement, challenge, difference, complaint, nonconformity, variance, opposition. (*ANT.*) *acquiesce, assent, compliance, concur, comply, acceptance, approval.*

**prototype** (*SYN.*) model, archetype, specimen, instance, illustration, example, pattern, sample. (*ANT.*) *rule, concept, precept.*

**protract** (*SYN.*) extend, strain, distend, expand, spread, stretch, elongate, distort, lengthen. (*ANT.*) *tighten, contract, loosen.*

**protuberance** (*SYN.*) prominence, projection, bulge, protrusion, swelling.

**proud** (*SYN.*) overbearing, vain, arrogant, haughty, stately, vain, glorious, disdainful, prideful, conceited, egotistical, self-important, supercilious. (*ANT.*) *humble, meek, ashamed, lowly.*

**prove** (*SYN.*) manifest, verify, confirm, demonstrate, establish, show, affirm, examine, corroborate, try, test. (*ANT.*) *contradict, refute, disprove.*

**proverb** (*SYN.*) maxim, byword, saying, adage, saw, motto, apothegm.

**proverbial** (*SYN.*) common, well-known.

**provide** (*SYN.*) supply, endow, afford, produce, yield, give, fit, equip, furnish. (*ANT.*) *strip, denude, divest, despoil.*

**provident** (*SYN.*) saving, thrifty, economical, frugal, sparing. (*ANT.*) *wasteful, lavish, extravagant.*

**provision** (*SYN.*) supply, fund, condition, arrangement, accumulation, reserve, store.

**provisions** (*SYN.*) stock, supplies, store.

**provoke** (*SYN.*) excite, stimulate, agitate, arouse, incite, stir up, vex, bother, disquiet, excite, irritate, annoy, anger. (*ANT.*) *quell, allay, pacify, calm, quiet.*

**prowess** (*SYN.*) fortitude, mettle, boldness, fearlessness, courage, chivalry, bravery. (*ANT.*) *fear, cowardice, timidity.*

**prowl** (*SYN.*) sneak, slink, lurk.

**proximate** (*SYN.*) nigh, imminent, adjacent, neighboring, bordering, close. (*ANT.*) *removed, distant, far.*

**proximity** (*SYN.*) vicinity, nearness.

**proxy** (*SYN.*) representative, equivalent, makeshift, alternate, deputy, substitute. (*ANT.*) *sovereign, head, principal, master.*

**prudence** (*SYN.*) watchfulness, care, heed, vigilance, wariness, carefulness, tact, judgment, wisdom, common, foresight, caution. (*ANT.*) *rashness, recklessness, abandon, foolishness, carelessness.*

**prudent** (*SYN.*) reasonable, sensible, sound, discreet, practical, judicious. (*ANT.*) *stupid, unaware, absurd.*

**pry** (*SYN.*) peer, peep, meddle, peek.

**prying** (*SYN.*) inquisitive, meddling, curious, inquiring, nosy, peering, searching, interrogative, snoopy. (*ANT.*) *unconcerned, incurious, indifferent, uninterested.*

**psyche** (*SYN.*) judgment, reason, understanding, brain, intellect, mentality, soul, mind, faculties, spirit. (*ANT.*) *materiality, body, matter, corporeality.*

**psychosis** (*SYN.*) derangement, insanity, madness, delirium, dementia, frenzy, lunacy, mania, aberration. (*ANT.*) *stability, rationality, sanity.*

**public** (*SYN.*) common, civil, governmental, federal, unrestricted, people, society, open.

**publish** (*SYN.*) distribute, issue, declare, announce, reveal, proclaim, publicize.

**pull** (*SYN.*) attract, induce, prolong, draw, tow, drag, remove, take out, persuade, allure, entice, extract. (*ANT.*) *shorten, alienate, drive, propel.*

**pulsate** (*SYN.*) beat, throb, palpitate.

**pummel** (*SYN.*) punish, correct, castigate, discipline,

chastise, strike. (*ANT.*) *release, acquit, free, exonerate.*

**pump** (*SYN.*) interrogate, question, ask, inquire, quiz, examine, query. (*ANT.*) *state, answer, respond, reply.*

**punctual** (*SYN.*) timely, prompt, exact, ready, precise. (*ANT.*) *laggardly, tardy, dilatory, late.*

**punish** (*SYN.*) correct, pummel, chasten, reprove, strike, castigate, chastise. (*ANT.*) *release, exonerate, reward, pardon, acquit, free.*

**puny** (*SYN.*) feeble, impaired, exhausted, infirm, unimportant, weak, decrepit. (*ANT.*) *strong, forceful, lusty, vigorous.*

**purchase** (*SYN.*) get, procure, buy, acquire, obtain. (*ANT.*) *sell, dispose of, vend.*

**pure** (*SYN.*) chaste, absolute, clean, immaculate, untainted, spotless, guiltless, modest, virgin, bare, unmixed, simple. (*ANT.*) *corrupt, mixed, defiled, foul, tainted, adulterated, polluted, tarnished.*

**puritanical** (*SYN.*) prim, stiff. (*ANT.*) *permissive.*

**purport** (*SYN.*) import, meaning, explanation, acceptation, drift, sense, significance, purpose, intent, gist.

**purpose** (*SYN.*) intention, end, goal, aim, objective, application, use, drift, object. (*ANT.*) *hazard, accident, fate.*

**pursue** (*SYN.*) persist, track, follow, hunt, hound, chase, trail. (*ANT.*) *evade, abandon, flee, elude.*

**pursuit** (*SYN.*) hunt, chase.

**push** (*SYN.*) jostle, urge, press, thrust, force, drive, crowd, hasten, shove, propel, promote. (*ANT.*) *ignore, falter, halt, drag, oppose.*

**pushy** (*SYN.*) impudent, abrupt, prominent, insolent, forward, brazen, conspicuous, bold, striking. (*ANT.*) *retiring, timid, cowardly, bashful.*

**put** (*SYN.*) set, place, state, express, say, assign, attach, establish.

**putrefy** (*SYN.*) disintegrate, decay, rot, waste, spoil, decompose. (*ANT.*) *grow, increase, luxuriate.*

**putrid** (*SYN.*) decayed, rotten, moldy, decomposed.

**puzzle** (*SYN.*) mystery, mystify, confound, perplex, riddle, conundrum, confusion, bewilder, enigma, dilemma. (*ANT.*) *key, solution, solve, explain, answer, resolution, illumine, clue.*

# Q

**quack** (SYN.) faker, fake, fraud, gaggle, clack, gabble, bluffer, cackle, dissembler, charlatan, impostor.

**quackery** (SYN.) charlatanism, deceit, make-believe, fakery, duplicity, dissimulation, pretense, fraudulence, sham, counterfeiting, show. (ANT.) integrity, probity, veracity, sincerity, honesty.

**quaff** (SYN.) swig, swill, swallow, lap up, sip, drink, ingurgitate, guzzle, imbibe.

**quagmire** (SYN.) swamp, bog, fen, ooze, morass, slough, marsh, plight, predicament, dilemma, impasse, fix, entanglement, quicksand, hole, quandary.

**quail** (SYN.) recoil, cower, flinch, blench, wince, falter, shrink, shake, hesitate, faint, droop. (ANT.) brave, resist, defy, withstand.

**quaint** (SYN.) odd, uncommon, old-fashioned, antique, antiquated, queer, unusual, curious, eccentric, peculiar, picturesque, singular, whimsical, droll, charming, fanciful, strange. (ANT.) usual, normal, common, navel, ordinary, modern, current, commonplace, familiar.

**quake** (SYN.) shake, tremble, shudder, quiver, pulsate, stagger, shiver, temblor, vibrate, quaver, throb, earthquake.

**qualification** (SYN.) efficiency, adaptation, restriction, aptness, skill, ability, faculty, talent, power, aptitude, competence, suitability, capability, fitness, condition, dexterity. (ANT.) unreadiness, incapacity, disability.

**qualified** (SYN.) clever, skillful, efficient, suitable, able, capable, fit, fitted, suited, bounded, limited, contingent, eligible, delimited, adept, circumscribed, equipped, modified, competent. (ANT.) deficient, inept, impotent, categorical, unlimited, unfitted, unfit, incapable, unsuitable, inadequate.

**qualify** (SYN.) fit, suit, befit, ready, prepare, empower, lessen, moderate, soften, capacitate, condition, adapt, label, designate, name, call, equip, train, restrict, limit, change. (ANT.) unfit, incapacitate, disable, disqualify, enlarge, reinforce, aggravate.

**quality** (SYN.) trait, feature, attribute, value, peculiarity, grade, caliber, character, distinction, rank, condition, status, characteristic, kind, nature, constitution, mark, type, property. (ANT.) nature, inferiority, mediocrity, triviality, indifference, inferior, shoddy, second-rate, being, substance, essence.

**qualm** (SYN.) doubt, uneasiness, anxiety, suspicion, skepticism, question, pang, compunction, twinge, regret, uncertainty, demur, fear, remorse, misgiving. (ANT.) security, comfort, confidence, easiness, invulnerability, firmness.

**quandary** (SYN.) predicament, perplexity, confusion, uncertainty, puzzle, plight, bewilderment, fix, difficulty, entanglement, impasse, doubt, dilemma. (ANT.) ease, relief, certainty, assurance.

**quantity** (SYN.) sum, measure, volume, content, aggregate, bulk, mass, portion, amount, number, multitude, extent. (ANT.) zero, nothing.

**quarantine** (SYN.) segregate, separate, confine, isolate, seclude.

**quarrel** (SYN.) contention, argument, affray, dispute, altercation, squabble, feud, difference, disagree, bicker, differ, spar, fight, bickering, tiff, argue, disagreement, spat. (ANT.) peace, friendliness, reconciliation, amity, agreement, sympathy, accord, concur, support, agree, unity, harmony.

**quarrelsome** (SYN.) testy, contentious, edgy, peevish, irritable, snappish, argumentative, disputatious, cranky, belligerent, combative, disagreeable. (ANT.) genial, friendly, peaceful, easygoing, peaceable, tempered.

**quarry** (SYN.) prey, quest, game, victim, goal, aim, prize, objective.

**quarter** (SYN.) place, source, fount, well, origin, mainspring, mercy, pity, compassion, clemency, spring, benevolence, forbearance. (ANT.) ruthlessness, brutality, cruelty, barbarity, harshness, ferocity.

**quarters** (SYN.) residence, rooms, lodgings, dwelling, flat, billets, chambers, accommodations.

**quash** (SYN.) void, annul, overthrow, nullify, suppress, cancel, quench, quell, repress, invalidate. (ANT.) reinforce, sustain, authorize, sanction, validate, incite.

**quasi** (SYN.) would-be, partial, synthetic, nominal, imitation, bogus, counterfeit, mock. (ANT.) certified, real, legitimate.

**quaver** (SYN.) tremble, shake, hesitate, trill, oscillate, waver, vibrate, shiver, quiver, falter, quake.

**quay** (SYN.) dock, wharf, pier, jetty, bank.

**queasy** (SYN.) sick, squeamish, nauseated, uneasy, queer, restless, nauseous, uncomfortable. (ANT.) untroubled, comfortable, easy, relaxed.

**queen** (SYN.) empress, diva, goddess, star.

**queer** (SYN.) odd, quaint, curious, unusual, droll, strange, peculiar, extraordinary, singular, uncommon, eccentric, weird, funny, nutty, screwy, wacky, deviant, whimsical. (ANT.) familiar, usual, normal, common, commonplace, plain, patent, ordinary.

**queerness** (SYN.) oddity, oddness, freakishness, strangeness, singularity, outlandishness, weirdness. (ANT.) normality, familiarity, commonness, standardization.

**quell** (SYN.) subdue, calm, pacify, quiet, cool, hush, appease, lull, mollify, reduce, crush, smother, suppress, stifle, extinguish. (ANT.) foment, arouse, foster, incite.

**quench** (SYN.) extinguish, stop, suppress, sate, allay, abate, stifle, slacken, put out, slake, satisfy (ANT.) set, light, begin, start, kindle.

**querulous** (SYN.) faultfinding, fretful, carping, critical, complaining, censorious, captious, petulant. (ANT.) pleased, easygoing, contented, carefree.

**query** (SYN.) inquire, interrogate, demand, investigate, probe, examine, question, inquiry, ask. (ANT.) answer.

**quest** (SYN.) investigation, interrogation, research, examination, search, question, exploration, seek, pursue, journey, hunt, pursuit, explore, query. (ANT.) negligence, inactivity, disregard.

**question** (SYN.) interrogate, quiz, doubt, ask, pump, challenge, inquiry, uncertainty, interview, suspect, inquire, dispute, demand, examine, query. (ANT.) accept, solution, reply, assurance, rejoinder, state, answer, result, response, attest, avow, confidence, respond.

**questionable** (SYN.) uncertain, doubtful, dubious, implausible, debatable, hypothetical, unlikely. (ANT.) obvious, assured, indubitable, proper, unimpeachable, seemly, conventional, sure, certain.

**queue** (SYN.) file, row, line, series, chain, tier, sequence, string.

**quibble** (SYN.) cavil, shift, evasion, equivocation, dodge, sophism, prevaricate.

**quick** (SYN.) rapid, touchy, shrewd, active, hasty, testy, nimble, irascible, discerning, fast, swift, precipitate, excitable, speedy, sharp, impatient, acute, abrupt, curt, brisk, clever, keen, sensitive, lively. (ANT.) inattentive, dull, gradual, patient, slow, unhurried, backward, deliberate, sluggish.

**quicken** (SYN.) expedite, forward, rush, hurry, accelerate, push, hasten, dispatch, facilitate, speed. (ANT.) slow, impede, hinder, hamper, delay, kill, deaden, retard, block.

**quickly** (SYN.) soon, rapidly, fast, at once, promptly, presently, swiftly, hastily, fleetly, headlong. (ANT.) deliberately, gradually.

**quickness** (SYN.) energy, vigor, intensity, action, movement, briskness, exercise, motion, rapidity, agility, enterprise. (ANT.) sloth, idleness, inertia, dullness.

**quick-witted** (SYN.) astute, shrewd, alert, keen, penetrating, quick, intelligent. (ANT.) slow, dull, unintelligent, plodding.

**quiescent** (SYN.) latent, resting, silent, tranquil, undeveloped, still, quiet, dormant, secret, unseen, inactive. (ANT.) visible, aroused, evident, active, patent, astir, manifest.

**quiet** (SYN.) meek, passive, hushed, peaceful, calm, patient, quiescent, motionless, tranquil, gentle, undisturbed, mild, peace, silent, quiescence, hush, modest, quietude, rest, tranquillity. (ANT.) disturbed, agitation, excitement, loud, disturbance, restless, noisy, boisterous, perturbed, noise, agitated.

**quietness** (SYN.) tranquillity, repose, calm, silence, quietude, stillness. (ANT.) flurry, disturbance, fuss, turbulence, agitation, uproar, tumult.

**quintessence** (SYN.) heart, soul, extract, essence, distillation, core. (ANT.) contingency, adjunct, excrescence, nonessential.

**quip** (SYN.) jest, sally, wisecrack,

witticism, joke, jibe, pleasantry.

**quirk** (SYN.) mannerism, idiosyncrasy, foible, peculiarity, oddity, quiddity, vagary, habit, trait, eccentricity.

**quirky** (SYN.) odd, weird, whimsical, peculiar, pixilated, erratic, kinky. (ANT.) normal, conventional, steady.

**quisling** (SYN.) collaborationist, traitor, subversive, betrayer. (ANT.) partisan, loyalist.

**quit** (SYN.) leave, stop, desist, depart, abandon, resign, withdraw, refrain, retreat, cease, vacate, end, relinquish, discontinue, halt, lay off, surrender. (ANT.) persevere, remain, stay, endure, persist, abide, continue.

**quite** (SYN.) somewhat, rather, completely, truly, absolutely, really, entirely. (ANT.) hardly, merely, barely, somewhat.

**quitter** (SYN.) shirker, dropout, defeatist, piker, loser, malingerer.

**quiver** (SYN.) quake, shake, shudder, tremble, vibrate, shiver.

**quixotic** (SYN.) unrealistic, romantic, visionary, impractical, idealistic, chimerical, lofty, fantastic, fey. (ANT.) pragmatic, realistic, practical.

**quiz** (SYN.) challenge, interrogate, inquire, pump, doubt, question, ask, dispute, test, query, examine. (ANT.) reply, say, inform, respond, accept, answer, state.

**quizzical** (SYN.) teasing, coy, mocking, derisive, insolent, arch, bantering, puzzled, questioning, baffled. (ANT.) respectful, obsequious, uninterested, normal, usual, serious, attentive.

**quota** (SYN.) share, portion, apportionment, ratio, proportion, allotment.

**quotation** (SYN.) quote, selection, excerpt, repetition, cutting, reference.

**quote** (SYN.) refer to, recite, paraphrase, adduce, repeat, illustrate, cite, echo. (ANT.) retort, contradict, refute.

# R

**rabble** (SYN.) throng, mob, horde, crowd.

**rabid** (SYN.) frantic, frenzied, violent, raging, raving, zealous, fanatical. (ANT.) normal, sound, sober, moderate.

**race** (SYN.) meet, run, clan, stock, lineage, strain, match, course, stream, hasten, compete, folk, competition. (ANT.) linger, dawdle, dwell.

**rack** (SYN.) frame, framework, bracket, scaffold, skeleton.

**racket** (SYN.) sound, cry, babel, noise, uproar, hubbub, clamor, fuss, disturbance, din, tumult, fracas, clatter. (ANT.) stillness, hush, silence, quiet, tranquillity, peace.

**racy** (SYN.) interesting, vigorous, lively, bawdy, lewd, shameless, spirited, animated, entertaining.

**radiance** (SYN.) luster, brilliancy, brightness, splendor, effulgence, glowing. (ANT.) gloom, darkness, obscurity.

**radiant** (SYN.) showy, superb, brilliant, illustrious, dazzling, grand, shining, bright, effulgent, beaming, sumptuous. (ANT.) dark, unimpressive, dull, dim, lusterless, ordinary.

**radiate** (SYN.) spread, emit, diffuse, shed, irradiate, shine, gleam, illuminate.

**radical** (SYN.) ultra, innate, essential, organic, complete, revolutionary, insurgent, natural, total, fundamental, extreme, basic, original, thorough. (ANT.) extraneous, moderate, conservative, superficial, shallow, established.

**radius** (SYN.) orbit, reach, extent, scope, sphere, range, sweep.

**raft** (SYN.) pontoon, platform, float.

**rag** (SYN.) dishcloth, dishrag, cloth.

**rage** (SYN.) passion, ire, exasperation, fashion, fad, vogue, craze, anger, temper, fury, irritation, mania, rave, rant, storm, fume, wrath. (ANT.) peace, forbearance, patience.

**ragged** (SYN.) tattered, torn, worn, shredded, seedy, threadbare, shabby.

**raging** (SYN.) raving, severe, boisterous, violent, fierce, wild, passionate, acute, intense, powerful. (ANT.) feeble, soft, calm, quiet.

**raid** (SYN.) assault, attack, invasion, arrest, invade, seizure, maraud, foray.

**rail** (SYN.) railing, fence, bar.

**railing** (SYN.) balustrade, banister, barrier, fence.

**rain** (SYN.) shower, drizzle, rainstorm, sprinkle, deluge, downpour.

**raise** (SYN.) grow, muster, elevate, heave, cultivate, awake, rouse, excite, enlarge, increase, rise, breed, hoist, bring up. (ANT.) destroy, decrease, lessen, cut, depreciate, lower, abase, debase, drop, demolish.

**rakish** (SYN.) dapper, dashing, smart, debonair, natty, swanky, showy.

**rally** (SYN.) muster, convoke, summon, convene, convention, assemblage.

**ramble** (SYN.) amble, wander, roam, saunter, walk, deviate. (ANT.) stop, linger, stay, halt, settle.

**rambling** (SYN.) incoherent, erratic. (ANT.) straightforward, coherent.

**rambunctious** (SYN.) stubborn, defiant, unruly, aggressive, contrary.

**ramification** (SYN.) aftermath, extension, branch, offshoot, result, consequence.

**rampage** (SYN.) tumult, outbreak, uproar, rage, frenzy, ebullition, storm.

**rampant** (SYN.) excessive, flagrant, boisterous, menacing. (ANT.) bland, calm, mild.

**ramshackle** (SYN.) rickety, decrepit, flimsy, dilapidated, shaky.

**rancid** (SYN.) spoiled, rank, tainted, sour, musty, putrid, rotten, putrescent. (ANT.) pure, fresh, wholesome, fragrant.

**rancor** (SYN.) spite, grudge, malice, animosity, malevolence, hostility. (ANT.) kindness, toleration, affection.

**random** (SYN.) haphazard, chance, unscheduled, unplanned, casual. (ANT.) intentional, specific, particular.

**range** (SYN.) expanse, extent, limit, area, grassland, pasture, plain, change, wander, roam, travel, rove.

**ransack** (SYN.) pillage, loot, rummage, plunder, despoil, ravish, search.

**ransom** (SYN.) release, deliverance, compensation, redeem.

**rant** (SYN.) declaim, rave, harangue.

**rap** (SYN.) thump, knock, blow, whack.

**rapacious** (SYN.) greedy, wolfish, avaricious, ravenous, grasping, predatory.

**rapid** (SYN.) speedy, quick, swift, fast. (ANT.) deliberate, halting, sluggish, slow.

**rapine** (SYN.) destruction, pillage, robbery, marauding, spoiling.

**rapport** (SYN.) harmony, fellowship, agreement, mutuality, accord, empathy.

**rapture** (SYN.) joy, gladness, ecstasy, bliss, transport, exultation, delight, happiness, enchantment, ravishment. (ANT.) woe, misery, wretch, depression.

**rare** (SYN.) unique, strange, precious, uncommon, infrequent, choice, singular, occasional, unusual, fine, matchless. (ANT.) worthless, common, commonplace, usual, everyday, customary.

**rarely** (SYN.) scarcely, hardly, infrequently, occasionally, sparingly, barely. (ANT.) usually, continually, often.

**rascal** (SYN.) scoundrel, villain, trickster, rogue, scamp, swindler, imp, prankster.

**rash** (SYN.) quick, careless, passionate, thoughtless, hotheaded, reckless, foolhardy, eruption, dermatitis, heedless. (ANT.) thoughtful, considered, prudent, reasoning, calculating, careful.

**raspy** (SYN.) gruff, harsh, dissonant, grinding, hoarse, grating, strident.

**rate** (SYN.) try, adjudicate, consider, decide, condemn, decree, estimate, speed, pace, measure, judge, arbitrate.

**ratify** (SYN.) validate, certify, confirm, establish, support, endorse, uphold.

**rating** (SYN.) assessment, position, assignment, status, classification.

**ration** (SYN.) portion, allowance, distribute, measure, allotment, share, percentage.

**rational** (SYN.) sound, wise, sane, intelligent, sober, sensible, judicious, sober. (ANT.) irrational, absurd, insane.

**rationality** (SYN.) cause, aim, intelligence, reason, basis, understanding, ground, argument, mind, sense.

**raucous** (SYN.) raspy, harsh, grating, hoarse, discordant, rowdy. (ANT.) pleasant, sweet.

**ravage** (SYN.) ruin, despoil, strip, waste, destroy, pillage, plunder, sack, havoc. (ANT.) conserve, save, accumulate.

**rave** (SYN.) rage, storm, laud, praise.

**ravenous** (SYN.) hungry, voracious, craving, starved,

gluttonous, famished. *(ANT.) replete, gorged, satiated, full.*

**ravine** *(SYN.)* chasm, gorge, crevasse, canyon, abyss.

**ravish** *(SYN.)* violate, debauch.

**ravishing** *(SYN.)* enchanting, captivating, bewitching, fascinating, alluring. *(ANT.) loathsome, disgusting, repulsive.*

**raw** *(SYN.)* harsh, rough, coarse, unrefined, undone, uncooked, unprocessed, crude, unpolished, natural. *(ANT.) finished, refined, processed.*

**ray** *(SYN.)* beam.

**raze** *(SYN.)* ravage, wreck, destroy, flatten, annihilate, obliterate, demolish. *(ANT.) erect, construct, preserve, establish, save.*

**reach** *(SYN.)* overtake, arrive at, extent, distance, scope, range, extend, attain, stretch. *(ANT.) fail, miss.*

**react** *(SYN.)* result, reply, respond. *(ANT.) overlook, disregard.*

**reaction** *(SYN.)* result, response, reception, repercussion.

**readable** *(SYN.)* understandable, distinct, legible, plain, clear, comprehensible. *(ANT.) obliterated, illegible, defaced.*

**readily** *(SYN.)* quickly, promptly, easily.

**ready** *(SYN.)* mature, ripe, complete, seasonable, done, arrange, prompt, prepared, completed, quick, mellow. *(ANT.) undeveloped, immature, green.*

**real** *(SYN.)* true, actual, positive, authentic, genuine, veritable. *(ANT.) counterfeit, unreal, fictitious, false, sham, supposed.*

**realization** *(SYN.)* completion, achievement, performance, accomplishment, comprehension, insight. *(ANT.) failure.*

**realize** *(SYN.)* discern, learn, comprehend, appreciate, perfect, actualize, understand, apprehend, know, see. *(ANT.) misunderstand, misapprehend.*

**really** *(SYN.)* truly, actually, honestly, undoubtedly, positively, genuinely. *(ANT.) questionably, possibly, doubtfully.*

**realm** *(SYN.)* land, domain, farm, kingdom, sphere, department, estate, world.

**reap** *(SYN.)* gather, harvest, gain, glean, produce, cut, pick, acquire, garner. *(ANT.) plant, seed, sow, lose, squander.*

**reaping** *(SYN.)* proceeds, result, crop, yield, fruit, produce.

**rear** *(SYN.)* posterior, raise, lift, train, nurture, rump, back, elevate, construct, build.

**reason** *(SYN.)* intelligence, objective, understanding, mind, aim, argument, cause, judgment, common sense, sanity, gather, assume, sake, motive.

**reasonable** *(SYN.)* prudent, rational, logical, sage, sound, moderate, intelligent, sensible, discreet. *(ANT.) unaware, insane, absurd, stupid, illogical, irrational.*

**rebel** *(SYN.)* revolutionary, traitor, mutineer, mutiny, revolt, disobey.

**rebellion** *(SYN.)* revolt, uprising, coup, overthrow, insurrection, revolution. *(ANT.) submission, obedience, repression, peace.*

**rebellious** *(SYN.)* unruly, forward, defiant, undutiful, disobedient. *(ANT.) obedient, compliant, submissive.*

**rebirth** *(SYN.)* renascence, renaissance, revival.

**rebuff** *(SYN.)* snub, oppose, resist, reject, refuse, slight, opposition. *(ANT.) welcome, encourage, support.*

**rebuild** *(SYN.)* restore, renew, refresh, reconstruct, renovate.

**rebuke** *(SYN.)* chide, scold, reproach, censure, upbraid, scolding, condemn. *(ANT.) praise, exonerate, absolve.*

**rebuttal** *(SYN.)* contradiction, defense, answer. *(ANT.) argument, validation, corroboration.*

**recall** *(SYN.)* recollect, remembrance, withdraw, retract, remember, recollection, reminisce, mind, memory, remind. *(ANT.) forget, overlook, ignore.*

**recede** *(SYN.)* withdraw, ebb, retire, retreat.

**receive** *(SYN.)* entertain, acquire, admit, accept, shelter, greet, obtain, welcome. *(ANT.) reject, offer, give, bestow, discharge.*

**recent** *(SYN.)* novel, original, late, new, newfangled, fresh, modern, current. *(ANT.) old, antiquated, ancient.*

**reception** *(SYN.)* gathering, party.

**recess** *(SYN.)* hollow, opening, nook, cranny, dent, respite, rest, break, pause. *(ANT.) gather, convene.*

**recession** *(SYN.)* slump, depression.

**recipe** *(SYN.)* instructions, formula, prescriptions, procedure, method.

**recital** *(SYN.)* history,

account, relation, chronicle, narrative, detail, narration. *(ANT.) distortion, confusion, misrepresentation.*

**recite** *(SYN.)* describe, narrate, declaim, rehearse, tell, mention, repeat, detail, recapitulate, report, list, relate, deliver.

**reckless** *(SYN.)* thoughtless, inconsiderate, careless, imprudent, rash, indiscreet, unconcerned. *(ANT.) careful, nice, accurate.*

**reclaim** *(SYN.)* reform, rescue, reinstate, regenerate, recycle.

**recline** *(SYN.)* stretch, sprawl, repose, rest, lounge, loll, incline.

**recluse** *(SYN.)* hermit, eremite, loner, anchorite.

**recognize** *(SYN.)* remember, avow, own, know, admit, apprehend, recollect, recall, concede, acknowledge, confess. *(ANT.) disown, ignore, renounce.*

**recollect** *(SYN.)* recall, remember, memory, reflect, call to mind, reminisce. *(ANT.) forget.*

**recollection** *(SYN.)* remembrance, retrospection, impression, recall. *(ANT.) forgetfulness, oblivion.*

**recommend** *(SYN.)* hind, refer, advise, commend, suggest, counsel, allude, praise, approve, intimate, advocate. *(ANT.) disapprove, declare, insist.*

**recommendation** *(SYN.)* instruction, justice, trustworthiness, counsel, admonition, caution, integrity, uprightness. *(ANT.) fraud, deceit, trickery, cheating.*

**reconcile** *(SYN.)* meditate, unite, adapt, adjust, settle, reunite, appease.

**recondition** *(SYN.)* rebuild, overhaul, restore, service.

**reconsider** *(SYN.)* ponder, reevaluate, mull over, reflect, reassess.

**record** *(SYN.)* enter, write, register, chronicle, history, account, document.

**recount** *(SYN.)* report, convey, narrate, tell, detail, recite, describe, repeat.

**recoup** *(SYN.)* regain, recover, repay, retrieve.

**recover** *(SYN.)* regain, redeem, recapture, retrieve, salvage, better, improve, mend, heal. *(ANT.) debilitate, succumb, worsen.*

**recreation** *(SYN.)* entertainment, amusement, enjoyment, diversion, fun.

**recrimination** *(SYN.)* vindication, reproach, dissension,

accusation, countercharge.

**recruit** *(SYN.)* trainee, beginner, volunteer, draftee, select, enlist, novice.

**recuperate** *(SYN.)* regain, retrieve, cure, recapture, redeem, rally, convalesce, recover, repossess, restore. *(ANT.) sicker, weaken, lose, regress, forfeit.*

**redeem** *(SYN.)* claim, recover, repossess, regain, reclaim, cash in, retrieve.

**reduce** *(SYN.)* lessen, decrease, lower, downgrade, degrade, suppress, abate, diminish. *(ANT.) enlarge, swell, raise, elevate, revive, increase, amplify.*

**reduction** *(SYN.)* shortening, abridgment, abbreviation. *(ANT.) amplification, extension, enlargement.*

**reek** *(SYN.)* odor, stench, stink, smell.

**refer** *(SYN.)* recommend, direct, commend, regard, concern, relate, suggest, mention.

**referee** *(SYN.)* judge, arbitrator, umpire, arbiter, moderator, mediator.

**reference** *(SYN.)* allusion, direction, mention, concern, respect, referral.

**refine** *(SYN.)* purify, clarify, improve, clean. *(ANT.) pollute, debase, muddy, downgrade.*

**refined** *(SYN.)* purified, cultured, cultivated, courteous, courtly. *(ANT.) rude, coarse, crude, vulgar.*

**refinement** *(SYN.)* culture, enlightenment, education, civilization. *(ANT.) vulgarity, ignorance, boorishness.*

**reflect** *(SYN.)* muse, mirror, deliberate, cogitate, think, reproduce, ponder, consider, reason, meditate, contemplate.

**reflection** *(SYN.)* warning, conception, intelligence, appearance, likeness, image, cogitation, notification.

**reform** *(SYN.)* right, improve, correction, change, amend, improvement, better, betterment, correct, rectify. *(ANT.) spoil, damage, aggravate, vitiate.*

**refresh** *(SYN.)* exhilarate, renew, invigorate. *(ANT.) exhaust, tire.*

**refreshing** *(SYN.)* bracing, cool, brisk, fresh.

**refreshment** *(SYN.)* food, snack, drink, nourishment, exhilaration, stimulation.

**refuge** *(SYN.)* safety, retreat, shelter, asylum, sanctuary, harbor. *(ANT.) peril,* exposure, jeopardy, danger.

**refuse** (SYN.) spurn, rebuff, decline, reject, trash, rubbish, withhold, disallow, waste, garbage, deny, demur. (ANT.) allow, accept, welcome, grant.

**refute** (SYN.) rebut, disprove, confute, falsify, controvert, contradict. (ANT.) prove, confirm, accept, establish.

**regain** (SYN.) redeem, retrieve, recover, repossess, recapture. (ANT.) lose.

**regalement** (SYN.) feast, dinner, celebration, entertainment.

**regard** (SYN.) estimate, value, honor, affection, notice, care, consideration, consider, relation, respect, attend, thought, reference, care, attention, esteem, concern, liking. (ANT.) neglect, disgust, antipathy.

**regards** (SYN.) salutation, greetings, good wishes, respects, remembrances.

**regenerate** (SYN.) improve, reconstruct, remedy, reestablish, rebuild.

**regime** (SYN.) direction, government, administration, management, dynasty, command, leadership.

**regimented** (SYN.) ordered, directed, controlled, orderly, rigid, disciplined. (ANT.) loose, free, unstructured.

**region** (SYN.) belt, place, spot, territory, climate, area, zone, locality, station, locale.

**register** (SYN.) catalog, record, book, list, roll, enter, roster, chronicle.

**regressive** (SYN.) revisionist, retrograde. (ANT.) progressive, civilized, advanced.

**regret** (SYN.) sorrow, qualm, lament, grief, compunction, bemoan, concern, scruple, misgiving, remorse, contrition. (ANT.) obduracy, complacency.

**regular** (SYN.) steady, orderly, natural, normal, customary, usual, habitual, even, uniform, systematic, unvaried, methodical, symmetrical. (ANT.) odd, exceptional, unusual, irregular, abnormal, rare.

**regulate** (SYN.) control, manage, govern, direct, legislate, set, adjust, systematize.

**regulation** (SYN.) method, rule, axiom, guide, control, standard, canon, precept, restraint, requirement. (ANT.) chaos, deviation, hazard, turbulence, confusion.

**rehabilitate** (SYN.) renew, restore, rebuild, reestablish, repair, reconstruct.

**rehearse** (SYN.) repeat, practice, train, learn, coach, prepare, perfect, direct.

**reign** (SYN.) dominion, power, rule, sovereignty, govern, domination.

**reimburse** (SYN.) recompense, remunerate, compensate, remit.

**rein** (SYN.) restriction, bridle, check, deterrent, curb, restraint, barrier, control.

**reinforce** (SYN.) brace, strengthen, fortify, intensify, support.

**reiterate** (SYN.) reproduce, recapitulate, duplicate, repeat, rephrase.

**reject** (SYN.) spurn, rebuff, decline, renounce, expel, discard, deny, refuse. (ANT.) endorse, grant, welcome, accept.

**rejection** (SYN.) dissent, nonconformity, variance, challenge, remonstrance, difference, noncompliance. (ANT.) assent, acceptance, compliance.

**rejoice** (SYN.) celebrate, delight, enjoy, revel, exhilarate, elate.

**rejuvenate** (SYN.) refresh, rekindle, overhaul, revitalize, animate, invigorate. (ANT.) deplete, weaken, exhaust.

**relapse** (SYN.) worsen, deteriorate, regress, weaken, fade, sink, fail. (ANT.) strengthen, progress, advance, get well.

**relate** (SYN.) refer, beat, report, describe, tell, correlate, narrate, recount, compare, connect.

**relation** (SYN.) entente, compact, coalition, alliance, connection, relationship, association, partnership, similarity, kinsman, treaty, marriage. (ANT.) separation, divorce.

**relationship** (SYN.) link, tie, alliance, connection, union, bond, affinity, conjunction. (ANT.) separation, disunion.

**relative** (SYN.) dependent, proportional, about, pertinent, regarding.

**relax** (SYN.) slacken, loosen, repose, rest, recline, unwind. (ANT.) increase, tighten, intensify.

**relaxation** (SYN.) comfort, ease, rest, enjoyment, lull, recess, breather, loafing.

**relaxed** (SYN.) welcome, pleasing, casual, acceptable, informal, restful, agreeable. (ANT.) formal, planned, wretched, distressing, troubling.

**release** (SYN.) liberate, emancipate, relinquish, proclaim, publish, liberation, announce,

deliver, free, discharge. (ANT.) restrict, imprison, subjugate.

**relegate** (SYN.) entrust, authorize, remand, refer, assign.

**relent** (SYN.) cede, yield, surrender, give, relax, abdicate, relinquish, waive. (ANT.) strive, assert, struggle.

**relentless** (SYN.) eternal, stubborn, tenacious, dogged, ceaseless, incessant, persistent, determined.

**relevant** (SYN.) related, material, apt, applicable, fit, relating, germane. (ANT.) foreign, alien, unrelated.

**reliable** (SYN.) trusty, tried, certain, secure, trustworthy, dependable. (ANT.) unreliable, eccentric, questionable, erratic, dubious.

**reliance** (SYN.) faith, confidence, trust. (ANT.) mistrust, doubt, skepticism.

**relic** (SYN.) remains, fossil, throwback, souvenir, keepsake, heirloom.

**relief** (SYN.) help, aid, comfort, ease, backing, patronage, alms, support. (ANT.) hostility, defiance, antagonism, resistance.

**relieve** (SYN.) diminish, soothe, calm, abate, pacify, ease, lessen, replace, spell, lighten, comfort, alleviate. (ANT.) disturb, irritate, agitate, trouble, aggravate, worry.

**religion** (SYN.) tenet, belief, dogma, faith, creed, persuasion.

**religious** (SYN.) godly, reverent, faithful, devout, zeal, pious, divine, holy, devoted, sacred, theological. (ANT.) profane, irreligious, skeptical, impious, lax, atheistic.

**religiousness** (SYN.) love, zeal, affection, devoutness, fidelity, ardor. (ANT.) indifference, apathy, unfaithfulness.

**relinquish** (SYN.) capitulate, submit, yield, abandon, cede, sacrifice, disclaim. (ANT.) overcome, conquer, rout, resist.

**relish** (SYN.) enjoyment, satisfaction, delight, gusto, appreciation, condiment, like, enjoy, enthusiasm. (ANT.) distaste, antipathy, disfavor, dislike.

**reluctance** (SYN.) disgust, hatred, repulsion, abhorrence, distaste, repugnance, aversion. (ANT.) enthusiasm, affection.

**reluctant** (SYN.) slow, averse, hesitant, unwilling, loath,

disinclined, balky. (ANT.) ready, eager, willing, disposed.

**rely** (SYN.) confide, trust, lean, depend. (ANT.) mistrust, disbelieve, question, distrust.

**remain** (SYN.) survive, rest, stay, abide, halt, endure, dwell, tarry, continue, linger. (ANT.) finish, leave, terminate, dissipate.

**remainder** (SYN.) leftover, residue, rest, surplus, balance, excess.

**remains** (SYN.) residue, balance, rest, remnants, relics, discards, waste, junk.

**remark** (SYN.) comment, state, utterance, mention, note, observe, observation, annotation, declaration, statement.

**remarkable** (SYN.) exciting, impressive, overpowering, unusual, affecting, thrilling, splendid, special, noteworthy, extraordinary, touching, august. (ANT.) ordinary, unimpressive, commonplace, average.

**remedy** (SYN.) redress, help, cure, relief, medicine, restorative, rectify, alleviate, medication, correct, reparation.

**remember** (SYN.) recollect, reminisce, recall, memorize, mind, retain, remind. (ANT.) forget, overlook, disregard.

**remembrance** (SYN.) monument, memory, recollection, memento, recall, keepsake, souvenir, retrospection.

**remiss** (SYN.) delinquent, lax, careless, negligent, oblivious, forgetful, absentminded, sloppy, irresponsible.

**remit** (SYN.) send, pay, forward, forgive, pardon, overlook, excuse, reimburse.

**remittance** (SYN.) payment.

**remnant** (SYN.) remains, remainder, rest, residue, trace, relic.

**remodel** (SYN.) remake, reshape, rebuild, redecorate, renovate, modify, change, alter, convert, refurbish, update.

**remonstrate** (SYN.) grouch, protest, complain, grumble, murmur, repine, dispute. (ANT.) rejoice, applaud, praise.

**remorse** (SYN.) sorrow, qualm, contrition, regret, compunction, repentance. (ANT.) obduracy, complacency.

**remorseless** (SYN.) savage, unrelenting, crude, barbaric, merciless, cruel, fiendish, brutal, callous. (ANT.) kind, refined, polite, civilized.

**remote** (SYN.) inconsiderable, removed, slight, far,

unlikely, distant, inaccessible, unreachable, isolated, sequestered. (*ANT.*) *visible, nearby, current, near, close.*

**remove** (*SYN.*) transport, eject, move, vacate, withdraw, dislodge, transfer, doff, displace, eliminate, murder, kill, oust, extract. (*ANT.*) *insert, retain, stay, keep.*

**removed** (*SYN.*) aloof, distant, cool, remote.

**remuneration** (*SYN.*) wages, pay, salary, compensation, reimbursement, reward.

**render** (*SYN.*) become, make, perform, do, offer, present, give, submit.

**rendition** (*SYN.*) interpretation, version, depiction, expression, characterization.

**renegade** (*SYN.*) defector, insurgent, dissenter, rebel, maverick, mutineer, betrayer.

**renege** (*SYN.*) let down, doublecross, deceive.

**renew** (*SYN.*) restore, renovate, overhaul, revise, modernize, reshape, redo.

**renounce** (*SYN.*) resign, disown, revoke, abandon, quit, retract, forgo, leave, forsake, abdicate, reject, relinquish, deny. (*ANT.*) *assert, uphold, recognize, maintain.*

**renovate** (*SYN.*) restore, rehabilitate, rebuild, refresh, renew, overhaul, redesign.

**renown** (*SYN.*) honor, reputation, eminence, acclaim, glory, repute, luster, fame, notability. (*ANT.*) *obscurity, anonymity.*

**renowned** (*SYN.*) noted, famous, distinguished, well-known, glorious, celebrated. (*ANT.*) *unknown, infamous, hidden, obscure.*

**rent** (*SYN.*) payment, rental, let, lease, hire.

**repair** (*SYN.*) rebuilding, mend, renew, linker, correct, patch, restore, adjust, reconstruction, remedy, amend, rehabilitation, retrieve. (*ANT.*) *harm, break.*

**repartee** (*SYN.*) badinage, banter.

**repast** (*SYN.*) feast, banquet, meal, refreshment, snack.

**repeal** (*SYN.*) end, cancel, nullify, annul, quash, abolish, cancellation, rescind, abolition, abrogate.

**repeat** (*SYN.*) reiterate, restate, redo, rehearse, quote, remake, relate, iterate, reproduce.

**repel** (*SYN.*) check, repulse, rebuff, reject, decline, discourage. (*ANT.*) *lure, attract.*

**repellent** (*SYN.*) sickening,

offensive, disgusting, nauseating, repugnant, obnoxious.

**repent** (*SYN.*) deplore, regret, rue, lament.

**repentance** (*SYN.*) penitence, remorse, sorrow, compunction, qualm, grief. (*ANT.*) *obduracy, complacency.*

**repentant** (*SYN.*) regretful, sorrowful, contrite, sorry, penitent. (*ANT.*) *remorseless, obdurate.*

**repented** (*SYN.*) continuous, frequent, recurrent, continual.

**repetitious** (*SYN.*) repeated, monotonous, boring, tiresome, humdrum.

**repine** (*SYN.*) protest, lament, complain, whine, regret, grouch, murmur, grumble. (*ANT.*) *rejoice, applaud, praise.*

**replace** (*SYN.*) alternate, return, reinstate.

**replacement** (*SYN.*) understudy, proxy, second, alternate, substitute, replica, surrogate.

**replenish** (*SYN.*) store, pervade, fill, stock, occupy, supply. (*ANT.*) *empty, void, deplete, exhaust.*

**replica** (*SYN.*) reproduction, copy, exemplar, imitation, duplicate, facsimile. (*ANT.*) *prototype.*

**reply** (*SYN.*) retort, rejoinder, answer, retaliate, respond, confirmation. (*ANT.*) *summoning, inquiry.*

**report** (*SYN.*) declare, herald, publish, announce, summary, publish, advertise. (*ANT.*) *suppress, conceal, withhold, bury.*

**reporter** (*SYN.*) journalist.

**repose** (*SYN.*) hush, quiet, tranquillity, rest, peace, slumber, calm, stillness, sleep, calmness. (*ANT.*) *tumult, excitement, agitation.*

**reprehensible** (*SYN.*) criminal, immoral, damnable, culpable, wrong, wicked.

**represent** (*SYN.*) picture, draw, delineate, portray, depict, denote, symbolize. (*ANT.*) *misrepresent, caricature.*

**representation** (*SYN.*) effigy, film, likeness, portrait, print, scene, appearance, drawing, scene, view, cinema.

**representative** (*SYN.*) delegate, agent, substitute, surrogate.

**repress** (*SYN.*) limit, stop, check, bridle, curb, restrain, constrain, suppress. (*ANT.*) *loosen, aid, incite, liberate, encourage.*

**reprimand** (*SYN.*) rate, scold, vituperate, berate, lecture,

blame, admonish, upbraid. (*ANT.*) *praise, approve.*

**reproach** (*SYN.*) defamation, dishonor, insult, profanation, abuse, disparagement, misuse, reviling. (*ANT.*) *respect, laudation, approval, plaudit.*

**reproduction** (*SYN.*) replica, copy, exemplar, transcript, duplicate, photocopy.

**reproof** (*SYN.*) rebuke, punishment, blame, censure, disapproval, scorn, disdain, admonition.

**repugnance** (*SYN.*) disgust, hatred, reluctance, abhorrence, aversion, loathing, antipathy, distaste, repulsion. (*ANT.*) *devotion, affection, enthusiasm, attachment.*

**repulsive** (*SYN.*) repellent, ugly, homely, deformed, horrid, offensive, plain, uncomely. (*ANT.*) *fair, pretty, attractive.*

**reputable** (*SYN.*) honest, upstanding, trustworthy, straightforward, upright, reliable. (*ANT.*) *notorious, corrupt, disreputable.*

**reputation** (*SYN.*) class, nature, standing, name, fame, kind, renown, prominence, character, distinction, disposition, repute.

**repute** (*SYN.*) class, nature, standing, kind, character, reputation, disposition, sort.

**request** (*SYN.*) sue, implore, petition, desire, appeal, question, entreaty, beseech, ask, pray, supplicate. (*ANT.*) *require.*

**require** (*SYN.*) exact, need, order, command, order, lack, claim, demand, want.

**requirement** (*SYN.*) demand, need, necessity, condition, provision, prerequisite.

**requisite** (*SYN.*) vital, necessary, basic, fundamental, indispensable, essential, needed. (*ANT.*) *casual, nonessential, peripheral.*

**rescind** (*SYN.*) annul, quash, revoke, abolish, invalidate, abrogate, withdraw.

**rescue** (*SYN.*) liberate, ransom, release, deliver, deliverance, liberation.

**research** (*SYN.*) exploration, quest, scrutiny, exploration, interrogation, query, examination, study, investigation. (*ANT.*) *inattention, disregard, negligence.*

**resemblance** (*SYN.*) parity, similitude, analogy, likeness, correspondence. (*ANT.*) *distinction, difference.*

**resemble** (*SYN.*) duplicate, mirror, look like.

**resentfulness** (*SYN.*) envy, jealousy, covetousness, suspicion. (*ANT.*) *liberality, geniality, tolerance, difference.*

**resentment** (*SYN.*) displeasure, bitterness, indignation, rancor, outrage, hostility. (*ANT.*) *complacency, understanding, good will.*

**reservation** (*SYN.*) skepticism, restriction, objection, limitation, doubt.

**reserve** (*SYN.*) fund, hold, keep, store, accumulation, save, stock, maintain, supply. (*ANT.*) *waste, squander.*

**reserved** (*SYN.*) cautious, fearful, timorous, wary, aloof, chary, sheepish, restrained, proper, unfriendly, bashful, diffident. (*ANT.*) *forward, bold, wild, immodest, brazen, abandoned, friendly.*

**reside** (*SYN.*) inhabit, dwell, abide, live, lie.

**residence** (*SYN.*) home, dwelling, stay, seat, abode, quarters, domicile, living quarters.

**residue** (*SYN.*) balance, remainder, rest, ashes, remnants, dregs, leftovers, ends.

**resign** (*SYN.*) vacate, withdraw, leave, surrender, quit.

**resignation** (*SYN.*) withdrawal, surrender, quitting, abdication, acquiescence. (*ANT.*) recalcitrance, defiance, resistance.

**resigned** (*SYN.*) forbearing, stoical, assiduous, passive, accepting, composed, uncomplaining, (*ANT.*) *turbulent, chafing.*

**resilience** (*SYN.*) rubbery, springy, buoyant, elasticity. (*ANT.*) *unresponsive, fixed, stolid.*

**resist** (*SYN.*) defy, attack, withstand, hinder, confront, oppose. (*ANT.*) *relent, allow, yield, accede.*

**resolute** (*SYN.*) firm, resolved, set, determined, decided. (*ANT.*) *irresolute, wavering, vacillating.*

**resolution** (*SYN.*) resolve, courage, determination, persistence, statement, verdict, recommendation, decision, steadfastness, dedication, perseverance. (*ANT.*) *indecision, inconstancy.*

**resolve** (*SYN.*) determination, resolution, courage, settle, decide, persistence, determine, confirm, decision, steadfastness. (*ANT.*) *integrate, indecision, inconstancy.*

**resort** (*SYN.*) motel, lodge, hotel, solve.

**resound** (*SYN.*) echo, ring,

reverberate.

**resource** *(SYN.)* store, source, supply, reserve.

**resourceful** *(SYN.)* inventive, ingenious, creative, clever, imaginative, skillful.

**respect** *(SYN.)* honor, approval, revere, heed, value, admire, esteem, point, detail, admiration, reverence, regard, feature, particular, venerate, consider. *(ANT.)* neglect, abuse, scorn, disregard, despise.

**respectable** *(SYN.)* becoming, respected, proper, seemly, tolerable, decent, acceptable, fair, adequate, passable, suitable, honorable, valuable. *(ANT.)* unsavory, vulgar, gross, disputable, reprehensible.

**respectful** *(SYN.)* courteous, polite, well-behaved, well-bred, compliant, submissive. *(ANT.)* disobedient, impertinent, rude.

**respite** *(SYN.)* deferment, adjournment, suspension.

**respond** *(SYN.)* rejoin, answer, reply, acknowledge, retort. *(ANT.)* overlook, disregard.

**response** *(SYN.)* reply, acknowledgment, answer, retort, rejoinder. *(ANT.)* summoning, inquiry.

**responsibility** *(SYN.)* duty, obligation, accountability, trustworthiness, trust, liability, commitment.

**responsible** *(SYN.)* answerable, chargeable, trustworthy, liable, accountable, able, capable, upstanding, reliable, solid, indebted, creditable. *(ANT.)* careless, free, negligent.

**rest** *(SYN.)* ease, intermission, calm, quiet, balance, surplus, repose, lounge, inactivity, motionlessness, immobility, standstill, relax, remainder, excess, relaxation, slumber, peace, tranquillity, leisure. *(ANT.)* tumult, commotion, motion, agitation.

**restful** *(SYN.)* peaceful, quiet, tranquil, calm. *(ANT.)* tumultuous, upsetting, agitated, disturbed.

**restitution** *(SYN.)* recompense, satisfaction, refund, amends, retrieval.

**restive** *(SYN.)* balky, disobedient, fractious, impatient, unruly, fidgety, uneasy.

**restless** *(SYN.)* sleepless, unquiet, transient, active, agitated, disturbed, jumpy, nervous, uneasy, disquieted, irresolute. *(ANT.)* quiet, tranquil, calm, peaceable.

**restore** *(SYN.)* repair, recover, rebuild, reestablish, renovate,

return, renew, mend, reinstall, revive, rehabilitate, replace.

**restrain** *(SYN.)* limit, curb, constraint, stop, bridle, control, constrain, repress, check, suppress, hinder. *(ANT.)* incite, aid, loosen.

**restraint** *(SYN.)* order, self-control, reserve, control, regulation, limitation, confinement. *(ANT.)* freedom, liberty.

**restrict** *(SYN.)* fetter, restrain, confine, limit, engage, attach, connect, link, tie, bind. *(ANT.)* broaden, enlarge, untie, loose, free.

**restriction** *(SYN.)* curb, handicap, check, boundary, ban, limitation, control, deterrent.

**result** *(SYN.)* effect, issue, outcome, resolve, end, consequence, happen, determination, conclusion, reward, aftermath. *(ANT.)* cause, beginning, origin.

**resume** *(SYN.)* restart, continue, recommence, reassume.

**resurgence** *(SYN.)* rebirth, comeback, recovery, revival, resuscitation, rejuvenation, renewal.

**resuscitate** *(SYN.)* restore, revive.

**retain** *(SYN.)* keep, hold, recall, remember, employ, hire, engage.

**retainer** *(SYN.)* aide, assistant, lackey, attendant, servant.

**retaliate** *(SYN.)* repay, revenge, return, avenge. *(ANT.)* condone, forgive, overlook, excuse, forget.

**retard** *(SYN.)* detain, slacken, defer, impede, hold back, delay, postpone. *(ANT.)* accelerate, speed, hasten, rush.

**retention** *(SYN.)* reservation, acquisition, holding, tenacity, possession.

**reticent** *(SYN.)* reserved, subdued, quiet, shy, withdrawn, restrained, bashful, silent. *(ANT.)* outspoken, forward, opinionated.

**retire** *(SYN.)* resign, quit, abdicate, depart, vacate.

**retiring** *(SYN.)* timid, bashful, withdrawn, modest, reticent, quiet, reserved. *(ANT.)* gregarious, assertive, bold.

**retort** *(SYN.)* reply, answer, response, respond, rejoin, rejoinder, retaliate. *(ANT.)* summoning, inquiry.

**retreat** *(SYN.)* leave, depart, retire, withdraw, retirement, withdrawal, departure, shelter, refuge. *(ANT.)* advanced.

**retrench** *(SYN.)* reduce, scrape, curtail.

**retribution** *(SYN.)* justice,

vengeance, reprisal, punishment, comeuppance, vindictiveness, revenge, retaliation.

**retrieve** *(SYN.)* regain, recover, recapture, repossess, reclaim, salvage, recoup.

**retrograde** *(SYN.)* regressive, backward, declining, deteriorating, worsening. *(ANT.)* onward, progression, advanced.

**return** *(SYN.)* restoration, replace, revert, recur, restore, retreat. *(ANT.)* keep, take, retain.

**reveal** *(SYN.)* discover, publish, communicate, impart, uncover, tell, betray, divulge, disclose. *(ANT.)* conceal, cover, obscure, cloak, hide.

**revel** *(SYN.)* rejoice, wallow, bask, enjoy, delight, savor, gloat, luxuriate, relish.

**revelation** *(SYN.)* hallucination, dream, prophecy, apparition, ghost, mirage, discovery, daydream, surprise, shocker.

**revelry** *(SYN.)* merriment, merry-making, carousal, feasting, gala, festival.

**revenge** *(SYN.)* vindictiveness, reprisal, requital, vengeance, repayment, repay, retribution, reparation. *(ANT.)* reconcile, forgive, pity.

**revenue** *(SYN.)* take, proceeds, income, profit, return.

**revere** *(SYN.)* admire, honor, worship, respect, venerate, adore. *(ANT.)* ignore, despise.

**reverence** *(SYN.)* glory, worship, homage, admiration, dignity, renown, respect, esteem, veneration, adoration, honor. *(ANT.)* dishonor, derision, reproach.

**reverent** *(SYN.)* honoring, respectful, adoring, pious, devout, humble. *(ANT.)* silent, disrespectful.

**reverse** *(SYN.)* overthrow, unmake, rescind, opposite, invert, contrary, rear, back, misfortune, defeat, upset, countermand, revoke. *(ANT.)* vouch, stabilize, endorse, affirm.

**revert** *(SYN.)* return, relapse, backslide, reverse, retreat, recur, go back. *(ANT.)* keep, take, appropriate.

**review** *(SYN.)* reconsideration, examination, commentary, retrospection, restudy, journal, synopsis, study, reexamine, critique, inspection.

**revile** *(SYN.)* defame, malign, vilify, abuse, traduce, asperse, scandalize, smear. *(ANT.)* honor, respect, cherish, protect.

**revise** *(SYN.)* change, alter, improve, correct, amend,

update, rewrite, polish.

**revision** *(SYN.)* inspection, survey, retrospection, commentary, critique.

**revival** *(SYN.)* renaissance, exhumation, resurgence, renewal, revitalization.

**revive** *(SYN.)* refresh, lessen, decrease, renew, reduce, lower, abate, reanimate, diminish, reawaken, rejuvenate, suppress. *(ANT.)* increase, amplify, intensify.

**revoke** *(SYN.)* nullify, cancel, abolish, quash, rescind, abrogate.

**revolt** *(SYN.)* mutiny, rebel, disgust, revolution, uprising, rebellion, upheaval, takeover, insurgence, abolish.

**revolting** *(SYN.)* hateful, odious, abominable, foul, vile, detestable, loathsome, repugnant, obnoxious, sickening. *(ANT.)* delightful, agreeable, pleasant.

**revolution** *(SYN.)* rebellion, mutiny, turn, coup, revolt, overthrow, cycle, spin, uprising.

**revolutionary** *(SYN.)* insurgent, extremist, radical, subversive, mutinous.

**revolve** *(SYN.)* spin, wheel, rotate, circle, turn, whirl, gyrate.

**revolver** *(SYN.)* gun, pistol.

**revulsion** *(SYN.)* dislike, distaste, aversion, repugnance, disgust. *(ANT.)* attraction, desire, fondness, preference.

**reward** *(SYN.)* bounty, premium, award, compensation, prize, recompense, bonus, remuneration, accolade. *(ANT.)* punishment, penalty, chastisement.

**rewarding** *(SYN.)* pleasing, productive, fruitful, profitable, favorable, satisfying, gratifying, fulfilling.

**rhetoric** *(SYN.)* style, verbosity, expressiveness, eloquence, fluency, flamboyance.

**rhyme** *(SYN.)* poem, verse, poetry, ballad, ditty, rhapsody, sonnet.

**ribald** *(SYN.)* suggestive, off-color, indecent, spicy, rude, vulgar.

**rich** *(SYN.)* ample, costly, wealthy, fruitful, prolific, abundant, well-off, affluent, plentiful, fertile, bountiful, luxuriant. *(ANT.)* poor, unfruitful, beggarly, barren, impoverished, scarce, scanty, unproductive, destitute.

**rickety** *(SYN.)* unsound, unsteady, flimsy, unstable, shaky, decrepit, wobbly. *(ANT.)* steady, solid, sturdy.

**ricochet** *(SYN.)* recoil, backfire,

rebound, bounce, deviate, boomerang.

**rid** *(SYN.)* free, clear, shed, delivered, eliminate, disperse, unload, purge.

**riddle** *(SYN.)* puzzle, mystery, conundrum, problem, question, enigma. *(ANT.)* key, solution, answer, resolution.

**ride** *(SYN.)* tour, journey, motor, manage, drive, control, guide.

**ridge** *(SYN.)* hillock, backbone, spine, crest, mound, hump.

**ridicule** *(SYN.)* gibe, banter, mock, jeering, deride, tease, taunt, satire, mockery, derision. *(ANT.)* praise.

**ridiculous** *(SYN.)* silly, nonsensical, absurd, accurate, inconsistent, farcical, proper, laughable, apt, preposterous, foolish. *(ANT.)* sound, reasonable, consistent.

**rife** *(SYN.)* widespread, abundant, innumerable, rampant, teeming.

**rifle** *(SYN.)* plunder, pillage, rummage, ransack, rob, steal.

**rift** *(SYN.)* crevice, fault, crack, flaw, fissure, split, breach, opening.

**right** *(SYN.)* correct, appropriate, suitable, ethical, fit, real, legitimate, justice, factual, just, directly, virtue, true, definite, straight, honorably, seemly. *(ANT.)* immoral, unfair, wrong, bad, improper.

**righteous** *(SYN.)* ethical, chaste, honorable, good, virtuous, noble. *(ANT.)* sinful, libertine, amoral, licentious.

**rigid** *(SYN.)* strict, unyielding, stiff, stern, austere, rigorous, inflexible, stringent, unbendable, severe, harsh, unbending. *(ANT.)* supple, flexible, mild, compassionate, pliable, limp, relaxed.

**rigorous** *(SYN.)* unfeeling, rough, strict, blunt, cruel, hard, severe, grating, coarse, jarring, stern, stringent. *(ANT.)* soft, mild, tender, gentle, smooth.

**rile** *(SYN.)* irritate, nettle, hector, exasperate, provoke, gripe.

**rim** *(SYN.)* verge, frontier, border, outskirts, edge, brink, lip, limit, termination, boundary, fringe, brim, margin. *(ANT.)* core, mainland, center.

**rind** *(SYN.)* layer, cover, skin, hide, peel, crust, bark.

**ring** *(SYN.)* fillet, band, loop, circlet, circle, surround, encircle, peal, sound, resound, jingle, tinkle.

**ringleader** *(SYN.)* provoker,

troublemaker, leader, instigator, chief, inciter, agitator.

**rinse** *(SYN.)* launder, cleanse, wash, soak, immerse, laundering, rinsing, bathe, clean.

**riot** *(SYN.)* disturbance, disorder, outburst, commotion, insurgence, uproar, panic, boisterousness, lark, hoot, sensation, caper, roister, frolic, eruption, confusion, tumult, revolt.

**riotous** *(SYN.)* boisterous, wild, rambunctious, tumultuous, turbulent, noisy, loud, rowdy, rollicking,

**rip** *(SYN.)* tear, rend, wound, rive, cleave, cut, slit, slash, lacerate, shred, scramble, dart, dash, split, disunite. *(ANT.)* mend, join, repair.

**ripe** *(SYN.)* ready, finished, mature, complete, full-grown, develop, mellow, seasonable, full-fledged, primed, disposed, keen, avid, consummate. *(ANT.)* raw, crude, undeveloped, premature, unprepared, unripe.

**ripen** *(SYN.)* grow, season, age, mature, mellow, develop, progress, maturate.

**rip into** *(SYN.)* assail, lash out at, attack, charge.

**rip-off** *(SYN.)* fraud, dishonesty, gyp, racket, swindle, exploitation, heist, theft, extortion, thievery, larceny, shakedown.

**riposte** *(SYN.)* rejoinder, comeback, quip, retort, response, reply, wisecrack.

**ripple** *(SYN.)* wave, ruffle, wavelet, gurgle, undulate, corrugation, rumple, crumple, dribble, bubble.

**rise** *(SYN.)* thrive, awaken, ascend, climb, mount, tower, arise, wake, scale, flourish, prosper, advance, proceed, soar. *(ANT.)* fail, drop, plunge, fade, slump, decline, sinking, depression, waning, comedown, setback, retrogression, descend.

**risk** *(SYN.)* hazard, peril, danger, endanger, chance, jeopardy, threat, vulnerability, contingency, precariousness, shakiness. *(ANT.)* protection, safety, immunity, defense.

**risky** *(SYN.)* menacing, chancy, threatening, critical, perilous, insecure, unsafe, dicey, unsound, dangerous. *(ANT.)* guarded, safe, certain, firm, secure.

**rite** *(SYN.)* pomp, solemnity, ceremony, observance, ceremonial, formality.

**ritual** *(SYN.)* pomp, solemnity, ceremony, parade, rite, ritualism, prescription, routine,

custom, tradition.

**rival** *(SYN.)* enemy, opponent, contestant, compete, foe, adversary, oppose, competitor, contest, antagonist. *(ANT.)* colleague, confederate, allay, collaborator, helpmate, teammate.

**rivalry** *(SYN.)* contest, struggle, duel, race, vying, opposition, contention, competition. *(ANT.)* alliance, collaboration, partnership, teamwork, coalition.

**river** *(SYN.)* brook, stream, headstream, watercourse, tributary, creek.

**rivet** *(SYN.)* weld, bolt, fasten, attach, secure, bind, join, staple, nail, couple.

**road** *(SYN.)* street, way, highway, pike, drive, expressway, boulevard.

**roam** *(SYN.)* err, saunter, deviate, rove, range, wander, digress, ramble, stroll. *(ANT.)* stop, linger, stay, halt, settle.

**roar** *(SYN.)* cry, bellow, yell, shout, yowl, howl, bawl, hoot, bang, boom, blast, blare, scream, whoop, holler, yelp.

**roast** *(SYN.)* deride, ridicule, kid, ride, mock, tease, twit, parody, burlesque.

**rob** *(SYN.)* fleece, steal, despoil, pilfer, pillage, sack, loot, plunder, burglarize, ransack, hold up, rip off, thieve.

**robbery** *(SYN.)* larceny, plundering, thievery, stealing, theft, pillage, swiping, caper, snatching, burglary, plunder.

**robe** *(SYN.)* housecoat, bathrobe, dressing gown, caftan, muumuu, smock, cape.

**robot** *(SYN.)* computer, android, automaton, pawn, workhorse, drudge, laborer.

**robust** *(SYN.)* well, hearty, hale, sound, healthy, strong, able-bodied, stalwart. *(ANT.)* fragile, feeble, debilitated, reserved, refined, puny, frail, delicate, infirm.

**rock** *(SYN.)* pebble, boulder, stone, gravel, granite, roll, sway, swagger, limestone.

**rocky** *(SYN.)* unstable, faint, rock-like, stony, pebbly, gravelly, rough, bumpy, formidable, quavering, challenging, unsteady, dizzy. *(ANT.)* effortless, easy, slight, simple, sound, rugged, stout, hardy, strong, robust.

**rod** *(SYN.)* bar, pole, wand, stick, pike, staff, billy, baton.

**rogue** *(SYN.)* criminal, rascal, outlaw, scoundrel, scamp, good-for-nothing, villain.

**roguish** *(SYN.)* prankish, playful, mischievous, elfish,

waggish, devilish, tricky. *(ANT.)* grave, humorless, solemn, staid.

**roil** *(SYN.)* muddy, rile, mire, disturb.

**roister** *(SYN.)* bluster, swagger, swashbuckle, vaunt, bluff, flourish, rollick.

**role** *(SYN.)* task, part, function, characterization, portrayal, face, character.

**roll** *(SYN.)* revolve, rotate, whirl, swing, rock, waver, reel, lumber, swagger, stagger, progress, proceed, turn, spin.

**rollicking** *(SYN.)* spirited, animated, frolicsome, exuberant, lighthearted, carefree.

**roll up** *(SYN.)* amass, collect, accumulate, gather.

**romance** *(SYN.)* affair, enchantment, novel, tale, adventure, enterprise, story.

**romantic** *(SYN.)* poetic, mental, dreamy, fanciful, imaginative, extravagant, impractical, exaggerated, wild, idealistic, mawkish, ideal, maudlin. *(ANT.)* homely, faint-hearted, familiar, unromantic, pessimistic, unemotional, cynical, literal, prosaic.

**romp** *(SYN.)* caper, gambol, frolic, play, conquer, triumph, horseplay, frisk. *(ANT.)* defeat, rout.

**room** *(SYN.)* enclosure, cell, chamber, space, stay, lodge, cubicle, reside.

**roomy** *(SYN.)* broad, large, wide, sizable, generous, capacious, ample, spacious, extensive, commodious, vast. *(ANT.)* tight, limited, crowded, confined, narrow.

**roost** *(SYN.)* coop, hen house, perch, hutch, residence, abode, hearth, lodgings.

**root** *(SYN.)* reason, bottom, groundwork, cause, support, base, underpinning, beginning, mainspring, source, basis. *(ANT.)* cover, top, building.

**rooted** *(SYN.)* fixed, fast, firm, steadfast, immovable, stationary.

**root for** *(SYN.)* back, support, boost, promote, bolster, encourage, hail, cheer.

**root out** *(SYN.)* dispose of, uproot, cut out, pluck out.

**rope** *(SYN.)* string, wire, cord, cable, line, strand, rigging, ropework, cordage.

**ropy** *(SYN.)* wiry, stringy, viscous, threadlike, viscoid.

**roster** *(SYN.)* list, census, muster, enrollment, listing, register.

**rosy** *(SYN.)* reddish, pink, healthy, fresh, cheerful,

bright, happy, glowing, flushed, promising, favorable. *(ANT.) pale, pallid, gray, wan, disheartening, ashen, unfavorable, gloomy.*

**rot** *(SYN.)* putrefy, waste, decay, mold, decompose, dwindle, spoil, decline, decomposition, wane, rotting, ebb. *(ANT.) increase, rise, grow.*

**rotary** *(SYN.)* axial, rotating, turning, gyrate, revolving, rolling, whirling, rotational.

**rotate** *(SYN.)* spin, twirl, wheel, circle, twist, orbit, invert, swivel, gyrate, wind, alternate, recur, intermit, pivot. *(ANT.) stop, arrest, stand.*

**rote** *(SYN.)* repetition, system, convention, routine, mechanization, habitude, habit, custom.

**rough** *(SYN.)* jagged, scratchy, crude, incomplete, severe, craggy, stormy, rugged, unpolished, approximate, uneven, irregular, bumpy, coarse. *(ANT.) calm, polished, civil, mild, refined, placid, gentle, smooth, sleek, sophisticated, suave.*

**round** *(SYN.)* rotund, chubby, curved, bulbous, entire, complete, spherical, circular, bowed. *(ANT.) slender, trim, slim, thin, lean.*

**rouse** *(SYN.)* waken, awaken, stimulate, excite, summon, arise, stir. *(ANT.) rest, calm, sleep, restrain, sedate.*

**rousing** *(SYN.)* exciting, galvanic, stimulating, electric, moving, exhilarating, stirring, breathtaking, inciting. *(ANT.) flat, uninteresting, drab, monotonous, boring, tiresome, slow, dull.*

**rout** *(SYN.)* defeat, beat, quell, vanquish, conquer, humble, subdue, scatter. *(ANT.) cede, retreat, surrender.*

**route** *(SYN.)* street, course, trail, way, avenue, passage, thoroughfare, track.

**routine** *(SYN.)* way, habit, use, custom, practice, fashion, method, system. *(ANT.) unusual, rate, uncommon.*

**rover** *(SYN.)* traveler, adventurer, wanderer, voyager.

**row** *(SYN.)* file, order, series, rank, progression, sequence, arrangement.

**rowdy** *(SYN.)* disorderly, unruly, brawling, roughneck, scrapper.

**royal** *(SYN.)* lordly, regal, noble, courtly, ruling, stately, dignified, supreme, majestic, sovereign, imperial, kingly.

*(ANT.) servile, common, low, humble, vulgar.*

**rub** *(SYN.)* shine, polish, scour, scrape.

**rubbish** *(SYN.)* debris, garbage, trash, waste, junk, clutter.

**ruddy** *(SYN.)* rosy, reddish, healthy, robust, blushing, sanguine.

**rude** *(SYN.)* gruff, impudent, blunt, impolite, boorish, insolent, saucy, rough, crude, unmannerly, coarse, impertinent. *(ANT.) courtly, civil, stately, calm, dignified, polished, courteous, cultivated, polite.*

**rudimentary** *(SYN.)* essential, primary, fundamental, original, imperfect.

**rue** *(SYN.)* lament, repine, sorrow, deplore, regret, bemoan.

**ruffian** *(SYN.)* crook, hoodlum, thug.

**ruffle** *(SYN.)* rumple, disarrange, disorder, disturb, trimming, frill.

**rug** *(SYN.)* floorcovering, carpet.

**rugged** *(SYN.)* jagged, craw, scratchy, irregular, uneven, harsh, severe, tough. *(ANT.) smooth, level, even.*

**ruin** *(SYN.)* wreck, exterminate, devastate, annihilate, raze, demolish, spoil. *(ANT.) save, establish, preserve.*

**rule** *(SYN.)* law, guide, order, regulation, dominion, sovereignty, control.

**ruler** *(SYN.)* commander, chief, leader, governor, yardstick.

**ruling** *(SYN.)* judgment, decision, decree.

**ruminate** *(SYN.)* brood, reflect, meditate, ponder, consider, speculate.

**rummage** *(SYN.)* root, scour, ransack.

**rumor** *(SYN.)* innuendo, hearsay, gossip.

**rumple** *(SYN.)* tousle, furrow, crease, wrinkle, dishevel.

**run** *(SYN.)* race, hurry, speed, hasten, sprint, dart, scamper, dash.

**runaway** *(SYN.)* refugee, deserter, fugitive.

**run-down** *(SYN.)* ramshackle, dilapidated, tumble-down, weakened.

**rupture** *(SYN.)* fracture, fissure, cleft, break, split, gash.

**rural** *(SYN.)* country, farm, rustic, backwoods. *(ANT.) citified, urban.*

**rush** *(SYN.)* dash, speed, hurry, hasten, run, scoot, hustle, scurry. *(ANT.) tarry, linger.*

**rut** *(SYN.)* routine, habit, groove, track.

# S

**sabotage** *(SYN.)* subversion, undermine, treason, treachery, damage, disable, subvert.

**sack** *(SYN.)* pouch, bag.

**sacrament** *(SYN.)* communion, fellowship, rite, association, participation, union. *(ANT.) nonparticipation, alienation.*

**sacred** *(SYN.)* consecrated, blessed, devout, divine, holy, hallowed, pious, religious, spiritual, saintly. *(ANT.) profane, evil, sacrilegious, worldly, secular, blasphemous, impious.*

**sad** *(SYN.)* dejected, cheerless, despondent, depressed, disconsolate, doleful, downhearted, downcast, dismal, melancholy, somber, glum, saddening. *(ANT.) happy, cheerful, glad, merry.*

**safe** *(SYN.)* dependable, certain, harmless, secure, snug, trustworthy. *(ANT.) hazardous, dangerous, unsafe, insecure, perilous.*

**sag** *(SYN.)* incline, bend, lean, slant, tend, depend, rely, trust, fail. *(ANT.) rise, raise, erect, straighten.*

**sagacity** *(SYN.)* erudition, discretion, foresight, insight, information, judgment, intelligence, knowledge, learning. *(ANT.) foolishness, imprudence, stupidity, nonsense.*

**sage** *(SYN.)* intellectual, disciple, learner, savant, scholar, pupil, student, wise, judicious, sagacious, rational, logical. *(ANT.) dunce, fool, dolt, idiot.*

**saintly** *(SYN.)* virtuous, moral, holy, devout, righteous, good.

**sake** *(SYN.)* motive, reason, purpose, benefit, advantage, welfare.

**salary** *(SYN.)* compensation, allowance, earnings, pay, fee, payment, recompense, wages. *(ANT.) gratuity, present, gift.*

**saloon** *(SYN.)* pub, bar.

**salubrious** *(SYN.)* healthy, hale, sound, robust, strong, well, hygienic, wholesome, salutary. *(ANT.) diseased, delicate, frail, injurious.*

**salutary** *(SYN.)* beneficial, advantageous, profitable, useful, wholesome. *(ANT.) destructive, deleterious, detrimental, injurious, harmful.*

**salute** *(SYN.)* receive, greet.

**salvage** *(SYN.)* retrieve, rescue,

recover.

**salvation** *(SYN.)* release, rescue, deliverance.

**same** *(SYN.)* equal, coincident, equivalent, like, indistinguishable. *(ANT.) disparate, contrary, dissimilar, opposed, distinct.*

**sample** *(SYN.)* example, case, illustration, model, instance, pattern, prototype, specimen, token.

**sanction** *(SYN.)* approval, approbation, authorization, authority, let, permit. *(ANT.) reproach, reprimand, stricture, censure, object, forbid, refuse, resist.*

**sanctuary** *(SYN.)* harbor, haven, asylum, refuge, retreat, shelter. *(ANT.) danger, hazard, exposure, jeopardy, peril.*

**sane** *(SYN.)* balanced, rational, normal, sound, reasonable. *(ANT.) crazy, insane, irrational.*

**sanitary** *(SYN.)* purified, clean, hygienic, disinfected. *(ANT.) soiled, fouled, unclean, dirty.*

**sap** *(SYN.)* exhausted, drain, weaken.

**sarcastic** *(SYN.)* biting, acrimonious, cutting, caustic, derisive, sardonic, satirical, ironic, sneering. *(ANT.) agreeable, affable, pleasant.*

**sardonic** *(SYN.)* bitter, caustic, acrimonious, severe, harsh. *(ANT.) mellow, pleasant, sweet.*

**satanic** *(SYN.)* demonic, fiendish, diabolic.

**sate** *(SYN.)* fill up, fill, occupy, furnish, pervade, stock, replenish, store, supply, content, gorge, satiate, stuff, satisfy. *(ANT.) empty, drain, deplete, void.*

**satire** *(SYN.)* cleverness, fun, banter, humor, irony, raillery, pleasantry. *(ANT.) platitude, sobriety, commonplace, solemnity.*

**satirical** *(SYN.)* biting, caustic, acrimonious, cutting, ironic, derisive, sarcastic, sneering, sardonic, taunting. *(ANT.) agreeable, affable, pleasant.*

**satisfactory** *(SYN.)* ample, capable, adequate, commensurate, enough, sufficient, fitting, suitable, okay. *(ANT.) scant, lacking, deficient, unsatisfactory, poor.*

**satisfy** *(SYN.)* compensate, appease, content, gratify, fulfill, suitable. *(ANT.) displease, dissatisfy, annoy, tantalize.*

**saturate** *(SYN.)* fill, diffuse, infiltrate, penetrate, permeate, run through.

**saucy** *(SYN.)* insolent, bold, impudent, impertinent. *(ANT.) shy, demure.*

**savage** *(SYN.)* brutal, cruel, barbarous, ferocious, inhuman, merciless. *(ANT.) compassionate, gentle, humane, kind, merciful, tame, cultivated.*

**save** *(SYN.)* defend, conserve, keep, maintain, guard, preserve, protect, safeguard, rescue, secure, uphold, spare. *(ANT.) abolish, destroy, abandon, impale, injure.*

**savory** *(SYN.)* delectable, delightful, delicious, palatable, luscious, tasty. *(ANT.) distasteful, nauseous, acrid, unpalatable, unsavory.*

**say** *(SYN.)* converse, articulate, declare, express, discourse, harangue, talk, speak, tell, utter, remark, state. *(ANT.) hush, refrain, be silent.*

**saying** *(SYN.)* aphorism, adage, byword, maxim, proverb, motto.

**scalding** *(SYN.)* hot, scorching, burning, torrid, warm, fervent, ardent, fiery. *(ANT.) cool, cold, freezing, passionless, frigid, bland.*

**scale** *(SYN.)* balance, proportion, ration, range, climb, mount.

**scamp** *(SYN.)* troublemaker, rascal.

**scan** *(SYN.)* examine, study.

**scandal** *(SYN.)* chagrin, humiliation, abashment, mortification, dishonor, disgrace, disrepute, odium. *(ANT.) glory, honor, dignity, praise.*

**scandalize** *(SYN.)* asperse, defame, abuse, disparage, revile, vilify, traduce. *(ANT.) honor, respect, cherish.*

**scandalous** *(SYN.)* disgraceful, discreditable, dishonorable, ignominious, disreputable, shameful. *(ANT.) honorable, renowned, esteemed.*

**scant** *(SYN.)* succinct, concise, terse, inadequate, deficient, insufficient. *(ANT.) ample, big, extended, abundant, protracted.*

**scarce** *(SYN.)* occasional, choice, infrequent, exceptional, incomparable, precious, singular, rare, uncommon. *(ANT.) frequent, ordinary, usual, customary, abundant, numerous, worthless.*

**scarcely** *(SYN.)* barely, hardly.

**scarcity** *(SYN.)* want, insufficiency, lack, need, dearth. *(ANT.) abundance.*

**scare** *(SYN.)* alarm, papal, affright, astound, dismay,

daunt, frighten, intimidate, horrify, terrorize, shock. *(ANT.) compose, reassure, soothe.*

**scared** *(SYN.)* apprehensive, afraid, faint-hearted, frightened, fearful, timid. *(ANT.) bold, assured, courageous, composed, sanguine.*

**scarf** *(SYN.)* kerchief.

**scatter** *(SYN.)* dispel, disperse, diffuse, disseminate, separate, dissipate, spread. *(ANT.) assemble, accumulate, amass, gather, collect.*

**scene** *(SYN.)* exhibition, view, display.

**scent** *(SYN.)* fragrance, fume, aroma, incense, perfume, odor, redolence, stench, stink, smell.

**schedule** *(SYN.)* program, timetable.

**scheme** *(SYN.)* conspiracy, cabal, design, machination, intrigue, plot, plan, chart.

**scholar** *(SYN.)* intellectual, pupil, learner, disciple, sage, student, savant, teacher. *(ANT.) dunce, idiot, fool, ignoramus.*

**scholarly** *(SYN.)* bookish, erudite, formal, academic, learned, pedantic, theoretical, scholastic. *(ANT.) practical, simple.*

**scholarship** *(SYN.)* cognizance, erudition, apprehension, information, learning, knowledge, science, wisdom. *(ANT.) illiteracy, stupidity, ignorance, misunderstanding.*

**science** *(SYN.)* enlightenment, discipline, knowledge, scholarship. *(ANT.) superstition, ignorance.*

**scoff** *(SYN.)* ridicule, belittle, mock.

**scold** *(SYN.)* berate, blame, lecture, rebuke, censure, admonish, reprehend, upbraid, reprimand, criticize. *(ANT.) commend, praise, approve.*

**scope** *(SYN.)* area, compass, expanse, amount, extent, magnitude, degree, measure, reach, size, range.

**scorch** *(SYN.)* burn, char, consume, blaze, incinerate, sear, singe, scald. *(ANT.) put out, quench, extinguish.*

**score** *(SYN.)* reckoning, tally, record, mark, rating.

**scorn** *(SYN.)* contumely, derision, contempt, detestation, hatred, disdain, despise, hate, spurn, refuse, reject. *(ANT.) esteem, respect, awe.*

**scornful** *(SYN.)* disdainful, contemptuous.

**scoundrel** *(SYN.)* rogue, villain,

cad.

**scour** *(SYN.)* wash, clean, scrub.

**scourge** *(SYN.)* affliction, lash, whip.

**scowl** *(SYN.)* glower, frown, glare.

**scramble** *(SYN.)* combine, mix, blend, hasten, clamber, climb.

**scrap** *(SYN.)* fragment, rag, apportionment, part, portion, piece, section, share, segment, crumb, junk. *(ANT.) whole, entirety.*

**scrape** *(SYN.)* difficulty, dilemma, condition, fix, predicament, plight, situation, strait, scour, rub, scratch. *(ANT.) comfort, ease, calmness.*

**scratch** *(SYN.)* scrape, scar.

**scrawny** *(SYN.)* gaunt, skinny, spindly. *(ANT.) husky, burly.*

**scream** *(SYN.)* screech, shriek, yell.

**screech** *(SYN.)* yell, cry, scream, shriek.

**screen** *(SYN.)* partition, cover, separation, protection.

**scrimp** *(SYN.)* skimp, save, economize, conserve.

**script** *(SYN.)* penmanship, hand, handwriting, text, lines.

**scrounge** *(SYN.)* sponge, borrow.

**scrub** *(SYN.)* cleanse, mop, purify, clean, sweep, wash, scour. *(ANT.) pollute, dirty, stain, sully.*

**scrupulous** *(SYN.)* conscientious, candid, honest, honorable, fair, just, sincere, truthful, upright, painstaking, critical. *(ANT.) dishonest, fraudulent, lying, deceitful, tricky.*

**scrutinize** *(SYN.)* criticize, appraise, evaluate, examine, inspect, analyze. *(ANT.) neglect, overlook, approve.*

**scurrilous** *(SYN.)* insulting, outrageous.

**scurry** *(SYN.)* scamper, scramble, hasten, hustle, hurry.

**scuttle** *(SYN.)* swamp, ditch, sink.

**seal** *(SYN.)* emblem, stamp, symbol, crest, signet.

**search** *(SYN.)* exploration, examination, investigation, inquiry, pursuit, quest, explore, scrutinize, investigate, hunt, probe, rummage, ransack, seek, scour. *(ANT.) resignation, abandonment.*

**searching** *(SYN.)* inquiring, inquisitive, interrogative, nosy, curious, peeping, peering, snoopy, prying. *(ANT.) indifferent, unconcerned, incurious, uninterested.*

**season** *(SYN.)* mature, perfect,

ripen, develop, age.

**seasoned** *(SYN.)* veteran, skilled.

**secede** *(SYN.)* quit, withdraw, resign.

**secluded** *(SYN.)* deserted, desolate, isolated, alone, lonely, lone, unaided, only, sole, solitary, single, separate, sheltered, hidden, secret. *(ANT.) surrounded, accompanied.*

**seclusion** *(SYN.)* insulation, isolation, loneliness, alienation, quarantine, segregation, separation, retirement. *(ANT.) fellowship, union, connection, association, communion.*

**secondary** *(SYN.)* minor, poorer, inferior, lower, subordinate. *(ANT.) greater, higher, superior.*

**secret** *(SYN.)* concealed, hidden, latent, covert, private, surreptitious, unknown. *(ANT.) disclosed, exposed, known, obvious, conspicuous, open, public.*

**secrete** *(SYN.)* clothe, conceal, cover, cloak, curtain, envelop, disguise, hide, mask, guard, protect, shroud, veil. *(ANT.) divulge, reveal, expose, unveil.*

**sect** *(SYN.)* segment, denomination, faction, group.

**section** *(SYN.)* district, country, domain, dominion, division, land, place, province, territory, subdivision.

**secular** *(SYN.)* lay, earthly, laic, mundane, temporal, profane, worldly, temporal. *(ANT.) religious, spiritual, unworldly, ecclesiastical.*

**secure** *(SYN.)* certain, definite, fixed, assured, indubitable, positive, inevitable, undeniable, sure, unquestionable, firm, *(ANT.) probable, questionable, uncertain, doubtful, loose, endangered, free.*

**security** *(SYN.)* bond, earnest, pawn, bail, guaranty, pledge, token, surety.

**sedate** *(SYN.)* controlled, serene, calm, composed, unruffled.

**sediment** *(SYN.)* residue, lees, dregs, grounds.

**see** *(SYN.)* contemplate, descry, behold, discern, espy, distinguish, glimpse, inspect, look at, observe, perceive, scan, watch, view, witness, regard, examine, study, notice, eye.

**seek** *(SYN.)* explore, hunt, examine, look, investigate, probe, ransack, search, scour, rummage, scrutinize.

**seem** *(SYN.)* look, appear,

assume, suggest, resemble, pretend. *(ANT.)* exist, be, disappear, withdraw, vanish.

**segment** *(SYN.)* apportionment, division, fragment, moiety, allotment, part, portion, piece, scrap, share, section, element, faction, ingredient, interest, side. *(ANT.)* whole, entirety.

**segregate** *(SYN.)* exclude, separate. *(ANT.)* include, combine.

**seize** *(SYN.)* check, detain, hinder, apprehend, arrest, obstruct, stop, restrain, withhold, grab, grasp, clutch. *(ANT.)* free, liberate, release, activate, discharge, loosen.

**seldom** *(SYN.)* infrequently, scarcely, rarely.

**select** *(SYN.)* cull, opt, pick, choose, elect, prefer. *(ANT.) reject, refuse.*

**selection** *(SYN.)* election, choice, alternative, option, preference.

**self-denial** *(SYN.)* abstinence, continence, abstention, forbearance, fasting, sobriety, moderation, temperance. *(ANT.) gluttony, excess, greed, intoxication, self-indulgence.*

**self-important** *(SYN.)* egotistical, proud, conceited, egocentric.

**self-indulgence** *(SYN.)* egotism, narrowness, self-centeredness, self-seeking, stinginess. *(ANT.) charity, magnanimity, altruism, liberality.*

**selfish** *(SYN.)* narrow, self-centered, self-seeking, mercenary, stingy, ungenerous, greedy, mean, miserly. *(ANT.) charitable.*

**self-satisfied** *(SYN.)* smug, complacent.

**sell** *(SYN.)* market, retail, merchandise, vend, trade, barter.

**send** *(SYN.)* discharge, emit, dispatch, cast, propel, impel, throw, transmit, forward, ship, convey, mail. *(ANT.) get, hold, retain, receive, bring.*

**senescence** *(SYN.)* dotage, senility, age, seniority. *(ANT.) infancy, youth, childhood.*

**senile** *(SYN.)* antiquated, antique, aged, ancient, archaic, obsolete, old, elderly, old-fashioned, venerable. *(ANT.) new, youthful, young, modern.*

**senior** *(SYN.)* superior, older, elder. *(ANT.) minor, junior.*

**sensation** *(SYN.)* feeling, image, impression, apprehension, sense, sensibility, perception, sensitiveness. *(ANT.) insensibility, torpor, stupor, apathy.*

**sensational** *(SYN.)* exciting, marvelous, superb, thrilling, startling, spectacular.

**sense** *(SYN.)* drift, connotation, explanation, gist, implication, intent, import, interpretation, purport, meaning, purpose, signification, significance, sensation, perception, feeling, awareness, insight, consciousness, appreciate, discern, perceive.

**senseless** *(SYN.)* dense, dull, crass, brainless, dumb, obtuse, foolish, stupid. *(ANT.) discerning, intelligent, alert, clever, bright.*

**sensibility** *(SYN.)* sensation, emotion, feeling, passion, tenderness, sentiment. *(ANT.) coldness, imperturbability, anesthesia, insensibility, fact.*

**sensible** *(SYN.)* apprehensible, perceptible, appreciable, alive, aware, awake, cognizant, comprehending, perceiving, conscious, sentient, intelligent, discreet, practical, judicious, prudent, sagacious, reasonable, sage, sober, wise, sound. *(ANT.) impalpable, imperceptible, absurd, stupid, unaware, foolish.*

**sensitive** *(SYN.)* perceptive, prone, impressionable, responsive, susceptible, sentient, tender, sore, delicate, tender, tense, touchy, nervous, keen. *(ANT.) dull, hard, callous, insensitive.*

**sensual** *(SYN.)* lascivious, earthy, lecherous, carnal, sensory, voluptuous, wanton, erotic, lustful, sexual, indecent. *(ANT.) chaste, ascetic, abstemious, virtuous, continent.*

**sentence** *(SYN.)* convict, condemn. *(ANT.) acquit, pardon, absolve.*

**sentiment** *(SYN.)* affection, emotion, sensation, feeling, sensibility, passion, tenderness, impression, opinion, attitude. *(ANT.) coldness, imperturbability, insensibility, fact.*

**sentimental** *(SYN.)* extravagant, fanciful, fantastic, dreamy, fictitious, idealistic, ideal, maudlin, imaginative, mawkish, poetic, romantic, picturesque. *(ANT.) literal, practical, prosaic.*

**separate** *(SYN.)* part, sever, sunder, divide, allot, dispense, share, distribute, disconnect, split, isolate, segregate, different, distinct, independent. *(ANT.) convene, join, gather, combine.*

**separation** *(SYN.)* insulation, isolation, loneliness, alienation, quarantine, seclusion, retirement, solitude, segregation, withdrawal. *(ANT.) communion, fellowship, union, association, connection.*

**sequence** *(SYN.)* chain, graduation, order, progression, arrangement, following, series, succession, train, string.

**serene** *(SYN.)* composed, imperturbable, calm, dispassionate, pacific, placid, peaceful, quiet, tranquil, still, undisturbed, unruffled. *(ANT.) frantic, turbulent, wild, excited, stormy, agitated, turbulent.*

**serenity** *(SYN.)* calmness, hush, calm, quiet, peace, quiescence, quietude, rest, repose, stillness, silence, tranquillity. *(ANT.) tumult, excitement, noise, agitation.*

**series** *(SYN.)* following, chain, arrangement, graduation, progression, order, sequence, train, string.

**serious** *(SYN.)* important, momentous, great, earnest, grave, sedate, sober, staid, alarming, solemn, critical, dangerous, risky, solemn. *(ANT.) trivial, informal, relaxed, small.*

**servant** *(SYN.)* attendant, butler, domestic, valet, manservant, maid.

**serve** *(SYN.)* assist, attend, help, succor, advance, benefit, forward, answer, promote, content, satisfy, suffice, supply, distribute, wait on, aid. *(ANT.) command, direct, dictate, mule.*

**service** *(SYN.)* advantage, account, avail, benefit, behalf, favor, good, gain, profit, interest. *(ANT.) distress, calamity, trouble, handicap.*

**serviceable** *(SYN.)* beneficial, good, helpful, advantageous, profitable, salutary, wholesome, useful. *(ANT.) destructive, deleterious, detrimental, injurious, harmful.*

**servile** *(SYN.)* base, contemptible, despicable, abject, groveling, dishonorable, ignominious, ignoble, lowly, low, menial, mean, sordid, vulgar, vile. *(ANT.) honored, exalted, lofty, esteemed, righteous, noble.*

**servitude** *(SYN.)* confinement, captivity, bondage, imprisonment, slavery. *(ANT.) liberation, freedom.*

**set** *(SYN.)* deposit, dispose, lay, arrange, place, put, position, pose, station, appoint, fix, assign, settle, establish. *(ANT.) mislay, misplace, disturb, remove, disarrange.*

**settle** *(SYN.)* close, conclude, adjudicate, decide, end, resolve, agree upon, establish, satisfy, pay, lodge, locate, reside, determine, abide, terminate. *(ANT.) suspend, hesitate, doubt, vacillate, waver.*

**settlement** *(SYN.)* completion, close, end, finale, issue, conclusion, termination, deduction, decision, inference. *(ANT.) commencement, prelude, start, inception, beginning.*

**sever** *(SYN.)* part, divide, sunder, split, cut, separate. *(ANT.) convene, connect, gather, join, unite, combine.*

**several** *(SYN.)* some, few, a handful.

**severe** *(SYN.)* arduous, distressing, acute, exacting, hard, harsh, intense, relentless, rigorous, sharp, stem, rigid, stringent, strict, cruel, firm, unyielding, unmitigated, difficult, unpleasant, dangerous, violent. *(ANT.) genial, indulgent, lenient, yielding, merciful, considerate.*

**sew** *(SYN.)* mend, patch, fix, stitch, refit, restore, repair.

**shabby** *(SYN.)* indigent, impecunious, needy, penniless, worn, ragged, destitute, poor, threadbare, deficient, inferior, scanty. *(ANT.) rich, wealthy, ample, affluent, opulent, right, sufficient, good.*

**shack** *(SYN.)* hovel, hut, shanty, shed.

**shackle** *(SYN.)* chain, fetter, handcuff.

**shade** *(SYN.)* complexion, dye, hue, paint, color, stain, pigment, darkness, shadow, tincture, dusk, gloom, blacken, darken, conceal, screen, tint, tinge. *(ANT.) transparency, paleness.*

**shadowy** *(SYN.)* dark, dim, gloomy, murky, black, obscure, dusky, unilluminated, dismal, evil, gloomy, sinister, indistinct, hidden, vague, undefined, wicked, indefinite, mystic, secret, occult. *(ANT.) bright, clear, light, pleasant, lucid.*

**shady** *(SYN.)* shifty, shaded, questionable, doubtful, devious.

**shaggy** *(SYN.)* hairy, unkempt, uncombed, woolly.

**shake** *(SYN.)* flutter, jar, jolt, quake, agitate, quiver, shiver, shudder, rock, totter, sway, tremble, vibrate, waver.

**shaky** (SYN.) questionable, uncertain, iffy, faltering, unsteady. (ANT.) *sure, definite, positive, certain.*

**shallow** (SYN.) exterior, cursory, flimsy, frivolous, slight, imperfect, superficial. (ANT.) *complete, deep, abstruse, profound, thorough.*

**sham** (SYN.) affect, act, feign, assume, pretend, simulate, profess. (ANT.) *exhibit, display, reveal, expose.*

**shame** (SYN.) chagrin, humiliation, abashment, disgrace, mortification, dishonor, ignominy, embarrassment, disrepute, odium, mortify, humiliate, abash, humble, opprobrium, scandal. (ANT.) *pride, glory, praise, honor.*

**shameful** (SYN.) disgraceful, dishonorable, disreputable, discreditable, humiliating, ignominious, scandalous. (ANT.) *honorable, renowned, respectable, esteemed.*

**shameless** (SYN.) unembarrassed, unashamed, brazen, bold, impudent. (ANT.) *demure, modest.*

**shape** (SYN.) create, construct, forge, fashion, form, make, produce, mold, constitute, compose, arrange, combine, organize, frame, outline, figure, invent, appearance, pattern, cast, model, devise. (ANT.) *disfigure, misshape, dismantle, wreck.*

**shapeless** (SYN.) rough, amorphous, vague.

**shapely** (SYN.) attractive, well-formed, curvy, alluring. (ANT.) *shapeless.*

**share** (SYN.) parcel, bit, part, division, portion, ration, piece, fragment, allotment, partake, apportion, participate, divide, section. (ANT.) *whole.*

**shared** (SYN.) joint, common, reciprocal, correlative, mutual.

**sharp** (SYN.) biting, pointed, cunning, acute, keen, rough, fine, cutting, shrill, pungent, witty, acrid, blunt, steep, shrewd. (ANT.) *gentle, bland, shallow, smooth, blunt.*

**sharpen** (SYN.) whet, hone, strop.

**shatter** (SYN.) crack, rend, break, pound, smash, burst, demolish, shiver, infringe. (ANT.) *renovate, join, repair, mend.*

**shattered** (SYN.) fractured, destroyed, reduced, separated, broken, smashed, flattened, rent, wrecked. (ANT.) *united, integral, whole.*

**shawl** (SYN.) stole, scarf.

**sheepish** (SYN.) coy, embarrassed, shy, humble, abashed, diffident, timid, modest, timorous. (ANT.) *daring, outgoing, adventurous, gregarious.*

**sheer** (SYN.) thin, transparent, clear, simple, utter, absolute, abrupt, steep, see-through.

**sheet** (SYN.) leaf, layer, coating, film.

**shelter** (SYN.) retreat, safety, cover, asylum, protection, sanctuary, harbor, guard, haven, security. (ANT.) *unveil, expose, bare.*

**shield** (SYN.) envelop, cover, clothe, curtain, protest, protection, cloak, guard, conceal, defense, shelter, hide, screen, veil, shroud. (ANT.) *unveil, divulge, reveal, bare.*

**shift** (SYN.) move, modify, transfer, substitute, vary, change, alter, spell, turn, transfigure. (ANT.) *settle, establish.*

**shifting** (SYN.) wavering, inconstant, changeable, fitful, variable, fickle. (ANT.) *uniform, stable, unchanging.*

**shiftless** (SYN.) idle, lazy, slothful. (ANT.) *energetic.*

**shifty** (SYN.) shrewd, crafty, tricky.

**shilly-shally** (SYN.) fluctuate, waver, hesitate, vacillate.

**shimmer** (SYN.) glimmer, shine, gleam. (ANT.) *dull.*

**shine** (SYN.) flicker, glisten, glow, blaze, glare, flash, beam, shimmer, glimmer, radiate, brush, polish, twinkle, buff, luster, gloss, scintillate, radiance, gleam.

**shining** (SYN.) dazzling, illustrious, showy, superb, brilliant, effulgent, magnificent, splendid, bright. (ANT.) *ordinary, dull.*

**shiny** (SYN.) bright, glossy, polished, glistening. (ANT.) *lusterless, dull.*

**shipshape** (SYN.) clean, neat. (ANT.) *sloppy, messy.*

**shiver** (SYN.) quiver, quake, quaver, tremble, shudder, shake, break, shatter.

**shock** (SYN.) disconcert, astonish, surprise, astound, amaze, clash, disturbance, bewilder, outrage, horrify, revolt, agitation, stagger, blow, impact, collision, surprise, startle, upset, stun.

**shocking** (SYN.) hideous, frightful, severe, appalling, horrible, awful, terrible, dire, fearful. (ANT.) *safe, happy, secure, joyous.*

**shore** (SYN.) seaside, beach, coast. (ANT.) *inland.*

**short** (SYN.) abrupt, squat, concise, brief, low, curtailed, dumpy, terse, inadequate, succinct, dwarfed, small, abbreviated, lacking, abridge, condensed, undersized, slight, little. (ANT.) *extended, protracted.*

**shortage** (SYN.) deficiency, deficit, shortfall. (ANT.) *surplus, enough.*

**shortcoming** (SYN.) error, vice, blemish, failure, flaw, omission, failing. (ANT.) *perfection, completeness.*

**shorten** (SYN.) curtail, limit, cut, abbreviate, reduce, abridge, lessen, restrict. (ANT.) *lengthen, elongate.*

**shortening** (SYN.) reduction, abridgment, abbreviation. (ANT.) *enlargement, amplification.*

**short-handed** (SYN.) understaffed.

**shortly** (SYN.) soon, directly, presently.

**shortsighted** (SYN.) myopic, nearsighted, unimaginative, unthinking, thoughtless.

**shout** (SYN.) ejaculate, cry, yell, roar, vociferate, bellow, exclaim. (ANT.) *whisper.*

**shove** (SYN.) propel, drive, urge, crowd, jostle, force, push, promote. (ANT.) *retreat, falter, oppose, drag, halt.*

**shovel** (SYN.) spade.

**show** (SYN.) flourish, parade, point, reveal, explain, array, movie, production, display, exhibit, note, spectacle, demonstrate, entertainment, tell, usher, guide, prove, indicate, present, lead, demonstration.

**showy** (SYN.) ceremonious, stagy, affected, theatrical, artificial. (ANT.) *unaffected, modest, unemotional, subdued.*

**shred** (SYN.) particle, speck, iota, mite, bit, smidgen, tear, slit, cleave, rip, disunite, wound, rend, mince, tatter, lacerate. (ANT.) *bulk, unite, quantity, mend, aggregate, repair.*

**shrewd** (SYN.) cunning, covert, artful, stealthy, foxy, astute, ingenious, guileful, crafty, sly, surreptitious, wily, tricky, clever, intelligent, clandestine. (ANT.) *frank, sincere, candid, open.*

**shriek** (SYN.) screech, scream, howl, yell.

**shrill** (SYN.) keen, penetrating, sharp, acute, piercing, severe. (ANT.) *gentle, bland, shallow.*

**shrink** (SYN.) diminish, shrivel, dwindle.

**shrivel** (SYN.) wizen, waste, droop, decline, sink, dry, languish, wither. (ANT.) *renew, refresh, revive, rejuvenate.*

**shun** (SYN.) escape, avert, forestall, avoid, forbear, evade, ward, elude, dodge, free. (ANT.) *encounter, confront, meet.*

**shut** (SYN.) seal, finish, stop, close, terminate, conclude, clog, end, obstruct. (ANT.) *begin, open, start, unbar, inaugurate, unlock, commence.*

**shy** (SYN.) reserved, fearful, bashful, retiring, cautious, demure, timid, shrinking, wary, chary. (ANT.) *brazen, bold, immodest, self-confident, audacious.*

**sick** (SYN.) ill, morbid, ailing, unhealthy, diseased, unwell, infirm. (ANT.) *sound, well, robust, strong.*

**sickness** (SYN.) illness, ailment, disease, complaint, disorder. (ANT.) *soundness, healthiness, vigor.*

**side** (SYN.) surface, face, foe, opponent, rival, indirect, secondary, unimportant.

**siege** (SYN.) blockade.

**sieve** (SYN.) screen, strainer, colander.

**sight** (SYN.) eyesight, vision, scene, view, display, spectacle, eyesore.

**sightless** (SYN.) unmindful, oblivious, blind, unseeing, heedless, ignorant. (ANT.) *sensible, discerning, aware, perceiving.*

**sign** (SYN.) omen, mark, emblem, token, suggestion, indication, clue, hint, approve, authorize, signal, gesture, symbol, portent.

**signal** (SYN.) beacon, sign, alarm.

**significance** (SYN.) connotation, drift, acceptation, explanation, implication, gist, importance, interpretation, intent, weight, meaning, purpose, purport, sense.

**significant** (SYN.) grave, important, critical, material, indicative, meaningful, crucial, momentous, telling, vital, weighty. (ANT.) *irrelevant, insignificant, meaningless, unimportant, negligible.*

**signify** (SYN.) designate, imply, denote, intimate, reveal, indicate, manifest, mean, communicate, show, specify. (ANT.) *distract, divert, mislead, conceal.*

**silence** (SYN.) motionless, peaceful, placid, hushed, stillness, quiescent, still, soundlessness, quiet, tranquil, noiselessness, hush, muteness, undisturbed. (*ANT.*) *strident, loud, racket, disturbed, clamor, agitated.*

**silent** (*SYN.*) dumb, hushed, mute, calm, noiseless, quiet, peaceful, still, soundless, speechless, tranquil, uncommunicative, taciturn. (*ANT.*) *communicative, loud, noisy, raucous, talkative, clamorous.*

**silhouette** (*SYN.*) contour, delineation, brief, draft, form, figure, outline, profile, plan, sketch.

**silly** (*SYN.*) asinine, brainless, crazy, absurd, foolish, irrational, witless, nonsensical, simple, ridiculous, stupid. (*ANT.*) *sane, wise, judicious, prudent.*

**similar** (*SYN.*) alike, akin, allied, comparable, analogous, correlative, corresponding, correspondent, parallel, resembling, like. (*ANT.*) *dissimilar, divergent, opposed, different, incongruous.*

**similarity** (*SYN.*) likeness, parity, analogy, correspondence, resemblance, similitude. (*ANT.*) *distinction, variance, difference.*

**simple** (*SYN.*) effortless, elementary, pure, easy, facile, mere, single, uncompounded, homely, humble, unmixed, plain, artless, naive, frank, natural, unsophisticated, open, asinine, foolish, credulous, silly. (*ANT.*) *artful, complex, intricate, adorned.*

**simpleton** (*SYN.*) idiot, fool, ignoramus.

**simulate** (*SYN.*) copy, counterfeit, duplicate, ape, imitate, impersonate, mock, mimic. (*ANT.*) *distort, diverge, alter, invent.*

**sin** (*SYN.*) evil, crime, iniquity, transgress, guilt, offense, ungodliness, trespass, vice, transgression, wickedness, wrong. (*ANT.*) *goodness, purity, virtue, righteousness.*

**sincere** (*SYN.*) earnest, frank, heartfelt, genuine, candid, honest, open, true, straightforward, faithful, truthful, upright, trustworthy, unfeigned. (*ANT.*) *hypocritical, insincere, affected, dishonest, untruthful.*

**sincerity** (*SYN.*) fairness, frankness, honesty, justice, candor, integrity, openness, responsibility, rectitude, uprightness. (*ANT.*) *deceit, dishonesty, cheating.*

**sinful** (*SYN.*) bad, corrupt,

dissolute, antisocial, immoral, licentious, profligate, evil, indecent, unprincipled, vicious. (*ANT.*) *pure, noble, virtuous.*

**sing** (*SYN.*) chant, croon, hum, carol, intone, lilt, warble.

**singe** (*SYN.*) burn, char, consume, blaze, incinerate, scorch, sear, scald. (*ANT.*) *put out, quench, extinguish.*

**single** (*SYN.*) individual, marked, particular, distinctive, separate, special, specific, lone, one, solitary, sole, unwed, unmarried, singular, unique. (*ANT.*) *ordinary, universal, general.*

**singular** (*SYN.*) exceptional, eccentric, odd, peculiar, rate, extraordinary, strange, unusual, striking, characteristic, remarkable, rare, individual, distinctive, uncommon, special. (*ANT.*) *normal, ordinary.*

**sink** (*SYN.*) diminish, droop, subside, hang, decline, fall, extend, downward, drop, descend. (*ANT.*) *mount, climb, soar, arise.*

**sinless** (*SYN.*) faultless, holy, immaculate, perfect, blameless, holy, consummate, ideal, excellent, superlative, supreme. (*ANT.*) *defective, faulty, imperfect.*

**sip** (*SYN.*) drink, taste, swallow.

**sire** (*SYN.*) breed, create, father, engender, beget, generate, procreate, originate, produce, propagate. (*ANT.*) *destroy, ill, extinguish, murder, abort.*

**site** (*SYN.*) place, position, location, situation, station, locality.

**situation** (*SYN.*) circumstance, plight, state, site, location, placement, locale, predicament, position, state, condition.

**size** (*SYN.*) bigness, bulk, dimensions, expanse, amplitude, measurement, area, extent, largeness, magnitude, mass, greatness, volume.

**skeptic** (*SYN.*) doubter, infidel, agnostic, deist, questioner, unbeliever. (*ANT.*) *believer, worshiper, adorer.*

**skepticism** (*SYN.*) hesitation, questioning, wavering, doubting, distrust, mistrust, suspicion. (*ANT.*) *confidence, reliance, trust.*

**sketch** (*SYN.*) draft, figure, form, outline, contour, delineation, drawing, picture, represent, silhouette, draw, profile.

**sketchy** (*SYN.*) indefinite, vague, incomplete, indistinct. (*ANT.*) *definite, detailed, complete.*

**skill** (*SYN.*) cunning, deftness, dexterity, ability, adroitness, cleverness, talent, readiness, skillfulness. (*ANT.*) *ineptitude, inability.*

**skillful** (*SYN.*) adept, clever, able, accomplished, competent, expert, ingenious, cunning, proficient, practiced, versed, skilled. (*ANT.*) *untrained, inept, clumsy, inexpert, bungling, awkward.*

**skimpy** (*SYN.*) cheap, scanty, meager. (*ANT.*) *abundant, generous.*

**skin** (*SYN.*) outside, covering, peel, rind, shell, pare.

**skinny** (*SYN.*) gaunt, thin, raw-boned. (*ANT.*) *fat, hefty, heavy.*

**skip** (*SYN.*) drop, eliminate, ignore, exclude, cancel, delete, disregard, omit, overlook, neglect, miss. (*ANT.*) *notice, introduce, include, insert.*

**skirmish** (*SYN.*) brawl, battle, conflict, combat, dispute, encounter, contend, quarrel, squabble, scuffle, wrangle.

**slack** (*SYN.*) lax, limp, indefinite, free, disengaged, unbound, untied, unfastened, vague, dissolute, heedless, careless, unrestrained, limp, lazy, loose, inactive, sluggish, wanton. (*ANT.*) *restrained, tied, right, stiff, taunt, rigid, fast, inhibited.*

**slander** (*SYN.*) libel, calumny, backbiting, aspersion, scandal, vilification. (*ANT.*) *praise, flattery, commendation, defense.*

**slang** (*SYN.*) jargon, dialect.

**slant** (*SYN.*) disposition, inclination, bias, bent, partiality, slope, tilt, pitch, penchant, prejudice, proneness, proclivity, turn, incline, lean, tendency. (*ANT.*) *justice, fairness, impartiality, equity.*

**slash** (*SYN.*) gash, cut, slit, lower, reduce.

**slaughter** (*SYN.*) butcher, kill, massacre, slay, butchering, killing.

**slave** (*SYN.*) bondservant, serf.

**slavery** (*SYN.*) captivity, imprisonment, serfdom, confinement, bondage, thralldom, servitude, enslavement. (*ANT.*) *freedom, liberation.*

**slay** (*SYN.*) assassinate, kill, murder.

**sleek** (*SYN.*) smooth, polished, slick. (*ANT.*) *blunt,*

harsh, rough, rugged.

**sleep** (*SYN.*) drowse, nap, nod, catnap, repose, doze, rest, slumber, snooze.

**sleepy** (*SYN.*) tired, drowsy, nodding.

**slender** (*SYN.*) lank, lean, meager, emaciated, gaunt, scanty, rare, skinny, scrawny, slight, spare, trim, slim, tenuous, thin. (*ANT.*) *fat, broad, overweight, thick, wide, bulky.*

**slide** (*SYN.*) glide, slip, skim, skid.

**slight** (*SYN.*) lank, lean, meager, emaciated, gaunt, fine, narrow, scanty, scrawny, skinny, sparse, small, rare, slender, spare, insignificant, tenuous, unimportant, slim, thin. (*ANT.*) *regarded, notice, enormous, large, major, huge, include.*

**slim** (*SYN.*) thin, slender, lank, slight, weak, insignificant, unimportant.

**slip** (*SYN.*) error, fault, inaccuracy, shift, err, slide, mistake, glide, blunder. (*ANT.*) *precision, truth, accuracy.*

**slipshod** (*SYN.*) sloppy, careless. (*ANT.*) *careful.*

**slit** (*SYN.*) slash, cut, tear, slot.

**slogan** (*SYN.*) catchword, motto.

**slope** (*SYN.*) incline, leaning, inclination, bending, slant.

**sloth** (*SYN.*) indolence, idleness, inactivity, inertia, sluggishness, torpidity. (*ANT.*) *alertness, assiduousness, diligence, activity.*

**slothful** (*SYN.*) indolent, idle, inactive, lazy, inert, supine, sluggish, torpid. (*ANT.*) *alert, diligent, active, assiduous.*

**slovenly** (*SYN.*) sloppy, bedraggled, unkempt, messy. (*ANT.*) *meticulous, neat.*

**slow** (*SYN.*) deliberate, dull, delaying, dawdling, gradual, leisurely, tired, sluggish, unhurried, behindhand, delayed. (*ANT.*) *rapid, quick, swift, speedy, fast.*

**sluggish** (*SYN.*) dull, deliberate, dawdling, delaying, laggard, gradual, leisurely, tired, slow, lethargic. (*ANT.*) *quick, raid, fast, speedy, swift, energetic, vivacious.*

**slumber** (*SYN.*) drowse, catnap, nod, doze, repose, sleep, rest, snooze.

**slump** (*SYN.*) drop, decline, descent.

**sly** (*SYN.*) covert, artful, astute, crafty, clandestine, foxy, furtive, cunning, insidious, guileful, stealthy, subtle, shrewd, tricky, surreptitious, underhand, wily, secretive.

(ANT.) *sincere, ingenuous, open, candid.*

**small** (SYN.) little, minute, petty, diminutive, puny, wee, tiny, trivial, slight, miniature. (ANT.) *immense, enormous, large, huge.*

**smart** (SYN.) dexterous, quick, skillful, adroit, apt, clever, bright, witty, ingenious, sharp, intelligent. (ANT.) *foolish, stupid, unskilled, awkward, clumsy, bungling, slow, dumb.*

**smash** (SYN.) burst, crush, demolish, destroy, break, crack, fracture, pound, fringe, rack, rupture, shatter, rend. (ANT.) *mend, renovate, restore, repair.*

**smear** (SYN.) wipe, rub, spread.

**smell** (SYN.) fragrance, fume, odor, perfume, incense, aroma, fetidness, stench, stink, scent, sniff, detect, bouquet.

**smidgen** (SYN.) crumb, mite, small, bit, particle, shred, speck, scrap. (ANT.) *bulk, mass, quantity, aggregate.*

**smile** (SYN.) grin. (ANT.) *frown.*

**smite** (SYN.) knock, hit, dash, beat, belabor, buffet, pound, punch, pummel, thrash, thump, defeat, overthrow, overpower, subdue, vanquish, rout. (ANT.) *surrender, fail, defend, shield, stroke.*

**smooth** (SYN.) polished, sleek, slick, glib, diplomatic, flat, level, plain, suave, urbane, even, unwrinkled. (ANT.) *rugged, harsh, rough, blunt, bluff, uneven.*

**smother** (SYN.) suffocate, asphyxiate, stifle.

**smutty** (SYN.) disgusting, filthy, impure, coarse, dirty, lewd, offensive, obscene, pornographic. (ANT.) *modest, refined, decent, pure.*

**snag** (SYN.) difficulty, bar, barrier, check, hindrance, obstruction. (ANT.) *assistance, help, encouragement.*

**snappish** (SYN.) ill-natured, ill-tempered, fractious, irritable, fretful, peevish, testy, touchy, petulant. (ANT.) *good-tempered, pleasant, good-natured, affable, genial.*

**snappy** (SYN.) quick, stylish, chic.

**snare** (SYN.) capture, catch, arrest, clutch, grasp, grip, lay, apprehend, seize, trap, net. (ANT.) *throw, release, lose, liberate.*

**snarl** (SYN.) growl.

**snatch** (SYN.) grasp, seize, grab.

**sneak** (SYN.) steal, skulk, slink.

**sneer** (SYN.) flout, jeer, mock, gibe, deride, taunt, scoff, scorn. (ANT.) *laud, flatter, praise, compliment.*

**sneering** (SYN.) derision, gibe, banter, jeering, mockery, raillery, sarcasm, ridicule, satire.

**sniveling** (SYN.) whimpering, sniffling, weepy, whining, blubbering.

**snobbish** (SYN.) uppity, conceited, snobby, snotty.

**snoopy** (SYN.) inquisitive, interrogative, curious, inquiring, meddling, peeping, prying, peering. (ANT.) *uninterested, incurious, unconcerned, indifferent.*

**snub** (SYN.) rebuke, insult, slight.

**snug** (SYN.) constricted, close, contracted, compact, firm, narrow, taut, tense, stretched, tight, cozy, comfortable, sheltered. (ANT.) *loose, lax, slack, relaxed, open.*

**soak** (SYN.) saturate, drench, steep, wet.

**soar** (SYN.) flutter, fly, flit, float, glide, sail, hover. (ANT.) *plummet, sink, fall, descend.*

**sob** (SYN.) weep, cry, lament.

**sober** (SYN.) sedate, serious, staid, earnest, grave, solemn, moderate. (ANT.) *ordinary, joyful, informal, boisterous, drunk, fuddled, inebriated.*

**sobriety** (SYN.) forbearance, abstinence, abstention, self-denial, moderation, temperance. (ANT.) *self-indulgence, excess, intoxication.*

**social** (SYN.) friendly, civil, gregarious, affable, communicative, hospitable, sociable, group, common, genial, polite. (ANT.) *inhospitable, hermitic, antisocial, disagreeable.*

**society** (SYN.) nation, community, civilization, organization, club, association, fraternity, circle, association, company, companionship.

**soft** (SYN.) gentle, lenient, flexible, compassionate, malleable, meek, mellow, subdued, mild, tender, supple, yielding, pliable, elastic, pliant. (ANT.) *unyielding, rough, hard, tough, rigid.*

**soften** (SYN.) assuage, diminish, abate, allay, alleviate, mitigate, relieve, soothe. (ANT.) *irritate, increase, aggravate, agitate.*

**soil** (SYN.) defile, discolor,

spot, befoul, blemish, blight, stain, sully, earth, dirt, loam, dirty. (ANT.) *purify, honor, cleanse, bleach, decorate.*

**solace** (SYN.) contentment, ease, enjoyment, comfort, consolation, relief, succor. (ANT.) *torture, torment, misery, affliction, discomfort.*

**sole** (SYN.) isolated, desolate, deserted, secluded, unaided, lone, alone, only, single, solitary. (ANT.) *surrounded, accompanied, attended.*

**solemn** (SYN.) ceremonious, imposing, formal, impressive, reverential, ritualistic, grave, sedate, earnest, sober, staid, serious, dignified. (ANT.) *ordinary, joyful, informal, boisterous, cheerful, gay, happy.*

**solicit** (SYN.) beg, beseech, request, seek, pray.

**solicitous** (SYN.) anxious, concerned.

**solicitude** (SYN.) concern, worry, anxiety, care, attention, regard, vigilance, caution, wariness. (ANT.) *indifference, disregard, neglect, negligence.*

**solid** (SYN.) hard, dense, compact, firm. (ANT.) *loose.*

**solitary** (SYN.) isolated, alone, lonely, deserted, unaided, secluded, only, single, lone, sole. (ANT.) *surrounded, attended, accompanied.*

**solitude** (SYN.) loneliness, privacy, refuge, retirement, seclusion, retreat, alienation, asylum, concealment. (ANT.) *publicity, exposure, notoriety.*

**solution** (SYN.) explanation, answer.

**solve** (SYN.) explain, answer, unravel.

**somatic** (SYN.) corporeal, corporal, natural, material, bodily, physical. (ANT.) *spiritual, mental.*

**somber** (SYN.) dismal, dark, bleak, doleful, cheerless, natural, physical, serious, sober, gloomy, grave. (ANT.) *lively, joyous, cheerful, happy.*

**sometimes** (SYN.) occasionally. (ANT.) *invariably, always.*

**soon** (SYN.) shortly, early, betimes, beforehand. (ANT.) *tardy, late, overdue, belated.*

**soothe** (SYN.) encourage, console, solace, comfort, cheer, gladden, sympathize, calm, pacify. (ANT.) *dishearten, depress, antagonize, aggravate, disquiet, upset, unnerve.*

**soothing** (SYN.) gentle, benign, docile, calm, mild, placid, peaceful, serene, soft, relaxed, tractable, tame. (ANT.) *violent, savage, fierce,*

harsh.

**sophisticated** (SYN.) cultured, worldly, blase, cultivated, urbane, cosmopolitan, suave, intricate, complex, advanced. (ANT.) *uncouth, ingenuous, simple, naive, crude.*

**sorcery** (SYN.) enchantment, conjuring, art, charm, black magic, voodoo, witchcraft, wizardry.

**sordid** (SYN.) vicious, odious, revolting, obscene, foul, loathsome, base, depraved, debased, vile, vulgar, abject, wicked, ignoble, despicable, mean, low, worthless, wretched, dirty, unclean. (ANT.) *upright, decent, honorable.*

**sore** (SYN.) tender, sensitive, aching, hurting, painful.

**sorrow** (SYN.) grief, distress, heartache, anguish, misery, sadness, mourning, trial, tribulation, gloom, depression. (ANT.) *consolation, solace, joy, happiness, comfort.*

**sorrowful** (SYN.) dismal, doleful, dejected, despondent, depressed, disconsolate, gloomy, melancholy, glum, moody, somber, sad, grave, aggrieved. (ANT.) *merry, happy, cheerful, joyous.*

**sorry** (SYN.) hurt, pained, sorrowful, afflicted, grieved, contrite, repentant, paltry, poor, wretched, remorseful, mean, shabby, contemptible, worthless, vile, regretful, apologetic. (ANT.) *delighted, impenitent, cheerful, unrepentant, splendid.*

**sort** (SYN.) class, stamp, category, description, nature, character, kind, type, variety. (ANT.) *peculiarity, deviation.*

**sound** (SYN.) effective, logical, telling, binding, powerful, weighty, legal, strong, conclusive, valid. (ANT.) *weak, null, counterfeit.*

**sour** (SYN.) glum, sullen, bitter, peevish, acid, rancid, tart, acrimonious, sharp, bad-tempered, unpleasant, cranky. (ANT.) *wholesome, kindly, genial, benevolent, sweet.*

**source** (SYN.) birth, foundation, agent, determinant, reason, origin, cause, start, incentive, motive, spring, inducement, principle, beginning. (ANT.) *product, harvest, outcome, issue, consequence, end.*

**souvenir** (SYN.) memento, monument, commemoration, remembrance.

**sovereign** (SYN.) monarch, king, emperor, queen.

**sovereignty** (SYN.) command, influence, authority,

predominance, control, sway. (ANT.) debility, incapacity, disablement, ineptitude, impotence.

**space** (SYN.) room, area, location.

**spacious** (SYN.) capacious, large, vast, ample, extensive, wide, roomy, large. (ANT.) limited, narrow, small, cramped.

**span** (SYN.) spread, extent.

**spare** (SYN.) preserve, safeguard, uphold, conserve, protect, defend, rescue, reserve, additional, unoccupied. (ANT.) impair, abolish, injure, abandon.

**sparing** (SYN.) economical, thrifty, frugal. (ANT.) lavish.

**sparkle** (SYN.) gleam, glitter, twinkle, beam, glisten, radiate, shine, blaze.

**spat** (SYN.) quarrel, dispute, affray, wrangle, altercation. (ANT.) peace, friendliness, agreement, reconciliation.

**spawn** (SYN.) yield, bear.

**speak** (SYN.) declare, express, say, articulate, harangue, converse, talk, utter. (ANT.) refrain, hush, quiet.

**special** (SYN.) individual, uncommon, distinctive, peculiar, exceptional, unusual, extraordinary, different, particular. (ANT.) general, widespread, broad, prevailing, average, ordinary.

**specialist** (SYN.) authority, expert.

**species** (SYN.) variety, type, kind, class, sort.

**specific** (SYN.) limited, characteristic, definite, peculiar, explicit, categorical, particular, distinct, precise. (ANT.) generic, general, nonspecific.

**specify** (SYN.) name, call, mention, appoint, denominate, designate, define. (ANT.) miscall, hint.

**specimen** (SYN.) prototype, example, sample, model, pattern, type.

**speck** (SYN.) scrap, jot, bit, mite, smidgen, crumb, iota, particle, spot. (ANT.) quantity, bulk, aggregate.

**spectacle** (SYN.) demonstration, ostentation, movie, array, exhibition, show, display, performance, parade, splurge.

**spectator** (SYN.) viewer, observer.

**speculate** (SYN.) assume, deduce, surmise, apprehend, imagine, consider, view, think, guess, suppose, conjecture. (ANT.) prove, demonstrate, conclude.

**speech** (SYN.) gossip, discourse, talk, chatter, lecture, conference, discussion, address, dialogue, articulation, accent. (ANT.) silence, correspondence, writing, meditation.

**speed** (SYN.) forward, push, accelerate, hasten, rapidity, dispatch, swiftness. (ANT.) impede, slow, block, retard.

**spellbound** (SYN.) fascinated, entranced, hypnotized, mesmerized, rapt.

**spend** (SYN.) pay, disburse, consume. (ANT.) hoard, save.

**spendthrift** (SYN.) squanderer, profligate.

**sphere** (SYN.) globe, orb, ball, environment, area, domain.

**spherical** (SYN.) round, curved, globular.

**spicy** (SYN.) hot, indecent, off-color, suggestive, indelicate.

**spin** (SYN.) revolve, turn, rotate, whirl, twirl, tell, narrate, relate.

**spine** (SYN.) vertebrae, backbone.

**spineless** (SYN.) weak, limp, cowardly. (ANT.) brave, strong, courageous.

**spirit** (SYN.) courage, phantom, verve, fortitude, apparition, mood, soul, ghost. (ANT.) listlessness, substance, languor.

**spirited** (SYN.) excited, animated, lively, active, vigorous, energetic. (ANT.) indolent, lazy, sleepy.

**spiritless** (SYN.) gone, lifeless, departed, dead, insensible, deceased, unconscious. (ANT.) stirring, alive, living.

**spiritual** (SYN.) sacred, unearthly, holy, divine, immaterial, supernatural. (ANT.) material, physical, corporeal.

**spite** (SYN.) grudge, rancor, malice, animosity, malevolence, malignity. (ANT.) kindness, toleration, affection.

**spiteful** (SYN.) vicious, disagreeable, surly, ill-natured. (ANT.) pretty, beautiful, attractive, fair.

**splendid** (SYN.) glorious, illustrious, radiant, brilliant, showy, superb, bright. (ANT.) ordinary, mediocre, dull.

**splendor** (SYN.) effulgence, radiance, brightness, luster, magnificence, display. (ANT.) darkness, obscurity, dullness.

**splinter** (SYN.) fragment, piece, sliver, chip, shiver.

**split** (SYN.) rend, shred, cleave, disunite, sever, break, divide, opening, lacerate. (ANT.) repair, unite, join, sew.

**spoil** (SYN.) rot, disintegrate, waste, decay, ruin, damage, mold, destroy. (ANT.) luxuriate, grow, flourish.

**spoken** (SYN.) verbal, pronounced, articulated, vocal, uttered, oral. (ANT.) written, documentary.

**spokesman** (SYN.) agent, representative.

**spontaneous** (SYN.) impulsive, voluntary, automatic, instinctive, willing, extemporaneous, natural, unconscious. (ANT.) planned, rehearsed, forced, studied, prepared.

**sport** (SYN.) match, play, amusement, fun, pastime, entertainment, athletics.

**sporting** (SYN.) considerate, fair, sportsmanlike.

**spot** (SYN.) blemish, mark, stain, flaw, blot, location, place, site, splatter.

**spotty** (SYN.) erratic, uneven, irregular, inconsistent. (ANT.) regular, even.

**spout** (SYN.) spurt, squirt, tube, nozzle.

**spray** (SYN.) splash, spatter, sprinkle.

**spread** (SYN.) unfold, distribute, open, disperse, unroll, unfurl, scatter, jelly. (ANT.) shut, close, hide, conceal.

**sprightly** (SYN.) blithe, hopeful, vivacious, buoyant, lively, light, nimble. (ANT.) hopeless, depressed, sullen, dejected, despondent.

**spring** (SYN.) commencement, foundation, start, beginning, inception, jump, cradle, begin, birth, bound, originate. (ANT.) issue, product, end.

**sprinkle** (SYN.) strew, spread, scatter, rain.

**spruce** (SYN.) orderly, neat, trim, clear, nice. (ANT.) unkempt, sloppy, dirty.

**spry** (SYN.) brisk, quick, agile, nimble, energetic, supple, alert, active, lively. (ANT.) heavy, sluggish, inert, clumsy.

**spur** (SYN.) inducement, purpose, cause, motive, impulse, reason, incitement. (ANT.) effort, action, result, attempt.

**squabble** (SYN.) bicker, debate, altercate, contend, discuss, argue, quarrel. (ANT.) concede, agree, assent.

**squalid** (SYN.) base, indecent, grimy, dirty, pitiful, filthy, muddy, nasty. (ANT.) wholesome, clean, pure.

**squander** (SYN.) scatter, lavish, consume, dissipate, misuse. (ANT.) preserve, conserve, save, accumulate.

**squeamish** (SYN.) particular, careful.

**stab** (SYN.) stick, gore, pierce, knife, spear, bayonet.

**stability** (SYN.) steadiness, balance, proportion, composure, symmetry. (ANT.) imbalance, fall, unsteadiness.

**stable** (SYN.) firm, enduring, constant, fixed, unwavering, steadfast, steady. (ANT.) irresolute, variable, changeable.

**stack** (SYN.) mass, pile, mound, heap, accumulate.

**staff** (SYN.) pole, stick, club, personnel, crew, employees.

**stage** (SYN.) frame, platform, boards, theater, scaffold, period, phase, step, direct, produce, present.

**stagger** (SYN.) totter, sway, reel, vary, falter, alternate.

**staid** (SYN.) solemn, sedate, earnest, sober, grave. (ANT.) joyful, informal, ordinary.

**stain** (SYN.) blight, dye, tint, befoul, spot, defile, mark, dishonor, disgrace, smirch, blot, tint, blemish, discolor, color, tinge. (ANT.) honor, bleach, decorate, purify.

**stair** (SYN.) staircase, stairway, steps.

**stake** (SYN.) rod, pole, picket, post, pale, bet, wager, concern, interest.

**stale** (SYN.) tasteless, spoiled, old, inedible, dry, uninteresting, trite, flat, dull, vapid, insipid. (ANT.) new, fresh, tasty.

**stalk** (SYN.) dog, follow, track, shadow, hunt.

**stall** (SYN.) hesitate, stop, delay, postpone.

**stammer** (SYN.) falter, stutter.

**stamp** (SYN.) crush, trample, imprint, mark, brand, block, seal, die.

**stand** (SYN.) tolerate, suffer, stay, stand up, endure, bear, abide, halt, arise, rise, remain, sustain, rest. (ANT.) run, yield, advance.

**standard** (SYN.) law, proof, pennant, emblem, touchstone, measure, example, gauge, model, banner, symbol, test. (ANT.) guess, chance, irregular, unusual, supposition.

**standing** (SYN.) rank, position, station, status.

**standpoint** (SYN.) position, viewpoint, attitude.

**staple** (SYN.) main, principal, chief, essential, necessary.

**stare** (SYN.) gaze.

**stark** (SYN.) utter, absolute, sheer, complete, rough, severe, harsh, grim.

**start** (SYN.) opening, source,

commence, onset, surprise, shock, beginning, origin, begin, initiate, jerk, jump, advantage, lead, commencement, outset. *(ANT.) end, completion, termination, close.*

**startle** *(SYN.)* astonish, disconcert, aback, alarm, shock, agitate, surprise, astound, amaze, stun. *(ANT.) caution, prepare, admonish, forewarn.*

**starved** *(SYN.)* longing, voracious, hungry, craving, avid, famished. *(ANT.) satisfied, sated, gouged, full.*

**state** *(SYN.)* circumstance, predicament, case, situation, condition, affirm, declare, express, nation, country, status, assert, recite, tell, recount. *(ANT.) imply, conceal, retract.*

**stately** *(SYN.)* lordly, elegant, regal, sovereign, impressive, magnificent, courtly, grand, imposing, majestic, noble, supreme, dignified. *(ANT.) low, common, mean, servile, humble, vulgar.*

**statement** *(SYN.)* announcement, mention, allegation, declaration, thesis, assertion, report.

**station** *(SYN.)* post, depot, terminal, position, place.

**statuesque** *(SYN.)* imposing, stately, regal, majestic, dignified.

**status** *(SYN.)* place, caste, standing, condition, state, rank, position.

**statute** *(SYN.)* law, ruling, decree, rule. *(ANT.) intention, deliberation.*

**staunch** *(SYN.)* faithful, true, constant, reliable, loyal, devoted. *(ANT.) treacherous, untrustworthy.*

**stay** *(SYN.)* delay, continue, hinder, check, hold, hindrance, support, brace, line, rope, linger, sojourn, abide, halt, stand, rest, remain, tarry, arrest, wait. *(ANT.) hasten, progress, go, depart, advance, leave.*

**stead** *(SYN.)* place.

**steadfast** *(SYN.)* solid, inflexible, constant, stable, unyielding, secure. *(ANT.) unstable, insecure, unsteady.*

**steadfastness** *(SYN.)* persistence, industry, tenacity, constancy, persistency. *(ANT.) laziness, sloth, cessation.*

**steady** *(SYN.)* regular, even, unremitting, stable, steadfast, firm, reliable, solid.

**steal** *(SYN.)* rob, swipe, burglarize, pilfer, shoplift, embezzle, snitch. *(ANT.) restore, buy, return, refund.*

**stealthy** *(SYN.)* sly, secret, furtive. *(ANT.) direct, open, obvious.*

**steep** *(SYN.)* sharp, hilly, sheer, abrupt, perpendicular, precipitous. *(ANT.) gradual, level, flat.*

**steer** *(SYN.)* manage, guide, conduct, lead, supervise, navigate, drive, control, direct.

**stem** *(SYN.)* stalk, trunk, arise, check, stop, originate, hinder.

**stench** *(SYN.)* odor, fetor, fetidness, stink, aroma, smell, fume, scent.

**step** *(SYN.)* stride, pace, stage, move, action, measure, come, go, walk.

**stern** *(SYN.)* harsh, rigid, exacting, rigorous, sharp, severe, strict, hard, unyielding, unmitigated, stringent. *(ANT.) indulgent, forgiving, yielding, lenient, considerate.*

**stew** *(SYN.)* ragout, goulash, boil, simmer.

**stick** *(SYN.)* stalk, twig, rod, staff, pole, pierce, spear, stab, puncture, gore, cling, adhere, hold, catch, abide, remain, persist.

**stickler** *(SYN.)* nitpicker, perfectionist, disciplinarian.

**sticky** *(SYN.)* tricky, delicate, awkward.

**stiff** *(SYN.)* severe, unbendable, unyielding, harsh, inflexible, unbending, rigid, firm, hard, solid, rigorous. *(ANT.) supple, yielding, compassionate, mild, lenient, resilient.*

**stifle** *(SYN.)* choke, strangle, suffocate.

**stigma** *(SYN.)* trace, scar, blot, stain, mark, vestige.

**still** *(SYN.)* peaceful, undisturbed, but, mild, hushed, calm, patient, modest, nevertheless, motionless, meek, quiescent, stationary, besides, however, quiet, hush, tranquil, serene, placid. *(ANT.) agitated, loud.*

**stimulate** *(SYN.)* irritate, excite, arouse, disquiet, rouse, activate, urge, invigorate, animate, provoke. *(ANT.) quell, calm, quiet.*

**stimulus** *(SYN.)* motive, goad, arousal, provocation, encouragement. *(ANT.) discouragement, depressant.*

**stingy** *(SYN.)* greedy, penurious, avaricious, mean, penny-pinching, cheap, selfish, miserly, tight, tightfisted. *(ANT.) munificent, generous, giving, extravagant, open-handed, bountiful.*

**stipend** *(SYN.)* payment, earnings, salary, allowance, pay, compensation, wages. *(ANT.) gratuity, gift.*

**stipulate** *(SYN.)* require, demand.

**stir** *(SYN.)* instigate, impel, push, agitate, induce, mix, rouse, move, propel. *(ANT.) halt, stop, deter.*

**stock** *(SYN.)* hoard, store, strain, accumulation, supply, carry, keep, provision, fund, breed, sort. *(ANT.) sameness, likeness, homogeneity, uniformity.*

**stoical** *(SYN.)* passive, forbearing, uncomplaining, composed, patient. *(ANT.) turbulent, chafing, hysterical.*

**stolid** *(SYN.)* obtuse, unsharpened, dull, blunt, edgeless. *(ANT.) suave, tactful, polished, subtle.*

**stone** *(SYN.)* pebble, gravel, rock.

**stony** *(SYN.)* insensitive, unsentimental, cold.

**stoop** *(SYN.)* bow, bend, lean, crouch.

**stop** *(SYN.)* terminate, check, abstain, hinder, arrest, close, bar, cork, halt, end, conclude, obstruct, finish, quit, pause, discontinue, stay, impede, cease. *(ANT.) start, proceed, speed, begin.*

**store** *(SYN.)* amass, hoard, collect, market, shop, reserve, supply, deposit, bank, save, accrue, increase, stock. *(ANT.) dissipate, waste, disperse.*

**storm** *(SYN.)* gale, tempest, tornado, thunderstorm, hurricane, rage, rant, assault, besiege.

**stormy** *(SYN.)* rough, inclement, windy, blustery, roaring, tempestuous. *(ANT.) quiet, calm, tranquil, peaceful.*

**story** *(SYN.)* yarn, novel, history, tale, falsehood, account, fable, anecdote, narrative, fabrication, lie, level, floor, fiction, report.

**stout** *(SYN.)* plump, obese, chubby, fat, paunchy, overweight, portly, heavy, sturdy, strong, pudgy, thickset. *(ANT.) thin, slender, flimsy, gaunt, slim.*

**straight** *(SYN.)* erect, honorable, square, just, direct, undeviating, unbent, right, upright, honest, uncurving, directly, moral, correct, orderly, vertical. *(ANT.) dishonest, bent, circuitous, twisted, crooked.*

**straightforward** *(SYN.)* forthright, direct, open, candid, aboveboard. *(ANT.)* devious.

**strain** *(SYN.)* stock, kind, variety, stretch, breed, tighten, harm, injure, screen, filter, sprain, sort.

**strainer** *(SYN.)* colander, sieve, filter.

**strait** *(SYN.)* fix, situation, passage, condition, dilemma, channel, trouble, predicament, difficulty, distress, crisis. *(ANT.) ease, calmness, satisfaction, comfort.*

**strange** *(SYN.)* bizarre, peculiar, odd, abnormal, irregular, unusual, curious, uncommon, singular, extraordinary, foreign, eccentric, unfamiliar, queer. *(ANT.) regular, common, familiar, conventional.*

**stranger** *(SYN.)* foreigner, outsider, newcomer, alien, outlander, immigrant. *(ANT.) friend, associate, acquaintance.*

**strap** *(SYN.)* strip, belt, thong, band.

**stratagem** *(SYN.)* design, ruse, cabal, plot, machination, subterfuge, trick, wile, conspiracy.

**strategy** *(SYN.)* technique, management, tactics, approach.

**stray** *(SYN.)* ramble, rove, deviate, lost, strayed, wander, digress, roam, stroll. *(ANT.) linger, stop, halt, settle.*

**stream** *(SYN.)* issue, proceed, flow, come, abound, spout, run, brook.

**street** *(SYN.)* way, road, boulevard, avenue.

**strength** *(SYN.)* power, might, toughness, durability, soundness, vigor, potency. *(ANT.) weakness, frailty, feebleness.*

**strengthen** *(SYN.)* verify, assure, confirm, fix, sanction, ratify, substantiate.

**strenuous** *(SYN.)* forceful, energetic, active, vigorous, determined.

**stress** *(SYN.)* urgency, press, emphasize, accentuate, accent, weight, strain, importance, compulsion, pressure. *(ANT.) relaxation, lenience, ease.*

**stretch** *(SYN.)* strain, expand, elongate, extend, lengthen, spread, distend, protract, distort. *(ANT.) tighten, loosen, slacken, contract.*

**strict** *(SYN.)* rough, stiff, stringent, harsh, unbending, severe, rigorous. *(ANT.) easygoing, lenient, mild.*

**strife** *(SYN.)* disagreement, conflict, discord, quarrel, difference, unrest. *(ANT.) tranquillity, peace, concord.*

# strike

**strike** *(SYN.)* pound, hit, smite, beat, assault, attack, affect, impress, overwhelm, sit down, walkout, slowdown.

**striking** *(SYN.)* arresting, imposing, splendid, august, impressive, thrilling, stirring, awesome, awe-inspiring. *(ANT.)* ordinary, unimpressive, commonplace, regular.

**stringent** *(SYN.)* harsh, rugged, grating, severe, gruff.

**strip** *(SYN.)* disrobe, undress, remove, uncover, peel, ribbon, band, piece.

**stripped** *(SYN.)* open, simple, bare, nude, uncovered, exposed, bald, plain, naked, barren, defenseless. *(ANT.)* protected, dressed, concealed.

**strive** *(SYN.)* aim, struggle, attempt, undertake, design, endeavor, try. *(ANT.)* omit, abandon, neglect, decline.

**stroke** *(SYN.)* rap, blow, tap, knock, feat, achievement, accomplishment, caress.

**stroll** *(SYN.)* amble, walk, ramble.

**strong** *(SYN.)* potent, hale, athletic, mighty, sturdy, impregnable, resistant. *(ANT.)* feeble, insipid, brittle, weak, bland, fragile.

**structure** *(SYN.)* construction, framework, arrangement.

**struggle** *(SYN.)* fray, strive, fight, contest, battle, skirmish, oppose, clash. *(ANT.)* peace, agreement, truce.

**stubborn** *(SYN.)* obstinate, firm, determined, inflexible, obdurate, uncompromising, pigheaded, contumacious, rigid, unbending, intractable. *(ANT.)* docile, yielding, amenable, submissive.

**student** *(SYN.)* pupil, observer, disciple, scholar, learner.

**studio** *(SYN.)* workroom, workshop.

**study** *(SYN.)* weigh, muse, master, contemplate, reflect, examination, examine.

**stuff** *(SYN.)* thing, subject, material, theme, matter, substance, fill, ram, cram, pack, textile, cloth, topic.

**stumble** *(SYN.)* sink, collapse, tumble, drop, topple, lurch, trip, fall. *(ANT.)* steady, climb, soar, arise.

**stun** *(SYN.)* shock, knock out, dumbfound, take, amaze, alarm. *(ANT.)* forewarn, caution, prepare.

**stunning** *(SYN.)* brilliant, dazzling, exquisite, ravishing. *(ANT.)* drab, ugly.

**stunt** *(SYN.)* check, restrict, hinder.

**stupid** *(SYN.)* dull, obtuse, half-witted, brainless, foolish, dumb, witless, idiotic. *(ANT.)* smart, intelligent, clever, quick, bright, alert, discerning.

**stupor** *(SYN.)* lethargy, torpor, daze, languor, drowsiness, numbness. *(ANT.)* wakefulness, liveliness, activity.

**sturdy** *(SYN.)* hale, strong, rugged, stout, mighty, enduring, hardy, well-built. *(ANT.)* fragile, brittle, insipid, delicate.

**style** *(SYN.)* sort, type, kind, chic, smartness, elegance.

**subdue** *(SYN.)* crush, overcome, rout, beat, reduce, lower, defeat, vanquish. *(ANT.)* retreat, cede, surrender.

**subject** *(SYN.)* subordinate, theme, case, topic, dependent, citizen, matter.

**sublime** *(SYN.)* lofty, raised, elevated, supreme, exalted, splendid, grand. *(ANT.)* ordinary, vase, low, ridiculous.

**submerge** *(SYN.)* submerse, dunk, sink, dip, immerse, engage, douse, engross. *(ANT.)* surface, rise, uplift, elevate.

**submissive** *(SYN.)* deferential, yielding, dutiful, compliant. *(ANT.)* rebellious, intractable, insubordinate.

**submit** *(SYN.)* quit, resign, waive, yield, tender, offer, abdicate, cede, surrender. *(ANT.)* fight, oppose, resist, struggle, deny.

**subordinate** *(SYN.)* demean, reduce, inferior, assistant, citizen. *(ANT.)* superior.

**subsequent** *(SYN.)* later, following. *(ANT.)* preceding, previous.

**subside** *(SYN.)* decrease, lower, sink, droop, hang, collapse, downward. *(ANT.)* mount, steady, arise, climb.

**subsidy** *(SYN.)* support, aid, grant.

**substance** *(SYN.)* stuff, essence, importance, material, moment, matter. *(ANT.)* spirit, immaterial.

**substantial** *(SYN.)* large, considerable, sizable, actual, real, tangible, influential. *(ANT.)* unimportant, trivial.

**substantiate** *(SYN.)* strengthen, corroborate, confirm.

**substitute** *(SYN.)* proxy, expedient, deputy, makeshift, replacement, alternate, lieutenant, representative, surrogate, displace, exchange, equivalent. *(ANT.)* sovereign, master, head.

**substitution** *(SYN.)* change, mutation, vicissitude, alteration,

modification. *(ANT.)* uniformity, monotony.

**subterfuge** *(SYN.)* pretext, excuse, cloak, simulation, disguise, garb, pretension. *(ANT.)* reality, truth, actuality, sincerity.

**subtle** *(SYN.)* suggestive, indirect. *(ANT.)* overt, obvious.

**subtract** *(SYN.)* decrease, reduce, curtail, deduct, diminish, remove, lessen. *(ANT.)* expand, increase, add, enlarge, grow.

**succeed** *(SYN.)* thrive, follow, replace, achieve, win, flourish, prevail, inherit. *(ANT.)* flop, miscarry, anticipate, fail, precede.

**success** *(SYN.)* advance, prosperity, luck. *(ANT.)* failure.

**successful** *(SYN.)* fortunate, favorable, lucky, triumphant.

**succession** *(SYN.)* chain, course, series, order, string, arrangement, progression, train, following.

**successive** *(SYN.)* serial, sequential.

**succinct** *(SYN.)* pithy, curt, brief, short, compendious, terse. *(ANT.)* prolonged, extended, long, protracted.

**succor** *(SYN.)* ease, solace, comfort, enjoyment, consolation. *(ANT.)* suffering, discomfort, torture, affliction, torment.

**sudden** *(SYN.)* rapid, swift, immediate, abrupt, unexpected, unforeseen, hasty. *(ANT.)* slowly, anticipated.

**suffer** *(SYN.)* stand, experience, endure, bear, feel, allow, let, permit, sustain. *(ANT.)* exclude, banish, overcome.

**suffering** *(SYN.)* distress, ache, anguish, pain, woe, misery, torment. *(ANT.)* ease, relief, comfort.

**sufficient** *(SYN.)* fitting, enough, adequate, satisfactory. *(ANT.)* scant, deficient.

**suffix** *(SYN.)* ending. *(ANT.)* prefix.

**suggest** *(SYN.)* propose, offer, refer, advise, hint, insinuate, recommend, allude. *(ANT.)* dictate, declare, insist.

**suggestion** *(SYN.)* exhortation, recommendation, intelligence, caution, admonition, warning, advice.

**suit** *(SYN.)* conform, accommodate, fit. *(ANT.)* misapply, disturb.

**suitable** *(SYN.)* welcome, agreeable, acceptable, gratifying. *(ANT.)* offensive, disagreeable.

**sullen** *(SYN.)* fretful, morose, dismal, silent, sulky, bitter,

sad, somber, glum, gloomy, dour, moody. *(ANT.)* pleasant, joyous, merry.

**sultry** *(SYN.)* close, hot, stifling.

**sum** *(SYN.)* amount, total, aggregate, whole, increase, append, add. *(ANT.)* sample, fraction, reduce, deduct.

**summarize** *(SYN.)* abstract, abridge. *(ANT.)* restore, add, unite, return.

**summary** *(SYN.)* digest, outline, abstract, synopsis, concise, brief, short, compact.

**summit** *(SYN.)* peak, top, head, crest, zenith, apex, crown, pinnacle. *(ANT.)* bottom, foundation, base, foot.

**summon** *(SYN.)* invoke, call, invite. *(ANT.)* dismiss.

**sundry** *(SYN.)* miscellaneous, several, different, various, divers. *(ANT.)* similar, identical, alike, same, congruous.

**sunny** *(SYN.)* cheery, cheerful, fair, joyful, happy, cloudless. *(ANT.)* overcast, cloudy.

**superannuated** *(SYN.)* old, archaic, aged, senile, ancient, venerable, elderly. *(ANT.)* youthful, modern, young.

**superb** *(SYN.)* splendid, wonderful, extraordinary, marvelous.

**supercilious** *(SYN.)* contemptuous, snobbish, overbearing, vainglorious, arrogant, haughty. *(ANT.)* meek, ashamed, lowly.

**superficial** *(SYN.)* flimsy, shallow, cursory, slight, exterior. *(ANT.)* thorough, deep, abstruse, profound.

**superintend** *(SYN.)* control, govern, rule, command, manage, direct, regulate. *(ANT.)* ignore, follow, submit, abandon.

**superintendence** *(SYN.)* control, oversight, surveillance, management.

**superintendent** *(SYN.)* manager, supervisor, overseer, director, administrator.

**superiority** *(SYN.)* profit, mastery, advantage, good, service, edge, utility. *(ANT.)* harm, detriment, impediment.

**superlative** *(SYN.)* pure, consummate, sinless, blameless, holy, perfect, faultless, ideal, unqualified, immaculate. *(ANT.)* lacking, defective, imperfect, deficient.

**supernatural** *(SYN.)* unearthly, preternatural, marvelous, miraculous. *(ANT.)* plain, human, physical, common.

**supervise** *(SYN.)* rule, oversee, govern, command, direct, superintend, manage. (*ANT.*) *submit, forsake, abandon.*

**supervision** (*SYN.*) oversight, inspection, surveillance, charge, management.

**supervisor** (*SYN.*) manager, boss, foreman, director.

**supplant** (*SYN.*) overturn, overcome. (*ANT.*) *uphold, conserve.*

**supple** (*SYN.*) lithe, pliant, flexible, limber, elastic, pliable. (*ANT.*) *stiff, brittle, rigid.*

**supplement** (*SYN.*) extension, complement, addition, extend, add.

**supplicate** (*SYN.*) beg, petition, solicit, adjure, beseech, entreat, ask, pray, crave. (*ANT.*) *cede, give, bestow, grant.*

**supplication** (*SYN.*) invocation, plea, appeal, request, entreaty.

**supply** (*SYN.*) provide, inventory, hoard, reserve, store, accumulation, stock, furnish, endow, give.

**support** (*SYN.*) groundwork, aid, favor, base, prop, assistance, comfort, basis, succor, living, subsistence, encouragement, backing, livelihood, help. (*ANT.*) *discourage, abandon, oppose, opposition, attack.*

**supporter** (*SYN.*) follower, devotee, adherent, henchman, attendant, disciple, votary. (*ANT.*) *master, head, chief.*

**suppose** (*SYN.*) believe, presume, deduce, apprehend, think, assume, imagine, speculate, guess, conjecture. (*ANT.*) *prove, demonstrate, ascertain.*

**supposition** (*SYN.*) theory, conjecture. (*ANT.*) *proof, fact.*

**suppress** (*SYN.*) diminish, reduce, overpower, abate, lessen, decrease, subdue. (*ANT.*) *revive, amplify, intensify, enlarge.*

**supremacy** (*SYN.*) domination, predominance, ascendancy, sovereignty.

**supreme** (*SYN.*) greatest, best, highest, main, principal, cardinal, first, chief, foremost, paramount. (*ANT.*) *supplemental, minor, subsidiary, auxiliary.*

**sure** (*SYN.*) confident, fixed, inevitable, certain, positive, trustworthy, reliable, unquestionable, convinced, steady. (*ANT.*) *probable, uncertain, doubtful.*

**surface** (*SYN.*) outside, exterior, cover, covering.

**surge** (*SYN.*) heave, swell, grow. (*ANT.*) *wane, ebb, diminish.*

**surly** (*SYN.*) disagreeable, hostile, unfriendly, ugly, antagonistic.

**surmise** (*SYN.*) judge, think, believe, assume, suppose, presume, guess.

**surpass** (*SYN.*) pass, exceed, excel, outstrip, outdo.

**surplus** (*SYN.*) extravagance, intemperance, superabundance, excess, immoderation, remainder, extra, profusion, superfluity. (*ANT.*) *want, lack, dearth.*

**surprise** (*SYN.*) miracle, prodigy, wonder, awe, phenomenon, marvel, bewilderment, wonderment, rarity. (*ANT.*) *expectation, triviality, indifference, familiarity.*

**surrender** (*SYN.*) relinquish, resign, yield, abandon, sacrifice, submit, cede. (*ANT.*) *overcome, rout, conquer.*

**surreptitious** (*SYN.*) sneaky, sneaking, underhand, sly, furtive. (*ANT.*) *openhanded, open, straightforward.*

**surround** (*SYN.*) confine, encompass, circle, encircle, girdle, fence, circumscribe, limit, envelop. (*ANT.*) *open, distend, expose, enlarge.*

**surveillance** (*SYN.*) inspection, oversight, supervision, management, control.

**survey** (*SYN.*) scan, inspect, view, examine, inspection, examination.

**survive** (*SYN.*) live, remain, continue, persist. (*ANT.*) *die, fail, succumb.*

**suspect** (*SYN.*) waver, disbelieve, presume, suppose, mistrust, distrust.

**suspend** (*SYN.*) delay, hang, withhold, interrupt, postpone, dangle, adjourn, poise. (*ANT.*) *persist, proceed, maintain.*

**suspicion** (*SYN.*) unbelief, distrust, suspense, uncertainty, doubt. (*ANT.*) *determination, conviction, faith, belief.*

**sustain** (*SYN.*) bear, carry, undergo, foster, keep, prop, help, advocate, back. (*ANT.*) *discourage, oppose, destroy.*

**sustenance** (*SYN.*) fare, food, diet, rations, nutriment, edibles, victuals. (*ANT.*) *hunger, want, drink.*

**swallow** (*SYN.*) gorge, eat, mouthful.

**swallow up** (*SYN.*) consume, absorb, engulf, assimilate. (*ANT.*) *exude, dispense, expel, discharge.*

**swarm** (*SYN.*) throng, horde, crowd.

**swarthy** (*SYN.*) sable, dark. (*ANT.*) *bright, light.*

**swear** (*SYN.*) declare, state, affirm, vouchsafe, curse, maintain. (*ANT.*) *demur, oppose, deny, contradict.*

**sweat** (*SYN.*) perspiration, perspire.

**sweeping** (*SYN.*) extensive, wide, general, broad, tolerant, comprehensive, vast. (*ANT.*) *restricted, confined.*

**sweet** (*SYN.*) engaging, luscious, pure, clean, fresh, melodious, pleasant. (*ANT.*) *bitter, harsh, nasty, irascible, discordant, irritable, acrid.*

**swell** (*SYN.*) increase, grow, expand, enlarge. (*ANT.*) *diminish, shrink.*

**swift** (*SYN.*) quick, fast, fleet, speedy, rapid, expeditious.

**swindle** (*SYN.*) bilk, defraud, con, deceive, cheat, guile, deception, deceit. (*ANT.*) *sincerity, honesty, fairness.*

**swing** (*SYN.*) rock, sway, wave.

**switch** (*SYN.*) shift, change, turn.

**swoon** (*SYN.*) faint.

**symbol** (*SYN.*) sign, character.

**sympathetic** (*SYN.*) considerate, compassionate, gentle, benevolent, good, tender, affable, merciful, thoughtful. (*ANT.*) *unkind, merciless, unsympathetic, indifferent, intolerant, cruel.*

**sympathy** (*SYN.*) compassion, agreement, tenderness, commiseration, pity. (*ANT.*) *indifference, unconcern, antipathy.*

**symptom** (*SYN.*) indication, sign.

**synopsis** (*SYN.*) outline, digest.

**synthetic** (*SYN.*) counterfeit, artificial, phony, unreal, bogus, sham. (*ANT.*) *natural, true, genuine.*

**system** (*SYN.*) organization, procedure, regularity, arrangement, mode, order. (*ANT.*) *confusion, chance, disorder.*

**systematic** (*SYN.*) orderly, organized. (*ANT.*) *irregular, random.*

# T

**table** (*SYN.*) catalog, list, schedule, postpone, chart, index, shelve, delay, put off.

**tablet** (*SYN.*) pad, notebook, capsule, sketchpad, pill, lozenge.

**taboo** (*SYN.*) banned, prohibited, forbidden, restriction.

(*ANT.*) *accepted, allowed.*

**tacit** (*SYN.*) understood, assumed, implied.

**taciturn** (*SYN.*) quiet, withdrawn, reserved.

**tack** (*SYN.*) add, join, attach, clasp, fasten.

**tackle** (*SYN.*) rigging, gear, apparatus, equipment, grab, seize, catch, down, throw, try, undertake.

**tacky** (*SYN.*) gummy, sticky, gooey.

**tact** (*SYN.*) dexterity, poise, diplomacy, judgment, saviorfaire, skill, finesse, sense, prudence, adroitness, address. (*ANT.*) *incompetence, vulgarity, blunder, rudeness, insensitivity, grossness.*

**tactical** (*SYN.*) foxy, cunning, proficient, deft, adroit, clever, expert. (*ANT.*) *blundering, gauche, clumsy, inept.*

**tactics** (*SYN.*) plan, strategy, approach, maneuver, course, scheme.

**tag** (*SYN.*) sticker, label, mark, identification, marker, name.

**tail** (*SYN.*) rear, back, follow, end, shadow, pursue, trail, heel.

**tailor** (*SYN.*) modest, couturier, modify, redo, shape, fashion.

**taint** (*SYN.*) spot, stain, tarnish, soil, mark, discolor. (*ANT.*) *cleanse, disinfect, clean.*

**tainted** (*SYN.*) crooked, impure, vitiated, profligate, debased, spoiled, corrupted, depraved, dishonest, contaminated, putrid, unsound.

**take** (*SYN.*) accept, grasp, catch, confiscate, clutch, adopt, assume, receive, bring, attract, claim, necessitate, steal, ensnare, capture, demand, select, appropriate, obtain, captivate, hold, seize, win, escort, note, record, rob, shoplift, get, remove, gain, choose.

**taking** (*SYN.*) charming, captivating, winning, attractive.

**takeover** (*SYN.*) revolution, merger, usurpation, confiscation.

**tale** (*SYN.*) falsehood, history, yarn, chronicle, account, fable, fiction, narration, story, narrative, anecdote.

**talent** (*SYN.*) capability, knack, skill, endowment, gift, cleverness, aptitude, ability, genius. (*ANT.*) *ineptitude, incompetence.*

**talented** (*SYN.*) skillful, smart, adroit, dexterous, clever, apt, quick-witted, witty, ingenious. (*ANT.*) *dull, clumsy, awkward, unskilled,* *stupid, slow.*

**talk** (SYN.) conversation, gossip, report, speech, communicate, discuss, confer, chatter, conference, preach, dialogue, reason, jabber, discourse, lecture, communication, consul, plead, argue, converse, rant, chat, mutter, speak, rumor, deliberate, discussion. (ANT.) *silence, correspondence, meditation, writing.*

**talkative** (SYN.) glib, communicative, chattering, loquacious, voluble, garrulous, chatty. (ANT.) *uncommunicative, laconic, reticent, silent.*

**tall** (SYN.) elevated, high, towering, big, lofty, imposing, gigantic. (ANT.) *tiny, low, short, small, stunted.*

**tally** (SYN.) score, count, compute, reckon, calculate, estimate, list, figure, correspond, agree, match, check.

**tame** (SYN.) domesticated, dull, insipid, docile, broken, uninteresting, gentle, subdued, insipid, flat, unexciting, boring, break, domesticate, mild, tedious, domestic, submissive. (ANT.) *spirited, savage, wild, exciting, animated, undomesticated.*

**tamper** (SYN.) mix in, interrupt, interfere, meddle, interpose.

**tang** (SYN.) zest, sharpness, tartness, taste.

**tangible** (SYN.) material, sensible, palpable, corporeal, bodily. (ANT.) *metaphysical, mental, spiritual.*

**tangle** (SYN.) confuse, knot, snarl, twist, ensnare, embroil, implicate.

**tangy** (SYN.) pungent, peppery, seasoned, sharp, tart.

**tantalize** (SYN.) lease, tempt, entice, titillate, stimulate, frustrate.

**tantrum** (SYN.) outburst, fit, fury, flare-up, conniption, rampage.

**tap** (SYN.) pat, rap, hit, strike, blow, faucet, spout, spigot, bunghole.

**tape** (SYN.) ribbon, strip, fasten, bandage, bind, record, tie.

**taper** (SYN.) narrow, candle, decrease.

**tardy** (SYN.) slow, delayed, overdue, late, belated. (ANT.) *prompt, timely, punctual, early.*

**target** (SYN.) aim, goal, object, objective.

**tariff** (SYN.) duty, tax, levy, rate.

**tarnish** (SYN.) discolor, blight, defile, sully, spot,

befoul, disgrace, stain. (ANT.) *honor, purify, cleanse, bleach, shine, gleam, sparkle.*

**tarry** (SYN.) dawdle, loiter, linger, dally, remain, delay, procrastinate.

**tart** (SYN.) sour, acrid, pungent, acid, sharp, distasteful, bitter. (ANT.) *mellow, sweet, delicious, pleasant.*

**task** (SYN.) work, job, undertaking, labor, chore, duty, stint.

**taste** (SYN.) tang, inclination, liking, sensibility, flavor, savor, try, sip, sample, zest, experience, undergo, appreciation, relish, discrimination, discernment, judgment. (ANT.) *indelicacy, disinclination, antipathy.*

**tasteful** (SYN.) elegant, choice, refined, suitable, artistic. (ANT.) *offensive, unbecoming.*

**tasteless** (SYN.) flavorless, insipid, unpalatable, rude, unrefined, uncultivated, boorish, uninteresting.

**tasty** (SYN.) delectable, delicious, luscious, palatable, tempting.

**tattered** (SYN.) ragged, torn, shoddy, shabby, frazzled, frayed, tacky, seedy.

**tattle** (SYN.) inform, divulge, disclose, blab, reveal.

**taunt** (SYN.) tease, deride, flout, scoff, sneer, mock, annoy, pester, bother, ridicule, jeer. (ANT.) *praise, compliment, laud, flatter.*

**taunting** (SYN.) ironic, caustic, cutting, sardonic, derisive, biting, acrimonious, sarcastic, satirical, sneering. (ANT.) *pleasant, agreeable, affable, amiable.*

**taut** (SYN.) tight, constricted, firm, stretched, snug, tense, extended. (ANT.) *slack, loose, relaxed, open, lax.*

**tavern** (SYN.) pub, bar, cocktail lounge.

**tawdry** (SYN.) pretentious, showy, vulgar, tasteless, sordid, garish.

**tax** (SYN.) duty, assessment, excise, levy, toll, burden, strain, tribute, tariff, assess, encumber, overload, impost, custom, exaction, rate. (ANT.) *reward, gift, remuneration, wages.*

**taxi** (SYN.) cab, taxicab.

**teach** (SYN.) inform, school, educate, train, inculcate, instruct, instill, tutor. (ANT.) *misinform, misguide.*

**teacher** (SYN.) tutor, instructor, professor, lecturer.

**team** (SYN.) company, band,

party, crew, gang, group.

**teamwork** (SYN.) collaboration, cooperation.

**tear** (SYN.) rend, shred, sunder, cleave, rip, lacerate, teardrop, disunite, divide, drop, wound, split, slit, sever. (ANT.) *mend, repair, join, unite, sew.*

**tearful** (SYN.) sad, weeping, crying, sobbing, weepy, lachrymose.

**tease** (SYN.) badger, harry, bother, irritate, nag, pester, taunt, vex, annoy, disturb, harass, worry, tantalize, plague, aggravate, provoke, torment. (ANT.) *please, delight, soothe, comfort, gratify.*

**technical** (SYN.) industrial, technological, specialized, mechanical.

**technique** (SYN.) system, method, routine, approach, procedure.

**tedious** (SYN.) boring, dilatory, humdrum, sluggish, monotonous, irksome, dreary, dull, tiring, burdensome, tiresome, wearisome, tardy. (ANT.) *interesting, entertaining, engaging, exciting, amusing, quick.*

**teem** (SYN.) abound, swarm.

**teeming** (SYN.) overflowing, bountiful, abundant, ample, profuse, plenteous, rich, copious. (ANT.) *scant, scarce, deficient, insufficient.*

**teeter** (SYN.) sway, hesitate, hem and haw, waver.

**telecast** (SYN.) broadcast.

**televise** (SYN.) telecast.

**tell** (SYN.) report, mention, state, betray, announce, recount, relate, narrate, rehearse, mention, utter, confess, disclose, direct, request, acquaint, instruct, notify, inform, determine, reveal, divulge.

**telling** (SYN.) persuasive, convincing, forceful, effective.

**telltale** (SYN.) revealing, informative, suggestive, meaningful.

**temerity** (SYN.) rashness, foolhardiness, audacity, boldness, recklessness, precipitancy. (ANT.) *prudence, wariness, caution, hesitation, timidity.*

**temper** (SYN.) fury, choler, exasperation, anger, passion, petulance, disposition, nature, rage, soothe, soften, wrath, indignation, irritation, pacify, animosity, mood, resentment. (ANT.) *peace, self-control, forbearance, conciliation.*

**temperament** (SYN.) humor, mood, temper, nature, disposition.

**temperamental** (SYN.) testy, moody, touchy, sensitive, irritable. (ANT.) *calm, unruffled, serene.*

**temperance** (SYN.) abstinence, sobriety, self-denial, forbearance, abstention. (ANT.) *intoxication, excess, self-indulgence, gluttony, wantonness.*

**temperate** (SYN.) controlled, moderate, cool, calm, restrained. (ANT.) *excessive, extreme, prodigal.*

**tempest** (SYN.) draft, squall, wind, blast, gust, storm, hurricane, commotion, tumult, zephyr. (ANT.) *calm, tranquillity.*

**tempo** (SYN.) measure, beat, cadence, rhythm.

**temporal** (SYN.) mundane, earthly, lay, profane, worldly, terrestrial, laic. (ANT.) *spiritual, ecclesiastical, unworldly, religious, heavenly.*

**temporary** (SYN.) brief, momentary, short-lived, fleeting, ephemeral, passing, short, transient. (ANT.) *lasting, permanent, immortal, everlasting, timeless, abiding.*

**tempt** (SYN.) entice, allure, lure, attract, seduce, invite, magnetize.

**tenacious** (SYN.) persistent, determined, unchanging, unyielding.

**tenable** (SYN.) correct, practical, rational, reasonable, sensible, defensible.

**tenacity** (SYN.) perseverance, steadfastness, industry, constancy, persistence, pertinacity. (ANT.) *laziness, rest, cessation, idleness, sloth.*

**tenant** (SYN.) renter, lessee, lodger, lease-holder, dweller, resident.

**tend** (SYN.) escort, follow, care for, lackey, watch, protect, take care of, attend, guard, serve.

**tendency** (SYN.) drift, inclination, proneness, leaning, bias, aim, disposition, predisposition, propensity, trend, impulse. (ANT.) *disinclination, aversion, deviation.*

**tender** (SYN.) sympathetic, sore, sensitive, painful, gentle, meek, delicate, fragile, proffer, bland, mild, loving, offer, affectionate, soothing, propose, moderate, soft. (ANT.) *rough, severe, fierce, chewy, tough, cruel, unfeeling, harsh.*

**tenderfoot** (SYN.) novice, apprentice, beginner, amateur.

**tenderhearted** (SYN.) kind, sympathetic, merciful, softhearted, understanding, sentimental, affectionate, gentle, sensitive.

**tenderness** *(SYN.)* attachment, kindness, love, affection, endearment. *(ANT.) repugnance, indifference, aversion, hatred.*

**tenet** *(SYN.)* dogma, belief, precept, doctrine, creed, opinion. *(ANT.) deed, conduct, practice, performance.*

**tense** *(SYN.)* strained, stretched, excited, tight, nervous. *(ANT.) loose, placid, lax, relaxed.*

**tension** *(SYN.)* stress, strain, pressure, anxiety, apprehension, distress.

**tentative** *(SYN.)* hypothetical, indefinite, probationary, conditional.

**tenure** *(SYN.)* administration, time, regime, term.

**tepid** *(SYN.)* temperate, mild, lukewarm. *(ANT.) boiling, scalding, passionate, hot.*

**term** *(SYN.)* period, limit, time, boundary, duration, name, phrase, interval, session, semester, expression, word.

**terminal** *(SYN.)* eventual, final, concluding, decisive, ending, fatal, latest, last, ultimate, conclusive. *(ANT.) original, first, rudimentary, incipient, inaugural.*

**terminate** *(SYN.)* close, end, finish, abolish, complete, cease, stop, conclude, expire, culminate. *(ANT.) establish, begin, initiate, start, commence.*

**terminology** *(SYN.)* vocabulary, nomenclature, terms, phraseology.

**terms** *(SYN.)* stipulations, agreement, conditions, provisions.

**terrible** *(SYN.)* frightful, dire, awful, gruesome, horrible, shocking, horrifying, terrifying, horrid, hideous, appalling. *(ANT.) secure, happy, joyous, pleasing, safe.*

**terrific** *(SYN.)* superb, wonderful, glorious, great, magnificent, divine, colossal, sensational, marvelous.

**terrify** *(SYN.)* dismay, intimidate, startle, terrorize, appall, frighten, petrify, astound, alarm, affright, horrify, scare. *(ANT.) soothe, allay, reassure, compose, embolden.*

**territory** *(SYN.)* dominion, province, quarter, section, country, division, region, domain, area, place, district.

**terror** *(SYN.)* fear, alarm, dismay, horror, dread, consternation, fright, panic. *(ANT.) calm, security, assurance, peace.*

**terse** *(SYN.)* concise, incisive, succinct, summary, condensed, compact, neat, pithy, summary. *(ANT.) verbose, wordy, lengthy, prolix.*

**test** *(SYN.)* exam, examination, trial, quiz, analyze, verify, validate.

**testify** *(SYN.)* depose, warrant, witness, state, attest, swear.

**testimony** *(SYN.)* evidence, attestation, declaration, proof, witness, confirmation. *(ANT.) refutation, argument, disproof, contradiction.*

**testy** *(SYN.)* ill-natured, irritable, snappish, waspish, fractious, fretful, touchy, ill-tempered, peevish, petulant. *(ANT.) pleasant, affable, good-tempered, genial, good-natured.*

**tether** *(SYN.)* tie, hamper, restraint, bridle.

**text** *(SYN.)* textbook, book, manual.

**textile** *(SYN.)* material, cloth, goods, fabric.

**texture** *(SYN.)* construction, structure, make-up, composition, grain, finish.

**thankful** *(SYN.)* obliged, grateful, appreciative. *(ANT.) thankless, ungrateful, resenting.*

**thaw** *(SYN.)* liquefy, melt, dissolve. *(ANT.) solidify, freeze.*

**theater** *(SYN.)* arena, playhouse, battlefield, stadium, hall.

**theatrical** *(SYN.)* ceremonious, melodramatic, stagy, artificial, affected, dramatic, showy, compelling. *(ANT.) unemotional, subdued, unaffected.*

**theft** *(SYN.)* larceny, robbery, stealing, plunder, burglary, pillage, thievery.

**theme** *(SYN.)* motive, topic, argument, subject, thesis, text, point, paper, essay, composition.

**theoretical** *(SYN.)* bookish, learned, scholarly, pedantic, academic, formal, erudite, scholastic. *(ANT.) practical, ignorant, commonsense, simple.*

**theory** *(SYN.)* doctrine, guess, presupposition, postulate, assumption, hypothesis, speculation. *(ANT.) practice, verity, fact, proof.*

**therefore** *(SYN.)* consequently, thence so, accordingly, hence, then.

**thick** *(SYN.)* compressed, heavy, compact, viscous, close, concentrated, crowded, syrupy, dense. *(ANT.) watery, slim, thin, sparse, dispersed, dissipated.*

**thief** *(SYN.)* burglar, robber, criminal.

**thin** *(SYN.)* diluted, flimsy, lean, narrow, spare, emaciated, diaphanous, gauzy, meager, slender, tenuous, slim, rare, sparse, scanty, lank, gossamer, slight. *(ANT.) fat, wide, broad, thick, bulky.*

**think** *(SYN.)* picture, contemplate, ponder, esteem, intend, mean, imagine, deliberate, recall, speculate, recollect, deem, apprehend, consider, devise, plan, judge, reflect, suppose, assume, meditate, muse. *(ANT.) forget, conjecture, guess.*

**thirst** *(SYN.)* appetite, desire, craving.

**thirsty** *(SYN.)* arid, dry, dehydrated, parched, craving, desirous. *(ANT.) satisfied.*

**thorn** *(SYN.)* spine, barb, prickle, nettle, bramble.

**thorough** *(SYN.)* entire, complete, perfect, total, finished, unbroken, careful, thoroughgoing, consummate, undivided. *(ANT.) unfinished, careless, slapdash, imperfect, haphazard, lacking.*

**thoroughfare** *(SYN.)* avenue, street, parkway, highway, boulevard. *(ANT.) byway.*

**though** *(SYN.)* in any case, notwithstanding, however, nevertheless.

**thought** *(SYN.)* consideration, pensive, attentive, heedful, prudent, dreamy, reflective, introspective, meditation, notion, view, deliberation, sentiment, fancy, idea, impression, reasoning, contemplation, judgment, regard. *(ANT.) thoughtlessness.*

**thoughtful** *(SYN.)* considerate, attentive, dreamy, pensive, provident, introspective, meditative, cautious, heedful, kind, courteous, friendly. *(ANT.) thoughtless, heedless, inconsiderate, rash, precipitous, selfish.*

**thoughtless** *(SYN.)* inattentive, unconcerned, negligent, lax, desultory, inconsiderate, careless, imprudent, inaccurate, neglectful, indiscreet, remiss. *(ANT.) meticulous, accurate, nice, careful.*

**thrash** *(SYN.)* whip, beat, defeat, flog, punish, strap, thresh.

**thread** *(SYN.)* yarn, strand, filament, fiber, string, cord.

**threadbare** *(SYN.)* shabby, tacky, worn, ragged, frayed.

**threat** *(SYN.)* menace, warning, danger, hazard, jeopardy, omen.

**threaten** *(SYN.)* caution, warning, forewarn, menace, intimidate, loom.

**threatening** *(SYN.)* imminent, nigh, approaching, impending, overhanging, sinister, foreboding. *(ANT.) improbable, retreating, afar, distant, remote.*

**threshold** *(SYN.)* edge, verge, start, beginning, doorsill, commencement.

**thrift** *(SYN.)* prudence, conservation, saving, economy.

**thrifty** *(SYN.)* saving, economical, sparing, frugal, provident, stingy, saving, parsimonious. *(ANT.) wasteful, spendthrift, intemperate, self-indulgent, extravagant.*

**thrill** *(SYN.)* arouse, rouse, excite, stimulation, excitement, tingle. *(ANT.) bore.*

**thrive** *(SYN.)* succeed, flourish, grow, prosper. *(ANT.) expire, fade, shrivel, die, fail.*

**throb** *(SYN.)* pound, pulsate, palpitate, beat, pulse.

**throe** *(SYN.)* pang, twinge, distress, suffering, pain, ache, grief, agony. *(ANT.) pleasure, relief, ease, solace, comfort.*

**throng** *(SYN.)* masses, press, crowd, bevy, populace, swarm, rabble, horde, host, mass, teem, mob, multitude.

**throttle** *(SYN.)* smother, choke, strangle.

**through** *(SYN.)* completed, done, finished, over.

**throughout** *(SYN.)* all over, everywhere, during.

**throw** *(SYN.)* propel, cast, pitch, toss, hurl, send, thrust, fling. *(ANT.) retain, pull, draw, haul, hold.*

**thrust** *(SYN.)* jostle, push, promote, crowd, force, drive, hasten, press, shove, urge. *(ANT.) ignore, falter, retreat, drag, oppose, halt.*

**thug** *(SYN.)* mobster, hoodlum, mugger, gangster, assassin, gunman.

**thump** *(SYN.)* blow, strike, knock, jab, poke, pound, beat, clout, bat, rap, bang.

**thunderstruck** *(SYN.)* amazed, astounded, astonished, awed, flabbergasted, surprised, dumbfounded, bewildered, spellbound.

**thus** *(SYN.)* hence, therefore, accordingly, so, consequently.

**thwart** *(SYN.)* defeat, frustrate, prevent, foil, stop, baffle, circumvent, hinder, obstruct, disappoint, balk, outwit. *(ANT.) promote, accomplish, fulfill, help, further.*

**ticket** *(SYN.)* stamp, label, tag, seal, token, pass, summons, certificate, ballot, sticker, slate, citation.

**tickle** *(SYN.)* delight, entertain, thrill, amuse, titillate, excite.

**ticklish** *(SYN.)* fragile, delicate, tough, difficult.

**tidings** *(SYN.)* message, report, information, word, intelligence, news.

**tidy** *(SYN.)* trim, clear, neat, precise, spruce, orderly, shipshape. *(ANT.)* disheveled, unkempt, sloppy, dirty, slovenly.

**tie** *(SYN.)* bond, join, relationship, bind, restrict, fetter, connect, conjunction, association, alliance, union, fasten, engage, attach, restrain, oblige, link, affinity. *(ANT.)* separation, disunion, unfasten, open, loose, untie, free, isolation.

**tier** *(SYN.)* line, row, level, deck, layer.

**tiff** *(SYN.)* bicker, squabble, argue, row, clash, dispute, altercation.

**tight** *(SYN.)* firm, taut, penny-pinching, constricted, snug, taut, parsimonious, secure, fast, strong, sealed, fastened, watertight, locked, close, compact, stingy. *(ANT.)* slack, lax, open, relaxed, loose.

**till** *(SYN.)* plow, work, money-box, depository, cultivate, vault.

**tilt** *(SYN.)* slant, slope, incline, tip, lean.

**timber** *(SYN.)* lumber, wood, logs.

**time** *(SYN.)* epoch, span, term, age, duration, interim, period, tempo, interval, space, spell, season.

**timeless** *(SYN.)* unending, lasting, perpetual, endless, immemorial. *(ANT.)* temporary, mortal, temporal.

**timely** *(SYN.)* prompt, exact, punctual, ready, precise. *(ANT.)* slow, tardy, late.

**timepiece** *(SYN.)* clock, watch.

**timetable** *(SYN.)* list, schedule.

**timid** *(SYN.)* coy, humble, sheepish, abashed, embarrassed, modest, bashful, diffident, shamefaced, retiring, fearful, faint-hearted, shy, timorous. *(ANT.)* gregarious, bold, daring, adventurous, fearless.

**tinge** *(SYN.)* color, tint, dye, stain, flavor, imbue, season, impregnate.

**tingle** *(SYN.)* shiver, chime, prickle.

**tinker** *(SYN.)* potter, putter, fiddle with, dawdle, dally, dabble.

**tinkle** *(SYN.)* sound, peal, ring, jingle, chime, toll.

**tint** *(SYN.)* color, tinge, dye, stain, hue, tone, shade.

**tiny** *(SYN.)* minute, little, petty, wee, slight, diminutive, miniature, small, insignificant, trivial, puny. *(ANT.)* huge, large, immense, big, enormous.

**tip** *(SYN.)* point, end, top, peak, upset, tilt, reward, gift, gratuity, clue, hint, suggestion, inkling.

**tirade** *(SYN.)* outburst, harangue, scolding.

**tire** *(SYN.)* jade, tucker, bore, weary, exhaust, weaken, wear out, fatigue. *(ANT.)* restore, revive, exhilarate, invigorate, refresh.

**tired** *(SYN.)* weary, exhausted, fatigued, run-down, sleepy, faint, spent, wearied, worn, jaded. *(ANT.)* rested, fresh, hearty, invigorated, energetic, tireless, eager.

**tireless** *(SYN.)* active, enthusiastic, energetic, strenuous. *(ANT.)* exhausted, wearied, fatigued.

**tiresome** *(SYN.)* dull, boring, monotonous, tedious. *(ANT.)* interesting.

**titan** *(SYN.)* colossus, powerhouse, mammoth.

**title** *(SYN.)* epithet, privilege, name, appellation, claim, denomination, due, heading, ownership, right, deed, designation.

**toast** *(SYN.)* salutation, pledge, celebration.

**toddle** *(SYN.)* stumble, wobble, shuffle.

**toil** *(SYN.)* labor, drudgery, work, travail, performance, business, achievement, employment, occupation, slave, sweat, effort. *(ANT.)* recreation, ease, vacation, relax, loll, play, leisure, repose.

**token** *(SYN.)* mark, sign, sample, indication, evidence, symbol.

**tolerant** *(SYN.)* extensive, vast, considerate, broad, patient, large, sweeping, liberal, wide. *(ANT.)* intolerant, bigoted, biased, restricted, narrow, confined.

**tolerate** *(SYN.)* endure, allow, bear, authorize, permit, brook, stand, abide. *(ANT.)* forbid, protest, prohibit, discriminating.

**toll** *(SYN.)* impost, burden, rate, assessment, duty, custom, excise, tribute, levy, burden, strain. *(ANT.)* reward, wages, gift, remuneration.

**tomb** *(SYN.)* vault, monument, catacomb, grave, mausoleum.

**tone** *(SYN.)* noise, sound, mood, manner, expression, cadence.

**tongs** *(SYN.)* tweezers, hook, grapnel, forceps.

**tongue** *(SYN.)* diction, lingo, cant, jargon, vernacular, dialect, idiom, speech, phraseology. *(ANT.)* nonsense, drivel, babble.

**too** *(SYN.)* furthermore, moreover, similarly, also, in addition, besides, likewise.

**tool** *(SYN.)* devise, medium, apparatus, agent, implement, utensil, agent, vehicle, instrument. *(ANT.)* preventive, hindrance, impediment, obstruction.

**top** *(SYN.)* crown, pinnacle, peak, tip, cover, cap, zenith, apex, crest, chief, head, summit. *(ANT.)* bottom, foundation, base, foot.

**topic** *(SYN.)* subject, thesis, issue, argument, matter, theme, point.

**topple** *(SYN.)* collapse, sink, fall, tumble.

**torrent** *(SYN.)* pain, woe, pester, ache, distress, misery, harass, throe, annoy, vex, torture, anguish, suffering, misery. *(ANT.)* relief, comfort, ease, gratify, delight.

**torpid** *(SYN.)* sluggish, idle, lazy, inert, inactive, supine, slothful, indolent, motionless, lethargic. *(ANT.)* alert, assiduous, diligent, active.

**torpor** *(SYN.)* lethargy, daze, numbness, stupor, drowsiness, insensibility, languor. *(ANT.)* wakefulness, liveliness, activity, alertness, readiness.

**torrent** *(SYN.)* flood, downpour, deluge.

**torrid** *(SYN.)* scorching, ardent, impetuous, passionate, scalding, warm, fiery, hot-blooded, sultry, tropical, intense, sweltering, burning, hot. *(ANT.)* passionless, impassive, cold, frigid, apathetic, freezing, phlegmatic, indifferent, temperate.

**torso** *(SYN.)* form, frame, body. *(ANT.)* soul, mind, spirit, intellect.

**torture** *(SYN.)* anguish, badger, plague, distress, ache, torment, pester, pain, hound, agony, woe, worry, vex, persecute, suffering, throe, afflict, misery. *(ANT.)* aid, relief, comfort, ease, support, encourage, mitigation.

**toss** *(SYN.)* throw, cast, hurl, pitch, tumble, thrust, fling, propel. *(ANT.)* retain, pull, draw, haul, hold.

**total** *(SYN.)* entire, complete, concluded, finished, thorough, whole, entirely, collection, aggregate, conglomeration, unbroken, perfect, undivided, consummate, full. *(ANT.)* part, element, imperfect, unfinished, ingredient, particular, lacking.

**tote** *(SYN.)* move, transfer, convey, drag, carry.

**totter** *(SYN.)* falter, stagger, reel, sway, waver, stumble, wobble.

**touch** *(SYN.)* finger, feel, handle, move, affect, concern, mention, hint, trace, suggestion, knack, skill, ability, talent.

**touch-and-go** *(SYN.)* dangerous, risky, perilous, hazardous.

**touching** *(SYN.)* pitiable, affecting, moving, sad, adjunct, bordering, tangent, poignant, tender, effective, impressive, adjacent. *(ANT.)* removed, enlivening, animated, exhilarating.

**touchy** *(SYN.)* snappish, irritable, fiery, choleric, testy, hot, irascible, nervous, excitable, petulant, sensitive, short-tempered, jumpy, peevish. *(ANT.)* composed, agreeable, tranquil, calm, serene, stolid, cool.

**tough** *(SYN.)* sturdy, difficult, trying, incorrigible, troublesome, hard, stout, leathery, strong, laborious, inedible, sinewy, cohesive, firm, callous, obdurate, vicious. *(ANT.)* vulnerable, submissive, easy, brittle, facile, weak, fragile, compliant, tender, frail.

**toughness** *(SYN.)* stamina, fortitude, durability, intensity, force, might, stoutness, power, sturdiness, vigor. *(ANT.)* weakness, feebleness, infirmity, frailty.

**tour** *(SYN.)* rove, travel, go, visit, excursion, ramble, journey, roam. *(ANT.)* stop, stay.

**tourist** *(SYN.)* traveler, sightseer, vagabond, voyager.

**tournament** *(SYN.)* tourney, match, contest, competition.

**tout** *(SYN.)* vend, importune, peddle, solicit, sell, hawk.

**tow** *(SYN.)* tug, take out, unsheathe, haul, draw, remove, extract, pull, drag. *(ANT.)* propel, drive.

**towering** *(SYN.)* elevated, exalted, high, lofty, tall, proud, eminent. *(ANT.)* base, mean, stunted, small, tiny, low.

**town** *(SYN.)* hamlet, village, community, municipality.

**toxic** *(SYN.)* deadly, poisonous,

fatal, lethal, harmful. (*ANT.*) *beneficial.*

**toy** (*SYN.*) play, romp, frolic, gamble, stake, caper, plaything, wager, revel.

**trace** (*SYN.*) stigma, feature, indication, trait, mark, stain, scar, sign, trail, trace, suggestion, characteristic, vestige.

**track** (*SYN.*) persist, pursue, follow, sign, mark, spoor, trace, path, route, road, carry, hunt, chase. (*ANT.*) *escape, evade, abandon, flee, elude.*

**tract** (*SYN.*) area, region, territory, district, expanse, domain.

**tractable** (*SYN.*) yielding, deferential, submissive, dutiful, compliant, obedient. (*ANT.*) *rebellious, intractable, insubordinate.*

**trade** (*SYN.*) business, traffic, commerce, dealing, craft, occupation, profession, livelihood, swap, barter, exchange.

**trademark** (*SYN.*) logo, brand name, identification, emblem, insignia, monogram.

**tradition** (*SYN.*) custom, legend, folklore, belief, rite, practice.

**traduce** (*SYN.*) defame, malign, vilify, revile, abuse, asperse, scandalize, disparage. (*ANT.*) *protect, honor, cherish, praise, respect, support, extol.*

**tragedy** (*SYN.*) unhappiness, misfortune, misery, adversity, catastrophe.

**tragic** (*SYN.*) miserable, unfortunate, depressing, melancholy, mournful. (*ANT.*) *happy, cheerful, comic.*

**trail** (*SYN.*) persist, pursue, chase, follow, drag, draw, hunt, track. (*ANT.*) *evade, flee, abandon, elude, escape.*

**train** (*SYN.*) direct, prepare, aim, point, level, teach, drill, tutor, bid, instruct, order, command. (*ANT.*) *distract, deceive, misguide, misdirect.*

**traipse** (*SYN.*) roam, wander, saunter, meander.

**trait** (*SYN.*) characteristic, feature, attribute, peculiarity, mark, quality, property.

**traitor** (*SYN.*) turncoat, betrayer, spy, double-dealer, conspirator.

**traitorous** (*SYN.*) disloyal, faithless, apostate, false, recreant, perfidious, treasonable, treacherous. (*ANT.*) *devoted, trite, loyal, constant.*

**tramp** (*SYN.*) bum, beggar, rover, hobo, march, stamp, stomp, vagabond, wanderer, vagrant. (*ANT.*) *laborer, worker, gentleman.*

**trample** (*SYN.*) crush, stomp,

squash.

**tranquil** (*SYN.*) composed, calm, dispassionate, imperturbable, peaceful, pacific, placid, quiet, still, serene, undisturbed, unruffled. (*ANT.*) *frantic, stormy, excited, disturbed, upset, turbulent, wild.*

**tranquillity** (*SYN.*) calmness, calm, hush, peace, quiet, quiescence, quietude, repose, serenity, rest, stillness, silence, placid. (*ANT.*) *disturbance, agitation, excitement, tumult, noise.*

**transact** (*SYN.*) conduct, manage, execute, treat, perform.

**transaction** (*SYN.*) business, deal, affair, deed, settlement, occurrence, negotiation, proceeding.

**transcend** (*SYN.*) overstep, overshadow, exceed.

**transcribe** (*SYN.*) write, copy, rewrite, record.

**transfer** (*SYN.*) dispatch, send, transmit, remove, transport, transplant, consign, move, shift, reassign, assign, relegate.

**transform** (*SYN.*) change, convert, alter, modify, transfigure, shift, vary, veer. (*ANT.*) *continue, settle, preserve, stabilize.*

**transgression** (*SYN.*) atrocity, indignity, offense, insult, outrage, aggression, injustice, crime, misdeed, trespass, sin, wrong, vice. (*ANT.*) *innocence, morality, gentleness, right.*

**transient** (*SYN.*) ephemeral, evanescent, brief, fleeting, momentary, temporary, short-lived. (*ANT.*) *immortal, abiding, permanent, lasting, timeless, established.*

**transition** (*SYN.*) change, variation, modification.

**translate** (*SYN.*) decipher, construe, decode, elucidate, explicate, explain, interpret, solve, render, unravel. (*ANT.*) *distort, falsify, misinterpret, misconstrue.*

**transmit** (*SYN.*) confer, convey, communicate, divulge, disclose, impart, send, inform, relate, notify, reveal, dispatch, tell. (*ANT.*) *withhold, hide, conceal.*

**transparent** (*SYN.*) crystalline, clear, limpid, lucid, translucent, thin, evident, manifest, plain, evident, explicit, obvious, open. (*ANT.*) *opaque, muddy, turbid, thick, questionable, ambiguous.*

**transpire** (*SYN.*) befall, bechance, betide, happen,

chance, occur.

**transport** (*SYN.*) carry, bear, convey, remove, move, shift, enrapture, transfer, lift, entrance, ravish, stimulate.

**transpose** (*SYN.*) change, switch, reverse.

**trap** (*SYN.*) artifice, bait, ambush, intrigue, net, lure, pitfall, ensnare, deadfall, snare, ruse, entrap, bag, trick, stratagem, wile.

**trash** (*SYN.*) refuse, garbage, rubbish, waste.

**trashy** (*SYN.*) insignificant, worthless.

**trauma** (*SYN.*) ordeal, upheaval, jolt, shock, disturbance.

**travail** (*SYN.*) suffering, torment, anxiety, distress, anguish, misery, ordeal.

**travel** (*SYN.*) journey, go, touring, ramble, rove, voyage, cruise, tour, roam. (*ANT.*) *stop, stay, remain, hibernate.*

**travesty** (*SYN.*) farce, joke, misrepresentation, counterfeit, mimicry.

**treachery** (*SYN.*) collusion, cabal, combination, intrigue, conspiracy, machination, disloyalty, betrayal, treason, plot. (*ANT.*) *allegiance, steadfastness, loyalty.*

**treason** (*SYN.*) cabal, combination, betrayal, sedition, collusion, intrigue, conspiracy, machination, disloyalty, treachery, plot.

**treasure** (*SYN.*) cherish, hold dear, abundance, guard, prize, appreciate, value, riches, wealth, foster, sustain, nurture. (*ANT.*) *disregard, neglect, dislike, abandon, reject.*

**treat** (*SYN.*) employ, avail, manipulate, exploit, operate, utilize, exert, act, exercise, practice, handle, manage, deal, entertain, indulge, host, negotiate, tend, attend, heal, use. (*ANT.*) *neglect, overlook, ignore, waste.*

**treaty** (*SYN.*) compact, agreement, pact, bargain, covenant, alliance, marriage. (*ANT.*) *schism, separation, divorce.*

**trek** (*SYN.*) tramp, hike, plod, trudge.

**tremble** (*SYN.*) flutter, jolt, jar, agitate, quake, quiver, quaver, rock, shake, shudder, shiver, totter, sway, vibrate, waver.

**trembling** (*SYN.*) apprehension, alarm, dread, fright, fear, horror, terror, panic. (*ANT.*) *composure, calmness, tranquility.*

**tremendous** (*SYN.*) enormous, huge, colossal, gigantic,

great, large.

**tremor** (*SYN.*) flutter, vibration, palpitation.

**trench** (*SYN.*) gully, gorge, ditch, gulch, moat, dugout, trough.

**trenchant** (*SYN.*) clear, emphatic, forceful, impressive, meaningful.

**trend** (*SYN.*) inclination, drift, course, tendency, direction.

**trendy** (*SYN.*) modish, faddish, stylish, voguish, popular, current.

**trepidation** (*SYN.*) apprehension, alarm, dread, fright, fear, horror, panic, terror. (*ANT.*) *boldness, bravery, fearlessness, courage, assurance.*

**trespass** (*SYN.*) atrocity, indignity, affront, insult, outrage, offense, aggression, crime, misdeed, injustice, vice, wrong, sin. (*ANT.*) *evacuate, vacate, relinquish, abandon.*

**trespasser** (*SYN.*) invader, intruder, encroacher.

**trial** (*SYN.*) experiment, ordeal, proof, test, examination, attempt, effort, endeavor, essay, affliction, misery, hardship, suffering, difficulty, misfortune, tribulation, trouble. (*ANT.*) *consolation, alleviation.*

**tribe** (*SYN.*) group, race, clan, bunch.

**tribulation** (*SYN.*) anguish, distress, agony, grief, misery, sorrow, torment, suffering, woe, disaster, calamity, evil, trouble, misfortune. (*ANT.*) *elation, delight, joy, fun.*

**tribunal** (*SYN.*) arbitrators, judges, decision makers, judiciary.

**trick** (*SYN.*) artifice, antic, deception, device, cheat, fraud, hoax, guile, imposture, ruse, ploy, stratagem, trickery, deceit, jest, joke, prank, defraud, subterfuge, wile, stunt. (*ANT.*) *exposure, candor, openness, honesty, sincerity.*

**trickle** (*SYN.*) drip, drop, dribble, leak, seep.

**tricky** (*SYN.*) artifice, antic, covert, cunning, foxy, crafty, furtive, guileful, insidious, sly, shrews, stealthy, surreptitious, subtle, underhand, wily. (*ANT.*) *frank, candid, ingenuous, sincere, open.*

**trifling** (*SYN.*) insignificant, frivolous, paltry, petty, trivial, small, unimportant. (*ANT.*) *momentous, serious, important.*

**trigger** (*SYN.*) generate, provoke, prompt, motivate, activate.

**trim** (*SYN.*) nice, clear, orderly,

precise, tidy, spruce, adorn, bedeck, clip, shave, prune, cut, shear, compact, neat, decorate, embellish, garnish. (ANT.) deface, deform, spoil, mar, serious, momentous.

**trimmings** (SYN.) accessories, adornments, decorations, garnish, ornaments.

**trinket** (SYN.) bead, token, memento, bauble, charm, knickknack.

**trio** (SYN.) threesome, triad, triple.

**trip** (SYN.) expedition, cruise, stumble, err, journey, jaunt, passage, blunder, bungle, slip, excursion, tour, pilgrimage, voyage, travel.

**trite** (SYN.) common, banal, hackneyed, ordinary, stereotyped, stale. (ANT.) modern, fresh, momentous, stimulating, novel, new.

**triumph** (SYN.) conquest, achievement, success, prevail, win, jubilation, victory, ovation. (ANT.) succumb, failure, defeat.

**triumphant** (SYN.) celebrating, exultant, joyful, exhilarated, smug.

**trivial** (SYN.) insignificant, frivolous, paltry, petty, trifling, small, unimportant. (ANT.) momentous, important, weighty, serious.

**troops** (SYN.) militia, troopers, recruits, soldiers, enlisted men.

**trophy** (SYN.) award, memento, honor, testimonial, prize.

**tropical** (SYN.) sultry, sweltering, humid, torrid.

**trouble** (SYN.) anxiety, affliction, calamity, distress, hardship, grief, pain, misery, sorrow, woe, bother, annoyance, care, embarrassment, irritation, torment, pains, worry, disorder, problem, disturbance, effort, exertion, toil, inconvenience, misfortune, labor. (ANT.) console, accommodate, gratify, soothe, joy, peace.

**troublemaker** (SYN.) rebel, scamp, agitator, demon, devil, ruffian.

**troublesome** (SYN.) bothersome, annoying, distressing, irksome, disturbing, trying, arduous, vexatious, arduous, difficult, burdensome, laborious, tedious. (ANT.) accommodating, gratifying, easy, pleasant.

**trounce** (SYN.) lash, flog, switch, whack, punish, whip, stomp.

**truant** (SYN.) delinquent, absentee, vagrant, malingerer.

**truce** (SYN.) armistice, cease-fire, interval, break, intermission, respite.

**trudge** (SYN.) march, trek, lumber, hike.

**true** (SYN.) actual, authentic, accurate, correct, exact, genuine, real, veracious, veritable, constant, honest, faithful, loyal, reliable, valid, legitimate, steadfast, sincere. (ANT.) erroneous, counterfeit, false, spurious, fictitious, faithless, inconstant, fickle.

**truly** (SYN.) indeed, actually, precisely, literally, really, factually.

**truncate** (SYN.) prune, clip, pare, shorten.

**truss** (SYN.) girder, brace, framework, shoring.

**trust** (SYN.) credence, confidence, dependence, reliance, faith, trust, depend on, rely on, reckon on, believe, hope, credit, commit, entrust, confide. (ANT.) incredulity, doubt, skepticism, mistrust.

**trusted** (SYN.) trustworthy, reliable, true, loyal, staunch, devoted.

**trustworthy** (SYN.) dependable, certain, reliable, secure, safe, sure, tried, trust. (ANT.) fallible, dubious, questionable, unreliable, uncertain.

**truth** (SYN.) actuality, authenticity, accuracy, correctness, exactness, honesty, fact, rightness, truthfulness, veracity, verisimilitude, verity. (ANT.) falsity, fiction, lie, untruth.

**truthful** (SYN.) frank, candid, honest, sincere, open, veracious, accurate, correct. (ANT.) misleading, sly, deceitful.

**try** (SYN.) endeavor, attempt, strive, struggle, undertake, afflict, test, prove, torment, trouble, essay, examine, analyze, investigate, effort, aim, design, aspire, intend, mean. (ANT.) decline, ignore, abandon, omit, neglect, comfort, console.

**trying** (SYN.) bothersome, annoying, distressing, disturbing, troublesome, arduous, vexatious, difficult, tedious. (ANT.) easy, accommodating, pleasant, gratifying.

**tryout** (SYN.) audition, trial, chance, test.

**tryst** (SYN.) rendezvous, meeting, appointment.

**tub** (SYN.) basin, vessel, sink, bowl.

**tube** (SYN.) hose, pipe, reed.

**tubular** (SYN.) hollow, cylindrical.

**tuck** (SYN.) crease, fold, gather, bend.

**tuft** (SYN.) bunch, group, cluster.

**tug** (SYN.) pull, wrench, tow, haul, jerk.

**tuition** (SYN.) instruction, schooling, teaching, education.

**tumble** (SYN.) toss, trip, fall, sprawl, wallow, lurch, flounder, plunge, topple.

**tumult** (SYN.) chaos, agitation, commotion, confusion, disarray, disarrangement, disorder, noise, hubbub, ferment. (ANT.) peacefulness, order, peace, tranquillity.

**tune** (SYN.) song, concord, harmony, air, melody, strain. (ANT.) aversion, discord.

**tunnel** (SYN.) passage, grotto, cave.

**turbid** (SYN.) dark, cloudy, thick, muddy, murky.

**turf** (SYN.) lawn, grassland, sod, grass.

**turmoil** (SYN.) chaos, agitation, commotion, confusion, disarray, disorder. (ANT.) order, peace, certainty, quiet, tranquillity.

**turn** (SYN.) circulate, circle, invert, rotate, revolve, spin, twist, twirl, whirl, wheel, avert, reverse, become, sour. (ANT.) fix, stand, arrest, stop, continue, endure, proceed.

**turncoat** (SYN.) renegade, defector, deserter, rat, betrayer, traitor. (ANT.) loyalist.

**turret** (SYN.) watchtower, belfry, steeple, tower, cupola, lookout.

**tussle** (SYN.) wrestle, struggle, contend, battle, fight, scuffle.

**tutor** (SYN.) instruct, prime, school, teach, train, prepare, drill.

**tweak** (SYN.) squeeze, pinch, nip.

**twig** (SYN.) sprig, branch, shoot, stem.

**twilight** (SYN.) sunset, sundown, nightfall, eventide, dusk.

**twin** (SYN.) lookalike, imitation, copy, double, replica.

**twine** (SYN.) string, cordage, rope, cord.

**twinge** (SYN.) smart, pang, pain.

**twinkle** (SYN.) shine, gleam, glisten, sparkle, glitter, shimmer, scintillate.

**twirl** (SYN.) rotate, spin, wind, turn, pivot, wheel, swivel, whirl.

**twist** (SYN.) bow, bend, crook, intertwine, curve, incline, deflect, lean, braid, distort, contort, warp, interweave, stoop, turn. (ANT.) resist, break, straighten, stiffen.

**twitch** (SYN.) fidget, shudder, jerk.

**two-faced** (SYN.) deceitful, insincere, hypocritical, false, untrustworthy. (ANT.) straightforward, honest.

**tycoon** (SYN.) millionaire, industrialist, businessman.

**tyke** (SYN.) rascal, urchin, brat, ragamuffin, imp.

**typhoon** (SYN.) hurricane, cyclone, storm, tornado, whirlwind, twister.

**typical** (SYN.) common, accustomed, conventional, familiar, customary. (ANT.) marvelous, extraordinary, odd, atypical, uncommon, strange.

**typify** (SYN.) symbolize, illustrate, signify, represent, incarnate, indicate.

**tyrannize** (SYN.) oppress, victimize, threaten, brutalize, coerce.

**tyrannous** (SYN.) arbitrary, absolute, authoritative, despotic. (ANT.) conditional, accountable, contingent, qualified, dependent.

**tyrant** (SYN.) dictator, autocrat, despot, oppressor, slave driver, martinet, disciplinarian, persecutor.

# U

**ugly** (SYN.) hideous, homely, plain, deformed, repellent, uncomely, repulsive, ill-natured, unsightly, nasty, unpleasant, wicked, disagreeable, spiteful, surly, vicious. (ANT.) beautiful, fair, pretty, attractive, handsome, comely, good.

**ultimate** (SYN.) extreme, latest, final, concluding, decisive, hindmost, last, terminal, utmost, greatest, maximum. (ANT.) foremost, opening, first, beginning, initial.

**umbrage** (SYN.) anger, displeasure.

**umpire** (SYN.) judge, referee, arbitrator.

**unadulterated** (SYN.) genuine, clear, clean, immaculate, spotless, pure, absolute, untainted, sheer, bare. (ANT.) foul, sullied, corrupt, tainted, polluted, tarnished, defiled.

**unalterable** (SYN.) fixed, unchangeable, steadfast, inflexible.

**unanimity** (SYN.) accord, unity, agreement.

**unannounced** (SYN.) hasty, precipitate, abrupt, unexpected. (ANT.) courteous, expected, anticipated.

**unassuming** *(SYN.)* humble, lowly, compliant, modest, plain, meek, simple, unostentatious, retiring, submissive, unpretentious. *(ANT.) haughty, showy, pompous, proud, vain, arrogant, boastful.*

**unattached** *(SYN.)* apart, separate, unmarried, single, free, independent. *(ANT.) committed, involved, entangled.*

**unavoidable** *(SYN.)* inescapable, certain, inevitable, unpreventible.

**unawares** *(SYN.)* abruptly, suddenly, unexpectedly, off guard.

**unbalanced** *(SYN.)* crazy, mad, insane, deranged.

**unbearable** *(SYN.)* insufferable, intolerable. *(ANT.) tolerable, acceptable.*

**unbeliever** *(SYN.)* dissenter, apostate, heretic, schismatic, nonconformist, sectary, sectarian.

**unbending** *(SYN.)* firm, inflexible, determined, obstinate. *(ANT.) flexible.*

**unbiased** *(SYN.)* honest, equitable, fair, impartial, reasonable, unprejudiced, just. *(ANT.) partial, fraudulent, dishonorable.*

**unbroken** *(SYN.)* complete, uninterrupted, continuous, whole.

**unburden** *(SYN.)* clear, disentangle, divest, free.

**uncanny** *(SYN.)* amazing, remarkable, extraordinary, strange.

**uncertain** *(SYN.)* dim, hazy, indefinite, obscure, indistinct, unclear, undetermined, unsettled, ambiguous, unsure, doubtful, questionable, dubious, vague. *(ANT.) explicit, lucid, specific, certain, unmistakable, precise, clear.*

**uncertainty** *(SYN.)* distrust, doubt, hesitation, incredulity, scruple, ambiguity, skepticism, suspense, suspicion, unbelief. *(ANT.) faith, belief, certainty, conviction, determination.*

**uncivil** *(SYN.)* impolite, rude, discourteous. *(ANT.) polite.*

**uncivilized** *(SYN.)* barbaric, barbarous, barbarian, brutal, crude, inhuman, cruel, merciless, rude, remorseless, uncultured, savage, unrelenting. *(ANT.) humane, kind, polite, civilized, refined.*

**unclad** *(SYN.)* exposed, nude, naked, bare, stripped, defenseless, uncovered, open, unprotected. *(ANT.) concealed, protected, clothed, covered, dressed.*

**uncommon** *(SYN.)* unusual, rare, odd, scarce, strange, peculiar, queer, exceptional, remarkable. *(ANT.) ordinary, usual.*

**uncompromising** *(SYN.)* determined, dogged, firm, immovable, contumacious, headstrong, inflexible, obdurate, intractable, obstinate, pertinacious, stubborn, unyielding. *(ANT.) docile, compliant, amenable, yielding, submissive, pliable.*

**unconcern** *(SYN.)* disinterestedness, impartiality, indifference, apathy, insensibility, neutrality. *(ANT.) affection, fervor, passion, ardor.*

**unconditional** *(SYN.)* unqualified, unrestricted, arbitrary, absolute, pure, complete, actual, authoritative, perfect, entire, ultimate, tyrannous. *(ANT.) conditional, contingent, accountable, dependent, qualified.*

**unconscious** *(SYN.)* lethargic, numb, comatose.

**uncouth** *(SYN.)* green, harsh, crude, coarse, ill-prepared, rough, raw, unfinished, unrefined, vulgar, rude, impolite, discourteous, unpolished, ill-mannered, crass. *(ANT.) well-prepared, cultivated, refined, civilized, finished.*

**uncover** *(SYN.)* disclose, discover, betray, divulge, expose, reveal, impart, show. *(ANT.) conceal, hide, cover, obscure, cloak.*

**undependable** *(SYN.)* changeable, unstable, uncertain, shifty, irresponsible. *(ANT.) stable, dependable, trustworthy.*

**under** *(SYN.)* beneath, underneath, following, below, lower, downward. *(ANT.) over, above, up, higher.*

**undercover** *(SYN.)* hidden, secret.

**undergo** *(SYN.)* endure, feel, stand, bear, indulge, suffer, sustain, experience, let, allow, permit, tolerate. *(ANT.) overcome, discard, exclude, banish.*

**underhand** *(SYN.)* sly, secret, sneaky, secretive, stealthy, crafty. *(ANT.) honest, open, direct, frank.*

**undermine** *(SYN.)* demoralize, thwart, erode, weaken, subvert, sabotage.

**underscore** *(SYN.)* emphasize, stress.

**undersigned** *(SYN.)* casual, chance, contingent, accidental, fortuitous, incidental, unintended. *(ANT.) decreed, planned, willed, calculated.*

**understand** *(SYN.)* apprehend, comprehend, appreciate, conceive, discern, know, grasp, hear, learn, realize, see, perceive. *(ANT.) misunderstand, mistake, misapprehend, ignore.*

**understanding** *(SYN.)* agreement, coincidence, concord, accordance, concurrence, harmony, unison, compact, contract, arrangement, bargain, covenant, stipulation. *(ANT.) variance, difference, discord, dissension, disagreement.*

**understudy** *(SYN.)* deputy, agent, proxy, representative, agent, alternate, lieutenant, substitute. *(ANT.) head, principal, sovereign, master.*

**undertake** *(SYN.)* venture, attempt.

**undertaking** *(SYN.)* effort, endeavor, attempt, experiment, trial, essay. *(ANT.) laziness, neglect, inaction.*

**undesirable** *(SYN.)* obnoxious, distasteful, objectionable, repugnant. *(ANT.) appealing, inviting, attractive.*

**undivided** *(SYN.)* complete, intact, entire, integral, total, perfect, unimpaired, whole. *(ANT.) partial, incomplete.*

**undoing** *(SYN.)* ruin, downfall, destruction, failure, disgrace.

**undying** *(SYN.)* endless, deathless, eternal, everlasting, ceaseless, immortal, infinite, perpetual, timeless. *(ANT.) transient, mortal, temporal, ephemeral, impermanent.*

**unearthly** *(SYN.)* metaphysical, ghostly, miraculous, marvelous, preternatural, superhuman, spiritual, foreign, strange, weird, supernatural. *(ANT.) physical, plain, human, natural, common, mundane.*

**uneducated** *(SYN.)* uncultured, ignorant, illiterate, uninformed, unlearned, untaught, unlettered. *(ANT.) erudite, cultured, educated, literate, formed.*

**unemployed** *(SYN.)* inert, inactive, idle, jobless, unoccupied. *(ANT.) working, occupied, active, industrious, employed.*

**uneven** *(SYN.)* remaining, single, odd, unmatched, rugged, gnarled, irregular. *(ANT.) matched, even, flat, smooth.*

**unexceptional** *(SYN.)* commonplace, trivial, customary.

**unexpected** *(SYN.)* immediate, hasty, surprising, instantaneous, unforeseen, abrupt, rapid, startling, sudden. *(ANT.) expected, gradual, predicted, anticipated, planned.*

**unfaithful** *(SYN.)* treacherous, disloyal, deceitful, capricious. *(ANT.) true, loyal, steadfast, faithful.*

**unfasten** *(SYN.)* open, expand, spread, exhibit, unbar, unlock, unfold, unseal. *(ANT.) shut, hide, conceal, close.*

**unfavorable** *(SYN.)* antagonistic, contrary, adverse, opposed, opposite, disastrous, counteractive, unlucky. *(ANT.) benign, fortunate, lucky, propitious.*

**unfeeling** *(SYN.)* hard, rigorous, cruel, stern, callous, numb, strict, unsympathetic, severe. *(ANT.) tender, gentle, lenient, humane.*

**unfold** *(SYN.)* develop, create, elaborate, amplify, evolve, mature, expand. *(ANT.) wither, restrict, contract, stunt, compress.*

**unfurnished** *(SYN.)* naked, mere, bare, exposed, stripped, plain, open, simple. *(ANT.) concealed, protected, covered.*

**ungainly** *(SYN.)* clumsy, awkward, bungling, clownish, gawky. *(ANT.) dexterous, graceful, elegant.*

**unhappy** *(SYN.)* sad, miserable, wretched, melancholy, distressed, depressed. *(ANT.) joyful, happy, cheerful.*

**unhealthy** *(SYN.)* infirm, sick, diseased, sickly. *(ANT.) vigorous, well, healthy, hale.*

**uniform** *(SYN.)* methodical, natural, customary, orderly, normal, consistent, ordinary, regular, unvarying, unchanging, systematic, steady, unvaried. *(ANT.) rare, unusual, erratic, abnormal, exceptional.*

**unimportant** *(SYN.)* petty, trivial, paltry, trifling, insignificant, indifferent, minor.

**uninformed** *(SYN.)* illiterate, uncultured, uneducated, ignorant, unlearned, untaught, unlettered. *(ANT.) informed, literate, erudite, cultured, educated.*

**uninhibited** *(SYN.)* loose, open, liberated, free. *(ANT.) constrained, tense, suppressed.*

**unintelligible** *(SYN.)* ambiguous, cryptic, dark, cloudy, abstruse, dusky, mysterious, indistinct, obscure, vague. *(ANT.) lucid, distinct, bright, clear.*

**uninteresting** *(SYN.)* burdensome, dilatory, dreary, dull, boring, slow, humdrum, monotonous, sluggish, tedious, tardy, wearisome, tiresome. (*ANT.*) *entertaining, exciting, quick, amusing.*

**union** (*SYN.*) fusion, incorporation, combination, joining, concurrence, solidarity, agreement, unification, concord, harmony, alliance, unanimity, coalition, confederacy, amalgamation, league, concert, marriage. (*ANT.*) *disagreement, separation, discord.*

**unique** (*SYN.*) exceptional, matchless, distinctive, choice, peculiar, singular, rare, sole, single, incomparable, uncommon, solitary, unequaled. (*ANT.*) *typical, ordinary, commonplace, frequent, common.*

**unison** (*SYN.*) harmony, concurrence, understanding, accordance, concord, agreeable, coincidence. (*ANT.*) *disagreement, difference, discord, variance.*

**unite** (*SYN.*) attach, blend, amalgamate, combine, conjoin, associate, connect, embody, consolidate, join, link, fuse, unify, merge. (*ANT.*) *sever, divide, separate, disrupt, disconnect.*

**universal** (*SYN.*) frequent, general, popular, common, familiar, prevailing, prevalent, usual. (*ANT.*) *scarce, odd, regional, local, extraordinary, exceptional.*

**unkempt** (*SYN.*) sloppy, rumpled, untidy, messy, bedraggled. (*ANT.*) *presentable, well-groomed, tidy, neat.*

**unkind** (*SYN.*) unfeeling, unsympathetic, unpleasant, cruel, harsh. (*ANT.*) *considerate, sympathetic, amiable, kind.*

**unlawful** (*SYN.*) illegitimate, illicit, illegal, outlawed, criminal, prohibited. (*ANT.*) *permitted, honest, legal, legitimate.*

**unlike** (*SYN.*) dissimilar, different, distinct, contrary, diverse, divergent, opposite, incongruous, variant, miscellaneous, divers. (*ANT.*) *conditional, accountable, contingent, qualified, dependent.*

**unlucky** (*SYN.*) cursed, inauspicious, unfortunate. (*ANT.*) *fortunate, blessed.*

**unmerciful** (*SYN.*) cruel, merciless, heartless, brutal.

**unmistakable** (*SYN.*) clear, patent, plain, visible, obvious.

**unnecessary** (*SYN.*) pointless, needless, superfluous, purposeless.

**unoccupied** (*SYN.*) empty, vacant, uninhabited.

**unparalleled** (*SYN.*) peerless, unequaled, rare, unique, unmatched.

**unpleasant** (*SYN.*) offensive, disagreeable, repulsive, obnoxious, unpleasing.

**unqualified** (*SYN.*) inept, unfit, incapable, incompetent, unquestioned, absolute.

**unreasonable** (*SYN.*) foolish, absurd, irrational, inconsistent, nonsensical, ridiculous, silly. (*ANT.*) *reasonable, sensible, sound, consistent, rational.*

**unruffled** (*SYN.*) calm, smooth, serene, unperturbed.

**unruly** (*SYN.*) unmanageable, disorganized, disorderly, disobedient. (*ANT.*) *orderly.*

**unsafe** (*SYN.*) hazardous, insecure, critical, dangerous, perilous, menacing, risky, precarious, threatening, (*ANT.*) *protected, secure, firm, safe.*

**unselfish** (*SYN.*) bountiful, generous, liberal, giving, beneficent, magnanimous, openhanded, munificent. (*ANT.*) *miserly, stingy, greedy, selfish, covetous.*

**unsightly** (*SYN.*) ugly, unattractive, hideous.

**unsophisticated** (*SYN.*) frank, candid, artless, ingenuous, naive, open, simple, natural. (*ANT.*) *sophisticated, worldly, cunning, crafty.*

**unsound** (*SYN.*) feeble, flimsy, weak, fragile, sick, unhealthy, diseased, invalid, faulty, false.

**unstable** (*SYN.*) fickle, fitful, inconstant, capricious, changeable, restless, variable. (*ANT.*) *steady, stable, trustworthy, constant.*

**unswerving** (*SYN.*) fast, firm, inflexible, constant, secure, stable, solid, steady, steadfast, unyielding. (*ANT.*) *sluggish, insecure, unsteady, unstable, loose, slow.*

**untainted** (*SYN.*) genuine, pure, spotless, clean, clear, unadulterated, guiltless, innocent, chaste, modest, undefiled, sincere, virgin. (*ANT.*) *polluted, tainted, sullied, tarnished, defiled, corrupt, foul.*

**untamed** (*SYN.*) fierce, savage, uncivilized, barbarous, outlandish, rude, undomesticated, wild, frenzied, mad, turbulent, impetuous, wanton, boisterous, wayward, stormy, extravagant, tempestuous, foolish, rash, giddy, reckless. (*ANT.*) *quiet, gentle, calm, civilized, placid.*

**untidy** (*SYN.*) messy, sloppy, disorderly, slovenly.

**untoward** (*SYN.*) disobedient, contrary, peevish, fractious, forward, petulant, obstinate, intractable, stubborn, perverse, ungovernable. (*ANT.*) *docile, tractable, obliging, agreeable.*

**unusual** (*SYN.*) capricious, abnormal, devious, eccentric, aberrant, irregular, variable, remarkable, extraordinary, odd, peculiar, uncommon, strange, exceptional, unnatural. (*ANT.*) *regular, usual, fixed, ordinary.*

**unyielding** (*SYN.*) fast, firm, inflexible, constant, solid, secure, stable, steadfast, unswerving, steady. (*ANT.*) *sluggish, slow, insecure, loose, unsteady, unstable.*

**upbraid** (*SYN.*) blame, censure, berate, admonish, rate, lecture, rebuke, reprimand, reprehend, scold, vituperate. (*ANT.*) *praise, commend, approve.*

**uphold** (*SYN.*) justify, espouse, assert, defend, maintain, vindicate. (*ANT.*) *oppose, submit, assault, deny, attack.*

**upright** (*SYN.*) undeviating, right, unswerving, direct, erect, unbent, straight, fair, vertical. (*ANT.*) *bent, dishonest, crooked, circuitous, winding.*

**uprising** (*SYN.*) revolution, mutiny, revolt, rebellion.

**uproar** (*SYN.*) noise, disorder, commotion, tumult, disturbance.

**upset** (*SYN.*) disturb, harass, bother, annoy, haunt, molest, inconvenience, perplex, pester, tease, plague, trouble, worry, overturn, topple, upend, capsize, fluster, agitate. (*ANT.*) *soothe, relieve, gratify.*

**urbane** (*SYN.*) civil, considerate, cultivated, courteous, genteel, polite, accomplished, refined, well-mannered. (*ANT.*) *rude, uncouth, boorish, uncivil.*

**urge** (*SYN.*) craving, desire, longing, lust, appetite, aspiration, yearning, incite, coax, entice, force, drive, prod, press, plead, coerce, persuade, implore, beg, recommend, advise. (*ANT.*) *loathing, hate, distaste, aversion, deter, dissuade, discourage.*

**urgency** (*SYN.*) emergency, exigency, pass, pinch, strait, crisis.

**urgent** (*SYN.*) critical, crucial, exigent, imperative, impelling, insistent, necessary, instant, serious, pressing, cogent, important, importunate,

immediate. (*ANT.*) *trivial, unimportant, insignificant.*

**usage** (*SYN.*) use, treatment, custom, practice, tradition.

**use** (*SYN.*) custom, practice, habit, training, usage, manner, apply, avail, employ, operate, utilize, exert, exhaust, handle, manage, accustom, inure, exploit, manipulate, spend, expend, consume. (*ANT.*) *disuse, neglect, waste, ignore, overlook, idleness.*

**useful** (*SYN.*) beneficial, helpful, good, serviceable, wholesome, advantageous. (*ANT.*) *harmful, injurious, deleterious, destructive, detrimental.*

**usefulness** (*SYN.*) price, merit, utility, excellence, virtue, worth, worthiness. (*ANT.*) *cheapness, valueless, uselessness.*

**useless** (*SYN.*) bootless, empty, idle, pointless, vain, valueless, worthless, abortive, fruitless, unavailing, ineffectual, vapid. (*ANT.*) *profitable, potent, effective.*

**usher** (*SYN.*) guide, lead.

**usual** (*SYN.*) customary, common, familiar, general, normal, habitual, accustomed, everyday, ordinary, regular. (*ANT.*) *irregular, exceptional, rare, extraordinary, abnormal.*

**utensil** (*SYN.*) instrument, tool, vehicle, apparatus, device, implement. (*ANT.*) *preventive, obstruction.*

**utilize** (*SYN.*) use, apply, devote, busy, employ, occupy, avail. (*ANT.*) *reject, banish, discharge, discard.*

**utopian** (*SYN.*) perfect, ideal, faultless, exemplary, supreme, visionary, unreal. (*ANT.*) *real, imperfect, actual, faulty.*

**utter** (*SYN.*) full, perfect, whole, finished, entire, speak, say, complete, superlative. (*ANT.*) *imperfect, deficient, lacking, faulty, incomplete.*

# V

**vacancy** (*SYN.*) void, emptiness, vacuum, hollowness, blankness, vacuity, depletion, nothingness. (*ANT.*) *plenitude, fullness, profusion, completeness.*

**vacant** (*SYN.*) barren, empty, blank, bare, unoccupied, void, vacuous. (*ANT.*) *filled, packed, employed, full, replete, busy, engaged.*

**vacate** (*SYN.*) abjure, relinquish, abdicate, renounce, abandon, resign, surrender, desert, waive, quit, leave.

*(ANT.) stay, support, uphold, maintain.*

**vacation** *(SYN.)* rest, holiday, recess, break. *(ANT.) labor, work, routine.*

**vacillate** *(SYN.)* hesitate, oscillate, undulate, change, fluctuate, vary, waver. *(ANT.) adhere, persist, stick, decide.*

**vacillating** *(SYN.)* contrary, illogical, contradictory, inconsistent, incongruous, incompatible, paradoxical, irreconcilable, unsteady, wavering. *(ANT.) correspondent, congruous, consistent, compatible.*

**vacuity** *(SYN.)* space, emptiness, vacuum, void, blank, nothingness, ignorance, unawareness, senselessness, mindlessness, chatter, nonsense, froth, absurdity. *(ANT.) matter, fullness, content, substance, knowledge, intelligence.*

**vacuous** *(SYN.)* dull, blank, uncomprehending, imbecilic, foolish, thoughtless, distracted, absent-minded. *(ANT.) responsive, alert, attentive, bright, intelligent, aware.*

**vacuum** *(SYN.)* void, gap, emptiness, hole, chasm, nothingness, abyss.

**vagabond** *(SYN.)* pauper, ragamuffin, scrub, beggar, mendicant, starveling, wretch, tatterdemalion, hobo, tramp. *(ANT.) responsible, established, rooted, installed, reliable.*

**vagary** *(SYN.)* notion, whim, fantasy, fancy, daydream, caprice, conceit, quirk, whimsy, impulse.

**vagrant** *(SYN.)* hobo, rover, tramp, beggar, bum, wanderer, vagabond. *(ANT.) settled, worker, laborer, rooted, ambitious, gentleman.*

**vague** *(SYN.)* indefinite, hazy, dim, indistinct, ambiguous, obscure, undetermined, unclear, unsure, unsettled. *(ANT.) certain, spelled out, specific, lucid, clear, definite, distinct, explicit, precise, unequivocal.*

**vain** *(SYN.)* fruitless, empty, bootless, futile, idle, abortive, ineffectual, unavailing, vapid, pointless, valueless, useless, trivial, unfruitful, worthless, unsuccessful, proud, conceited. *(ANT.) meek, modest, potent, rewarding, self-effacing, diffident, profitable, effective, humble.*

**vainglory** *(SYN.)* conceit, pride, self-esteem, arrogance, self-respect, superciliousness, haughtiness, vanity. *(ANT.)*

shame, modesty, meekness, humility, lowliness.

**valet** *(SYN.)* groom, dresser, attendant, manservant.

**valiant** *(SYN.)* bold, brave, courageous, adventurous, audacious, chivalrous, daring, fearless, heroic, gallant, magnanimous, intrepid, unafraid, valorous, dauntless. *(ANT.) weak, fearful, cowardly, timid.*

**valid** *(SYN.)* cogent, conclusive, effective, convincing, binding, efficacious, logical, powerful, legal, sound, weighty, well-founded, real, genuine, actual, true, trustworthy, strong, telling, authentic. *(ANT.) weak, unconvincing, void, unproved, null, spurious, counterfeit.*

**validate** *(SYN.)* corroborate, substantiate, support, confirm, prove, uphold, sustain, authenticate. *(ANT.) disprove, contradict, cancel.*

**valise** *(SYN.)* satchel, bag, baggage.

**valley** *(SYN.)* dale, dell, lowland, basin, gully, vale, ravine. *(ANT.) highland, hill, upland, headland.*

**valor** *(SYN.)* courage, heroism, bravery, boldness, intrepidity, fearlessness.

**valuable** *(SYN.)* profitable, useful, costly, precious, dear, expensive, worthy, important, high-priced, esteemed. *(ANT.) trashy, poor, cheap, worthless.*

**value** *(SYN.)* price, merit, usefulness, value, virtue, utility, appreciate, prize, hold dear, treasure, excellence, benefit, cost, rate, evaluate, appraise, esteem, importance, worth, worthiness. *(ANT.) valueless, uselessness, cheapness.*

**vanish** *(SYN.)* evaporate, disappear. *(ANT.) appear.*

**vanity** *(SYN.)* complacency, egotism, pride, self-esteem, conceit, caprice, fancy, idea, conception, notion, haughtiness, self-respect, whim, smugness, vainglory, arrogance, imagination. *(ANT.) meekness, humility, diffidence.*

**vanquish** *(SYN.)* defeat, crush, humble, surmount, master, beat, conquer, overcome, rout, quell, subjugate, subdue. *(ANT.) surrender, cede, lose, retreat, capitulate.*

**vapid** *(SYN.)* hackneyed, inane, insipid, trite, banal, commonplace. *(ANT.) striking, novel, fresh, original, stimulating.*

**vapor** *(SYN.)* steam, fog, mist, smog, haze, steam.

**variable** *(SYN.)* fickle, fitful, inconstant, unstable, shifting, changeable, unsteady, wavering, vacillating. *(ANT.) unchanging, uniform, stable, unwavering, steady, constant.*

**variant** *(SYN.)* dissimilar, different, distinct, contrary, diverse, divergent, opposite, unlike, incongruous, divers, sundry, various, miscellaneous. *(ANT.) similar, same, congruous, identical, alike.*

**variation** *(SYN.)* change, alternation, alteration, substitution, variety, substitute, mutation, exchange, vicissitude. *(ANT.) uniformity, stability, monotony.*

**variety** *(SYN.)* dissimilarity, diversity, heterogeneity, assortment, change, difference, medley, mixture, miscellany, form, type, class, breed, sort, kind, strain, stock. *(ANT.) likeness, monotony, uniformity, sameness, homogeneity.*

**various** *(SYN.)* miscellaneous, sundry, divers, several, contrary, distinct, dissimilar, divergent, unlike, incongruous, opposite, different. *(ANT.) identical, similar, same, alike, congruous.*

**vary** *(SYN.)* exchange, substitute, alter, change, modify, shift, convert, transform, transfigure, diversify, veer. *(ANT.) settle, stabilize, continue, establish, preserve.*

**vassalage** *(SYN.)* confinement, captivity, imprisonment, slavery, thralldom. *(ANT.) liberation, freedom.*

**vast** *(SYN.)* big, capacious, extensive, huge, great, ample, immense, wide, unlimited, enormous, measureless, large. *(ANT.) tiny, small, short, little.*

**vault** *(SYN.)* caper, jerk, jump, leap, bound, crypt, sepulcher, hop, spring, safe, start, tomb, grave, catacomb, skip.

**vaunt** *(SYN.)* crow, flaunt, glory, boast. *(ANT.) minimize, humble, deprecate, apologize.*

**vaunting** *(SYN.)* flourish, display, ostentation, parade, show, pomp. *(ANT.) modesty, reserve, humility.*

**vehement** *(SYN.)* excitable, fervent, ardent, burning, fiery, glowing, impetuous, hot, irascible, passionate. *(ANT.) calm, quiet, cool, apathetic, deliberate.*

**veil** *(SYN.)* clothe, conceal, cover, cloak, web, hide, curtain, disguise, gauze, envelop, screen, mask, shield, film. *(ANT.) reveal, unveil, bare,*

divulge.

**velocity** *(SYN.)* quickness, rapidity, speed, swiftness.

**venal** *(SYN.)* greedy, mercenary, sordid, corrupt. *(ANT.) liberal, honorable, generous.*

**venerable** *(SYN.)* antiquated, aged, antique, ancient, elderly, old, superannuated, old-fashion. *(ANT.) young, new, youthful, modern.*

**venerate** *(SYN.)* approve, esteem, admire, appreciate, wonder, respect. *(ANT.) dislike, despise.*

**vengeance** *(SYN.)* requital, reprisal, reparation, retribution, revenge. *(ANT.) forgiveness, remission, pardon, mercy.*

**venom** *(SYN.)* toxin, poison, bitterness, spite, hate.

**vent** *(SYN.)* eject, emit, expel, shoot, spurt, emanate, hurl, shed, belch, discharge, breathe.

**venture** *(SYN.)* speculate, attempt, test, dare, hazard, gamble, chance, risk. *(ANT.) insure, secure, protect.*

**verbal** *(SYN.)* oral, spoken, literal, unwritten, vocal. *(ANT.) printed, written, recorded.*

**verbose** *(SYN.)* communicative, glib, chattering, chatty, garrulous, loquacious, talkative. *(ANT.) uncommunicative, silent.*

**verbosity** *(SYN.)* long-windedness, verboseness, redundancy, wordiness. *(ANT.) terseness, laconic, conciseness.*

**verdict** *(SYN.)* judgment, finding, opinion, decision.

**verge** *(SYN.)* lip, rim, edge, margin, brink, brim.

**verification** *(SYN.)* confirmation, demonstration, evidence, proof, test, experiment, testimony, trial.

**verify** *(SYN.)* confirm, substantiate, acknowledge, determine, assure, establish, approve, fix, settle, ratify, strengthen, corroborate, affirm, sanction.

**veritable** *(SYN.)* authentic, correct, genuine, real, true, accurate, actual. *(ANT.) false, fictitious, spurious, erroneous, counterfeit.*

**versed** *(SYN.)* conversant, familiar, intimate, knowing, acquainted, aware. *(ANT.) untrained, unaccomplished.*

**version** *(SYN.)* interpretation, rendition.

**vertical** *(SYN.)* erect, perpendicular, upright. *(ANT.) horizontal.*

**very** *(SYN.)* exceedingly, extremely, greatly, considerably.

**vessel** *(SYN.)* craft, boat, ship.

**vestige** (*SYN.*) stain, scar, mark, brand, stigma, characteristic, trace, feature, trait, symptom, hint, token, suggestion, indication.

**veto** (*SYN.*) refusal, denial, refuse, deny, negate, forbid, prohibit. (*ANT.*) approve, approval.

**vex** (*SYN.*) embitter, exasperate, aggravate, annoy, chafe, bother, provoke, pester, plague, anger, nettle. (*ANT.*) soften, soothe, palliate, mitigate.

**vexation** (*SYN.*) chagrin, irritation, annoyance, mortification, irritation, pique. (*ANT.*) comfort, pleasure, appeasement, gratification.

**vibrate** (*SYN.*) flutter, jar, quake, jolt, quaver, agitate, transgression, wickedness, ungodliness, tremble.

**vice** (*SYN.*) iniquity, crime, offense, evil, guilt, sin, ungodliness, wickedness, depravity, corruption, wrong. (*ANT.*) righteousness, virtue, goodness, innocence, purity.

**vicinity** (*SYN.*) district, area, locality, neighborhood, environs, proximity, nearness, adjacency. (*ANT.*) remoteness, distance.

**vicious** (*SYN.*) bad, evil, wicked, sinful, corrupt, cruel, savage, dangerous.

**victimize** (*SYN.*) cheat, dupe, swindle, deceive, take advantage of.

**victor** (*SYN.*) champion, winner. (*ANT.*) loser.

**victory** (*SYN.*) conquest, jubilation, triumph, success, achievement, ovation. (*ANT.*) defeat, failure.

**view** (*SYN.*) discern, gaze, glance, behold, eye, stare, watch, examine, witness, prospect, vision, vista, sight, look, panorama, opinion, judgment, belief, impression, perspective, range, regard, thought, observation, survey, scene, conception, outlook, inspect, observe. (*ANT.*) miss, overlook, avert, hide.

**viewpoint** (*SYN.*) attitude, standpoint, aspect, pose, disposition, position, stand, posture.

**vigilant** (*SYN.*) anxious, attentive, careful, alert, circumspect, cautious, observant, wary, watchful, wakeful. (*ANT.*) inattentive, neglectful, careless.

**vigor** (*SYN.*) spirit, verve, energy, zeal, fortitude, vitality, strength, liveliness. (*ANT.*) listlessness.

**vigorous** (*SYN.*) brisk, energetic, active, blithe, animated, frolicsome, strong, spirited, lively, forceful, sprightly, vivacious, powerful, supple. (*ANT.*) vapid, dull, listless, insipid.

**vile** (*SYN.*) foul, loathsome, base, depraved, debased, sordid, vulgar, wicked, abject, ignoble, mean, worthless, sinful, bad, low, wretched, evil, offensive, objectionable, disgusting. (*ANT.*) honorable, upright, decent, laudable, attractive.

**vilify** (*SYN.*) asperse, defame, disparage, abuse, malign, revile, scandalize. (*ANT.*) protect, honor, praise, cherish.

**village** (*SYN.*) hamlet, town. (*ANT.*) metropolis, city.

**villain** (*SYN.*) rascal, rogue, cad, brute, scoundrel, devil, scamp.

**villainous** (*SYN.*) deleterious, evil, bad, base, iniquitous, unsound, sinful, unwholesome, wicked. (*ANT.*) honorable, reputable, moral, good, excellent.

**vindicate** (*SYN.*) clear, assert, defend, absolve, excuse, acquit, uphold, support. (*ANT.*) accuse, convict, abandon.

**violate** (*SYN.*) disobey, invade, defile, break, desecrate, pollute, dishonor, debauch, profane, deflower, ravish.

**violence** (*SYN.*) constraint, force, compulsion, coercion. (*ANT.*) weakness, persuasion, feebleness, impotence, frailty.

**violent** (*SYN.*) strong, forceful, powerful, forcible, angry, fierce, savage, passionate, furious. (*ANT.*) gentle.

**virgin** (*SYN.*) immaculate, genuine, spotless, clean, clear, unadulterated, chaste, untainted, innocent, guiltless, untouched, modest, maid, maiden, sincere, unused, undefiled, pure. (*ANT.*) foul, tainted, defiled, sullied, polluted, corrupt.

**virile** (*SYN.*) hardy, male, mannish, lusty, bold, masculine, strong, vigorous. (*ANT.*) feminine, unmanly, weak, effeminate, womanish, emasculated.

**virtue** (*SYN.*) integrity, probity, purity, chastity, goodness, rectitude, effectiveness, force, honor, power, efficacy, quality, strength, merit, righteousness. (*ANT.*) fault, vice, lewdness, corruption.

**virtuous** (*SYN.*) good, ethical, chaste, honorable, moral, just, pure, righteous, upstanding, upright, scrupulous. (*ANT.*) licentious, unethical, amoral, sinful, libertine, immoral.

**virulent** (*SYN.*) hostile, malevolent, malignant, bitter, spiteful, wicked. (*ANT.*) kind, affectionate, benevolent.

**vision** (*SYN.*) dream, hallucination, mirage, eyesight, sight, fantasy, illusion, specter, revelation, phantom, spook. (*ANT.*) verity, reality.

**visionary** (*SYN.*) faultless, ideal, perfect, unreal, supreme. (*ANT.*) real, actual, imperfect, faulty.

**visit** (*SYN.*) attend, see, appointment.

**visitor** (*SYN.*) caller, guest.

**vista** (*SYN.*) view, scene, aspect.

**vital** (*SYN.*) cardinal, living, paramount, alive, essential, critical, basic, indispensable, urgent, life-and-death. (*ANT.*) lifeless, unimportant, inanimate, nonessential.

**vitality** (*SYN.*) buoyancy, being, life, liveliness, existence, spirit, vigor. (*ANT.*) death, lethargy, dullness, demise.

**vitiate** (*SYN.*) allay, abase, corrupt, adulterate, debase, defile, depress, deprave, degrade, impair, humiliate, pervert.

**vivacious** (*SYN.*) lively, spirited.

**vivid** (*SYN.*) brilliant, striking, clear, bright, intense, lively, strong, graphic. (*ANT.*) dim, dusky, vague, dull, dreary.

**vocal** (*SYN.*) said, uttered, oral, spoken, definite, outspoken, specific.

**vocation** (*SYN.*) commerce, employment, business, art, job, profession, trade, occupation, career, calling, work, trading. (*ANT.*) pastime, hobby, avocation.

**void** (*SYN.*) barren, emptiness, space, annul, cancel, empty, bare, unoccupied, meaningless, invalid, useless, invalidate, worthless, vacant, barren. (*ANT.*) employed, full, replete, engaged.

**volatile** (*SYN.*) effervescent, resilient, buoyant, animated, cheerful, hopeful, lively, sprightly, spirited, vivacious. (*ANT.*) depressed, sullen, hopeless, dejected, despondent.

**volition** (*SYN.*) desire, intention, pleasure, preference, choice, decision, resolution, testament, wish, will. (*ANT.*) disinterest, compulsion, indifference.

**voluble** (*SYN.*) glib, communicative, verbose, loquacious, chatty, chattering. (*ANT.*) uncommunicative, laconic, taciturn, silent.

**volume** (*SYN.*) capacity, loudness, sound, magnitude, mass, book, dimensions, quantity, amount, size.

**voluntary** (*SYN.*) extemporaneous, free, automatic, spontaneous, offhand. (*ANT.*) forced, planned, required, rehearsed, compulsory, prepared.

**volunteer** (*SYN.*) extend, offer, present, advance, propose, tender, sacrifice. (*ANT.*) receive, spurn, reject, accept, retain.

**voracious** (*SYN.*) insatiable, ravenous.

**vow** (*SYN.*) oath, pledge, swear, promise.

**voyage** (*SYN.*) tour, journey, excursion.

**vulgar** (*SYN.*) ordinary, popular, common, general, crude, coarse, low, rude. (*ANT.*) polite, refined, select, aristocratic.

**vulnerable** (*SYN.*) unguarded, defenseless, unprotected.

# W

**wacky** (*SYN.*) strange, crazy, peculiar.

**wad** (*SYN.*) hunk, clump, chunk.

**wafer** (*SYN.*) cracker, lozenge.

**waft** (*SYN.*) convey, glide, sail, float.

**wage** (*SYN.*) conduct, pursue, make.

**wager** (*SYN.*) stake, bet, play, gamble, speculate, risk, chance.

**wages** (*SYN.*) payment, compensation, fee, allowance, pay, salary, earnings, rate, recompense.

**wagon** (*SYN.*) carriage, buggy, cart, surrey, stagecoach.

**waif** (*SYN.*) guttersnipe, ragamuffin, tramp, vagrant, urchin.

**wail** (*SYN.*) mourn, moan, cry, bewail, lament, bemoan, sorrow.

**wait** (*SYN.*) linger, tarry, attend, bide, watch, delay, await, abide, stay, serve, pause, remain, rest, minister, expect. (*ANT.*) hasten, act, leave, expedite.

**waive** (*SYN.*) renounce, abandon, surrender, relinquish, forgo. (*ANT.*) uphold, maintain.

**wake** (*SYN.*) awaken, rouse,

waken, arouse, stimulate, activate. (ANT.) doze, sleep.

**waken** (SYN.) wake, arouse, rouse, awaken, stimulate, activate. (ANT.) doze, sleep.

**walk** (SYN.) step, stroll, march, amble, saunter, hike, lane, path, passage.

**wall** (SYN.) barricade, divider, partition, panel, stockade.

**wallow** (SYN.) plunge, roll, flounder, grovel.

**wan** (SYN.) colorless, haggard, gaunt, pallid, pasty, pale.

**wander** (SYN.) rove, stroll, deviate, ramble, digress, roam, traipse, range, err, meander, saunter. (ANT.) linger, stop, settle.

**wane** (SYN.) abate, weaken, fade, ebb, decrease, wither, subside.

**want** (SYN.) penury, destitution, crave, desire, requirement, poverty, wish, require, need, privation. (ANT.) wealth, plenty, abundance.

**wanton** (SYN.) lecherous, immoral, loose, lewd, salacious, lustful.

**war** (SYN.) battle, hostility, combat, fight, strife, contention. (ANT.) peace, calm, friendship, harmony.

**warble** (SYN.) sing, trill, chirp.

**ward** (SYN.) annex, wing, section.

**warden** (SYN.) custodian, guard, guardian, keeper, turnkey, jailer, curator.

**wares** (SYN.) merchandise, staples, inventory, commodities, goods.

**wariness** (SYN.) heed, care, watchfulness, caution, vigilance. (ANT.) carelessness, abandon.

**warlike** (SYN.) hostile, unfriendly, combative, belligerent, antagonistic, pugnacious, bellicose, opposed, aggressive. (ANT.) cordial, peaceful, amicable.

**warm** (SYN.) sincere, cordial, hearty, earnest, sympathetic, ardent, heated, gracious, temperate, enthusiastic, lukewarm, tepid, eager, sociable. (ANT.) cool, aloof, taciturn, brisk, indifferent.

**warmhearted** (SYN.) loving, kind, kindhearted, friendly, generous.

**warmth** (SYN.) friendliness, cordiality, geniality, understanding, compassion.

**warn** (SYN.) apprise, notify, admonish, caution, advise, inform.

**warning** (SYN.) advice, information, caution, portent,

admonition, indication, notice, sign.

**warp** (SYN.) turn, bend, twist, distort, deprave.

**warrant** (SYN.) pledge, assurance, warranty, guarantee, authorize, approve, mandate, sanction.

**warrior** (SYN.) combatant, fighter, soldier, mercenary, guerrilla.

**wary** (SYN.) careful, awake, watchful, heedful, attentive, alive, mindful, cautious, thoughtful. (ANT.) unaware, indifferent, careless, apathetic.

**wash** (SYN.) launder, cleanse, rub, wet, clean, scrub, bathe. (ANT.) soil, dirty, stain.

**washed-out** (SYN.) bleached, dull, faded, pale, discolored, pallid.

**waspish** (SYN.) irritable, petulant, fractious, ill-tempered, testy, snappish, touchy. (ANT.) pleasant, genial.

**waste** (SYN.) forlorn, bleak, wild, solitary, dissipate, abandoned, spend, deserted, bare, consume, dwindle, decay, misspend, decrease, wither, wear, effluent, useless, unused, garbage, rubbish, refuse, trash, squander, uninhabited. (ANT.) cultivated, attended.

**wasteful** (SYN.) wanton, costly, lavish, extravagant.

**watch** (SYN.) inspect, descry, behold, distinguish, guard, attend, observe, contemplate, espy, perceive, look at, protect, chronometer, timepiece, patrol, vigil, duty, shift, regard, note, view, scan, sentinel, watchman, sentry, discern.

**watchdog** (SYN.) lookout, guard, sentinel, sentry.

**watchful** (SYN.) alert, careful, attentive, vigilant, wary, cautious.

**waterfall** (SYN.) cascade, cataract.

**watertight** (SYN.) impregnable, firm, solid.

**wave** (SYN.) ripple, whitecap, undulation, breaker, surf, swell, sea, surge, tide, flow, roll.

**waver** (SYN.) question, suspect, flicker, deliberate, doubt, distrust, hesitate, falter, stagger. (ANT.) confide, trust, believe, decide.

**wavering** (SYN.) fickle, shifting, variable, changeable, vacillating, fitful. (ANT.) unchanging, constant, uniform.

**wavy** (SYN.) rippling, serpentine, curly.

**wax** (SYN.) raise, heighten,

expand, accrue, enhance, extend, multiply, enlarge, augment, amplify. (ANT.) contract, reduce, atrophy, diminish.

**way** (SYN.) habit, road, course, avenue, route, mode, system, channel, track, fashion, method, walk, approach, manner, technique, means, procedure, trail, proceed, progress, path, style.

**waylay** (SYN.) surprise, accost, ambush, attack, pounce, intercept.

**wayward** (SYN.) stubborn, headstrong, contrary, obstinate, naughty, disobedient, rebellious, refractory.

**weak** (SYN.) frail, debilitated, delicate, poor, wavering, infirm, bending, lame, defenseless, vulnerable, fragile, pliant, feeble, watery, diluted, undecided, assailable, irresolute, unsteady, yielding, tender. (ANT.) strong, potent, sturdy, powerful.

**weaken** (SYN.) exhaust, sap, disable, devitalize.

**weakling** (SYN.) sissy, namby-pamby, milksop, milquetoast.

**weakness** (SYN.) incompetence, inability, impotence, handicap, fondness, liking, affection, disability, incapacity, feebleness. (ANT.) strength, ability, power.

**wealth** (SYN.) fortune, money, riches, possessions, means, abundance, opulence, affluence, property, quantity, profession, luxury. (ANT.) want, need.

**wealthy** (SYN.) rich, exorbitant, prosperous, affluent, successful. (ANT.) poverty-stricken, poor, indigent, impoverished, beggarly, destitute, needy.

**wear** (SYN.) erode, fray, grind, apparel, clothes, garb, attire.

**wearied** (SYN.) weak, languid, faint, irresolute, feeble, timid. (ANT.) brave, vigorous.

**weary** (SYN.) faint, spent, worn, tired, fatigued, exhausted, tiresome, bored, wearied, tedious, jaded. (ANT.) rested, hearty, fresh.

**weasel** (SYN.) cheat, traitor, betrayer.

**weave** (SYN.) lace, interlace, plait, intertwine, braid, knit.

**web** (SYN.) netting, network, net, cobweb, trap, entanglement.

**wed** (SYN.) espouse, marry.

**wedge** (SYN.) chock, jam, lodge.

**wedlock** (SYN.) marriage, union, espousal, wedding, matrimony.

**wee** (SYN.) small, tiny, miniature, petite, microscopic, minute.

**weep** (SYN.) mourn, sob, bemoan, cry, lament, whimper, wail.

**weigh** (SYN.) heed, deliberate, consider, study, ponder, contemplate, reflect, evaluate. (ANT.) neglect, ignore.

**weight** (SYN.) importance, emphasis, load, burden, import, stress, influence, heaviness, pressure, value, gravity, significance. (ANT.) triviality, levity, insignificance, lightness, buoyancy.

**weird** (SYN.) odd, eerie, strange, unnatural, peculiar, spooky.

**welcome** (SYN.) entertain, greet, accept, receive, reception, gain, greeting, shelter. (ANT.) reject, bestow, impart, discharge.

**weld** (SYN.) solder, connect, fuse, bond.

**welfare** (SYN.) good, well-being, prosperity.

**well** (SYN.) hearty, happy, sound, hale, beneficial, good, convenient, expedient, healthy, favorably, fully, thoroughly, surely, adequately, satisfactorily, competently, certainly, completely, trim, undoubtedly, fit, profitable. (ANT.) infirm, depressed, weak.

**well-being** (SYN.) delight, happiness, satisfaction, contentment, gladness. (ANT.) sorrow, grief, sadness, despair.

**well-bred** (SYN.) cultured, polite, genteel, courtly, refined, cultivated. (ANT.) crude, vulgar, boorish, rude.

**well-known** (SYN.) famous, illustrious, celebrated, noted, eminent, renowned. (ANT.) unknown, ignominious, obscure, hidden.

**wet** (SYN.) moist, dank, soaked, damp, drenched, dampen, moisten. (ANT.) arid, dry, parched.

**wharf** (SYN.) pier, dock.

**wheedle** (SYN.) coax, cajole, persuade.

**whim** (SYN.) fancy, notion, humor, quirk, caprice, whimsy, inclination, vagary.

**whimsical** (SYN.) quaint, strange, curious, odd, unusual, droll, queer, eccentric, peculiar. (ANT.) normal, common, usual, familiar.

**whine** (SYN.) whimper, cry, moan, complain.

**whip** (SYN.) scourge, thrash, beat, lash.

**whirl** (SYN.) rotate, twirl, spin, revolve, reel.

**whole** (SYN.) total, sound, all, intact, complete, well, hale, integral, unimpaired, healed, entire, uncut, undivided, unbroken, undamaged, perfect. (ANT.) partial, defective, imperfect, deficient.

**wholesome** (SYN.) robust, well, hale, healthy, sound, salubrious, good, hygienic, salutary, nourishing, healthful, strong, nutritious, hearty. (ANT.) frail, noxious, infirm, delicate, injurious, diseased.

**wicked** (SYN.) deleterious, iniquitous, immoral, bad, evil, base, ungodly, unsound, sinful, bitter, blasphemous, malicious, evil-minded, profane, baleful, hostile, rancorous, unwholesome. (ANT.) moral, good, reputable, honorable.

**wide** (SYN.) large, broad, sweeping, extensive, vast, expanded. (ANT.) restricted, narrow.

**width** (SYN.) wideness, extensiveness, breadth.

**wield** (SYN.) handle, brandish.

**wild** (SYN.) outlandish, uncivilized, untamed, irregular, wanton, foolish, mad, barbarous, rough, waste, desert, uncultivated, boisterous, unruly, savage, primitive, giddy, unrestrained, silly, wayward, uncontrolled, impetuous, crazy, ferocious, undomesticated, desolate. (ANT.) quiet, gentle, placid, tame, restrained, civilized.

**will** (SYN.) intention, desire, volition, decision, resolution, wish, resoluteness, choice, determination, pleasure. (ANT.) disinterest, coercion, indifference.

**willful** (SYN.) intentional, designed, contemplated, studied, premeditated. (ANT.) fortuitous.

**willing** (SYN.) agreeing, energetic, enthusiastic, consenting, agreeable, eager.

**wilt** (SYN.) sag, droop, weaken.

**wily** (SYN.) cunning, foxy, sly, crafty.

**win** (SYN.) gain, succeed, prevail, achieve, thrive, obtain, get, acquire, earn, flourish. (ANT.) lose, miss, forfeit, fail.

**wind** (SYN.) gale, breeze, storm, gust, blast, air, breath, flurry, puff, blow, hurricane, typhoon, cyclone, tornado, suggestion, hint, clue, zephyr,

squall, coil, crank, screw, meander, wander, twist, weave, draft.

**winsome** (SYN.) winning, charming, agreeable.

**wisdom** (SYN.) insight, judgment, learning, sense, discretion, reason, prudence, erudition, foresight, intelligence, knowledge, information, sagacity. (ANT.) nonsense, foolishness, stupidity, ignorance.

**wise** (SYN.) informed, sagacious, learned, penetrating, enlightened, advisable, prudent, profound, deep, erudite, scholarly, knowing, sound, intelligent, expedient, discerning. (ANT.) simple, shallow, foolish.

**wish** (SYN.) crave, hanker, long, hunger, yearning, lust, craving, yearn, want, appetite, covet, longing, desire, urge. (ANT.) hate, aversion, loathing, distaste.

**wit** (SYN.) sense, humor, pleasantry, satire, intelligence, comprehension, understanding, banter, mind, wisdom, intellect, wittiness, fun, drollery, humorist, wag, comedian, raillery, irony, witticism. (ANT.) solemnity, commonplace, sobriety.

**witch** (SYN.) magician, sorcerer, enchanter, sorceress, enchantress, warlock.

**witchcraft** (SYN.) enchantment, magic, wizardry, conjuring, voodoo.

**withdraw** (SYN.) renounce, leave, abandon, recall, retreat, go, secede, desert, quit, retire, depart, retract, remove, forsake. (ANT.) enter, tarry, abide, place, stay.

**wither** (SYN.) wilt, languish, dry, shrivel, decline, fade, decay, sear, waste, wizen, weaken, droop, sink, fail, shrink. (ANT.) renew, refresh, revive.

**withhold** (SYN.) forbear, abstain, repress, check, refrain. (ANT.) persist, continue.

**witness** (SYN.) perceive, proof, spectator, confirmation, see, attestation, watch, observe, eyewitness, notice, testimony. (ANT.) refutation, contradiction, argument.

**witty** (SYN.) funny, talented, apt, bright, adroit, sharp, clever. (ANT.) foolish, slow, dull, clumsy, awkward.

**wizard** (SYN.) magician, conjuror, sorcerer.

**wizardry** (SYN.) voodoo, legerdemain, conjuring, witchcraft, charm.

**woe** (SYN.) sorrow, disaster, trouble, evil, agony, suffering, anguish, sadness, grief, distress, misery, torment, misfortune. (ANT.) pleasure, delight, fun.

**womanly** (SYN.) girlish, womanish, female, ladylike. (ANT.) mannish, virile, male, masculine.

**wonder** (SYN.) awe, curiosity, miracle, admiration, surprise, wonderment. (ANT.) expectation, familiarity, indifference, apathy, triviality.

**wonderful** (SYN.) extraordinary, marvelous, astonishing, amazing, remarkable, astounding.

**wont** (SYN.) practice, use, custom, training, habit, usage, manner. (ANT.) inexperience, disuse.

**word** (SYN.) phrase, term, utterance, expression, articulate.

**wordy** (SYN.) talkative, verbose, garrulous.

**work** (SYN.) opus, employment, achievement, performance, toil, business, exertion, occupation, labor, job, product. (ANT.) recreation, leisure, vacation, ease.

**working** (SYN.) busy, active, industrious. (ANT.) lazy, dormant, passive, inactive.

**world** (SYN.) globe, earth, universe.

**worn** (SYN.) tired, jaded, exhausted, wearied, faint, weary. (ANT.) invigorated, fresh, rested.

**worry** (SYN.) concern, trouble, disquiet, anxiety, fear, pain, harry, gall, grieve. (ANT.) console, comfort, contentment, satisfaction, peace.

**worship** (SYN.) honor, revere, adore, idolize, reverence, glorify, respect. (ANT.) curse, scorn, blaspheme, despise.

**worth** (SYN.) value, price, deserving, excellence, usefulness, utility, worthiness. (ANT.) uselessness, valueless, cheapness.

**worthless** (SYN.) empty, idle, abortive, ineffectual, bootless, vain, unavailing. (ANT.) effective, valuable, potent.

**wound** (SYN.) mar, harm, damage, hurt, dishonor, injure, injury, spoil, wrong. (ANT.) compliment, preserve, help.

**wrap** (SYN.) cover, protect, shield, cloak, mask, clothe, curtain, guard, conceal. (ANT.) reveal, bare, unveil, expose.

**wrath** (SYN.) fury, anger,

irritation, rage, animosity, passion, temper, petulance. (ANT.) patience, conciliation, peace.

**wreck** (SYN.) ravage, devastation, extinguish, destroy, annihilate, damage, raze. (ANT.) construct, preserve, establish.

**wrench** (SYN.) tug, jerk, twist.

**wrestle** (SYN.) fight, tussle, grapple.

**wretch** (SYN.) cad, scoundrel, rogue.

**wretched** (SYN.) forlorn, miserable, comfortless, despicable, paltry, low. (ANT.) contented, happy, significant.

**wring** (SYN.) twist, extract.

**writer** (SYN.) creator, maker, author, composer.

**writhe** (SYN.) twist, squirm.

**wrong** (SYN.) awry, incorrect, improper, amiss, naughty, inappropriate, criminal, faulty, erroneous, bad, evil, imprecise. (ANT.) proper, true, correct, suitable.

**wry** (SYN.) amusing, witty, dry, droll.

# Y

**yacht** (SYN.) sailboat, boat, cruiser.

**yank** (SYN.) pull, wrest, draw, haul, tug, jerk, wrench, heave, extract.

**yap** (SYN.) howl, bark.

**yard** (SYN.) pen, confine, court, enclosure, compound, garden.

**yardstick** (SYN.) measure, criterion, gauge.

**yarn** (SYN.) wool, tale, narrative, thread, story, fiber, anecdote.

**yaw** (SYN.) tack, change course, pitch, toss, roll.

**yawn** (SYN.) open, gape.

**yearly** (SYN.) annually.

**yearn** (SYN.) pine, long for, want, desire, crave, wish.

**yearning** (SYN.) hungering, craving, desire, longing, appetite, lust, urge, aspiration, wish. (ANT.) distaste, loathing, abomination, hate.

**yell** (SYN.) call, scream, shout, whoop, howl, roar, holler, wail, bawl.

**yellow** (SYN.) fearful, cowardly, chicken. (ANT.) bold, brave.

**yelp** (SYN.) screech, squeal, howl, bark.

**yen** (SYN.) longing, craving, fancy, appetite, desire, lust, hunger.

**yet** (SYN.) moreover, also,

additionally, besides.

**yield** *(SYN.)* produce, afford, breed, grant, accord, cede, relent, succumb, bestow, allow, permit, give way, submit, bear, surrender, supply, fruits, give up, abdicate, return, impart, harvest, permit, accede, acquiesce, crop, capitulate, pay, concede, generate, relinquish. *(ANT.) assert, deny, refuse, resist, struggle, oppose, strive.*

**yielding** *(SYN.)* dutiful, submissive, compliant, obedient, tractable. *(ANT.) rebellious, intractable, insubordinate.*

**yoke** *(SYN.)* tether, leash, bridle, harness.

**yokel** *(SYN.)* hick, peasant, hayseed, innocent.

**young** *(SYN.)* immature, undeveloped, youthful, underdeveloped, juvenile, junior, underage. *(ANT.) old, mature, elderly.*

**youngster** *(SYN.)* kid, lad, stripling, minor, youth, child, fledgling. *(ANT.) adult, elder.*

**youthful** *(SYN.)* childish, immature, young, boyish, childlike, callow, girlish, puerile. *(ANT.) old, elderly, senile, aged, mature.*

**yowl** *(SYN.)* yell, shriek, cry, wail, whoop, howl, scream.

# Z

**zany** *(SYN.)* clownish, comical, foolish, silly, scatterbrained.

**zap** *(SYN.)* drive, vim, pep, determination.

**zeal** *(SYN.)* fervor, eagerness, passion, vehemence, devotion, intensity, excitement, earnestness, inspiration, warmth, ardor, fanaticism, enthusiasm. *(ANT.) unconcern, ennui, apathy, indifference.*

**zealot** *(SYN.)* champion, crank, fanatic, bigot.

**zealous** *(SYN.)* enthusiastic, fiery, keen, eager, fervid, ardent, intense, vehement, fervent, glowing, hot, impassioned, passionate. *(ANT.) cool, nonchalant, apathetic.*

**zenith** *(SYN.)* culmination, apex, height, acme, consummation, top, summit, pinnacle, climax, peak. *(ANT.) floor, nadir, depth, anticlimax.*

**zero** *(SYN.)* nonexistent, nil, nothing, none.

**zest** *(SYN.)* enjoyment, savor, eagerness, relish, satisfaction, gusto, spice, tang, pleasure, exhilaration.

**zestful** *(SYN.)* delightful, thrilling, exciting, stimulating, enjoyable.

**zip** *(SYN.)* vigor, vim, energy, vitality, spirited, animation, provocative.

**zone** *(SYN.)* region, climate, tract, belt, sector, section, district, locality, precinct, territory.

**zoo** *(SYN.)* menagerie.

**zoom** *(SYN.)* zip, fly, speed, whiz, roar, race.

# Writer's Handbook

# Getting Started With the Writing Process

The writing process can be considered as five parts: **select, connect, draft, revise,** and **proofread.** These parts are constantly flowing into and influencing one another without any clear line between them. Writing does not proceed in nice, neat steps. As the writer, you might get an idea for the conclusion while writing the introduction.

The more you use the writing process, the more it becomes automatic to you. It is like riding a bike. When you first learn to ride, you are a little unsteady and unsure of yourself. With practice, riding a bike becomes more and more automatic. The writing process becomes automatic in the same way.

To begin the writing process, look through your writing folder for topics. You may get topics from television or the newspaper. Then, decide if your purpose will be to explain, describe, or convince your reader before you narrow your general topic. If your topic covers too much ground, pick the part that interests you most. You can select a narrower form of the topic by clustering.

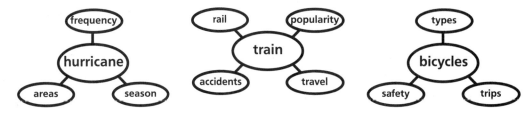

Write your clusters. Add all ideas that come to mind. Choose two or three ideas that interest you the most or that you want to learn more about. Create a new word cluster for each one. Review your new clusters. Select one to write about, and save the others for other projects. Now connect all ideas that go together. Draw lines from one circle to another within your cluster. Draft your ideas into paragraphs. Most likely, this will be the body of your writing. Next, write an introduction or beginning, and add a conclusion or ending. Remember, while you are writing the body of your paper, you might have an idea for an introduction or conclusion. Your writing evolves. Your revision stage can be part of your drafting stage. Read your paper aloud to yourself. Check for spelling and mechanics. Have another student read your work during the revision phase. Proofread your paper, make corrections, and write your final copy.

## Tips for Your Own Writing

- Know whether your purpose is to explain, describe, or convince.
- Select a topic; it may help to cluster ideas you get from reading, observing, or watching television.
- Connect ideas and details within a cluster. If you need to, read about the topic for further details.
- Draft the ideas in your cluster by writing them as sentences and paragraphs.
- Revise with the help of a friend; proofread, revise, and proofread again.

# Getting Ideas

The best source of ideas comes from you. However, you may need a *push* to get you started. Look for ideas and then revert back to what **you** like best or are most interested in. When you write, always consider your resources.

There are many resources to consider when you write; however, your own experiences can bring an outlook to your topic unmatched by any other resource. The key is to choose a topic that you know or would like to know more about. When you know the subject well, you can focus your writing and describe details more distinctly. Brainstorm or cluster special hobbies, talents or skills, travel or other experiences, and people you know. They are good subjects for writing. Experiences, impressions, and perceptions that you have had are the best material for writing.

Imagine a story you would like to write. If you need more information, go to the library or glance through newspapers or magazines. As you preview the information, make a list of topics that interest you. Go through books. Pay attention to the table of contents. Watch information channels on television. The news is a good source of ideas. Again, take notes. Eventually, write down all the ideas and information you gained from previewing the different resources.

Think about your purpose, explore your topic, come up with a narrowed topic, gather material for the details, and decide on who your audience will be and how to appeal to that audience. Develop some sort of method for organizing your information.

Getting ideas involves deciding upon a general topic, and then limiting, or narrowing, that general topic. Then you need to gather details. Go to the library. Brainstorm or cluster by yourself or with others. Make a list of ideas. Group your ideas under related headings. Drop ideas that don't seem to fit in anywhere. Not only do you have ideas, but you now have details that are somewhat organized.

## Tips for Your Own Writing

- Tap your greatest resource by imagining what might happen if . . ., or by thinking about special hobbies, talents or skills, travel or other experiences, and people you know.
- Go to the library and read books, magazines, and newspapers, or watch television for ideas.

# Writer's Handbook

# Writing a Paragraph

A sentence is a group of words that has a subject and a verb. The verb indicates past, present, or future tense. A paragraph is a group of sentences that belongs together. When you begin a new idea or paragraph, start on a new line and indent the first word several spaces from the left margin like the first word in this paragraph you are reading. A composition is a group of paragraphs about one topic. Sometimes a composition is so short that it is only one paragraph long. No matter how many paragraphs you write, you develop them in the same way unless you are writing dialogue in a story. Remember, all sentences in the paragraph have a close relationship to each other.

First, determine whether your purpose is to entertain, explain, describe, or convince. Second, develop your main idea according to a specific order. Your sentences may be written according to **time, space,** or **order of importance.** Words used to show order include *first, last, second, next, finally, then, tomorrow, before, after, least, smallest,* or *most importantly.*

A paragraph may consist of an introductory sentence that tells the main idea. Supporting sentences add details. The concluding sentence of a composition usually draws together the supporting details and restates the main idea.

Once you know your purpose and order, write smooth-flowing, supporting sentences. They give details, reasons, examples, or likenesses and/or differences.

**Details** help the reader form a clearer picture. See how the details help you picture Robin's skateboard:

Robin enjoys her new skateboard.

Robin enjoys her shiny red skateboard with the turned-up, pointed front.

**Reasons** are used when the writer wants to persuade the reader. Sometimes writers show how their topic is like something the reader knows. Vocabulary used to show likenesses includes *also, just as, in the same manner, resembles,* and *similarly.* To develop a paragraph that shows differences, you might include words like *by contrast, on the other hand, unlike, on the contrary,* and *but.*

## Tips for Your Own Writing

- Know your purpose and make your writing fit that purpose.
- Organize sentences or paragraphs by using some type of order.
- Support the topic with details, reasons, or examples.

# Staying on Topic

If you narrow your subject by clustering, it will not be difficult to stay on topic. Cluster, cluster, cluster! Cluster to find your general topic; cluster to find your narrowed topic; cluster to find the details. This will help your writing be more focused. Once you have a specific subject in mind, decide whether your purpose is to describe, inform, persuade, or entertain. That type of planning helps you stick with your topic. Determining the audience you are writing for will also help you remain on topic.

To stay on topic, think in terms of the whole picture and then parts of that picture. In a one-paragraph composition, the whole picture is the one main idea. The parts of that picture are the sentences that support that one idea. The final sentence completes or ends your piece.

The whole picture of a composition is its subject or main idea. The parts of that picture include the paragraphs that support that one idea. Each paragraph contains reasons, examples, details, or facts. The sentences in the paragraphs are also parts of the bigger picture. Clustering will help you come up with the details for those sentences. Don't forget to eliminate and add details to that cluster. Connect ideas that relate to each other. An introduction and a conclusion will help your subject be even more unified and organized.

One test to determine whether you have stayed on topic is to ask yourself, "What is the main idea of this paragraph?" Read each sentence and ask yourself, "Does this sentence give a reason, example, detail, or fact that directly relates to the main idea of the paragraph?"

Another test to help you stay on topic involves remembering the Ws of writing: *who, what, where, when,* and *why.* Answering those questions will help you identify some very basic information related only to your topic. It will help even more if you add *how* to that list.

## Tips for Your Own Writing

- Narrow your general subject by clustering.
- Select the purpose and audience for your writing.
- Continue to cluster to support the different areas of your topic with details.
- Ask yourself *who, what, where, when, why,* and *how,* and you will identify very basic information that relates only to your subject.
- Ask yourself *why* about your subject until you completely run out of answers.

# Writer's Handbook

# *Proofreading Checklist*

Sometimes you think you wrote one thing but actually did not. This makes it difficult for you to find mistakes in your own writing. You read what you meant to say rather than the actual words on the page. It helps to put the writing away overnight. This gives your brain time to forget what you wrote. Later, you will be able to see the words that are actually on the page. It helps to read your work aloud, word for word. Listen to see whether it makes sense. Try to identify missing or extra words. Read your work again, silently. Look carefully for mistakes in punctuation, spelling, and grammar. Find punctuation mistakes by reading the sentences aloud and backwards. Start with the last sentence, then read the next-to-last sentence, and so on. If what you read doesn't sound like a sentence, check the punctuation. Page 3 of this thesaurus lists the basic proofreading marks you can use to mark mistakes.

Proofread for mistakes in spelling, punctuation, capitalization, and verb usage. It is best to check your work for no more than two items at a time. Be sure that your composition is clear, unified, and complete.

The paragraph below shows how to use these proofreading marks.

Would I make the team or would the coach pick someone else? that was the

question. I knew that Ben, Lamar, and Carlos had already been chosen. Was I next?

Just then Jana came and stood in the doorway of the gym. she seemed to be looking

for someone. I hopped she was looking for me, but I didn't want her to see me me

fail. What pressure!

## *Tips for Your Own Writing*

Your proofreading checklist:
**I. Mechanics**
   **A.** Spelling
   **B.** Capitalization
      **1.** Start all sentences with a capital letter including sentences inside dialogue.
      **2.** Capitalize specific names of people, places, and things.
   **C.** Punctuation
      **1.** Punctuate the end of each sentence properly.
      **2.** Place commas in compound sentences and in items listed in a series.
      **3.** Punctuate dialogue or conversation with quotation marks and commas.
**II. Usage**
   **A.** Verify your use of commonly misused words.
   **B.** Check for correct usage of verbs and plurals.
**Read your writing to make sure the meaning is clear, unified, and complete.**

# Stories

Every story needs a problem to be met and dealt with or solved, a setting, and interesting characters. It should also have a beginning, a middle, and an end. Actually, the most important part of many stories is the characters. You want readers to care about your characters or people (or sometimes animals). You write about characters in three ways: by what the character says and does; by what other characters say about the character; and by what you, the writer, show us about the character.

Good writers show; they don't tell. See the difference below in *telling* what a character is like and *showing* what a character is like.

| How a character— | Telling | Showing |
| --- | --- | --- |
| Looked: | He was strong. | Muscles bulged under his shirt. |
| Felt: | He felt sad. | A dark cloud seemed to have settled over him. |
| Acted: | She was friendly. | She smiled and waved every time she saw me. |
| Talked: | She said a car was coming. | She screamed, "Watch out for that car!" |

Write so your reader knows what the characters look like, say, do, think, and feel. The best way to do this is to include sensory details that draw upon any of the five senses—sight, sound, smell, touch, and even taste. Help the reader experience the situation just as the character did. Bring your characters to life. "The outside of the spacecraft looked bad" is not as descriptive as "The outside of the spacecraft was scorched and scratched."

The setting of a story is the time (the "when") and place (the "where") of the story. The reader can visualize the setting when you describe it well.

What happens in a story is the plot, or plan. Most likely, the beginning contains a problem of some kind, and the ending has a solution. The solution may be that there is no solution, but at least the character or characters have gained a new insight about the situation. The plot is the heart of the story. Think of an interesting or funny problem, then think of a solution. Don't forget to explain and develop the events or episodes of the story in the proper sequence. That would be the middle of your story. It helps to show the reader a clear connection between the problem, the main character, and the character's feelings.

## Tips for Your Own Writing

- Each story has characters, setting (time and place), and plan, or plot.
- The plan, or plot, of the story has a beginning, a middle, and an end.
- Develop a character by what the character says and does, what other characters say about the character, and/or what you, the writer, tell us about the character.
- Use sensory words and details to describe a character.

# Expository Writing – Planning a Report

Expository reports give information about a subject using description, facts, or examples. Reports inform and explain. In a report that informs, the writer gives information about a topic. In a report that explains, the writer explains how to do something. Once you have chosen a narrowed topic and decided whether you need to inform or explain, make a K-W-L chart.

| K-<br>What I **K**now | W-<br>What I **W**ant to Know | L-<br>What I Have **L**earned |
|---|---|---|

First, list all the things you know about your topic in the **K** column. Next, list all the questions you have about your topic under the **W** column. Then, research the topic. List the most important things you learned about your topic in the **L** column.

Take notes regarding the subject. If you want, you may use note cards. Put one fact or detail on a card with a note as to the source of the information. Add as much information as necessary in case you need to find the source again.

Review all your note cards once again. Choose the fact or detail that you find most interesting, and use that as your main idea. Go through your note cards again, and choose the facts and details that support your main idea. Eliminate unnecessary notes.

Sort your cards into three or four categories. Those categories will be the main points of your report. If your teacher requires an outline, these main points may be used as the main headings of your outline. Write each main point on a different sheet of paper with one main point at the top of each sheet. Each main point should support your main topic. Arrange the note cards in some sort of logical order. Next, write under each main point all the notes from the cards that support the main idea on the top of the paper. Write each note in the proper order. Work with one paper and one stack of note cards at a time. The discussion on the next page will show you how to draft or shape the details and facts from each sheet of paper into paragraphs. You have done most of the difficult work in the planning stage of your report.

## Tips for Your Own Writing

- Choose a topic and narrow it according to the first two topics in the *Writer's Handbook* on pages 110 and 111.
- Gather facts and details by reading and taking notes about your topic.
- Choose the most interesting fact as your main point.
- Arrange notes in a logical order to support your main idea.
- Draft details and facts into paragraphs.

# Expository Writing – Writing a Report

In the previous lesson, you were asked to organize your notes in some logical order and then to write them on one of three or four sheets of paper with one main idea at the top of each sheet of paper. Next, look at the notes on that paper and decide how to organize the information. Here are three possible choices:

1. **Time order:** Use this approach if you are writing about something that happened over time, such as a war, a famous person's life, the life cycle of an animal, or changes in climate. You will describe the events in the order they happened.

2. **Order of importance:** This is a good approach if you are writing about the causes of something (such as allergies), the uses of something (such as gold), or a scientist's inventions. Start with the most important item and proceed to the least important items.

3. **Problem-cause-solution:** This approach is helpful for topics such as ways to avoid skin cancer, better ways to distribute the world's food, ways to save energy, or ways to solve another problem. Describe the problem, explain the cause, and conclude with the solution.

Work with one sheet of paper at a time. That is, work with one main idea at a time. Organize the notes in the order of your choice, and draft sentences and paragraphs with the examples, facts, or details from those notes. After writing all the paragraphs, draft an introduction and a conclusion. Remember, this is merely a draft; it can be revised at any time. Go through your paper to determine whether any part of it needs more development. If so, add more details, facts, or examples in the margins. You may decide to use carets ( ∧ ) where you want to insert new information and write it at the bottom of the page. Delete parts that do not support or relate to the main idea or the main points. Add charts or illustrations if needed. Use your proofreading list from page 114 to proofread your paper, and ask someone to review your paper. Make revisions again before writing your final copy. Proofread one more time, and your report is finished.

## Tips for Your Own Writing

- Decide whether to organize your report by **time, importance, problem-cause-solution,** or some other type of order, and arrange your notes accordingly.
- Keep in mind the main idea listed at the top of each paper, and draft sentences and paragraph(s) using the examples, facts, or details from your notes.
- Draft an introduction and conclusion for your report.
- Revise the paper by deleting or adding information.
- Proofread, revise, write your final copy, and proofread again.

# Writing a Persuasive Composition

When you write a composition, you are putting together a written message. The message in a *persuasive* composition is that you want to *coax* or talk someone into believing or acting a certain way. Write a letter to that person asking him or her to let you do something. Your letter is a form of persuasive writing.

In a persuasive composition, first decide *what* you want to talk someone into doing or believing. Narrow your topic as you have learned to do in earlier in this handbook. Next, think *who* your audience or readers will be. Will your composition be read only by your peers or by adults?

Gather evidence to support your belief, or gather evidence and then formulate an opinion. Evidence includes *facts and information*. A *fact* can be proved and checked. On the other hand, an *opinion* is a belief or feeling. It cannot be proved or checked.

**Fact:** Northville city government plans to tear down the old school. (If you check with city officials, they will tell you that they do plan to tear down the school.)

**Opinion:** The old school is very beautiful, and it should be preserved. (That is your opinion as a writer. Not everyone would agree with you.)

You need to learn about your subject to make a convincing argument. Go to the library and read, interview people, or write for information to gather evidence. Determine *why* you believe what you do about your subject. Make note of your source if necessary. Sometimes noting your source strengthens your argument. It backs up your opinion with the opinions of authorities.

Organize your notes or ideas in a specific order. Write a conclusion and include a general statement that can be logically drawn from the information you have collected. Your conclusion needs to be supported by the evidence you have gathered.

Now draft the remainder of the composition. The introduction needs to present your position with a strong statement about your stand on the issue. The body of the composition simply supports your position with clear reasons, facts, and examples as to *why* you believe as you do.

You have completed your first draft. Revise and edit your paper. Ask someone to help you edit it. Revise as many times as necessary. Proofread your final copy.

## Tips for Your Own Writing

- Decide *what* you want someone else to believe or do, and *who* you want to convince.
- Gather evidence and learn more about your topic.
- Ideas are organized as to how they support your position.
- The introduction presents your position with a strong statement on the issue.
- The conclusion makes a general statement that is supported by the evidence.

# Word Lists

**VERBS: Forms of some irregular verbs.**

| PRESENT Today I... | PAST Yesterday I... | PAST PARTICIPLE I have... |
|---|---|---|
| ★be | ★was/were | ★been |
| become/becomes | became | become |
| begin/begins | began | begun |
| burn/burns | burned/burnt | burned/burnt |
| burst | burst | burst |
| dive/dives | dived/dove | dived |
| drink/drinks | drank | drunk |
| forget/forgets | forgot | forgotten/forgot |
| lay/lays | laid | laid |
| lead/leads | led | led |
| lend/lends | lent | lent |
| lie (recline)/lies | lay | lain |
| lose/loses | lost | lost |
| rise/rises | rose | risen |
| see/sees | saw | seen |
| shake/shakes | shook | shaken |
| strike/strikes | struck | struck/stricken |
| swim/swims | swam | swum |

| ★conjugation of to be: | Singular | Plural |
|---|---|---|
| | I **am** | we **are** |
| | you **are** | you **are** |
| | he, she, *or* it **is** | they **are** |

**VIVID VERBS**

| | | | | | |
|---|---|---|---|---|---|
| absorb | ebb | inspect | praise | sandbag | smack |
| bolt | glance | laud | rattle | scream | swoop |
| decline | glare | peek | rip | screech | zoom |

**ADJECTIVES**

| | | | | |
|---|---|---|---|---|
| beaming | dark | featherbrained | inviting | quizzical |
| beefy | deceitful | glossy | lustrous | sinister |
| bulky | enchanting | immense | magnificent | vast |
| curious | engrossing | intriguing | moldy | wicked |

**PREPOSITIONS: Below is a partial list of some common prepositions.**

| | | | | |
|---|---|---|---|---|
| aboard | considering | from between | in regard to | outside |
| alongside | despite | from under | inside | over to |
| away from | down from | in addition to | instead of | regarding |
| behind | except for | in front of | on account of | underneath |
| besides | from among | in place of | on behalf of | within |

## Postal State and Possession Abbreviations

### States

| | | | |
|---|---|---|---|
| Alabama | AL | New Jersey | NJ |
| Alaska | AK | New Mexico | NM |
| Arizona | AZ | New York | NY |
| Arkansas | AR | North Carolina | NC |
| California | CA | North Dakota | ND |
| Colorado | CO | Ohio | OH |
| Connecticut | CT | Oklahoma | OK |
| Delaware | DE | Oregon | OR |
| Florida | FL | Pennsylvania | PA |
| Georgia | GA | Rhode Island | RI |
| Hawaii | HI | South Carolina | SC |
| Idaho | ID | South Dakota | SD |
| Illinois | IL | Tennessee | TN |
| Indiana | IN | Texas | TX |
| Iowa | IA | Utah | UT |
| Kansas | KS | Vermont | VT |
| Kentucky | KY | Virginia | VA |
| Louisiana | LA | Washington | WA |
| Maine | ME | West Virginia | WV |
| Maryland | MD | Wisconsin | WI |
| Massachusetts | MA | Wyoming | WY |
| Michigan | MI | | |
| Minnesota | MN | | |
| Mississippi | MS | District of Columbia | DC |
| Missouri | MO | | |
| Montana | MT | | |

### U.S. Possessions

| | |
|---|---|
| Nebraska | NE |
| Nevada | NV |
| New Hampshire | NH |

| | |
|---|---|
| American Samoa | AS |
| Guam | GU |
| Puerto Rico | PR |
| Virgin Islands | VI |

# WEIGHTS AND MEASURES

## ENGLISH

### Length

| | |
|---|---|
| 12 inches | = 1 foot |
| 3 feet | = 1 yard |
| 220 yards | = 1 furlong |
| 8 furlongs | = 1 mile |
| 5280 feet | = 1 mile |
| 1760 yards | = 1 mile |

### Area

| | |
|---|---|
| 144 square inches | = 1 square foot |
| 9 square feet | = 1 square yard |
| 4840 square yards | = 1 acre |
| 640 acres | = 1 square mile |
| 1 square mile | = 1 section |
| 36 sections | = 1 township |

### Volume

| | |
|---|---|
| 1728 cubic inches | = 1 cubic foot |
| 27 cubic feet | = 1 cubic yard |

### Capacity (Dry)

| | |
|---|---|
| 2 pints | = 1 quart |
| 8 quarts | = 1 peck |
| 4 pecks | = 1 bushel |

### Capacity (Liquid)

| | |
|---|---|
| 16 fluid ounces | = 1 pint |
| 4 gills | = 1 pint |
| 2 pints | = 1 quart |
| 4 quarts | = 1 gallon (8 pints) |

### Mass

| | |
|---|---|
| 437.5 grains | = 1 ounce |
| 16 ounces | = 1 pound (7000 grains) |
| 14 pounds | = 1 stone |
| 100 pounds | = 1 hundredweight [cwt] |
| 20 cwt | = 1 ton (2000 pounds) |

### Troy Weights

| | |
|---|---|
| 24 grains | = 1 pennyweight |
| 20 pennyweights | = 1 ounce (480 grains) |
| 12 ounces | = 1 pound (5760 grains) |

### Measures

| | |
|---|---|
| 60 minims | = 1 fluid dram |
| 8 fluid drams | = 1 fluid ounce |
| 16 fluid ounces | = 1 pint |

### Apothecaries' Weights

| | |
|---|---|
| 20 grains | = 1 scruple |
| 3 scruples | = 1 dram |
| 8 drams | = 1 ounce (480 grains) |
| 12 ounces | = 1 pound (5760 grains) |

## METRIC

### Length

| | |
|---|---|
| 1 millimeter | = 1000 micrometers |
| 1 centimeter | = 10 millimeters |
| 1 meter | = 1000 millimeters |
| 1 meter | = 100 centimeters |
| 1 kilometer | = 1000 meters |

### Area

| | |
|---|---|
| 1 square centimeter | = 100 square millimeters |
| 1 square meter | = 10,000 square centimeters |
| 1 square meter | = 1,000,000 square millimeters |
| 1 square kilometer | = 1,000,000 square meters |

### Volume

| | |
|---|---|
| 1 milliliter | = 1 cubic centimeter |
| 1 liter | = 1000 milliliters |
| 1 liter | = 0.001 cubic meter |

### Mass

| | |
|---|---|
| 1 gram | = 1000 milligrams |
| 1 kilogram | = 1000 grams |
| 1 metric ton | = 1000 kilograms |

# APPROXIMATE CONVERSIONS FROM ENGLISH TO METRIC

| Symbol | When You Know | Multiply by | To Find | Symbol |
|---|---|---|---|---|
| **LENGTH** | | | | |
| in | inches | 2.5 | centimeters | cm |
| ft | feet | 30 | centimeters | cm |
| yd | yards | 0.9 | meters | m |
| mi | miles | 1.6 | kilometers | km |
| **AREA** | | | | |
| $in^2$ | square inches | 6.5 | square centimeters | $cm^2$ |
| $ft^2$ | square feet | 0.09 | square meters | $m^2$ |
| $yd^2$ | square yards | 0.8 | square meters | $m^2$ |
| $mi^2$ | square miles | 2.6 | square kilometers | $km^2$ |
| | acres | 0.4 | hectares | ha |
| **MASS** | | | | |
| oz | ounces | 28 | grams | g |
| lb | pounds | 0.45 | kilograms | kg |
| ST | short tons (2000 lb) | 0.9 | metric ton | t |
| **VOLUME** | | | | |
| tsp | teaspoons | 5 | milliliters | mL |
| tbsp | tablespoons | 15 | milliliters | mL |
| $in^3$ | cubic inches | 16 | milliliters | mL |
| fl oz | fluid ounces | 30 | milliliters | mL |
| c | cups | 0.24 | liters | L |
| pt | pints | 0.47 | liters | L |
| qt | quarts | 0.95 | liters | L |
| gal | gallons | 3.8 | liters | L |
| $ft^3$ | cubic feet | 0.03 | cubic meters | $m^3$ |
| $yd^3$ | cubic yards | 0.76 | cubic meters | $m^3$ |
| **TEMPERATURE** | **(exact)** | | | |
| °F | Fahrenheit | subtract 32 and multiply by 5/9 | Celsius | °C |

# APPROXIMATE CONVERSIONS FROM METRIC TO ENGLISH

| Symbol | When You Know | Multiply by | To Find | Symbol |
|---|---|---|---|---|
| **LENGTH** | | | | |
| mm | millimeters | 0.04 | inches | in |
| cm | centimeters | 0.4 | inches | in |
| m | meters | 3.3 | feet | ft |
| m | meters | 1.1 | yards | yd |
| km | kilometers | 0.6 | miles | mi |
| | | | | |
| **AREA** | | | | |
| cm² | square centimeters | 0.16 | square inches | in² |
| m² | square meters | 1.2 | square yards | yd² |
| km² | square kilometers | 0.4 | square miles | mi² |
| ha | hectares (10,000 m) | 2.5 | acres | a |
| | | | | |
| **MASS** | | | | |
| g | grams | 0.035 | ounces | oz |
| kg | kilograms | 2.2 | pounds | lb |
| t | metric ton (1,000 kg) | 1.1 | short tons | ST |
| | | | | |
| **VOLUME** | | | | |
| mL | milliliters | 0.03 | fluid ounces | fl oz |
| mL | milliliters | 0.06 | cubic inches | in³ |
| L | liters | 2.1 | pints | pt |
| L | liters | 1.06 | quarts | qt |
| L | liters | 0.26 | gallons | gal |
| m³ | cubic meters | 35 | cubic feet | ft³ |
| m³ | cubic meters | 1.3 | cubic yards | yd³ |
| | | | | |
| **TEMPERATURE** | **(exact)** | | | |
| °C | Celsius | subtract 9/5 and add 32 | Fahrenheit | °F |

# COOKING CONVERSIONS

| | | |
|---|---|---|
| A few grains/pinch/dash, etc. (dry) | = | Less than 1/8 tsp |
| A dash (liquid) | = | A few drops |
| 3 teaspoons | = | 1 tablespoon |
| 1/2 tablespoon | = | 1-1/2 teaspoons |
| 1 tablespoon | = | 3 teaspoons |
| 2 tablespoons | = | 1 fluid ounce |
| 4 tablespoons | = | 1/4 cup |
| 5-1/3 tablespoons | = | 1/3 cup |
| 8 tablespoons | = | 1/2 cup |
| 8 tablespoons | = | 4 fluid ounces |
| 10-2/3 tablespoons | = | 2/3 cup |
| 12 tablespoons | = | 3/4 cup |
| 16 tablespoons | = | 1 cup |
| 16 tablespoons | = | 8 fluid ounces |
| 1/8 cup | = | 2 tablespoons |
| 1/4 cup | = | 4 tablespoons |
| 1/4 cup | = | 2 fluid ounces |
| 1/3 cup | = | 5 tablespoons plus 1 teaspoon |
| 1/2 cup | = | 8 tablespoons |
| 1 cup | = | 16 tablespoons |
| 1 cup | = | 8 fluid ounces |
| 1 cup | = | 1/2 pint |
| 2 cups | = | 1 pint |
| 2 pints | = | 1 quart |
| 4 quarts (liquid) | = | 1 gallon |
| 8 quarts (dry) | = | 1 peck |
| 4 pecks (dry) | = | 1 bushel |
| 1 kilogram | = | approximately 2 pounds |
| 1 liter | = | approximately 4 cups or 1 quart |
| 1 cup | = | 275 milliliters |
| 1 pint | = | 550 milliliters |
| 1 quart | = | 900 milliliters |

# NOTES

# NOTES

# NOTES

# NOTES